GEO

THE
Family Tree
Guide Book

EVERYTHING YOU NEED TO KNOW
TO TRACE YOUR GENEALOGY ACROSS NORTH AMERICA

THE EDITORS OF FAMILY TREE MAGAZINE

BETTERWAY BOOKS
CINCINNATI, OHIO

www.familytreemagazine.com

Portions of this book have previously appeared in *Family Tree Magazine*, © 2001, 2002 F&W Publications Inc.

07   06   05   04   03   5   4   3   2   1

Library of Congress Cataloging-in-Publication Data

The family tree guide book : everything you need to know to trace your genealogy across North America / the editors of Family Tree Magazine.
    p. cm.
Includes bibliographical references and index.
ISBN 1-55870-647-X (pbk. : alk. paper)
  1. United States—Genealogy—Handbooks, manuals, etc. 2. Canada—Genealogy—Handbooks, manuals, etc. I. Family tree magazine (Cincinnati, Ohio)
CS49 .F353 2003
929'.1'072073—dc21   2002151681
                                                         CIP

Edited by David A. Fryxell, Brad Crawford, and Erin Nevius
Cover design by Brian Roeth
Interior design by Clare Finney

Contents

NEW ENGLAND 23
Connecticut, Maine, Massachusetts, New Hampshire, Rhode Island, Vermont

If you have New England roots, give thanks that our Pilgrim forefathers and those who came after them left a cornucopia of records.

MID-ATLANTIC 46
Delaware, Maryland, New Jersey, New York, Pennsylvania

The Mid-Atlantic states have been at the heart of American history—and American ancestry—from the very beginning.

COURTESY NEW ENGLAND HISTORIC GENEALOGICAL SOCIETY

Discovering the New England Historic Genealogical Society can help you trace your "Yankee" roots.

SOUTH 78

Alabama, Arkansas, Florida, Georgia, Kentucky, Louisiana, Mississippi, North Carolina, South Carolina, Tennessee, Texas, Virginia, West Virginia

Did your ancestors make their stand in Dixie? The South *will* rise again—in your family tree, if you follow these tips and use these resources for researching your Southern roots.

COURTESY GEORGIA DEPARTMENT OF INDUSTRY, TRADE, AND TOURISM

Civil War sites such as Georgia's Kennesaw Civil War Museum can help you connect with your heritage.

MIDWEST 144

Illinois, Indiana, Iowa, Michigan, Minnesota, Missouri, Ohio, Wisconsin

Follow your pioneer ancestors' migrations across the frontier with this expert advice and these extensive resources.

GREAT PLAINS & ROCKIES 193

Colorado, Idaho, Kansas, Montana, Nebraska, North Dakota, Oklahoma, South Dakota, Utah, Wyoming

Discover your ancestors' "manifest destiny" in the states of the Great Plains and the Rocky Mountain region.

Salt Lake City's genealogical riches make it the top research destination for family history.

Your ancestors' frontier past is celebrated in places such as Fort Worth, Texas, where the Old West lives.

Foreword

BY SHARON DEBARTOLO CARMACK

Genealogy used to be the third most popular hobby, falling behind stamp collecting and coin collecting. With about 120 million people interested in tracing their roots these days, I suspect those stamps and coins are now gathering dust under beds. So what's all the fuss about? Why is there such a growing obsession with "collecting" dead relatives and needing to know who came before us? Many of us probably have some deep psychological reasons for starting the climb up the family tree, but the simple answer is, it's fun. It's like a mystery that needs solving.

Genealogy is more than just names and dates; it's the story of your past.

WHAT'S IT ALL ABOUT?

Genealogy is addictive. Once you begin searching for your ancestors, you'll be hooked. You'll think about it night and day. It will become your reason for living. You will begin to bore your friends, neighbors, relatives, and other genealogists with stories of your dead relatives. But don't worry; we've all done it. At first, the challenge is to see how far back you can trace a lineage. Then, that's no longer enough. What were your ancestors' lives like? You'll take a new path and want to discover intimate details about your ancestors: how they dressed, what kind of houses they lived in, what they ate.

Genealogy is a never-ending hobby. You will always have a new line to trace or a new problem to solve. Think about it: Each generation doubles the number of ancestors. You have two parents; your parents had two parents, giving you four grandparents; and they each had two parents, giving you eight great-grandparents. By the time you count back to the tenth generation—your eighth great-grandparents—you have 2,046 ancestors, 1,024 of whom are in that tenth generation alone! So you always have something to do. Usually, one family or one individual grabs your interest or proves more challenging, and you may find that you spend most of your research time on that branch.

Genealogy is time consuming. Tracing your ancestry to the 1500s is not something you can do on the Internet on a rainy Saturday afternoon. You'll wait weeks for a vital records office to respond to your request for a death certificate. You'll wait days for a roll of microfilm you ordered to arrive at the library. You'll wait months to visit a distant research repository and look for a will. You'll spend hours cranking the handle of a microfilm reader to find your great-grandfather on a census. But, frankly, you won't mind. It's all part of the fun.

Genealogy is more than just collecting names and dates. Yes, your initial goal may be to trace your lineage back to an immigrant ancestor or to see how far back in time you can take a line. But let's face it: Even to another person interested in genealogy, names and dates on a chart are rather dull. Adding flesh to the bones—the family stories, the skeletons, and the historical perspective—is what makes genealogy interesting to everyone.

Genealogy isn't always cheap (but try to name a hobby that is free). The first book I read on how to do genealogy was Gilbert H. Doane's *Searching for Your Ancestors*. I opened the cover and read, "All you need is a notebook, a few pencils, an inquisitive mind, a willingness to ask questions and dig for facts...." Doane was correct to a degree, but he left off one important requisite: money. In 1974, when Doane's book was published, the cost to obtain a copy of a birth or death certificate was about one dollar to three dollars. Today, you may pay as much as twenty dollars. You'll discover books you want to buy; research trips you want to take; computer and office equipment you want to purchase; classes, institutes, and conferences you want to attend. On the other hand, many people trace their family trees within the confines of a tight budget. You can make genealogy as expensive or inexpensive as you want.

Genealogy isn't always easy. Tracing your ancestry requires searching in historical documents such as censuses, wills, deeds, military records, tax lists, immigration papers, and ships' passenger lists, to name a few. Many of these records aren't online yet, so you'll have to visit libraries, courthouses, historical societies, town halls, and archives to examine them. You must accurately connect each generation to the next, so reviewing these documents is a requirement. You certainly don't want to claim the wrong ancestors!

Genealogy is frustrating, yet challenging. While it seems like the ancestors in some lineages just fall into place in the course of research, others require more diligence.

Historical documents weren't created with genealogists in mind. You may get only one tiny piece of information from a record after you've waited for weeks for the record to arrive in your mailbox. Worse yet, it may not tell you anything you didn't already know about an ancestor. Some records—such as the censuses of the twentieth century—contain extensive data on people; other records—such as the first federal census, taken in 1790—contain only scant information.

Genealogically valuable documents are not always available for research. Some records have been inadvertently destroyed due to neglect, fires and floods, and other natural disasters; such was the fate of most of the 1890 federal census.

Even if the documents you want to consult are accessible, you may not find your ancestor in them at all. You have to learn to become creative and find other records showing activities in which your ancestor may have been a part. It's like putting together the pieces of a jigsaw puzzle: When all the pieces fit together, you feel you've accomplished something. When they don't fit, though you may be frustrated, you just keep at it until it blends to make a pretty scene. Though the puzzle may not be easy to complete, as you progress, you can more easily deduce what probably goes in the empty spaces.

Genealogical research isn't already complete and posted on the Internet. No question, the

Internet is a fabulous tool for genealogists, and more and more images of actual records are becoming available online. Keep in mind, however, that more than five million family-history sites are on the Internet, and several million of them have information that hasn't been proven or verified by anyone except maybe the Web master. Use the information you find on the Internet as clues, then track down the original documents where that data came from. You'll be glad you did.

Genealogy is one of the most rewarding things you can do. Through genealogy, you'll meet all kinds of people, most notably cousins and other relatives you had no idea were out there. Some may be distantly related—that fourth cousin, three generations removed. You'll reunite with lost relatives and friends. And you'll leave a legacy for your children, grandchildren, and the many generations to come. Genealogy has the power to bring family members together, closing the gap between generations.

Genealogy is about constant learning. New sources and methods for finding your ancestors are released almost daily. In 2001, the Ellis Island Passenger Arrival List database came online. In 2002, a major record group—the 1930 census—became available to the public. Tomorrow will bring even more records for you to search. What about when you reach a stumbling block in your research? Each year, new guidebooks are published to help you find your ancestors in all these records.

WHAT *THE FAMILY TREE GUIDE BOOK* IS ALL ABOUT

So where do you begin? Do you feel overwhelmed? That's where *The Family Tree Guide Book* comes in. It can help you begin the search for your ancestors across the United States and Canada and take away that overwhelming feeling. Emily Anne Croom, the best-selling author of *Unpuzzling Your Past*, takes you step-by-step through beginning the climb up your family tree. Next, David Fryxell, editor in chief of *Family Tree Magazine*, explains how you can find your ancestors across North America. The rest of *The Family Tree Guide Book* is conveniently arranged into sections on six U.S. regions and Canada, each section giving you sources, travel information, and tips for finding and using records. But that's not all. If you have Native American or African-American roots, check out the specialized help for those topics at the end of this book. Some of the leading genealogical authors have contributed to this book, sharing their insights and advice to help you successfully trace your lineage.

Genealogy is fun and flexible. You can spend every day of the week or just one day a month finding your ancestors. Genealogy is a hobby where you can have a passing interest or get totally involved. You can travel and walk the lands your ancestors owned, or you can stay at home and surf the Web. You can write to libraries and courthouses for records, or you can crank the handle of a microfilm reader in a research repository. You can buy books or borrow them from a library. You can use books and museums to travel back in time. You can put your genealogy away for several months or years, and your ancestors will patiently wait for you to return. Regardless of your reasons for hunting out the past or of how much or little time and money you devote to it, *The Family Tree Guide Book* is here when you need it!

Getting Started Tracing Your Ancestors

BY EMILY ANNE CROOM

Have you ever considered that a tree's root system is much more extensive than its combined trunk, branches, and leaves? The same is true of family trees. On your family tree, you have more ancestors than you have parents, siblings, and children. Discovering your family roots means uncovering those ancestors—solving the puzzles of genealogy.

Maybe you like working puzzles or outguessing detectives in mystery stories; genealogy is another form of puzzle and mystery. Or maybe you enjoy reading historical novels; genealogy is a family-made adventure in history, sometimes better than a novel. If you're curious about your family history and combine this curiosity with the challenge of finding solutions plus the adventure of history, you'll love "doing genealogy."

That involves
• looking for ancestors
• trying to identify the events, names, places, dates, and relationships that shaped their lives
• trying to learn about their place and experience in the history and geography that surrounded them

"Doing genealogy" means starting with yourself and working back, one generation at a time, toward the unknown. Sometimes, the identification process is as easy as looking in a family Bible, interviewing older relatives, and reading newspaper obituaries. At other times, discovering the names of the next generation of ancestors is not so straightforward. That's when you need to probe deeper for clues, ask more questions, and look for more cousins. You have to study everything you can find and try to draw logical, reasonable, and documented conclusions. Eventually, all of us hit the proverbial brick wall in every family—that's a given. It's often possible, however, with enough curiosity and determination, to get around those walls. Every success, large or small, keeps you in the hunt for that next ancestor. A dedicated genealogist will go to great lengths to prove one great-grandmother's maiden name or one great-grandfather's real birthplace.

Why? We're curious, and we want the best possible answer to the puzzle. It does little good to accept the wrong ancestor. Little good comes from working a jigsaw puzzle where the pieces *almost* fit. In a jigsaw puzzle, it's a funny-looking cat that ends up with a church spire where its tail should be, just because the colors are the same. In genealogy, it's a funny-looking family where names match but the mother is thirty years old, the father is eight, and the son is twenty-two.

GATHERING THE PIECES AT HOME

Start under your own roof, before even the first visit to the library. Here are four keys to getting started on your own puzzle:

1. Vital statistics are vital. First, gather names and vital statistics: birth, marriage, and death dates and places. Include your immediate family, parents, grandparents, aunts, uncles, and cousins. This information is often tucked away in boxes under the bed, in the attic, or in Aunt Hattie's old trunk. It could be in scrapbooks, family Bibles or birth, marriage, and death certificates.

Interviewing relatives is another way to discover information on several generations. Ask Grandma about her parents and grandparents. Uncle Henry might supply names of children who died young, whom no one else thought to mention. Aunt Clara may fill in gaps on Aunt Sally's family, with whom everyone else has lost contact. The more different the contributions, the more thorough the picture. You may also get discrepancies: two different marriage dates for Uncle Albert and Aunt Jane. Keep both. That's something to resolve as you research.

2. Focus your search. When you've gathered names, relationships, and vital statistics for several generations using materials at home and from relatives, choose a focus ancestor for concentrated study. Maybe it will be a grandparent you were named after, or a great-grandparent about whom you know very little.

You had eight great-grandparents, four couples. Each couple probably created records of the kind found in courthouses or archives. These records may contain your missing information. They also may lead you to the parents, grandparents, and other forebears of your focus couple. Try to focus on one family at a time. Otherwise, too many names dilute the search and you don't really study each family. It's in-depth study that leads to breakthroughs.

3. Chart your findings. Over the years, genealogists have developed helpful charts for displaying vital statistics and relationships. Most genealogy computer software allows users to print out a variety of nice-looking chart formats. A book with many kinds of pre-printed forms for the genealogist is *The Unpuzzling Your Past Workbook* (Betterway Books, $15.99). Or you can download blank versions of the forms on these pages, and many more, from the Toolkit section of the *Family Tree Magazine* Web site <www.familytreemagazine.com>.

One basic genealogy form is the pedigree chart *(next page)*. This multi-generation chart reads backward in time to show the ancestors of one person. It's a good reference, something like a road map of ancestor names, dates and places. Most pedigree charts show four or five generations, although versions are available for naming many more. Another useful chart is the family group sheet *(see page 12)*, a record of three generations. Broader in scope than the pedigree chart, it details one nuclear family: parents and their children, with names of grandparents. You should start one of these charts for every family you study: yourself as both child and parent, your siblings and their families, your parents as children, their siblings and families, and so forth. These two charts are not meant to be filled out as you research. They don't take the place of research notes. Instead, they're the products of research: vital statistics, names, and relationships that are established and shown to be correct.

4. Get organized. Genealogy research consists of two basic components: methods and sources. Part of good methodology is getting and staying

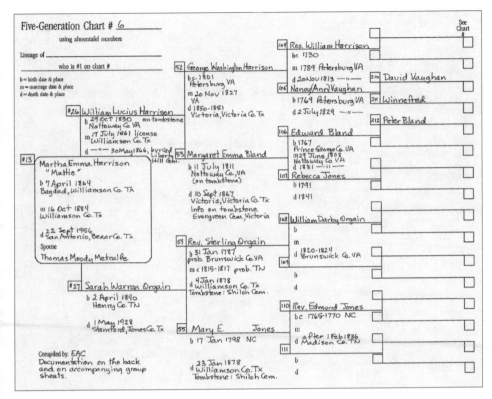

Five-Generation Chart # 6
using ahnentafel numbers

Lineage of _____
who is #1 on chart # _____

b = birth date & place
m = marriage date & place
d = death date & place

#13
Martha Emma Harrison
"Mattie"

b 7 April 1864
Bagdad, Williamson Co. Tx

m 16 Oct 1884
Williamson Co. Tx

d 22 Sept 1956
San Antonio, Bexar Co. Tx

Spouse
Thomas Moody Metcalfe

#26 William Lucius Harrison
b 29 Oct 1830   on tombstone
Nottoway Co. VA
m 17 July 1861 license
Williamson Co. Tx
d —"— 30 May 1866, buried
Liberty Hill Cem.

#27 Sarah Warren Orgain
b 2 April 1840
Henry Co. TN
d 1 May 1928
Stamford, Jones Co. Tx

52 George Washington Harrison
b c 1801
Petersburg, VA
m 20 Nov 1827
VA
d 1850-1851
Victoria, Victoria Co. Tx

53 Margaret Emma Bland
b 11 July 1811
Nottoway Co., VA
(on tombstone)
d 10 Sept 1867
Victoria, Victoria Co. Tx
Info on tombstone
Evergreen Cem. Victoria

54 Rev. Sterling Orgain
b 31 Jan 1787
prob. Brunswick Co VA
m c 1815-1817 prob. TN
d 4 Jan 1878
Williamson Co. Tx
Tombstone: Shiloh Cem.

55 Mary E.   Jones
b 17 Jan 1798 NC
d 23 Jan 1878
Williamson Co. Tx
Tombstone: Shiloh Cem.

104 Rev. William Harrison
b c 1730
m 1789 Petersburg VA
d 20 Nov 1813 —"—

105 Nancy (Ann) Vaughan
b 1769 Petersburg VA
d 2 July 1829 —"—

106 Edward Bland
b 1767
Prince George Co. VA
m 29 June 1808
Nottoway Co VA
d 1831 —"—

107 Rebecca Jones
b 1791
d 1841

108 William Darby Orgain
b
m
d 1820-1824
Brunswick Co. VA

109
b
d

110 Rev. Edmund Jones
b c 1765-1770 NC
m
after 1 Feb 1836
d Madison Co. TN

111
b
d

210 David Vaughan

211 Winnefred

212 Peter Bland

See
Chart
#

Compiled by: EAC
Documentation on the back
and on accompanying group
sheets.

A pedigree chart shows one person's ancestors.

organized. This means deciding how to record your research notes and how to file them so you can find them easily. There's no right or wrong way: Do what works best for you. There are probably twice as many ways to organize as there are genealogists, because nearly everybody changes procedures at some point. Some people work best with file folders stored in boxes or cabinets. Others work best with three-ring binders housed in bookcases. Many use a combination of these. Some find index cards useful for master lists. Most genealogists agree, however, that spiral notebooks aren't a good choice and the dining room table isn't the best option for holding our stuff. Yes, everybody usually tries the table and learns that Thanksgiving dinner or Mother's Day brunch creates a real kink in the filing system.

Whether using folders or binders, most genealogists keep all papers pertaining to a given ancestor or couple in one folder or notebook. Even those who store notes and documents in file folders at home may use notebooks for research. Many genealogists sort research notes first by surname or individual, then by location, then by topic or type of source where information is found. For example, let's say your focus ancestor is named Polk, so you have a notebook dedicated to Polk research. When you find this ancestor in North Carolina and then, earlier in life, in Delaware, you divide the notebook into a section for each state. If the ancestor lived in more than one county in North Carolina, you'll probably subdivide the North Carolina section by county. Behind the county dividers are subdivisions for land, marriage, cemetery, and other kinds of records. As notes accumulate, you may need a separate binder for each state. The same ideas can apply to file folders.

Another important but easily overlooked

Family Group Sheet of the <u>Robertson-Arnold</u> **Family**

	Source #			Source #
<u>Thomas Roberson</u> Full name of husband This is the way he signed his name.	1, 3, 10, 12	Birth date c. 1807-1809		10, 11
		Birth place		
His father		Death date c. June 30-July 1, 1842	}	12
		Death place Putnam Co. Georgia		
His mother with maiden name		Burial place		
<u>Elizabeth C. Arnold</u> Full maiden name of wife	1, 3, 10	Birth date c. 1808-1809		7, 10
Arnold		Birth place Georgia		7, 14
Her father		Death date 1857-1868		15, 16, 17, 21
<u>Elizabeth Allen</u>	2	Death place probably Caddo Parish, Louisiana		
Her mother with maiden name daughter of James Allen	2	Burial place		

Other Spouses She m 2nd Isaac Croom, Sr., Caddo Parish LA, bond dated 22 June 1846. By Isaac, she had daughter Louisiana, in 1848 Source #s 4, 7, 15, 17	Marriage date, place, etc. 18 August 1833, Putnam Co. Georgia Source #s 3

Children of this marriage	Birth date & place	Death date, place, & burial place	Marriage date, place & spouse
1. Ann Maria Robertson Source #s 19	1835-1836 probably in Putnam Co. GA #7,8	1873-1880 probably in Madison Co. TN #13, 20	Isaac Croom, Jr. 15 Sept. 1856 Caddo Parish LA #5
2. Thomas James Robertson Source #s 18	1841-1842 probably in Putnam Co GA #7, 9	after 1871 possibly in Arkansas #18	M.A. Gerrald 28 Dec 1865 Caddo Parish LA #6
  Source #s			
  Source #s			

aspect of organizing is consistency in the size of paper you use. Standard 8½" x 11" paper works best. If you can avoid using notepads and backs of envelopes, you'll have better luck keeping up with your notes.

Some researchers prefer taking notes on laptop computers instead of paper. Others transcribe all their notes to the computer when they return home from researching. Whether paper or electronic, your notes need to be filed for later study by name, location, and source. You may try several filing ideas to determine what works best for you. Whatever you choose needs to be easy for you to maintain and use—after all, unpuzzling your past is an adventure that may span many years.

FILLING IN THE BLANKS

Some basic research techniques and tips can help make sure that your puzzle pieces come together. Here are nine principles to keep in mind as you start digging into your roots:

1. Names. Always look for names: full names, middle names, parents' names, and spouses' and children's names. Names can be important clues to the past. Family surnames, for example, have long been adopted as given names: Blalock, Vincent, Major, and so on. Middle names can also be clues, often to the maiden name of a mother or grandmother—but only clues, because there's no guarantee that Hardy Green Carter had an ancestor named Hardy or Green. If Hardy and cousins had the middle name Green, there's a reason. You'd want to find out why this pattern exists and what it may mean in discovering your ancestors.

Regardless of names in vogue at any given time, plenty of children in the English-speaking world (perhaps too many from the genealogical point of view) have been called Mary, Sarah, Elizabeth, James, John, and William, especially when these were "family" names. You'll become acutely aware of names when trying to sort out ancestors. Is the William Smith who keeps appearing in the county records one man or three? Did Samuel Stone have one wife named Mary or two? Just because the name is the same, you can't assume it's your ancestor.

For female ancestors, search for maiden names because they help identify the parent generations; use maiden names on charts instead of married names. When genealogists speak of the children of James Brown and Melissa Gray, we're not implying that the couple had children out of wedlock; we're identifying the wife's maiden name.

Spelling of names varies. If one brother dropped the *e* from the end of his surname (Brown) and the other brother kept the *e* (Browne), you have to look for both. A person in the records with or without the *e* could belong to either branch. Remember, many of your ancestors couldn't read and write, or spell their own names. Regional accents and accents of those for whom English was a second language also meant that clerks didn't always understand spoken names and had to guess the spelling. Clerks wrote down what they heard

and sometimes spelled words phonetically and creatively: *Right* for Wright and *Eldridge* for Heldreth. Before working on a focus ancestor in documents and publications, list ways the name might be pronounced and spelled. Look for all the variations in indexes and records as you research. Don't ignore something just because the name is spelled differently from what you expect.

2. Family stories. Interviewing relatives and friends is a good way to collect family stories and oral traditions. Some are simply fun and add a human quality to the family history. Others have a genealogical character: where folks came from and when, who a great-great-grandparent was, how one ancestor became the hero of a certain battle, how we are descended from a certain general or president. These tales often contain some truth, but many are simply a matter of "creative remembering." The "hero" may have participated in that battle, or the family may have lived near the battlefield when the "hero" was five. The general or president may have the same name as an ancestor with no kinship whatsoever. Your job is to use such stories as clues for research to try to determine the truth.

3. Cluster genealogy. Your ancestors didn't live in a vacuum but in a family, an extended family, and a community. They lived, worked, and worshiped with, fought beside, served on juries with, did business with, married and were buried near relatives, friends, and neighbors. To trace your ancestors successfully, you'll eventually need to develop and study a cluster of their relatives and associates. Make a habit of collecting information on other known relatives, especially siblings, and those suspected of being related.

4. Networking. Finding cousins, even distant ones, is often a way to increase your knowledge of a focus ancestor. Many researchers use genealogical periodicals and the Internet, with its thousands of genealogy Web sites, to find other people working on the same surname, the same ancestor, or the same county. Computerized databases and electronic products contain millions of names, and many genealogists search them for ancestors.

The answers found in such periodicals, Web sites, and databases vary greatly. Much depends on the quality of work done by the people who compiled the information. The best researchers consider the information they find in this way to be clues. They try to track down the original source of the information, evaluate it, compare it with other sources, and be convinced of its accuracy before accepting it. Less cautious researchers swallow the findings whole, even if they say that two siblings were born four months apart and a year after their mother died. Many such databases give "family trees" going back a thousand years or more. These are usually more wishful thinking than fact. Even though people may want Charlemagne as an ancestor, proving that he actually was will be next to impossible. It's much better to work carefully backward through fewer generations and know that what you have is solid, in-depth, documented, and still interesting.

5. Continuing education. Genealogists have many opportunities to learn as they go. You can join genealogical societies, including ones in the state or county where your focus ancestors lived. You can attend local, regional, and national conferences. You can begin to assemble your own library of reference books, or read genealogy periodicals. Through societies, at conferences and research facilities, and on the Internet, you can meet, share with, and learn from other genealogists.

6. Sources and evidence. Sources abound. The ones genealogists love most are the sources that give a direct statement of a genealogical fact—a name, date, place, or relationship: "I, John Stephens Barker, give to my grandson John Barker Tomlinson the farm where I now live, at Pearson's Crossroads." "I, Stanley Griggs, con-

sent for my daughter Melissa Jane, age 15, to marry James Roberts." These kinds of statements are often found in such sources as land, military, probate, marriage, and court records. When you can't find direct evidence of this kind, look for clues again. Investigate sources that may lead you indirectly to the facts. Genealogists frequently use such "circumstantial evidence" to establish relationships. But you must not jump to conclusions. Your goal is to establish genealogical facts from the best available sources, using as many as it takes to make a convincing "case."

The best sources are usually the ones closest in time to the events they report, especially firsthand accounts. A clerk's recording of a marriage, land transaction, or will is usually the closest we can come to these events. But even these official records can contain copying errors. Published books are at least one more step away from the most original record and therefore have added potential for human error. So you can't automatically accept the handwritten or printed word as absolute truth.

7. After "home work," then what? You won't find all your answers at home, or in any one place. After your initial "home work," you should visit genealogy collections in libraries, history and reference sections of university libraries, cemeteries, and courthouses. You might start your outside research in the federal census records. Every ten years since 1790, the United States government has counted the population to apportion seats in the House of Representatives. Census records through 1930 are widely accessible on microfilm, and some are on CD-ROM. Ask about availability at your local library or at a Family History Center operated by the Church of Jesus Christ of Latter-day Saints. (You can find the center nearest you online at <www.familysearch.org/Eng/Library/FHC/frameset_fhc.asp>.)

Information in the census records varies. The most comprehensive for genealogists are those for 1850 and afterward because they name members of free households and indicate ages, birthplaces, occupations, and other details. Like other records, they can contain mistakes and omissions, but they're great and fascinating resources.

Genealogy books and microfilm copies of newspapers and county records are sometimes available on interlibrary loan through local public libraries. Many state historical societies or state libraries lend these kinds of sources within their own state. One large rental library is the American Genealogical Lending Library (AGLL), part of the Heritage Quest genealogy publishing company [(800) 760-2455; <www.heritagequest.com>]. Some genealogical societies, such as the New England Historic Genealogical Society [(888) 906-3447; <www.newenglandancestors.org>], allow members to rent books from the society library.

If you have a Family History Center within reach, you have access to the resources of the church's monumental Family History Library in Salt Lake City. Renting microfilm and microfiche is easy, and coverage is virtually worldwide. Volunteer staff at the centers can also show you how to use their computerized and electronic databases. Many of the Family History Library's resources are also available via the FamilySearch Web site <www.familysearch.org>.

8. Plan, research, and review. Written plans for research help keep you on target. From the unknowns in your information, decide what you want to look for, and list your research questions before you go to research. Other tips:

- Don't try to reach back too quickly by skipping a generation.
- Be open to discarding preconceived ideas and oral tradition.
- Follow up on leads and clues. A valuable clue, for example, might be a seemingly unimportant list of jurors with your ancestor's name on it. To the genealogist, this proves the ancestor was alive and in that place on that date.
- Think as you research: Is this the right time and place for this ancestor? Does the information make sense for this ancestor? What makes me believe this really is my ancestor?
- Each time you research, review and analyze what you have found as you plan what to do next. Did you get any direct answers? What clues did each record give you? What conclusion do the facts support? Or what further research do you need to do before you can reach a conclusion?

9. How do you know? As you research, make note of where you find each piece of information. This process of documenting your research is essential. If you found Aunt Mattie's birthdate on the back of her baby picture in Grandma's handwriting, say so. If Grandpa's death certificate names his parents, note it. For any source you use, write down as much identifying information as possible, including page numbers. You need enough for a complete footnote or bibliography entry (remember those from back in school?). Why bother? First, you may need to look at the information again later to check details. Second, others may want to look at the same source to see whether it helps their research. And finally, you need to be able to defend your answer to the questions, "How do you know?" and "Where did you get that?"

Whether or not you're new to genealogy, these suggestions will help you research within your family or in public records. Genealogists who are focused, organized, cautious, thorough, continually learning, thinking as they research, explicit in documenting their work, and patient are more successful. They're the ones who get the most out of—and have the most fun— unpuzzling their past.

Finding Your Family Tree Across the U.S. and Canada

BY DAVID A. FRYXELL

So you've caught "roots mania," as *Time* magazine called the genealogy boom in a cover story several years ago, but you're not sure how to get started. Or maybe you've dabbled in researching your family history, but you're not certain about your next steps. You might even have gone a long way in your genealogy, only to hit the notorious "brick wall."

In any case, the family tree facts you need lie outside your front door and even beyond your local library and courthouse. Whether you plan to visit archives and other remote repositories in person or virtually, by way of the Internet, *The Family Tree Guide Book* has what you need to plan your search for ancestral answers. To make the most of any trip, use this book's advice on everything from places to stay and dine to historic attractions along the way.

The Mid-Continent Public Library in Independence, Missouri

But before you start packing—even before you fire up your modem and start traveling in cyberspace—make sure you're really prepared for your journey into your past. Don't waste valuable research time on the road doing tasks that you could have accomplished at your leisure from the comfort of your own home. Don't find yourself at last at the archive that has the records you need, only to discover that you didn't do the homework necessary to make the most of this treasure trove.

SEVEN STEPS TO SUCCESS

Start your exploration for ancestors across the United States and Canada with these seven simple steps:

1. Gather what you already know about your family. Yes, your journey begins right at home. Take a shoebox or file folder and collect family records, old photos, letters, diaries, photocopies from family Bibles, even newspaper clippings.

You'll be surprised at how much you already know about your family history. Obituaries clipped from old newspapers can give you vital clues about your ancestors' names, their siblings, key dates in their lives, and places where they lived—and where you might track down more facts later. Letters and diaries can give you not only family facts but also a dramatic feel for what your ancestors' lives were like. Photographs can be filled with clues, even if they're not part of the image. For example, old professional portraits typically have the photographer's name somewhere on them. Directories are available to help you find out where a photographer worked and when, which can help you set your pictured ancestors in time and place.

As you research these "home sources," pay particular attention to clues about places. This book, organized by place, will become much more valuable to you as you discover exactly where your ancestors lived, died, and (most important to the genealogist!) left records.

2. Talk to your relatives. Ask your parents, grandparents, aunts, and uncles about their memories. Don't ask just about facts and dates—get the stories about their growing up and the ancestors they remember. Try to phrase questions with *why, how* and *what*. Bring along props, such as old photos, to get the conversation going.

Since interview sessions longer than an hour or so can be pretty tiring, you may need several sessions to get what you're after. Focus on interviewing one person at a time. You'll want to tape-record your interviews, but take notes as well so you won't have to transcribe the entire tape.

3. Put it on paper. Write down what you know so you can decide what you don't know yet. Start with a five-generation **pedigree chart,** which you can download for free from <www.familytreemagazine.com/forms/download.html>. This will help you record your ancestors' names and the dates and places—don't forget those places!—of their birth, marriage, and death.

Another helpful form is the **family group sheet,** which you can also download for free on the *Family Tree Magazine* Web site. You should start one of these for every family—father, mother, and children—that you research.

You can annotate your charts with simple footnotes and note the sources of your information on the back. Keeping track of where you got what piece of information is important as you later try to evaluate sometimes-conflicting data about your ancestors and avoid going over the same ground more than once. And it's a lot easier to start recording your sources right from the beginning than to go back later and try to reconstruct where you got Aunt Harriet's birth date or Great-Grandpa Joe's birthplace.

Eventually, you may want to transfer the data from your paper charts to one of the many popular genealogy software programs. You might even choose to skip the paper and jump right to the computer. Either way, look for a program that lets you sort data and generate reports by location, so you can easily create a list of all the research you need to do in any place you visit.

4. Focus your search. What are the blanks in your family tree? Don't try to fill them in all at once—focus on someone from the most recent generation where your chart is missing information. Try to solve that mystery first, then work backward in time.

5. Search the Internet. The Internet is a terrific place to find leads and share information—but don't expect to "find your whole family tree" online. Some of the most exciting and popular databases on the Web let you search for files called **GEDCOM** files. GEDCOM, short for Genealogical Data Communication, is a universal file format for family trees in electronic form. All of the popular genealogy software programs let you create and import GEDCOM files. Someone may have already researched a branch of your family history and shared it as a GEDCOM file. Besides genealogy Web sites, you can also try searching for surnames using general search engines such as Google <www.google.

com> and Alta Vista <www.altavista.com>.

Don't assume that everything you find in a pedigree database or elsewhere online is accurate. No one checks or validates this uploaded data. Try to find corroborating evidence for every fact you download from the Internet. Don't pick up someone else's mistakes and pass them on to future generations!

You can also network online with other researchers tracing your surname. This can be an excellent way to virtually "visit" your ancestral stomping grounds before you trek there in person.

6. Explore specific Web sites. Once you've searched for your family surnames, try Web sites specifically about your ethnic heritage or the parts of the country where your relatives lived. You may even find Web sites about your family created by distant relatives researching the same family tree. *Family Tree Magazine*'s annual guide to the 101 best family-history Web sites, posted online at <www.familytreemagazine. com>, is a great place to start.

Throughout this book, you'll find hundreds of Web site addresses (URLs). Note that they all appear within angle brackets—< >—to make it easy to tell where the Web addresses begin and end. Not all URLs begin with "www" or end in ".com," so always type exactly what you see between the brackets. If a Web site doesn't seem to work, first make sure you've typed it correctly. If you have, then simply wait a few hours or a day and try again; the site's server may be temporarily on the fritz. If the URL still doesn't work, remember that Web site addresses do change—check the *Family Tree Magazine* Web site for updates, or try searching for the name of the site in a general search engine to track down the new location. You can also check The Internet Archive <www.archive.org>, which has more than 10 billion archived Web pages from 1996 to the present.

Many of the Web sites in this book are useful for gathering background information, checking on facilities' hours, and otherwise preparing for visits in person. Make sure you take advantage of the online catalogs of libraries and archives to find what you want before you go; save your precious research time for looking at actual records, books, and documents.

Increasingly, too, you can access real records as well as abstracts and transcripts of real records online. The popular site for Ellis Island's immigration records <www.ellisisland.org>, discussed in the Mid-Atlantic section, is the best-known such online database; look for others throughout this book. The important thing isn't how you trace your ancestors from coast to coast; it's finding the answers you're after!

7. Discover your local Family History Center. Since 1938, members of the Church of Jesus Christ of Latter-day Saints, popularly known as the Mormons, have been gathering and archiving millions of genealogical records about people of all faiths. Church archivists travel the world in pursuit of original documents in churches, courthouses, and libraries and microfilming them to add to the storehouse of data in the church's Granite Mountain Record Vault. The church makes copies of this vast archive—information on some two billion people—available to the public at its five-story, 142,000-square-foot Family History Library in Salt Lake City. You can plan your visit to this mecca for genealogists with our in-depth guide on page 202.

But you don't have to trek to Salt Lake City to tap the world's largest genealogical library. You can search its catalog via the Web at <www.familysearch.org>, and you can borrow materials from the main library in Salt Lake City via any of the more than thirty-four hundred Family History Centers located around the globe. Chances are, there's one right in your own backyard. We list all the Family History Centers in the United States and Canada geographically throughout this book, so it's easy to find one near where you live—or when you're on the road.

You don't have to be a Church member to use the Family History Centers, which are staffed by knowledgeable, friendly volunteers who can help you get started. Call before you visit, or check the hours of operation online at <www.familysearch.org>; hours vary widely.

PUTTING IT ON THE MAP

When you're ready to hit the trail and start retracing your ancestors' footsteps, once again planning is the key to success. Preparing for a family history research trip starts, of course, with the choice of destination. Gather what you know about where your ancestors lived and how they migrated across the country. Consider actually mapping your family tree to help plan your trip; some genealogy software will do this for you.

Work backward in time, starting with the present day and what you know and pushing into the past. If you live in Arkansas and you think your ancestors got there from Virginia by way of North Carolina and Tennessee, look for clues in Tennessee first; don't skip their in-between stops and try to find them in Virginia right away. Similarly, before you can trace your immigrant ancestors "across the pond"—to the old country in Europe, for example—you need to complete your research in North America. (That's one reason this book is so important! Whether your roots go back to Italy or Ireland, Africa or Asia, or a country you have yet to determine, you need to first explore your ancestry in the United States and Canada.)

Focus on the questions you want to answer and where those answers might be. Organize your family tree "targets" by location and then, with the help of this book, by specific resource in each city or county. Try to group together everything you might want to research at the courthouse in your great-grandmother's home-town, for example.

Next, advises professional genealogist and author Christine Rose, reduce everything to a single page. "Don't try to go into a courthouse or other records location with a thick file of papers," says Rose, who spends six months a year on the road doing genealogical research. "Focus on what exactly you're trying to find—parents' birth dates? A maiden name?"

Make sure the records you want are really where you expect them to be. Even something as seemingly straightforward as county vital records (birth, marriage, and death certificates, for example) may not be in the county court-house. As the United States grew westward and its population boomed, many large counties spun off new counties and redrew boundaries. If a county was created in, say, 1850, that county's pre-1850 records may be stored in the court-house of the original, "parent" county. See the resources at the end of this chapter for help in puzzling out what county was what when.

Smart planning also means checking whether the courthouses and other places you want to visit will be open when you're there. Don't assume! Arriving at last only to find a "Sorry, We're Closed" sign is a sure way to wreck a family history trip. Remember, for example, that some Southern states still celebrate Robert E. Lee's birthday (January 19) as a holiday. Use the phone numbers and Web sites throughout this book to make sure you can find answers instead of locked doors. It's also worth asking in advance whether you need to make an appoint-ment or reserve equipment, such as microfilm readers.

Your big genealogical research trip is not the time to test your skills for the first time, by the way. Don't wait until you're standing in front of great-grandpa's farm to learn how to use that new camera, for instance. Or if you've never done a tombstone rubbing, practice before you get to the ancestral resting place.

FACT-FINDING DESTINATIONS

Here are some key stops for your family history research, and how to get the most out of your visit at each:

• **Courthouses:** Keep in mind that helping traveling genealogists is not the primary duty of courthouse clerks. "Never tell clerks you're there for genealogical purposes," advises Rose. "They're busy, and as soon as a genealogist comes in the door they may become antagonistic, thinking they're going to encounter some long-winded story."

Start by asking for the indexes to the records for the period you're researching. Be pleasant and professional, and respect the clerk's time. "Sometimes later on the clerk gets curious and comes to ask me what I'm doing," says Rose. If that happens to you, then you might make an ally. Be prepared for that: Go to the courthouse armed with self-addressed stamped envelopes (SASEs) to leave behind in case a clerk comes across something useful to you after you've gone home.

Don't limit your courthouse search to vital records. The person you're seeking might be named in old civil case records, perhaps because he sued (or got sued by) someone. Witnesses to real estate transactions sometimes were family members, so scour these records for names.

• **Local genealogical societies and libraries with genealogy collections:** Remember to consult the online catalog from home so you can arrive prepared with a list of books and documents you want to see. At the library, look beyond the obvious genealogical archives: City directories, for example, can be essential tools for finding your relatives.

• **Cemeteries and funeral homes:** You may have to do other on-site research—looking at death records in the courthouse or obituaries in old newspapers, for example—to find the right cemetery. Once you do, don't just eye the old tombstones; visit the cemetery office, if there is one. There and at the funeral home, try to learn who bought the burial plot and paid for the funeral; chances are, they're your relatives, too.

• **Churches:** Before you visit the old family church, find out if that's where records are kept. You might need to visit a denominational office or a diocesan archive instead. Besides baptismal, marriage, and funeral records, check old church newsletters, Sunday school rosters, and even church committee minutes.

• **Newspapers:** Preparation is a must here— don't assume you can stroll in and help yourself to a newspaper's "morgue." These files are primarily for the paper's staff, after all. Policies on public access vary, so call first. The old newspapers you need may not even be archived at the newspaper's offices any more, but they may be housed at local libraries or historical societies. Again, go beyond the obvious birth announcements and obits: Look for your ancestors' names in news stories, business updates, and (especially in small-town papers) chatty reports of trips taken and parties hosted.

These resources are only the beginning of what you can tap on a research trip. Try school records and college alumni files (as much as privacy regulations allow), local veterans clubs and service clubs, and places your ancestors may have worked. Think of yourself as a detective out to solve a case—the mystery of your past.

BRINGING HISTORY TO LIFE

A family-history trip can be more than just a research trip. If your itinerary allows, take the opportunity not only to find your ancestors but also to learn what it was like to walk in their shoes. Museums and historic sites across the country re-create the past, from immigrant tenements to frontier forts; we've listed scores of examples throughout this book and spotlighted dozens in our city guides.

Visiting battlefields and other war-related sites can be a fascinating and moving experience, especially if your ancestors fought in the Civil War or Revolutionary War. To explore beyond what's included in this book, consult the Civil War Preservation Trust [(202) 367-1861; <www.civilwar.org/cwtsites.htm>]. It can help lead you to more than six hundred historic sites in twenty-eight states, ranging from famous battlefields such as Gettysburg to cemeteries and even lighthouses. The National Park Service <www.nps.gov> also has an excellent series of Web sites and guides to battlefields.

When you visit a battlefield, start at the visitors center, advises Carole C. Mahoney, former director of heritage tourism for the Civil War Preservation Trust. Take advantage of the National Park Service guides there who are trained in history, and pick up maps and brochures to orient yourself. In touring the actual site, Mahoney says, "Be respectful of the place. You're on hallowed ground. Often soldiers who fell there are buried there or nearby." Don't get too caught up in the military details, she adds: "It's a nice spot for quiet reflection. Close your eyes, stand quietly, and try to imagine what it was like."

PACK WISELY

Ready to go? Remember to pack smart. First, here's what *not* to take along on your family history trip: your original files, photos, and documents. But *do* make room in your suitcase for these family-history "road warrior" essentials:

- Paper for note taking (some archives don't allow spiral-bound notebooks)
- Pens *and* pencils with a pencil sharpener or a mechanical pencil with lead refills (pens are forbidden in many libraries)
- File folders
- Camera, flash, tripod, batteries, and (unless you have a digital camera) film; consider investing in a close-up lens for photographing documents (ask permission before photographing in archives)
- Maps
- Essential charts and lists of what information you want to find and where
- Self-addressed stamped envelopes to leave behind

- Change for photocopiers, phones, and vending machines
- Comfortable shoes
- Magnifying glass

Other handy items to pack include:
- Insect repellent and an umbrella (if you plan to explore cemeteries and other outdoor sites)
- Rice paper and crayons for tombstone rubbings (again, ask permission before touching the tombstones)
- Tape recorder for dictating notes or for taping an on-site translator
- Camcorder
- Laptop computer or personal digital assistant (PDA) with copies of your files
- Portable scanner
- Gloves and trowel for clearing debris from around tombstones, plus a plastic trash bag to kneel on
- Business cards with your name and address to leave behind

And don't forget to pack your copy of *The Family Tree Guide Book!*

Smart packing can help you get better results from your family history research trips.

GENERAL U.S. AND CANADIAN RESOURCES

(Also see the Canada section for specific Canadian resources.)

Maps and Finding Your Way

Library of Congress Map Collections, 1500–1999 <memory.loc.gov/ammem/gmdhtml/gmdhome.html>: A wealth of historic maps.

MapBlast <www.mapblast.com>: Free, customizable U.S. and Canadian maps.

MapQuest <www.mapquest.com>: Free, customizable U.S. maps.

Maps on Us <www.mapsonus.com>: Free, customizable U.S. maps.

RootsWeb Canadian Resources <www.rootsweb.com/roots-l/canada.html>

RootsWeb United States Resources <www.rootsweb.com/roots-l/usa.html>: Links to RootsWeb resource pages on all fifty states, plus a list of all U.S. counties and other resources.

Tiger Mapping Service <tiger.census.gov>: Search for U.S. place names and generate free maps from census data.

TopoZone.com <www.topozone.com>: Interactive topographic maps of the United States, perfect for getting the lay of your ancestors' land.

United States Geological Survey National Mapping Information <mapping.usgs.gov>: Atlas, geographic names information, and more map links.

State, Province, and County Facts

Cyndi's List <www.cyndislist.com>: Includes hundreds of links to sites about researching in the United States <www.CyndisList.com/ usa.htm> and Canada <www.CyndisList.com/ canada.htm>.

FamilySearch Research Outlines and Guides <www.familysearch.org>: Click on "Search" then "Research Helps," and select a place from the list to find in-depth research outlines and other resources for all fifty states and all Canadian provinces, as well as helpful information on researching in U.S. and Canadian territories.

USGenWeb Project <www.usgenweb.org>: Links for genealogical information in all fifty states, with many individual counties represented.

Vital Records Information <www.vitalrec.com>: Locations of vital records throughout the United States, plus links to foreign data.

Where to Write for Vital Records <www.cdc.gov/nchs/howto/w2w/w2welcom.htm>: U.S. government guide to vital records locations in all fifty states.

New England

REGIONAL GUIDE
BY MAUREEN A. TAYLOR

New England may be small—a mere 66,000 square miles compared to Alaska's 591,000 square miles—but what it lacks in size, it makes up for in variety. Mark Twain once said of New England, "In the spring I have counted 136 different kinds of weather inside of four-and-twenty hours." Besides the rapidly changing weather, each state has a distinct mix of character and history. Forget the stereotypic small-town New England of *Peyton Place* or *Murder, She Wrote* and the horrific happenings of Stephen King's *Maine*. Start researching your New England roots, and you'll discover the true diversity of the region.

To uncover your New England family history you need to shake off everything (well, almost everything) you've heard about the area and acquire a basic historical background on the six New England states: Connecticut, Maine, Massachusetts, New Hampshire, Rhode Island, and Vermont. As every schoolchild knows, the *Mayflower* landed at Plymouth Rock in 1620 in what's now Massachusetts, and the Boston Tea Party and Paul Revere's ride helped launch the American Revolution there. But unless you live in New England, you may not know much more than these fundamentals about the region.

Much of American history started here, and so did many American families. More than one-quarter of the people living in the United States today have some New England connection. That means a lot of people need to know how to find genealogical treasure in the area—and you can find it if you know where to look.

AMERICA'S CRADLE
The classic task in New England genealogy is, of course, tracing a lineage back to the *Mayflower*. In fact, 25 percent of Americans believe they have *Mayflower* ancestry, a 1999 Scripps Howard/Ohio University poll found.

According to the General Society of *Mayflower* Descendants, however, thirty-five million people worldwide may be able to count at least one of the twenty-six original Pilgrims as an ancestor; this means that roughly half the number of Americans who think they're *Mayflower* descendants actually are. And the society has only about twenty-five thousand members who've actually been able to document their *Mayflower* ancestry. (For more information, see the society's Web site at <www.mayflower.org>. You can find links to other Pilgrim genealogy sites online at <pilgrims.net/plymouth/ROOTS>.)

While not everyone has *Mayflower* roots, most families have ancestors with a restless spirit like that of the Pilgrims. When you look at the genealogy of an early New England family, you can find lots of young men who went "west." Back then, west simply meant west of where they were presently living—Vermont, for example, was part of the "west" then. The promise of new land and economic opportunity lured ambitious men and women to spread throughout New England and eventually beyond.

Be sure to start by retracing your family's migration patterns, working backward in time from the present. Even if you have an old New England surname and an oral tradition of *Mayflower* lineage, it's still necessary to take your research step-by-step rather than leaping to what could be a wrong conclusion. I've seen researchers decide to skip a century trying to make a link to an early New England settler. Don't do it! You just might end up in the wrong family tree entirely. Take time to examine home sources, interview relatives, and look carefully at each document you find.

RELIGION AND CIRCUMSTANCE

You can increase your chances of discovering family information by studying the time periods and areas in which your ancestors lived. Don't confine your research to military conflicts or political happenings. Religion formed the foundation of many seventeenth-century New England communities, and religious records are some of the earliest resources available.

The Pilgrims weren't the only religious refugees to populate the region. Since the founders of Massachusetts had a habit of banishing religious leaders who disagreed with them, these founders were in part responsible for the settlement of the rest of the region. Individuals branching out from the original English settlements in Massachusetts settled Maine, Connecticut, New Hampshire, and Rhode Island.

Several banished ministers, including one woman, founded Rhode Island's four original towns—Providence, Portsmouth, Warwick, and Newport. Other religious dissenters who sought refuge in Rhode Island included members of the Society of Friends, known as Quakers. Society of Friends records are among some of the best for genealogists because of the amount of detail included. (You can learn all about the records on deposit at the Rhode Island Historical Society Library, for example, in Richard Stattler's *Guide to the Records of the Religious Society of Friends (Quakers) in New England* [Rhode Island Historical Society, $22]). Most of the eighteenth-century Rhode Islanders were Quakers, so you may have Quaker roots you don't even know about.

Other ministers from Massachusetts settled Connecticut. Thomas Hooker established Hartford in 1635, then banded together with the inhabitants of Wethersfield and Windsor to form the colony of Connecticut. Essentially, early Connecticut had two separate governmental units: The New Haven area remained distinct from Hooker's Congregationalist stronghold. Throughout the Colonial period, only about a dozen families controlled most political offices, strengthening their dominance through intermarriage.

Maine was actually a part of Massachusetts for almost two centuries, until 1820, with towns clustered along the seacoast and the northern border. If you have early Maine ancestors, you may find material on them in Massachusetts records. On the other hand, your Maine ancestors might have been closet Canadians: Great Britain disputed the ownership of the northern edge of Maine until the Webster-Ashburton Treaty of 1842 finally set the boundary between Maine and Canada.

Samuel de Champlain and a group of French people tried to settle in Maine in 1604 but later moved into Vermont (that state's largest body of water, Lake Champlain, is named for him). Later migrants to Vermont arrived in the colony from Connecticut, traveling northward along the Connecticut River and settling in the valleys surrounding the Green Mountains. Independent-minded Vermonters fought off land claims from New York and actually formed an independent republic from 1777 to 1791. Vermont was also the first state to provide voting rights to all males regardless of race or religion and to abolish the land-ownership requirement for voting.

As in Vermont, geography dictated the settlement patterns of New Hampshire. Initially, migrants from Essex County, Massachusetts, grouped around the Piscatagua River or the seacoast. Later immigrants, including many Ulster Scots, came from overseas. Much like the other New England states, New Hampshire became increasingly ethnically diverse, attracting French Canadians, Poles, Greeks, and others.

NEW ENGLAND RESEARCH

Once you have a grasp on New England's history and geography, you will be ready to explore the region's genealogical riches. These include Colonial census records, court documents, vital records, and religious papers, all extending back to the 1600s. All you need to know to discover your family's unique place in New England's past is what's available and where to look.

Some research is easier in New England because, unlike other areas of the country, all

New England states enacted civil registration by 1866. According to Ralph Crandall in *Genealogical Research in New England* (NEHGS), "Englishmen were deeply rooted in the habit of record keeping at the parish, county and national level." The early settlers brought with them their need for civil as well as religious records. Starting with the earliest settlements, to create order in their communities in the wilderness, town and city clerks maintained records of births, marriages, and deaths. Unfortunately, the Boston clerk neglected to record vital records for the late eighteenth century, leaving a large gap for genealogists.

A variety of census records for the New England states is available. Federal census records, including an 1890 veterans census, exist for 1790 to 1920 for every state except Vermont, which got started a year late. Vermont joined the United States in 1791 and then undertook a census of its citizens. Records of Colonial censuses and state censuses also exist for most New England states. For example, Rhode Island enumerated residents on its own every ten years from 1865 to 1935, and Massachusetts took state censuses in 1855 and 1865. Only fragments of Maine's first state census in 1837 still exist.

Since military service was a requirement in seventeenth-century New England, extensive materials can help the research of anyone with an ancestor who served. Rhode Island took a special military census for 1777, and Connecticut has one for 1917. A fire destroyed Vermont's original military records from before 1920.

Newspaper coverage for New England is also extensive. More than 447 newspapers flourished here from 1690 to 1820. Transcriptions of many of the personal notices of genealogical interest that appeared in these papers have been collected by two publishers that specialize in New England materials: the New England Historic Genealogical Society (NEHGS) and Picton Press.

IMMIGRANT NATION

The influx of new immigrant groups and the advent of the Industrial Revolution changed the character of the region—and created new records for genealogists to tap. An English immigrant, Samuel Slater, started the first factory to manufacture cotton thread in Pawtucket, Rhode Island, in 1790. Soon after, textile factories began appearing in towns across New England. Many immigrants came here to work in shipbuilding, whaling, the lumber industry (which supplied masts for English ships), marble and granite quarries, or even in the tobacco industry that flourished in the Connecticut River Valley. The occupational history of your ancestor can direct you to new resources to study your family.

You may also need to consult immigration records. Immigrants arrived not only at Ellis Island <www.ellisisland.org> but also through many of New England's coastal seaports such as Providence, Portland, and Boston, as well as along the border between New England and Canada. You can consult several National Archives and Records Administration <www.archives.gov> publications, including *Copies of Lists of Passengers Arriving at Miscellaneous Ports on the Atlantic and Gulf Coasts 1820-1873* (M575) and Canadian border entries known as the *St. Albans Arrival Records* (M1461-M1465). Researchers with early ancestors need to use *The Great Migration* series by Robert Charles Anderson.

Don't forget that New Englanders did more than their share to create today's industrialized, technological world. Among New England inventors are Eli Whitney (cotton gin), Charles Thurber (typewriter), Charles Goodyear (rubber), and Russian immigrant Igor Sikorsky (helicopter). If you have New England roots you should investigate patent records to see if anyone in your family developed an invention. See the U.S. Patent and Trademark Office's Web site for information <www.uspto.gov/main/patents.htm>.

Of course, the first "immigrants" to New England were the native populations who already lived there when the Puritans arrived in 1620. Even before then, Europeans established trade with many of the tribes, including the Algonquin, Abnaki, Mahican, and Pennacook. Settlers lived alongside these tribes and fought beside these native people in Colonial conflicts. For more on researching Native American roots, see the special section at the end of this book.

Slavery was not unknown in New England. The "triangle trade" of sugar, rum, and slaves made the fortunes of many prominent merchant families. New England abolitionists, however, were prominent in advocating the end of the slave trade, and each New England state abolished slavery before the Civil War. Barbara W. Brown and James M. Rose's *Black Roots in Southeastern Connecticut, 1650-1900* (New London County Historical Society, $35) is a valuable resource for researchers of African-American roots, as is Franklin A. Dorman's *Twenty Families of Color in Early Massachusetts, 1742-1998* (NEHGS, $35). See the special section later in this book for some specifics on researching African-American roots.

MAKING THE PILGRIMAGE

Once you've gathered all the information you can from home, you may want to go to New England to research your roots there. Many genealogists plan spring and fall trips to the area to take advantage of the beautiful scenery. Whenever you visit, make sure you go prepared.

First, create a list of publications and records that you want to consult. To do this, use online card catalogs, Web sites, and the resources listed in this book. A quick check of the Family History Library catalog <www.familysearch.org/Eng/Library/FHLC/frameset_fhlc.asp> before you leave home can provide sources. Many early New England records are on microfilm and available through Family History Centers in your area.

New England boasts some of the oldest and largest research facilities in the country, from the extensive collections of the Boston Public Library and the New England Historic Genealogical Society to the Connecticut State Library in Hartford. Connecticut, Rhode Island, Massachusetts, and New Hampshire have large groups of records in centralized locations, but keep in mind that many records are also located in the town halls and public libraries in small towns. Since some repositories operate with only limited hours, always call ahead to verify when they're open; also check on their policies for researchers. Connecticut researchers, for instance, need to present a genealogical society membership card before many clerks will let them use material.

Unfortunately, one of the most persistent myths about New England research is that everything is already published. While many of the early town vital records and histories are in book form, on CD-ROM, or on the Web, there is still a tremendous amount of material held at the town or county level. Look at everything available to you at home before you leave, then spend your time in New England mining these primary records.

MAKING THE MOST OF RESOURCES

Despite New England's unusual wealth of records, don't expect to find all your ancestors instantly. The geographic and political divisions of the area can challenge even experienced genealogists. Use a good gazetteer to locate tiny places and pronounce place names often derived from Native American languages. Rhode Island, for instance, has just thirty-nine cities and towns but more than one hundred villages.

The inaccuracy of early maps and land grants often created land disputes in New England's Colonial era. At one time Connecticut and Massachusetts both claimed ownership of part of Rhode Island, which means records from the southern part of that state can be found in all

three states. Most of the New England states had similar boundary disputes with their neighbors. Once you identify the name of the town or village in which your ancestor lived, consult Marcia Melnyk's *Genealogist's Handbook of New England Research* to discover the proper place to look for records.

New Englanders come to understand the quirkiness of their region and learn to live with the unpredictable weather. New England genealogists love tapping the wealth of resources here and easily following their ancestral wanderings with day trips—nothing is very far apart, and the scenery in-between is beautiful. Whether your ancestors came here on the *Mayflower* or arrived to enlist in the Industrial Revolution, finding your New England roots can give you much cause for thanksgiving.

ORGANIZATIONS & ARCHIVES

American Antiquarian Society
185 Salisbury St.
Worcester, MA 01609
(508) 755-5221
<www.american antiquarian.org>

Boston Public Library
700 Boylston St.
Boston, MA 02116
(617) 536-5400
<www.bpl.org>

National Archives-New England Region
380 Trapelo Rd.
Waltham, MA 02452
(781) 647-8104
Fax: (781) 647-8088
<www.archives.gov/ facilities/ma/boston.html>

New England Historic Genealogical Society (NEHGS)
101 Newbury St.
Boston, MA 02116
(617) 536-5740 or

(888) 286-3447
Fax: (617) 536-7307
<www.newengland ancestors.org>

RESOURCES

Bible Records from the ManuscriptCollections of the New England Historic Genealogical Society
(NEHGS, $39.99), CD-ROM

Digging for Genealogical Treasure in New England Town Records
by Ann Smith Lainhart (NEHGS, $15)

Genealogical Dictionary of Maine and New Hampshire
by Sybil Noyes, Charles T. Libby, and Walter G. Davis (Genealogical Publishing Co., out of print)

Genealogical Dictionary of the First Settlers of New England
by James Savage (Genealogical Publishing Co., $150)

Genealogical Research in New England
edited by Ralph J. Crandall (Genealogical Publishing Co., out of print)

Genealogist's Handbook of New England Research,
4th ed., by Marcia Melnyk (NEHGS, $19.95)

The Great Migration Begins: Immigrants to New England, 1620-1633
(3 vols.) by Robert Charles Anderson (NEHGS, $125)

The Great Migration: Immigrants to New England, 1634-1635
(6 vols. to be published; first 2 vols. available at press time) by Robert Charles Anderson (NEHGS, $45 per volume)

Great Migration Begins: Immigrants to New England, 1620-1633
(NEHGS, $59.95), CD-ROM

New England Marriages Prior to 1700
by Clarence A. Torrey (NEHGS, $89.99), CD-ROM

PERIODICALS

The New England Historical and Genealogical Register
(1847-) and *New England Ancestors*, New England Historic Genealogical Society, 101 Newbury St., Boston, MA 02116

WEB SITES

Descendants of *Mayflower* Passengers mailing list
To subscribe, send e-mail to MAYFLOWER-L-request@rootsweb.com with the single word "subscribe" in the message subject and body.

New England Archivists: Archives in New England
<www.lib.umb.edu/newengarch/nearch.html>: Contains a list of archives arranged by state.

NEW-ENGLAND-HISTO-RY-L mailing list
To subscribe, send e-mail to NEW-ENGLAND-HIS-TORY-L-request@rootsweb.com with the single word "subscribe" in the message subject and body.

BOSTON

BY MAUREEN A. TAYLOR

Boston is the third-largest genealogical research center in the country (after Washington, DC, and Salt Lake City) because of the high concentration of libraries and archives in the area. Many of them are located either within walking distance of each other or on public transportation lines. The oldest public transportation system in the United States, the **Massachusetts Bay Transportation Authority** (MBTA; <www.mbta.com>), affectionately known as the "T" by residents, is organized by color and easy to use. Rail lines connect to Logan Airport and Amtrak, and the MBTA offers a special visitor package ($6 a day) that you can purchase online. So leave your car at home and save on parking.

A first stop in Boston for any genealogist is

COURTESY OF THE NEW ENGLAND HISTORIC GENEALOGICAL SOCIETY

The New England Historic Genealogical Society's library features five floors of books and resources.

the astounding hub of facilities in the Back Bay neighborhood. **The New England Historic Genealogical Society** [101 Newbury Street; (617) 536-5740; <www.newenglandancestors.org>] has extensive holdings on New England, of course, but it also has one of the largest collections of Canadian materials in the United States and a reading room dedicated to British resources. This membership organization collects genealogies and local histories from across the country. Visitors pay a $15-per-day fee applicable to a membership. Recently renovated, the library features five floors of books, manuscripts, CDs, and microfilm packed into one building with librarians on every floor.

A very short walk—not bad even in winter—from the NEHGS deposits you on the steps of the **Boston Public Library** [700 Boylston Street; (617) 536-5400; <www.bpl.org>], the first public library in the United States. The Research Library can keep genealogists enthralled for days with the breadth of its contents: everything from patent materials, U.S. census records, newspapers, and city directories to collection-specific reference desks. You can find genealogical resources in the social sciences reading room and in the microtext division. To use microfilm, apply for a library card in the main section of the library.

A longer walk down Boylston Street takes you to the **Massachusetts Historical Society** [1154 Boylston Street; (617) 536-1608; <www.masshist.org>], which has collections dating from the seventeenth century.

Located outside the city proper are the **Massachusetts State Archives** [220 Morrissey Boulevard; (617) 727-2816; <www.state.ma.us/sec/arc/arcgen/genidx.htm>] and the **Northeast Regional Branch of the National Archives** [380 Trapelo Road, Waltham; (781) 647-8104; <www.archives.gov/facilities/ma/boston.html>]. Both archives are worth the trip. The Massachusetts State Archives is on the MBTA Red Line. You can take a T bus to the National

Archives, but its distance from downtown makes renting a car to travel there worthwhile.

So many resources are open to researchers in Boston that it's important to carefully plan your trip beforehand. Try the list on **BostonFamilyHistory.com** <www.bostonfamilyhistory.com>, a Web site developed especially for genealogists. It includes a directory of research materials and facilities as well as neighborhood history.

Boston is known as an Irish city, and indeed 26 percent of the people in the state of Massachusetts—that's 1.6 million people—claim Irish ancestry. The city even has a rich history of Irish political figures including the Kennedys. But the ethnic diversity of Boston surprises visitors. It's important to remember that Boston was one of the largest ports of immigration in the nineteenth century and that those immigrants

Boston's Dreams of Freedom museum celebrates the city's rich heritage of immigration.

At the Dreams of Freedom museum, you can relive the experiences of your immigrant ancestors.

settled in the city's neighborhoods. Even today, different parts of the city reflect their ethnic heritage. You can learn more about your immigrant ancestors' experiences in Boston by visiting the new **Dreams of Freedom** museum [1 Milk Street; (617) 338-6022; <www.dreamsoffreedom.org>].

To experience the city's rich history firsthand, walk in your ancestor's footsteps. Irish Americans may be especially interested in following the city's **Irish Heritage Trail** <www.irishheritagetrail.com>. You can see on the **Freedom Trail** <www.thefreedomtrail.org> what your Revolutionary ancestors were up to. More options appear in *Boston Neighborhoods: A Food Lover's Walking, Eating and Shopping Guide to Ethnic Enclaves in and Around Boston* by Lynda Morgenroth and Carleen Moira Powell (Globe Pequot Press, $15.95).

If you're hungry after all that research and walking, try the culinary treats that beckon visitors, from the tony cafés of Newbury Street in the Back Bay to the tourist spots of Fanueil Hall Marketplace. Restaurant reviews appear every Thursday in the *Boston Globe* "Calendar" section <www.boston.com/globe/calendar> and monthly in the pages of *Boston Magazine* <www.bostonmagazine.com>.

Be sure to take time to enjoy some of the finest museums in the country. Try the **Museum of Fine Arts** [465 Huntington Avenue; (617) 267-9300; <www.mfa.org>] or the **Isabella Stewart Gardner Museum** [280 The Fenway; (617) 566-1401; <www.gardnermuseum.org>], which remains just as Mrs. Gardner arranged it back in 1903.

The lodging options may help you decide when to travel to Boston. As in most major cities, lodging is expensive here. Peak visiting seasons in Boston are spring and fall, and hotel rates drop in the winter. Don't be scared away by the winter weather: With everything so close, you won't mind the cold. For help finding accommodations, contact the **Boston Convention and Visitors Bureau** [(888) SEE-BOSTON (733-2678); <www.bostonusa.com>] to receive a free lodging guide.

HARTFORD

BY MAUREEN A. TAYLOR

Located on the Connecticut River, Hartford was settled first by the Dutch in the seventeenth century and then by Rev. Thomas Hooker, who left Massachusetts to establish a religious colony. The Connecticut River, with its connections to major transportation routes, transformed the community from agricultural pursuits to international trade. This capital city became known as the Insurance Capital of the World because of the insurance industry founded by local merchants to protect their cargo. In the late nineteenth century, Hartford was one of the nation's richest cities.

In the nineteenth and twentieth centuries, industry provided economic stability to Connecticut. Samuel Colt built his firearm factories in a part of the city that became known as Coltsville. Hartford also became known for the Columbia bicycle, developed here by A.A. Pope, and Pratt and Whitney supplied engines to the airline and defense industries from here. Industrial growth encouraged immigrants to settle in the area, and Hartford attracted a diverse population from all over the world.

Today, Hartford is rich in history as well. Its **Old State House** [800 Main Street; (860) 522-6766] was the scene of the original *Amistad* trial featured in the movie of the same name. Noah Webster, compiler of the first *Dictionary of the American Language* <www.ctstateu.edu/noahweb>, once lived here. The country's oldest art museum, the **Wadsworth Athenaeum** [600 Main Street; (860) 278-2670; <www.wadsworth athenaeum.org>] is a local cultural icon, as is **Mark Twain's house** [351 Farmington Avenue; (860) 247-0998; <www.marktwainhouse.org>], a wonderful example of Gothic architecture.

While the majority of people who work in Hartford commute from surrounding communities, genealogists don't need to travel far to find the resources they need. The single largest collection of material is at the **Connecticut State Library's History and Genealogy Unit** [231 Capitol Avenue; (860) 757-6580; <www.cslib.org/handg.htm>]. With the library's helpful staff and wealth of resources such as cemetery, Bible, and church records, as well as an extensive manuscript collection, you're unlikely to leave empty handed. Before you visit, use the research guides at the library's Web site to prepare a list of items to look at.

The library is close to hotels of most of the major chains, including Hilton, Sheraton, Crowne Plaza, and Residence Inn. For a bit of history in your hotel, try the turn-of-the-century **Goodwin Hotel** [1 Haynes Street; (860) 522-4935; <www.goodwinhotel.com>].

Just a few miles away, the **Connecticut Historical Society** [1 Elizabeth Street; (860) 236-5621; <www.chs.org>] has a good general reference collection and a large manuscript department that includes genealogical manuscripts. The society's online catalog is part of the state's union catalog, reQuest <www.chs.org/library/default.htm>, which helps you locate material in any participating library in the state. A complete run of the *Hartford Courant*, the oldest continuously published paper in the United States, is on microfilm at the historical society. Out-of-state members can borrow volumes from the circulating collection of local histories of Connecticut cities and towns.

The **Connecticut Society of Genealogists** [175 Maple Street; (860) 569-0002; <www.csginc.org>] is an active group with its own research library. The society sponsors an annual genealogical writing contest, and it has an Ancestry Service to notify members of common ancestors. Since town clerks in Connecticut must see proof of genealogical society membership before allowing access to local resources such as land records, joining the Connecticut Society of Genealogists can help you gain access to such material. You may also check the list of town historical societies on the University of Connecticut Web site <www.lib.uconn.edu/ConnState/connhistsoc.html>.

No visit to Hartford is complete without a stroll through downtown West Hartford, with its trendy restaurants and shops. Established as a separate community in 1854, West Hartford is located close to the Connecticut Historical Society. West Hartford's handy Web site <www.west-hartford.com> has a calendar of events and an index of services. After working hard knocking down those genealogical brick walls, take some time to relax before tackling another

Industrial activity drew people from all over the world to make their home in Hartford.

research problem. Hartford will still be waiting for you, as it has for hundreds of years.

PROVIDENCE

BY MAUREEN A. TAYLOR

A trip to the State of Rhode Island and Providence Plantations—the smallest state in the United States but the one with the longest official name—offers genealogists who have Rhode Island roots a bountiful feast of research, culture, and some of the best restaurants in the country. The state name actually dates to the Colonial period, when *Rhode Island* referred only to Aquidneck Island in Narragansett Bay. Whether your ancestors founded one of the original four towns—Providence, Newport, Portsmouth, or Warwick—or came with the nineteenth-century influx of immigrants, you can find most of what you need to discover your family history and explore your ethnic origins, as well.

Start your search in the capital city, Providence, where the major research libraries are a short walk—up or down one of the seven hills the city is famous for—away from each other. You won't need public transportation; just bring a comfortable pair of shoes. Begin your research at the **Rhode Island Historical Society Library** [121 Hope Street; (401) 331-8575; <www.rihs.org>], located on College Hill near Brown University. The society's collection has books, manuscripts, published and unpublished genealogies, photographs, microfilms, and any type of research document a genealogist would require for finding Rhode Island roots, including microfilm copies of city and town records, census documents, and all the Rhode Island newspapers ever published. It's a one-stop shop for family historians. The helpful staff knows the resources of their library; if they don't have what you need, they can direct you to the right facility. The library is open to the public free of charge (donations accepted), but call to verify the hours and to make appointments to see items in the manuscript and graphics departments.

Take a walk down College Hill, admire the Brown University campus, and visit its **John Hay Library** [20 Prospect Street; (401) 863-2146; <www.brown.edu/Facilities/University_Library/libs/hay>]. Before you go, consult the online card catalog, Josiah <library.brown.edu/screens/opacmenu.html>. While primarily an academic library, the Hay Library also has special collections, including a manuscript department, relating to Rhode Island families.

Down the hill and across the city's new walking bridges is the **Rhode Island Archives** [337 Westminster Street; (401) 222-2353; <www.state.ri.us/archives>]. The archives has the only index to the 1875 state census, along with materials from Colonial governments and state agencies. Birth and marriage records are open to the public after a century; death records, after fifty years. Once again, a helpful staff is on hand to direct you to the appropriate material and offer advice.

Court documents are a short drive away in neighboring Pawtucket in the **Rhode Island Judicial Records Center** [5 Hill Street; (401) 721-2640; <www.judicial-records.state.ri.us>]. There you can find all the dirt on litigious Rhode Islanders in the depositions and court documents for civil and criminal cases from the seventeenth century to 1900 (divorce case records exist from 1749).

Initially settled in 1636 by individuals, led by Roger Williams, escaping from religious persecution in Massachusetts, the Rhode Island area was the first colony to offer refuge for people with different religious beliefs. Quakers, Huguenots, Jews, and others began to settle towns around Narragansett Bay, and they left a treasure trove of documents. Today, immigrants from all over the world live in Providence and the rest of the state, offering visitors and residents an amazing cultural variety within a few square miles. Providence's new **Heritage Harbor**

Museum [350 Eddy Street; (401) 751-7979; <www.heritageharbor.org>] will showcase the ethnic diversity of the state and bring nineteen historical and cultural organizations together under one roof to tell the story of all Rhode Islanders. The museum will transform the decommissioned South Street Power Plant on the riverfront and ultimately encompass more than 250,000 square feet of exhibit, public, office, collections, and library space spanning four floors. Renovation of the power plant building began in July 2000, and a phased opening is planned to begin in late 2003.

Genealogists sometimes tend to forget to venture out of the libraries and experience the life of each city they visit. In Providence, all the libraries close around 5 P.M., so there's no excuse to not embrace this colorful city and explore where your ancestors once lived. The size of the state makes it possible to conduct research in Providence in the morning, have lunch in the village where your ancestor settled, go to the southern part of the state (or even Boston) for additional research, and return to Providence for dinner.

Be sure to explore your heritage through the city's stellar ethnic restaurants, such as

- **Cassarino's Restaurant** [177 Atwells Avenue; (401) 751-3333]—award-winning Italian cuisine on Federal Hill
- **Spain of Narragansett** [1144 Ocean Road, Narragansett; (401) 783-9770]—Spanish and Mediterranean food in an oceanfront castle-like setting

- **Hemenway's Seafood Grill & Oyster Bar** [One Providence Washington Plaza; (401) 351-8570]—for a taste of Providence's seafaring tradition

Make sure you get a taste of the city as well as its cuisine. After stuffing yourself with specialty pastry, homemade pasta, and grilled seafood, walk it off by following the **River Walk** in downtown Providence; you can learn about the history of the city through the signs and pictures found along the way. Plan your visit around the internationally renowned **Waterfire** <www.waterfire.com> and enjoy an evening of light and sound along the waterfront. Also in Providence, the **Rhode Island School of Design Museum** [224 Benefit Street; (401) 454-6500; <www.risd.edu/museum.cfm>] is worth a visit due to its outstanding art collection and period rooms. If you want to see the gardens and houses of your ancestors, purchase tickets in advance and arrive in time for the annual **Festival of Historic Houses** sponsored by the **Providence Preservation Society** [21 Meeting Street; (401) 831-7440; <www.ppsri.org>].

Centrally located lodging makes your trip even easier. You might choose the elegant **Biltmore Hotel** [11 Dorrance Street; (401) 598-8000] or the modern **Westin** [1 West Exchange Street; (401) 598-8170]. If you prefer to opt for truly historic lodgings, stay at the **1863 Old Court Bed & Breakfast** [144 Benefit Street; (401) 751-2002; <www.oldcourt.com/home.htm>], next to the old Rhode Island Courthouse.

ORGANIZATIONS & ARCHIVES

Connecticut Ancestry Society
P.O. Box 249
Stamford, CT 06904

Connecticut Historical Society
1 Elizabeth St.
Hartford, CT 06105
(860) 236-5621
Fax: (860) 236-2664
<www.chs.org>

Connecticut Society of Genealogists, Inc.
P.O. Box 435
2106 Main St.
Glastonbury, CT 06033
(860) 569-0002
<www.csginc.org>

Connecticut State Library
History and Genealogy Unit
231 Capitol Ave.
Hartford, CT 06106
(860) 757-6580
Fax: (860) 757-6677
<www.cslib.org/handg.htm>

Stamford Genealogical Society
P.O. Box 249
Stamford, CT 06904

RESOURCES

"Connecticut Genealogical Research" lecture by Thomas Kemp (Audiotapes.com, $8.50)

Early Connecticut Marriages: As Found on Ancient Church Records Prior to 1800 by Frederic W. Bailey (Genealogical Publishing Co., $55)

New England Family Histories: State of Connecticut by LuVerne V. Hall and Donald O. Virdin (Heritage Books, $24.50)

PERIODICALS

Connecticut Ancestry, formerly **Stamford Genealogical Society Bulletin** (1958-), Stamford Genealogical Society, P.O. Box 249, Stamford, CT 06904

Connecticut Maple Leaf (1983-), French-Canadian Genealogical Society of Connecticut, P.O. Box 929, Tolland, CT 06084

The Connecticut Nutmegger (1968-), Connecticut Society of Genealogists, Inc., P.O. Box 435, 175 Maple St., Glastonbury, CT 06033

WEB SITES

Connecticut Genealogy Forum
<genforum.genealogy.com/ct>: Post and search Connecticut-related queries.

Connecticut GenWeb Project
<www.rootsweb.com/~ctgenweb>: Links to county pages and a list of Connecticut research helps.

Connecticut History Online
<www.lib.uconn.edu/cho>: Searchable site with historical photos.

Connecticut Mailing Lists
<www.rootsweb.com/~jfuller/gen_mail_states-ct.html>: Network with other researchers through state and county lists.

Connecticut Resources at RootsWeb
<resources.rootsweb.com/USA/CT>: Multiple search engines, surnames, archives.

Connecticut State Library
<www.cslib.org/indexsch.htm>: Offers for a fee a limited genealogical index search service.

New England Genealogy
<pages.prodigy.net/kathyb/home.htm>: Links to several Connecticut online resources.

New England Genealogy by Ray Brown
<freepages.genealogy.rootsweb.com/~rbrown>: Links to birth and marriage records.

Vital Records Information
<vitalrec.com/ct.html>: Where to obtain copies of birth and death certificates, marriage licenses, and divorce decrees.

FAMILY HISTORY CENTERS

Goshen
122 N St.
(860) 491-5227

Groton
1230 Flander Rd.
(860) 536-5102

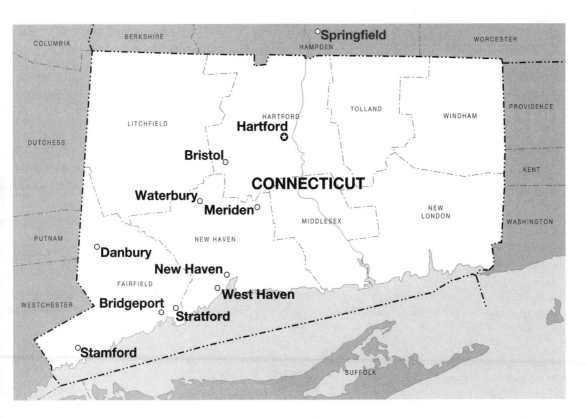

Hartford
1000 Mountain Rd.
(860) 242-1607

Madison
275 Warpas Rd.
(203) 245-8267

Manchester
34 Woodside St.
(860) 643-4003

New Canaan
682 South Ave.
(203) 966-8475

New Haven
990 Racebrook Rd.
(203) 387-2012

Newtown
16 Saw Mill Rd.
(203) 426-1752

Southington
750 Meriden Waterbury
Turnpike
(860) 628-0617

Stamford
834 Stillwater Rd.

MAINE

ORGANIZATIONS & ARCHIVES

Bangor Public Library
145 Harlow St.
Bangor, ME 04401-4900
(207) 947-8336
Fax (207) 945-6694
<www.bpl.lib.me.us>

The Center for Maine History
485 Congress St.
Portland, ME 04101
(207) 774-1822
<www.mainehistory.com>

Maine Genealogical Society
P.O. Box 221
Farmington, ME 04938

Maine Historical Society
485 Congress St.
Portland, ME 04101
(207) 774-1822
Fax: (207) 775-4301

Maine Old Cemetery Association
P.O. Box 641
Augusta, ME 04332
<www.rootsweb.com/
~memoca/moca.htm>

Maine State Archives
State House, Station 84
Augusta, ME 04333-0084
(207) 287-5795
Fax: (207) 289-5739
<www.state.me.us/
sos/arc>

Maine State Library
State House, Station 64
Augusta, ME 04333
(207) 287-5600
Fax: (207) 287-5615
<www.state.me.us/msl>

University of Maine at Orono
Raymond H. Fogler
Library, Special
Collections
P.O. Box 5729
Orono, ME 04469
(207) 581-1688
Fax: (207) 581-1653

RESOURCES

"Genealogical Resources in Maine"
lecture by Joseph
Anderson
(Audiotapes.com, $8.50)

Maine Genealogy: A Bibliographical Guide
(Maine Historical Society,
$4)

"Maine Town and Court Records"
lecture by Steve Seames
(Audiotapes.com, $8.50)

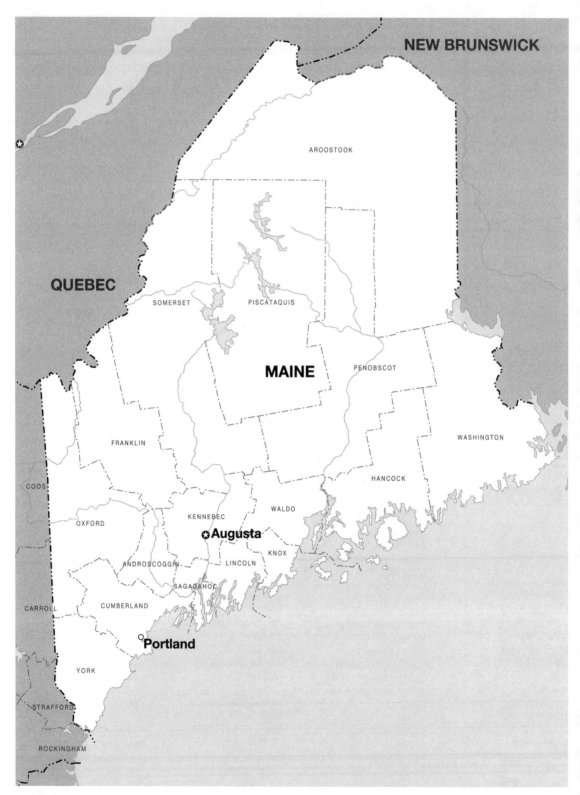

NEW BRUNSWICK

QUEBEC

AROOSTOOK

SOMERSET

PISCATAQUIS

MAINE

PENOBSCOT

WASHINGTON

FRANKLIN

COOS

HANCOCK

OXFORD

KENNEBEC

WALDO

Augusta

KNOX

ANDROSCOGGIN

LINCOLN

SAGADAHOC

CARROLL

CUMBERLAND

Portland

YORK

STRAFFORD

ROCKINGHAM

MAINE

Statehood: 1820
Statewide Birth and Death Records Begin: 1892
Statewide Marriage Records Begin: 1892
Address for Vital Statistics:
   Department of Human Services
   Office of Vital Statistics
   State House, Station 11
   Augusta, ME 04330
   (207) 287-3184

Available Censuses: U.S. federal censuses 1790, 1800, 1810, 1820, 1830, 1840, 1850, 1860, 1870, 1880, 1900, 1910, and 1920 with these exceptions: some of York county for 1800, half of Oxford county for 1810, some of Washington county for 1820. Although the 1890 census was destroyed, the 1890 Union veterans schedule and index are available. Statewide indexes exist for the 1790, 1800, 1810, 1820, 1830, 1840, and 1850 censuses.

City Directories at the Family History Library Include: Portland 1823-1934

PERIODICALS

The Bangor Historical Magazine
(1885-1894), 1993 reprint. 10 vols. Picton Press, Camden, ME

Downeast Ancestry
(1977-), News-Journal, 60 Court St., Machias, ME 04654

The Maine Seine
(1980-1990), Maine Genealogical Society, P.O. Box 221, Farmington, ME 04938

WEB SITES

Jean's Maine Genealogy Page
<www.mnopltd.com/jean>: Index of deaths and marriages, 1851 through 1865.

Maine GenWeb Project
<www.rootsweb.com/~megenweb>: Links to state and county resources.

Maine Mailing Lists
<www.rootsweb.com/~jfuller/gen_mail_states-me.html>: Subscribe to Maine state or county mailing lists.

Maine Resources at RootsWeb
<resources.rootsweb.com/USA/ME/>: Archived resources, search engines.

Marriage History Search Form
<thor.ddp.state.me.us/archives/plsql/archdev.Marriage_Archive.search_form>: Search for Maine marriages from 1892 to 1996.

New England Old Newspaper Index Project of Maine
<www.rootsweb.com/~megenweb/newspaper/project/>: Maine newspapers with indexes.

Vital Records Information
<vitalrec.com/me.html>: Obtain copies of birth and death certificates, marriage licenses, and divorce decrees.

FAMILY HISTORY CENTERS

Augusta
4 Hasson St.
(207) 582-1827

Bangor
639 Grandview Ave.
(207) 947-5624

Caribou
67 Paris Snow Dr.
(207) 492-4381

Farmington
Woodfield Drive
(207) 778-4038

Oxford
Skeetfield Road
(207) 743-8125

Portland
29 Ocean House Rd.
(207) 767-5000

Rockland
Old County Road
(207) 594-1018

Topsham
Pinewood Drive
(207) 725-8427

Waterville
50 Washington St.
(207) 873-0054

ORGANIZATIONS & ARCHIVES

Boston Public Library
700 Boylston St.
Copley Square
Boston, MA 02117
(617) 536-5400
Fax: (617) 536-4306
<www.bpl.org>

Massachusetts Historical Commission
220 Morrissey Blvd.
Boston, MA 02125
(617) 727-8470
<www.state.ma.us/sec/mhc>

JERRY JACKSON

Maine's Portland Head Light, established in the 1790s, is a reminder of the state's maritime heritage.

**Massachusetts Historical
Society Library**
1154 Boylston St.
Boston, MA 02215
(617) 536-1608
Fax: (617) 536-1608
<www.masshist.org/
library.html>

**Massachusetts Society of
Genealogists**
P.O. Box 215
Ashland, MA 01721
(508) 792-5066
<www.rootsweb.com/
~masgi/msog>

**Massachusetts State
Archives**
220 Morrissey Blvd.
Boston, MA
(617) 727-9150
<www.state.ma.us/sec/
arc/arcgen/genidx.htm>

Peabody Essex Museum
132 Essex St.
Salem, MA 01970
(508) 744-3390
Fax: (508) 744-0036

**State Library of
Massachusetts**
State House, Room 341
Beacon St.
(617) 727-2590
Fax: (617) 727-5819
<www.state.ma.us/lib>

RESOURCES

*"From the Safe to Your
Shelf: Massachusetts
Vital Records"*
lecture by Jay Holbrook
(Audiotapes.com, $8.50)

*The History of Land Titles
in Massachusetts*
by James Sullivan (Ayer
Co., $25.95)

*Massachusetts
Genealogical Research*
by George K. Schweitzer
(Genealogical Sources
Unlimited, $15)

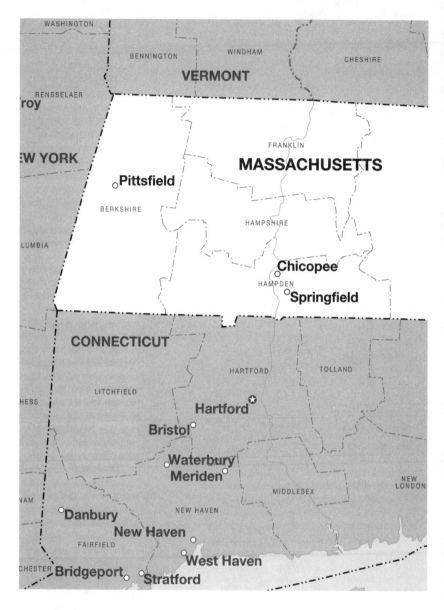

*Pioneers of
Massachusetts (1620-
1650): A Descriptive List,
Drawn From the Records
of the Colonies, Towns
and Churches*
by Charles Henry Pope
(Genealogical Publishing
Co., $35)

*"The Records of
Massachusetts Bay: An
In-Depth View"*

lecture by Ralph Crandall
(Audiotapes.com, $8.50)

PERIODICALS

Essex Antiquarian
(1897-1909, 13 vols.)
Salem, MA

*The Mayflower
Descendant*
(1899-1937, 1985-),
Massachusetts Society of

Mayflower Descendants,
376 Boylston St., Boston,
MA 02116; (617) 266-
1624

The Mayflower Quarterly
(1935-), General Society
of *Mayflower*
Descendants, P.O. Box
3297, Plymouth, MA
02361; (508) 746-3188

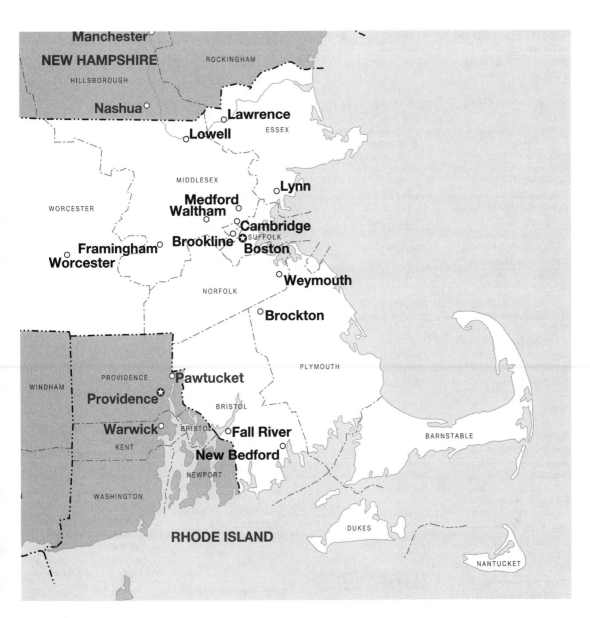

WEB SITES

BostonFamilyHistory.com
<www.bostonfamily
history.com>: Explore the
history of Boston's neighborhoods or use a mes-
sage board.

**Massachusetts Cemetery
Directory**
<mass-doc.com/mass_
cemetery_guide.htm>:

Links to Massachusetts
cemeteries and their
locations on U.S.
Geological Survey maps.

**Massachusetts Civil War
Research Center**
<fitzware.com>: Search a
database of more than
150,000 soldiers, sailors,
and marines who served
in Massachusetts units.

**Massachusetts Civil War
Web Sites**
<masshome.com/
histcwar.html>: Links to
Massachusetts Civil War
resources and regimental
histories.

**Massachusetts
Genealogy Books**
<www.genealogy-books.
com/books/massachusetts.
html>: Descriptive list of

history and genealogy
books on New England.

**Massachusetts
Genealogy Links**
<genealogylinks.net/usa/
massachusetts>: Links to
census, cemetery, mili-
tary, and ship records.

**Massachusetts GenWeb
Project**
<www.rootsweb.com/

~magenweb>: Subscribe to a Massachusetts genealogy list or research a particular town.

Massachusetts Mailing Lists
<www.rootsweb.com/ ~jfuller/gen_mail_ states-ma.html>: Free subscriptions to state and county mailing lists.

Massachusetts Resources at RootsWeb
<resources.rootsweb. com/USA/MA>: Personal Web pages, search engines, and online records.

The *Mayflower* Web Pages
<members.aol.com/ calebj/mayflower.html>: *Mayflower* passenger lists and documents.

Researching Your Family's History at the Massachusetts Archives
<www.state.ma.us/sec/ arc/arcgen/genidx.htm>: Description of the archives' holdings and how to access them.

Vital Records Information
<vitalrec.com/ma.html>: Where to obtain copies of birth and death certificates, marriage licenses, and divorce decrees.

FAMILY HISTORY CENTERS

Amherst
376 Maple St.
(413) 731-8792

Belmont
15 Ledgewood Pl.
(617) 489-9375

Boston
150 Brown St.
(781) 235-2164

Brewster
94 Freeman's Way
(508) 896-9863

Cambridge
2 Longfellow Park
(617) 491-4749

Cape Cod
County Road
(508) 564-5437

Foxboro
76 N. Main St.
(508) 543-0298

Hingham
379 Gardner St.
(781) 749-9835

Lynnfield
400 Essex St.
(781) 334-5586

Martha's Vineyard
2 Merchants Mart
(508) 693-8642

North Dartmouth
400 Cross Rd.
(508) 994-8215

Worcester
67 Chester St.
(508) 852-7000

NEW HAMPSHIRE

ORGANIZATIONS & ARCHIVES

New Hampshire Department of State
Division of Records Management and Archives
71 S. Fruit St.
Concord, NH 03301
(603) 271-2236
Fax: (603) 271-2272
<www.state.nh.us/state/>

MASSACHUSETTS

Statehood: 1788
Statewide Birth and Death Records Begin: 1841
Statewide Marriage Records Begin: 1841
Address for Vital Statistics:
Massachusetts State Archives at Columbia Point
220 Morrissey Blvd.
Boston, MA 02125
(617) 727-2816

Available Censuses: U.S. federal censuses 1790, 1800, 1810, 1820, 1830, 1840, 1850, 1860, 1870, 1880, 1900, 1910, and 1920. Indexes exist for 1790, 1800, 1810, 1820, 1830, 1840, 1850, 1860, 1900, and 1920. State and Territorial Censuses 1779, 1855, 1865.

City Directories at the Family History Library Include: Boston 1789-1860, 1861-1935, 1905, 1909, 1941, 1951

New Hampshire Historical Society
The Tuck Library
30 Park St.
Concord, NH 03301
(603) 228-6688
Fax: (603) 224-046
<www.nhhistory.org>

New Hampshire Society of Genealogists
P.O. Box 152
Rindge, NH 03461
<www.nhsog.org>

New Hampshire State Library
20 Park St.
Concord, NH 03301
(603) 271-2392
Fax: (603) 271-6826
<www.state.nh.us/nhsl>

The University of New Hampshire Library
Dimond Library Special Collections
18 Library Way
Durham, NH 03824
(603) 862-2714
<www.izaak.unh.edu>

RESOURCES

Directory of Repositories of Family History in New Hampshire
by Scott Green (Clearfield Co., $10.95)

New England Family Histories and Genealogies: States of New Hampshire and Vermont
by LuVerne V. Hall and Donald Virdin (Heritage Books, $18.50)

"Research in New Hampshire"
lecture by George Sanborn (Audiotapes.com, $8.50)

PERIODICALS

American-Canadian Genealogist: Official Journal of the American-Canadian Genealogical Society of New Hampshire

(1975-), American-Canadian Genealogical Society, P.O. Box 6478, Manchester, NH 03108

The Granite Monthly (1877-1930, 51 vols.)

Historical New Hampshire (1944-), New Hampshire Historical Society, 30 Park St., Concord, NH 03301

New Hampshire Genealogical Record (1903-April 1910; 1990-), New Hampshire Society of Genealogists, P.O. Box 152, Rindge, NH 03461

WEB SITES

Books on New Hampshire Genealogy <waynesworld.org/My-Ancestors/GenealogyBooks-3>: List of genealogy and history books on New Hampshire.

New Hampshire Almanac <www.state.nh.us/nhinfo/guide.html>: A guide to research in the history of New Hampshire towns, 1780-1800, part of the "After the Revolution" project.

New Hampshire Civil War History and Genealogy Project <www.usgennet.org/usa/nh/topic/civilwar>: Regimental histories and rosters for New Hampshire soldiers.

New Hampshire Genealogy Forum <genforum.genealogy.com/nh>: Post queries on your New Hampshire research.

New Hampshire GenWeb Project <www.rootsquest.com/~usgwnhus>: Court records, deeds, images, and historical gazetteers are being added to this site.

New Hampshire Mailing Lists <www.rootsweb.com/~jfuller/gen_mail_states-nh.html>: Subscribe to county and state mailing lists.

New Hampshire Resources at RootsWeb <resources.rootsweb.com/USA/NH>: Personal Web pages, search engines, online records.

NEW HAMPSHIRE

Statehood: 1788
Statewide Birth and Death Records Begin: 1901
Statewide Marriage Records Begin: 1901
Address for Vital Statistics:
Bureau of Vital Records and Health Statistics
Health and Welfare Building
6 Hazen Dr.
Concord, NH 03301
(603) 271-4651
<www.dhhs.state.nh.us/DHHS/
BVR/default.htm>

Available Censuses: U.S. federal censuses 1790, 1800, 1810, 1820, 1830, 1840, 1850, 1860, 1870, 1880, 1900, 1910, and 1920. Strafford County: 1800 federal census is missing for Alton, Barnstead, Brookfield, Effingham, Gilmantown, Middleton, New Durham, Ossipee, Tuftonborough, Wakefield, and Wolfeborough; the 1798 Direct Tax serves as a census substitute for many of these towns. Most of the 1820 census is also missing except for Centre Harbor, Gilford, Moultonborough, New Hampton, and Sanbornton. Rockingham County: 1800 census is missing for Aktinson, Greenland, Hampton, Hampton Falls, Londonderry, Northampton, Pelham, Plaistow, Salem, Seabrook, Stratham, and Windham . Grafton County: 1820 census is missing. Rockingham County: 1820 census is missing for Gosport, Greenland, New Castle, Newington, Portsmouth, and Rye. Colonial censuses for 1732 to 1742 are available. Statewide indexes are available for 1790, 1800, 1810, 1820, 1830, 1840, 1850, 1860, 1870, 1880, 1900 and 1920.

City Directories at the Family History Library Include: Concord 1830-1935 (gaps); Dover 1830-1935 (gaps); Great Falls (now Somersworth) 1848; Keene 1827, 1830, 1831, 1871-1935 (gaps); Manchester 1844-1935 (gaps); Nashua 1841-1935 (gaps); New Hampshire 1849; New Ipswich 1858; Peterborough 1830; Portsmouth 1817-1935 (gaps)

New Hampshire Sources for Genealogy Research <familylineage.com/research_pages/newhampshire.html>: Links to people, places, events, archives, and lookups.

Vital Records Information <vitalrec.com/nh.html>: Where to obtain copies of birth and death certificates, marriage licenses, and divorce decrees.

FAMILY HISTORY CENTERS

Concord
90 Clinton St.
(603) 225-2848

Exeter
55 Hampton Falls Rd.
(603) 778-2509

Lebanon
Route 4
(603) 448-4374

Nashua
110 Concord St.
(603) 594-8888

Randolph
Gorham Hill Route 2 on town line
(603) 466-3417

RHODE ISLAND

ORGANIZATIONS & ARCHIVES

American-French Genealogical Society
P.O. Box 2010
78 Earle St.
Woonsocket, RI 02895
(401) 765-6141
Fax: (401) 765-6141
<www.afgs.org>

Rhode Island Genealogical Society
P.O. Box 433
Greenville, RI 02828
<users.ids.net/~ricon/rigs.html>

Rhode Island Historical Society
110 Benevolent St.
Providence, RI 02906
(401) 331-8575
Fax: (401) 351-0127
<www.rihs.org>

Rhode Island State Archives
337 Westminster St.
Providence, RI 02903
(401) 222-2353
Fax: (401) 222-3199
<www.state.ri.us/archives>

Rhode Island Supreme Court Judicial Records Center
5 Hill St.
Pawtucket, RI 02860
(401) 721-2640
< www.judicial-records.state.ri.us/main.htm>

RESOURCES

Rhode Island: Biographical and Genealogical Sketch Index
by J. Carlyle Parker
(Marietta Publishing Co., $29.95)

"Rhode Island Court Records"
lecture by Stephen Grimes (Audiotapes.com, $8.50)

"Rhode Island Genealogy on the Web"
lecture by Jennifer A. Schmidt
(Audiotapes.com, $8.50)

RHODE ISLAND

Statehood: 1790
Statewide Birth and Death Records Begin: 1853
Statewide Marriage Records Begin: 1853
Address for Vital Statistics:
Rhode Island Department of Health
Vital Records
#3 Capitol Hill, Room 101
Providence, RI 02908
(401) 222-2231
<www.health.state.ri.us>

Available Censuses: U.S. federal censuses 1790, 1800, 1810, 1820, 1830, 1840, 1850, 1860, 1870, 1880, 1900, 1910, and 1920. Statewide indexes are available for 1790, 1800, 1810, 1820, 1830, 1840, 1850, 1860, 1870, 1880, 1900, 1910, and 1920. Colonial censuses (or equivalents) exist for 1747 to 1754, 1774, and 1782. State and territorial censuses 1747, 1770, 1774, 1777, 1779, 1782, 1865, 1875, 1885, 1905, 1915, 1925 and 1935. An index exists for the 1865 state census.

City Directories at the Family History Library Include: Providence 1798, 1826, 1856-1860, 1861-1933

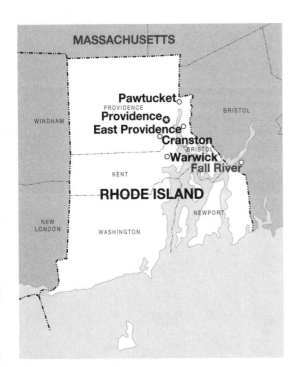

PERIODICALS

Rhode Island Genealogical Register (1978-), Rhode Island Families Association, P.O. Box 585, East Princeton, MA 01517

Rhode Island History (1942-), Rhode Island Historical Society, 110 Benevolent St., Providence, RI 02906

Rhode Island Roots (1973-), Rhode Island Genealogical Society, P.O. Box 433, Greenville, RI 02828

WEB SITES

Rhode Island and Providence Plantations
<www.usgennet.org/usa/ri/state>: Many links to Rhode Island information, counties, historical topics, and more.

Rhode Island Consortium of Genealogical and Historical Societies
<users.ids.net/~ricon>: Calendar of events from participating organizations.

Rhode Island Genealogy Forum
<genforum.genealogy.com/ri>: Post queries for help on Rhode Island research.

Rhode Island GenWeb Project
<www.rootsweb.com/~rigenweb>: Search the database for the state's Historical Cemeteries Transcription Project, plus state facts, resources, links, transcriptions, and more.

Rhode Island Mailing Lists
<www.rootsweb.com/~jfuller/gen_mail_states-ri.html>: Free subscriptions to state and county mailing lists.

Rhode Island Resources at RootsWeb
<resources.rootsweb.com/USA/RI>: Search engines, personal Web pages, archives, and mailing lists.

Vital Records Information
<vitalrec.com/ri.html>: Where to obtain copies of birth and death certificates, marriage licenses, and divorce decrees.

FAMILY HISTORY CENTERS

Providence
1000 Narragansett Pkwy.
(401) 463-8150

VERMONT

ORGANIZATIONS & ARCHIVES

Genealogical Society of Vermont
P.O. Box 1553
St. Albans, VT 05478
<www.rootsweb.com/~vtgsv>

Vermont Historical Society
Vermont History Center
60 Washington St.
Barre, VT 05641
(802) 479-8500
Fax: (802) 479-8510
<www.state.vt.us/vhs>

Vermont State Archives
26 Terrace St.
Drawer 9
Montpelier, VT 05609
(802) 828-1135

VERMONT

Statehood: 1791
Statewide Birth and Death Records Begin: 1955
Statewide Marriage Records Begin: 1955
Address for Vital Statistics:
Vermont Department of Health
Vital Records Section
P.O. Box 70
108 Cherry Street
Burlington, VT 05402
(802) 828-3286
<www.state.vt.us/health/_hs/vitals/
records/vitalrecords.htm>

Available Censuses: U.S. federal censuses 1790, 1800, 1810, 1820, 1830, 1840, 1850, 1860, 1870, 1880, 1900, 1910, and 1920. Statewide indexes are available for 1790, 1800, 1810, 1820, 1830, 1840, 1850, 1860, 1870, 1880, 1900, and 1920.

City Directories at the Family History Library Include: County directories 1881-1888.

Fax: (802) 828-2465
<vermont-archives.org >

RESOURCES

New England Family Histories and Genealogies: States of New Hampshire and Vermont
by LuVerne V. Hall and Donald Virdin (Heritage Books, $18.50)

"Vermont Research" lecture by Alice Eichholz (Audiotapes.com, $8.50)

"Vermont Sources: Where They Are and How to Use Them" lecture by George Sanborn (Audiotapes.com, $8.50)

PERIODICALS

Across the Border (1988), Diana Hibbert Bailey, Carlton Place, Ontario, Canada

Branches and Twigs (1972-1995), Genealogical Society of Vermont, P.O. Box 1553, St. Albans, VT 05478

Vermont Genealogy (1996-), Genealogical Society of Vermont, P.O. Box 1553, St. Albans, VT 05478

Vermont History (1954-), Vermont Historical Society, Vermont History Center 60 Washington St. Barre, VT 05641

WEB SITES

Genealogy Researchers in Vermont
<www.state.vt.us/vhs/genames.htm>: A list compiled by the Vermont Historical Society Library.

Vermont Genealogy
<www.middlebury.edu/~lib>: Genealogy resources at the Middlebury College Library.

Vermont Genealogy Resources
<freepages.genealogy.rootsweb.com/~vermontgenealogyresources>: Links to Vermont history and maps.

Vermont GenWeb
<www.rootsquest.com/~usgwvtus>: Basic overview of Vermont's genealogical resources. General state resources.

Vermont in the Civil War
<vermontcivilwar.org>: Search the largest online repository of information documenting Vermont's Civil War participation.

Vermont Mailing Lists
<rootsweb.com/~jfuller/gen_mail_states-vt.html>: State and county mailing lists.

Vermont Resources at RootsWeb
<resources.rootsweb.com/USA/VT>: Personal Web pages, archives, search engines.

Vital Records Information
<vitalrec.com/vt.html>: Where to obtain copies of birth and death certificates, marriage licenses, and divorce decrees.

FAMILY HISTORY CENTERS

Bennington
Houghton Lane
(802) 442-8126

Montpelier
Hersey Road
(802) 229-0482

Rutland
637 N. Shrewsbury Rd.
(802) 773-8346

South Royalton
Dairy Hill Road
(802) 763-7784

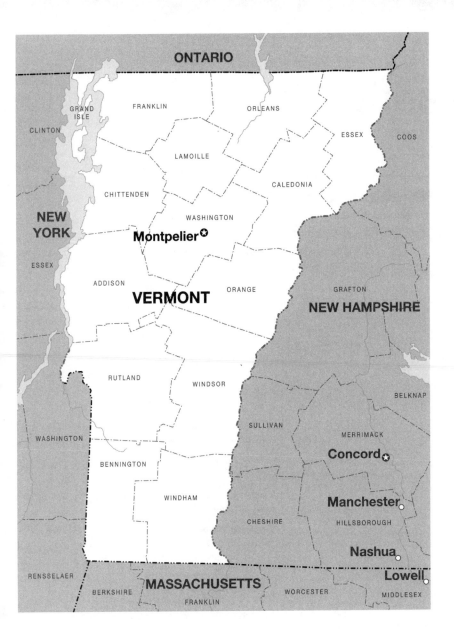

ONTARIO

GRAND
ISLE

FRANKLIN

ORLEANS

ESSEX

COOS

CLINTON

LAMOILLE

CALEDONIA

CHITTENDEN

**NEW
YORK**

WASHINGTON

ESSEX

Montpelier ✪

ADDISON

VERMONT

ORANGE

GRAFTON

NEW HAMPSHIRE

RUTLAND

WINDSOR

BELKNAP

SULLIVAN

MERRIMACK

WASHINGTON

Concord ✪

BENNINGTON

Manchester ○

WINDHAM

CHESHIRE

HILLSBOROUGH

Nashua ○

Lowell ○

RENSSELAER

MASSACHUSETTS

WORCESTER

MIDDLESEX

BERKSHIRE

FRANKLIN

Mid-Atlantic

Delaware
Maryland
New Jersey
New York
Pennsylvania

REGIONAL GUIDE
BY MAUREEN A. TAYLOR

The Mid-Atlantic states—Delaware, Maryland, New Jersey, New York, and Pennsylvania—are as central to America's legacy as, well, Uncle Sam. That American icon originated in Troy, New York, where a meatpacker named Samuel Wilson stamped each of his boxes with "U.S. Beef"—misinterpreted by consumers who thought "U.S." was short for "Uncle Sam." From New York City's Statue of Liberty to Philadelphia's Liberty Bell and Independence Hall to Baltimore's Fort McHenry—whose War of 1812 siege inspired "The Star Spangled Banner"—scenes of American history are splashed across the canvas that is this region. Delaware, "The First State," led the way in ratifying the Constitution. Key battles of the American Revolution were settled in New Jersey. Millions of immigrants first set foot in America at Ellis Island, off the shores of New York and New Jersey. Women's suffrage got its spark at Seneca Falls, New York.

The Mid-Atlantic states have given us many of the best-known names in our history, too, from Benjamin Franklin and Alexander Hamilton to Babe Ruth and Wilt Chamberlain. New York alone has supplied six U.S. presidents—Martin Van Buren, Millard Fillmore, Chester Alan Arthur, Grover Cleveland, Theodore Roosevelt, and Franklin Delano Roosevelt. The region has given birth to classic American authors such as Washington Irving, Herman Melville, and Walt Whitman and was home to many of the nineteenth century's wealthiest citizens—Vanderbilt, Rockefeller, Du Pont, Carnegie, and Mellon.

If your ancestors have roots in Maryland, Delaware, Pennsylvania, New York, or New Jersey, you'll discover a wealth of genealogical resources for tracing them. Genealogist and area expert Gary Boyd Roberts offers these tips for getting started:

- The best published county sources of information are county and biographical encyclopedic histories known as "mug books" because of their combination of data and photographs supplied by individuals who "paid to have their mugs put in." You can find these mug books in most local history collections. Who knows? You may even discover a photo of your ancestor.

- Take advantage of the many in-depth reference books on the various states, many of them listed in the resource guides in this section.

- For published genealogies of area families, consult family histories printed in journals such as *The New York Genealogical and Biographical Record, The National Genealogical Society Quarterly*, and *The American Genealogist*. Use the *Periodical Source Index* (PERSI)—available at larger libraries, on CD-ROM, and as part of the Ancestry.com database subscription at <www.ancestry.com>—to find these family histories.

- Use the Family History Library research helps for each state (see <www.familysearch.org>) as genealogical guidebooks to truly understand the region and focus your efforts.

THE FIRST ARRIVALS

Unlike New England, which was settled primarily by the English, the Mid-Atlantic region boasts early Dutch, Swedish, Germans, French, English, and a variety of religious refugees. The Dutch settled New York as New Netherland; Jews also began settling in New Amsterdam (New York City) in the 1650s. In 1664 the British took over New Netherland and renamed it, though the area's Dutch heritage persisted enough to flavor the works of Washington Irving.

New Jersey was spun off after the British takeover of New Netherland, when the Duke of York rewarded two faithful supporters with their own colony. The new colony owners promptly began advertising for settlers, and they even lured away New Englanders. Newark, for example, was founded in 1666 by Puritan families from New Haven, Connecticut.

Maryland's English immigrants typically arrived as indentured servants and convicts. The colony, chartered in 1632 by Lord Baltimore, also came to offer refuge to many Roman Catholics.

Delaware was briefly the heart of New Sweden and the only Swedish colony in America, founded in 1638. The Dutch soon took control, but a semi-independent "Swedish Nation" of Swedes and Finns remained until 1681, when William Penn received his charter for Pennsylvania and three counties that became Delaware. The future state's boundaries weren't finally settled until 1750.

Pennsylvania, with its Quaker roots and good documentation adhered to by the Society of Friends, delights researchers with its meeting records complete with vital records. Penn began Pennsylvania as a colony based on religious freedom, so a variety of faiths and cultures settled here under the toleration taught by Penn's Quaker faith. Use William Wade Hinshaw's *Encyclopedia of Quaker Genealogy* (Genealogy.com CD #192, $59.99; also available as part of a GenealogyLibrary.com online subscription, $49.99 per year) to trace Quaker family histories and migrations.

For finding other early settlers, useful resources include P. William Filby's *Passenger and Immigration Lists Index* (Genealogy.com CD #354, $59.99; also available as part of the International and Passenger Records Collection online subscription, $79.99 per year) and Peter Wilson Coldham's *The Complete Book of Emigrants, 1607-1776* (Genealogy.com CD #350, $29.99) and *The Complete Book of Emigrants in Bondage, 1614-1775* (printed volume, $36).

When most researchers think of immigration, the first thing that comes to mind is Ellis Island in New York City's harbor, but the Mid-Atlantic region actually had several other ports of arrival, including Baltimore and Philadelphia. If your ancestor arrived after Ellis Island opened in 1892, then check the vast database on its Web site <www.ellisisland.org> to find a passenger list showing your ancestor's arrival.

The National Archives and Records Administration (NARA) has several different microfilm sets for arrivals at Atlantic ports. Consult the Immigrant and Passenger Arrivals information on the NARA Web site <www.archives.gov> or visit one of the regional facilities to search Soundex indexes (which group similarly spelled names) to

- Passenger Lists of Vessels Arriving at Baltimore, Maryland, 1820-1897 (M327)
- Passenger Lists of Vessels Arriving at Baltimore, Maryland, 1891-1909 (T844)
- Passenger Lists of Vessels Arriving at New York, New York, 1820-1897 (M237)
- Passenger Lists of Vessels Arriving at Philadelphia, 1800-1882 (M425)
- Passenger Lists of Vessels Arriving at Philadelphia, 1883-1945 (T840)

So many immigrants came to the area in the late nineteenth century that between 1860 and 1900 the population of New York City tripled.

THE PUSH WESTWARD

Researchers looking for ancestors in upstate and western New York and Pennsylvania might long to be Rip Van Winkle in reverse—instead of going forward twenty years, they'll want to travel backwards in time to unravel the mystery of missing records that plagues most researchers. When a branch of the family tree from New England is noted in print as having "gone west," west refers to territories west of their starting point—not the West of cowboys and Indians. In the eighteenth century west could mean New York or Pennsylvania. Henry Hoff, editor of the *New England Historical and Genealogical Register* and former editor of *The New York Genealogical and Biographical Record*, reminds researchers looking for elusive ancestors to check for interaction in and emigration from the neighboring states. For instance, settlers of upstate New York came from New England; early Philadelphians moved west following old Indian trails; emigrants from Pennsylvania and Maryland settled Delaware.

Westward migration was further encouraged through Revolutionary War land grants that offered parcels in New York and Pennsylvania. To see if your ancestor received one of these grants, consult Virgil D. White's *Genealogical Abstracts of Revolutionary War Pension Files* (4 volumes, National Historical Publishing Co., out of print, available in libraries) or Lloyd DeWitt Bockstruck's *Revolutionary War Bounty Land Grants Awarded by State Governments* (Genealogical Publishing Co., $45).

The western parts of the Mid-Atlantic region also expanded through the new transportation and trade routes offered by man-made canals. The Erie Canal took eight years to build, but this water route from the Hudson River to Lake Erie helped make New York City a major port. The canal also provided transportation to individuals seeking to settle in the west. Find out more about this fascinating waterway at <www.history.rochester.edu/canal>, or consult the Guide to Canal Records in the New York State Archives <www.archives.nysed.gov/holding/aids/canal/content.htm>. While the Erie Canal is of course famous, other states also built canals. In Pennsylvania, for instance, the Union Canal Company of Pennsylvania and The Susquehanna Canal Company operated from 1835 to 1897.

FAST FACTS

Like most genealogical endeavors, finding your ancestors in the Mid-Atlantic region becomes a lot easier once you know some of the details and quirks of what you're researching. The more you know about the area and its history, the easier it gets. To help you jump-start your genealogical quest in this region, here are some key facts about each state to keep in mind:

Delaware

- You can find county and municipal records as well as an extensive collection of manuscript material at the Delaware State Archives.
- Delaware has only three counties: Kent, New Castle, and Sussex. Most of the county records are held at the Delaware State Archives.

Maryland

- Although the Maryland Assembly mandated the recording of vital records in 1654, few such records exist. In 1695, the responsibility of registering births and marriages was given to the Protestant Episcopal Church.
- Land patents from 1634 forward are at the Maryland State Archives.
- Records for the city of Baltimore are separate from those of the state's twenty-three counties.

New Jersey

- Statewide registration of births, marriages, and deaths began in May 1848.
- State censuses were taken every ten years from 1855 through 1915; these records are kept at the New Jersey State Archives.
- No federal census records for 1790 through 1820 exist for New Jersey, but tax lists from 1773 through 1822 are available.
- Gravestone transcriptions by the Genealogical Society of New Jersey are kept at Rutgers University.

New York

- Surrogate's Courts have been set up to handle probate in every county since 1787.
- Starting in 1830, every probate had to have a petition that listed the next of kin.
- Vital records registration began in 1880.
- State census records exist for every tenth year from 1825 through 1875 and for 1892, 1905, 1915, and 1925.

Pennsylvania

- Western Pennsylvania was owned by the French until after the French and Indian War.
- Statewide registration of vital records began in 1906.
- Land records under the Bureau of Land Records, now the Land Records Office, started in 1682.

CITY SEARCH

Another inescapable fact of the Mid-Atlantic region is that it includes some of the largest cities in North America. Your research strategy here is likely to become at some point an urban genealogical hunt, so it makes sense to learn some techniques for finding ancestors in densely populated areas:

- **Learn the history of the city.** Each city has a different growth pattern and population. By studying the history, you'll save yourself time and money looking for records.
- **Use directories.** Take advantage of city and telephone directories whenever they're available to help you sort through individuals of the same name and identify street addresses to assist with census research.
- **Locate a local resource.** Most metropolitan areas feature a historical society, and many public libraries have a local history collection. Take advantage of these resources to efficiently find what you're looking for. Library and archive staff can be ideal sources of genealogical reference help in these repositories.
- **Find maps.** Urban maps such as the Sanborn Insurance Atlases (available at many large public libraries) contain a phenomenal amount of information, including even the composition of the building your ancestor owned or rented. Maps also help orient you to various parts of a city.
- **Read the paper.** Metropolitan areas usually had at least one English-language newspaper (often there were several) and one published by each ethnic group that assimilated in the

area. Look for newspaper indexes and special collections of newspapers to help understand your ethnic roots—you may even find a published vital record or business notice about your ancestor.

- **Hire a professional researcher.** If you're trying to do long-distance research and the wait for records is interminable, consider enlisting a professional researcher in that area. While staffing is an issue at many archives, a walk-in patron can usually expedite the request process. The Association of Professional Genealogists has on its Web site <www.apgen.org> a list of members to help you find a researcher with relevant expertise.

OVERCOMING CHALLENGES

Don't be discouraged by nonexistent vital records, ink-smeared census documents, and the all-too-common "all the records were burned in a fire" scenario. Those black holes in your research sometimes can be overcome through patience and perseverance. Professional genealogist Edward Steele offers to regional researchers advice that has universal application: Success "requires an understanding of how records were initiated, by what legal or civic bodies they were created, and where they are now kept. Also, counties were changing their boundaries at the time that many families were passing through, so researchers may be searching in the wrong jurisdiction. And finally, many families did simply 'pass through,' staying for perhaps a generation or two (or not even that long) during the period before civil registration of vital events."

So get out there and consult research guides, hire researchers, do whatever will help you break the problem down into small pieces. Remember to create a timeline of your ancestors' lives, consider what types of records they created in their lifetimes, and think creatively. Consult church records, business records, and court documents, and read anything on paper or online that resembles your research problem.

You never know where a solution will appear, but looking in as many places as possible improves your odds of finding it.

After all, your Uncle Sam wants you—to find him, your Great-Great-Aunt Sally, your Quaker fifth-great-grandfather, the great-grandmother who passed through Ellis Island, and all the others whose stories make up your Mid-Atlantic heritage.

ORGANIZATIONS & ARCHIVES

Daughters of the American Revolution Library
1776 D St. NW
Washington, DC 20006
(202) 879-3229
<www.dar.org/library/default.html>

The Library of Congress
101 Independence Ave. SE
Washington, DC 20540
(202) 707-5000
<www.loc.gov>

National Institute on Genealogical Research
P.O. Box 14274
Washington, DC 20044
<www.rootsweb.com/~natgenin>

National Archives and Records Administration, Mid-Atlantic Region (Center City Philadelphia)
900 Market St.
Philadelphia, PA 19107
(215) 597-3000
Fax: (215) 597-2303
<www.archives.gov/facilities/pa/philadelphia_center_city.html>

National Archives and Records Administration, Mid-Atlantic Region (Northeast Philadelphia)
14700 Townsend Rd.
Philadelphia, PA 19154

(215) 671-9027
Fax: (215) 671-0273
<www.archives.gov/facilities/pa/philadelphia_northeast.html >

National Archives Library
Pennsylvania Avenue at Eighth Street NW
Washington, DC 20408
(202) 501-5415
<www.archives.gov>

National Archives and Records Administration, Northeast Region
201 Varick St.
New York, NY 10014
(212) 337-1300
<www.archives.gov/facilities/ny/new_york_city.html>

National Archives and Records Administration, Washington National Records Center
4205 Suitland Rd.
Suitland, MD 20746
(202) 501-5415
Fax: (202) 501-7006
<www.archives.gov/facilities/md/suitland.html>

RESOURCES

American Genealogical Research at the DAR, Washington, DC
by Eric G. Grundset and Steven B. Rhodes
(National Society,

Daughters of the American Revolution, $25)

Black History: A Guide to Civilian Records in the National Archives compiled by Debra L. Newman (National Archives and Records Administration, $15)

The Chesapeake Book of the Dead: Tombstones, Epitaphs, Histories, Reflections, and Oddments of the Region by Helen Chappell, Starke Jett ($24.95)

The Guide to Federal Records in the National Archives of the United States (National Archives and Records Adminstration, $95): Volumes 1 and 2 describe the record groups and much of what they contain. They also help you determine which facility might house the records you seek. Volume 3 indexes the descriptions. This publication is also available free online at <www.archives.gov/research_room/federal_records_guide/>

Guide to Genealogical Research in the National Archives Third ed. (National Archives and Records Administration, $25)

Guide to Records in the National Archives Relating to American Indians compiled by Edward E. Hill (National Archives and Records Administration, $25)

PERIODICALS

Prologue National Archives and Records Administration, 700 Pennsylvania Ave. NW, Washington, DC 20408. Some articles from past issues are online.

WEB SITES

American Family Immigration History Center <www.ellisisland.org>: Searchable database of passengers arriving at Ellis Island.

Canal People <lists.rootsweb.com/index/other/Occupations/CANAL-PEOPLE.html>

Mid-Atlantic Roots Network <midatlantic.rootsweb.com/>

Palatines to America <www.genealogy.org/~palam>

The Quaker Corner <www.rootsweb.com/~quakers/>

BALTIMORE
BY DARIN PAINTER

Two parts hydrogen, one part oxygen, and you have the element of choice for Marylanders. Perhaps that's why more than half of them live in Baltimore, the fifth-busiest port on the East Coast and widely known for its **National Aquarium** [Pier 3, 501 East Pratt Street; (410) 576-3800; <www.aqua.org>] and vibrant Inner Harbor. Watermen still prowl the Chesapeake Bay in flat-bottom skipjacks to catch Maryland blue crabs and drudge for "arshters" (oysters). You can cast your own net and feast on the city's bountiful genealogy resources.

The catch of the day is the **Maryland Historical Society Library** [201 West Monument Street; (410) 685-3750; <www.mdhs.org>], which showcases more than six million objects detailing the history of Maryland and its people. In its History and Genealogy Reading Room, you can plunge into immigration records; obituaries and marriage announcements extracted from newspapers; dozens of eighteenth- and nineteenth-century church registers; more than 400,000 photographs; donated Bible records and family group sheets; and issues of *The Bulletin*, the quarterly journal of the Maryland Genealogical Society <www.mdgensoc.org>. The Historical Society's museum also includes the original manuscript of "The Star-Spangled Banner," which Baltimorean Francis Scott Key wrote after the British bombardment of Fort McHenry during the War of 1812.

Another key to unlocking your family history in Baltimore is the **Central Branch of the Enoch Pratt Free Library** [400 Cathedral Street; (800) 492-5626; <www.pratt.lib.md.us>], the nation's first free-circulation public library. The Periodicals Department has a microfilm collection of census records for 1790 through 1930, slave schedules for 1850 and 1860, Port of Baltimore passenger lists for September 1820 through 1948, city directories for 1796 through 1937, and telephone directories for 1898 through 1972. Examine the microfilm collection "Genealogy and Local History: Parts 1-3," which catalogs more than five hundred family histories. The library's Maryland Department includes indexes of deaths from 1727 through 1915, marriages from 1727 through 1875, church and cemetery records, and more than two thousand Baltimore maps, dating back to 1630.

From there, you won't need a large map to find the **Baltimore Museum of Industry** [1415 Key Highway; (410) 727-4808; <www.charm. net/~bmi/>], a short walk (or water taxi ride) from the southern side of the Inner Harbor. Experience the city's rich history firsthand by strolling through an 1886 bank; operating a machine workshop circa 1900; or viewing past financial ledgers, correspondence books, payroll cards, union contracts, patents, and blueprints of local companies. In true Baltimore fashion, the museum building is a former oyster cannery.

Speaking of seafood, take a break and enjoy some. On a pier at the southwestern tip of the Inner Harbor, the **Rusty Scupper** [402 Key Highway; (410) 727-3678] offers a terrific view of the waterfront. **Windows** [Renaissance Harborplace Hotel, 202 East Pratt Street; (410) 547-1200] offers a panoramic view of the Inner Harbor and creative seafood entrees. If you'd rather dine on something that didn't swim, take a stroll east from the Inner Harbor toward Little Italy and try **La Tavola** [248 Albemarle Street; (410) 685-1859], renowned for its homemade pastas. A few blocks southeast of Little Italy is the cobblestone neighborhood of Fell's Point. Two great restaurants there are **Hamilton's** [888 South Broadway; (410) 522-2195], which serves flavorful contemporary cuisine, and **O'Bryckis Crab House** [1727 East Pratt Street; (410) 732-6399], *the* place to go in Baltimore for steamed crabs. (It's closed from mid-December to early March.)

If you're discovering your Baltimore roots with the next generation of family-history sleuths (your kids), open the door at **Port Discovery—The Baltimore Children's Museum** [35 Market Place; (410) 727-8120; <www. portdiscovery.com>]. The new, thirty million-dollar interactive museum includes Miss Perception's Mystery House, where children can help solve a mystery surrounding the disappearance of a fictitious family.

Solidarity, even among some families, was a real problem for Marylanders during the Civil War: The Southern state's loyalty was gray because many of its citizens sided with the blue. For a glimpse into the violence and divided loyalties your ancestors may have endured, check out the **Baltimore Civil War Museum—President Street Station** (601 President Street; (410) 385-5188; <www.mdhs.org/explore/baltcivilwar. html>).

Names of ancestors devoted to their faiths might appear in collections at Baltimore's religious sites. Three valuable ones are the **Jewish Historical Society of Maryland** [15 Lloyd Street; (410) 732-6400; <www.jhsm.org/>], **The United Methodist Historical Society of the Baltimore-Washington Conference** [2200 St. Paul Street; (410) 889-4458], and the **Archdiocese of Baltimore Archives** [320 Cathedral Street; (410) 547-5443].

Two sites are off the beaten path—but worth your while. The **Great Blacks in Wax Museum** [1601 East North Avenue; (410) 563-3404, <www.greatblacksinwax.org>] is America's first and only wax museum of African-American history and culture. **Westminster Cemetery and Catacombs** [West Fayette and Greene Streets; (410) 706-2072] is the city's oldest cemetery and the final resting place of Edgar Allan Poe (who lived in Baltimore when he wrote his first short story).

No genealogical journey to Baltimore is complete without taking a twenty-mile trip south to Annapolis to visit the newly constructed **Maryland State Archives** [I-97 South to Route 50 East to Exit 24 to 350 Rowe Boulevard; (410)

260-6400; <www.mdarchives.state.md.us>]. Its vital holdings date from the founding of the colony in 1634. They include complete birth, marriage, divorce, and death records; colonial and state executive, legislative, and judicial records; county probate, land, and court records; church records; business records; county and municipal government records; and special collections of private papers, maps, photographs, and newspapers. The archives' search room is closed on Sundays and Mondays. (For records of births after 1978, deaths after 1987, and marriages after 1973, you'll need to visit the **Department of Health and Mental Hygiene's Division of Vital Records** in Baltimore [6550 Reisterstown Road; (800) 832-3277; <www.dhmh.state.md.us/>].)

Near the Maryland State Archives is the **Maryland State Law Library** [361 Rowe Boulevard; (410) 260-1430; <www.lawlib.state.md.us>], which boasts a complete microfilm file of the *Baltimore Sun* from 1837 to the present.

For a quick bite here in America's Sailing Capital, stroll down Annapolis's Main Street to the City Dock and try **McGarvey's Saloon and Oyster Bar** [8 Market Space, (410) 263-5700] for the locally famous crab dip appetizer. (Don't mind the large tree growing inside the restaurant.)

Wherever you plan to visit, before booking a hotel room for your trip, make a stop online at <www.MarylandGenealogy.com>. The site posts discounted hotel rates for genealogists through its reservation service (powered by Lodging.com). Several hotels are within walking distance of the Maryland Historical Society and Inner Harbor; these include the Victorian-style **Biltmore Suites Hotel** [206 West Madison Street; (410) 728-6550; <www.biltmoresuites.com>], the 622-room **Renaissance Harborplace Hotel** [202 East Pratt Street; (410) 547-1200], and the economical **Days Inn Inner Harbor** [100 Hopkins Place; (410) 576-1000].

NEW YORK CITY

BY AMY LEIBROCK

Washington, DC, may hold the keys to our nation's political history, but New York City embodies our nation's character. Tens of millions of immigrants passed through the Port of New York in search of a better life, which means at least 40 percent of all Americans can trace their roots to the Big Apple. You can do plenty of research here, but save time to visit some of the outstanding sites that provide a glimpse into what life was like for your immigrant ancestors in this ever-evolving metropolis.

Begin your trip as more than twelve million immigrants did, with a ferry ride to **Ellis Island** ($8 per ferry ticket). Go early: In addition to doing research at the **American Family Immigration History Center** [<www.ellisisland.org>; $5 admission; (212) 883-1986 for reservations], you'll want to spend a few hours perusing the exhibits at the **Ellis Island Immigration Museum** [<www.nps.gov/elis>; (212) 363-3200]. At the history center, you can search ships' passenger records for 1892 to 1924 and obtain reproductions of original ship manifests and photos of ships of passage. The museum takes visitors through the very rooms immigrants were shuffled through; these rooms are now full of photos, artifacts, and text and recorded interviews chronicling the immigrants' journeys from their homelands to the lives they found in America.

On the ferry to Ellis Island, which departs from **Battery Park** (by subway, 4, 5 to Bowling Green; 1, 9 to South Ferry), you may be tempted to stop at the **Statue of Liberty** [(212) 363-3200; <www.nps.gov/stli>]. If you devote only one day to these sites, you might want to settle for taking photos of the statue from the ferry—it takes at least three hours to get through the Immigration Museum's mesmerizing exhibits. For more on Ellis Island, see the next article.

If your ancestors immigrated through New York before 1892, you can search for their records at the **National Archives** in the West Village [201 Varick Street; (212) 337-1300; <www.archives.gov/facilities/ny/new_york_city.html>; 1, 9 to Houston Street; E to Spring Street]. The archives' highlights include ships' passenger records for the Port of New York for 1820 to 1957, naturalization records for most of New York and New Jersey, and census records for 1790 through 1920.

One of the country's largest genealogical and local history collections that is open to the public is at the **New York Public Library's Irma and Paul Milstein Division of United States History, Local History and Genealogy** [Fifth Avenue and Forty-second Street, Room 121; (212) 930-0828; <www.nypl.org/research/chss/lhg/genea.html>; D, F, S to Forty-second Street; 4, 5, 6, S to Grand Central/Forty-second Street]. The division collects materials documenting American history on the national, state, and local levels, as well as visual resources and international genealogical materials.

A much different body of materials is accessible at the **New York Family History Center** [125 Columbus Avenue at Sixty-fifth Street, Second Floor; (212) 873-1690; 1, 9 to Sixty-sixth Street/Lincoln Center]. This noteworthy branch of Salt Lake City's Family History Library has more than 8,500 microfiche and microfilms and more than 900 books focusing on British, Eastern European, Caribbean, Puerto Rican, and Canadian information.

If your ancestors were among the one-third of Ellis Island immigrants to settle in New York, you can visit several places to research their stories. Start with the **Municipal Reference and Research Center** [31 Chambers Street, Room 112; (212) 788-8590; <www.ci.nyc.ny.us/html/doris/html/dorisref.html>; R to City Hall; 4, 5, 6 to Brooklyn Bridge/City Hall; A, C to Chambers Street; 2, 3 to Park Place], which houses vital records for 1795 to 1948, various city directories dating from 1796, a wealth of city government records, and photographs of every building in all five boroughs taken from 1939 to 1941 by the Department of Taxes.

The library collections at the **New York Historical Society** [$5 suggested donation; 2 W. Seventy-seventh Street at Central Park West; (212) 873-3400; <www.nyhistory.org>; B, C to 81st Street] consist of approximately 500,000 books and pamphlets, two million manuscripts, and more than ten thousand newspaper titles. Visitors can also access one of the world's largest collections of orderly books from the American Revolution and an array of publications and manuscripts from the Civil War.

It may be worth the $50 out-of-New York membership fee to join the **New York Genealogical & Biographical Society** [122-126 E. Fifty-eighth Street between Park Avenue and Lexington Avenue; (212) 755-8532; <www.nygbs.org>; 4, 5, 6 to Fifty-ninth Street]. The society's library houses more than 75,000 books; thirteen hundred periodicals; thirty thousand manuscripts; nearly 22,000 microforms; and computer media focusing mainly on New York state genealogy and local history.

For an authentic look at how New York's immigrants lived, visit the **Lower East Side Tenement Museum** [90 Orchard Street; (212) 431-0233; <www.tenement.org>; F to Delancey]. There you can learn about the lives of past residents of the building that was home from 1863 to 1935 to an estimated seven thousand people from more than twenty nations. Call ahead for tour tickets ($8 and $9). You can combine this with a tour of the **Merchant's House Museum** [$5 admission; 29 E. Fourth Street between Bowery and Lafayette Streets; (212) 777-1089; <www.merchantshouse.com>; 6 to Astor Place]. Built in 1832, it's the city's only family home preserved intact from the nineteenth century.

If you're especially interested in a particular neighborhood, consider taking a guided walking tour. **Big Onion Walking Tours** [(212) 439-1090; <www.bigonion.com>] and **NYC Discovery**

Walking Tours [(212) 465-3331] offer a range of interestingly themed tours led by knowledgeable guides.

At $1.50 per ride, the quickest and most economical way to traverse the city is by subway. Tokens are still sold, but most people now use Metrocards, which are also good on buses and can be bought at token booths or self-serve machines in stations. Depending on how much you'll use the trains, you may choose to put money on a Metrocard or buy a one-day ($4) or seven-day ($17) unlimited-ride card.

The lines are denoted by letters and numbers. Directions in stations are almost always indicated by "uptown" and "downtown," so be sure you know before you enter a station which way you're going and then double-check the signs above the platforms. Maps are free at token booths.

New York's continual influx of cultures makes for a stellar culinary scene. If you're up for Italian, try Little Italy's **Il Cortile** [125 Mulberry Street between Canal and Hester Streets; (212) 226-6060; 6, N, R, J, M, Z to Canal Street]. Pick any one of the eateries in "Little India" (E. Sixth Street between First and Second Avenues) for savory and economical Indian fare. The **2nd Avenue Deli** [156 Second Avenue and Tenth Street; (212) 677-0606; 6 to Astor Place] is a New York kosher classic.

If you're in the mood to splurge, call for reservations at **Jean Georges** in the Trump International Hotel [jacket required; 1 Central Park West between Sixtieth and Sixty-first Streets; (212) 299-3900; A, B, C, D, 1, 9 to 59th St./Columbus Circle]. And for the best American mac 'n cheese, take a seat at **Chat 'n Chew** [10 E. Sixteenth Street, one block west of Union Square; (212) 243-1616; L, N, R, 4, 5, 6 to Union Square]. Visit <www.zagat.com> or <newyork.citysearch.com> for more restaurant ideas.

As for lodging, with so many hotels (and such high prices) to pick from, where to start?

For easy access to Ellis Island, the National Archives, and the Municipal Archives, consider downtown's **Marriott Financial Center** [85 West Street; (800) 242-8685] or the **Millennium Hilton** [55 Church Street; (800) 774-1500].

Within walking distance of the public library, the literary landmark **Algonquin Hotel** [59 W. Forty-fourth Street, between Fifth and Sixth Avenues; (212) 840-6800] offers 165 rooms that drip with classic New York style. For a more economical choice, stay at the **Quality Hotel and Suites Midtown** [59 W. Forty-sixth Street, between Fifth and Sixth Avenues; (800) 567-7720].

ELLIS ISLAND

BY DAVID A. FRYXELL

Annie Moore was lucky. Because the thirteen-year-old Irish girl was the first immigrant to pass through Ellis Island, on January 1, 1892, she was treated more like a celebrity than one of the "huddled masses yearning to breathe free" described on the nearby Statue of Liberty. Fresh off the boat from County Cork, Annie entered America bearing a ten-dollar gold coin from the state immigration commissioner.

The twelve million immigrants who came after her over the next thirty-two years hardly received a red-carpet introduction to America.

Twelve million immigrants passed through Ellis Island between 1892 and 1924.

Herded like animals, probed by doctors, interrogated, tested, sometimes separated from their families, and sometimes even turned away, the "wretched refuse" of Europe's teeming shores came to think of Ellis Island as the "island of hope, island of tears." But they made it, most of them, following Annie Moore to the promised land and remaking America in their image. Today, more than 100 million Americans have at least one ancestor who came through Ellis Island.

A trip to Ellis Island is a perfect way to explore your own immigrant heritage. You can relive your ancestors' experiences in a state-of-the-art museum. You can look for your family's name on the **American Immigration Wall of Honor,** the largest wall of names in the world. You can hear seventeen hundred oral-history interviews of immigrants and former Ellis Island employees. And now, thanks to the $22.5 million **American Family Immigration History Center** that opened in 2001, you can find your immigrant ancestors' actual passenger records and create a multimedia scrapbook of your heritage.

Since the abandoned and dilapidated Ellis Island was restored and reopened as a national monument in 1990, visitors have enjoyed the re-creation of the immigrant experience—and yet they've gone away frustrated at the inability to access their ancestors' records there. Until recently, genealogists and historians interested in the records of Ellis Island's immigrants had to squint at National Archives microfilm. The new center, developed and funded by the **Statue of Liberty-Ellis Island Foundation**, puts these pages from our history at the fingertips of Ellis Island visitors as well as Web surfers who visit <www.ellisisland.org>.

Your visit to Ellis Island will be a good deal more comfortable than your immigrant ancestor's was. To get there, take the same ferries that serve the nearby **Statue of Liberty**. Ferries depart from **Battery Park** in Manhattan (tickets are sold at **Castle Clinton**) and **Liberty State Park** in New Jersey from 9 A.M. to 3:50 P.M. daily, with extended hours in the summer. Round-trip tickets are $8 for adults, $6 for seniors, and $3 for children. If you want to include a climb to the Statue of Liberty's crown in your trip, catch the first ferry of the day to get a place in line. For more information on the ferry, call (212) 269-5755 for New York or (201) 435-9499 for New Jersey information. Admission to Ellis Island is free.

Like millions of immigrants did, you'll begin by entering the ornate, red-brick and limestone Beaux Arts main immigration processing facility. Restored in 1990 at a cost of $170 million, it's now a 200,000-square-foot museum filled with artifacts and historic images. Two theaters feature *Island of Hope, Island of Tears*, a thirty-minute movie documentary. A small stage showcases a play, *Embracing Freedom*, based on interviews with immigrants and Ellis Island inspectors. The movie is free; play tickets cost $3 for adults and $2.50 for seniors and children. The museum also includes a bookstore, a gift shop, and a cafeteria.

Entrance to the new American Family Immigration History Center costs $5 per session. You should make advance reservations for the center's interactive kiosks; call (212) 883-1986 or use the Web site <www.ellisisland.org>.

Each visitor to the new center gets a swipe card; use the card to log in to "Your Ellis Island File," where you can store your genealogical findings. After a multimedia introduction to the island and its history, you will be led through the steps to search for your ancestors. It's easy to flip back and forth between a digitized version of the passenger files—the fruits of more than 5.6 million volunteer hours of painstaking input and cross-checking—and more than three million scanned images of actual handwritten ship manifests. You can also view an image of the ship that brought your family to America.

The center enables members of the Statue of Liberty-Ellis Island Foundation ($45 annual fee) to create digital family history scrapbooks. Special scrapbooking rooms, designed to hold up to seven family members, provide a scanner, microphone, camera, and keyboard so you can capture family stories, take a group picture, scan in an image of grandpa's pocket watch, or record a favorite family song. An on-screen "host" walks patrons through the whole process. Once family members review their creation, after having selected from four different page formats and various cover designs, they can receive a free printout of their scrapbook or get a multimedia version on CD-ROM.

For your immigrant ancestors, having their names on that ship's manifest was the culmination of a dream—and often the beginning of a nightmare. A steerage ticket to America cost about twenty-five dollars, which might have been two years' wages. That bought passage on a crowded, three thousand-mile voyage of two weeks to a month as human cargo, suffering seasickness and unsanitary conditions on a diet of thin soup and bread.

Harder still than the voyage was leaving behind everything and everyone they knew. Julia Gonipow, who emigrated from Lithuania in 1899, remembered, "The day I left home, my mother came with me to the railroad station. When we said 'good-bye,' she said it was just like seeing me go into my casket. I never saw her again."

But they said their good-byes and endured the trip to reach, as one British cartoon now hanging in the Ellis Island museum put it, "the U.S. Ark of Refuge," where they'd find "free education, free land, free speech, free ballot, free lunch." They left behind joblessness, poverty, conscription, and persecution. Although English, Irish, Germans, and Scandinavians had led the migration to America for most of the nineteenth century, by the time Ellis Island opened in 1892, immigrants from Italy, Russia, and Austria-Hungary had joined the flood. By 1907, these three groups accounted for 75 percent of the traffic through Ellis Island.

On the ship's arrival, immigration officials cleared first- and second-class passengers aboard. Steerage passengers were hustled onto a ferry to Ellis Island. According to one of the most often told tales about Ellis Island, the harried immigration inspectors routinely changed newcomers' names through misspelling or simplification. But Sharon DeBartolo Carmack, author of *A Genealogist's Guide to Discovering Your Immigrant & Ethnic Ancestors* (Betterway Books, $18.99), debunks this legend: "No evidence whatsoever exists to suggest this ever occurred, and I have challenged countless people who insist their ancestor's name was changed on Ellis Island to provide me with proof. So far, no one has been able to…. Inspectors compared the names the immigrants told them against what was recorded on the passenger lists. These lists were created at the ports of departure. There was no reason to record or change anyone's surname once they arrived. More likely, immigrants themselves changed their names after they settled in America to avoid prejudice and to blend more easily into American society."

At its peak in 1907, Ellis Island saw more than eleven thousand immigrants a day. Wearing numbered tags that matched a page of the ship's manifest, the immigrants entered the Baggage Room. Here they could check their meager possessions, a sampling of which can be seen today in the "Treasures From Home" exhibit: wool gloves from Norway; eyeglasses from Scotland; an apron from Romania; a ladies' fan from Italy; a battered teddy bear that came to America from Switzerland with Gertrude Schneider, age ten.

From the Baggage Room, the immigrants went up to the Registry Room, the great, two-story main hall with its American flags and vaulted, terra-cotta-tiled ceiling. Even as the immigrants mounted the stairs, Public Health Service doctors watched for signs of infirmity. In what became known as "the six-second physical," the doctors scanned for ailments that might disqualify a newcomer. Chalk marks on the clothes identified those to be detained for further examination: "H" for heart problems, "L" for lameness, "E" for eye disease. Intelligence was tested, too. A typical question might be "Would you wash stairs from the top down or from the bottom up?"—which once brought the sharp response, "I didn't come to America to wash stairs."

At the far end of the Registry Room waited the legal inspectors. Working with an army of interpreters, they tried to weed out anarchists, polygamists, and immigrants unable to support themselves in their new land (these were coded "S.I.-L.P.C.": "special inquiry—likely to become a public charge"). About 10 percent of immigrants were held for a hearing; today, visitors to Ellis Island can relive this experience by serving as a mock hearing board, deciding an immigrant's fate in a reenactment.

The average stay at Ellis Island was less than a day. Some immigrants, however, had to stay overnight in crowded dormitories or be quarantined in the island's hospital. Families got separated, and anxious parents might have waited weeks to be reunited with their children. More than 3,500 immigrants died on Ellis Island, and more than 350 babies were born there. Ultimately, about two out of every hundred would-be new Americans were turned away.

Most immigrants who came to Ellis Island, however, went down from the Registry Room to the railroad ticket office and the free ferries to a new life. Immigrants bound for Manhattan met their relatives—many of whom they'd never seen—at the "kissing post." Katherine Beychok, a Russian Jewish immigrant in 1910, remembered meeting her father for the first time: "I saw a man coming forward, and he was so beautiful.... And I fell in love with him and he with me." Gaining entrance to America, another immigrant recalled, "was as if God's great promise had been fulfilled."

Once beyond the gateway of Ellis Island, though, immigrants found that life could be every bit as hard as it had been back home. An old Italian story posted in today's Ellis Island museum puts it this way: "I came to America because I heard the streets were paved with gold. When I got here, I found out three things: First, the streets were not paved with gold. Second, they weren't paved at all. Third, I was expected to pave them."

But pave them they did—and build our cities and make our laws and enrich our culture. Irving Berlin came through Ellis Island from Russia in 1893; Al Jolson, from Lithuania in 1894. Knute Rockne arrived from Norway in 1893. Felix Frankfurter came from Austria in 1894. Sol Hurok came from the Ukraine in 1906. Isaac Asimov came from Russia in 1923.

They gave America their children, too. For example, among the 600,000 names inscribed on Ellis Island's American Immigrant Wall of Honor are the parents of one Francis Albert Sinatra.

The wall, a row of gleaming slabs of names outside the museum, honors all who came and built America. Whether your immigrant ancestors entered through Ellis Island, through another port, or forcibly as slaves, you can memorialize them here for a contribution of $100 to the Statue of Liberty-Ellis Island Foundation.

Computer kiosks let you search for names on the wall. You can find notables ranging from George Washington's great-grandfather and John F. Kennedy's great-grandparents to the ancestors of Gregory Peck, Cicely Tyson, and Jay Leno. (For more information on the Wall of Honor, call (212) 561-4500, or write Ellis Campaign, 292 Madison Ave., Floor 14, New York, NY 10017. You can also register a name online at <www.wallofhonor.com/names>.)

"It touches a human chord in the great spirit of adventure," says Stephen Briganti, president of the Statue of Liberty-Ellis Island Foundation, "how these people made it possible for us to be Americans. They are our history."

Though immigrants entered through other ports, by far the greatest influx during the greatest human migration in history came through Ellis Island. And today, Ellis Island is the only national monument dedicated to the immigrant experience shared by so many of our ancestors.

Like thirteen-year-old Annie Moore, who's immortalized in a statue in Ellis Island's museum, our ancestors sailed under the Statue of Liberty's lamp and to this "golden door." Most weren't as lucky as Annie, and it was a long time before many of them saw a ten-dollar gold piece.

But we're all lucky that they came.

PHILADELPHIA

BY LAUREN EISENSTODT

Home of the Liberty Bell. First capital of the United States. Birthplace of the Declaration of Independence and the Constitution. Philadelphia is where our nation began—what better place to uncover your roots? Founded in 1682 by William Penn, an English Quaker, the city grew to be the second-largest English-speaking city in the world during the eighteenth century. Called the Athens of the Americas, it has remained a cultural center as the fifth-largest city in the United States and the second-largest city on the East Coast.

Philadelphia's old-world charm can be found in the cobblestone streets and Colonial-era homes of the Historic and Waterfront District, located a couple of blocks east of the Convention Center between Sixth Street and Penn's Landing on the banks of the Delaware River. This is where you're likely to spend much of your visit as you explore your American heritage. Take a day or two to wander around Old City, a historic hub of Philadelphia. Here you can find the **Betsy Ross House**, the **U.S. Mint**, and a number of historic churches and synagogues. You should also stroll down **Elfreth's Alley**, the nation's oldest residential street. While you're in

the neighborhood, grab a hoagie for lunch. You'll find coupons for these Philly-born sandwiches—as well as a number of area attractions—at Historic Philadelphia Inc.'s Web site <historic.philly.com>.

Just south of Old City, past Market Street, is **Independence National Historic Park**, where you can see the **Liberty Bell** and tour **Independence Hall**, in which our forefathers created the country's most important documents. The forty-five-acre park has some twenty buildings open to the public. Most offer free tours, but some charge a $2 interpretive fee. Independence Hall is a popular tourist attraction, so get there early to avoid the wait for a free tour. For current hours and other information, call (215) 597-8974 or visit the Web site <www.nps.gov/inde>.

Need a break from the crowds? Begin your

You can trace the "genealogy" of the United States back to Independence Hall in Philadelphia.

serious genealogical research with the **Historical Society of Pennsylvania**'s (HSP) extensive Civil War resources and collection of forty thousand published and unpublished genealogies. HSP's library [1300 Locust Street; (215) 732-6200] is open Tuesday through Saturday. Admission is $5 for adults and $2 for students who have current student identification cards. Check the Web site <www.hsp.org> for detailed directions and library rules.

Another resource is the **National Archives and Records Administration's Mid-Atlantic Region** facility [900 Market Street; (215) 597-3000; <www.archives.gov/facilities/pa/philadelphia_center_city.html>], which holds World War I draft registration cards and naturalization records and indexes for Delaware, Maryland, Pennsylvania, Virginia, and West Virginia.

For naturalization and vital records as well as city directories, visit the **Philadelphia City Archives** [3101 Market Street, Suite 150; (215) 685-9401; <apps.phila.gov/phils/records.htm>]. But if you're looking for records of births and deaths that occurred after June 30, 1915, you'll have to apply to the **Pennsylvania Division of Vital Records** [1400 Spring Garden Street, Room 1009; (215) 560-3054].

You won't want to leave the City of Brotherly Love without visiting at least one of its museums, which will further your appreciation for your heritage or that of your neighbor. In 2000, the **National Liberty Museum** [321 Chestnut Street; (215) 925-2800; <www.libertymuseum. org/browse.htm>] was created to celebrate "our nation's heritage of freedom and the wonderful diverse society it has produced" by paying tribute to more than 350 heroes of democracy from America and abroad. Admission is $5 for adults, $4 for seniors, and $3 for students.

Celebrate black heritage at the **African American Museum of Philadelphia** [701 Arch Street; (215) 574-0380; <aampmuseum.org>]. Admission is $6 for adults and $4 for seniors, students, children, and those with disabilities.

In the eighteenth century, Philadelphia was the world's second-largest English-speaking city.

The **National Museum of American Jewish History** [55 N. Fifth Street; (215) 923-3811; <www.nmajh.org>] charges $3 for adults and $2 for seniors, students, and children.

Climb into immigrant ship bunks and chart a course for Penn's Landing at the **Independence Seaport Museum** [211 S. Columbus Boulevard and Walnut Street; (215) 925-5439; <seaport.philly.com>]. With hands-on exhibits and a research library containing maps, ship plans, and logbooks, this is the place to explore Philadelphia's maritime history. Admission is $8 for adults, $6.50 for seniors, and $4 for children.

The best way to see Philadelphia is to walk it, but you have alternatives. You can reach just about any area by public transit: bus, subway, or trolley. Your best bet, though, is the tourist-friendly **PHLASH** bus [<www.phillyphlash.net>; (215) 4-PHLASH], which will shuttle you for just $4 a day to thirty-two stops near area attractions.

Philadelphia has been named the number-one restaurant city, and for good reason. Whether you crave curry or cheese steak, you'll find it here. Start sampling with these restaurants, which you'll find near the above attractions:

- **Fork** [306 Market Street; (215) 625-9425; <www.forkrestaurant.com>]—hip, classy spot for the over-thirty crowd

- **Rococo** [123 Chestnut Street; (215) 629-1100]—multiethnic cuisine recognized by *Gourmet Magazine*
- **City Tavern** [132 S. Second Street; (215) 413-1443]—colonial tavern with an impressive selection of beer
- **Lamberti's Cucina** [212 Walnut Street; (215) 238-0499; <www.lambertis.com>]—moderately priced Italian cuisine; near Independence Seaport Museum
- **Blue Angel** [706 Chestnut Street; (215) 925-6889]—voted "best French fries" by *Philadelphia Magazine*
- **Warmdaddy's** [Front and Market Streets; (215) 627-8400; <www.warmdaddys.com>]—jazz, blues, and Southern cookin'

While researching your ancestors, why not stay in a restored eighteenth-century bed-and-breakfast? Step back into the Federal Period at the **Thomas Bond House** [129 S. Second Street; (800) 845-2663; <www.winston-salem-inn.com/philadelphia>], the only bed-and-breakfast in Independence National Historic Park. Rooms run between $95 and $175 per night. You might also try **Penn's View Inn** [14 N. Front Street; (215) 922-7600], a nineteenth-century bed-and-breakfast with prices ranging from $120 to $200 per night.

The **Best Western Inn** [235 Chestnut Street; (215) 922-4443] in Old City also offers plenty of charm. It's in an old Victorian townhouse just minutes from landmarks and restaurants; rooms run from $135 to $200 per night.

If you're on a budget, the **Comfort Inn** [100 N. Christopher Columbus Boulevard; (215) 627-7900] doesn't offer a lot of frills, but it does have a great view of the Delaware River. And it's just a few blocks from Old City.

PITTSBURGH

BY JESSICA YEREGA

You probably think of Pittsburgh simply as the "Steel City" of the Industrial Revolution. But while maintaining the quaint, close-knit ethnic neighborhoods that were once mill towns and the historic landmarks that were once simply functional, the city has slowly grown into a clean, safe, and cultural travel destination.

The **Carnegie Library of Pittsburgh** [4400 Forbes Avenue; (412) 622-3114; <www.clpgh.org>] is one of the nation's original public libraries, dating back to 1895. Its walls house more than four million resources. For histories, records, and directories of regional genealogical information, check the library's Pennsylvania Department of Genealogy <www.clpgh.org/clp/Pennsylvania/pagen.html>. Resources here, to name just a few, include directories for Pittsburgh and surrounding cities dating back as far as 1815; census records; immigration and passenger lists; and historic data on deeds, maps, and cemeteries. When you're in this massive building, make sure you don't miss the library and offices of the **Western Pennsylvania Genealogical Society** [(412) 687-6811; <www.wpgs.org/wpgs.html>], which boasts regional records unavailable elsewhere. Out-of-town membership in this society is available.

The library is not the only genealogical game in town. If you're still hungry for local information, visit **The Senator John Heinz Pittsburgh Regional History Center** [1212 Smallman Street; (412) 454-6000; <www.pghhistory.org>].

If you dare to delve back into history as far as the French and Indian War, take a stroll through scenic **Point State Park** [(412) 471-0235], where the city's three rivers—the Allegheny, the Monongahela, and the Ohio—meet, and stop by the park's **Fort Pitt Museum** [(412) 281-9284]. This was the key to what was then "the west" for both the French and the British, just as Pittsburgh later became an important departure point for settlers heading to the Northwest Territory.

If this gets you in the mood to go museum hopping, you've come to the right place. The Carnegie Institute was established in 1895 by local steel tycoon Andrew Carnegie. Today four

Carnegie Museums of Pittsburgh <www.carnegiemuseums.org> thrive: the **Carnegie Museum of Art**, the **Carnegie Museum of Natural History** [both adjacent to the library at 4400 Forbes Avenue; (412) 622-3131; $8 adult admission at each facility], the **Carnegie Science Center** [1 Allegheny Avenue; (412) 237-3400; $14 adult admission], and **The Andy Warhol Museum** [117 Sandusky Street; (412) 237-8300; $8 adult admission], celebrating the works of another of Pittsburgh's famous sons.

Take a historic tour of the city from a different angle on "America's largest and most successful inland riverboat company": the **Gateway Clipper Fleet** [Station Square, (412) 355-7980; <www.gatewayclipper.com>], whose boats have skirted the city since 1958. Select the Narrated Historical Three Rivers Sightseeing Cruise, or choose from a number of other cruises stopping off at places such as the rivers' locks and dams, the zoo, the aviary, the Carnegie Science Center, **PNC Park** (home of the Pittsburgh Pirates) and **Heinz Field** (home of the Steelers). Cruise prices start at $4.50. Special educational tours for children are also available.

Once you've walked the libraries and sailed the rivers, consider climbing the mountain. Beginning in 1870, inclines—cable-powered boxes resembling trolley cars—transported mill workers from their homes atop Mount Washington, which overlooks the city from across the rivers, down the steep slope to their jobs at the riverside mills. Two remain in operation today: the **Monongahela Incline** [Station Square; (412) 442-2000] and the **Duquesne Incline** [1197 West Carson Street; (412) 381-1665].

If your ancestors lived in Pittsburgh, they probably either worked in the steel mills or lived in a community of people who did. The **Steel Industry Heritage Corporation** [623 East Eighth Avenue; (412) 464-5119; <www.riversofsteel.com>] offers tours of the remaining mills. These tours run May through November, and you can choose to tour by bus or boat. Be sure to make reservations in advance. To preface your trip with a historical fictional account of what it was like to live and work in Pittsburgh while immigrants were flocking to the city's booming steel industry, read *Out of This Furnace* by Thomas Bell (University of Pittsburgh Press, $14.95).

Today the **Nationality Rooms** at the **University of Pittsburgh's Cathedral of Learning** [1209 Cathedral of Learning; (412) 624-6000; <www.pitt.edu/~natrooms>] showcase the legacy of these immigrants. Construction began on the forty-two-story Gothic cathedral in 1926, and the twenty-six Nationality Rooms were completed between 1938 and 2000. Each room is dedicated to a different heritage. Adult admission to these rooms, on the ground floor in the nation's tallest academic building, is $3. As you leave, stop for a look at the breathtaking 1938 **Heinz Memorial Chapel** on the cathedral's lawn [Fifth and South Bellefield Streets; (412) 624-4157].

The railroad was also key to the thriving city's economy in the late 1800s and early 1900s. Today the city honors and celebrates that history at the restored **Station Square** <www.stationsquare.com> across from downtown. This historic site originally served as the yards of the Pittsburgh and Lake Erie Railroad, but today it houses along the tracks an outdoor museum, a hotel, and more than forty specialty shops (many of which feature art and other regional items) and restaurants. Both inclines and the Gateway Clipper Fleet are also easily accessible from the station. The outdoor amphitheater at Station Square provides entertainment in seasonable temperatures. See the sights by taking a ride on the Gray Line Sightseeing Trolley or by enjoying a twilight horse-drawn carriage ride.

To let your inner child in on your historical trip, spend a day at one of the city's two historic amusement parks, open May through September. The first roller coaster at **Kennywood Park** [4800 Kennywood Boulevard; (412) 461-0500; <www.kennywood.com>] was built in

1902, and the park still features restored wooden rides. General admission is $8, and ride-all-day passes range from $22.95 to $27.95. If you care to venture a bit farther from city limits, visit **Idlewild Park** [fifty miles from Pittsburgh on Route 30 East; (724) 238-6544; <www.idlewild.com>], originally built in 1878. The park features a water park and Story Book Forest, begun in 1956 to bring nursery rhymes to life. Fun Day passes are $19.95.

For accommodations within walking distance of the Carnegie Library, try the **Holiday Inn University Center** [100 Lytton Avenue; (412) 682-6200]. If you prefer to stay in the heart of downtown, consider the **Ramada Plaza Suites and Conference Center** [1 Bigelow Square; (800) 225-5858; <www.plazasuites.com>]. The **Sheraton Station Square Hotel** [7 Station Square Drive; (888) 729-7705] offers an up-close view of the city from just across the river.

For a low-budget meal with a regional flavor, try one of the **Primanti Brothers** locations across the city [central downtown location: 2 South Market Place; (412) 261-1599]. Here you can experience "The Original Pittsburgh Sandwich," featuring french fries and coleslaw in-between the bread with the rest of your fixings. To check out *Pittsburgh Magazine*'s choice for "Best steak in Pittsburgh" in a casual downtown atmosphere, visit **Ruth's Chris Steak House** [6 PPG Place; (412) 391-4800]. You can pick from a full menu of American cuisine at **The Ruddy Duck** [1 Bigelow Square; (412) 281-3825]. You can combine upscale dining and a taste of history at the **Grand Concourse** [Station Square; (412) 261-1717], a former train station that has been converted into an elegant restaurant along the railroad tracks and offers its diners a chance to "take a step back in time."

WASHINGTON, DC

BY JIM FABER

Nothing beats a trip to the nation's capital for putting you in touch with history, family and otherwise. And don't let your research quest keep you from seeing a bit of the city while you're there. Washington, after all, is perhaps the only city in the world to list government and tourism as its top two industries.

Maybe you've been to one of the National Archives' regional facilities, but you'll want to make a trip to the **National Archives Building** (700 Pennsylvania Avenue NW; <www.archives.gov/research_room/genealogy>), which holds our government's most cherished documents: the Declaration of Independence and the Constitution. There's plenty of information to keep you busy; there's also plenty of information to get lost in, so plan ahead. Visit NARA's Genealogy Page to view the archives' holdings. For research tips, see the Research Room Web site at <www.archives.gov/research_room>, or call (800) 234-8861.

When visiting Washington, it makes sense to leave your car at home. Parking is tough to come by legally, and the city's good things come in clusters. Plan to walk a lot and use the city's subway system, the **Metro**. The Metro is clean, cost efficient ($5 for an all-day pass), and will get you to most places that you want to go. The National Archives Building is right off the Archives/Navy Memorial stop on the yellow or green line. You can find a map on the Metro's Web site <www.wmata.com>. The only drawback of the Metro is that the system shuts down around midnight on most weeknights. Late nights will require springing for a cab, and you'll pay based on an archaic zones-traveled-through system instead of a time or distance fare.

Some monuments, such as the FDR memorial, are a hike from the Metro, though. Your best bet for these is a **Tourmobile** pass, which lets you get on and off at any of its twenty-four stops (see <www.tourmobile.com>).

Other must-sees for family history buffs are the **Library of Congress** and the Smithsonian Institution. The library holds more than 120 million items on 530 miles of bookshelves in its three massive buildings, which are named after Library of Congress founder Thomas Jefferson, John Adams, and James Madison. It's located at 101 Independence Avenue SE; use the Capitol South Metro stop (blue and orange lines). Researchers should use the Second Street entrance to the Jefferson Building, Admission is free. For further information, call (202) 707-5000 or visit the Web site at <www.loc.gov>.

The **Smithsonian Institution** <www.si.edu> includes fourteen museums in Washington, DC, and the National Zoo. Its **National Museum of American History** [Fourteenth Street and Constitution Avenue Northwest; (202) 357-2700; <americanhistory.si.edu>] has a collection ranging from the "Star-Spangled Banner" flag to Judy Garland's *The Wizard of Oz* ruby slippers. It's truly "the nation's attic." Use the Smithsonian or Federal Triangle Metro stops (blue and orange lines). Admission is free.

Take time to explore the 150,000 volumes and 53,000 microforms of genealogical material at the **Daughters of the American Revolution Library** [1776 D Street NW; (202) 879-3229; <www.dar.org/library/default.html>]. The library is open to researchers weekdays and Sunday afternoons for a fee of $5 (except during holidays and the group's annual meeting in mid-April). Use the Farragut West Metro stop (blue and orange lines).

Among the city's newer museum attractions is the **United States Holocaust Memorial Museum** [100 Raoul Wallenberg Place Southwest; Smithsonian Metro stop; (202) 488-0400; <www.ushmm.org>], which offers a somber but important look at history. Admission is free but timed. Since all tickets frequently are gone by noon, consider reserving them in advance [<tickets.com> or (800) 400-9373] for a small fee. Please think twice before taking small children to this powerful, harrowing museum.

Check out <www.washingtonpost.com/wp-srv/entertainment/art/museumlist.htm> for a handy guide to Washington's museum riches.

After a hard day of research or museum-hopping, you'll need to eat. Fortunately, Washington is a glutton's paradise. Food of any origin—Thai, Ethiopian, Indian, and Vietnamese, among many others—can be found in this international town. To hobnob with the city's journalists and congressional staffers, try the **Hawk and Dove** [329 Pennsylvania Avenue SE; (202) 543-3300], which has a publike atmosphere and food and prices to match. To dine with political power brokers, try the pricier **Monocle** [107 D Street NE; (202) 546-4488].

For those who don't understand what a gourmand is but know the letters *B*, *B*, and *Q*, the **Capital Q** [707 H Street NW; (202) 347-8396] will hit the spot. The local city magazine, *The Washingtonian*, named it one of the best bargains in town. (But go for lunch, not dinner, as it's not the best neighborhood at night.)

For those looking for a restaurant within a mile or so of the National Archives, longtime *Washington Post* critic Phyllis Richman has recommended the following establishments. (Most require reservations. Expect price tags to match the quality; these are a splurge.)

- **Café Atlantico** [405 Eighth Street NW; (202) 393-0812]—Caribbean and Latin American cuisine

The Library of Congress, home to more than 120 million items, celebrated its 200th birthday in 2000.

- **DC Coast** [1401 K Street NW; (202) 216-5988]—seafood
- **Georgia Brown's** [950 Fifteenth Street NW; (202)393-4499]—Southern cooking
- **Jaleo** [480 Seventh Street NW; (202) 628-7949]—famous for tapas
- **Morrison-Clark Inn** [1015 L Street NW; (202) 898-1200]—American cuisine
- **Ruppert's** [1017 Seventh Street NW; (202) 783-0699]—inventive seasonal specialities

For lodging not far from the archives, try the **Hotel George** [15 E Street NW; (800) 576-8331]. The adjoining restaurant, **bis**, is popular with politicos and TV journalists. Also handy to the archives is **Lowe's L'Enfant Plaza** [480 L'Enfant Plaza SW; (202) 484-1000]. Cost-conscious visitors might try the **Best Western Downtown** near Capitol Hill [724 Third Street NW; (800) 242-4831]. The rooms here are standard hotel fare but offer a good deal for nearly the same convenience. Safety is a concern near Capitol Hill, especially at night. Your best bet for lodging might lie someplace such as nearby Rosslyn, a quick Metro ride away.

If you're researching ancestors who actually lived in the District of Columbia itself, you'll want to visit the **Historical Society of Washington, D.C.,** [1307 New Hampshire Avenue NW; (202) 785-2068; <www.hswdc.org>] and the **District of Columbia Public Library** [901 G Street NW; (202) 727-1101; <www.dclibrary.org>]. Federal censuses are available for the District of Columbia for 1800 (eastern part only), 1820, 1830, 1840, 1850, 1860, 1870, 1880, 1900, 1910, 1920, and 1930, with indexes for all but part of 1880, 1910, and 1930. The Family History Library has city directories for 1822-1860, 1862-1935, 1941, 1956, and 1960.

DELAWARE

ORGANIZATIONS & ARCHIVES

The Delaware Genealogical Society
505 N. Market St.
Wilmington, DE 19801
<www.delgensoc.org>

Delaware Public Archives
121 Duke of York St.
Dover, DE 19901
(302) 744-5000
<www.archives.state.de.us>

Hagley Museum and Library
P.O. Box 3630
Wilmington, DE 19807
(302) 658-2400
Fax: (302) 658-0568
<www.hagley.lib.de.us>

The Historical Society of Delaware
505 N. Market St.
Wilmington, DE 19801
(302) 655-7161
Fax: (302) 655-7844
<www.hsd.org>

University of Delaware Library
181 South College Ave.
Newark, DE 19717
(302) 831-2965

RESOURCES

The Chesapeake Book of the Dead: Tombstones, Epitaphs, Histories, Reflections, and Oddments of the Region
by Helen Chappell and Starke Jett (Johns Hopkins University Press, $24.95)

Delaware Genealogical Research Guide
edited by Thomas P. Doherty (Delaware Genealogical Society, $10)

DELAWARE

STATE STATS

Statehood: 1787
Statewide Birth and Death Records Begin: 1861; stopped in 1863, and resumed in 1881
Statewide Marriage Records Begin: 1847
Address for Vital Statistics:
Bureau of Vital Statistics
Jesse S. Cooper Memorial Building
William Penn St.
Dover, DE 19901

Available Censuses: U.S. federal censuses 1800, 1810, 1820, 1830, 1840, 1850, 1860, 1870, 1880, 1900, 1910, and 1920. Statewide indexes are available for 1800, 1810, 1820, 1830, 1840, 1850, 1860, 1870, 1880, 1900, and 1920.

City Directories at the Family History Library Include: 1814, 1845, 1853, 1857, 1859/1860, 1862-1901, 1934

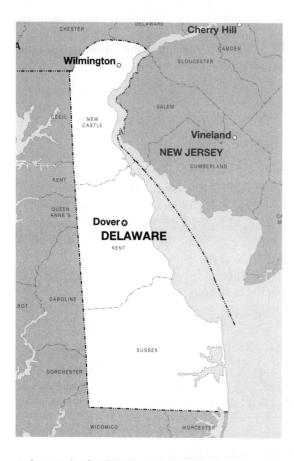

exhibits, educational materials, historical markers, and "This Day in Delaware History."

Delaware Resources at RootsWeb
<resources.rootsweb.com/USA/DE>: Links and search engine for cemeteries, surnames, and resources.

Genealogical Information and Repositories
<delgensoc.org/delrep.html>: Guide to research libraries and archives.

Vital Records Information
<vitalrec.com/de.html>: Where to obtain copies of birth and death certificates, marriage licenses, and divorce decrees.

FAMILY HISTORY CENTERS

Dover
Route 10, between 13 & Route 113A
(302) 697-2700

Newark
500 W. Chestnut Hill Rd.
(302) 456-9301

Wilmington
143 Dickinson Ln.
(302) 654-1911

MARYLAND

ORGANIZATIONS & ARCHIVES

Baltimore City Archives
211 E. Pleasant St., Room 201
Baltimore, MD 21202
(410) 396-4861

Enoch Pratt Free Library
400 Cathedral St.
Baltimore, MD 21201
(410) 396-5430

Fax: (410) 837-0582
<www.pratt.lib.md.us>

Genealogical Council of Maryland
c/o Jean Brandau, Secretary
3603 Monterey Rd.
Baltimore, MD 21218

Johns Hopkins University
George Peabody Library
17 E. Mount Vernon Pl.
Baltimore, MD 21202
(410) 659-8197
Fax: (410) 659-8137
<peabody-events.mse.jhu.edu>

Maryland Genealogical Society
201 W. Monument St.
Baltimore, MD 21201
(410) 685-3750, extension 360
<www.mdgensoc.org>

Maryland Historical Society Library
201 W. Monument St.
Baltimore, MD 21201
(410) 685-3750, extension 359
Fax: (410) 385-0487
<www.mdhs.org>

Maryland State Archives
Hall of Records Building
350 Rowe Blvd.
Annapolis, MD 21401
(410) 260-6400 or (800) 235-4045
Fax: (410) 974-3895
<www.mdarchives.state.md.us>

Maryland State Law Library
Robert C. Murphy Courts of Appeal Building
361 Rowe Blvd.
Annapolis, MD 21401
(410) 260-1430 or (888) 216-8156
Fax: (410) 974-2063 or (877) 233-3871
<www.lawlib.state.md.us>

Index to Scharf's History of Delaware, 1609-1888
Historical Society of Delaware, $19.50)

PERIODICALS

Delaware Genealogical Society Journal
(1980-), The Delaware Genealogical Society, 505 N. Market St., Wilmington, DE 19801

The Maryland and Delaware Genealogist
(1959-1990), Raymond B. Clark Jr., ed.

WEB SITES

Books We Own
<rootsweb.com/~bwo/delaware.html>: Find vol-

unteers to do lookups in Delaware resources, including out-of-print books.

Delaware GenWeb Project
<www.rootsweb.com/~degenweb/>: Features an online gazetteer and a search engine for the site's archives.

Delaware Mailing Lists
<rootsweb.com/~jfuller/gen_mail_states-de.html>: Lists that cover Delaware censuses, lookups, resources, and research.

Delaware Public Archives
<www.state.de.us/sos/dpa>: Collections,

Statehood: 1788
Statewide Birth and Death Records Begin: 1898
Statewide Marriage Records Begin: 1950
Address for Vital Statistics:
   Division of Vital Records
   4201 Patterson Ave.
   P.O. Box 13146
   Baltimore, MD 21203
   (800) 832-3277 or (410) 764-3038
   Fax: (410) 358-7381

Available Censuses: U.S. federal censuses 1790, 1800, 1810, 1820, 1830, 1840, 1850, 1860, 1870, 1880, 1900, 1910, and 1920. Allegany, Calvert, and Somerset counties: Original 1790 schedules are missing. Baltimore County: 1800 census, the original schedules outside of Baltimore City missing. Montgomery, Prince Georges, Queen Annes, St. Marys, and Somerset: Original 1830 schedules are missing. Statewide indexes are available for the 1790, 1800, 1820, 1830, 1840, and 1850, 1880, 1900, and 1920 federal censuses. The 1860 index includes only areas outside Baltimore City.

City Directories at the Family History Library Include: Baltimore 1752, 1796-1860, 1863-1930, 1914, 1940, 1956

University of Maryland College Park Libraries
Theodore R. McKeldin Library
College Park, MD 20742
(301) 405-0800
Fax: (301) 314-9408
<www.lib.umd.edu/MCK/mckeldin.html>

RESOURCES

British Roots of Maryland Families
by Robert Barnes
(Genealogical Publishing Co., $49.50)

"Genealogical Research in Maryland"
lecture by Mary K. Meyer
(Audiotapes.com, $8.50)

Maryland Genealogies: A Consolidation of Articles From the Maryland Historical Magazine
with an introduction by Robert Barnes (2 volumes; Genealogical Publishing Co., $52.50)

PERIODICALS

The Maryland and Delaware Genealogist
(1959-1990), Raymond B. Clark Jr., ed.

Maryland Genealogical Society Bulletin
(1961-), Maryland Genealogical Society, 201 W. Monument St., Baltimore, MD 21201

Maryland Historical and Genealogical Bulletin
(1930-50), Roland F. Hayes Jr., ed.

Maryland Historical Magazine
(1906-), Maryland Historical Society, 201 W. Monument St., Baltimore, MD 21201

Maryland Magazine of Genealogy
(1978-), Maryland Historical Society, 201 W. Monument St., Baltimore, MD 21201

WEB SITES

Immigrant Communities in Maryland
<www.cip.umd.edu/
~mddlmddl/791/
communities/html/>:
Ethnic links, including
African-American, Irish,
and Italian.

Maryland Genealogy
<delmarweb.com/
maryland/genealogy.
html>: Links to counties
and vital records.

Maryland Genealogy Resources
<mdgenealogy.com>: A
guide to researching
Maryland genealogy and
history.

Maryland GenWeb Project
<www.mdgenweb.org>:
Cemetery data, statewide
and county resources,
and useful links.

Maryland Mailing Lists
<rootsweb.com/~jfuller/
gen_mail_states-md.
html>: State- and county-
level lists.

Maryland Resources at RootsWeb
<resources.rootsweb.
com/USA/MD>: Queries,
archived messages,
search engines.

Maryland State Archives
<mdarchives.state.md.us/
msa/homepage/html/
refserv.html>: Description
of records and how to
obtain them.

Vital Records Information
<vitalrec.com/md.html>:
Get copies of birth and
death certificates, mar-
riage licenses, and
divorce decrees.

FAMILY HISTORY CENTERS

Annapolis
1875 Ritchie Highway
(410) 757-4173

Baltimore
120 Stemmers Run Rd.
(410) 686-8481

Columbia
4100 St. John's Ln.
(410) 465-1642

Cumberland
12205 Gramlick Rd. SW
(301) 724-1609

Frederick
199 N Pl.
(301) 698-0406

Hampstead
4117 Lower Beckysville
Rd.
(410) 239-2461

Hancock
200 Douglas St. Ext
(301) 678-6007

Lexington Park
Old Rolling Rd.
(301) 863-8002

Salisbury
106 Greenlawn Ln.
(410) 742-8568

Seneca
18900 Kingsview Rd.
(301) 972-5897

Suitland
5300 Auth Rd.
(301) 423-8294

Washington, DC
10000 Stoneybrook Dr.
(301) 587-0042

NEW JERSEY

ORGANIZATIONS & ARCHIVES

The Genealogical Society of New Jersey
P.O. Box 1291
New Brunswick, NJ 08903
(732) 932-7510
<www.rootsweb.com/
~njgsnj/main.htm>

Gloucester County Historical Society Library
17 Hunter St.
P.O. Box 409
Woodbury, NJ 08096
(609) 845-4771
<www.rootsweb.com/
~njglouce/gchs>

New Jersey Historical Society Library
52 Park Pl.
Newark, NJ 07102
(973) 596-8500 or (800)
852-7899
Fax: (973) 596-6957
<www.jerseyhistory.org>

New Jersey Information Center
Newark Public Library
5 Washington St.
P.O. Box 630
Newark, NJ 07102
(973) 733-7775
Fax: (973) 733-4870
<www.npl.org/Pages/
Collections/njic.html>

New Jersey State Archives
Department of State
Building
225 W. State St., Level 2
P.O. Box 307
Trenton, NJ 08625
(609) 292-6260
<www.state.nj.us/state/
darm/links/archives.html>

New Jersey State Library
Genealogy and Local
History Collection
185 W. State St., CN 520
P.O. Box 520
Trenton, NJ 08625
(609) 292-6200, (609) 292-
6274
Fax: (609) 984-7901
<www.njstatelib.org/
aboutus/SGIS/libgene.
htm>

Rutgers University Libraries
Special Collections and
University Archives
Archibald Stevens
Alexander Library
169 College Ave.
New Brunswick, NJ 08901
(732) 932-7006
Fax: (732) 932-7012
<www.libraries.rutgers.
edu/rul/libs/special_coll/
special_coll.shtml>

RESOURCES

*Colonial New Jersey
Source Records CD-ROM*
(Genealogical Publishing
Co., $29.99)

*Genealogies of New
Jersey Families From the
Genealogical Magazine
of New Jersey*
(2 volumes; Genealogical
Publishing Co., $150.00)

*"New Jersey: Garden
State Research"*
lecture by Michael
Strauss (Audiotapes.com,
$8.50)

*New Netherland Vital
Records, 1600s*
by David M. Riker
(Genealogy.com, $29.99),
CD-ROM

*Official Register of the
Officers and Men of New
Jersey in the
Revolutionary War*
by William S. Stryker
(Genealogical Publishing
Co., $65)

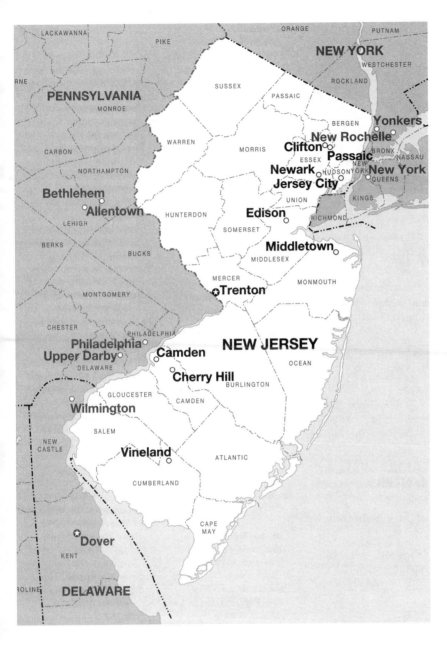

(1845-1966), New Jersey Historical Society, 52 Park Pl., Newark, NJ 07104

Somerset County Historical Quarterly (1912-1919), edited by A. Van Doren Honeyman and published by the Somerset County Historical Society, 9 Van Veghten Dr., Bridgewater, NJ 08807.

Vineland Historical Magazine (1916-), Vineland Historical and Antiquarian Society, 108 S. Seventh St., P.O. Box 35, Vineland, NJ 08360

WEB SITES

Civil War Rosters <geocities.com/Area51/ Lair/3680/cw/cw-nj.html>: Links to names and other information about Civil War soldiers.

Genealogical Resources on the Web <www.njstatelib.org/ cyberdesk/genealog. htm>: New Jersey State Library site with links to online collections.

The New Jersey Churchscape <njchurchscape.com>: Database and photos of eighteenth- and nine- teenth-century churches.

New Jersey Genealogy Resource Center <accessgenealogy.com/ newjersey>: Links to archives, libraries, vital records, cemeteries, cen- suses, military records.

New Jersey GenWeb Project <rootsweb.com/

PERIODICALS

The Cape May County Magazine of History and Genealogy (1931), Cape May County Historical and Genealogical Society, 504 Rt. 9 North, Cape May Court House, NJ 08210

The Genealogical Magazine of New Jersey (1925-), Genealogical Society of New Jersey

The Jerseyman (1891-1905), Hunterdon County Historical Society, 114 Main St., Flemington, NJ 08822

The New Jersey Genesis (1953-1971), published first by Harold A. Sonn and later by Carl M. Williams

New Jersey History (1967-), formerly *Proceedings of the New Jersey Historical Society*,

Statehood: 1787
Statewide Birth and Death Records Begin: 1848
Statewide Marriage Records Begin: 1848
Address for Vital Statistics:
Bureau of Vital Statistics
P.O. Box 370
Trenton, NJ 08625
(609) 292-4087 (information)
(609) 633-2860 (to order records)
Fax: (609) 392-4292

Available Censuses: U.S. federal censuses 1830, 1840, 1850, 1860, 1870, 1880, 1900, 1910, and 1920. Statewide indexes are available for the 1800 (Cumberland County), 1830, 1840, 1850, 1860, 1880 (partial), 1900, and 1920 censuses.

City Directories at the Family History Library Include: Hoboken 1852-1859, 1859-1860, 1861-1901, 1902-1926; Jersey City 1849-1860, 1861-1901, 1902-1926; Newark 1835-1860, 1861-1901, 1902-1935, 1938; Trenton 1844-1845, 1854, 1857, 1859, 1867-1935 (intermittent years), 1930

~njgenweb>: Links to state and county resources.

New Jersey Mailing Lists
<rootsweb.com/~jfuller/gen_mail_states-nj.html>: State and county lists.

New Jersey Resources at RootsWeb
<resources.rootsweb.com/USA/NJ>: Personal pages and other New Jersey links.

Vital Records Information
<vitalrec.com/nj.html>: Where to obtain copies of birth and death certificates, marriage licenses, and divorce decrees.

FAMILY HISTORY CENTERS

Caldwell
209 Mountain Ave.
(973) 226-8975

Cherry Hill
260 E. Evesham Rd.
(856) 795-8841

Clinton
9 Red Schoolhouse Rd.
(908) 713-0292

East Brunswick
303 Dunhams Corner Rd.
(732) 254-1480

Eatontown
14 Reynolds Dr.
(732) 542-2691

Emerson
840 Soldier Hill Rd.
(201) 262-7357

Fardale
30 Youngs Rd.
(201) 327-1940

Irvington
1064 Clinton Ave.

Ledgewood
156 Mountain Rd.
(973) 347-2856

Morristown
283 James St.
(973) 539-5362

Paterson
42-48 E. Thirty-ninth St.

Princeton
610 Alexander Rd.
(609) 452-0802

Scotch Plains
1781 Raritan Rd.
(908) 889-0628

Short Hills
140 White Oak Ridge Rd.
(973) 379-7315

Toms River
1350 Old Freehold Rd.
(732) 349-5947

Union City
2500 New York Ave.
(201) 866-8118

Vineland
110 Highland Ave.
(856) 696-5002

NEW YORK

ORGANIZATIONS & ARCHIVES

Brooklyn Historical Society
128 Pierrepont St.
Brooklyn, NY 11201
(718) 222-4111
Fax: (718) 222-3794
<www.brooklynhistory.org>

Montgomery County Department of History and Archives
Old Court House
P. O. Box 1500
Fonda, NY 12068
(518) 853-8186
Fax: (518) 853-8392
<www.amsterdam-ny.com/mcha>

New York City Department of Records and Information Services
Municipal Archives
31 Chambers St., Room 103
New York, NY 10007
(212) 788-8580
Fax: (212) 385-0984
<www.ci.nyc.ny.us/html/doris/html>

New York Genealogical and Biographical Society Library
122 E. Fifty-eighth St.
New York, NY 10022
(212) 755-8532
Fax: (212) 754-4218
<www.nygbs.org>

New-York Historical Society
2 W. Seventy-seventh St.
New York, NY 10024
(212) 873-3400
Fax: (212) 875-1591
<www.nyhistory.org>

The New York Public Library
The Irma and Paul Milstein Division of United States History, Local History and Genealogy
Fifth Avenue and Forty-second Street, Room 121
New York, NY 10018
(212) 930-0828
<www.nypl.org/research/chss/lhg/genea.html>

The New York State
Archives
New York State
Education Department
Cultural Education
Center
Empire State Plaza,
Eleventh Floor
Albany, NY 12230
(518) 474-8955
Fax: (518) 473-9985
<www.archives.nysed.gov>

New York State Council
of Genealogical
Organizations
P.O. Box 2593
Syracuse, NY 13220

The New York State
Library
Local History and
Genealogy Section
Cultural Education
Center

Empire State Plaza,
Seventh Floor
Albany, NY 12230
(518) 474-5355 or
(518) 474-5161
Fax: (518) 474-5786
<www.nysl.nysed.gov/
gengen.htm>

Olin, Kroch and Uris
Libraries
Cornell University
Ithaca, NY 14853
(607) 255-3319
Fax: (607) 255-9346
<www.library.cornell.edu
/ okuref/refleft.html>

RESOURCES

*Early New York Families
1600s-1900s*
(Genealogy.com, $39.99)

*"Finding Naturalization
Records in New York
City"*
lecture by Estelle M.
Guzik (Audiotapes.com,
$8.50)

*Gazetteer of the State of
New York (1860)*
by J.H. French; reprinted
with an index of names
compiled by Frank Place
(Genealogical Publishing
Co., $60)

*New York Genealogy
Research Manual*
by Bill Madon (Self-pub-
lished, $12 from
<treesearch.com/
treesearch.html>)

*New York State Probate
Records: A Genealogist's
Guide to Testate and
Intestate Records*
by Gordon L. Remington
(New England Historic
Genealogical Society,
$19.95)

*Index to Upstate New
York Source Records,
1685-1910*
(Genealogy.com, $39.99)

*New York State Towns,
Villages, and Cities: A
Guide to Genealogical
Sources*
by Gordon L. Remington
(New England Historic
Genealogical Society,
$17.95)

PERIODICALS

The Capital
(1986-), Arthur C.M. Kelly,
60 Cedar Heights Rd.,
Rhinebeck, NY 12572

De Halve Maen
(1922-), Holland Society
of New York, 122 E. Fifty-
eighth St., New York, NY
10022

*Dorot: The Journal of the
Jewish Genealogical
Society*
(1979-), Jewish
Genealogical Society of
New York, P.O. Box 6398,
New York, NY 10128

*Early Settlers of New
York State: Their
Ancestors and
Descendants*
(1934-42), T.J. Foley,
Akron, NY

Lifelines
(1984-), Northern New
York American-Canadian
Genealogical Society, P.O.
Box 1256, Plattsburgh,
NY 12901

The Mohawk
(1984-), Arthur C.M. Kelly,
60 Cedar Heights Rd.,
Rhinebeck, NY 12572

New York State Queries
(1987-), Carolyn Wilson
Weinder, 2206 W.
Borden Rd., Spokane, WA
99204

*The Patents: The
Northeastern New York
Genealogical Society
Newsletter*
(1982-), Northeastern
New York Genealogical
Society, 9 Lydia St., South
Glens Fall, NY 12803

Tree Talks
(1961-), Central New York
Genealogical Society, P.O.
Box 104, Colvin Station,
Syracuse, NY 13205

*Western New York
Genealogical Society
Journal*
(1974-), Western New
York Genealogical
Society, P.O. Box 338,
Hamburg, NY 14075

Ottawa

ONTARIO

Kingston

JEFFERSON

Toronto

LEWIS

OSWEGO

ONEIDA

NIAGARA

ORLEANS

Rochester

WAYNE

Niagara Falls

MONROE

Utica

GENESEE

Syracuse

ONONDAGA

MADISON

Buffalo

West Seneca

ONTARIO

ERIE

WYOMING

SENECA

CAYUGA

LIVINGSTON

YATES

CORTLAND

CHENANGO

SCHUYLER

TOMPKINS

CHAUTAUQUA

CATTARAUGUS

ALLEGANY

STEUBEN

CHEMUNG

TIOGA

BROOME

Binghamton

ERIE

PENNSYLVANIA

WARREN

MCKEAN

POTTER

TIOGA

BRADFORD

SUSQUEHANNA

CRAWFORD

WAYNE

FOREST

WYOMING

LACKAWANNA

VENANGO

ELK

CAMERON

SULLIVAN

Scranton

LYCOMING

CLARION

JEFFERSON

CLINTON

LUZERNE

Wilkes-Barre

COLUMBIA

MONROE

CLEARFIELD

CENTRE

UNION

MONTOUR

CARBON

BUTLER

ARMSTRONG

NORTHUMBERLAND

NORTHAMPTON

INDIANA

SNYDER

SCHUYLKILL

MIFFLIN

Allentown

BLAIR

JUNIATA

LEHIGH

CAMBRIA

Altoona

DAUPHIN

BERKS

PERRY

Reading

WESTMORELAND

HUNTINGDON

Harrisburg

LEBANON

MONTGOMERY

CUMBERLAND

WEB SITES

New York Biography Project
<nybiographies.org>:
Historical biographies of New York citizens and settlers (from various sources).

New York Family History
<geocities.com/~agiroux>:
Links to New York City and Long Island churches, cemeteries, and vital records.

New York GenWeb Project
<www.rootsweb.com/~nygenweb>: Links to state and county resources.

New York Mailing Lists
<rootsweb.com/~jfuller/gen_mail_states-ny.html>: State- and county-level mailing lists.

New York Resources at RootsWeb
<resources.rootsweb.com/USA/NY>:
GEDCOMs, queries, Bibles, records.

Tribes and Villages of New York
<hanksville.org/sand/contacts/tribal/NY.html>:
Links to Native American reservations.

Vital Records Information
<vitalrec.com/ny.html>:
Where to obtain copies of birth and death certificates, marriage licenses, and divorce decrees.

FAMILY HISTORY CENTERS

Albany
411 Loudon Rd.
(518) 463-2566

Auburn
63 Kearney Ave.
(315) 253-0670

Brockport
4088 Lake Rd.
(716) 637-2030

Bronx
211 E. Kingsbridge Rd.
(718) 561-7824

Brooklyn
1212 Glenwood Rd.
(718) 434-8245

Buffalo
1424 Maple Rd.
(716) 688-2439

Cortland
111 Fairview Dr.
(607) 753-6418

Elmira
1060 W. Broad St.
(607) 739-8002

Fayette
1455 Aunkst Rd.
(315) 539-8167

Fredonia
1718 Chestnut Rd.
(716) 673-1718

Gloversville
Ext Steele Ave.
(518) 725-4417

Herkimer
Gross Boulevard

Ithaca
114 Burleigh Dr.
(607) 257-1334

Jamestown
851 Forest Ave.
(716) 487-0830

Kingston
Fording Place Road
(845) 382-2170

Lake Placid
Old Military & John
Brown Roads
(518) 523-2889

Lowville
E. State Street
(315) 376-9386

Lynbrook
10 Peninsula Blvd.
(516) 599-8079

Middletown
790 Silverlake
Scotchtown Rd.
(845) 692-0364

New York City
125 Columbus Ave. at
Sixty-fifth Street
(212) 873-1690

Newburgh
Mt. Airy Road
(845) 564-6785

Norwich
Cole and Chirlin Drives
(607) 336-6341

Olean
1935 Windfall Rd.
(716) 372-5515

Oneonta
Balmoral Drive
(607) 432-8195

Orchard Park
4005 Baker Rd.
(716) 662-3117

Owego
Montrose Turnpike
(607) 687-5137

Plainview
160 Washington Ave.
(516) 433-0122

Syracuse
4889 Bear Rd.
(315) 457-5172

Terryville
372 Terryville Rd.
(631) 642-2096

Utica
8439 Clark Mills Rd.
(315) 736-7414

Vestal
305 Murray Hill Rd.
(607) 797-3900

Watertown
20065 Route 65, Ives
Street Rd.
(315) 788-4161

Wellsville
100 Crescent Ln.
(585) 593-3481

Westchester
60 Wayside Ln.
(914) 472-3186

PENNSYLVANIA

ORGANIZATIONS & ARCHIVES

Carnegie Library of Pittsburgh
4400 Forbes Ave.
Pittsburgh, PA 15213
(412) 622-3114
Fax: (412) 621-1267
<www.carnegielibrary.
org>

City Archives of Philadelphia
Department of Records
3101 Market St.,
Suite 150
Philadelphia, PA 19104
(215) 685-9401
Fax: (215) 685-9409
<apps.phila.gov/phils/
carchive.htm>

Genealogical Society of Pennsylvania
215 S. Broad St.,

Plattsburg
22 Dennis Ave.
(518) 561-1092

Potsdam
21 Castle Dr.
(315) 265-6228

Poughkeepsie
204 Spakenkill Rd.
(845) 462-2470

Pulaski
53 Nelson Ave.
(315) 298-4422

Queens
86-16 Sixtieth Rd.
(718) 478-5337

Rochester
1400 Westfall Rd.
(585) 271-5040

Rochester (Palmyra)
460 Kreag Rd.
(716) 248-9930

Schoharie Valley
Church Street
(518) 868-2049

Staten Island
913 Rockland Ave.
(718) 698-0668

Seventh Floor
Philadelphia, PA 19107
(215) 545-0391
Fax: (215) 545-0936
<libertynet.org/gspa>

Historical Society of Pennsylvania
1300 Locust St.
Philadelphia, PA 19107
(215) 732-6200
Fax: (215) 732-2680
<www.hsp.org>

Historical Society of Western Pennsylvania
1212 Smallman St.
Pittsburgh, PA 15222
(412) 454-6000
Fax: (412) 454-6028
<www.pghhistory.org>

Pennsylvania German Society
P.O. Box 244
Kutztown, PA 19530
(610) 894-9551
Fax: (610) 894-9808

Pennsylvania State Archives
Reference Section
350 North St.
Harrisburg, PA 17120
(717) 783-3281
<www.phmc.state.pa.us/
bah/dam/overview.
htm?secid=31>

State Library of Pennsylvania
Department of Education
Commonwealth Libraries
Commonwealth and
Walnut Streets
P.O. Box 1601
Harrisburg, PA 17105
(717) 783-5950
Fax: (717) 783-5420
<www.statelibrary.state.
pa.us/libraries/site/
default.asp>

Western Pennsylvania Genealogical Society
4400 Forbes Avenue
Pittsburgh, PA 15213

(412) 687-6811
<www.wpgs.org>

RESOURCES

Genealogies of Pennsylvania Families from the Pennsylvania Magazine of History and Biography [1 vol.] and the Pennsylvania Genealogical Magazine
3 vols. CD-ROM
(Genealogical Publishing Co.,$39.99)

Pennsylvania Genealogical Research
by George K. Schweitzer
(Genealogical Sources Unlimited, $15.00)

Pennsylvania Land Records: A History and Guide for Research
by Donna Bingham Munger (Scholarly Resources, $29.95)

PERIODICALS

Keystone Kuzzins
(1972-), Erie Society for Genealogical Research, P.O. Box 1403, Erie, PA 16512

Mennonite Family History
(1982-), Mennonite Family History, 10 W. Main St., P. O. Box 171, Elverson, PA 19520

The Pennsylvania Dutchman
(1949-1957, 8 vols.)

The Pennsylvania Genealogical Magazine
(1895-), Genealogical Society of Pennsylvania, 1305 Locust St., Philadelphia, PA 19107

The Pennsylvania-

German
(1900-1911)

The Pennsylvania Magazine of History and Biography
(1877-), Historical Society of Pennsylvania, 1300 Locust St., Philadelphia, PA 19107

The Pennsylvania Traveler-Post,
formerly *Pennsylvania Ancestors and Their Descendants Today*
(1964-), Richard and Mildred Williams, P.O. Box 776, Newtown, PA 18940

Western Pennsylvania Genealogical Quarterly
(1974-), Western Pennsylvania Genealogical Society, 4338 Bigelow Blvd., Pittsburgh, PA 15213

Your Family Tree
(1948-1983), Floyd G. Hoenstine, 414 Montgomery St., P.O. Box 208, Hollidaysburg, PA 16648

WEB SITES

Brenda's Guide to PA Genealogy
<www.keynet.net/users/
oron/palinks.htm>:
Resources for everything from Bible records to the Underground Railroad.

Pennsylvania Dutch Family History and Genealogy
<midatlantic.rootsweb.
com/padutch>: Surname boards and FAQs, plus links to other Pennsylvania Dutch sites.

Pennsylvania GenWeb Project
<www.pagenweb.org>:

Select a county resource link and explore the queries posted.

Pennsylvania Mailing Lists
<rootsweb.com/~jfuller/gen_mail_states-pa.html>

Pennsylvania Resources at RootsWeb
<resources.rootsweb.com/USA/PA>: Variety of family and general Pennsylvania-related genealogy links.

Pennsylvania State Archives
<www.digitalarchives.state.pa.us>: Online access to 200,000 Pennsylvania records.

Tim's Tips on PA German Research
<geocities.com/Heartland/Plains/3816/how2.html>: For county records and histories.

Vital Records Information
<vitalrec.com/pa.html>: Where to obtain copies of birth and death certificates, marriage licenses, and divorce decrees.

FAMILY HISTORY CENTERS

Allentown
1881 Van Buren Dr.
(610) 799-3522

Altoona-Ward
Lower Brush Mountain Road
(814) 696-0341

Beaver Valley
Church Street
(724) 774-3670

Berwick
School House Road
(570) 759-1637

Butler
365 Sawmill Run Rd.
(724) 482-2129

Carlisle
Skyline Drive
(717) 796-6085

Chambersburg
50 Ragged Edge Rd.
(717) 263-8679

Doylestown
Chapman and Ferry Roads
(215) 348-0645

Dubois-Ward
RD 1, Route 322
(814) 583-5837

Dubois-Kane
30 Chestnut St.
(814) 837-9729

Erie
1101 S. Hill Rd.
(814) 866-3611

Fairview
11887 Mentzer Gap Rd.
(717) 762-2268

Franklin
1449 Thompson Rd.
(814) 437-5561

Gettysburg
Kohler Mill and Irish Town Roads
(717) 624-7634

Harrisburg
1210 E. King St.
(717) 295-1719

Harrisburg/Hershey
4788 Union Deposit Rd.
(717) 545-3021

Indiana
1580 Old Route 119 N
(724) 349-1337

Johnstown
609 Walters Ave.
(814) 269-4652

Lock Haven
Route 64
(814) 726-6704

Meadville
597 N. Park Ave.
(814) 336-5064

Morrisville
1204 Pine Grove Rd.
(215) 295-9628

Nazareth
Rose Inn Avenue
(610) 759-9486

Philadelphia
5236 Rising Sun Ave.
(215) 329-3692

Pittsburgh
46 School St.
(412) 921-2115

Pottstown
93 Maugers Mill Rd.
(610) 327-3166

Reading
3344 Reading Crest Ave.
(610) 929-0235

Scranton
505 Griffin Pond Rd.
(570) 587-5123

Sharon
855 Woodland Rd.
(724) 962-0623

State College
842 Whitehall Rd.
(814) 238-4560

Sunbury
Ridge Road RR 1
(570) 473-9946

Towanda
605 Ann St.
(570) 265-5181

Valley Forge
721 Paxon Hollow Rd.
(610) 356-8507

Warren
Route 6 (east of Glade Bridge)
(814) 726-2455

Washington
525 Fairway Dr.
(724) 222-9474

Williamsport
82 Rader Rd.
(570) 494-1699

York
2100 Hollywood Dr.
(717) 846-4539

South

Alabama
Arkansas
Florida
Georgia
Kentucky
Louisiana
Mississippi
North Carolina
South Carolina
Tennessee
Texas
Virginia
West Virginia

REGIONAL GUIDE

BY DAVID A. FRYXELL

I n the geography of our imagination, the South is as constant as a Moon Pie. Forever under fluttering Stars and Bars, the stereotypical land of cotton is a drawling amalgam of *Gone With the Wind* and *The Andy Griffith Show*, *To Kill a Mockingbird* and the Grand Ole Opry, *In the Heat of the Night* and *Inherit the Wind*, bound together with grits and washed down with a cool mint julep out on the veranda, y'all. In the popular mind, Southern history began at Fort Sumter and ended when the Dixie of George Wallace gave way to the New South of Ted Turner.

But if you go looking for your Southern ancestors in Tara, you're likely to be disappointed. The reality of the South is much more complex than those stereotypes. Indeed, if you try to trace your Southern roots back more than three or four generations, you'll quickly stumble across a South that looks more like the Wild West than Mayberry. You'll find pioneers and Indians and families headed west—the frontier South of Daniel Boone, where the fever for land was hotter than Atlanta in August. Change was the constant here, with populations on the move and state and county borders melting like ice cubes in sweet tea. For example, I always thought of my maternal ancestors as being strictly from Alabama, where my mother grew up. But our family tree actually runs from Virginia to North Carolina to South Carolina, with offshoots in Georgia, before becoming firmly planted in the red dirt of Alabama.

Even the definition of "the South" isn't as solid as the Mason-Dixon line. That famous boundary, after all, put Maryland and Delaware down South—yet neither seceded, and we now think of both as mid-Atlantic states. Kentucky was a "border state" during the recent unpleasantness, but its settlement patterns are deeply Dixie. Certainly "the South" encompasses the eleven states of the Confederacy, yet Confederate Texas has a split personality, both Southern and Western.

SOUTHBOUND

So where do you start in this surprisingly complicated region? Like any genealogical quest, Southern genealogy begins in your own backyard: Start with sources in your own home and family, then work backward from today, one step at a time. Emily Anne Croom, author of the best-selling *Unpuzzling Your Past* (Betterway Books, $18.99) and an expert on Southern roots, advises, "Each family has its own starting point in Southern research. For those families still in the South, the starting point of research is where they are now. For those families no longer in the South, that starting point is when they left the region."

For many families who left the South, Croom says, the trigger was World War II military service or postwar job opportunities. Others moved away a few years earlier, seeking relief from the Great Depression and the Dust Bowl. In the late nineteenth and early twentieth centuries, the lure of cities replaced the promise of cheap farmland and tugged families away from the South, which remained heavily rural.

So your first challenge is to learn when, where, and why an ancestor or family moved to a city, left the South, or chose to remain in the rural South. Interview family members and pore over family papers. Consult city directories and the federal censuses from 1930 backward. Take advantage of the records from the many states that also had state censuses that can supplement or fill the gaps in federal enumerations. Study vital records beginning with the most recent birth, marriage, and death certificates.

Once you've identified an ancestor's last known Southern location, learn all you can about that state and even the county. The books and Web sites listed in this chapter can help you get started. Also search the Family History Library catalog <www.familysearch.org/Eng/Library/FHLC/frameset_fhlc.asp> for state and county records, which you can often borrow through a local Family History Center.

AGRARIAN ROOTS

As you work your way back from your last known Southern ancestor into the past, you'll probably stumble over some special challenges and puzzles. To get past them, it helps to know a little history.

Just as New Englanders proudly trace their roots to the *Mayflower*, the story of Southern families starts with the arrival of 105 settlers in Jamestown, Virginia, in 1607—well before the Pilgrims. In 1617, these nascent Southerners shipped their first tobacco back to England, starting an economic boom that would make wealthy Virginia the envy of other colonies. By 1700, Virginia already boasted fifty-eight thousand people. The restoration of the British monarchy in 1660, with Charles II, sparked a second wave of colonization. The crown gave a land grant to eight supporters who became the Lords Proprietors of the new colony of Carolina (from the Latin for *Charles*) in 1670. What tobacco was to Virginia, rice eventually became to Carolina, beckoning immigrants from the English colony of Barbados who emulated that island's plantation economy. French Huguenots seeking religious freedom also came, beginning in the 1680s. By 1730, the population in the Charleston area alone had reached thirty thousand.

North Carolina saw tentative settlements even before 1650, when it was dubbed Albemarle, but didn't really take off until 1691, when settlers from Virginia arrived and renamed it. That migration set the pattern for the next century and a half, as settlers pushed ever west and south in search of land and opportunity. Huguenots and Swiss Protestants came as well, and by 1730 North Carolina had thirty thousand colonists.

The last of the original Southern colonies (apart from the arguable Maryland and Delaware) was Georgia, chartered in 1732 with an unusual two-pronged mission: to serve as a barrier against Florida, which Spain had settled way back in 1565, and to welcome debtors and other castoffs from mother England. James Oglethorpe landed at Savannah with the first 115 settlers in 1733. In Georgia's early years it did attract eighteen hundred "charity colonists," along with a number of Scots and Germans, but the colony never quite lived up to its original intent, and Georgians envied the prosperity of neighboring South Carolina. By 1752, with little more than five thousand people, Georgia dropped its charter and became a royal colony.

If your ancestors stopped in one of these original colonies or if you can trace them back to Virginia, the Carolinas, or coastal Georgia, tap the wealth of genealogical resources dating to Colonial times. For example, Genealogical Publishing Company <www.genealogical.com> has published dozens of highly specific compilations such as *Virginia Northern Neck Land Grants, 1694-1742* and *South Carolina Marriages, 1688-1799*. Many of these works can be found in larger public libraries. The richness of Colonial records is also reflected in the CD-ROMs (such as Colonial America, 1607-1789 Census Index [#310, $29.99]) from Genealogy.com <www.genealogy.com> and in the databases at Ancestry.com <www.ancestry.com>.

Of course, these original states were also included in the very first U.S. census, in 1790, but the records for Virginia and Georgia were burned in the War of 1812 (as were censuses for the future Southern states of Kentucky and Tennessee). Your Southern Colonial ancestors may have fought in the Revolutionary War (though not necessarily on the winning side!). These military records are available on microfilm from the Family History Library (FHL; <www.familysearch.org>) and the National Archives and Records Administration (NARA; <www.archives.gov>). The National Society, Daughters of the American Revolution maintains a library of 160,000 books; 300,000 genealogical files; and 60,000 microforms in Washington, DC. You can search this library's catalog online at <www.dar.org/library/onlinlib.html>.

PRE-MANIFEST DESTINY

If your ancestors pushed on beyond the Colonial South, try picturing them not so much as characters from *Gone With the Wind* but as the pioneers following Daniel Boone in George Caleb Bingham's famous painting of the crossing of the Cumberland Gap. They were motivated by an impulse later called manifest destiny, succinctly expressed by Boone as: "Now is the time to secure all this country; we've got it, let's keep it!" Land lured eighteenth- and early-nineteenth-century Southerners as powerfully as gold later called people to California.

First they settled the western parts of the original colonies. Your Scotch-Irish ancestors may have settled the rolling, forested Piedmont of Virginia; some moved south from Pennsylvania in the mid-1700s, while others arrived directly in Southern ports and headed west. Your German ancestors may have headed for the Shenandoah Valley of Virginia or for the area near Salem, North Carolina. Other settlers took advantage of land bounties for veterans of the French and Indian War.

After Boone and others brought back word of the riches to be found in Kentucky and Tennessee, settlement rapidly pushed farther west. One early settler, upon seeing Kentucky, described, "So Rich a Soil, Covered in Clover in full Bloom, the Woods alive in wild game . . . It appeared that nature in the profusion of her Bounties had spread a feast for all that lives." Those who hadn't yet found their fortunes in the original colonies found those bounties irresistible. In early-nineteenth-century Virginia, if someone asked after the whereabouts of a man it was common to get the answer, "He's gone to hell or Kentucky."

Land speculators fueled the expansion, as did land bounties offered to North Carolinians and

Virginians who fought in the Revolutionary War. If your North Carolina ancestor served as a private, he got six hundred acres out west; if he was a colonel, seven thousand acres or more.

By 1783, Kentucky already had twelve thousand people. After gaining statehood in 1792, the population expanded from the "bluegrass country" around Lexington southward and westward, fueled first by state homestead acts and then by tobacco farming. Tennessee followed with statehood in 1796.

Historian Frank L. Owsley Sr. likened the settlement pattern itself to genealogy: "The Carolinas settled Georgia and, with considerable aid from Virginia, settled Tennessee. The remainder of the states of the Lower South were the children and grandchildren of the Carolinas, Georgia, and Tennessee."

Indian treaties and displacements, soil exhaustion in the east, public land sales, and the invention of the cotton gin all combined to fuel the next wave of settlement. In one of the fastest settlements in history, the population of Mississippi more than doubled from 1810 to 1820, and that of Alabama grew sixteenfold (from about 9,000 to 144,000).

If your ancestors caught "Alabama fever," look for them to have headed west and south during this mass exodus. Leaders in older states fretted over the depopulating effects of this fever, as illustrated by this 1817 lament from North Carolina Congressman James Graham: "The Alabama Feever [sic] rages here with great violence and has carried off vast numbers of our Citizens... . There is no question that this feaver is contagious ... for as soon as one neighbor visits another who has just returned from Alabama he immediately discovers the same symptoms which are exhibited by the one who has seen alluring Alabama."

CONSIDER ALL THE POSSIBILITIES

As you trace your Southern ancestors backward across what once was the frontier of "the Old Southwest," don't look for them to have simply uprooted from, say, Virginia and then settled for good in Alabama. Migrating families typically tried several new homesteads, possibly in several states. Historian Owsley compares this fickle migration pattern to "a great drove of blackbirds lighting in a grain field"—one gust of wind and they were aloft again, only to settle in the next field over.

You can look for patterns, however. Migrating families often went due west, and they looked to settle in valleys that reminded them of the place they'd just left. They moved in clusters, with one family member or even a neighbor being the first to try a new area and others in the cluster following later. Children of migrating families were more likely to eventually migrate again themselves. If you can't trace your ancestors' migrations, try tracing those of their siblings and other kin. Look, too, for unrelated people who lived near your ancestors; they may have lived near your ancestors in their previous home, too.

Census records can be valuable tools here, since federal censuses go back to 1810 for Louisiana, Kentucky, and parts of Tennessee; to 1820 for Mississippi; and to 1830 for Alabama and Arkansas. Territorial censuses were taken for some areas even earlier. Texas, not a state until 1845, had its own census in years ranging from 1829 to 1836. You can access the records of these through Family History Centers, the National Archives, and larger libraries. Census records are also becoming available online at subscription sites such as those at <www.ancestry.com> and <www.genealogy.com>, as well as through volunteer efforts at <www.usgenweb.org>.

Don't check for your Southern ancestors in just one county or even one state, however. If you can't find them in Alabama, for example, maybe they weren't there long enough to be counted before heading for greener pastures in Mississippi or Texas.

The 1850 U.S. census was the first to list not only the names of all free inhabitants in a household but also their birthplaces, so it gives a valuable snapshot of Southerners' migrating ways—and it may help you find patterns in your family's past. That enumeration found almost 400,000 people born in Virginia, Georgia, Tennessee, and the Carolinas who had landed in Alabama, Georgia (non-Georgia natives), Mississippi, and Louisiana.

You can also explore records of what likely drew your ancestors to this part of the South in the first place—public land. More than 2 million title records for public land sales (called "patents") are searchable online at the Bureau of Land Management's Web site <www.glorecords. blm.gov>. The records from 1820 to 1908 cover all the Southern states except the original colonies and Kentucky, Tennessee, and Texas. This is a great way to find not only your ancestors but also their neighbors, whose names might help you take the next step backward.

SHIFTING BOUNDARIES

A little history lesson is also helpful in finding your ancestors' vital records, probate records, and other state and local paperwork such as court cases and land transactions. Because of the shifting boundaries of the expanding frontier, your family may have switched from one county to another, or even changed states, without ever leaving home.

In 1750, remember, Virginia encompassed everything to the west of today's state. Tennessee was largely claimed by North Carolina until 1784. Mississippi and Alabama were part of the Mississippi Territory from 1798 until statehood in 1817 and 1819, while Georgia claimed parts of Alabama and Florida until 1802.

More problematic for family historians is the shifting of county lines that has occurred. In 1740, for example, all of noncoastal North Carolina was divided into just three counties; today, the state has one hundred counties, and those in the western three-quarters have been subdivided several times. Orange County, for instance, was formed in 1752 from parts of Bladen, Granville, and Johnston counties. And lines weren't redrawn just way back when: As recently as 1861, Mitchell County, North Carolina, was created from five other counties.

Some counties have simply been renamed. In 1858, for example, Benton County, Alabama, became Calhoun County, for John C. Calhoun.

USGenWeb's state pages <www.usgenweb. org/statelinks-table.html> can help you unscramble your ancestors' county lines and figure out what was which county when. The especially Byzantine evolution of South Carolina counties and districts is painstakingly traced on that state's USGenWeb site at <www.geocities.com/ Heartland/Hills/3837>.

History also created special challenges for researching genealogy in Louisiana, where the counties are called "parishes." That state's diverse heritage means that some records are in Spanish, French, and even Latin.

Once you do place your ancestors, you might take advantage of county heritage books. Sharon Williamson, former North Carolina USGenWeb coordinator <www.rootsweb.com/~ncgenweb>, says, "These books contain a combination of genealogy and history and make it much easier to get a picture of what early life was like in a particular place." The county pages on USGenWeb sites are a good place to find out whether your ancestor's county has such a book.

AFRICAN AMERICANS IN THE SOUTH

Of course, not everyone in the South came from Europe, and hundreds of thousands "migrated" against their will. The first African slaves came to the South in 1619, not long after the first settlers. Though slavery took several decades to become widespread, by 1710 South Carolina had more blacks than whites, and by 1800, the United States had almost one million slaves.

Tracing your Southern slave ancestors back

past 1870, the year of the first post-Civil War census, typically requires identifying the slave-holding family and locating that family's records. For an in-depth, seven-step guide to getting started on African-American roots, see the special section later in this book.

If you are researching slave ancestors, you should also consult an important new resource. In February 2001, the records of more than 480,000 ex-slaves, extracted from the Reconstruction-era records of the Freedman's Savings and Trust Co., were released on a searchable CD-ROM database. Depositors often named other relatives and their whereabouts, and early records included names of former slave owners and their plantations. You can search this CD-ROM free of charge at any Family History Center, or you can buy it for $6.50 at <www.familysearch.org> (click "Order/Download Products" then "Software Products").

American Indians lived throughout the South as well: Among these were the Powhatan in Virginia; the Tuscarora in North Carolina; the Cherokee in the Carolinas and Georgia; the Yamassee in South Carolina and Georgia; the Creek in Alabama, Georgia, and Florida; the Choctaw in Mississippi; the Seminoles in Florida; and the Chickasaw in Mississippi and Alabama. White settlers, wars, treaties, and mass relocations gradually drove most of them west to what became the Indian Territory, today's Oklahoma. See the guide to Native American roots at the end of this book.

A DIFFERENT COUNTRY

The Civil War marks a sharp boundary in the history and the genealogy of the South. Beginning with South Carolina's secession in December 1860, your Southern ancestors lived in a different country for more than four years.

For those tracing families back to the South of the 1860s, Croom emphasizes the importance of studying—before trying to push further back in time—the history of where the ancestors lived during and after the war. Like other historic disruptions, the war may have prompted your ancestors to move.

You can find valuable information in Confederate military records and state pension files. (Unlike Union troops, who earned federal pensions, those on the losing side had to rely on their states for pensions.) The best source for finding your ancestor's regiment is the sixteen-volume *Roster of Confederate Soldiers, 1861-1865* edited by Janet B. Hewett and available in major libraries. Once you find the right regiment, you may find firsthand reports of your ancestor's unit in *War of the Rebellion: A Compilation of the Official Records of the Union and Confederate Armies* (known as the "OR" for "Official Records") and its companion naval volumes. For pension records, consult individual state archives; Henry Putney Beers' *The Confederacy: A Guide to the Archives of the Confederate States of America* is a good starting point. Also look for old issues of *Confederate Veteran* magazine, published from 1893 to 1932, and its two-volume index.

Not all Southern men served in the military. Some also sympathized with or joined the Union cause, and many families were divided by the war just as the nation was.

Gradually, painfully, in fits and starts, the post-Civil War South became more a part of the American mainstream. Researching your ancestors that were in the South after 1865 is not so different from researching anywhere else in the United States. Today's Dixie is home to CNN, "America's Team," Coke, NASA, Disney World, and President George W. Bush—hard to believe it was ever a separate, rebellious nation, much less an untamed frontier.

Little did Scarlett O'Hara dream what tomorrow would bring to the South when she opined, "Tomorrow is another day." We are that tomorrow, and frankly, it's up to us to give a damn about how we got here.

ORGANIZATIONS & ARCHIVES

Birmingham Public Library
2100 Park Pl.
Birmingham, AL 35203
(205) 226-3600
<www.bham.lib.al.us/sou/genealogy.htm>

Center for the Study of Southern Culture
University of Mississippi
P.O. Box 1848
University, MS 38677
(662) 915-5993
<www.olemiss.edu/depts/south/>

Clayton Library
Center for Genealogical Research
5300 Caroline
Houston, TX 77004
(832) 393-2600
<www.houstonlibrary.org/clayton>

Confederate Research Center
Hill College
Harold B. Simpson
History Complex
P.O. Box 619
Hillsboro, TX 76645
(254) 582-2555 ext. 258
<www.hill-college.cc.tx.us/museum/mainpage/research/research.html>

Earl Gregg Swem Library
Reference Department
College of William and Mary
Williamsburg, VA 23187
(757) 221-3050
<www.swem.wm.edu/Resources/subject/VaGenealogy/>

Institute of Genealogy and Historical Research
Samford University
Library
800 Lakeshore Dr.
Birmingham, AL 35229

(205) 726-2198
<www.samford.edu/schools/ighr/ighr.html>

International Society of Sons and Daughters of Slave Ancestry
P.O. Box 436937
Chicago, IL 60643
<www.rootsweb.com/~ilissdsa>

Library of Virginia
800 E. Broad St.
Richmond, VA 23219
(804) 692-3500
<www.lva.lib.va.us>

National Archives and Records Administration–Southeast Region
1557 St. Joseph Ave.
East Point, GA 30344
(404) 763-7474
<www.archives.gov/facilities/ga/atlanta.html>

National Archives and Records Administration–Southwest Region
501 W. Felix St.,
Building 1
P.O. Box 6216
Fort Worth, TX 76115
(817) 334-5515
<www.archives.gov/facilities/tx/fort_worth.html>

Sons of Confederate Veterans
P.O. Box 59
Columbia, TN 38402
(800) 380-1896
<www.scv.org>

Southern Oral History Program
Campus Box 3195
406 Hamilton Hall
UNC-Chapel Hill
Chapel Hill, NC 27599
(919) 962-0455
<www.unc.edu/depts/sohp/sohpnew/>

United Daughters of the Confederacy
328 North Blvd.
Richmond, VA 23220
(804) 355-1636
<www.hqudc.org>

United States Civil War Center
Louisiana State University
Raphael Semmes Dr.
Baton Rouge, LA 70803
(225) 578-3151
<www.cwc.lsu.edu>

RESOURCES

The American South: A History
by William J. Cooper Jr. and Thomas E. Terrill (McGraw-Hill, $46.55)

Black Roots: A Beginners Guide to Tracing the African American Family Tree
by Tony Burroughs (Fireside, $16)

The Dixie Frontier: A Social History
by Everett Dick (University of Oklahoma Press, $19.95)

Frontiers in Conflict: The Old Southwest, 1795-1830
by Thomas D. Clark and John D.W. Guice (University of New Mexico Press, out of print)

A Genealogist's Guide to Discovering Your African-American Ancestors
by Franklin Carter Smith and Emily Anne Croom (Betterway Books, $21.99)

In Search of Confederate Ancestors: The Guide
by J.H. Segars (Southern

Heritage Press, $10.95)

The Routledge Historical Atlas of the American South
by Andrew K. Frank (Routledge, $17.95)

Slave Genealogy: A Research Guide With Case Studies
by David H. Streets (Heritage Books, $19.50)

The Sleuth Book for Genealogists
by Emily Anne Croom (Betterway Books, $18.99): All but one of the examples in this book are Southern.

The Southern Frontier, 1670-1732
by Verner W. Crane (W.W. Norton, out of print)

Tracing Your Civil War Ancestor
by Bertram Hawthorne Groene (Ballantine, $10)

Unpuzzling Your Past
by Emily Anne Croom (Betterway Books, $18.99): Many of the examples in this essential beginner's guide are Southern.

PERIODICALS

Southern Footprints
P.O. Box 16611,
Hattiesburg, MS 39404;
<www.SouthernFootprints.com>

WEB SITES

AfriGeneas
<www.afrigeneas.com>: African-American genealogy.

Appalachianfamily
An Appalachian roots mailing list. To subscribe, e-mail "subscribe" to appalachianfamily-sub-scribe@yahoogroups.com.

Carolina Cuzins
<www.carolinacuzins.org>

Deep-South-Roots-L
An Internet mailing list covering Georgia, Alabama, Florida, and Mississippi. To subscribe, e-mail "SUB DEEP-SOUTH-ROOTS-L *first-name lastname*" in the body of a message to listserv@listserv.indiana.edu.

Early Families in Southern States
An Internet mailing focusing on Colonial Maryland, Virginia, and the Carolinas. To sub-scribe, e-mail "subscribe" to efss-l-request@rootsweb.com.

The Freedmen's Bureau Online
<freedmensbureau.com>: Records of freed slaves.

Mid-Atlantic Roots Network
<midatlantic.rootsweb.com>: Includes Virginia and North Carolina.

National Archives Confederate Pension Records information
<www.archives.gov/research_room/genealogy/military/confederate_pension_records.html>

The-Road
Mailing list focuses on Scots and Germans along the "Philadelphia Road," including Virginia and the Carolinas. E-mail "subscribe" to the-road-l-request@rootsweb.com.

Southern Trails
<homepages.rootsweb.com/~south1/trails1.htm>

Traveller Southern Families
<misc.traveller.com/genealogy>

ATLANTA
BY SUSAN WENNER JACKSON

As the phoenix of the South, Atlanta rose from the ashes of the Civil War to become one of the region's largest, most dynamic cities and the "capital of the New South." Despite its modern attitudes and appearance, though, the city harbors a long and complicated past. Atlanta now serves as a major repository of the South's history stored on paper and microfilm.

The mother lode of southeastern US genealogical records awaits you at the **National Archives and Records Administration Southeast Region** [1557 St. Joseph Avenue; (404) 763-7474; <www.archives.gov/facilities/ga/atlanta.html>]. Located between downtown and the Hartsfield Atlanta Airport, this facility specializes in federal records dating to 1716 from Alabama, Florida, Georgia, Kentucky, Mississippi, North Carolina, South Carolina, and Tennessee. Regional holdings include indexes of passenger arrival lists for eastern and Gulf Coast ports and naturalization records from federal courts throughout the Southeast. Also look for military service records and indexes (including World War I draft registration cards) and pension and bounty land warrant applications. For general U.S. research, you can find federal census records and indexes for 1790 to 1920.

Before you go, check out the Guide to Archival Holdings at NARA's Southeast Region (Atlanta) at <www.archives.gov/facilities/ga/atlanta/holdings.html>. To get to the archives by public transportation, take the Metropolitan Atlanta Rapid Transit Authority (MARTA) train to the East Point or Lakewood station and catch

The Atlanta History Center brings the area's past to life through exhibits as well as archives.

COURTESY OF GEORGIA DEPARTMENT OF INDUSTRY, TRADE & TOURISM

The Atlanta History Center's Tullie Smith Farm offers a glimpse of 1840s life in rural Georgia.

bus 20 for a five-minute ride to the facility. [For help navigating MARTA, see the Web site <www.itsmarta.com> or call (404) 848-5000.] Once you're there, you'll need to apply for a researcher identification card (similar to a library card) in order to use the archival holdings. Nearby hotels include **Hampton Inn and Suites-Atlanta Airport** [3450 Bobby Brown Parkway; (404) 767-9300] and **Holiday Inn Atlanta Airport** [1380 Virginia Avenue; (404) 762-9482]. Your choices for something to eat around here are mostly chain restaurants and cafés.

The place for Georgia-specific research is the **Georgia Department of Archives and History** [330 Capitol Avenue SE; (404) 656-2393; <www.sos.state.ga.us/archives>]. At the Ben W. Fortson Archives and Records Building, you can tap state and local records, as well as private manuscripts and photographs, dating to 1732. The archives' Surveyor General Collection includes Georgia's 1.5 million land grants and plats from 1775 to 1909, plus more than ten thousand county and state maps. In the nongovernment section, you can find family letters and papers, business records and account books, records of organizations and churches, and photographs.

Before your visit to the state archives, take a look at Documenting Family History in Georgia at <www.sos.state.ga.us/archives/rs/dfhg.htm>. If you take MARTA, use the Georgia State University station; the state archives is three blocks south of it. Upon arrival, apply for a research card, which you must wear at all times while in the building.

Also downtown is the **Atlanta-Fulton Public Library's Local & Family History Department** [1 Margaret Mitchell Square; (404) 730-4636; <www.af.public.lib.ga.us/central/gagen>]. Located on the main library's fifth floor, this department has books on the history of Atlanta, Georgia, and the neighboring region, plus genealogical sources for Georgia as well as some for North Carolina, South Carolina, Virginia, Tennessee, and other states. Highlights include Atlanta city directories from 1867, Atlanta telephone directories from 1946, crisscross directories from 1946, microfilmed archives of *The Atlanta Georgian* and neighborhood community papers, a biographical index card file of prominent Georgians of the past, and indexes of Georgia vital records.

The library is at the corner of Forsyth Street and Carnegie Way. (Take MARTA to the Peachtree Center station.) Pick up the genealogy

Atlanta commemorates its Civil War heritage at the Kennesaw Civil War Museum.

"pathfinder" guides for beginners, African-American research, Native American research, and missing persons at the service desk.

If you want to stay near the state archives and the downtown public library, you can choose from plenty of hotels in the vicinity:

- **Atlanta Hilton and Towers** [255 Courtland Street NE; (800) 774-1500]
- **Best Western American Hotel** [160 Spring Street NW; (800) 780-7234]
- **Days Inn Downtown** [300 Spring Street NW; (800) 544-8313]
- **Ramada Hotel Downtown** [450 Capitol Avenue SE; (800) 298-2054]

Restaurants, too, abound:

- **Mumbo Jumbo Café** [89 Park Place NE; (404) 523-0330]—continental but spicy
- **Loaf and Kettle** [57 Forsyth Street NW; (404) 525-8624]—sandwich shop
- **Pacific Rim Bistro** [303 Peachtree Center Avenue NE; (404) 893-0018]—Asian cuisine

A good stop for both state and regional research is the **Atlanta History Center** [130 West Paces Ferry Road NW; (404) 814-4000; <www.atlhist.org>]. Its general collections include a special library dedicated to the American Revolution, cemetery and census records, insurance maps, and city directories. The manuscript collections include private papers, institutional records, and business documents. The history center's visual collection portrays the South through photographic prints, negatives, miscellaneous graphics, maps, and architectural drawings, as well as film, audio, and video.

To get to the Atlanta History Center, take MARTA to the Lenox station. Transfer to bus 23 to Peachtree and West Paces Ferry Road. Walk three blocks west on West Paces Ferry Road to reach the pedestrian entrance in front. Be sure to register before you begin researching.

Places to stay in this area include:

- **Embassy Suites** [3285 Peachtree Road; (800) 362-2779]
- **Summerfield Suites** [505 Pharr Road; (877) 999-3223]
- **Hampton Inn Buckhead** [3398 Piedmont Road NE; (800) 531-0202]

Buckhead is Atlanta's restaurant district, so you can find plenty of eateries nearby to choose from. A few suggestions:

- **Horseradish Grill** [4320 Powers Ferry Road; (404) 255-7277]—Southern
- **Seeger's** [111 West Paces Ferry Road; (404) 846-9779]—contemporary
- **Eclipse di Luna** [764 Miami Circle; (404) 846-0449]—Mediterranean

For a break from microfilm and copy machines, explore some of Atlanta's rich heritage. The battles and soldiers of the Civil War are still remembered at the **Kennesaw Mountain National Battlefield** [900 Kennesaw Mountain Drive; (770) 427-4686; <www.nps.gov/kemo>] and the **Kennesaw Civil War Museum** [2829 Cherokee Street; (800) 742-6897]. And what would a visit to Atlanta be without a little *Gone With the Wind*? Visit the **Margaret Mitchell House & Museum** [990 Peachtree Street; (404) 249-7015; <www.gwtw.org>] in midtown Atlanta to celebrate the famous book's author. To learn about the city's more recent history, stop by the **Martin Luther King Jr. National Historic Site** [450 Auburn Avenue NE; (404) 331-6922; <www.nps.gov/malu>], where you can walk in the footsteps of the slain civil rights leader.

CHARLESTON
BY DARIN PAINTER

A crown jewel of the South, Charleston has more church spires than skyline, more hospitality than hustle. Known as the "Holy City," its religious relics—and dignified citizens—have survived three centuries of epidemics, fires, wars, and hurricanes. Perhaps that's why graciousness is the everyday mood in this charming, antebellum spot, which offers (thank you very much) a heavenly heap of heritage sites.

Located near the hub of Charleston's historic downtown, by the corner of Broad and Meeting streets, is the **South Carolina Historical Society** [100 Meeting Street; (843) 723-3225; <www.schistory.org>]. Formed in 1855, it includes an extensive collection of rare manuscripts, books, letters, maps, journals, and periodicals, as well as a photo archive of more than forty thousand images.

Just northwest of the Historical Society near the Ashley River, Charleston's past comes to life at **The Citadel Archives & Museum** [171 Moultrie Street; (843) 953-6846; <www.citadel.edu/archivesandmuseum>]. Arranged chronologically from 1842 to the present, its permanent exhibits display the military, academic, athletic, and social aspects of your cadet ancestors' lives. Collections include personal papers, letters, diaries, reports, minutes, speeches, films, and videotapes.

From The Citadel, go a few blocks south to visit the nationally recognized **Avery Research Center for African-American History and Culture** [125 Bull Street; (843) 953-7609; <www.cofc.edu/~averyrsc/>], founded in 1865 and located west of the main campus of the College of Charleston. The center traces the heritage of South Carolina's low-country African Americans and contains one of the best series of manuscript collections documenting the civil rights movement.

One of the best aspects of Charleston is its 181 churches, representing twenty-five denominations. Church records abound. The largest collection is at the **Archives of the Diocese of Charleston** [114 Rear Broad Street; (843) 724-8372; <www.catholic-doc.org/archives/archives.html>], established in 1820. Its holdings date from 1789 and include the papers of bishops; administrative records of diocesan offices; chancery correspondence; and records of various agencies, religious orders, programs, and

Middleton Place near Charleston was the home of the president of the First Continental Congress.

churchgoers. The archives also include parish histories, property records, deed and construction files, some architectural drawings, cemetery records, newspapers, and photographs. Original registers containing sacramental records aren't held in the archives, but it does contains numerous microfilm copies of parish registers prior to 1930.

The easiest form of transportation in downtown Charleston is the **Downtown Area Shuttle** [DASH; (843) 724-7420]. You can purchase a ride-all-day ticket for $3 at the **Charleston Visitor Reception and Transportation Center**, also called the "Visitors Center" [375 Meeting Street; (843) 853-8000].

Across the street is **The Charleston Museum** [360 Meeting Street; (843) 722-2996; <www.charlestonmuseum.org>], America's oldest museum, founded in 1773. Exhibits focus on Colonial trade and commerce, the plantation system, and more. The museum's Discover Me Room has hands-on exhibits for children. Two historic homes are part of the museum: **The Joseph Manigault House** (350 Meeting Street), built in 1803, is a historic landmark that captures the lifestyle of a wealthy, rice-planting family. The **Heyward-Washington House** (87 Church Street), built in 1772, was the home of Thomas Heyward Jr., a signer of the Declaration of Independence.

Two other downtown sites are worth seeing: **Market Hall** [88 Meeting Street; (843) 723-1541] is a landmark built in 1841 that houses the Confederate Museum's collection of flags, uniforms, swords, and other Civil War memorabilia. **Old Powder Magazine** [79 Cumberland Street; (843) 805-6730] contains a bevy of artifacts from eighteenth-century Charleston.

During that century, more Revolutionary War battles were fought in South Carolina than in any other state. Charleston, though, is better known for its role in the Civil War, which began on April 12, 1861, at Fort Sumter. Later, from 1863 to 1865, the Confederates at Fort Sumter withstood a twenty-two-month siege by Union forces. About sixty-three thousand South Carolinians served in the Confederate army, and you can acknowledge their bravery at **Fort Sumter National Monument** (Charleston Harbor; <www.nps.gov/fosu>). Ferries to the fort depart from the city's Municipal Marina on Lockwood Boulevard and from Patriot's Point, located east of the Cooper River in the community of Mount Pleasant.

To enjoy some living history, travel ten minutes northwest to **Middleton Place** [4300 Ashley River Road; (800) 782-3608; <www.middletonplace.org>], a plantation built in 1741. It was the home of Henry Middleton, president of the First Continental Congress. In the stable yard, craftspeople use authentic tools and equipment to demonstrate spinning, blacksmithing, and other domestic skills from the plantation era. Middleton Place, which plays host to "Plantation Days" on Saturdays in November, also is home to America's oldest landscaped gardens.

Chefs in the Holy City can't turn water into wine, but you should see what they can do with she-crab soup, sautéed shrimp, and other low-country cuisine. Try the crispy flounder at **Anson** [12 Anson Street; (843) 577-0551], a charming restaurant framed by about a dozen French windows. A contemporary, elegant choice is

McCrady's [2 Unity Alley; (843) 577-0025], where locals go for tuna tartare. **Magnolias** [185 East Bay Street; (843) 577-7771] is located in the city's former Customs House and specializes in Deep South dinners. **Hominy Grill** [207 Rutledge Avenue; (843) 937-0930] serves tasty, distinctly Southern dishes. If you're in the mood for shellfish and oysters to go (or to sit—this place has six dining rooms), check out **Hyman's Seafood Company Restaurant** [215 Meeting Street; (843) 723-6000].

The city's best-known hotel is the upscale **Charleston Place** [205 Meeting Street; (843) 722-4900; <www.charlestonplace.com>]. It's within walking distance of the South Carolina Historical Society, as are the charming **Mills House Hotel** [115 Meeting Street; (800) 874-9600; <www.millshouse.com>] and **Meeting Street Inn** [173 Meeting Street; (843) 723-1882; <www.meetingstreetinn.com>]. One block from the Battery (the southern point of Charleston, where the Cooper and Ashley Rivers meet) is **Hayne House** [30 King Street; (843) 577-2633; <www.haynehouse.com>], built in 1755. Another good choice is the more moderate **Anchorage Inn** [26 Vendue Range; (800) 421-2952; <www.anchoragencharleston.com>], built in the 1840s as a cotton warehouse.

South Carolina's most comprehensive collection of genealogy resources is located in the capital city of Columbia, a worthwhile two-hour trip northwest on I-26. If you go, visit the **South Carolina Department of Archives and History** [Archives & History Center, 8301 Parklane Road; (803) 896-6100; <www.state.sc.us/scdah/>]. Its holdings include vital records, church records, court records, Colonial petitions and correspondence, military records, newspapers, tax records, cemetery records, probate records, maps, federal census records from 1790 through 1910, and local histories. The **Division of Vital Records** [J. Marion Sims Building, 2600 Bull Street; (803) 898-3630; <www.scdhec.net/vr>], part of the South Carolina Department of

Health and Environmental Control, houses state birth records since January 1915, state marriage records since July 1950, and state divorce records since July 1962.

DALLAS-FORT WORTH

BY ALLISON STACY

True to the city's nickname—the Big D—bigger is better in Dallas. Boasting more restaurants per person than New York City, a greater concentration of shopping centers than any U.S. metropolis, and an airport bigger than the entire island of Manhattan, the town that President John F. Kennedy and J.R. Ewing made famous is Texas's top visitor destination. So it should come as no surprise that Dallas-Fort Worth (DFW) is also among the state's biggest family history hot spots, its genealogical riches flowing like the Texas crude that turned Dallas into one of the nation's financial centers. While you're drilling for your roots here, have fun exploring the area's heritage of oil, railroads, cowboys, and outlaws.

Many historical and genealogical attractions are close to downtown, which means you can take advantage of the city's excellent public transportation system, **DART** [(214) 979-1111; <www.dart.org>]. Light-rail serves several downtown stops as well as the DFW airport. Buses can take you just about anywhere else. You pay only $2 for a local one-day pass.

The **Dallas Public Library** [1515 Young Street; (214) 670-1400; <dallaslibrary.org>] is within walking distance of downtown rail stations. Its genealogy collection is one of the South's biggest: eighty thousand volumes; forty-two thousand rolls of microfilm; seventy-seven thousand microfiche; and more than seven hundred maps and charts that cover all U.S. states and parts of Canada, the British Isles, and Germany. Visit the Texas/Dallas History and Archives here, too, for more than fifteen hundred newspapers and periodicals, Sanborn fire insurance maps, yearbooks, membership directories, oral

The colorful Old Red Courthouse has been a Dallas landmark since 1892.

history interviews, and government records.

Shopping is a favorite Dallas pastime, and a quick walk down Ervay Street will lead you to the original **Neiman Marcus** store [1618 Main Street; (214) 741-6911]. A few blocks away at the corner of Commerce and Akard Streets, the Baroque stylings of the **Hotel Adolphus** [1321 Commerce Street; (241)742-8200; <www.hoteladolphus.com>] are as dazzling—and expensive—as the wares at Neiman Marcus. Established by beer baron Adolphus Busch in 1912, this luxurious landmark has hosted many of Dallas's celebrity visitors. It's also renowned for its French Room restaurant. For more affordable lodging downtown, try the **Hampton Inn** [1015 Elm Street; (800) 531-0202], the **Grand Hotel** [1914 Commerce Street; (214) 747-7000], or the historic **Holiday Inn Aristocrat** [1933 Main Street; (800) 465-4329].

From Akard Street you can hop on light-rail for a quick ride to the **West End Historic District** <www.dallaswestend.org>. Warehouses that were originally spawned by late-nineteenth-century railroad and commercial growth have been transformed into restaurants, shops, and clubs, including the **West End Marketplace** in the former Sunshine Biscuit building. Among the neighborhood's other historical buildings are the **Old Red Courthouse**, built in 1892, and a replica of Dallas founder **John Neely Bryan's log cabin**.

West End's best-known locale is **Dealey Plaza**, the site of President John F. Kennedy's assassination on November 22, 1963. Today, Dallas remembers him at the **Kennedy Memorial** and **The Sixth Floor Museum at Dealey Plaza** [411 Elm Street; (214) 747-6660; <www.jfk.org>], located in the Texas School Book Depository building, where Lee Harvey Oswald is said to have fired the fatal shots.

Just east of downtown is **Fair Park** <www.fairparkdallas.com>, site of the Cotton Bowl and more genealogical destinations. Look for Texas Methodist ancestors at **Southern Methodist University's Bridwell Library** [6005 Bishop Boulevard; (214) 768-2481; <www2.smu.edu/bridwell>], or explore the **DeGolyer Library's** history collections [6404 Hilltop Lane; (214) 768-2012; <www2.smu.edu/cul/degolyer>]. You can find the Archives of Women of the Southwest, railroad and immigration ephemera, collections from railroad companies, and three hundred U.S. and Mexican newspapers covering 1810 to 1939. To learn more about Texas's railroading history, take a ride into the past at the **Age of Steam Railroad Museum** [1105 Washington Street; (214) 428-0101; <www.dallasrailwaymuseum.com>].

Within Fair Park's **Hall of State** <www.hallofstate.com> is the **Dallas Historical Society's G.B. Dealey Library** [3939 Grand Avenue; (214) 421-4500; <www.dallashistory.org>]. Its three million documents, eight thousand photographs, and ten thousand volumes on Texas history include Sam Houston's handwritten account of the Battle of San Jacinto. You'll need to schedule a research appointment in advance.

After the Civil War, many former slaves, lured by the burgeoning railroad industry, came to Dallas and built Freedman's Towns. Explore the area's black heritage at Fair Park's **African-American Museum** [3536 Grand Avenue; (214) 565-9026; <www.dallasblack.com/channel1/aam>], which has one of the country's largest African-American folk art collections. For black roots research, check out the historical collection and archives, which houses archives of Texas women, Dallas county politics, and *Sepia* magazine, as well as a Freedman's Cemetery collection. This graveyard, located just north of downtown at Lemmon Avenue and the Central Expressway, had been almost completely covered by buildings when the Texas Department of Transportation discovered it in 1986. Thousands of African Americans were buried there between 1860 and the early 1900s. As archaeologists began excavating and relocating graves in 1991, they discovered wooden markers; clothing; and seashells from the Atlantic, the Caribbean, and even Africa.

You can turn back the clock more than a century by going a few miles west of Fair Park on I-30. On the south side of downtown Dallas, **Old City Park** [1717 Gano Street; (214) 421-

The Sixth Floor Museum at Dealey Plaza recalls the tragic events of John F. Kennedy's assassination.

5141; <www.oldcitypark.org>] re-creates pioneer and Victorian life in a village of authentic buildings from 1840 to 1910, along with a working 1860s farm. You can enjoy soups, salads, and sandwiches in an 1876 farmhouse at **Brent Place Restaurant** [(214) 421-5141].

Getting to Fort Worth is easier and cheaper than ever—the completion of the Trinity Rail Express line means you can ride directly from downtown Dallas to downtown Fort Worth for a few bucks. It's a small price to pay for the genealogical fortune you can find at the **National Archives and Records Administration Southwest Region** on the south side of Fort Worth [501 West Felix Street, Building 1; (817) 334-5515; <www.archives.gov/facilities/tx/fort_worth.html>]. Get there by bus, or take the South Freeway. After you get your researcher ID, you can dig into federal records from Arkansas, Louisiana, Oklahoma, and Texas, plus you can examine the entire U.S. census and passenger records. Of special note: This branch has extensive American Indian materials, including Dawes census cards and enrollment jackets for the Five Civilized Tribes and Bureau of Indian Affairs records (Record Group 75).

After a long day of research, revel in Fort

The Fort Worth Stockyards National Historic District celebrates the city's cowboy culture.

Worth's cowboy culture at the **Stockyards National Historic District** [130 East Exchange Avenue; (817) 624-4741; <www.fortworth stockyards.org>]. As a stop on the Old Chisolm Trail, Fort Worth earned its "Cowtown" moniker from its booming cattle business. Today, you can catch a rodeo or cattle drive (still done daily) and take a guided tour.

You can also find plenty of the Old West in the district's lodging and restaurants. **Cattlemen's Steakhouse** [2458 North Main Street; (817) 624-3945; <www.cattlemenssteakhouse.com>] and **Riscky's BBQ** [140 East Exchange Avenue; (817) 626-7777; <www.risckys.com>] serve up famous Texas fare. **Miss Molly's Hotel** [1091/2 West Exchange Avenue; (800) 996-6559; <www.missmollys.com>] is a former brothel turned bed-and-breakfast. The **Stockyards Hotel** [109 East Exchange Avenue; (800) 423-8471; <www.stockyardshotel.com>] once hosted Bonnie and Clyde.

They weren't the only outlaws in town. Butch Cassidy and the Sundance Kid and Wyatt Earp and Doc Holiday once frequented the saloons and gambling parlors of "Hell's Half Acre," now known as **Sundance Square** [512 Main Street, Suite 1500; (817) 339-7777; <www.sundancesquare.com>]. Considering the area's rowdy past, family historians who hope to find a horse thief or bank robber among their Texas ancestors just might get lucky in Dallas-Fort Worth.

HOUSTON

BY EMILY ANNE CROOM

Located at the junction of the South, Southwest, world community, and outer space, Houston is a diverse city at the center of a large metropolitan area reaching into seven surrounding counties.

Everyone knows Houston is Space City and a world hub for the petroleum industry. But did you know that the city boasts one of the nation's premier genealogy libraries? While the genealogist explores the world of ancestors, family members can explore exciting museums and beautiful parks near the library.

This crown jewel is **Clayton Library, Center for Genealogical Research** [5300 Caroline; (832) 393-2600; <www.houstonlibrary.org/clayton>]. The genealogy unit of Houston Public Library, Clayton Library houses a magnificent concentration of research materials that include microprint collections, books, periodicals, maps, CD-ROMs, and more than ten thousand published and unpublished family histories. Located in the heart of the city's Museum District and near the world-renowned Texas Medical Center, the library attracts researchers from all parts of the United States its diverse and extensive collection. Whether your ancestors were from New England, the South, or the Midwest, and whether they arrived in the United States in the seventeenth century or the twentieth, this library has research opportunities for you.

An example of the broad scope of the library's resources is that it holds all available federal census and Soundex microfilm from 1790 through 1920, as well as much of the 1930 film, with related indexes and finding aids. In addition to the population schedules, the library has the slave schedules, numerous mortality and agriculture schedules, and the complete 1890 special census of Union veterans and widows.

Serious researchers understand the importance of primary source materials, and these are a principal focus of Clayton Library's print and microprint holdings. Examples include:

- an impressive collection of military records and passenger lists
- the Dawes rolls, Indian tribal censuses and enrollment cards, and other sources for Native American research
- Freedmen's Bureau records for Texas and Louisiana, all the existing Freedman's Savings and Trust Company depositor records and indexes to deposit ledgers, and other materials for African-American research
- a large nationwide collection of nineteenth- and early-twentieth-century city directories, including many 1930 directories to aid in researching the 1930 census
- vital records or related indexes for many states, including Connecticut's Hale and Barbour collections
- county records for a number of states
- Colonial and Revolution-era records for the original states, plus the papers of the Continental Congress
- eighteenth- and nineteenth-century research materials such as the Draper and Shane manuscript collections and a large collection of the Territorial Papers of the United States
- the entire Republic of Texas Claims
- the extensive microfiche GRO (General Register Office) Vital Records Indexes—Births, Marriages and Deaths for England and Wales, 1837-1930

Clayton Library also holds histories of U.S. states and counties; a growing foreign collection, including European, Canadian, and Latin American materials; and more than two thousand genealogy and local history periodical titles from the United States and other countries.

The library offers special interlibrary loan opportunities with Canadian provincial archives and the **Texas Regional Historical Resource Depository** <www.tsl.state.tx.us/arc/local>. Full-time trained staff members are available to assist patrons with developing research strategies and using the library's resources effectively. Visit the Clayton Library Web site for more information.

The **Central Library complex of the Houston Public Library** [500 McKinney; (832) 393-1313; <www.houstonlibrary.org>] houses three facilities of interest to genealogists: the Texas Room, the Houston Metropolitan Research Center, and the Bibliographic Information Center.

The Texas Room, or **Texas and Local History Department** [Ideson Building, 500 McKinney; (832) 393-1658; <www.houstonlibrary.org/hpl/txr.html>], focuses on Houston and Texas history. The department holds a number of microfilm collections for research in the Spanish and Mexican periods of Texas history, including the Bexar, Nacogdoches, and Laredo Archives, and *Texas As Province and Republic*, more than two thousand works published from 1795 to 1845.

The Texas Room also holds early Texas newspaper titles, the Sanborn Fire Insurance maps for Texas cities from the 1880s forward, Houston telephone directories from 1903, Houston and other Texas city directories, more than fifteen hundred Houston and Texas maps, some yearbooks from local schools and colleges, the Freedmen's Bureau records for Texas, and an extensive collection of Houston and Texas photographs. Overlapping somewhat with Clayton Library, the Texas Room also holds a number of Texas county, town, and church histories. Another important research collection is the Texas and Louisiana portions of the microfilm *Records of Ante-Bellum Southern Plantations From the Revolution Through the Civil War.*

This department is also the Texas Regional Historical Resource Depository for Harris and Galveston counties, with microfilm of county tax, deed, court, and other records, which are also available for interlibrary loan.

The **Houston Metropolitan Research Center** [Ideson Building, 500 McKinney; (832) 393-1658; <www.houstonlibrary.org/hpl/hmrc.html>] holds manuscripts and archives, including business, family, and religious institution records. Research can be done only by appointment.

The **Bibliographic Information Center** [Jesse Jones Building, 500 McKinney, First Floor; (832) 393-1313; <www.houstonlibrary.org>] holds newspapers on microfilm for Houston and other cities.

These academic libraries also have research collections of interest to genealogists:

• **Fondren Library of Rice University** [6100 Main; (713) 348-5698; <www.rice.edu/fondren>] holds the microfilm collection *Southern Women and Their Families*, most of the microfilm series *Records of Ante-Bellum Southern Plantations From the Revolution Through the Civil War*, and the same series *From Emancipation to the Great Migration.*

• **Neumann Library at the University of Houston-Clear Lake** [2700 Bay Area Boulevard; (281) 283-3910; <nola.cl.uh.edu>] has the microfilm collection *Confederate Imprints*—materials published in or by any of the Confederate states, 1861 to 1865—as well as *Texas as Province and Republic*, *History of Women* and *Western Americana.*

• **M.D. Anderson Library of the University of Houston-Central Campus** [114 University Libraries; (713) 743-1050; <info.lib.uh.edu>] also holds special collections on African Americans in Houston and women in Texas before 1900.

In addition, the libraries of **South Texas College of Law**, the **University of Houston Law Center**, and **Texas Southern University School of Law** contain materials of use in genealogy, such as the U.S. Statutes at Large, laws of the states, legal directories, and reports of appellate courts throughout the country.

The Houston area includes several cities whose public libraries have good genealogy departments, including Conroe and Richmond (see <www.rootsweb.com/~txharri2>). In addition, the following facilities are worth a visit for early Texas or southeast Texas research:

• **Rosenberg Library**, Galveston's public library, houses state and federal documents and the **Galveston and Texas History Center** [2310 Sealy Avenue, Galveston; (409) 763-8854; <www.rosenberg-library.org/gthc/rosenhis.html>]. Although its primary focus is history, the history center holds Texas federal census records from 1850 through 1920; Galveston County tax records; passenger lists from the Port of Galveston; Galveston city vital registers, mortuary and cemetery records, telephone and city directories, Sanborn fire insurance maps, and newspaper indexes; a Subject File of Galveston Island genealogies; and a sizable manuscripts collection. The center also provides a limited research service; call or write for details.

• The **Texas Seaport Museum** [Pier 21 at Harborside Drive, Galveston; (409) 763-1877; <www.tsm-elissa.org>] features an in-house and online database of more than 133,000 passengers who first entered the United States through the Port of Galveston. The list was created from National Archives records and other sources.

• The **Herzstein Library at the San Jacinto Monument** [1 Monument Circle, LaPorte; (281) 479-2421; <www.sanjacinto-museum.org>] houses an early Texas collection. The library is open by appointment.

Houston and Galveston are the county seats of Harris and Galveston Counties, respectively, and their courthouses contain numerous records, but the archives mentioned here are collectively a better first choice for most research. Call for the location of the records you need before making a trip [1001 Preston; (713) 755-6405; <www.cclerk.hctx.net>].

In Houston and its environs, you'll probably prefer a car for transportation. For more information, contact the **Houston Convention and Visitors Bureau** [901 Bagby; (713) 437-5200; <www.houston-guide.com>]. For details on museums, see <www.worldartantiques.com/TexasHouston.html> and <www.houston.tx.us/arts/museums.html>. For Galveston information, see <www.galveston.com> and <www.galvestonislandtx.com>.

NASHVILLE
BY DAVID A. FRYXELL

Nashville may be best known as the capital of the country music industry, but it's also the capital of Tennessee, making it as much of a mecca for those interested in genealogy as it is for fans of the Grand Ole Opry. Long before Nashville got its famous twang, it resonated with pioneers settling the old Southwest.

A hardy band led by James Robertson (who's buried here) founded the city in 1779 as "Fort Nashborough," which today is reconstructed at 170 First Avenue North in **Riverfront Park** downtown [(615) 862-8400]. The fort was the northern terminus of the Natchez Trace, so even if your migrating Dixie ancestors didn't settle here, they likely passed through.

Start looking for traces of them at the **Tennessee State Library and Archives** [403 Seventh Avenue North; (615) 741-2764; <www.state.tn.us/sos/statelib>], an imposingly columned building immediately west of the state capitol. (Arrive early to snag one of a handful of visitor parking spots at the front and side.) Get a feel for the place first with a ten-minute orientation tour by a staff member, then dive into the wealth of resources here. You can find Tennessee military records from the War of 1812 to Vietnam, with a particular emphasis on the Civil War, including pension applications, soldiers' home applications, veterans' questionnaires, and unit rosters. Microfilmed county records include chancery court, circuit court, and county court minutes; deeds; marriage records; and probate records. Most of the South is covered in census records on microfilm, and index books for Tennessee from 1820 to 1880 are available. City directories encompass Nashville from 1853, Memphis from 1850, Knoxville from 1859, and many smaller places. A vast newspaper collection on microfilm preserves almost every extant newspaper published in the state. If you have Cherokee ancestors, check here for files on the 1817-1819 and 1835-1838 removals of the Cherokee to Oklahoma, including censuses of Indians from Tennessee, Alabama, Georgia, and North Carolina. You may also find in the library's collection of Tennessee postcards your ancestral hometown the way it once looked.

Official state registration of vital records didn't begin until 1908, but the library does have some earlier birth records from Chattanooga (1879-), Knoxville (1881), and

Nashville (1881-) and death records from Chattanooga (1872-), Knoxville (1881-), Nashville (1874-), and Memphis (1848-). The library's Web site has an index to Tennessee death records from 1908 to 1912 and for thirty-four counties from 1914 to 1925. Birth records from 1914 forward and death records from 1952 forward are at the **Office of Vital Records** [421 Fifth Avenue North; (615) 741-1763; <www.state.tn.us/health/vr>].

Over on the south side of the capitol, the **War Memorial Building** is home to the **Tennessee Historical Society** [(615) 741-8934; <www.tennesseehistory.org>]. Its collections are housed at the state library and archives, however.

For a different view of Tennessee's past in the capitol area, continue south to the **Tennessee State Museum** [505 Deaderick Street; (800) 407-4324; <www.tnmuseum.org>] in the lower level of the **James K. Polk Cultural Center**. Permanent exhibits cover the state's Indians, the frontier era, the age of Andrew Jackson, antebellum Tennessee, the Civil War and Reconstruction, and the New South. Across the street is the **Military Museum**, where you can see the medals presented to Tennessee hero Sgt. Alvin York and a deck gun from the USS *Nashville*, which fired the first shots in the Spanish-American War. You can also tour the **State Capitol** itself, completed in 1859 and the crowning achievement of architect William Strickland. Tour information is available from the state museum.

Nashville's new **Main Public Library** is just a few blocks away [615 Church Street; (615) 862-5800; <www.nashv.lib.tn.us/Library/Branches/BenWest.html>]. Its Nashville Room [(615) 862-5782] holds books, photographs, pamphlets, and newspaper clippings on the city's history, plus early census materials and an index of obituaries from local newspapers.

Hotels within walking distance of the state library and archives include:

- **Sheraton Nashville Downtown** [623 Union Street; (888) 625-5144]

- **Hermitage Hotel** [231 Sixth Avenue North; (888) 888-9414]
- **Doubletree Hotel** [315 Fourth Avenue North; (615) 244-8200]
- **Days Inn Downtown** [711 Union Street; (800) 544-8313]

In-between microfilm reels, you can grab a taste of the South (the traditional "meat 'n' three"—three vegetables, that is) at **Monell's** [530 Church Street; (615) 248-4744] or get burgers at **Wolfy's** [425 Broadway; (615) 251-1621]. A bit farther away but worth the jaunt for dinner is **Jimmy Kelly's** [217 Louise Avenue; (615) 329-4349], which has been serving steak to Nashville since 1934. Barbecue, of course, is Nashville's favorite nosh, and you can start an argument trying to pick the best. Rest assured that you can find the real deal at **Mary's Pit Bar-B-Que** [1108 Jefferson Street; (615) 256-7696], a walk-up stand.

Once you start exploring greater Nashville, you can find other archives of interest. These include the **Metropolitan Nashville-Davidson County Archives** [3801 Green Hills Village Drive; (615) 862-5880; <www.geocities.com/metroarchives>] and **Vanderbilt University's Special Collections and University Archives** [419 Twenty-first Avenue South; (615) 322-2807; <www.library.Vanderbilt.edu/speccol/schome.html>]. If you have a prominent Baptist ancestor, look for clues at the **Southern Baptist Historical Library and Archives** [901 Commerce Street, #400; (615) 244-0344; <www.sbhla.org/familyhistory.htm>].

To give your eyes a rest from records, feast them on **Belle Meade Plantation** [5025 Harding Road; (800) 270-3991; <www.bellemeadeplantation.com>], known as the "Queen of the Tennessee Plantations." Costumed guides re-create Belle Meade's heyday as a thoroughbred farm as you tour the 1853 Greek Revival mansion and stables.

The Italianate **Belmont Mansion** [1900 Belmont Boulevard; (615) 460-5459; <www.

belmontmansion.com>], on the campus of Belmont University, was built in 1850 by Adelicia Acklen, one of the wealthiest women in America. Later, she furnished the mansion and added the elegant grand salon with proceeds from secretly conspiring with both the Union and the Confederacy during the Civil War. (Many Civil War battlefields are also within easy driving distance of Nashville; see the Web site of the **National Heritage Area on the Civil War in Tennessee** <chp.mtsu.edu/tncivwar> for a guide.)

Nashville's oldest plantation home open to the public is **Travellers Rest** [636 Farrell Parkway; (615) 832-8197; <www.travellersrest plantation.org>], whose original construction dates back to 1799.

The city's most famous mansion is, of course, **The Hermitage** [4580 Rachel's Lane; (615) 889-2941; <www.thehermitage.com>], the home of Andrew Jackson. Completely restored to its 1837 appearance, the house contains almost all original furnishings. In the summer you can watch archaeologists at work nearby excavating the 1804 slave cabins.

A bit of Nashville history that is slightly more recent but equally emblematic of the city's heritage is **The Parthenon** [West End and Twenty-fifth Avenues, Centennial Park; (615) 862-8431; <www.nashville.gov/parthenon>], built for the 1897 Tennessee Centennial Exposition. The world's only full-scale replica of the famous Greek temple, it holds the city's art museum and is home to a forty-two-foot statue of Athena— the largest indoor sculpture in the Western world.

Of course, Nashville's most famous "monument" today—one with its own bit of history— is the **Grand Ole Opry**. Since 1974, the world's longest-running radio show, an icon of country music, has been performed at the forty-four hundred-seat **Grand Ole Opry House** [2804 Opryland Drive; (615) 889-3060; <www.opry.com>]. Next door, the **Grand Ole Opry Museum** [2802 Opryland Drive; (615) 889-3060] celebrates country music from the days of Patsy Cline and Little Jimmy Dickens to Garth Brooks and Reba McEntire. If you plan to spend much time here, spend a night in the spectacular **Opryland Hotel** [2800 Opryland Drive; (615) 889-1000; <www. oprylandhotels.com>], set among nine acres of indoor gardens, waterfalls, and an indoor lake and river.

To see the original, historic home of the "opry," however, head back to **Music Row** on the edge of downtown. Built in 1892, the **Ryman Auditorium** [116 Fifth Avenue North; (615) 254-1445; <www.ryman.com>] now hosts theater and music from bluegrass to rock, but this stage is where the Grand Ole Opry was born in 1943. Nashville is also home to the **Country Music Hall of Fame** [222 Fifth Avenue South; (615) 416-2096; <www.halloffame.org>]. In short, the roots of country music are right here, and there's no better way to relax after finding your own roots than to get "a little bit country."

NEW ORLEANS

BY SUSAN WENNER JACKSON

Genealogy is more than just a hobby in New Orleans. For the people of this historic city, who your ancestors are determines who you are. Over the past three centuries, a person's lineage placed him as part of the city's Creole elite, a Garden District American, a *Gens de Couleur Libres* (free person of color), or a slave. Today, the distinctions aren't quite so dramatic. But the past lives on here, and the city's lifelong residents still know whose families go way back— and whose don't. Jan Voitier Dean was born and raised in New Orleans, and she says it's the perfect place to get in touch with your roots: "I've had the pleasure of going into several of my ancestors' nearly-two-hundred-year-old homes. What a thrill that was—I could practically feel my skirts swishing!"

New Orleans's long history (the city was settled in 1718) and its reverence for genealogy can give you a leg up if you're researching your

Louisiana roots. The place is packed with archives, libraries, cemeteries, and old buildings to help you climb your family tree. Probably the most difficult part of your trip will be determining which of the many places you should visit!

A good general place to start is the **New Orleans Public Library** [219 Loyola Avenue; (504) 529-READ (7323); <nutrias.org>], which also serves as the city archives. "They have a vast collection of material that is tremendously useful," says New Orleans professional genealogist Ellen Cleary <home.earthlink.net/~ellencleary>. "[The collection] includes an index to the obituary notices in New Orleans newspapers up to 1985; a biographical index; an index of justice of the peace marriages here; an index of birth, marriage, and death records; and marriage and death certificates."

The library also offers probate and succession records, divorce records, voting records, conveyance and real estate tax assessment records, Louisiana censuses, an index of tombstone inscriptions in many of the New Orleans cemeteries, and cemetery interment and ownership records. For a guide to the library's genealogical collections, visit <nutrias.org/~nopl/guides/genguide/ggcover.htm> or order a printed copy for $12 from the Friends of the New Orleans Public Library.

Another prime resource is the **Louisiana Historical Research Center** [400 Esplanade Avenue; (504) 568-6968]. The center carries French and Spanish translations in chronological order with a table of contents. It also has records dating from 1727 to about 1752 for the Little Red Church. "These are primarily [records] of the first Germans to colonize the area," says Shirley Bourquard, a certified genealogist in New Orleans. Other holdings include armorial records, genealogies, city directories, a *Louisiana Historical Quarterly* index, card files, cemetery files, tombstone inscriptions, and more. You need an appointment to research in this facility.

Next stop: the **Historic New Orleans Collection** [533 Royal Street; (504) 523-4662; www.hnoc. org]. Located in the heart of the historic French Quarter, this museum houses a "wonderful manuscript collection that includes family papers, letters, diaries, financial and legal documents, and records of New Orleans organizations," says Cleary. "This is *the* place to do research on colonial Louisiana." It also offers a survey of old New Orleans cemeteries that includes inscriptions and photographs of burial sites in St. Louis I & II, Lafayette I & II, St. Joseph I & II, Cypress Grove, Odd Fellows Rest, and Greenwood cemeteries.

Looking for early legal records? Try the **Notarial Archives** [421 Loyola Avenue; (504) 568-8577; <www.notarialarchives.org>], which contains all records of New Orleans notaries—important in the city's French-inspired culture. "If you can find out which notary someone in your family in New Orleans used, [that notary's] records can be a wealth of information about the family," Cleary notes. "The Notarial Archives also has some wonderful information about the old houses here in New Orleans."

If you have African-American ancestors, don't miss the **Amistad Center at Tulane**

The French Quarter epitomizes the colorful heritage of New Orleans.

University [6823 St. Charles Avenue; (504) 865-5535; <www.tulane.edu/~amistad>]. It specializes in African-American papers, as well as records of organizations and institutions in the African-American community. The center also has a smaller collection of holdings regarding Native Americans, Puerto Ricans, Chicanos, Asian-Americans, European immigrants, and Appalachian whites.

While you're there, you might also visit the Louisiana Collection at the **Tulane University Library** [Jones Hall; (504) 865-5685; <www.tulane.edu/~lmiller/LaCollection.html>]. This is a research collection of printed materials relating to Louisiana history and culture, including the state's best collection of nineteenth-century Louisiana books. In addition to thirty-five thousand books and pamphlets, the collection contains maps, photographs, illustrations from popular nineteenth-century magazines, sheet music, newspapers, and more.

While the many genealogical resources of New Orleans could occupy your entire trip, the city's historical attractions are enticing, too. Give in to the temptation—at least a few times during your visit—and soak up the heritage all around you. Nearly every archive or library has interesting places to see nearby. If you stay at the **Holiday Inn** [330 Loyola Avenue; (800) 535-7830; <www.basshotels.com/holiday-inn?_franchisee=MSYDT>] across from the public library, you can walk not only to your main research destination but also to the French Quarter. Other convenient places to hang your hat are the **Monteleone Hotel** [214 Royal Street; (800) 535-9595; <www.hotelmonteleone.com>], the **Olde Victorian Inn** [914 Rampart Street; (800) 725-2446; <www.oldevictorianinn.com>], and the **Omni Royal Crescent** [535 Gravier Street; (800) 843-6664; <www.omnihotels.com>].

A key attraction for history lovers is the **Louisiana State Museum** [751 Chartres; (504) 568-6968; <lsm.crt.state.la.us>], a complex of national landmarks that house thousands of artifacts and works of art reflecting Louisiana's legacy of historic events and cultural diversity. The museum operates five properties in the French Quarter: the **Cabildo**, the **Presbytère**, **1850 House**, the **Old U.S. Mint**, and **Madame John's Legacy**. Also take a tour of the **Hermann-Grima House** [820 St. Louis Street; (504) 525-5661; <www.gnofn.org/~hggh>], which represents one of the largest and best-preserved examples of American architecture in the French Quarter.

And don't forget about the "cities of the dead." New Orleans's cemeteries "are really worth seeing," says Cleary. "Because New Orleans is below sea level, the dead are buried above the ground here. The inscriptions on burial sites often give you a capsule picture of the members of a family, when they were born and when they died." Don't try this on your own, however: Your best bet is a walking tour, since the cemeteries have a reputation for muggings. Try **Magic Talking Tours** [(504) 588-9693], led by local historians.

Whether you're a hard-core genealogist or you're just along for the ride, you'll have to eat while you're in New Orleans, which is a food lover's paradise. The selection is not just limited to Cajun food, either—the city's restaurants run the gamut from world-renowned gourmet at **Commander's Palace** [1403 Washington Avenue; (504) 899-8221] to down-home country cookin' at **West End Café** [8536 Pontchartrain Boulevard; (504) 288-0711] on Lake Pontchartrain. If you visit the state museum or do a bit of shopping around Jackson Square, pop in at **Café du Monde** [Decatur and St. Ann Streets; (504) 525-4544] for chicory café au lait and beignets heavily dusted with powdered sugar. For brunch, treat yourself to a traditional Creole meal at **Brennan's** [417 Royal Street; (504) 525-9711], located in a gorgeous nineteenth-century building graced with a lovely tropical courtyard.

RALEIGH

BY DARIN PAINTER

Along with neighboring college towns Durham and Chapel Hill, the pine tree-spotted city of Raleigh is a corporate hub that attracts scientists, professors, and business gurus from around the world. What better place to look up your roots than the Research Triangle? More than just trees and Ph.D.s, the Triangle is a growing haven for genealogy.

From Bicentennial Plaza, Raleigh's main base, walk one block north to Jones Street, and turn ninety degrees to the right. Continue until you see the **North Carolina Office of Archives and History** [109 East Jones Street; (919) 733-7305; <www.ah.dcr.state.nc.us>]. It's the best place in the Triangle to discover your roots—not stopping here would be downright obtuse. The archives feature a vast collection of state and county holdings, including census records (1790 through 1920, except 1890), court records, land grants, estate records, marriage bonds (1741 to 1868), military records, and tax records. Holdings also include death certificates (1913 to 1929), cemetery records (prior to 1914), passenger lists (mostly since 1820), copies of federal and foreign government materials, maps, sound recordings, and photographs. Before visiting the archives, you can acquire the free brochure *Genealogical Research in the North Carolina State Archives* by writing to the North Carolina State Archives (Public Services Branch, 4614 Mail Service Center, Raleigh, NC 27699).

Independent from the archives but located in the same building, the **State Library of North Carolina** [109 East Jones Street; (919) 733-7222; <statelibrary.dcr.state.nc.us/ncslhome.htm>] includes the Genealogical Services Branch on its west mezzanine floor. There, you can inspect books of family histories; abstracts of federal, county, and state records; indexes of census records; periodicals; and bibliographies of significant North Carolinians. Remember this research tip: The archives have *records*; the state library has *books*. The same building also is home to the **North Carolina Genealogical Society** [Box 22, Greenville, NC 27835; (919) 733-7222; <www.ncgenealogy.org>].

Birth certificates since 1913, death certificates since 1930, marriage records since 1962, and divorce records since 1958 are housed a few blocks west at the **Vital Records Unit of the North Carolina Center for Health Statistics** [Cooper Building, 225 North McDowell Street; (919) 733-3526; <www.schs.state.nc.us/SCHS/certificates>]. Deeds, military discharges, Uniform Commercial Code filings, and pre-1962 marriage records are located at the **Wake County Register of Deeds** [Garland Jones Building, 300 South Salisbury Street; (919) 856-5460; <web.co.wake.nc.us/rdeeds>].

After you examine records here in the Triangle, it will be time for a tangent. You can find one while walking to the state-of-the-art **North Carolina Museum of History** [5 East Edenton Street; (919) 715-0200; <www.ncmuseumofhistory.org>], located between the **State Capitol** [1 East Edenton Street; (919) 733-4994; <www.ah.dcr.state.nc.us/sections/capitol>] and the **State Legislative Building** [16 W. Jones Street; (919) 733-7928; <www.ncga.state.nc.us>]. Take a peek at the capitol's west wing steps: Shortly after the Civil War, they were nicked permanently by unruly (tipsy) legislators who rolled whiskey barrels in and out of the building. North Carolina lost more native sons in the Civil War than any other state in the Confederacy. At the museum, you can see artifacts such as a captured Union flag, the vest of a fallen Confederate major, and an 1856 railroad spike.

To witness impressive Victorian architecture your ancestors may have helped build, take a self-guided walking tour of **Oakwood Historic District**, which encompasses twenty blocks. Maps are available at the **Capital Area Visitor Center** [301 North Blount Street; (919) 733-3456; <www.ah.dcr.state.nc.us/sections/

capitol/vc/vc.htm>]. Adjacent to this historic district is **Oakwood Cemetery** [701 Oakwood Avenue; (919) 832-6077], established in 1869. Also worth seeing is Raleigh's oldest dwelling—built in the 1760s—the **Joel Lane Museum House** [728 West Hargett Street at St. Mary's Street; (919) 833-3431], where costumed guides teach onlookers about Raleigh's growth.

A testament to that growth is the city's slick **Capital Area Transit** public transportation system [(919) 828-7228], which is the most convenient way to get around if you don't have a car. **Triangle Transit Authority** [(919) 549-9999] links Raleigh to the other two points in the Triangle, Durham and Chapel Hill—you should visit both of them.

Durham, twenty-three miles west of Raleigh, is home to Duke University's **Rare Book, Manuscript and Special Collections Library** [103 Perkins Library; (919) 660-5822; <scriptorium. lib.duke.edu>]. Its holdings, which are available for use in the Dalton-Brand Research Room, include nineteenth-century family histories and a variety of materials written by twentieth-century African-American women. While in Durham, stop by the **Hayti Heritage Center** [804 Old Fayetteville Street; (919) 683-1709], which celebrates African-American art and culture, and the **Duke Homestead State Historic Site** [2828 Duke Homestead Road; (919) 477-5498], a national historic landmark that's billed as the "living museum of tobacco history." Whether or not you indulge in what tobacco farmers here dub the "golden weed," you can take your vices to another level a few blocks away at **The Down Under Pub** [802 West Main Street; (919) 682-0039], which sells beer in half-yard-sized glasses. (Go easy, of course; to get the most out of your research in the Triangle, you can't be seeing stars.)

Chapel Hill, twelve miles southwest of Durham, is home to the University of North Carolina's **Louis Round Wilson Library** [South Road; (919) 962-0114; <www.lib.unc.edu>], which boasts the largest collection of state literature in the country. Its North Carolina Collection includes more than 120,000 books and 78,000 pamphlets detailing four centuries of colonial and state life. Of particular interest to genealogists are local histories and *The North Carolina Newspaper Project Union List*, an index to all newspapers ever published in the state (this index is located behind the main desk). The Southern Oral History Program Collection, a compilation of more than two thousand interviews of significant Southerners, is another heritage gem.

When visiting Raleigh, you have plenty of lodging options close to the archives and state library. Three good ones are:
- the **Velvet Cloak Inn** [1505 Hillsborough Street; (919) 828-0333]
- the nine-story **Brownstone Hotel** [1707 Hillsborough Street; (919) 828-0811]
- the quaint **Oakwood Inn** [411 North Bloodworth Street; (919) 832-9712]

Raleigh also has plenty of restaurants, several of which are along the cobblestone streets of City Market, located a few blocks southeast of Bicentennial Plaza. Try the biscuits at **Big Ed's City Market Restaurant** [220 Wolfe Street; (919) 836-9909], whose decor is a blend of farm equipment and political memorabilia. If you like charbroiled steak, try **Angus Barn** [9401 Glenwood Avenue, Highway 70 at Aviation Parkway, (919) 781-2444], an award-winning restaurant housed in a large, nineteenth-century barn. A more inexpensive, locally famous option is **Clyde Cooper's Barbecue** [109 East Davie Street; (919) 832-7614].

RICHMOND
BY JONATHAN ROLLINS

History records that in 1609, Capt. John Smith purchased land from Chief Powhatan and called the settlement "None Such." That settlement eventually evolved into Richmond, but today there still is nonesuch place as this capital of

Virginia and former capital of the Confederacy. Where else can you drive along one of America's most beautiful avenues and gaze up at imposing memorials dedicated to war heroes from the *losing* side? **Monument Avenue** takes its name from the stately statues of Confederate Generals Robert E. Lee, Stonewall Jackson, and J.E.B. Stuart and President Jefferson Davis. African-American tennis champion Arthur Ashe, a Richmond native, also is represented.

The James River, which offers up to Class V rapids, gives Richmond claim to the only urban whitewater run in the United States. The city also has the largest intact Victorian neighborhood (Fan District), the oldest continuously operated farmers market (Seventeenth and Main Streets), and the second-oldest working state capitol in the nation. The capitol's designer, Thomas Jefferson, lends his name to the **National Historic Landmark Jefferson Hotel** [101 West Franklin Street; (804) 788-8000; <www.jefferson-hotel.com>], whose famous "guests" have included alligators that resided in the lobby's reflecting pools until 1948. This grandest of Richmond hotels also features a lavish marble staircase, which many locals proudly claim was the model for the one in *Gone With the Wind*.

There also may be nonesuch place for genealogists, especially those whose roots run deep in the Old South. Begin at the **Library of Virginia** [800 East Broad Street; (804) 692-3500; archives research, (804) 692-3888; <www.lva.lib.va.us/index.htm>], the repository for all the commonwealth's records from the colony's founding to the present day. Among its vast resources are wills, deeds, and marriage bonds; military service, church, land office, tax, and census records; and genealogical notes and charts. Plan ahead by utilizing the library's Web site (which also has many digitized and transcribed documents for remote research) and ordering the free pamphlet *Genealogical Research at the Library of Virginia*.

Despite its modern skyline, Richmond remains rich in history, particularly of the Revolution and Civil War.

At the **Virginia Historical Society** [428 North Boulevard; (804) 358-4901; <www.vahistorical.org>] you can find genealogical notes and charts, family papers, Bible records, county histories, and some census records. Researchers must fill out call slips to request materials. The society's Web site <www.vahistorical.org/research/genealogy.htm> includes a handy comparison of the records kept here to those at the Library of Virginia. When you need a break from research, relive Virginia's rich history by wandering through the museum's extensive galleries.

Civil War enthusiasts have abundant choices in Richmond. Most people visit the **Museum of the Confederacy** [1201 East Clay Street; (804) 649-1861; <www.moc.org>] to view the world's largest collection of artifacts associated with the Confederacy. *The Washington Post* says the neighboring **White House of the Confederacy**, where Jefferson Davis lived during the Civil War, "probably is second only to Mount Vernon among restorations of historic American dwellings." But genealogists also should take advantage of the museum's Eleanor S. Brockenbrough Library (accessible by appointment only) to examine personal papers, government documents, journals, letters, and rare books. If this only whets your appetite for Civil War history, visit the **Chimborazo Visitor Center** [3215 East Broad Street; (804) 226-1981], where a hospital complex built in 1861 treated more than seventy-five thousand soldiers. This also is a great place to grab tour maps of nearby battlefields. Historians estimate that one-fourth of the Civil War's battles and more than half of its casualties took place within a seventy-five-mile radius of Richmond.

Another enticing stop for genealogists and history buffs is the **Valentine Richmond History Center** [1015 East Clay Street; (804) 649-0711; <www.valentinemuseum.com>]. The museum's decorative and fine arts, industrial artifacts, and archaeological finds document Richmond's past. While the majority of the center's holdings are not on display, books, photos, diaries, and letters are available for research by appointment.

In its prime, Richmond's Jackson Ward neighborhood was called the cultural mecca of Southern black society and the Wall Street of black America. Today, it's home to the **Black History Museum and Cultural Center of Virginia** [00 Clay Street; (804) 780-9093; <www.blackhistorymuseum.org>], which collects oral and written records, photographs, and other artifacts commemorating the lives of African Americans.

The **Beth Ahabah Museum and Archives** [1109 West Franklin Street; (804) 353-2668; <www.bethahabah.org/museum/museum.html>] highlights Jewish culture in Richmond since 1789 with congregational documents, genealogies, Civil War correspondence, and immigration photos. Beth Ahabah also operates **Hebrew Cemetery** (Fourth and Hospital Streets), which includes a section that holds Confederate soldiers; it is thought to be the only Jewish military cemetery outside of Israel.

Another notable burial ground is **Hollywood Cemetery** [412 South Cherry Street; (804) 648-8501; <www.hollywoodcemetery.org>]. Movie stars aren't buried here (the cemetery takes its name from surrounding holly trees), but you can see plenty of famous names nonetheless, among them President James Monroe and President John Tyler, Founding Father John Randolph, Jefferson Davis, and J.E.B. Stuart. A ninety-foot granite pyramid completed in 1869 serves as a memorial to the estimated eighteen thousand Confederate soldiers buried nearby. With scores of intriguing memorials sitting on a bluff overlooking the James River and Belle Isle, the cemetery is one of Richmond's most beautiful and serene spots.

St. John's Church [2401 East Broad Street; (804) 649-7938], Richmond's oldest, was the site of Patrick Henry's "Give me liberty or give me death" speech. This most famous of patriotic pep talks is reenacted at 2 P.M. each Sunday, Memorial Day through Labor Day.

Take time to admire the architecture of and stroll through the statue-laden grounds around **Capitol Square** (Ninth and Grace Streets). You can also take a free tour of the **Virginia State Capitol** [(804) 698-1788].

Don't pass up a visit to **Maymont** [2201 Shields Lake Drive; (804) 358-7166; <www.maymont.org>], a one hundred-acre country estate along the James River. Mansion tours are available by reservation, but simply wandering the grounds is one of the truest pleasures in Richmond. Attractions include lovely Italian and Japanese gardens, a petting zoo, and wildlife habitats containing animals native to Virginia.

If you prefer a tamer setting, visit the **Virginia Museum of Fine Arts** [2800 Grove Avenue; (804) 340-1400; <www.vmfa.state.va.us>]. The museum houses one of the largest art collections in the South and features works by Dégas, Monet, and John Singer Sargent, among others. Another prized exhibit is the largest public collection of Fabergé eggs outside of Russia.

Don't miss whatever film is playing at the **Byrd Theatre** [2908 West Cary Street; (804) 353-9911]. Known fondly as Richmond's movie palace (you'll see why when you step inside), this National Historic Landmark opened in 1928. Consider yourself especially fortunate if you're in town on a Saturday night, when the movie is preceded by a song or two performed on the mighty Wurlitzer organ that rises out of the orchestra pit. Splurge and sit in the balcony for an extra dollar ($2.99 total).

Here's a tip to make the sight-seeing a little easier: Purchase a Richmond Pass for $15. Available at city visitors centers and all participating attractions, the pass covers admission for your choice of any five of seventeen museums, historic homes, and gardens.

You're likely to have to do some driving in Richmond, but if you visit on a weekend from June to November, use the **Richmond Cultural Connection** [(804) 783-7450], which shuttles between various attractions, shopping spots, and restaurants. One dollar pays for an entire day of unlimited transfers; Richmond Pass holders ride for free.

As for places to kick off your shoes, the **Commonwealth Park Suites Hotel** [901 Bank Street; (888) 343-7301] across from Capitol Square and the **Richmond Marriott** [500 East Broad Street; (800) 228-0265] both are within three blocks of the Library of Virginia. The **Linden Row Inn** [100 East Franklin Street; (800) 348-7424] offers reasonable rates that include a deluxe continental breakfast, afternoon wine and cheese, downtown transportation, and free use of a YMCA. If you want to live like a Virginia aristocrat, stay at the previously mentioned five-diamond Jefferson Hotel and eat at its renowned restaurant, **Lemaire** [(804) 788-8000].

For very good food at very good prices, head to the Fan District, where top choices include the heaping helpings of baked spaghetti at **Joe's Inn** [205 North Shields Avenue; (804) 355-2282] and the spicy Southern delicacies at **Southern Culture** [2229 West Main Street; (804) 355-6939]. If you're looking for something a little more upscale, head down to the cobblestone streets of Shockoe Slip, where **Sam Miller's** [1210 East Cary Street; (804) 644-5465] specializes in seafood. Another popular option is the **Tobacco**

Company Restaurant [1201 East Cary Street; (804) 782-9555], a converted tobacco warehouse featuring Virginia-inspired specialties and a downstairs club. **Third Street Diner** [218 East Main Street; (804) 788-4750] isn't known for its haute cuisine, but you can get breakfast twenty-four hours a day, and the cast of characters this downtown institution regularly attracts rivals even the most eccentric of family trees.

SAN ANTONIO
BY PATRICIA MCMORROW

Definitely remember the **Alamo** while searching for your ancestors in San Antonio. The "Cradle of Texas Liberty," in the heart of downtown, is a fitting place for genealogists to start researching their Texas roots. After paying respects to Bowie, Crockett, Travis, and all the brave souls who battled Santa Ana's Mexican Army for thirteen days in 1836, visit the **Daughters of the Republic of Texas Library** [300 Alamo Plaza; (210) 225-1071; <drtl.org>]. The library, just south of the Alamo Church, houses some of Texas's earliest records, including original documents relating to the Revolution of 1835. You may be interested in the history of the Daughters of the Republic of Texas, too: As descendants of the courageous Alamo defenders, the daughters have faithfully guarded the heritage of the Revolution since 1891.

Just a quick walk west from the Alamo along the Riverwalk will take you to the **San Antonio Public Library** [600 Soledad; (210) 207-2500; <www.sanantonio.gov/library>]. You can't miss the enchilada-red building "decorated" with boldly colored geometric shapes. Designed by Mexican architect Ricardo Legorreta, the library's postmodern facade garnered national notice upon the opening in 1995.

Once you're inside, head to the Texana Collection on the sixth floor, and delve into the impressive collection of cemetery records, marriage licenses, and county and local histories. The collection has considerable information on

Czech settlers in Texas, too. Library staffers and volunteers are happy to answer questions and point you in the right direction.

To get a full grounding in the ethnic and cultural history of Texas, though, turn to the **Institute of Texan Cultures** [801 South Bowie Street; (210) 458-2300; <www.texancultures. utsa.edu/public >]. A quick bus, streetcar, or taxi ride south from downtown, the institute's library is heaven for genealogists. Oral histories, personal papers, books, and thousands of documents focus on the ethnic heritage and cultural facets of Texas's history. The institute's impressive photo archives include more than 3.5 million images from the city's newspapers and the well-known Zintgraff photographs of San Antonio from the 1930s through 1987. Admission to the library is free, but appointments are encouraged if you plan to seriously dig.

Here are some other important sources for your family research in San Antonio:

• The **Bexar Archives** [Bexar County Courthouse, Main Plaza; (210) 335-2216; <www.co.bexar.tx.us>]. Between 1717 and 1836, the governments of Spain and Mexico documented practically every aspect of life in what is now San Antonio. From the arrival of the Canary Islanders from Spain in 1731 and shipwrecks off the Gulf Coast to the price of livestock on any given day, the massive collection includes more than 250,000 pages of translated manuscripts and four thousand pages of printed materials. There's no charge to study the microfilm records, but it's a good idea to call for an appointment. The holdings of the Bexar Archives are also available on microfilm at the **University of Texas at San Antonio Library** [6900 North Loop 1604 West; (210) 458-4573; <www.lib.utsa.edu>].

• **Catholic Archives at the San Antonio Chancery** [2718 West Woodlawn; (210) 734-2620; <www.archdiosa.org>]. The San Fernando Archive represents the bulk of the chancery's eighteenth- and early-nineteenth-century holdings. These include baptism, marriage, and funeral records and many government documents created between 1731 and 1903.

• **San Antonio Conservation Society Foundation Library** [107 King William Street; (210) 224-6143; <www.saconservation.org>]. Learn about San Antonio's past through its architecture and social customs via the conservation society's library, just south of downtown in the historic King William District.

If your schedule permits a quick field trip, visit the **National Museum of the Pacific War** [340 East Main Street, Fredericksburg; (830) 997-4379; <www.nimitz-museum.org>]. Just seventy miles west of San Antonio in historic Fredericksburg, the museum tells the story of the Pacific Theater battles of World War II. Of particular note here are the **Admiral Nimitz Museum, Japanese Garden of Peace**, and the **Veterans' Walk of Honor**.

To keep yourself in the historic groove, consider staying at the **Menger Hotel** [204 Alamo Plaza; (800) 345-9285or (210) 223-4361; <www.historicmenger.com>]. Built in 1859, the Menger is a stone's throw from the Alamo and features a guest registry with names including Robert E. Lee, Ulysses Grant, Teddy Roosevelt, Dwight Eisenhower, Oscar Wilde, Sara Bernhardt, and Mae West. Be sure to pop into the Roosevelt Bar, where Teddy Roosevelt recruited many of his famous Rough Riders for service in the Spanish-American War.

Since all work and no play is a no-no in San Antonio, make time to stroll the city's Paseo del Rio, a.k.a. **Riverwalk**. This 2.5-mile meander along the cypress-and-palm-shaded San Antonio River is the postcard-picture image of the River City. If you're in the mood for exercise, start power walking at the north end of the Riverwalk, across from the **San Antonio Municipal Auditorium** [100 Auditorium Circle; (210) 207-8511]. If cafés and restaurants are higher on your agenda, entertain your choices ranging from the **Hard Rock Café** [111 West

Crockett Street; (210) 224-7625] to the venerable **Casa Rio** [430 East Commerce Street; (210) 225-6718]. Shopping options are plentiful, too. Wander through the shops of **La Villita** [418 Villita Street; (210) 207-8610], where jewelers, painters, and glassblowers work right on the premises.

Another must-see part of San Antonio, on the near west side of the city, is **El Mercado** [514 West Commerce Street; (210) 207-8600], home to about a hundred small shops and vendors. You can spend hours browsing through handcrafted folk art, clothing, and more. Afterward, enjoy sizzling fajitas—and margaritas!—at **La Margarita** [120 Produce Row; (210) 227-7140] or **Mi Tierra** [218 Produce Row; (210) 225-1262]. Both restaurants—owned by the same family—offer outdoor seating and strolling mariachis.

A less boisterous locale that exposes San Antonio's German roots is the **Guenther House** [205 East Guenther Street; (210) 227-1061] at the edge of the King William District. The 1860 home of Carl Hilmar Guenther, who made his fortune by creating Pioneer Flour Mills, is now a museum, restaurant, and shop featuring Pioneer products.

One warning about family research in San Antonio: You can get so busy with the city's food and fun that you need to muster extra discipline to focus on your genealogy.

ALABAMA

ORGANIZATIONS & ARCHIVES

Alabama Department of Archives and History
624 Washington Ave.
Montgomery, AL 36130
(334) 242-4435
Fax: (334) 240-3433
<www.archives.state.al.us>

Mailing address:
P.O. Box 300100
Montgomery, AL 36130

Alabama Genealogical Society
c/o Samford University Library
P.O. Box 2296
Birmingham, AL 35229

Alabama Historical Commission
468 S. Perry St.
Montgomery, AL 36130
(334) 230-2668
Fax: (334) 240-3477
<www.preserveala.org>

Auburn University
Special Collections Department
Ralph Brown Draughon Library
231 Mell St.
Auburn, AL 36849-5606
(334) 844-1732
Fax: (334) 844-1703
<www.lib.auburn.edu/sca>

Birmingham Public Library
2100 Park Place
Birmingham, AL 35203
(205) 226-3600

Mobile Public Library
Local History Department
701 Government St.
Mobile, AL 36602
(251) 208-7093
Fax: (251) 208-5866
<www.mplonline.org>

Samford University Library
Special Collection Department
800 Lakeshore Dr.
Birmingham, AL 35229
(205) 726-2748
Fax: (205) 726-2642
<library.samford.edu/about/special.html>

William Stanley Hoole Special Collections Library
University of Alabama
500 Hackberry Ln.
Tuscaloosa, AL 35487
(205) 348-0500
Fax: (205) 348-1699
<www.lib.ua.edu/libraries/hoole>
Mailing address:

P.O. Box 870266
Tuscaloosa, AL 35487

RESOURCES

"Research in Alabama and the Old Mississippi Territory"
lecture by Robert Scott Davis Jr.
(Audiotapes.com, $8.50)

Research in Alabama: A Genealogical Guide
by Marilyn Davis Barefield (University of Alabama Press, $19.95)

PERIODICALS

The Alabama Genealogical Register
(1959-1968), Elizabeth W. Thomas, ed., Tuscaloosa, Alabama

Alabama Genealogical Society Magazine
(1967-), Alabama Genealogical Society, c/o Samford University Library, P.O. Box 2296, Birmingham, AL 35229

AlaBenton Genealogical Society Quarterly
(1984-), AlaBenton Genealogical Society, c/o Anniston-Calhoun County Public Library, P.O. Box 308, Anniston, AL 36202

Central Alabama Genealogical Society Quarterly
(1974-), Central Alabama Genealogical Society, P.O. Box 125, Selma, AL 36702

Deep South Genealogical Quarterly
(1963-), Mobile Genealogical Society, P.O. Box 6224, Mobile, AL 36660

MCNAIRY HARDIN WAYNE LAWRENCE GILES MOORE SEQUATCHIE MCMINN

TENNESSEE LINCOLN FRANKLIN HAMILTON BRADLEY POLK

Chattanooga

MARION

ALCORN LAUDERDALE LIMESTONE MADISON JACKSON DADE CATOOSA FANNIN

TISHOMINGO WALKER WHITFIELD

PRENTISS COLBERT Huntsville MURRAY GILMER

MISSISSIPPI CHATTOOGA GORDON PICKENS

FRANKLIN LAWRENCE MORGAN DE KALB

LEE ITAWAMBA MARSHALL FLOYD BARTOW CHEROKEE

MARION WINSTON CULLMAN CHEROKEE GEORGIA

ETOWAH GWINNET

MONROE BLOUNT POLK COBB

PAULDING

LAMAR FAYETTE WALKER ST. CLAIR CALHOUN HARALSON Atlanta DA
KA

CLAY DOUGLAS

LOWNDES CLEBURNE CARROLL FULTON

OKTIBBEHA PICKENS TUSCALOOSA Birmingham TALLADEGA FAYETTE HEI
JEFFERSON COWETA

NOXUBEE Tuscaloosa SHELBY CLAY RANDOLPH HEARD SPALDI

ALABAMA PIKE

TROUP MERIWETHER LAM

KEMPER GREENE BIBB COOSA CHAMBERS UPSC

HALE CHILTON TALLAPOOSA HARRIS TALBOT

PERRY ELMORE LEE MUSCOGEE TAYL

SUMTER AUTAUGA MARION

LAUDERDALE Columbus

DALLAS Montgomery MACON CHATAHOOCHEE SCHLI

MARENGO MONTGOMERY RUSSELL

CLARKE LOWNDES BULLOCK STEWART SUMT

WEBSTER

CHOCTAW WILCOX BARBOUR QUITMAN RANDOLPH TERRELL

WAYNE CLARKE BUTLER CRENSHAW PIKE Alba

MONROE HENRY CLAY CALHOUN DOUGHER

WASHINGTON CONECUH COFFEE DALE EARLY BAKER

GREENE COVINGTON MILLER MITCHI

ESCAMBIA GENEVA HOUSTON

MOBILE SEMINOLE DECATUR GRA

GEORGE ESCAMBIA HOLMES

BALDWIN FLORIDA JACKSON GADSDEN

Mobile SANTA ROSA

JACKSON OKALOOSA WALTON WASHINGTON Tallahassee

Pensacola CALHOUN LEON

BAY LIBERTY WAKULLA

Natchez Trace Traveler
(1981-), Natchez Trace
Genealogical Society, P.O.
Box 420, Florence, AL
35631

Pioneer Trails
(1959-), Birmingham
Genealogical Society, P.O.
Box 2432, Birmingham,
AL 35201

**Settlers of Northeast
Alabama**
(1962-1980), Northeast
Alabama Genealogical
Society, P.O. Box 674,
Gadsden, AL 35902

Tap Roots
(1963-), Genealogical
Society of East Alabama,
P.O. Box 2892, Drawer
1351, Opelika, AL 36830

Valley Leaves
(1966-),Tennessee Valley
Genealogical Society, P.O.
Box 1568, Huntsville, AL
35807

Wiregrass Roots
(1997-), Southeast
Alabama Genealogical
Society, P.O. Box 246,
Dothan, AL 36302

WEB SITES

**The Alabama Civil War
Roots Homepage**
<rootsweb.com/
~alcwroot>: Tips on
locating Civil War
records.

Alabama GenWeb Project
<rootsweb.com/
~algenweb>: Links to
online census transcrip-
tions, county resources.

Alabama Mailing Lists
<rootsweb.com/~jfuller/
gen_mail_states-al.html>:
Subscribe to state or
county mailing lists.

**Alabama Resources at
RootsWeb**
<resources.rootsweb.
com/USA/AL>: Search
engines and links to per-
sonal Web pages contain-
ing Alabama resources.

Historic Alabama Maps
<alabamamaps.ua.edu/
alabama/historical>:
These historical maps
from the University of
Alabama show the evolu-
tion of county lines; the
locations of the iron,
steel, and coal mining
industries; and railroad
growth from 1860 to
1950.

Vital Records Information
<vitalrec.com/al.html>:
Where to obtain copies
of birth and death certificates, marriage licenses,
and divorce decrees.

FAMILY HISTORY
CENTERS

Anniston
1217 Lenlock Ln.
(256) 820-5828

Athens
1716 W. Market St.
(256) 232-1873

Atmore
308 Old Bratt Rd.
(334) 368-5130

Bessemer
831 Briarwood Dr.
(205) 424-0196

Birmingham
2780 Altadena Rd.
(205) 967-7279

Byrd Springs
2110 Byrd Springs Rd. SW
(256) 881-4461

ALABAMA

Statehood: 1819
Statewide Birth and Death Records Begin: 1908
Statewide Marriage Records Begin: 1936
Address for Vital Statistics:
  Center for Health Statistics Record Services
  State Department of Public Health
  P.O. Box 5625
  Montgomery, AL 36103
  (334) 206-5418
  Fax: (334) 262-9563
  <www.alapubhealth.org>

Available Censuses: U.S. federal censuses 1790
through 1840, 1850, 1860, 1870, 1900, 1910,
and 1920. Indexes exist for the 1820, 1830,
1840, 1850, 1860, 1870, 1900, 1910, and 1920
censuses. Colonial census records for 1706,
1721, and 1725 French settlements in or near
Mobile, Alabama. Censuses also exist for 1786,
1787, 1789, and 1805. Territorial censuses exist
from 1795 through 1810. State censuses exist
for 1820, 1850, 1855, and 1866.

**City Directories at the Family History Library
Include:** Birmingham 1902-1935 and 1940;
Huntsville 1850-1859 and 1931; Mobile 1835-
1837; Montgomery 1859-1860, 1878, 1902-
1935, and 1940.

Cullman
910 St. Joseph Dr.
(256) 739-0891

Decatur
2006 Modaus Rd. SW
(256) 350-6586

Demopolis
600 U.S. Highway 80
West
(334) 289-2660

Dothan
3199 Ross Clark Circle NW
(334) 793-7425

Enterprise
310 Shellfield Rd.
(334) 347-3631

Eufaula
Highway 131, Bakerhill
Highway
(334) 687-6146

Florence
1828 Broadway Blvd.
(256) 766-5553

Fort Payne
6611 Banks Dr. NW
(256) 845-0467

Gadsden
2001 Noccalulu Rd.
(256) 546-0746

Grove Hill
Highway 43 South
(334) 275-3009

Guntersville
4961 Spring Creek Dr.
(256) 582-6861

Huntsville
1804 Sparkman Dr.
(256) 721-0905

Indian Springs
2720 Cahaba Valley Rd.
Highway 1
(256) 988-5282

Jasper
1612 Eighteenth Ave.

Madison-Harvest
1297 Slaughter Rd.
(256) 722-9450

Mobile
5520 Zeigler Blvd.
(334) 344-9270

Monroe
430 Goodway Rd.
(334) 862-2937

Montgomery
3460 Carter Hill Rd.
(334) 269-9041

Opelika
510 Groce St.
(334) 745-2140

Ozark
Mixon School Road
(334) 774-9405

Robertsdale
18845 E. Silverhill Ave.
(251) 974-7400

Scottsboro
Bob Jones Road and
Greenwood Drive
(256) 259-1501

Toxey
Highway 17
(205) 673-2626

Tuscaloosa
2015 Third Ave. North
(205) 758-4820

Wetumpka
1405 Chapel Rd.
(334) 567-8339

ARKANSAS

ORGANIZATION & ARCHIVES

Arkansas Genealogical Society
P.O. Box 908
Hot Springs, AR 71902
<www.rootsweb.com/~args>

Arkansas Historical Association
History Department,
University of Arkansas
Old Main 416
Fayetteville, AR 72701
(479) 575-5884
Fax: (479) 575-2775
<www.uark.edu/depts/arkhist/home>

Arkansas History Commission
One Capitol Mall
Little Rock, AR 72201
(501) 682-6900
<www.ark-ives.com>

Little Rock Public Library
100 Rock St.
Little Rock, AR 72201
(501) 918-3000
Fax: (501) 375-7457
<www.cals.lib.ar.us/locations/lr.html>

Southwest Arkansas Regional Archives
Old Washington Historic
State Park
Box 134
Washington, AR 71862
(501) 983-2633

University of Arkansas
Special Collections
Library
Fayetteville, AR 72701
(479) 575-5577
<dante.uark.edu/specialcollections>

RESOURCES

Confederate Arkansas
by Michael B. Dougan
(University of Alabama
Press, $14.95)

"Razorbackers and Rackensachers: A Guide to Genealogical Research in Arkansas"
lecture by Russell Pierce
Baker (Audiotapes.com,
$8.50)

PERIODICALS

The Arkansas Family Historian
(1962-), Arkansas
Genealogical Society, P.O.
Box 908, Hot Springs, AR
71902

Backtracker
(1972-), Northwest
Arkansas Genealogical
Society, P.O. Box 796,
Rogers, AR 72757

Flashback
(1951-), Washington
County Historical Society,
118 E. Dickson,
Fayetteville, AR 72701

The Melting Pot Quarterly
(1978-), The Melting Pot
Genealogical Society, P.O.
Box 936, Hot Springs, AR
71902

WEB SITES

Arkansas Civil War Information
<rootsweb.com/~arcivwar>: Find rosters
and regimental histories
for Arkansas units.

Arkansas GenWeb Project
<rootsweb.com/~argenweb>: Links to
county and state
resources, including a
guide to Arkansas
research.

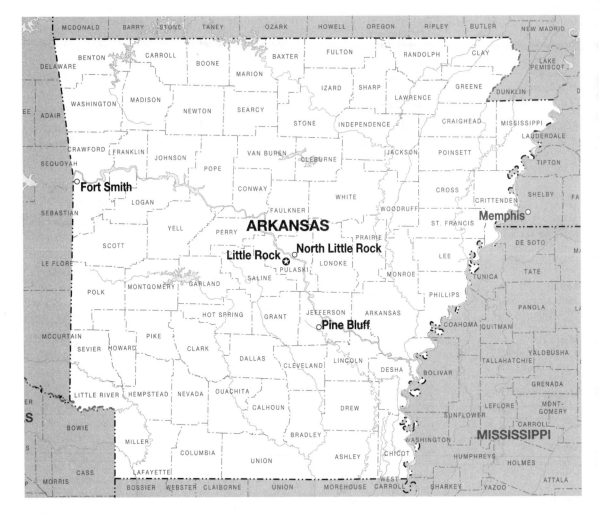

Arkansas Mailing Lists
<rootsweb.com/~jfuller/
gen_mail_states-ar.html>:
Network with other
Arkansas researchers
using state or county
mailing lists.

**Arkansas Resources at
RootsWeb**
<resources.rootsweb.
com/USA/AR>: Personal
Web sites and search
engines.

The Civil War in Arkansas
<civilwarbuff.org>:
Discover where battles
were fought and how

the war affected
Arkansans, and find links
to Civil War history and
records.

Vital Records Information
<vitalrec.com/ar.html>:
Where to obtain copies
of birth and death certificates, marriage licenses,
and divorce decrees.

FAMILY HISTORY CENTERS

Blytheville
1308 Mockingbird Lane
(870) 763-2657

Clarksville
S .5 mile Country Club
Rd.
(479) 705-8111

Conway
2045 Dave Ward Dr.
(501) 327-1200

El Dorado
28 N. Calion Rd.
(870) 863-7463

Fort Smith
8712 Horan Dr.
(479) 484-5373

Harrison
Highway 7 South
(870) 741-3850

Hot Springs
2765 Malvern Rd.
(501) 262-5640

Jacksonville
6110 T.P. White Dr.
(501) 985-2501

Jonesboro
301 E. Highland at 1-B
(870) 935-3400

Little Rock
13901 Quail Run Dr.
(501) 455-4998

Magnolia
2504 Pearce St.
(870) 234-7609

Mena
2590 Highway 88 East
(501) 394-4380

Monticello
519 Glenwood Rd.
(870) 367-5817

Mountain Home
100 Western Hills Dr.
(870) 425-7744

North Little Rock-Mountain View
612 S. Peabody Ave.
(870) 269-4139

Pocahontas
4187 Country Club Rd.
(870) 892-4187

Quitman
6556 Heber Springs Rd.
(501) 589-3628

Rogers
2805 N. Dixieland Rd.
(501) 636-0740

Russellville
200 S. Cumberland
(501) 968-3114

Springdale
922 E. Emma
(501) 756-8090

FLORIDA

ORGANIZATIONS & ARCHIVES

Alma Clyde Field Library of Florida History
435 Brevard Ave.
Cocoa, FL 32922
(321) 690-1971
<www.florida-historical-soc.org>

Florida Department of State
Division of Library & Information Services
Bureau of Archives and Records Management
500 S. Bronough St.

Tallahassee, FL 32399
(850) 245-6700
Fax: (904) 488-4894
<dlis.dos.state.fl.us/barm>

Florida Historical Society
1320 Highland Ave.
Melbourne, FL 32935
(321) 254-9855
<www.florida-historical-soc.org>

Florida State Genealogical Society
P.O. Box 10249
Tallahassee, FL 32302
(813) 872-0280
<www.rootsweb.com/~flsgs>

University of Florida
Department of Special and Area Studies Collections
208 Smathers Library
P.O. Box 117007
Gainesville, FL 32611
(352) 392-9075
Fax: (352) 392-4788
<web.uflib.ufl.edu/spec/general.html>

Orange County Library System
101 E. Central
Orlando, FL 32801
(407) 835-7323
Fax: (407) 648-0523
<www.ocls.lib.fl.us>

University of Miami
1300 Memorial Dr.
Otto G. Richter Library
P.O. Box 248214
Coral Gables, FL 33124
(305) 284-3551
Fax: (305) 284-4027
<www.library.miami.edu>

University of West Florida
John Chandler Pace Library
11000 University Parkway
Pensacola, FL 32514
(850) 474-2492

Fax: (850) 474-3338
<library.uwf.edu>

RESOURCES

"Genealogical Research in Florida"
lecture by Brian E. Michaels
(Audiotapes.com, $8.50)

Searching in Florida: A Reference Guide to Public and Private Records
by Diane C. Robie (lsc, out of print)

PERIODICALS

Ancestry
(1966-), The Palm Beach County Genealogical Society, P.O. Box 1746, West Palm Beach, FL 33402

The Florida Armchair Researcher
(1984-), Armchair Publications, 810 McDonough Rd., Hampton, GA 30228

The Florida Genealogist
(1977-), Florida State Genealogical Society, P.O. Box 10249, Tallahassee, FL 32302

Jacksonville Genealogical Society Quarterly
(1973-), Jacksonville Genealogical Society, P.O. Box 60756, Jacksonville, FL 32236

South Florida Pioneers
(1974-), Richard M. Livingston, P.O. Box 3749, North Fort Myers, FL 33918

WEB SITES

Civil War Military Units in Florida
<psy.fsu.edu/~thompson/cw/units.html>: Browse transcriptions of Civil War rosters.

Florida Genealogy Resources
<thesouthernedge.com/gen/flmisc.htm>: Links to land records and obituaries.

Florida GenWeb Project
<www.rootsweb.com/~flgenweb>: Surname registry, marriage and tombstone transcription databases, links to county resources.

Florida in the Civil War
<dhr.dos.state.fl.us/museum/civwar/>: Online "exhibit" adapted from the Museum of Florida History.

Florida Mailing Lists
<rootsweb.com/~jfuller/gen_mail_states-fl.html>: Free subscriptions to county and state mailing lists.

Florida Resources at RootsWeb
<resources.rootsweb.com/USA/FL/>: Florida Web sites and search engines.

Vital Records Information
<vitalrec.com/fl.html>: Where to obtain copies of birth and death certificates, marriage licenses, and divorce decrees.

WPA Life Histories From Florida
<memory.loc.gov/ammem/wpaintro/flcat.html>: Read first-person accounts of Civil War

memories, slavery, and history.

FAMILY HISTORY CENTERS

Apalachicola
270 Prado St.
(850) 653-8501

Arcadia
1760 N.E. Gibson St.
(863) 993-0996

Belle Glade
601 N.E. Avenue A
(561) 996-6355

Boca Raton
1530 W. Camino Real
(561) 395-6644

Bonifay
North Ride Road South
Highway 79
(850) 547-4557

Bradenton
3400 Cortez Rd.
(941) 755-6909

Brandon
4806 Bell Shoals Rd.

Bristol
Myers Ann Street
(904) 643-5600

Brooksville
21043 Yontz Rd.
(352) 796-7403

Bunnell
402 N. Palmetto St.
(386) 437-7881

Clermont
14600 Greenvalley Blvd.
(352) 242-6363

Cocoa
1803 Fiske Blvd. South
(321) 636-2431

Coral Springs
10148 N.W. Thirty-first St.
(954) 341-1725

Dade City
9016 Fort King Rd.
(813) 788-4826

Daytona Beach
1125 Sixth St.
(386) 257-9223

DeFuniak Springs
550 Lakeview Dr.
(850) 892-3167

Deland
1345 S. Aquarius Ave.
(386) 822-9695

Fort Myers
3105 Broadway
(941) 275-0001

Fort Pierce
2900 Virginia Ave.
(561) 464-0600

Fort Walton Beach
339 Lake Dr.
(850) 244-3338

Gainesville
10600 S.W. Twenty-fourth Ave.
(352) 331-8542

Hialeah Gardens
4300 W. Fourth Ave.
(305) 828-3460

Homestead
29600 SW 167th Ave.
(305) 246-4194

Jacksonville-East
7665 Fort Caroline Rd.
(904) 743-0527

Jacksonville-West
461 Blanding Blvd.
(904) 272-1150

Jupiter
6400 Roebuck Rd.
(561) 626-7989

Key West
3424 Northside Dr.
(305) 294-9400

Lake Butler
State Road 238
(904) 496-2245

Lake City
706 Country Club Rd.
(386) 755-9432

Lake Mary
2255 Lake Emma Rd.
(407) 333-0137

Lakeland
5850 Lakeland Highlands Rd.
(863) 709-0800

Lecanto
3474 W. Southern St.
(352) 746-5943

Leesburg
1875 S. Mount Vernon Rd.
(352) 787-3990

Live Oak
1310 Irvin St.
(904) 362-3573

MacClenny
Highway 228 and South Boulevard
(904) 259-6910

Marathon
6700 Overseas Highway
(305) 743-9016

Marianna
3141 College St.
(850) 482-8159

Mexico Beach
318 Robin Ln.
(850) 648-2049

Miami
9900 W. Flagler St.
(305) 485-8174

Miami Shores
2603 N.E. 163rd St.
(305) 756-5049

Naples
4935 Twenty-third Court SW
(941) 348-2229

Navarre
1751 Sea Lark Lane
(850) 939-3035

Newport Richey
10606 Hilltop Dr.
(727) 868-8225

Ocala
1831 S.E. Eighteenth Ave.
(352) 351-4163

Okeechobee
310 S.W. Sixth St.
(863) 467-2425

Orlando
45 E. Par Ave.
(407) 895-4832

Orlando-South
3001 Apopka-Vineland Rd.
(407) 876-8135

Palatka
1414 Husson Ave.
(386) 329-9317

Palm Beach
1710 Carandis Rd.
(561) 533-8803

Panama City
3140 State Ave.
(850) 785-9290

Pensacola
9490 Fox Run Rd.
(850) 969-1254

Plantation
851 N.W. 112th Ave.
(Hiatus Rd.)
(954) 472-0524

Port Charlotte
1303 Forrest Nelson Blvd.
(941) 627-6446

Sarasota
7001 S. Beneva
(941) 921-5932

Sebring
3235 Grand Prix Blvd.
(863) 382-1822

South Chase
701 Wethervee Rd.

St. Augustine
500 Deltona Blvd.
(904) 797-4515

St. Cloud
2821 Old Canow Creek Rd.

St. Petersburg
9000 106th Ave. N
(727) 399-8018

Starke
1404 Bessent Rd.
(904) 964-8145

Stuart
2401 S.W. Matheson Ave.
(561) 287-0167

Tallahassee
312 Stadium Dr.
(850) 222-8870

Tampa
4106 E. Fletcher Ave.
(813) 971-2869

Vero Beach
3980 Twelfth St.
(561) 569-5122

Wauchula
630 Hanchey Rd.
(941) 773-3532

Winter Haven
1958 Ninth St. SE
(941) 299-1691

GEORGIA

ORGANIZATIONS & ARCHIVES

Georgia Department of Archives and History
330 Capitol Ave. SE
Atlanta, GA 30334
(404) 656-2393
<www.sos.state.ga.us/archives>

Georgia Genealogical Society
P.O. Box 54575
Atlanta, GA 30308
<www.gagensociety.org>

Georgia Historical Society Library
501 Whitaker St.
Savannah, GA 31401
(912) 651-2128
<www.georgiahistory.com>

John E. Ladson Jr. Genealogical Library
119 Church St.
Vidalia, GA 30474
(912) 537-8186
<www.toombs.public.lib.ga.us/ladson.htm>

National Archives and Records Administration-Southeast Region (Atlanta)
1557 St. Joseph Ave.
East Point, GA 30344
(404) 763-7474
Fax: (404) 763-7059
<www.archives.gov/facilities/ga/atlanta.html>

Washington Memorial Library
Middle Georgia Regional Library
1180 Washington Ave.
Macon, GA 31201
(478) 744-0800
Fax: (478)742-3161
<www.co.bibb.ga.us/library>

RESOURCES

Georgia Genealogical Research
by George K. Schweitzer (Genealogical Sources Unlimited, $11.95 from <www.heritagequest.com>)

Georgia Genealogy and Local History: A Bibliography
by James E. Dorsey (out of print)

PERIODICALS

Georgia Genealogical Magazine
(1961-), La Bruce Lucas, 375 W. Broad St., P.O. Box 1267, Greenville, SC 29602

Georgia Genealogical Society Quarterly
(1964-), Georgia Genealogical Society, P.O. Box 54575, Atlanta, GA 30308

Georgia Genealogist
(1969-85), Heritage Papers, Danielsville, Georgia

Georgia Pioneers Genealogical Magazine
(1964-1987), Georgia Pioneers Genealogical Society, P.O. Box 1028, Albany, GA 31702

Huxford Genealogical Society Quarterly
(1974-), Huxford Genealogical Society, P.O. Box 595, Homerville, GA 31634

Northwest Georgia Historical and Genealogical Society Quarterly
(1976-), Northwest Georgia Historical and

GEORGIA

Statehood: 1788
Statewide Birth and Death Records Begin: 1919
Statewide Marriage Records Begin: 1952
Address for Vital Statistics:
Georgia Department of Human Resources
Vital Records Unit
47 Trinity Ave. SW, Room 217-H
Atlanta, GA 30334

Available Censuses: U.S. federal censuses 1820, 1830, 1840, 1850, 1860, 1870, 1880, 1900, 1910, and 1920. Statewide census indexes are available for the 1820, 1830, 1840, 1850, 1860, 1880, 1900, 1910 and 1920 censuses. State censuses conducted in various years from 1786 to 1890 have survived for some Georgia counties.

City Directories at the Family History Library Include: Atlanta 1859-1860, 1867-1935; Columbus 1859-1960, 1906-1934; Savannah 1848-1860, 1866-1934.

Genealogical Society Quarterly, P.O. Box 5063, Rome, GA 30162

WEB SITES

The Civil War in Georgia <www.cviog.uga.edu/Projects/gainfo/civilwar.htm>: Online books, diaries, and photographs, along with histories and rosters of Georgia military units.

Documenting Family History in Georgia: How to Begin <www.sos.state.ga.us/archives/rs/dfhg.htm>: Tips from the Georgia secretary of state detailing the scope and locations of Georgia records.

Georgia Genealogy Books <gagenbooks.com>: Browse a wide selection of books and CD-ROMs by county or author.

Georgia Genealogy Links <www.grapevine.net/~dthomas2/galinks.htm>: No-frills list of links to library, government, and organization Web sites.

Georgia GenWeb Project <www.rootsweb.com/~gagenweb>: Queries, records, county resources.

Georgia History <www.cviog.uga.edu/Projects/gainfo/gahist.htm>: Follow Georgia history from early Indian tribes through colonization and the Revolutionary War to Reconstruction and the twentieth century.

Georgia Mailing Lists <www.rootsweb.com/~jfuller/gen_mail_states-ga.html>: Network with other Georgia researchers using state or county mailing lists.

Georgia Resources at RootsWeb <resources.rootsweb.com/USA/GA>: Georgia-related personal Web sites and online documents.

Georgia Roots Gateway <geocities.com/Heartland/Plains/3956>: Links to genealogy in the Piedmont region and southern Georgia.

Vital Records Information <vitalrec.com/ga.html>: Where to obtain copies of birth and death certificates, marriage licenses, and divorce decrees.

FAMILY HISTORY CENTERS

Albany
2700 Westgate Blvd.
(229) 888-7588

Athens
706 Whitehead Rd.
(706) 543-3052

Atlanta
1463 Lee St. SW
(404) 755-7624

Augusta
835 N. Belair Rd.
(706) 860-1024

Cochran
502 Ann St.
(478) 934-7212

Columbus
4400 Reese Rd.
(706) 563-7216

Conyers
1275 Flat Shoals Rd.
(770) 760-7941

Dahlonega
Highway 9 South
(706) 265-2314

Douglas
200 N. Chester Ave.
(912) 384-0607

Douglasville
3027 Chapel Hill Rd.
(770) 949-5168

Hinesville
220 Sandy Run Dr.
(912) 368-2519

Jesup
510 Sunset Blvd.
(912) 427-4469

Jonesboro
2100 Lake Jodeco Rd.
(770) 477-5985

Kingsland
2911 Community Rd.
(912) 265-4363

Kingsland-Ward
1711 Laurel Island Parkway
(912) 673-0571

La Grange
115 Clark St.
(706) 882-2201

Lawrenceville
3355 Sugarloaf Pkwy.
(770) 962-5650

Lilburn
1150 Cole Rd.
(770) 931-3370

Macon
1624 Williamson Rd.
(478) 788-5885

Marietta-East
3195 Trickum Rd.
(770) 973-4510

Milledgeville
1700 N. Jefferson
(478) 454-4090

Moultrie
100 West
Blvd./Seventeenth Ave.
SW
(229) 985-5671

Newnan
821 Old Atlanta Highway
(770) 254-9857

Perry
1799 Houston Lake Rd.
(478) 987-0030

Powder Springs
2595 New Macland Rd.
(770) 943-9393

Rome
3300 Garden Lakes Pkwy.
(706) 235-2281

Roswell
500 Norcross St.
(770) 594-1706

Savannah
1200 King George Blvd.
(912) 927-6543

Statesboro
Highway 67

Sugar Hill
1234 Riverside Dr.
(770) 536-4391

Sugar Hill-Ward
4833 Suwanee Dam Rd.
(770) 271-3450

Swainsboro
463 W. Meadowlake
Pkwy.
(912) 237-2645

Thomaston
201 W. Church St.
(706) 647-2420

Tifton
402 W. Twenty-fourth St.
(229) 382-4202

Tucker
1947 Brockett Rd.
(770) 723-9941

Valdosta
2500 Jerry Jones Dr.
(229) 242-3264

Waycross
2095 Central Ave.
(912) 283-2661

Waynesboro
192 Timberwood Dr.
(706) 554-6570

KENTUCKY

ORGANIZATIONS & ARCHIVES

Department for Libraries and Archives
Public Records Division
300 Coffee Tree Rd.
Frankfort, KY 40602
(502) 564-8300
Fax: (502) 564-5773
<www.kdla.net>
Mailing address:
P.O. Box 537
Frankfort, KY 40602

Eastern Kentucky Library
Crabbe Library
Special Collections and
Archives
Libraries Complex,
Room 126
521 Lancaster Ave.
Richmond, KY 40475
(859) 622-1792
Fax: (859) 622-1174
<www.library.eku.edu/
SCA>

Forrest C. Pogue Special Collections Library
Murray State University
Murray, KY 42071
(270) 762-6152
<www.mursuky.edu/
msml/Pogue.html>

Kenton County Public Library
502 Scott Blvd.
Covington, KY 41011
(859) 491-7610
<www.kenton.lib.ky.us/
genealogy.html>

Kentucky Genealogical Society
P.O. Box 153
Frankfort, KY 40602
<kygs.org>

Kentucky Historical Society
100 W. Broadway
Frankfort, KY 40601
(502) 564-1792
<www.kyhistory.org>

Kentucky Libraries
1 Big Red Way
Western Kentucky University
Bowling Green, KY 42101
(270) 745-2905
Fax: (270) 745-6422
<www.wku.edu/Library>

Kentucky Room
Lexington Public Library
140 E. Main St.
Lexington, KY 40507
(859) 231-5520
<www.lexpublib.org/
reference/kyroom.html>

Margaret I. King Library-North
Department of Special Collections and Archives
University of Kentucky
Lexington, KY 40506
(859) 257-8611
Fax: (606) 257-6311
<www.uky.edu/libraries/
special>

RESOURCES

Cumulative Index to Bluegrass Roots, 1973-1984
by Brian D. Harney (Kentucky Genealogical Society)

Kentucky Ancestry: A Guide to Genealogical and Historical Research
by Roseann Reinemuth Hogan (Ancestry, $24.95)

Kentucky Marriage Records From the Register of the Kentucky Historical Society
(Genealogical Publishing Co., $55)

PERIODICALS

Bluegrass Roots
(1973-), Kentucky Genealogical Society, P.O. Box 153, Frankfort, KY 40602

The Bulletin
(1968-), West-Central Kentucky Family Research Association, P.O. Box 1932, Owensboro, KY 42302

The East Kentuckian: A Journal of History and Genealogy
(1965-), Hall Printing, P.O. Box 24202, Lexington, KY 20524

Martin, Morgan, and Pike counties.

Kentucky Genealogy Queries
<members.aol.com/kygenweb/kyquer.htm>: Post and read queries indexed by county.

Kentucky GenWeb Project
<www.rootsweb.com/~kygenweb>: Kentucky research sources and county links.

Kentucky History
<louisville.edu/library/ekstrom/govpubs/states/kentucky/kyhistory/kyhistory.html>: Kentucky history from the University of Louisville.

Kentucky History and Genealogy Information
<louisville.edu/~easchn01/kentucky/1hist.html>: Historical maps, biographies, census books.

Kentucky Mailing Lists
<www.rootsweb.com/~jfuller/gen_mail_states-ky.html>: State and county mailing lists.

Kentucky Resources at RootsWeb
<resources.rootsweb.com/USA/KY>: Online documents, Kentucky personal Web pages, search engines.

Kentucky Vital Records Index
<ukcc.uky.edu/~vitalrec>: Searchable Kentucky death index covering 1911 to 1992, and divorce and marriage indexes for 1973 to 1993.

The Filson Club History Quarterly
(1927-), Filson Club Historical Society, 1310 S. Third St., Louisville, KY 40208

Kentucky Ancestors
(1965-), Kentucky Historical Society, 100 W. Broadway, Frankfort, KY 40601

The Kentucky Genealogist
(1959-1986), Martha Porter Miller, Washington, D.C.

Kentucky Pioneer Genealogy and Records: A Genealogical Journal

Devoted to Kentucky
(1979-), Society of Kentucky Pioneers, 11129 Pleasantville Rd., Utica, KY 42376

The Register of the Kentucky State Historical Society
(1902-), Kentucky Historical Society, 100 W. Broadway, Frankfort, KY 40601

Traces of South Central Kentucky
(1982-), formerly *South Central Kentucky Historical and Genealogical Society Quarterly* (1974-1981) South Central

Genealogical and Historical Society, P.O. Box 80, Glasgow, KY 12141

Western Kentucky Journal
(1994-), B.J. Jerome, P.O. Box 325, Newburgh, IN 47629

WEB SITES

Eastern Kentucky Genealogy and History Connections
<bright.net/~kat>: Resources for genealogy in Boyd, Carter, Elliott, Floyd, Greenup, Johnson, Lawrence, Magoffin,

KENTUCKY

STATE STATS

Statehood: 1792
Statewide Birth and Death Records Begin: 1911
Statewide Marriage Records Begin: 1958
Address for Vital Statistics:
Cabinet for Health Services
Office of Vital Statistics
Department for Health Services
275 E.Main St.
Frankfort, KY 40621-0001
(502) 564-4212
Fax: (502) 227-0032
<publichealth.state.ky.us/vital.htm>

Available Censuses: U.S. federal censuses 1790, 1800, 1810, 1820, 1830, 1840, 1850, 1860, 1870, 1880, 1890, 1900, 1910, and 1920. Surname indexes exist for 1810, 1820, 1830, 1840, 1850, 1860, 1870, 1880, 1900, 1910, and 1920.

City Directories at the Family History Library Include: 1861, 1864-1935, and 1980-1984; Lexington 1806-1935 and 1980-1984; Covington and Newport from the mid-1800s to the 1930s.

Vital Records Information
<vitalrec.com/ky.html>:
Where to obtain copies of birth and death certificates, marriage licenses, and divorce decrees.

FAMILY HISTORY CENTERS

Ashland
1001 Kenwood Dr.
(606) 836-1272

Beattyville
Grand Avenue &
Highway 11
(606) 464-3378

Bowling Green
2938 Smallhouse Rd.
(502) 842-7148

Brandenburg
1412 Old Ekron Rd.
(270) 422-3656

Corbin
Browning Acres
Subdivision
(606) 528-2898

Elizabethtown
2950 Shepherdsville Rd.
(270) 737-5037

Fulton
501 Wells Ave.
(270) 472-3634

Glasgow
748 W. Cherry St.
(270) 651-5858

Hopkinsville
1118 Pin Oak Dr.
(270) 886-1616

Lebanon
Springfield Road
Highway 55
(270) 692-9878

Lexington
1789 Tates Creek Pk.
(859) 269-2722

Louisville
1000 Hurstbourne Ln.
(502) 426-8174

Madisonville
N. Main Street
(270) 825-1070

Martin
Highway 80
(606) 285-3133

Morgantown
108 Meadowlark Dr.
(270) 728-3491

Northern Kentucky Wards
144 Buttermilk Pk.
(859) 341-3866

Owensboro
3337 U.S. 60
(502) 685-3396

Owingsville
1954 E. Highway 36
(606) 674-6626

Paducah
320 Birch St.
(270) 443-8947

Tompkinsville
3000 Radio Station Rd.
(270) 487-6977

LOUISIANA

ORGANIZATIONS & ARCHIVES

Hill Memorial Library
Louisiana State University
Libraries
Baton Rouge, LA 70803
(225) 578-6568
Fax: (225) 578-9425
<www.lib.lsu.edu/
special>

Howard Tilton Memorial Library
Manuscripts & Rare
Books Department
Tulane University
7001 Freret St.
New Orleans, LA 70118
(504) 865-5685
Fax: (504) 865-5761
<www.tulane.edu/
~lmiller/Manuscripts
Home.html>

Louisiana Genealogical and Historical Society
P.O. Box 82060
Baton Rouge, LA 70884
(504) 766-3018
<www.rootsweb.com/
~la-lghs>

Louisiana Historical Association
University of
Southwestern Louisiana
929 Camp St.
New Orleans, LA 70130
(318) 482-6871
Fax: (318) 482-6028
<www.louisiana.edu/
Academic/LiberalArts/CLS/
lahist.html>
Mailing address:
P.O. Box 42808
Lafayette, LA 70504

Louisiana State Archives
3851 Essen Ln.
Baton Rouge, LA 70884
(225) 922-1000
<www.sec.state.la.us/
archives/archives/
archives-index.htm>

State Library of Louisiana
701 N. Fourth St.
Baton Rouge, LA 70802
(225) 342-4923
Fax: (225) 219-4804
<www.state.lib.la.us>
Mailing address:
P.O. Box 131
Baton Rouge, LA 70821

Louisiana State Museum/Louisiana Historical Center Library
400 Esplanade Ave.
New Orleans, LA 70176
(504) 568-8214
Fax: (504) 568-4995
<lsm.crt.state.la.us>
Mailing address:
P.O. Box 2448
New Orleans, LA 70176

New Orleans Public Library
219 Loyola Ave.
New Orleans, LA 70112
(504) 529-READ
<nutrias.org>

Orleans Parish Notarial Archives
Civil Courts Building
421 Loyola Ave.,
Room B-4
New Orleans, LA 70112

(504) 568-8577
Fax: (504) 568-8599
<www.orleanscdc.gov>

The Williams Research Center of the Historic New Orleans Collection
410 Chartres St.
New Orleans, LA 70130
(504) 598-7171
Fax: (504) 598-7168
<www.hnoc.org>

RESOURCES

"Way Down Yonder: Research on the Gulf Coast of Louisiana, Mississippi, and Alabama"
lecture by Emory C. Webre (Audiotapes.com, $8.50)

LOUISIANA

STATE STATS

Statehood: 1812
Statewide Birth and Death Records Begin: 1914
No statewide marriage registration: parish only
Address for Vital Statistics:
Vital Records Registry
Office of Public Health
P.O. Box 60630
New Orleans, LA 70160
(504) 568-5152
<oph.dhh.state.la.us/recordsstatistics/vitalrecords>

Available Censuses: U.S. federal censuses 1810, 1820, 1830, 1840, 1850, 1860, 1870, 1880, 1900, 1910, and 1920. Statewide indexes are available for the 1810, 1820, 1830, 1840, 1850, 1860, 1870, 1880, 1900, 1910, and 1920 censuses. Various military and local censuses, 1699 and 1805. New Orleans: Special census 1805.

City Directories at the Family History Library Include: New Orleans: 1805-1811, 1822-1824, 1832-1861, 1861-1935, 1874-1900, 1917, 1945, and 1965.

PERIODICALS

L'Heritage
(1978-), St. Bernard Genealogical Society, P.O. Box 271, Chalmette, LA 70044

The Louisiana Genealogical Register
(1954-), Louisiana Genealogical and Historical Society, P.O. Box 82060, Baton Rouge, LA 70884

The New Orleans Genesis
(1962-), Genealogical Research Society of New Orleans, P.O. Box 51791, New Orleans, LA 70151

Terrebonne Life Lines
(1982-), Terrebonne Genealogical Society, P.O. Box 295, Station 2, Houma, LA 70360

WEB SITES

Acadian-Cajun Genealogy and History
<www.acadian-cajun.com>: Maps, a timeline, data from Acadian censuses from 1671 to 1752, passenger lists for ships that brought the Acadians to Louisiana, and detailed descriptions of every kind of record available for Acadian and Cajun research.

Confederate Pension Applications Index Database
<sec.state.la.us/archives/gen/cpa-alpha.htm>: The Louisiana State Archives's searchable index contains more than forty-nine thousand names from eighteen thousand applications.

Digging Up Roots in the Mud Files
<nutrias.org/~nopl/inv/cdcdemo/text2.htm>: The online version of this 1998 seminar outlines sources for research in Orleans parish civil court records.

Genealogy Links
<nutrias.org/~nopl/links/genlinks/genlinks.htm>: Excellent compilation of Louisiana records.

A Guide to African-American Genealogical Research in New Orleans and Louisiana
<nutrias.org/~nopl/info/aarcinfo/guide.htm>: This page's excellent research tips cover records specific to African-American research, such as emancipation, slave, and Freedman's Bureau records.

Index to New Orleans Indentures, 1809-1843
<nutrias.org/~nopl/inv/indentures/ind-intr.htm>: Alphabetical list of names from five indenture books kept by the New Orleans mayor. Each entry tells the volume and number of the original record, which the city library has on microfilm.

Index to New Orleans Marriages in the *Daily Picayune*, 1837-1857
<nutrias.org/~nopl/info/louinfo/newsmarr/newsmarr.htm>: Look through marriages listed alphabetically; the New Orleans Public Library will photocopy the newspaper article for $2.

Louisiana GenWeb Project
<www.rootsweb.com/~lagenweb>: Archives project, lookups and links to county resources.

Louisiana Mailing Lists
<rootsweb.com/~jfuller/gen_mail_states-la.html>: Network with other Louisiana researchers with state or county mailing lists.

Louisiana Resources at RootsWeb
<resources.rootsweb.com/USA/LA>: Online documents, Louisiana personal Web pages, search engines.

Vital Records Information
<vitalrec.com/la.html>: Where to obtain copies of birth and death certificates, marriage licenses, and divorce decrees.

FAMILY HISTORY CENTERS

Alexandria
611 Versailles St.
(318) 448-1842

Baker
4901 Harding St.
(225) 775-0383

Baton Rouge
10335 Highland Rd.
(225) 769-8913

Denham Springs
25367 Riverton Ave.
(225) 664-8979

Gonzales
520 Highway 30
(225) 644-0581

Lafayette
116 E. Bluebird Dr.
(318) 984-7182

Monroe
Thirty-third and
Evangeline
(318) 322-7009

New Orleans
5025 Cleveland Pl.
(504) 885-3936

Opelousas
430 Plantation Rd.
(318) 942-8081

Ruston
205 W. Woodhaven Rd.
(318) 255-8379

Shreveport
200 Carroll St.
(318) 868-5169

Slidell
112 Rue Esplanade
(504) 641-3982

Thibodaux
3415 Little Bayou Black
Dr.
(985) 876-0221

Winnfield
8991 Highway 501
(318) 628-6945

MISSISSIPPI

ORGANIZATIONS & ARCHIVES

Mississippi Department of Archives and History
100 S. State St.
P.O. Box 571
Jackson, MS 39205
(601) 359-6850 or (601) 359-6975
<www.mdah.state.ms.us>

Mississippi Genealogical Society
P.O. Box 5301
Jackson, MS 39216

Mississippi Historical Society
P.O. Box 571
Jackson, MS 39205
<www.mdah.state.ms.us/admin/mhistsoc.html>

Mississippi State University
Mitchel Memorial Special Collections Genealogical Library
P.O. Box 5408
Mississippi State, MS 39762
(601) 325-7679
Fax: (601) 325-3560
<library.msstate.edu/sc>

University of Southern Mississippi
McCain Library and Archives
P.O. Box 5148
Hattiesburg, MS 39406
(601) 266-4345
Fax: (601) 266-6269
<www.lib.usm.edu/mccain.html>

MISSISSIPPI

Statehood: 1817
Statewide Birth and Death Records Begin: 1912
Statewide Marriage Records Begin: 1926
Address for Vital Statistics:
   Vital Records
   State Department of Health
   2423 N. State St.
   Jackson, MS 39216
   (601) 960-7981

Available Censuses: U.S. federal censuses 1820, 1830, 1840, 1850, 1860, 1870, 1880, 1900, 1910, and 1920. Statewide indexes are available for the 1820, 1830, 1840, 1850, 1860, 1870, 1880, 1900, 1910, and 1920 censuses. Territorial and state censuses were taken often between 1792 and 1866.

City Directories at the Family History Library Include: Vicksburg 1860.

RESOURCES

Tracing Your Mississippi Ancestors
by Anne S. Lipscomb
(University Press of Mississippi, $14.95)

PERIODICALS

Itawamba Settlers
(1981-), Itawamba Historic Society, P.O. Box 7, Mantachie, MS 38855

Mississippi Coast Historical and Genealogical Society Quarterly
(1981-), Mississippi Coast Historical and Genealogical Society Quarterly, P.O. Box 513, Biloxi, MS 39533

Mississippi Genealogical Exchange
(1955-), Mississippi Genealogical Exchange,
P.O. Box 16609, Jackson, MS 39236

Mississippi Genealogy and Local History
(1969-1979), Irene S. Gillis, P.O. Box 9114, Shreveport, LA 71109

Mississippi State Courier
(1984-1985), Courier Productions, P.O. Box 1320, Winnfield, LA 71483

The Northeast Mississippi Historical and Genealogical Society Quarterly
(1980-), Northeast Mississippi Historical and Genealogical Society, P.O. Box 434, Tupelo, MS 38802

WEB SITES

Mississippi Civil War Information
<misscivilwar.org>: Links to units, personal accounts, and battles—including maps—fought in Mississippi.

Mississippi GenWeb Project
<www.rootsweb.com/~msgenweb>: County maps, archived data, and queries.

Mississippi Mailing Lists
<www.rootsweb.com/~jfuller/gen_mail_states-ms.html>: Subscribe to free mailing lists for Mississippi state and county research.

Mississippi Resources at RootsWeb
<resources.rootsweb.com/USA/MS>: Mississippi personal Web pages, online transcriptions, and search engines.

Vital Records Information
<vitalrec.com/ms.html>:
Where to obtain copies
of birth and death certificates, marriage licenses,
and divorce decrees.

FAMILY HISTORY CENTERS

Booneville
204 George E. Allen Dr.
(662) 728-9011

Columbia
805 W. Lakeview Dr.
(601) 736-5846

Columbus
2808 Ridge Rd.
(601) 328-2788

Greenville
Wilcox at Highway 1
South
(601) 332-8176

Gulfport
11148 Klein Rd.
(228) 832-0195

Hattiesburg
2215 Broadway Dr.
(601) 268-1250

Jackson
1301 Pinehaven Rd.
(601) 924-2628

Liberty
213 W. Blalock Circle
(601) 657-8903

Meridian
Bounds Road Ext
(601) 483-7426

Natchez
Lower Woodville Road
Natchez, Adams County,
Mississippi
(601) 442-1893

Oxford
3501 S. Lamar
(662) 234-7586

Philadelphia
1033 Bounds Ave.
(601) 677-2131

Raytown
703 Highway 17
(601) 859-3591

Red Star
2174 Mormon Trail NW
(601) 833-6693

Senatobia
943 W. Tate St.
(662) 562-7161

Tupelo
1085 S. Thomas St.
(662) 844-2056

NORTH CAROLINA

ORGANIZATIONS & ARCHIVES

Duke University
William R. Perkins Library
217 Perkins Library
Durham, NC 27708
(919) 660-5880
Fax: (919) 684-2855
<www.lib.duke.edu>

**North Carolina Office of
Archives and History**
109 E. Jones St.
Raleigh, NC 27601
(919) 733-7305
Fax: (919) 733-8807
<www.ah.dcr.state.nc.us>
Mailing address:
4610 Mail Service Center
Raleigh, NC 27699

**North Carolina
Genealogical Society**
P.O. Box 22
Greenville, NC 27835
<www.rootsweb.com/
~ncgs>

**North Carolina State
Archives**
109 E. Jones St.
Raleigh, NC 27601
(919) 733-3952
Fax: (919) 733-1354

NORTH CAROLINA

Statehood: 1789
Statewide Birth and Death Records Begin: 1913
Statewide Marriage Records Begin: 1962
Address for Vital Statistics:
    Department of Environment, Health,
    and Natural Resources
    Vital Records Section
    225 N. McDowell St.
    P. O. Box 29537
    Raleigh, NC 27626-0537
    (919) 733-3526
    <www.schs.state.nc.us/SCHS/certificates>

Available Censuses: U.S. federal censuses 1790,
1800, 1810, 1820, 1830, 1840, 1850, 1860, 1870,
1880, 1900, 1910, and 1920. Caswell, Granville,
and Orange: 1790 missing (reconstructed from
tax lists: Caswell 1780, 1784; Granville, 1786-
1791; Orange, 1784-1793). Craven, Greene,
New Hanover, and Wake: 1810 missing.
Currituck, Franklin, Martin, Montgomery,
Randolph, and Wake: 1820 missing. Statewide
indexes are available for 1790, 1800, 1810,
1820, 1830, 1840, 1850, 1860, 1870, 1880, 1900,
1910, and 1920 censuses. 1784-1787 count for
the U.S. Continental Congress available for
twenty-four of the fifty counties then existing.

**City Directories at the Family History Library
Include:** Charlotte 1876, 1879-1880, 1893-1894,
1896-1900, 1902-1910; Greensboro 1903-1910,
1912-1931, 1933-1935; Raleigh 1903, 1905-
1906, 1909-1924, 1926, and 1928-1935.

<www.ah.dcr.state.nc.us/
sections/archives>
Mailing address:
North Carolina State
Archives
4614 Mail Service Center
Raleigh, NC 27699

**North Carolina State
Library**
109 E. Jones St.
Raleigh, NC 27601
(919) 733-7222
<statelibrary.dcr.state.nc.
us/iss/gr/genealog.htm>
Mailing address:
Genealogical Services

State Library of North
Carolina
4647 Mail Service Center
Raleigh, NC 27699

**University of North
Carolina at Chapel Hill**
Wilson Library
CB 3930
Chapel Hill, NC 27514
(919) 962-1172
Fax: (919) 962-4452
<www.lib.unc.edu/
wilson>

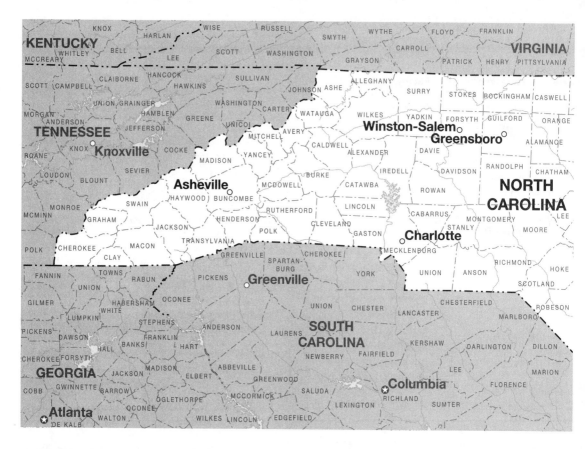

RESOURCES

Carolina Scots: An Historical and Genealogical Study of Over 100 Years of Emigration by Douglas F. Kelly (1739 Publications, $29.95)

"Genealogical Research in North Carolina's Military Bounty Land Records" lecture by Albert Bruce Pruitt (Audiotapes.com, $8.50)

North Carolina Genealogical Research by George K. Schweitzer (Genealogical Sources Unlimited, $11.95)

PERIODICALS

Bulletin of the Genealogical Society of Old Tryon County (1973-), Genealogical Society of Old Tryon County, P.O. Box 938, Forest City, NC 28043

Bulletin of the Wilkes Genealogical Society (1972-), Wilkes Genealogical Society, P.O. Box 1629, North Wilkesboro, NC 28659

The Carolina Genealogist (1969-), Heritage Papers, Danielsville, GA 30633

Journal of North Carolina Genealogy, formerly *The North*

Carolinian (1955-1972), W.P. Johnson, Raleigh, NC

North Carolina Genealogical Society Journal (1975-), North Carolina Genealogical Society, P.O. Box 1492, Raleigh, NC 27511

The North Carolina Historical Review (1924-), North Carolina Historical Commission, 109 E. Jones St., Raleigh, NC 17611

The North Carolina Historical Review: Fifty-Year Index (1924-1973), North Carolina Division of Archives and History,

Department of Cultural Resources

The Quarterly Review (1974-), Eastern North Carolina Genealogical Society, P.O. Box 395, New Bern, NC 28560

WEB SITES

Genealogical Research in North Carolina <statelibrary.dcr.state.nc. us/iss/gr/genealog.htm>: Tips on getting started, a table tracing county development, and a list of reference books from the state library.

North Carolina GenWeb Project <www.rootsweb.com/

~ncgenweb>: Links to North Carolina military project, map illustrating county formation, North Carolina questions and answers, and county and state resources.

North Carolina Mailing Lists
<www.rootsweb.com/~jfuller/gen_mail_states-nc.html>: County and state mailing lists.

North Carolina Resources at RootsWeb
<resources.rootsweb.com/USA/NC>: Personal Web sites and search engines.

North Carolina Vital Records Information
<vitalrec.com/nc.html>

Western North Carolina Genealogy Resource Center
<www.goldenbranches.com/nc-state>: Excellent source of western North Carolina county information.

FAMILY HISTORY CENTERS

Albemarle
1718 Ridge St.
(704) 982-2018

Albemarle, Va.
Corner of N.C. 32 and N.C. 37
(252) 482-8688

Asheville
3401 Sweeten Creek Rd.
(828) 684-6646

Boone
604 Poplar Grove Rd.
(704) 262-1376

Caswell
1401 Rascoe Dameron Rd.
(336) 421-0394

Charlotte-Central
2500 Rocky River Rd.
(704) 509-6407

Charlotte-South
5815 Carmel Rd.
(704) 541-1451

Cherokee
Highway 441 South
(828) 497-7651

Durham
1050 Airport Rd.
(919) 967-0988

Eden
4751 State Highway 14
(336) 623-1797

Elizabeth City
602 W. Ehringhaus St.
(252) 335-7892

Fayetteville
6420 Morganton Rd.
(910) 860-1350

Forest City
250 Mt. Pleasant Church Rd.
(828) 245-8561

Franklin
Bryson City Road
(828) 369-8329

Gastonia
2710 Redbud Dr.
(704) 865-6704

Goldsboro
1000 Eleventh St.
(919) 731-2130

Greensboro
3719 Pinetop Rd.
(336) 288-0321

Greenville
307 Martinsborough Rd.
(252) 756-3370

Harkers Island
1007 Island Rd.
(252) 728-2260

Hickory
Highway 127 North
(828) 324-2823

Kannapolis
1601 Cooper St.
(704) 932-4436

Kinston
3006 Carey Rd.
(252) 522-2116

Lake Norman
148 Lazy Ln.
(704) 664-7127

Lincolnton
105 Old Tram Rd.
(704) 748-6939

Lumberton
450 Liberty Hill Rd.
(910) 738-3461

Marion
4103 U.S. 70 West
(828) 652-2820

Morehead City
3606 Country Club Rd.
(252) 726-7812

Morganton
901 Bethal Rd.
(828) 433-5734

Murphy
Highway 141
(828) 837-8509

Nags Head
Windjammer Drive
(252) 441-5925

New Bern
1207 Forest Dr.
(252) 638-5341

North Wilkesboro
3314 N.C. Highway 115
South
(336) 667-2832

Pinehurst
Highway 15-501
(910) 692-2879

Raleigh
5060 Six Forks Rd.
(919) 783-7752

Roanoke Rapids
901 Park Ave.
(252) 535-2989

Rocky Mount
3224 Woodlawn Ave.
(252) 937-4086

Sparta
151 S. Main St.
(336) 372-7308

Statesville
Jane Sowers Road
(704) 872-9056

Wilmington
514 S. College Rd.
(910) 395-4456

Winston-Salem
4780 Westchester Dr.
(336) 768-8878

SOUTH CAROLINA

ORGANIZATIONS & ARCHIVES

Charleston Library Society
164 King St.
Charleston, SC 29401
(843) 723-9912
<www.sciway.net/lib/cls_home.html>

South Carolina Department of Archives and History
8301 Parklane Rd.
P.O. Box 11669
Capitol Station
Columbia, SC 29223
(803) 896-6100
Fax: (803) 896-6198
<www.state.sc.us/scdah/homepage.htm>

South Carolina Genealogical Society
P.O. Box 492
Colombia, SC 29202
<www.scgen.org>

South Carolina Historical Society
100 Meeting St.
Charleston, SC 29401
(803) 723-3225
Fax: (803) 723-8584
<www.schistory.org>

Thomas Cooper Library
University of South Carolina
1322 Greene St.
Columbia, SC 29208-0103
(803) 777-3142

Fax: (803) 777-4661
<www.sc.edu/library/tcl.html>

RESOURCES

A Guide to South Carolina Genealogical Research and Records
by Brent H. Holcomb
(Brent H. Holcomb, $15)

Research in South Carolina
by GeLee Corley Hendrix
(National Genealogical Society, $6.50)

PERIODICALS

Carolina Genealogist
(1969-1984), Mary Bondurant Warren, Danielsville, GA 30633

Carolina Herald and Newsletter
(1974-), South Carolina Genealogical Society, Inc., P.O. Box 492, Columbia, SC 29202

Names in South Carolina
(1954-), Department of English, University of South Carolina, Columbia, SC 29208

South Carolina Genealogical Register
(1963-1968), Elizabeth Wood Thomas, ed., Pass Christian, MS 39571

South Carolina Historical Magazine,
formerly *South Carolina Historical and Genealogical Magazine*
(1900-), South Carolina Historical Society, Fireproof Building, 100 Meeting St., Charleston, SC 29401

South Carolina Magazine of Ancestral Research

(1973-), Brent Holcomb, P.O. Box 21766, Columbia, SC 29221

Transactions of the Huguenot Society of South Carolina
(1888-), Huguenot Society of South Carolina, 138 Logan St., Charleston, SC 29401

WEB SITES

Index to South Carolina Civil War Soldiers
<www.researchonline.net/sccw/mastindx.htm>: Each page of this alphabetical index lists soldiers' names, units, and companies.

The Revolutionary War in South Carolina
<sciway.net/hist/periods/revolwar.html>: Links to maps, battles, and biographies of Revolutionary-era South Carolinians.

Selected South Carolina Archives
<www.scroots.org/archive.html>: Outlines the location, contact information, and operating hours of several South Carolina archives and summarizes the repositories' holdings.

Ship Passenger Lists
<www.rootsweb.com/~usgenweb/sc/sca_ship.html>: Passenger-list transcriptions for Charleston (1768) and the Carolinas (1774).

South Carolina Genealogy Books
<www.scmar.com>: Compilations of vital records, tombstone transcriptions, deed and will

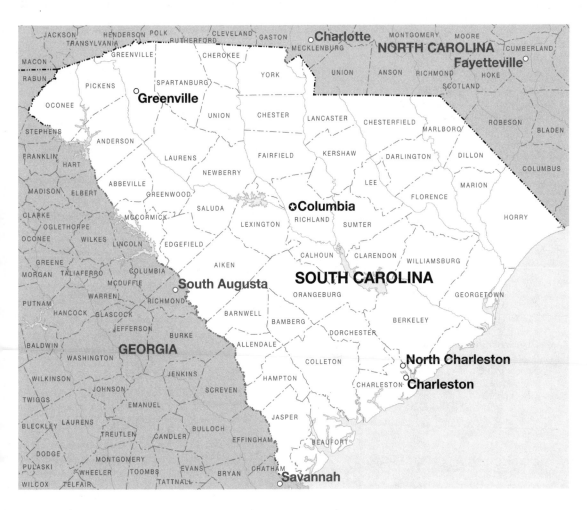

abstracts, and religious records.

South Carolina Mailing Lists
<www.rootsweb.com/~jfuller/gen_mail_states-sc.html>: Network with other researchers using state and county mailing lists.

South Carolina Marriage Records
<www.rootsweb.com/~usgenweb/sc/sca_marr.html>: Indexes of marriages beginning in 1641, many from the *South Carolina Magazine of Ancestral Research*.

SCGenWeb
<www.geocities.com/Heartland/Hills/3837>: Historical background, maps, state and county resources and links.

South Carolina Resources at RootsWeb
<resources.rootsweb.com/USA/SC/>: Search engines, personal Web pages, and user-submitted resources.

Vital Records Information
<vitalrec.com/sc.html>: Where to obtain copies of birth and death certificates, marriage licenses, and divorce decrees.

FAMILY HISTORY CENTERS

Aiken
358 E. Pine Log Rd.
(803) 648-0726

Beaufort
703 Parris Island Gateway
(843) 525-1823

Camden
34 Chestnut Ferry
(803) 432-7038

Charleston
1519 Sam Rittenberg Blvd.
(843) 766-6017

Columbia
4440 Fort Jackson Blvd.
(803) 782-7141

Florence
600 Maynard
(843) 662-2967

Gaffney
701 W. Buford St.
(864) 489-2615

Greenville
1301 Boiling Springs Rd.
(864) 627-0553

Greenwood
250 A Cokesbury Rd.
(864) 223-0937

SOUTH CAROLINA

Statehood: 1788
Statewide Birth and Death Records Begin: 1915
Statewide Marriage Records Begin: 1950
Address for Vital Statistics:
Office of Vital Records and Public Health
Statistics
2600 Bull St.
Columbia, SC 29201
(803) 734-4830
Fax: (803) 799-0301

U.S. federal censuses 1790, 1800, 1810, 1820, 1830, 1840, 1850, 1860, 1870, 1880, 1900, 1910, and 1920. Statewide indexes are available for the 1790, 1800, 1810, 1820, 1830, 1840, 1850, 1860, 1870, 1880, 1900, 1910, and 1920 censuses. No colonial censuses have been preserved. An 1848 census for the city of Charleston also exists.

City Directories at the Family History Library Include: Columbia 1859, 1860, 1903-1932, 1934-1935, 1931; Charleston 1796, 1866-1934, 1782, 1785, 1794, 1806-1807, 1809, 1824, 1836, 1856, and 1860.

Moncks Corner
319 W. Main St.
(843) 761-8671

Myrtle Beach
Forty-eighth Ave. North
and Highway 17 Bypass
(843) 449-1166

Newberry
2 Glenn St.

Orangeburg
1740 Broughton St. NE

Ridgeland
Grays Highway (278
West)
(843) 726-8241

Seneca
5003 Wells Highway
(864) 882-3147

Spartanburg
121 Quail Dr.
(864) 585-5943

Sumter
Highway 15 South
(803) 481-8300

TENNESSEE

ORGANIZATIONS & ARCHIVES

Chattanooga-Hamilton County Bicentennial Library
1001 Broad St.
Chattanooga, TN 37402
(423) 757-5310
Fax: (423) 757-5090
<www.lib.chattanooga.gov>

East Tennessee Historical Society
600 Market St.
P.O. Box 1629
Knoxville, TN 37901
(865) 215-8824
<www.east-tennessee-history.org>

McClung Historical Collection
East Tennessee Historical Center
314 W. Clinch Ave.
Third Floor
Knoxville, TN 37902
(865) 215-8801
<www.knoxlib.org/mcclung.htm>
Mailing address:
McClung Historical Collection
Knox County Archives
500 W. Church Ave.
Knoxville, TN 37902

Memphis/Shelby County Public Library and Information Center
3030 Poplar Ave.
Memphis, TN 38111
(901) 415-2742
Fax: (901) 725-8814
<www.memphislibrary.lib.tn.us>

Nashville Public Library
615 Church St.
Nashville, TN 37219
Tel: 615-862-5800
Fax: (615) 862-5771

Tennessee Genealogical Society
9114 Davies Plantation Rd.
Brunswick, TN 38014
<www.rootsweb.com/~tngs>

The Tennessee Historical Commission
2941 Lebanon Rd.
Nashville, TN 37243
(615) 532-1550
<www.state.tn.us/environment/hist>

Tennessee State Library and Archives
403 Seventh Ave. North
Nashville, TN 37243
(615) 741-2764
Fax: (615) 741-6471
<www.state.tn.us/sos/statelib/tslahome.htm>

University of Memphis Library
Special Collections Department
Campus Box 526500
Memphis, TN 38152
(901) 678-2210
Fax: (901) 678-8218
<www.lib.memphis.edu/speccoll.htm>

University of Tennessee, Knoxville
Hoskins Library, Special Collections
1401 Cumberland Ave.
Knoxville, TN 37996
(423) 974-4480
<www.lib.utk.edu>

RESOURCES

"5 Ts of Tennessee Research"
lecture by Barbara Renick
(Audiotapes.com, $8.50)

Research in Tennessee
by Gale Williams Bamman (National Genealogical Society, $6.50)

PERIODICALS

Ansearchin News
(1954-), Tennessee Genealogical Society, 9114 Davies Plantation Rd., Brunswick, TN 38014

East Tennessee Roots
(1984-), Thomas Edward Roach, Rutledge, TN

Family Findings
(1969-), Mid-West Tennessee Genealogical

Society, P.O. Box 3343, Jackson, TN 38303

The Journal of East Tennessee History: A Publication of the East Tennessee Historical Society (1929-),East Tennessee Historical Society, P.O. Box 1629, Knoxville, TN 37901

Middle Tennessee Journal of Genealogy and History (1995-), Middle Tennessee Genealogical Society, P.O Box 330948, Nashville, TN 37203

Tennessee Ancestors (1985-), East Tennessee Historical Society, P.O. Box 1629, Knoxville, TN 37901

Tennessee Historical Quarterly (1942-), Tennessee Historical Society, Ground Floor, War Memorial Building, Nashville, TN 37243

WEB SITES

Index to Tennessee Death Records, 1908-1912
<www.state.tn.us/sos/statelib/pubsvs/death2.htm>: Nearly ninety-eight thousand deaths are listed alphabetically. An index for 1914 to 1925 lists deaths by county. (No statewide death records exist for 1913.)

Tennessee Genealogy and History Web Site
<web.utk.edu/~kizzer/genehist/mainpage.htm>: This site's best resources are a primer on Tennessee land laws, a map of pre-1800 roads, and online biographies and journals.

Tennessee GenWeb Project
<tngenweb.org>: Tennessee genealogists are busy putting records—census, newspaper abstracts, marriages, county histories, Bible records, and more—online by county.

Tennessee History and Genealogy
<www.state.tn.us/sos/statelib/pubsvs/intro.htm>: State library and archives guide to finding Tennessee records, including vital, military, and census.

Tennessee Mailing Lists
<www.rootsweb.com/~jfuller/gen_mail_states-tn.html>: Network with other researchers using state and county mailing lists.

Tennessee Marriages
<members.tripod.com/~rosters/index-8.html>: County-by-county marriage databases contributed to USGenWeb.

Tennessee Resources at RootsWeb
<resources.rootsweb.com/USA/TN>: Search for your ancestor in multiple RootsWeb databases and personal Web pages.

Vital Records Information
<vitalrec.com/tn.html>: Where to obtain copies of birth and death certificates, marriage licenses, and divorce decrees.

FAMILY HISTORY CENTERS

Athens
508 Cedar Springs Rd.
(423) 745-0102

Chattanooga
8119 E. Brainerd Rd.
(423) 892-7632

Clarksville
3242 Highway 41A South
(931) 358-9635

Clinch River
111 Executive Park Dr.
(865) 494-6532

Columbia
1608 Hampshire Pk.
(931) 381-3650

Cookeville
981 Bunker Hill Rd.
(931) 526-3116

Crossville
1550 Genesis Rd.
(931) 484-2507

Cumberland Gap
Highway 63 East
(423) 869-2481

Fayetteville
40 Hilltop Rd.
(931) 433-6296

Franklin
1100 Grey Fox Ln.
(615) 794-4251

Gallatin
1360 E. Main St.
(615) 452-2741

Grove Park
6024 Grove Dr.
(865) 688-7411

Haywood 364 Haywood Ln. (615) 834-1318	**Memphis** 8150 Walnut Grove Rd. (901) 754-2545	**Smyrna** 316 Mayfield Dr. (615) 355-9268	**Clayton Library** Center for Genealogical Research 5300 Caroline

Haywood
364 Haywood Ln.
(615) 834-1318

Jackson
923 Pipkin Rd.
(901) 664-2274

Jamestown
516 N. Main
(615) 879-7356

Kingsport
100 Canongate Rd.
(423) 245-2321

Knoxville
400 Kendall Rd.
(865) 693-8252

Loudon
1005 Mulberry
(865) 458-2165

Maryville
706 Amerine Rd.
(865) 982-9080

McMinnville
183 Underwood Rd.
(931) 473-1053

Memphis
8150 Walnut Grove Rd.
(901) 754-2545

Memphis-North
4195 Kirby-Whitten Rd.
(901) 388-9974

Morristown
6301 Hiawatha
(423) 586-0901

Murfreesboro
902 E. Clark Blvd.
(615) 893-1349

Nashville
107 Twin Hill Dr.
(615) 859-6926

Oak Ridge
140 S. Jefferson Circle
(865) 483-6401

Paris
1921 Lone Oak Rd.
(901) 642-2285

Sevierville
401 Hardin Ln.
(865) 428-8550

Smyrna
316 Mayfield Dr.
(615) 355-9268

Tullahoma
Old Shelbyville Highway
130
(931) 455-5230

TEXAS

ORGANIZATIONS & ARCHIVES

Baylor University
Texas Collection
P.O. Box 97142
Waco, TX 76798
(254) 710-1268
<www3.baylor.edu/
Library/Texas>

**Center for American
History**
2.101 Sid Richardson Hall
The University of Texas at
Austin
Austin, TX 78712
(512) 495-4515
Fax: (512) 495-4542
<www.cah.utexas.edu>

Clayton Library
Center for Genealogical
Research
5300 Caroline
Houston, TX 77004
(832) 393-2600
<www.houstonlibrary.
org/clayton>

Dallas Public Library
1515 Young St.
Dallas, TX 75201
(214) 670-1400
<dallaslibrary.org/
central.htm>

**Daughters of the
Republic of Texas Library**
P.O. Box 1401
San Antonio, TX 78295
(210) 225-1071
Fax: (210) 212-8514
<www.drtl.org>

Houston Public Library
Houston Metropolitan
Research Center
500 McKinney St.
Houston, TX 77002
(713) 236-1313
<www.hpl.lib.tx.us/hpl/
hmrc.html>

National Archives and
Records Administration-
Fort Worth Branch
501 W. Felix St.
Building 1, Dock 1
P.O. Box 6216
Fort Worth, TX 76115
(817) 334-5515
Fax: (817) 334-5511
<www.archives.gov/
facilities/tx/fort_worth.
html>

**Rosenberg Library
Archives**
2310 Sealy Ave.
Galveston, TX 77550
(409) 763-8854
Fax: (409) 763-0275
<www.rosenberg-
library.org>

**Texas State Genealogical
Society**
Box 7
Sulphur Springs, TX
75483
<www.rootsweb.com/
~txsgs>

**Texas State Historical
Association**
2.306 Sid Richardson Hall

University of Texas
Austin, TX 78712
(512) 471-1525
Fax: (512) 471-1551
<www.tsha.utexas.edu>

Texas State Library
State Archives and
Library Building
1201 Brazos St.
P.O. Box 12927
Austin, TX 78711
(512) 463-5480
Fax: (512) 463-5436
<www.tsl.state.tx.us>

RESOURCES
*Genealogical Records in
Texas*
by Imogene and Leon
Kennedy (Genealogical
Publishing Co., $35)

**"Gone to Texas:
Migration Patterns to the
Lone Star State"**
lecture by Sammie
Townsend Lee
(Audiotapes.com, $8.50)

Research in Texas
by Lloyd Dewitt

Bockstruck (National
Genealogical Society,
$6.50)

PERIODICALS
Footprints
(1968-), Fort Worth
Genealogical Society, P.O.
Box 9767, Ft. Worth, TX
76147

Heart of Texas Records,
formerly *Central Texas
Genealogical Society
Bulletin* (1958-), Central
Texas Genealogical
Society, 1717 Austin Ave.,
Waco, TX 76701

Our Heritage
(1959-), San Antonio
Genealogical and
Historical Society, P.O.
Box 17461, San Antonio,
TX 78217

The Roadrunner
(1974-1991), Chaparral
Genealogical Society, P.O.
Box 606, Tomball, TX
77377

Stalkin' Kin
(1973-), San Angelo
Genealogical and
Historical Society, P.O.
Box 3453, San Angelo, TX
76902

Stirpes
(1961-), Texas State
Genealogical Society, c/o
Doris Cozart, Box 143,
Chillicothe, TX 79225

Yellowed Pages
(1971-), Southeast Texas
Genealogical and
Historical Society, c/o
Tyrrell Library, Box 3827,
Beaumont, TX 77704

WEB SITES
**Handbook of Texas
Online**
<tsha.utexas.edu/
handbook/online>:
Search more than twen-
ty-three thousand articles
on Texas history and
culture.

Lone Star Junction
<lsjunction.com>: The
"Texians" database docu-
ments more than ten
thousand early Texans
(1835 to statehood in
1845) through land and
voter records.

Republic of Texas Claims
<www.tsl.state.tx.us/arc/
repclaims>: Search for
your ancestor in this
index of more than forty-
eight thousand names of
citizens who submitted
payment, restitution, or
reimbursement claims
between 1835 and 1846.

Texas GenWeb Project
<www.rootsweb.com/
~txgenweb>: Offers tran-
scriptions of the 1850
census, as well as county

TEXAS

STATE STATS

Statehood: 1845
Statewide Birth and Death Records Begin: 1903
Statewide Marriage Records Begin: 1966
Address for Vital Statistics:
   Bureau of Vital Statistics
   Texas Department of Health
   1100 W. Forty-ninth St.
   Austin, TX 78756-3191
   (512) 458-7111
   <www.tdh.state.tx.us/bvs>

Available Censuses: U.S. federal censuses 1850, 1860, 1870, 1880, 1900, 1910, and 1920. Statewide indexes are available for 1850, 1860, 1870, 1880, 1900, 1910, and 1920 censuses. Some records from pre-statehood censuses also survive.

City Directories at the Family History Library Include: Austin 1857, 1881, 1885-1900, 1903-1916, 1918-1920, 1922, 1924, 1927, 1929-32, 1935, 1941, 1955, 1965, and 1969; Dallas 1875-1935, 1916, 1918, 1941, 1960, 1964, 1970, 1975, and 1979; Fort Worth 1877, 1878, 1885, 1888, 1892-1914, 1916, 1918, 1920, 1922-1935, 1941, 1960, 1965, 1970, 1972; Galveston 1856-1935, 1971, and 1982; Houston 1866, 1882-1913, 1915, and 1917-1935; San Antonio 1877-1934, 1940, 1941, 1960, 1965, and 1970

resources and research helps.

Texas Mailing Lists
<www.rootsweb.com/~jfuller/gen_mail_states-tx.html>: Network with other researchers using state and county mailing lists.

The Texas Ranger Research Center
<texasranger.org/Library/Genealogy.htm>: Was your ancestor a Texas Ranger? For a small fee, this center will look for you.

Texas Resources at RootsWeb
<resources.rootsweb.com/USA/TX>: Search for your ancestor in multiple databases.

Vital Records Information
<vitalrec.com/tx.html>: Where to obtain copies of birth and death certificates, marriage licenses, and divorce decrees.

FAMILY HISTORY CENTERS

Abilene
3325 N. Twelfth St.
(915) 673-8836

Alvin
2700 Lehi Ln.
(281) 585-3033

Amarillo
2101 N. Coulter St.
(806) 352-2409

Arlington
3809 Curt Dr.
(817) 446-7088

Austin
1000 E. Rutherford Ln.
(512) 837-3626

Austin-Oak Hills
5201 Convict Hill Rd.
(512) 892-6483

Azle
1010 Timber Oaks
(817) 444-6351

Bastrop
1635 Tahitian Dr.
(512) 321-4142

Bay City
2813 Sixteenth St.
(979) 245-3152

Baytown
1010 Birdsong Dr.
(281) 428-5141

Beaumont
3939 Turtle Creek Dr.
(409) 727-3548

Beaumont-Ward
7785 Weaver Dr.
(409) 866-1399

Beeville
100 E. Crocket
(512) 358-7313

Big Spring
1803 Wasson Rd.
(915) 263-4411

Boerne
203 Stonegate Rd.
(210) 249-9197

Bonham
Texas Highway 78 South
(903) 583-4949

Borger
1300 Roosevelt St.
(806) 274-4685

Brownsville
114 E. Price Rd.
(956) 546-6422

Brownwood
4503 E. Fourth
(915) 643-6635

Canyon Lake
41301 FM 3159
(830) 899-3224

Clear Lake
1802 Gunwale
(281) 488-4406

Cleburne
303 S. Nolan River Rd.
(817) 645-0566

Cleveland
1100 Southline
(281) 592-6364

College Station
2500 Barak Ln.
(979) 846-3516

The Colony
6800 Anderson Dr.
(972) 370-3537

Conroe
1516 Wilson Rd.
(409) 756-4004

Corpus Christi
6630 Wooldridge Rd.
(361) 993-2970

Corsicana
3800 Emhouse Rd.
(903) 872-4760

Cypress
16535 Kleinwood Dr.
(281) 251-5931

Dallas
1019 Big Stone Gap
(972) 709-0066

Dallas-East
10701 Lake Highlands Dr.
(214) 342-2642

Decatur
202 E. Thompson
(940) 627-2037

Del Rio
1315 Kings Way
(830) 775-4511

Denton
3000 Old North Rd.
(940) 387-3065

Eagle Pass
2355 Maria Del Refugio
(830) 773-2753

El Paso
1212 Sumac
(915) 599-8565

El Paso-First and Third
3651 Douglas Ave.
(915) 565-4323

El Paso-Mount Franklin
7315 Bishop Flores Dr.
(915) 581-8849

Fort Worth
5001 Altamesa Blvd.
(817) 292-8393

Fredericksburg
106 E. Driftwood
(210) 997-5018

Friendswood
505 Deseret
(281) 996-9346

Gainesville
1703 W. California St.
(940) 668-8055

Galveston
3114 Seventy-seventh St.
(409) 744-7938

Georgetown
218 Serenada Dr.
(512) 863-8221

Gilmer
1122 W. Pine St.
(903) 843-5805

Graham
Highway 380 East
(940) 549-5512

Granbury
708 Briarwood
(817) 573-6825

Greenville
5309 Utah Dr.
(903) 455-1614

Harlingen
2320 Hain Dr.
(956) 421-2028

Hondo
2910 Avenue Q
(830) 426-4203

Hondo Pass
5510 Hondo Pass Ave.
(915) 757-1215

Houston
1101 Bering Dr.
(713) 785-2105

Houston-East
4202 Yellowstone Dr.
(281) 991-8479

Houston-North
16331 Hafer Rd.
(281) 893-5381

Houston-South
602 Eldridge Rd.
(281) 240-1524

Hurst
4401 E. Loop 820 North
(817) 284-4472

Jasper
905 Shady Ln.
(409) 628-3046

Katy
1603 Norwalk
(281) 578-8338

Kerrville
202 Coronado Dr.
(830) 895-3909

Killeen
1410 S. Second St.
(254) 526-2918

Kingsville
2100 E. General Cavazos
Blvd.
(512) 592-3630

Kingwood
4021 Deerbrook
(281) 360-1352

Lake Jackson
502 Southern Oaks Dr.
(979) 297-8454

Laredo
1520 E. Hillside
(956) 753-9249

League City
4655 S. Shore Blvd.
(281) 538-1283

Lewisville
615 MacArthur Blvd.
(972) 393-6976

Livingston
2023 N. Houston St.
(936) 327-5680

Longview
1700 Blueridge Pkwy.
(903) 297-1349

Lubbock
3211 Fifty-eighth St.
(806) 792-5040

Lufkin
606 Bending Oak
(936) 637-7750

Magnolia
31705 Michael Rd.
(713) 521-9728

Marble Falls
200 Via Viejo
(830) 693-6545

McAllen
200 W. La Vista Ave.
(956) 682-1061

McKinney
2801 W. Eldorado Pkwy.
(972) 547-0019

Midland
4805 Gateway
(915) 694-3830

Mission Trail/Socorro
11300 N. Loop Rd.

Monahans
S. Eric Ave. at I-20 Access
Rd.
(915) 943-4549

Odessa
2011 N. Washington
(915) 337-3112

Old Katy
1928 Drexel
(281) 391-7689

Orange
6108 Hazelwood
(409) 883-7969

Pampa
411 E. Twenty-ninth St.
(806) 669-9547

Paris
3060 Pine Mill Rd.
(903) 784-0788

Pecos Ward
1901 S. Texas St.
(915) 447-6222

Pine Trails
14404 Kimtock Dr.
(281) 458-1526

Plainview
4211 S.W. Second St.
(806) 293-5897

Plano
2700 Round Rock Trail
(972) 867-6479

Pleasanton
636 Oak Haven
(830) 569-5703

Queen City
1806 S. Boggie St.
(903) 796-5376

Raymondville
490 N. First St.
(956) 689-5408

Richardson
900 S. Bowser Rd.
(972) 680-8654

Rockdale
310 Calhoun
(512) 446-6371

Rockwall
8901 Garner
(972) 475-8606

Round Rock
8140 Racine Trail
(512) 388-1160

San Angelo
4475 Southwest Blvd.
(915) 949-0740

San Antonio
9626 Adams Hill
(210) 673-9404

San Antonio-East
8801 Midcrown
(210) 656-4111

San Antonio-Fifth and Tenth
655 Castroville Rd.
(210) 431-9854

San Antonio-North
2103 St. Cloud
(210) 736-2940

San Antonio-West
6240 UTSA Blvd.
(210) 691-0594

San Marcos
120 Suncrest
(512) 353-8672

Sealy
600 West St.
(979) 885-1471

Seguin
1111 College St.
(830) 372-5212

Shadowdale
4703 Shadowdale
(713) 466-7706

Silsbee
W. Highway 418 at
Autumn Shadows
(409) 385-9692

Stephenville
1355 N. Dale
(254) 968-6294

Stone Oak
945 Knights Cross Dr.
(210) 497-7762

Texarkana-New Boston
3701 Moores Ln.
(903) 831-5225

Tyler
1617 Shiloh Rd.
(903) 509-8322

Uvalde
420 Ham Ln.
(830) 278-1501

Victoria
3408 N. Ben Wilson
(361) 575-0055

Waco
7201 Viking Dr.
(254) 776-4860

Waller
2325 Myer-Waller Rd.
(936) 372-5738

Weatherford
1802 S. Bowie Dr.
(817) 594-4064

Weslaco/Mercedes
321 S. Virginia
(956) 514-2438

Wharton
1906 Briar Ln.
(979) 532-5302

Wichita Falls
4325 York St.
(940) 696-9811

Wills Point
Farm to Market Road 47
(903) 873-4361

Woodville
Highway 287 and Pine St.
(409) 283-2236

Yorktown Kenedy
N. Riedel Street
(361) 564-3884

VIRGINIA

ORGANIZATIONS & ARCHIVES

College of William and Mary
Earl Gregg Swem Library
P.O. Box 8794
Williamsburg, VA 23187
(757) 221-3050
Fax: (757) 221-2635
<www.swem.wm.edu>

Handley Regional Library
P.O. Box 58
Winchester, VA 22604
(540) 662-9041
Fax: (540) 722-4769
<166.67.151.100/
handley/default.asp>

Jones Memorial Library
2311 Memorial Ave.
Lynchburg, VA 24501
(434) 846-0501
Fax: (434) 846-1572
<www.jmlibrary.org>

Library of Virginia (formerly Virginia State Library and Archives)
800 E. Broad St.

Richmond, VA 23219
(804) 692-3500
Fax: (804) 692-3556
<www.lva.lib.va.us>

University of Virginia
Alderman Library
Box 400114
Charlottesville, VA 22904
(804) 924-3021
Fax: (804) 924-1431
<www.lib.virginia.edu/
alderman>

Virginia Genealogical Society
5001 W. Broad St.
Suite 115
Richmond, VA 23230
(804) 285-8954
<www.vgs.org>

Virginia Historical Society
428 North Blvd.
Richmond, VA 23220
(804) 358-4901
<www.vahistorical.org>
Mailing address:
Box 7311
Richmond, VA 23221

RESOURCES

Atlas of County Boundary Changes in Virginia, 1634-1895
by Michael F. Doran
(Iberian Publishing Co., $26.95)

Research in Virginia
by Eric Grundset
(National Genealogical Society, $6.50)

Virginia Genealogical Research
by George K. Schweitzer
(Genealogical Sources Unlimited, $11.95 from <www.heritagequest.com>)

Virginia Genealogy: Sources and Resources
by Carol McGinnis

(Genealogical Publishing Co., $35)

PERIODICALS

The Huguenot
(1924-), Huguenot Society of the Founders of Manakin in the Colony of Virginia, Inc., 981 Huguenot Trail, Midlothian, VA 23113; (804) 794-5702

Magazine of Virginia Genealogy,
formerly *Quarterly of the Virginia Genealogical Society* (1963-), Virginia Genealogical Society, 5001 W. Broad St., Suite 115, Richmond, VA 23230

Sons of the Revolution in the State of Virginia Quarterly Magazine
(1922-1932) Sons of the Revolution in the State of Virginia

The Southside Virginian
(1982-), Lyndon H. Hart and J. Christian Kolbe, P.O. Box 118, Richmond, VA 23201

Tyler's Quarterly Historical and Genealogical Magazine
(1919-1952), Mrs. Lyon G. Tyler

Virginia Appalachian Notes
(1977-), Southwestern Virginia Genealogical Society, P.O. Box 12485, Roanoke, VA 24026

Virginia Genealogist
(1957-), John Frederick Dorman, P.O. Box 4883, Washington, DC 20008

Virginia Magazine of History and Biography
(1894-), Virginia Historical Society, P.O. Box 7311, Richmond, VA 23221

Virginia Tidewater Genealogy (1970-), Tidewater Genealogical Society, P.O. Box 7650, Hampton, VA 23666

William and Mary Quarterly, formerly *William and Mary College Quarterly Historical Magazine* (1892-), Institute of Early American History and Culture, P.O. Box 8781, Williamsburg, VA 23187

WEB SITES

1835 Virginia Pension List <www.rootsweb.com/~usgenweb/va/vapensio.htm>: Alphabetical entries for more than four thousand pensioners that list age, rank, county of residence, type of service, date and amount of the pension, and how much was paid out.

Genealogical Resources <www.lva.lib.va.us/whatwehave/gene>: A guide to the Library of Virginia's genealogical research holdings.

Iberian Publishing Company <www.iberian.com>: Publisher specializing in Virginia record compilations.

Library of Virginia Digital Library Program <www.lva.lib.va.us/dlp>: Search in more than eighty databases with more than 2.2 million original documents, photos, and maps, including court records, Bible and vital records, military history, newspapers, land records, and business records.

A List of the Parishes in Virginia, June the 30th, 1680 <lineages.com/archives/VAPSH680.HTM>: Parishes and their ministers by county.

Virginia Civil War Home Page <members.aol.com/jweaver300/grayson/vacwhp.htm>: Assortment of Confederate and Union resources, along with information on hospitals, Libby Prison, secession, and elections.

Virginia GenWeb Project <www.rootsweb.com/~vagenweb>: Join the surname registry, follow county boundary changes, view historical maps and photos, and link to county pages.

Virginia Mailing Lists <www.rootsweb.com/~jfuller/gen_mail_states-va.html>: Network with other researchers using state and county mailing lists.

Virginia Quit Rent Rolls, 1704 <lineages.com/vault/rents_1704_results.asp>: Search for an exact or Soundexed name; results give acreage and county.

Virginia Resources at RootsWeb <resources.rootsweb.com/USA/VA>: Search for your ancestor in multiple databases and personal Web pages.

Vital Records Information <vitalrec.com/va.html>: Where to obtain copies of birth and death certificates, marriage licenses, and divorce decrees.

FAMILY HISTORY CENTERS

Annandale
3900 Howard St.
(703) 256-5518

Ashburn
21015 Claiborne Parkway
(703) 858-5930

Bennetts Creek
4759 Bennetts Pasture Rd.
(757) 538-3610

Buckingham
U.S. Route 60
(804) 969-2034

Buena Vista
Highway 60
(540) 261-6446

Centreville
14150 Upper Ridge Dr.
(703) 830-5343

Charlottesville
Hydraulic Road
(804) 975-3866

Chesapeake
412 Scarborough Dr.
(757) 482-9612

Danville
3058 N. Main St.
(804) 836-6212

Deep Creek/Portsmouth
1115 Cherokee Rd.
(757) 485-3884

Eastern Shore
26133 Onley Rd.
(757) 787-1850

Fredericksburg
1710 Bragg Rd.
(540) 786-5641

Front Royal
7145 Browntown Rd.
(540) 636-6599

Gloucester
6846 Short Ln.
(804) 695-1162

Hamilton
Corner of Old Route 7 and Reid St.
(540) 338-9526

Harrisonburg
210 South Ave.
(540) 433-2945

Kilmarnock
Devils Bottom Road
(804) 435-9238

Lynchburg
110 Melinda Dr.
(434) 239-4744

Martinsville
Riverside Drive State Highway 57 A
(540) 629-7617

McLean
2034 Great Falls St.
(703) 532-9019

Mount Vernon
2000 George Washington Parkway
(703) 799-3071

New River
Route 460
(540) 626-7264

Newport News
902 Denbigh Blvd.
(757) 874-2335

Oakton
2719 Hunter Mill Rd.
(703) 281-1836

Richmond
5600 Monument Ave.
(804) 288-8134

Richmond-Chesterfield
4601 N. Bailey Bridge Rd.
(804) 763-4318

Roanoke
6311 Wayburn Dr.
(540) 562-2052

Tappahannock
995 Winston Rd.
(804) 443-3165

Virginia Beach
4780 Princess Anne Rd.
(757) 467-3302

Waynesboro
2825 Jefferson Ln.
(540) 942-1036

Winchester
399 Apple Pie Ridge
(540) 722-6055

Woodbridge
3000 Dale Blvd.
(703) 670-5977

WEST VIRGINIA

ORGANIZATIONS & ARCHIVES

Archives and History Library
Division of Culture and History
The Cultural Center
1900 Kanawha Blvd.

East Charleston, WV
25305
(304) 558-0230
Fax: (304) 558-2779
<www.wvculture.org/history>

West Virginia and Regional History Collection
West Virginia University Library
Colson Hall
P.O. Box 6069
Morgantown, WV 26506
(304) 293-4040
Fax: (304) 293-6923
<www.libraries.wvu.edu/history/westvirginia.htm>

West Virginia Genealogical Society
P.O. Box 249
Elkview, WV 25071
<www.rootsweb.com/~wvgs>

RESOURCES

Timesaving Aid to Virginia-West Virginia Ancestors,
vols. 1-4, by Patrick G. Wardell (Iberian Publishing Co., $36)

West Virginia Genealogy: Sources and Resources
by Carol McGinnis

(Genealogical Publishing Co., $20)

PERIODICALS

The Journal of the Kanawha Valley Genealogical Society (1977-), Kanawha Valley Genealogical Society, P.O. Box 8555, South Charleston, WV 25303

Tri-County Researcher (1976-), Linda Goddard Stout, P.O. Box 196, Proctor, WV 26055

West Augusta Historical and Genealogical Society Newsletter (1944-), West Augusta Historical and Genealogical Society, 2515 Tenth Ave., Parkersburg, WV 26101

West Virginia History: A Quarterly Magazine (1939-), West Virginia Division of Culture and History, Cultural Center, 1900 Kanawha Blvd. East, Charleston, WV 25305

WEB SITES

Early Virginia/WVA Genealogy <www.sonic.net/~melvaw>: Collection of early Monroe County settlers' family trees; also available as a GEDCOM file.

Vital Records Information <vitalrec.com/wv.html>: Where to obtain copies of birth and death certificates, marriage licenses, and divorce decrees.

West Virginia Genealogy Helplist <www.cybercomm.net/~freddie/helplist/wv.htm>: County-by-county list of volunteers and the sources in which they'll look up information for you.

West Virginia GenWeb Project <www.rootsweb.com/~wvgenweb>: Use the table to find out about your ancestor's county: when was formed, its parent counties, and the county seat. Check out the site's West Virginia Coal Mines project, which includes history, photos, and miners' memorials and obits.

West Virginia in the Civil War <wvcivilwar.com>: Links to regimental histories, battlefields, historic sites, and reenactment groups.

West Virginia Mailing Lists <www.rootsweb.com/~jfuller/gen_mail_states-wv.html>: Network with other researchers using state and county mailing lists.

West Virginia Resources at RootsWeb <resources.rootsweb.com/USA/WV/>: Search for your ancestor in RootsWeb databases and personal Web pages.

FAMILY HISTORY CENTERS

Buckhannon
179 S. Kanawha St.
(304) 472-5213

WEST VIRGINIA

Statehood: 1863
Statewide Birth and Death Records Begin: 1917
Statewide Marriage Records Begin: 1964
Address for Vital Statistics:
Vital Registration Office
State Capitol Complex No. 3, Room 516
Charleston, WV 25305
(304) 558-2931
Fax: (304) 558-1051
<www.wvdhhr.org/bph/oehp/hsc/vr/birtcert.htm>

Available Censuses: U.S. federal censuses 1810, 1820, 1830, 1840, 1850, 1860, 1870, 1880, 1900, 1910, and 1920. Part of Virginia in census prior to 1870 censuses. Indexes are available for the 1810, 1820, 1830, 1840, 1850, 1860, 1870, 1880, 1900, 1910, and 1920 censuses.

City Directories at the Family History Library Include: Charleston 1899-1900, 1922, 1930, 1940; Huntington 1899-1900, 1930; Wheeling 1839, 1851, 1899-1900, 1903/4-1934, and 1921-1922.

Charleston
2007 McClure Parkway
(304) 984-9333

Elkins
Route 219-250 South of
Elkins
(304) 636-7750

Fairmont
Route 73 North
(Meadowdale)
(304) 363-0116

Franklin
One-half mile north of
Franklin Route 220
(304) 358-7005

Harpers Ferry
343 Carriage Dr.

Huntington
5640 Shawnee Dr.
(304) 736-0250

Masontown
Highway 7
(304) 864-5377

Morgantown
Imperial Wood Meadow
Lane
(304) 594-1176

New Martinsville
130 Paddock Green Dr.
(304) 455-1413

Parkersburg
2515 Capitol Dr.
(304) 428-2857

Midwest

Illinois
Indiana
Iowa
Michigan
Minnesota
Missouri
Ohio
Wisconsin

REGIONAL GUIDE
BY PAULA STUART WARREN

Mention the Midwestern part of the United States and most people immediately think of cornfields, cows, pigs, lakes, and flat land. But the Midwestern states also include major cities, leading universities, Fortune 500 companies, scenic valleys, ski hills, operas, symphonies, museums, five-star hotels, historic sites, and—best of all for family historians—a wealth of genealogical resources. The Midwest is home to America's auto industry and that staple of genealogical research, the 3M Post-it brand note. In this region you can find the halls of fame for rock and roll and polka as well as pro football and U.S. hockey.

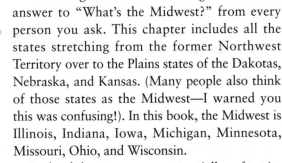

Exactly what states are we talking about? You could get a different answer to "What's the Midwest?" from every person you ask. This chapter includes all the states stretching from the former Northwest Territory over to the Plains states of the Dakotas, Nebraska, and Kansas. (Many people also think of those states as the Midwest—I warned you this was confusing!). In this book, the Midwest is Illinois, Indiana, Iowa, Michigan, Minnesota, Missouri, Ohio, and Wisconsin.

Each of these states was essentially a frontier area at some point in time as the population migrated westward. Each joined the Union in turn in the years between 1803 and 1858. The first people living in these states were the Native Americans of many different tribes, and their lands and living style were gradually pushed ever farther westward with the influx of new settlers in the 1800s. Some have since returned to their native areas.

The next wave of settlers to many of these states was the French-Canadian and British fur traders and military. The subsequent migrations were not just east to west, although those trails brought many New Englanders to the region. Many Southerners and others came into and down the Ohio River Valley. Other folks came up the Mississippi from the port of New Orleans. Still others came across the Canadian border, which had no restrictions before the 1890s.

Each Midwestern state is a melting pot of ethnic groups and religions. In the popular mind, Minnesota, for example, is made up of only Scandinavian Lutherans. Actually the Irish, Germans, and people of many other nationalities—including today a large influx of Hmong from Southeast Asia—are represented in large numbers, as is just about every religious denomination. Missouri may have a lot of Germans, but my husband's Missouri ancestors were English and Irish. And, yes, Wisconsin does have German beer and bratwurst, but that's where my French-Canadian and Scottish ancestors settled. Did you know that many early Ohio settlers were from Virginia and many early Illinois and Indiana settlers were from New England? Many Quakers migrated westward to Iowa. Today we find just about every ethnic group and religion in each of these Midwestern states.

To learn more about the ethnic groups in this region, study individual state and county histories. Publications such as *They Chose Minnesota* (Minnesota Historical Society Press, $24.95) detail many of the ethnic groups that settled a state.

OVER THE BORDERLINE

In your research, you must pay attention to state and county boundaries and formation dates. That geography class you groaned about in school is now of utmost importance! For example, the land that was to become Missouri was variously under the control of Spain, France, England, and the United States. If you research early pioneers in these Midwestern states, you may have to look for records in a state that had jurisdiction over one or more of the others before they were officially established. Early residents of what was to become Minnesota might be found in the records of Illinois, Iowa, Michigan, or Wisconsin, depending upon the

year. Note also how the rivers and the Great Lakes have been important to the settlement and growth of this region. Another variable is that some counties that once existed are now defunct. You can get help from the many map guides, place-name books, and atlases, such as *Indiana Place Names* by Ronald L. Baker and Marvin Carmony (Indiana University Press, out of print).

Now is the time to benefit if you paid attention in history class, too. The migrations into and out of the states affected the records created in each. The Upper Peninsula of Michigan and southern Illinois, for example, are extremely different from the rest of their respective states in terrain and population sources. Some people think that upper Michigan had only miners and fur traders, while others regard southern Illinois as basically a Southern state.

Ohio lands present another interesting research twist. Virginians who settled in an area of southwestern Ohio received the land for their Revolutionary War service. But did you know that some of northern Ohio was originally claimed by Connecticut?

Many Revolutionary War soldiers and their families migrated into other parts of the Midwest. Most of these states had many residents who served in the Civil War; in Missouri, these included soldiers of the Confederate and the Union forces.

Whether you have ancestors in all of these states or just a couple of them, you can enjoy a vast array of resources and libraries for researching your Midwestern roots. Join genealogical and historical societies to keep up-to-date on the ever-growing research and resources in these states. As an example, the Iowa Genealogical Society (IGS) works with its chapters all around the state who assist them in publishing indexes and abstracts of records. In its *Hawkeye Heritage*, IGS has run a series of articles about researching Iowa ancestors. You'll find details on societies in this chapter's state listings.

COUNTING THE POPULATION

A good place to start researching your Midwestern roots, as is true with any U.S. genealogy, is the census. The good news is that the federal censuses for these states still exist, for the most part, from the time of their territorial formation. Some early Ohio censuses are no longer available, and the same is true for some individual counties or parts of counties in all these states for particular years. You can find printed indexes to the federal censuses for these states for most years as well as a growing online and CD-ROM collection of indexes and actual census images. The Library of Michigan has a free online index to the Michigan 1870 federal census at <envoy.libraryofmichigan.org/1870_census>.

Many of these states also took state censuses; the majority of these were for years ending with 5. Iowa has state census records for as late as 1925; that census lists everyone in the household, the maiden name of the mother of each person enumerated, and even the county of birth for those born in Iowa. Wisconsin and Minnesota have enumerations of everyone in the state as late as 1905. Minnesota Historical Society volunteers and staff are indexing the 1895 every-name state census. Michigan has an 1894 state census, which for each woman tells how many children she had had and how many of them were still living. The rest of the states didn't collect this detail until the 1900 federal census. The 1894 Michigan census also tells how many years a person had been in the state and in the country.

If you have Ohio, Indiana, Missouri, or Illinois ancestry, you won't have such good fortune in state census research. Ohio and Indiana have some scattered enumerations of free white males. Missouri has some scattered state enumerations for early years. Illinois has some early state censuses, but many no longer exist. The most recent one is for 1865; that year's and the 1855 enumeration survive for most counties.

VITAL RECORDS, ONLINE AND OFF

Ohio became a state way back in 1803, and Indiana followed in 1816, but these states did not keep birth or death registrations in their early years. All of the Midwestern states now have state-level vital records offices (see state listings); other vital records can be found at the local registrar level. Some of these states' larger cities, such as St. Louis, also kept separate birth and death records.

During the Work Projects Administration (WPA) years, county and state vital records indexes were created for some of these states. Checking a variety of library catalogs may yield those for your ancestral areas. You can also find a variety of state, county, and local vital records for Midwestern states in the Family History Library's catalog <www.familysearch.org>. Checking these on microfilm via your local Family History Center saves you some costs of obtaining copies from a government office.

The registration of births and deaths in these states varies by state and time period. For example, roughly half of these events in Wisconsin were registered before the autumn of 1907. In contrast, the state health department of Minnesota was still urging local registrars in the 1940s to better comply with laws to register all births and deaths. Marriage records were generally kept in a more orderly fashion and usually begin with the formation of a county or in the years shortly thereafter.

Some of the vital records for these states have more than the basic details. For example, some Illinois counties have applications from the bride and groom that list place of birth and mother's maiden name.

Increasingly, Midwestern vital records indexes are going online. For Illinois, you can click on a statewide death index for 1916 to 1950 <www.cyberdriveillinois.com/departments/archives/databases.html>. Once you've found an ancestor in the online index, you can obtain birth and death records from 1916 forward from the Department of Public Health. Some Illinois counties have a scattering of earlier birth and death records dating back to the late 1870s. An ongoing statewide marriage index up through 1900 is also online at the same Web address, the result of cooperation between the state archives and the Illinois State Genealogical Society.

The Ohio Historical Society Web site <www.ohiohistory.org/dindex/search.cfm> offers a searchable death certificate index covering 1913 to 1937. Additional years are available at the society. The late 1860s saw the beginning of some county-level birth and death registrations in Ohio; late in 1908 this moved to the state level with copies also kept at the county level.

The Wisconsin State Genealogical Society has an online index to Wisconsin delayed and affidavit birth registrations from before 1 October 1907 <www.rootsweb.com/~wsgs/delayed_birth.htm>.

The Minnesota Historical Society hosts an online index to death certificates covering 1908 through 1959 <people.mnhs.org/dci/Search.cfm>, which received more than five thousand requests for death records in just one month after it went online.

Iowa's vital records begin in 1880, though some county records predate this. Indiana has birth and death records at the county level since the early 1880s, but these records do not include everyone. The state department of health has birth records from 1907 and death records from 1900. You can search databases of many Iowa marriages to 1850 and from 1851 to 1900 on the subscription Ancestry.com site.

Michigan researchers will appreciate the ongoing Genealogical Death Indexing System that currently covers 1867 to 1897 <www.mdch.state.mi.us/pha/osr/gendisx/search2.htm>. Genealogists across the state are entering the data.

Missouri has been steadily recording birth and death records at the state level since 1910.

Before 1881, a marriage could have been recorded at any courthouse; for a marriage after that time, a records can be found in the county where the license was obtained. A database of Missouri marriages to 1850 is available on Ancestry.com.

Indiana researchers can thank the WPA for its extensive work indexing the state's births and marriages. Today this data, covering 1880 to 1920 for births and 1845 to 1920 for marriages, can be searched on Ancestry.com, along with a separate database of marriages to 1850.

OTHER INDEXES AND DATABASES

State archives and historical societies throughout the Midwest offer many online and in-house databases, covering not only the vital records noted above but also military service and biographies. Those mentioned here are only the tip of the iceberg. More can be found via the USGenWeb site <www.usgenweb.org>; others are hosted at commercial sites such as Ancestry.com.

For example, the Illinois State Archives Databases Web site, previously mentioned, has a long list of military databases related to service in different wars, dating to the War of 1812. The state archives and historical society have in-house indexes to many local histories.

Indiana researchers should use the *Indiana Biographical Index*, which indexes many published items. This index and many of the books it indexes are found in many larger libraries.

Iowa members of the Grand Army of the Republic (GAR—that is, Union soldiers) are listed in a vast microfilmed index. Many of the actual GAR post records have also been filmed.

A detailed Michigan County Clerks Genealogy Directory is online via the state archives <www.sos.state.mi.us/history/archive/archgene.html>. Earlier editions are in booklet format in many libraries.

The Minnesota Historical Society has several military indexes, and it holds indexed 1918 alien registration records. The Iron Range Research

Center in Chisholm, Minnesota, offers census records for several states as well as a statewide naturalization index for the records of the eighty-seven Minnesota counties.

The Missouri State Archives has published a useful *Guide to County Resources on Microfilm*, which is also searchable online <www.sos.state. mo.us/CountyInventory>. This tells what records the archives have for each county; these are available for sale on microfilm and at the Family History Library (FHL) in Salt Lake City. The World War I Military Service Cards for Missouri have been indexed online <www.sos. state.mo.us/archives/ww1/default.asp> and cover 145,000 names. These may tell your military ancestor's place and date of birth.

Ohio researchers will appreciate the microfilmed every-name index to the biography sections of Ohio county histories. This index includes the names of 450,000 people.

The Wisconsin Historical Society has online searchable Local History and Biography Articles primarily from the years 1860 to 1940 <www. wisconsinhistory.org/wlhba/>. At the library itself, you'll find Wisconsin Necrology, which consists of thousands of obituaries.

Many of these states are mounting lists and indexes relating to Civil War and other service-related materials online. State and local histories and regimental histories are found in most historical societies, and some are accessible online. Keep checking, as new material is indexed and digitized all the time.

Each of the Midwestern states also participated in the United States Newspaper Program to identify, locate, catalog, and preserve newspapers across the country. Check the program's Web site <www.neh.gov/projects/usnp.html> for links to the information for each of these states, including newspaper titles and places where you can find copies. Most of the Midwestern states' newspapers are now on microfilm and available through interlibrary loan. The Illinois and Michigan projects are still in progress.

It's also worth noting that the Wisconsin Historical Society has the largest newspaper collection after the Library of Congress. The society's holdings include newspapers for Wisconsin, of course, and also for many other states, as well as special-interest newspapers: military, ethnic, Colonial, women, unions, and other subjects.

RANGE OF RESEARCH REPOSITORIES

The Midwest, with its progressive tradition and historic commitment to education, is rich in libraries, historical societies, archives, and special collections filled with materials helpful to family historians. For example, the Minnesota Historical Society's library's holdings contain loads of material for genealogists, including state and federal census records; naturalization papers; information on patriotic, fraternal, and veterans organizations; township histories; cemetery records; and city directories. In addition, this Minnesota archive holds the findings of an unusual group of reports done in one year only, 1918. These reports detail information on non-United States citizens who lived in the state, on farm crops and labor, and on the working women of Ramsey County. Holdings also include records of the Great Northern and Northern Pacific Railroads. In some cases, only an index of railroad workers exists; in others, actual payroll records are available.

You can find online or published holdings guides to many of these repositories or to research in the state or a major city. Check the Minnesota Historical Society's *Genealogical Resources of the Minnesota Historical Society: A Guide* or *Chicago and Cook County Sources: A Guide to Research*. Another city-specific guide is *Guide to Genealogical Research in St. Louis*. (These books and more are listed later in this chapter.) For each repository you plan to visit, be sure to call ahead or check the Web site to determine hours, fees, parking, and other details.

Several Midwestern states have statewide networks of research repositories that house records related to a county or group of counties. These may include both governmental and private records, though coverage varies by state. The Illinois Regional Archives Depositories (IRAD) house county records; the state archives Web site <www.cyberdriveillinois.com/departments/archives/irad/iradhome.html> provides access to the online listing of these and their holdings. Minnesota has Regional Research Centers, while Ohio has the Ohio Network of American History Research Centers. Wisconsin has Area Research Centers (ARC); the Wisconsin Historical Society Web site <www.wisconsinhistory.org/archives/arcnet> has details on these and links to their sites.

The Library of Michigan has the Abrams Foundation Historical Collection as well as other significant research resources. It has online and print discussions of many of its holdings <www.libofmich.lib.mi.us>. The Burton Historical Collection at the Detroit Public Library is a delight for researchers with Detroit and Michigan interests.

The Wisconsin Historical Society library covers the United States and Canada. Much of its collection is housed in open stacks that researchers can browse.

Iowa has two locations for its state historical society. Some items, such as census records and newspapers, are found at each, and each has its own specialties. The Iowa City location has many personal, organizational, and business manuscript collections, while the Des Moines location has the state archives. The Iowa Genealogical Society library is another gem for researchers.

In Ohio, the Public Library of Cincinnati and Hamilton County has a renowned History and Genealogy Department. The Western Reserve Historical Society in Cleveland is also well known. These are two places where you can research far beyond Ohio.

Similarly, the Newberry Library in Chicago has some great Chicago resources, but the holdings cover much more than its host city. The Mid-Continent Public Library in Independence, Missouri, boasts one of the nation's best genealogy collections.

In Fort Wayne, Indiana, the Allen County Public Library's genealogy department is home to materials related to all states, and it also has many foreign resources. See "Fort Wayne" later in this chapter for details on this unusual genealogical resource, second only to the Family History Library.

The Minnesota Historical Society has a wealth of Minnesota county and local resources, many indexes, and the state archives collection of local and state governmental records.

Minnesota's Iron Range Research Center, mentioned earlier, is a vacation destination. You can take your relatives or friends along on your research trip, and they can view the mining exhibits, listen to oral histories, have lunch, and visit an open-pit mine while you check out the research area.

Also in Minnesota, the Immigration History Research Center in Minneapolis serves many ethnic groups. It focuses on records created by immigrants from eastern, central, and southern Europe and from the Near East who settled in the Midwest.

The Swenson Center at Augustana College in Rock Island, Illinois, is the nation's leading repository for Swedish immigrant research. It's the only place outside of Sweden where you can access the fruits of a vast microfilming project of Swedish-American church records. If your Midwestern roots stretch back to Norway instead, head for the Vesterheim Center in Madison, Wisconsin.

As mentioned earlier, you can find just about every religious denomination in these states. Most of the church records remain with individual churches if they are still operating. Some older records or microfilmed records might be found at a historical society or a religious archive. The FHL has many, but certainly not all, church records for these states. Among the region's religious archives is the Evangelical Lutheran Church in America, near Chicago. Its Web site <www.elca.org/os/archives/geneal. html> includes research and access policies.

If you can't go yourself, most of these repositories offer research services for a fee or have lists of area researchers for hire.

The National Archives and Records Administration (NARA) of the United States also has many resources for Midwestern states. Many are in Washington, DC, and others are at regional locations. For the Midwest, check the regional archives in Chicago and Kansas City.

No matter which Midwestern states hold the records of your ancestors, you're in for a pleasing historical and genealogical research experience. Many records have survived and can be found in a variety of libraries, courthouses, and archives. The wealth of places to research in the Midwest can keep you busy for a long time. Plan to take that genealogical research tour in person, online, or long-distance with some on-site assistance. You'll be rewarded with wonderful information on the hardy Midwestern folks you descend from.

ORGANIZATIONS & ARCHIVES

Allen County Public Library
Historical Genealogy Department
900 Webster St.
P.O. Box 2270
Fort Wayne, IN 46801
(260) 421-1225
Fax: (260) 422-9688
<www.acpl.lib.in.us/genealogy>
Interim location (2003-approximately 2005 or 2006):
200 East Berry St.
Fort Wayne, IN 46801

Evangelical Lutheran Church in America Archives
321 Bonnie Ln.
Elk Grove Village, IL 60007
(847) 690-9410
<www.elca.org/os/archives/geneal.html>

Immigration History Research Center
University of Minnesota
311 Andersen Library
222 Twenty-first Ave. South
Minneapolis, MN 55455
(612) 625-4800
Fax: (612) 626-0018
<www1.umn.edu/ihrc>

International Society of Sons and Daughters of Slave Ancestry
P.O. Box 436937
Chicago, IL 60643
<www.rootsweb.com/~ilissdsa>

Iron Range Research Center
Highway 169 West
P.O. Box 392
Chisholm, MN 55719
(218) 254-7959 or (800) 372-6437
Fax: (218) 254-5235
<www.ironrangeresearchcenter.org>

Mid-Continent Public Library
317 W. 24 Highway
Independence, MO 64050
(816) 252-7228
<www.mcpl.lib.mo.us>

National Archives and Records Administration (NARA)-Great Lakes Region
7358 S. Pulaski Rd.
Chicago, IL 60629
(773) 581-7816
Fax: (312) 353-1294
<www.archives.gov/facilities/il/chicago.html>

National Archives and Records Administration-Central Plains Region (Kansas City)
2312 E. Bannister Rd.
Kansas City, MO 64131
(816) 926-6920
Fax: (816) 926-6982
<www.archives.gov/facilities/mo/kansas_city.html>

Newberry Library
60 W. Walton St.
Chicago, IL 60610
(312) 943-9090
<www.newberry.org>

Public Library of Cincinnati and Hamilton County
800 Vine St.
Cincinnati, OH 45202
(513) 369-6900
<www.cincinnatilibrary.org>

Swenson Swedish Immigration Research Center
Augustana College
639 38th St.
Rock Island, IL 61201
(309) 794-7204
Fax: (309) 794-7443
<www.augustana.edu/administration/SWENSON>

Vesterheim Genealogical Center and Naeseth Library
415 W. Main St.
Madison, WI 53703
(608) 255-2224
Fax: (608) 255-6842
<www.vesterheim.org/genealogy.html>

Western Reserve Historical Society
10825 East Blvd.
Cleveland, OH 44106
(216) 721-5722 or (216) 721-5727
<www.wrhs.org>

WEB SITES

Bureau of Land Management General Land Office Records
<www.glorecords.blm.gov>: All the Midwestern states were "public land states," so they are included in this database of land patents covering 1820 to 1908.

Downward Bound: Honoring Those Who Worked the Great Lakes
<www.mfhn.com/glsdb>

CHICAGO

BY MELANIE RIGNEY

You'll be blown away by the Windy City's family research opportunities. Chicago remains a city of neighborhoods, and a number of them have, just steps from public transportation, places where you can find out what your ancestors in the old country wore, ate, and did.

Any genealogist's trip to Chicago has to start at the **Newberry Library** [60 West Walton Street; (312) 943-9090; <www.newberry.org>], and when you get there, you're likely to never want to leave. Its local history collection includes works from across this country as well as Canada and the British Isles. Copies of every federal census nationwide from 1790 to 1850 and every state census through 1850 are available; for Midwest states, federal census holdings are complete through 1880. You also can find more than seventeen thousand genealogies. The amazing thing is that access to all this information is free; all you need for a reader's card is a photo ID and proof of current address. The Newberry does encourage donations—$50 for an adult to become an associate for a year. The library offers free tours on Thursdays and Saturdays. Take the Red Line subway to the Chicago Avenue stop; the Newberry is just a short walk away, and parking is rare and expensive here.

It's just a short cab or bus ride north to the **Chicago Historical Society** [Clark Street at North Avenue; (312) 642-4600; <www.chicagohs. org>]. The society has some twenty million photos, drawings, diaries, letters, and costumes representing Chicago's history.

Just a few miles away from the Newberry (take the Chicago Avenue bus west if you're comfortable with big-city environments) but in an entirely different world is the **Polish Museum of America** [984 North Milwaukee Avenue; (773) 384-3352; <pma.prcua.org>]. While many Eastern Europeans lived in the area at the turn of the century, it's now primarily a Latino com-

Chicago's Newberry Library houses one of the nation's leading genealogy collections.

munity. Nonetheless, the museum is a paean to all things Polish, from costumes and uniforms to a painting of Casimir Pulaski, the Pole who's known as the father of the American cavalry. (Chicago has the largest Polish population outside of Warsaw and celebrates Pulaski Day each March). Around the corner in the same building is the **Polish Genealogical Society of America** <www.pgsa.org>.

Not to worry if your roots aren't Polish. There's plenty more digging to be done in Chicago. The **DuSable Museum of African-American History** [740 East Fifty-sixth Place; (773) 947-0600; <www.dusablemuseum.org>] is the nation's oldest nonprofit institution devoted to African-American history. The permanent collection of photographs, art objects, and memorabilia has more than thirteen thousand items. You won't be far from Chicago's terrific **Museum of Science and Industry** [Fifty-seventh

Street and Lake Shore Drive; (773) 684-3323; <www.msichicago.org>] and the prestigious University of Chicago, but if you choose to visit these fine attractions, rent a car rather than relying on public transportation.

The **Balzekas Museum of Lithuanian Culture** [6500 South Pulaski Road; (773) 582-6500] focuses on the period from 1918 to World War II when Lithuania was independent and also documents the successful independence movement of the 1990s. You can see armor and other objects collected by the founder and learn about the process of carving those beautiful eggs. Balzekas also has a Children's Museum of Immigrant History that gives the kids an idea of what their ancestors would have worn when they came from Lithuania and elsewhere. The museum also serves as the postal address for the Lithuanian American Genealogy Society.

Speaking of Easter eggs, you can find out more about the colored variety at the **Ukrainian National Museum** [721 North Oakley Boulevard; (312) 421-8020; <www.ukrntlmuseum.org>]. It also has information about folk arts, musical instruments, and other artifacts and a collection of more than sixteen thousand books.

The Irish found a comfy home in Chicago and still have a major impact in city politics. (Hizzoner Rich Daley and his father, who was mayor practically forever, both have Irish roots.)

The Windy City also boasts endless cultural attractions, such as the renowned Art Institute of Chicago.

It's no surprise that the city is home to the **Irish American Heritage Center** on the Northwest Side [4626 North Knox; (773) 282-7035; <www.irishamhc.com>]. There's a small museum with a nice collection of Irish lace and maps that show Ireland's contributions to the world back to the sixth century.

Don't let the Minnesotans tell you they're the only ones who know about Swedish immigration. The **Swedish American Museum Center** [5211 North Clark Street; (773) 728-8111; <www.samac.org>] celebrates the history and culture of these immigrants, especially the ones who came to Chicago. The museum is located in the heavily Swedish pocket of Andersonville. Be sure to check out the marzipan princess torte at the nearby **Swedish Bakery** [5348 North Clark Street; (773) 561-8919; <www.swedishbakery.com>] and the famous cinnamon rolls at **Ann Sather** [5207 North Clark Street; (773) 271-6677; <www.annsather.com>].

Much of Chicago's Greek community had to relocate due to the University of Illinois-Chicago expansion decades ago, though you can still find some excellent Greek restaurants in the area if you take the Blue Line train to Halsted or exit the Eisenhower Expressway at Halsted and head north. But if it's Greek history you seek, you don't need to leave downtown. The **Hellenic Museum and Cultural Center** [168 North Michigan Avenue, Fourth Floor; (312) 726-1234; <www.hellenicmuseum.org>] is a short walk from the **Art Institute of Chicago** <www.artic.edu> and aims to preserve the Greek immigration experience.

We're just scratching the surface of the Second City's ethnic resources. Within an hour's drive or train ride of downtown, you can find even more resource centers for Assyrians to Slovenes and practically everyone in between. For more information on Chicago's ethnic museums and special events, see the Convention and Tourism Bureau's Web site <chicago.il.org>—the office doesn't help individual travelers with trips.

Of course, you can also find resources at the **National Archives and Records Administration Great Lakes Region** [7358 South Pulaski Road; (773) 581-7816; <www.archives.gov/facilities/il/chicago.html>], which maintains retired records from federal agencies and courts in Illinois, Indiana, Michigan, Minnesota, Ohio, and Wisconsin. And don't miss the main public library, the **Harold Washington Library Center** [400 South State Street; (312) 747-4300; <www.chipublib.org>].

Because driving in downtown Chicago and nearby areas isn't for the fainthearted, you may want to stay downtown. We especially like the **Embassy Suites Chicago** [600 North State Street; (312) 943-3800; <www.embassysuites.com>] because it's close to the Red Line subway's Grand Avenue stop, which can then take you to a White Sox or Cubs game easily or at least connect you with most other areas where you want to go in the city. **Papagus Greek Taverna** [(312) 642-8450], located in the hotel, is an excellent Greek restaurant, owned by Chicago's biggest restaurant company, Lettuce Entertain You. Lettuce has more than two dozen restaurants in the metro area, and the themes range from Italian to seafood to fine and casual dining; check out <www.lettuceentertainyou.com> for more information.

If you'd like to do some power shopping on North Michigan Avenue while you're in town, soak up eighty-plus years of history at the **Drake Hotel** [140 East Walton Place; (312) 787-2200], and be sure to take time out for high tea at its Palm Court. For something smaller and a little less pricey, consider the **Raphael Hotel** [201 East Delaware; (312) 943-5000], near the **Museum of Contemporary Art** [220 E. Chicago Avenue; (312) 280-2660, <www.mcachicago.org>].

Many of us are familiar with poet Carl Sandburg's characterization of Chicago as "hog butcher for the world . . . city of the big shoulders." But in that same poem, Sandburg challenged Chicago's detractors to "show me another city with lifted head singing/so proud to be alive and coarse and strong and cunning." It's a fitting tribute for a city that's grown to greatness through its immigrants.

CINCINNATI

BY SUSAN WENNER JACKSON

People with roots in the city of Cincinnati should consider themselves lucky—I know I do. Three-quarters of my ancestors settled in the Queen City during the mid- to late-nineteenth century, and most of their offspring have stayed here into the twenty-first century. A few years ago, when I began researching my family history, I realized just how wealthy this area is in genealogical resources. Among these are a top-rate, major public library with a genealogy department and a historical society with impressive research collections.

The best place to start searching for your Cincinnati roots (or your roots almost anyplace else, for that matter) is the **Public Library of Cincinnati and Hamilton County** [800 Vine Street; (513) 369-6900; <www.cincinnatilibrary.org>]. Located in the heart of downtown, the library offers a dizzying array of resources for genealogists. Head up to the third floor and begin with the History and Genealogy Department. Here you can find special collections, electronic resources, publications, and locator materials. Pick up at the reference desk free brochures that cover both general research and specific interests, such as German family history resources and the Civil War collection. The library's special collections include African-American books and microfilm records, atlases and maps (such as Sanborn fire insurance maps), all U.S. census records from 1790 to 1930, Cincinnati history materials, city directories from across the country, ten thousand compiled family histories, fourteen hundred genealogical magazines and newsletters (plus PERSI), military records, passenger lists, and travel guides.

Professional genealogist Carol Mahan, who

The Public Library of Cincinnati and Hamilton County boasts a top-10 genealogy collection.

specializes in Cincinnati research, points out a few other library resources that may be particularly helpful: "Be sure to check out the Bicentennial Microfilming Project of Hamilton County churches, cemeteries, and funeral home records for local Cincinnati research. For Catholic church research in Cincinnati, check out Jeffrey Herbert's restored marriage, church burial, and cemetery books. For German research, check out Herbert's German newspaper indexes."

Just about any Cincinnati researcher will benefit from a visit to the library, but what next? It all depends on how far back your family settled here; what countries they came from; and their religious, professional, and other affiliations. Most locals will tell you to order a copy of the *Guide to Genealogical Resources in Cincinnati and Hamilton County, Ohio* compiled by Connie Stunkel Terheiden and Kenny R. Burck (Hamilton County Chapter of the Ohio Genealogical Society, $6.50). "I cannot recommend this forty-two-page book enough," says Theresa Bengel, a professional genealogist in Cincinnati. "It is just filled with oodles of information that is a must for all family and professional genealogists and well worth the cost." The guide includes local historical maps, census roll numbers, a list of newspapers, church

genealogies, record locations and availability, Web sites, books, and much more. To order this book, print and fill out the form at <members.aol.com/ogshc/pubform.htm>, and mail it with a check for $8 to the **Hamilton County Chapter of the Ohio Genealogical Society** [P.O. Box 15865, Cincinnati, Ohio 45215, (513) 956-7078, <members.aol.com/ogshc>].

Vital records are likely to be at the top of your list of things to do, particularly regarding those ancestors who lived in Cincinnati in 1874 or later. Birth and death records are held at several offices, each with varying public access and covering different time periods. If your ancestors lived inside the city limits, their birth and death records are most likely at the **Cincinnati Elm Street Health Center** [1525 Elm Street; (513) 352-3120; <www.cincinnatihealth.org/VitalStat.htm>]. To access birth records for 1874 to the present and death records for 1865 to the present, call ahead to make an appointment. For ancestors who lived in Hamilton County but outside Cincinnati, check the **Hamilton County General Health District** [250 William Howard Taft Road; (513) 946-7804; <www.hamilton-co.org/boh>] for birth records for 1875 to the present and death records for 1891 to the present. Call ahead to make an appointment for research.

At the **William Howard Taft Center** [230 East Ninth Street; (513) 946-3600], otherwise known as the Hamilton County Courthouse, key family history documents are held by both the **Common Pleas Clerk of Courts** [(513) 946-5666] and the **Hamilton County Probate Court** [(513) 946-3600]. The clerk's office has microfilmed records of naturalization, declaration of intent, court dockets, judgments, lawsuits, divorces, and criminal and civil court cases. The probate court holds marriage records, administration index and estate records, guardianship records, wills, and marriage banns.

Nearby on Court Street, you may want to stop by the **Hamilton County Administration**

Building (138 East Court Street). Inside, the **Recorder's Office** [(513) 946-4600] has deeds, leases, mortgages, military grave locations and discharge records, and county atlases and maps. The **Auditor's Office** [(513) 946-4000] offers access to plat maps (1940 to the present), owners and addresses, and field cards indicating when buildings were constructed.

Don't forget that Cincinnati is located on the banks of the Ohio River, so your ancestors may have been Kentuckians at some point. "It was not uncommon for families to traverse back and forth across the Ohio," Bengel says. The **Kenton County Public Library** [502 Scott Boulevard, Covington, Kentucky; (859) 491-7610; <www.kenton.lib.ky.us>] is just across the river and can be helpful if you have any northern Kentucky roots to trace. Ask the Local History Department for a copy of the library's *Local History and Genealogical User Guide* to get you started.

When visiting the Queen City, your best bets for lodging are in the downtown area. That's where the bulk of the city's genealogical resources are located, as well as many of the city's other attractions. For a bit of luxury and history combined, the **Cincinnatian Hotel** [601 Vine Street; (513) 381-3000; <www.cincinnatianhotel.com>] is an excellent choice. Built in 1882, this grand building is a National Trust Historic Hotel, and it's located in the center of downtown. If you have an afternoon free, reserve your spot in the Cricket Lounge for a lovely English tea service. Other convenient lodging options are the **Westin** [21 East Fifth Street; (513) 621-7700; <www.starwood.com/westin/search/hotel_detail.html?propertyID=1044>] and the **Millennium Hotel Cincinnati** [141 West Sixth Street; (513) 352-2100].

If you need an activity that will please both genealogists and nongenealogists, definitely visit the **Cincinnati Museum Center** [1301 Western Avenue; (800) 733-2077; <www.cincymuseum.org>]. Housed in Cincinnati's former railroad terminal, the museum center houses the Cincinnati History Museum, the Museum of Natural History and Science, and the Cinergy Children's Museum. It's also home to the **Cincinnati Historical Society** and all its vast research collections of materials relating to the Greater Cincinnati area, the state of Ohio, and the Old Northwest Territory. While your kids or spouse watch an Omnimax film or explore a glacier exhibit, you can consult the society's printed works collection of books, pamphlets, periodicals, and maps; manuscript collection; and audiovisual collection in the library's reading room.

Ground was broken in June 2002 on the Cincinnati riverfront for the **National Underground Railroad Freedom Center** [(513) 412-6900; <www.undergroundrailroad.org>]. When completed in 2004, this center will be an important monument to the struggle to abolish slavery.

Cincinnati is home to other fascinating historical attractions. The **Cincinnati Fire Museum** [315 West Court Street; (513) 621-5571; <www.cincyfiremuseum.com>] preserves and displays two hundred years' worth of artifacts of firefighting in the greater Cincinnati area (such as the oldest surviving fire engine in Cincinnati). See where the author of *Uncle Tom's Cabin* lived: the **Harriet Beecher Stowe House** [2950 Gilbert Avenue; (513) 632-5120; <www.ohiohistory.org/places/stowe>]. Tour the boyhood home of a Cincinnati-born U.S. president: the **William Howard Taft National Historic Site** [2038 Auburn Avenue; (513) 684-3262; <www.nps.gov/wiho>].

DETROIT

BY CANDACE L. DORIOTT

As much as Detroit seems to be a city of the modern age, pistoning at the pace of the automobile, it actually celebrated its three hundredth birthday in 2001.

Antoine Cadillac founded the city as D'étroit

The Detroit Historical Museum demonstrates the Motor City's most famous industry.

in 1701. Ruled by the French until 1760, Detroit was then under British control before finally becoming part of the United States in 1796. When the Michigan Territory was created in 1805, Detroit was still mostly a French-speaking community.

You can immerse yourself in the city's past at the **Detroit Historical Museum** [5401 Woodward Avenue; (313) 833-1805; <www.detroit historical.org>]. Admission is $4.50 for adults. There you can walk the Streets of Old Detroit, from log to cobblestone to brick, and visit shops and businesses from past eras.

Neighbors of the museum in the city's Cultural Center include Wayne State University, The Detroit Institute of Arts, and the **Detroit Public Library** [5201 Woodward Avenue; (313) 833-1000; <www.detroit.lib.mi.us>]. The "DPL," open Tuesday through Saturday, should be the genealogist's headquarters in Detroit.

The DPL's **Burton Historical Collection** [(313) 833-1480; <www.detroit.lib.mi.us/burton>] is a treasury of primary and secondary source materials for family researchers. Among its holdings are U.S. and Canadian county and local histories, federal censuses for all states and some Canadian provinces, land and military records, genealogies, and photographs. The thirty-eight-volume set of *American State Papers* is here, as

are many city directories. Church holdings include microfilmed records of **Ste. Anne de Detroit** [1000 Ste. Anne; (313) 496-1701], founded in 1701 and the only area church until after the War of 1812. Protestants also used its services for baptism, marriage, and burial.

Manuscripts, including family papers, correspondence, ledgers, scrapbooks, voyageur licenses, and Detroit's earliest Colonial records, make up a significant share of Burton's holdings. Since many individuals prominent in Michigan history moved here from other places, it's not unusual for family papers such as wills, marriage registers, and slaveholders' inventories to have originated elsewhere. City archives and those of Wayne County and Michigan Territory provide probate, tax, and other early records. Children's Aid Society and Children's Home of Detroit records may also provide information on an orphaned ancestor.

Unfortunately, most of Burton's collection is not included in DPL's online catalog, except for material acquired since 1987. You need to rely on published guides to locate the rest of the material. Burton is a reference library, so material must be used on-site. If you can't get there, contact someone from the available list of researchers for help.

Three other DPL departments hold material of interest. Old newspapers are available on microfilm in the General Information Department. The Great Lakes Patent & Trademark Center is useful for finding inventive ancestors. The Map Collection contains wonderful old maps. If your forebears owned property in Wayne County outside of Detroit in 1855, look for their names on John Farmer's Map of Wayne County Michigan. Some maps from the 1700s name earlier property owners in Detroit and Macomb County.

Kitty-corner from DPL is the **Walter Reuther Library at Wayne State University** [5401 Cass Avenue; (313) 577-4024; <www.reuther. wayne.edu>]. Its focus is the development of labor unions and related social, economic, and political reform movements. Besides union archives, the holdings include personal papers, family correspondence, and audiovisuals, such as photographic collections from Detroit newspapers back to the early 1900s. Oral history projects include Women and Work, minorities, and Depression-era artists and writers.

If your ancestors owned property in Detroit or Wayne County, visit the **Wayne County Register of Deeds Office** [International Center Building, 400 Monroe Street, Sixth Floor; (313) 224-5854; <www.waynecountylandrecords.com>]. Its index of land transactions goes back to 1703; the office is working on an online database you can search from home. Ribbon farms of early Detroit settlers extended up the shoreline into what became Macomb County, so some records are at the **Macomb County Clerk's Office** [40 North Main Street, First Floor, Mount Clemens; (810) 469-5120; <www.libcoop.net/sabaugh/clerkindex.htm>]. Macomb separated from Detroit in 1818; the clerk's office has vital records since 1867 and marriage records since 1819.

If your research reveals ancestors who died in Detroit, check out **Mount Elliott Cemetery** [1701 Mount Elliott Road; (313) 567-0048] or **Elmwood Cemetery** [1200 Elmwood Avenue; (313) 567-3453]. Elmwood also offers black heritage tours highlighting historic grave sites.

The Streets of Old Detroit exhibit at the historical museum recaptures life in your ancestors' era.

If you're coming to Detroit to do research, staying at **Hotel St. Regis** [3071 West Grand Boulevard; (313) 873-3000], within a mile of the libraries, is particularly convenient. The downtown and riverfront areas offer accommodation options, but these are a bit farther away.

The closest dining, if you're at the Detroit Public Library, is across the street in **The Detroit Institute of Arts** [5200 Woodward Avenue; (313) 833-7900; <www.dia.org>] or at the **Small World Café** in the International Institute [111 East Kirby Street; (313) 874-2233].

Other recommended restaurant options are

- **Twingo's Café** [4710 Cass Avenue; (313) 832-3832]—French inspired
- **Traffic Jam & Snug Restaurant** [511 West Canfield; (313) 831-9470]—always interesting
- **Deli Unique** [3663 Woodward Avenue; (313) 833-8810]—cafeteria style
- **Duet** [3663 Woodward Avenue; (313) 831-3838]—expensive, but worth the splurge
- **JaDa** [546 East Larned Street; (313) 965-1700]—upscale BBQ and southern
- **Blue Nile Ethiopian Restaurant** [508 Monroe Street; (313) 964-6699]—something a little different
- Any Greektown restaurant

Unfortunately for out-of-towners, the Motor City lifestyle has prevented development of rapid transit. The Detroit People Mover, a monorail system circling the downtown and riverfront area, is the only useful public transportation for visitors. (See a handy unofficial transit map at <members.aol.com/wingsrgr8/DPM>.) If you stay at a downtown hotel, the People Mover is a great way to get to restaurants and the Register of Deeds, but it doesn't extend up Woodward Avenue to the library. To get around to all the research spots, you need one of the things Detroit is most famous for—an automobile.

A sweeping renovation will make the Allen Couunty Public Library even better for genealogists.

FORT WAYNE

BY ALLISON STACY

Roots researchers reserve the term *mecca* for Salt Lake City, home of the Family History Library (FHL). But when they describe genealogical nirvana, another destination quickly comes to mind: Fort Wayne, Indiana.

Family history is a top tourist attraction in this Midwestern metropolis—nearly 110,000 people travel here each year just to trace their roots. The reason it's on every researcher's radar: Indiana's second-largest city boasts the second-largest genealogy library in the world, the **Fred J. Reynolds Historical Genealogy Department** at the **Allen County Public Library** [900 Webster Street; (260) 421-1225; <www.acpl.lib.in.us/genealogy>]. The department has amassed a whopping 317,000-plus printed volumes, including 49,000 family histories and more than 306,000 microform records.

The Allen County Public Library's (ACPL) collection is surpassed only by that of the FHL, and ACPL's tops among public libraries.

If you're planning a trip any time soon, note that in January 2003 the library moves to an interim location at 200 East Berry Street, known locally as Renaissance Square. This temporary headquarters, necessary while the library undergoes a two-to-three-year renovation, is five blocks east of the regular library. You'll find some free parking as well as a pay parking garage across the street and more than 150 nearby metered spaces. For genealogists, the interim location also means getting your hands on the library's collection more readily: It will be a browsing collection of open shelves, no need to request materials.

When you arrive at the library, register and pick up PathFinder research guides. These thirteen pamphlets outline resources for ethnic ancestries, source types, and special topics. Ask to watch the orientation video, which explains library materials and procedures.

Besides its numerous compiled genealogies, the department owns more than 150,000 local history books. Look for these sources in either the online catalog or the card catalog.

If another researcher published an article about your family, you're in the right place to find it—the ACPL has the world's biggest English-language collection of family and local history periodicals. To help patrons tap these publications' contents, genealogy staff developed the *Periodical Source Index* (PERSI), accessible through Ancestry.com, on CD-ROM, and in print. All the indexed articles are at the library.

Of course, genealogy's trademark is microfilm, and the library has plenty of that, too. This is one of the few public libraries that has the entire U.S. census. Here you can also dig into state and territorial censuses covering eighteen states. For finding ancestors from up north, the ACPL has every Canadian census taken from 1666 to 1891. The library holds most National Archives passenger lists and indexes, as well most military service and pension records. Use the microtext catalog—a separate directory of filmed materials—to locate these sources.

ACPL offers plenty of electronic resources, too. All the FHL's FamilySearch databases are available here on CD-ROM, along with a long list of reference databases. Like the other genealogical materials, these electronic sources can be used only on-site, so prepare to spend much of your Fort Wayne visit cramming in research.

Still, there's plenty of historical fun to be had when you tire of scouring the umpteenth *Johnson Family History*. At the **Firefighter's Museum** [226 West Washington Boulevard; (260) 426-0051] you can tour an 1893 engine house and eat lunch amidst relics of fire fighting at the museum's **Old No. 3 Firehouse Café**.

On the east side of downtown, the **History Center** [302 East Berry Street; (260) 426-2882] houses the Old City Hall Historical Museum, Fort Wayne's historical seat of government and criminal detainment (it was also the local jail). Here you can see Gen. "Mad" Anthony Wayne's camp bed, Miami chief Little Turtle's watch, and sundry other artifacts. If you have roots in this area, make an appointment to research in the **Allen County Historical Society**'s archives, also in the History Center.

Civil War buffs should head across the street to the **Lincoln Museum** [200 East Berry Street; (260) 455-3864; <www.thelincolnmuseum. org>]. Honest Abe didn't have personal ties to this area, but the city is home to the Lincoln National Life Insurance Company. Arthur Hall, the company's founder and a lifelong Lincoln admirer, established the research foundation that created this museum in 1931. Interactive exhibits are there to teach you what life was like for Lincoln—and your ancestors. You can read the president's mail, decorate the White House,

or fight a Civil War battle. As you follow Berry Street back toward the library, you'll spy the **Allen County Courthouse** [715 Calhoun Street; (260) 449-4246], one of the city's architectural gems.

Fort Wayne's best-known historical claim to fame is that it's the burial site of John Chapman, a.k.a. Johnny Appleseed. Each fall, the city honors the legendary tree planter in a festival at **Johnny Appleseed Park**.

Of course, you'll also need places to rest and refuel for your next big day of research. Two downtown hotels are within walking distance of the ACPL, and both cater to family historians with a "genealogy package" discount. The **Hilton Fort Wayne Convention Center** [1020 South Calhoun Street; (260) 420-1100; <www. hilton.com>], at the corner of Calhoun Street and Washington Boulevard, sits a mere two blocks from the library's permanent location. The **Holiday Inn Downtown** [300 East Washington Boulevard; (260) 422-5511; <www.sixcontinentshotels.com/holiday-inn>] is three blocks farther down Washington.

Outside downtown, the **Fort Wayne Marriott** [305 East Washington Center Road; (800) 228-0265] and **Travelodge** [4606 Lincoln Highway East; (260) 422-9511] also offer family-history discounts. Bed-and-breakfast buffs can sojourn at the **Carole Lombard House** [704 Rockhill Street; (260) 426-9896] in the historic West Central neighborhood.

Fort Wayne has been called "the city of restaurants," so you won't have a tough time achieving dining nirvana. These eateries serve up a slice of the past:

- **Catablu** [2441 Broadway; (260) 456-6563]— casual cuisine in a historic theater
- **Don Hall's Old Gas House** [305 East Superior Street; (260) 426-3411; <www.donhalls.com/ pages/gashouse>]—prime rib, seafood, steaks, and Cajun cuisine in a circa-1907 building
- **Fort Wayne's Famous Coney Island Wiener Stand** [131 West Main Street; (260) 424-

2997]—serving hot dogs since 1914

- **Toast & Jam** [426 East Wayne Street; (260) 422-4JAM (422-4526), <homepages.msn.com/StageSt/toastnjam>]—Victorian dining and acoustic music in an 1888 treasure house turned coffeehouse

Once you get your fill of Hoosier history, rest up for more research. A trip to Fort Wayne will only increase your appetite for family history.

KANSAS CITY

BY CRYSTAL CONDE

Kansas City, the "Heart of America," is less than two thousand miles from virtually any location in the continental United States. For much of the nineteenth century, the traffic through the Kansas City area was mostly westward: Many pioneers and famous explorers such as Lewis and Clark passed through here on their way to the frontier. That left the area teeming with history for you to tap.

Your first stop, though, might actually be about thirty minutes east of Kansas City, in Independence, Missouri. The **Mid-Continent Public Library** [317 West 24 Highway, Independence; (816) 252-7228; <www.mcpl.lib.mo.us>] houses twelve thousand square feet of resources in its genealogy and local history branch, making it one of the best libraries for genealogy in the country. It's huge, so ask for a tour on your first visit to get acquainted.

Once you have a grasp of all the library has to offer, you can begin researching. You can find an abundance of records on microfilm, including the recently released 1930 census. Other riches include U.S. land sales in Missouri for 1818 through 1903, Missouri State Penitentiary records from 1836 through 1931, papers of the St. Louis fur trade, service records of Missouri Union and Confederate soldiers, Native American sources, the *Independence Examiner*, and the *Kansas City Star* and *Times*.

The library's **North Independence Branch**, next door, makes its more than six thousand genealogy and local history books available on interlibrary loan to residents of the Kansas City area. You can write the library for a free copy of *Genealogy From the Heartland*, a guide to the titles in its genealogy circulation collection.

The library offers free monthly classes on a variety of subjects ranging from getting started in genealogy to using the Internet for research. Basic charts and helpful worksheets are also available on the library's Web site.

Are your roots buried in Jackson County, Missouri? If so, while in Independence you should also visit the **Jackson County Historical Society Archives & Research Library** [Independence Square Courthouse, 112 West Lexington Avenue, Suite 103, Independence; (816) 252-7454; <www.jchs.org>]. The society's library houses wonderful historical artifacts to help you learn more about how your ancestors lived. Although it's not a major genealogical library, some materials in the society's collection are helpful and date back to 1826, when the county was formed. A sample of the collection includes city directories, indexes to Jackson County marriages from 1851 through 1892, U.S. census indexes from 1830 to 1870, and death records for Kansas City from 1874 through 1895. The historical society's library has a bookshop with more than one thousand titles for sale.

If your ancestors journeyed westward via the Santa Fe, Oregon, California, or Mormon Trail, you can research them and their migration at the **Merrill J. Mattes Research Library** at the **National Frontier Trails Center** in Independence [318 West Pacific, Independence; (816) 325-7575; <www.frontiertrailscenter.com>]. The research facility has manuscripts, thousands of maps, periodicals, photos, drawings, and microfilm records pertaining to the American West. Other collections range from archaeology to the Pony Express, mining, buffalo, military history, and Native Americans. Reference materials and artifacts date primarily from 1800 to 1880. More than twenty-three hundred trail diaries and letters offer a glimpse into the past. Call to set up an appointment to conduct research.

After you exhaust your research opportunities in Independence, head west to the big city itself and the **Kansas City Public Library** [311 E. Twelfth Street (new location at Tenth and Baltimore Streets by mid-2003); (816) 701-3505; <www.kclibrary.org>]. Historical materials and documents relating to the city and its surrounding area date to when the library was established in 1873. The local history collection boasts a newspaper clipping file of more than 200,000 articles dating to 1900; it's stored on microfilm and microfiche. Archival collections include photos, scrapbooks, letters, diaries, postcards, and personal documents that might give you a glimpse into your ancestor's life.

The library's special collections department has a unique series of out-of-print, nineteenth-century county histories of the Midwest and emigration areas in Missouri. It also boasts an excellent Western Americana series, with nineteenth-century publications containing pioneers' journal and diary transcripts.

Not far from the public library lies one of the most comprehensive collections of pre-Civil War steamboat cargo. The *Arabia* **Steamboat Museum** [400 Grand Boulevard; (816) 471-1856; <www.1856.com>] is home to more than 200,000 artifacts recovered from the steamboat *Arabia*, which was excavated from a farmer's crop field in 1988. View thousands of printed calico buttons, glass trade beads, boots, and other treasures.

The museum-hopping continues at the nearby **Kansas City Museum** [Union Station; (816) 483-8300; <www.kcmuseum.com>], where interactive history exhibits let you relive the past. Regional history displays illustrate a trading post, a log cabin, a blacksmith's shop, an old-fashioned soda fountain, and more.

The other must in your itinerary as you search for facts about your Kansas City ancestors is a stop at the **National Archives and Research Administration Central Plains Region** research facility [2312 East Bannister Road; (816) 926-6920; <www.archives.gov/facilities/mo/kansas_city.html>]. You can find the federal censuses for all states for 1790 to 1930; indexes for the 1880, 1900, 1910, and 1920 censuses; and some military service records and indexes. Censuses and land allotment files for Native Americans are also on microfilm here. To get a taste of Kansas City's history, check out the original records, which include photos, maps, and architectural drawings.

Before you make a trip to NARA's Kansas City branch, check to make sure the documents and records you want to view are housed there. In your correspondence, include your address and phone number.

With all that research, you can work up quite an appetite. Try these centrally located restaurants:

- **Trago** [1108 Grand Boulevard; (816) 221-2055]
- **Tio's** [1317 Grand Boulevard; (816) 221-8646]
- **Italian Gardens** [1110 Baltimore Avenue; (816) 221-9311]
- **Park View Café** [901 Locust Street; (816) 471-6677]

For a real taste of Kansas City culinary history, of course, you need to detour to **Arthur Bryant's BBQ** [1727 Brooklyn Avenue; (816) 231-1123], perhaps the nation's most famous barbecue establishment.

For lodging, try these convenient hotels:

- **Holiday Inn** [1215 Wyandotte Street; (800) 465-4329]
- **Doubletree Hotel** [1301 Wyandotte Street; (800) 222-TREE]
- **Savoy Hotel** [219 West Ninth Street; (816) 842-3575]
- **Historic Suites of America** [612 Central Street; (816) 842-6544]

MILWAUKEE

BY DAVID A. FRYXELL

If you have roots in Wisconsin and the upper Midwest, you need to know that there's more to Milwaukee than beer. Yes, it is the home of **Miller Brewing** [4251 West State Street; (414) 931-BEER (931-2337)]. Yes, the sudsy legacy of Capt. Frederick Pabst lives on in such historic sites as the **Pabst Theater**, an 1895 Baroque historic landmark [144 East Wells Street; (414) 286-3663], and the thirty-seven-room, fourteen-fireplace, 1892 **Pabst Mansion** [2000 West Wisconsin Avenue; (414) 931-0808]. And, sure, Milwaukee has days when the perfume of brewer's yeast tempts I-94 commuters to roll down their windows and take a deep sniff.

But Milwaukee also boasts a rich ethnic heritage (perhaps not unrelated to the origins of its brewing industry). Germans helped build the city in the nineteenth century, and the city remains home to some of the nation's best German restaurants, including **Karl Ratszch's** [320 East Mason Street; (414) 276-2720] and **Mader's** [1037 North Old World Third Street; (414) 271-3377]. Milwaukee has also seen influxes of Irish, Poles, and Italians, who similarly contributed mightily to the dining scene, as evidenced by the richly authentic **Mimma's** [1307 East Brady Street; (414) 271-7337]. Milwaukee is even home to one of the country's few fine Serbian restaurants, the **Old Town Serbian Gourmet House** [522 West Lincoln Avenue; (414) 672-0206].

Beneath the suds you can see a city rich in historical and genealogical resources. The best place to start, even before you travel, is the online guide to genealogical collections compiled by the Library Council of Metropolitan Milwaukee <www.uwm.edu/Library/arch/lcomm>; just use the pull-down menus at the bottom of the page to locate the records you're after. The site is hosted by the University of Wisconsin-Milwaukee, whose Golda Meir Library is home to the **Milwaukee Urban Archives** [2311 East Hartford Avenue; (414) 229-5402; <www.uwm.edu/Dept/Library/arch/genie.htm>]. You can find more than one hundred series of local governmental records, plus more than five hundred collections of papers and records, including those of civic clubs and unions.

Be sure to visit the **Milwaukee County Historical Society** [910 North Old World Third Street; (414) 273-8288; <www.milwaukeecountyhistsoc.org>]. Its handsome old museum has exhibits as well as archives of government and naturalization records and a photo collection. The **Milwaukee Public Library**'s 1898 landmark central library [814 West Wisconsin Avenue; (414) 286-3000; <www.mpl.org>] is home to the Great Lakes Marine Collection of logbooks and wreck reports, plus a collection of 3,192 photos of area World War I military personnel—maybe including one of your ancestors.

Take advantage of Milwaukee's specialized resources, too. If you have Catholic ancestors who might be buried in one of the eight cemeteries of the Archdiocese of Milwaukee, which

Modern Milwaukee was built by many ethnicities, including Germans, Italians, Irish, Poles, and Serbs.

covers southeastern Wisconsin, you can find them in a database at <www.cemeteries.org/genealogy/genealogy01.asp>. You can search for your Irish ancestors at the **Irish Cultural and Heritage Center of Wisconsin** [2133 West Wisconsin Avenue; (414) 345-8800], located in an 1887 national historic landmark.

Look for other genealogical help for the region from the **Milwaukee County Genealogical Society** [P.O. Box 270326, Milwaukee, Wisconsin 53227; <www.execpc.com/~mcgs>]. You may also want to consider a field trip to Madison, just ninety interstate minutes away, where the **Wisconsin Historical Society Library** [816 State Street, Madison; (608) 264-6535; <www.wisconsinhistory.org/library>] houses one of the nation's finest genealogical collections.

When you start to go cross-eyed from ogling microfilm, try sampling some of the area's ethnic and historical attractions. The **Milwaukee Public Museum** [800 West Wells Street; (414) 278-2702; <www.mpm.edu>] is best known for its dinosaurs and its re-creation of a tropical rain forest, but history buffs should walk the Streets of Old Milwaukee exhibit. This three-quarter-sized reproduction of a swath of turn-of-the-nineteenth-century Milwaukee includes twenty-five shops, restaurants, businesses, and bars your ancestors might have patronized. For a different take on business way back when, tour the **William F. Eisner Museum of Advertising and Design** [208 North Water Street; (414) 847-3290; <www.eisnermuseum.org>], the only museum of its kind in the country.

Milwaukee's (and the nation's) black heritage is preserved at the **Wisconsin Black Historical Society Museum** [2620 West Center Street; (414) 372-7677; <www.wbhsm.org>] and **America's Black Holocaust Museum** [2233 North Fourth Street; (414) 264-2500].

If your ancestors were clowns—literally—explore the **International Clown Hall of Fame** [161 West Wisconsin Avenue; (414) 319-0848; <www.clownmuseum.org>].

Best known for its brewing legacy, Milwaukee celebrates its sudsy past in landmarks old and new.

Two historical attractions are worth field trips out of town. Just thirty-five miles west in Eagle is **Old World Wisconsin** [S103 W37890 Highway 67, Eagle; (262) 594-6300; <www.wisconsinhistory.org/sites/oww/>], a re-creation of a nineteenth-century farm village. Costumed interpreters show life the way it was for your immigrant ancestors on six hundred acres little changed from the 1870s. About eighty miles north of Milwaukee, in the Lake Michigan port of Manitowoc, the **Wisconsin Maritime Museum** [75 Maritime Drive, Manitowoc; (920) 684-0218; <www.wimaritimemuseum.org>] celebrates the history of Great Lakes shipping.

When you're exhausted from exploring Milwaukee's genealogy resources and heritage, take a break with a favorite local product. No, we're not talking about beer again—Wisconsin is, after all, the Dairy State. Sample its bounty in frozen form at **Kopp's Frozen Custard** [three locations, <www.kopps.com>]. Trust us: One lick and you'll be looking for more Wisconsin ancestors, just to give you an excuse to return.

MINNEAPOLIS/ST. PAUL
BY DAVID A. FRYXELL

Despite what you may have seen in the movie *Fargo*, there's more to the Twin Cities of Minneapolis and St. Paul than ice, snow, and the Mall of America. And not everyone here has

The American Swedish Institute in Minneapolis is housed in a thirty-three-room former mansion.

(both state and federal), and local and church histories. New England researchers should check this surprising source, too, since the early founders of the Minnesota Historical Society were Yankees who left the society their papers and books.

If you get hungry while digging into the past, visit **Café Minnesota** [(651) 297-4859; <www.mnhs.org/market/cafemn>] inside the Minnesota History Center. This stylish restaurant is several cuts above standard cafeteria fare.

Across the river in Minneapolis, the **American Swedish Institute** [2600 Park Avenue; (612) 871-4907; <www.americanswedishinst.org>] celebrates the region's Swedish immigrant heritage in a style far grander than most Swedish newcomers ever knew. It's housed in a thirty-three-room mansion that once belonged to Swedish self-made millionaire Swan J. Turnblad. Exhibits range from immigrants' trunks to more than six hundred pieces of Swedish art glass. The institute's archives and library, which include records from Swedish ports, are open to the public by appointment; see <www.americanswedishinst.org/genealgy.htm> for more on the collection.

Another big draw is the **Immigration Research Center at the University of Minnesota** [311 Andersen Library, 222-21st Avenue; (612) 625-4800; <www.umn.edu/ihrc>]. The center collects records on immigration and ethnicity from across the country and is especially helpful for those with ancestors from southern, central, and eastern Europe and from the Near East.

For a look at how the other-richer-half lived, visit the house of railroad baron **James J. Hill** [240 Summit Avenue, St. Paul; (651) 297-2555; <www.mnhs.org/places/sites/jjhh>], who once boasted that if you gave him enough Swedish workers he could build a railroad straight to hell. His house, which cost nearly one million dollars in 1891, is now open for tours and doubles as a museum. (While you're on Summit Avenue, drive up and down to admire the mansions, and be sure to pause at the more modest

roots in Scandinavia, dontcha know, though the cities are indeed a rich resource for Viking genealogists (and home to the Sons of Norway fraternal order <www.sofn.com>).

The handsome, modern **Minnesota History Center** [345 West Kellogg Boulevard, St. Paul; (651) 296-6126; <www.mnhs.org/places/historycenter>] is a good place to start, whatever your ethnic roots. From a huge birch-bark canoe reminiscent of Minnesota's voyageur days to a twenty-four-ton boxcar recalling railroad history to Prince's *Purple Rain* costume, exhibits trace the state's historic high points. Don't miss the extensive library <www.mnhs.org/library>, the world's largest repository of Minnesota materials. The collection of the state's newspapers here is unmatched (including the archives of the *St. Paul Pioneer Press*, Minnesota's oldest newspaper). You can also find civil case files, tax and poll lists, school lists, all of Minnesota's censuses house, number 599, where F. Scott Fitzgerald lived.)

Other museums of interest include the **Hennepin History Museum** [2303 Third Avenue South, Minneapolis; (612) 870-1329; <www.hhmuseum.org>], strong on local history as well as Indian artifacts; the **Bakken Museum** [3537 Zenith Avenue South, Minneapolis; (612) 926-3878; <www.thebakken.org>], an unusual tribute to the history of electricity; and the **Science Museum of Minnesota**, which now also houses the equally unusual Questionable Medical Device Collection [120 W. Kellogg Boulevard, St. Paul; (651) 221-9444; <www.smm.org>], so you can see how your ancestors tried to cure what ailed them.

At the 1836 **Sibley House Historic Site** [on Highway 13 in Mendota; (651) 452-1596; <www.mnhs.org/places/sites/shs>] you can relive Minnesota's fur trading days. Just across the river in St. Paul at the 1820s **Fort Snelling** [(612) 726-1171; <www.mnhs.org/places/sites/hfs>] you can see what it was like to guard the frontier. Both are closed November through April. Farther to the south, in suburban Shakopee, **Murphy's Landing** is a living history museum that re-creates life in the 1840s to the 1890s along the Minnesota River [2187 East Highway 101; (952) 445-6901; <www.murphyslanding.org>].

For less wild and woolly exploration of the past, you can tap the **Minneapolis Public Library**'s main branch downtown [300 Nicollet Mall; (612) 630-6000; <www.mplib.org>] or the **St. Paul Public Library**'s main branch [90 West Fourth Street; (651) 266-7000; <www.stpaul.lib.mn.us/>]. The library of the **Minnesota Genealogical Society** [5768 Olson Memorial Highway, Golden Valley; (763) 595-9347; <www.mtn.org/mgs>] is open to the public; non-members pay $5 admission.

Because of the Minnesota History Center, visiting genealogists generally want to stay in downtown St. Paul. The historic, handsomely renovated **St. Paul Hotel** [350 Market Street;

The **Minnesota History Center** houses materials ranging from pioneers to Prince.

(651) 292-9292] is the clear choice here if your budget can bear it; likewise, for dining, opt for the hotel's **St. Paul Grill** [(651) 224-7455]. The **Radisson Hotel** [11 East Kellogg Boulevard; (651) 292-1900] is another solid choice, and its revolving rooftop **Carousel Restaurant** offers a panoramic view of the Mississippi River. Also consider the newer **Radisson City Center** [411 Minnesota Street; (651) 291-8800] and the more budget-friendly **Best Western Kelly Inn** [161 St. Anthony Avenue; (651) 227-8711], which is closest to the History Center and to the Minnesota State Capitol.

Other St. Paul restaurants worth noting include **W.A. Frost & Company** [374 Selby Avenue; (651) 224-5715], in the nineteenth-century Dacotah Building near the magnificent St. Paul Cathedral, and, when the season permits, the **No Wake Café** [Pier 1, Harriet Island; (651) 292-1411], a floating restaurant with a lovely view.

For those who don't want their choices to be limited, there's always the **Mall of America** [(952) 883-8800; <www.mallofamerica.com>], just a few minutes away in Bloomington, near the airport. This mall has forty-nine restaurants in addition to its 520 shops, its aquarium, and its indoor amusement park. (You can have fun even in the infamous Minnesota ice and snow—you betcha.)

The soaring Gateway Arch symbolizes the history of St. Louis as the "Gateway to the West."

ST. LOUIS

BY CRYSTAL CONDE

If your ancestors were lured west by the notion of abundant land and riverfront trade, chances are they settled in or near St. Louis, or at least passed through. Known as "The Gateway to the West," St. Louis is a city rich in genealogical treasures. With so many historical resources, deciding where to look can be a tricky task. So grab your city map, gather your research materials, and don't forget to take this handy guide on your pilgrimage.

First, explore the archives of the **St. Louis Mercantile Library** [8001 Natural Bridge Road, in the Thomas Jefferson Library Building; (314) 516-7240; <www.umsl.edu/mercantile>]. Located on the north campus of the University of Missouri-St. Louis, the library is the oldest west of the Mississippi River. Mercantile Library has one of the largest transportation collections in the region, with information such as passenger lists pertaining to waterways, railroads, and airlines. Original clippings from early-1900s issues of the *St. Louis Globe-Democrat*, as well as other historical newspapers on hard copy and microfilm, add to the library's genealogical appeal. Check Mercantile Library files to see if your ancestors were members. Membership is not mandatory in order to do research, but it

does have its perks. Copies cost thirty cents for nonmembers and only fifteen cents for members. Members are also allowed to check out materials. When you visit Mercantile Library, keep in mind that parking on campus can be tricky. If you plan to do extensive research, call the campus police department [(314) 516-5155] ahead of time to obtain a one-day parking permit.

Next, stop by the **Missouri Historical Society Library and Research Center** (225 South Skinker Boulevard; (314) 746-4599; <www.mohistory. org/LRC.html>). Here you can find extensive collections documenting the history of St. Louis, the state of Missouri, the Mississippi and Missouri Valleys, the Louisiana Purchase territory, and the American West.

The Research Center is divided into six collections. No appointment is necessary to use the general library and manuscript collections. Library collections include books, periodicals, newspapers, maps, and microfilms on topics such as American fur trade and the 1904 St. Louis World's Fair (immortalized in the movie and musical *Meet Me in St. Louis*). Among the Manuscript Collections, you can find papers relating to Lewis and Clark's 1804-1806 expedition, as well as records of free African Americans in St. Louis and elsewhere in Missouri.

To access the photographs and prints collections, broadcast media archives, architecture collections, or museum collections, call ahead to schedule an appointment. When you arrive, speak to one of the professional librarians or archivists for help accessing records. They can also assist you with photocopying, which costs twenty-five cents per page. The Library and Research Center is closed on Sundays and Mondays, so you might want to reserve those days for traveling.

For more genealogical resources, visit the **St. Louis County Library** [1640 South Lindbergh Boulevard; (314) 994-3300; <www.slcl.lib. mo.us>]. Tier 5 here is home to the library's special collections. Research tools include microfiche readers, two photocopiers, five computers, and six microfilm readers with printers. The prices for copies range from ten cents to twenty-five cents. Three-ring binders, purses, briefcases, bags, and personal or library books are prohibited in this facility.

You can search the Freedman's Bank records (on CD-ROM); World War I draft registration cards; city directories; and census, church, and cemetery records. The special collections department is also home to the Julius K. Hunter & Friends African-American Research Collection and the holdings of the **St. Louis Genealogical Society** [(314) 647-8547; <www.rootsweb.com/~mostlogs/stsociet.htm>]. For an in-depth look at tracing your roots in St. Louis, consult *Guide to Genealogical Research in St. Louis*, published by the society and available for sale on its Web site or at the county library.

Finally, dig in to one of the most comprehensive genealogy collections in St. Louis at the **St. Louis Public Library** downtown [1301 Olive Street; (314) 241-2288; <www.slpl.lib.mo.us>]. Park at one of the many metered spaces, and don't worry about what you take into the library—there are no restrictions. The history and genealogy department is on the second floor of the library. The department has census information available on microfilm, Soundex, plus city directories for the city of St. Louis from 1821 to 1980 and for St. Louis County from 1893 to 1979.

One of the most significant research resources the library has to offer is an electronic database called MapFind. The staff uses this program to access the library's enormous map collection. Find the information you need from the large-scale topographic maps of Missouri and Illinois, the historical St. Louis maps, and the medium-scale European maps. If you still can't find what you're looking for, ask the staff to retrieve one of the 100,000 maps from the basement.

Of course, while you're in St. Louis you should also visit the **St. Louis Gateway Arch** [(877) 982-1410; <www.stlouisarch.com>], located in the Jefferson National Expansion Memorial Park on the banks of the Mississippi. Designed by Eero Saarinen and dedicated in 1966, the stainless steel arch rises 630 feet high from a 60-foot foundation—making it the nation's tallest memorial. An underground visitor center features galleries celebrating America's westward expansion. Trams take you to an observation room at the top of the arch ($7 for adults, $3 for children ages three to twelve).

No matter what else you do, you'll need to eat. Try these centrally located restaurants:

- **Tequila's Mexican Restaurant** [116 North Sixth Street; (314) 621-1214]
- **Lorenzo's Trattoria on the Hill** [1933 Edwards Street; (314) 773-2223]
- **China Royal Restaurant** [5911 North Lindbergh Boulevard; (314) 731-1313]

For lodging, try these hotels:

- **Drury Inn** [201 South Twentieth Street; (314) 231-3900]
- **Holiday Inn** [811 North Ninth Street; (800) 465-4329]
- **Marriott Hotels & Resorts** [1 South Broadway; (800) 228-0265]
- **Travelodge** [9645 Natural Bridge Road; (314) 890-9000]

You can find more information on St. Louis travel and tourism online at Explore St. Louis <www.st-louis-cvc.com>. Also, check out the St. Louis Attractions site <www.stlouisattractions.com>. For restaurant and entertainment guides, see <www.geocities.com/HotSprings/2846/stlouis.html#CE>.

ILLINOIS

Statehood: 1818
Statewide Birth and Death Records Begin: 1916
Statewide Marriage Records Begin: 1962
Address for Vital Statistics:
Illinois Department of Public Health
Division of Vital Records
605 W. Jefferson St.
Springfield, IL 62702-5097
(217) 782-6553
<www.idph.state.il.us/vital/vitalhome.htm>

Available Censuses: U.S. federal censuses 1820, 1830, 1840, 1850, 1860, 1870, 1880, 1900, 1910, and 1920. Statewide surname indexes for the 1820, 1830, 1840, 1850, 1860, 1880, 1900, 1910, and 1920 censuses. Indexes for the 1870 census for Chicago and Cook County also available. Collected index to the 1810 to 1855 territorial, state, and federal censuses available. Records of many counties for the 1825, 1835, and 1845 state censuses missing or incomplete.

City Directories at the Family History Library Include: Chicago and Cook County 1839-1860, 1844-1901, and 1861-1929; Joliet 1872, 1875, 1877, 1881, 1884-1893, 1895-1906, 1908, 1909, 1912, 1914-1916, 1918, 1920, 1921, 1923, 1925, 1927, 1929, 1930, and 1932-1935; Moline 1855-58, 1901, and 1905-1935; Peoria 1844, 1850, 1856-1935, and 1972; Rockford 1857, 1859, 1865, 1880, and 1902-1935; Rock Island 1855-1859, 1882-1892, 1895-1897, 1899-1901, and 1905-1935; Springfield, 1849, 1855-1935

ILLINOIS

ORGANIZATIONS & ARCHIVES

Illinois Regional Archives Depository System (IRAD)
Margaret Cross Norton Building
Springfield, IL 62756
(217) 785-1266
Fax: (217) 524-3230
<www.sos.state.il.us/departments/archives/irad/iradholdings.html>

Illinois State Archives
Margret Cross Norton Building
Springfield, IL 62756
(217) 782-4682
Fax: (217) 524-3930
<www.sos.state.il.us/departments/archives/archives.html>

Illinois State Genealogical Society
P.O. Box 10195
Springfield, IL 62791
(217) 789-1968
<www.rootsweb.com/~ilsgs>

Illinois State Historical Library
1 Old State Capitol Plaza
Springfield, IL 62701
(217) 524-7216
Fax: (217) 785-6250
<www.state.il.us/hpa/lib>

Illinois State Historical Society
Old State Capitol
Springfield, IL 62701
(217) 525-2781
Fax: (217) 525-2783
<www.historyillinois.org>

Illinois State Library
300 S. Second St.
Springfield, IL 62701
(217) 782-7596
<www.library.sos.state.il.us/library/isl/isl.html>

RESOURCES

Chicago and Cook County Sources: A Guide to Research
by Loretto Dennis Szucs
(Ancestry Publishing Co., $16.95)

"Research in Illinois"
lecture by Sandra Hargreaves Luebking
(Audiotapes.com, $8.50)

Revolutionary Soldiers Buried in Illinois
by Harriet J. Walker
(Everton Publishers, out of print)

Roots on the Prairie: Tracing Your Illinois Ancestors
by Patricia A. Hamilton
(McLean County Historical Society, $5)

A Summary Guide to Local Governmental Records in the Illinois Regional Archives
(Illinois State Archives, $6)

PERIODICALS

Branching Out From St. Clair County
(1973-), Marissa Historical and Genealogical Society, P.O. Box 47, Marissa, IL 62257

Chicago Genealogist
(1968-),Chicago Genealogical Society, P.O. Box 1160, Chicago, IL 60690

The Circuit Rider
(1973-), Sangamon County Genealogical Society, P.O. Box 1829, Springfield, IL 62705

The Illiana Genealogist: Quarterly Publication of the Illiana Genealogical and Historical Society
(1965-), Illiana Genealogical and Historical Society, P.O. Box 207, Danville, IL 61834

Illinois State Genealogical Society Quarterly
(1969-), Illinois State Genealogical Society, P.O. Box 10195, Springfield, IL 62791

Prairie Roots
(1973-), Peoria Genealogical Society, P.O. Box 1489, Peoria, IL 61655

St. Clair County Genealogical Society Quarterly
(1978-), St. Clair County Genealogical Society, P.O. Box 431, Belleville, IL 62222

Where the Trails Cross
(1970-), South Suburban Genealogical and Historical Society, P.O.

Box 96, South Holland, IL 60473

WEB SITES

Genealogy and Family History Research in Illinois
<outfitters.com/illinois/history/family>: Links to searchable database, Illinois newspapers, and Quaker information.

Illinois GenWeb Project
<www.rootsweb.com/~ilgenweb>: County maps, Civil War project, research aids.

Illinois Mailing Lists
<www.rootsweb.com/~jfuller/gen_mail_states-il.html>: State and county lists.

Illinois Resources at RootsWeb
<resources.rootsweb.com/USA/IL>: Searchable databases and links to Illinois research-related personal Web pages.

Illinois Statewide Marriage Index, 1763-1900
<cyberdriveillinois.com/departments/archives/genealogy/marrsrch.html>: Searchable database with information for obtaining original marriage records.

Illinois Trails
<www.iltrails.org>: Links to maps, biographies, and research help.

Records in the Illinois State Archives
<cyberdriveillinois.com/departments/archives/databases.html>: Searchable databases of public land sales, military records, and emancipation records.

Vital Records Information
<vitalrec.com/il.html>: Where to obtain copies of birth and death certificates, marriage licenses, and divorce decrees.

FAMILY HISTORY CENTERS

Alton
6500 Humbert Rd.
(618) 466-4352

Bourbonnais
1091 Stratford Dr. East
(815) 939-2528

Buffalo Grove
15 E. Port Clinton
(847) 913-5387

Carbondale
7168 Old Highway 13 West
(618) 549-3034

Centralia
Airport & Calumet Road
(618) 532-3484

Champaign
604 W. Windsor Rd.
(217) 352-8063

Chicago Heights
402 Longwood Dr.
(708) 756-1280

Crystal Lake
5209 N. Walkup
(815) 459-7475

Danville
1949 N. Bowman Ave.
(217) 446-5887

Decatur
3955 Lourdes Dr.
(217) 875-9396

Dekalb
675 Fox Ave.
(815) 895-5460

Eldorado
103 Grayson Rd.
(618) 273-8172

Foxcroft
17947 Route 37 South
(618) 937-4755

Hyde Park
5200 S. University Ave.
(773) 493-1830

Jacksonville
1053 E. Vandalia
(217) 245-8113

Joliet
655 Springfield Ave.
(815) 725-8621

Litchfield
123468 Roberson Rd.
(217) 324-2396

Macomb
2000 W. Adams
(309) 836-3201

Mattoon
7256 Country Club Rd.
(217) 234-3362

Morris
1414 W. Du Pont Ave.
(815) 941-4133

Naperville
1320 Ridgeland Ave.
(630) 505-0233

Nauvoo
165 N. Wells St.
(217) 453-6347

Normal
1700 W. Hovey Ave.
(309) 454-4794

O'Fallon
255 Fairwood Hills Rd.
(618) 632-0210

Orland Park
13150 S. Eighty-eighth Ave.
(708) 361-5474

Ottawa
1377 Adams
(815) 433-9322

Peoria
3700 W. Reservoir Blvd.
(309) 682-4073

Quincy
210 Cardinal Terr.
(217) 224-3220

Rockford
620 N. Alpine Rd.
(815) 399-2660

Schaumburg
1320 W. Schaumburg Rd.
(847) 885-4130

Springfield
3601 Buckeye Dr.
(217) 529-7930

Sterling
2709 Sixteenth Ave.
(815) 625-1229

Westchester
1550 Haase
(708) 562-8679

Wilmette
2727 Lake Ave.
(847) 251-9818

INDIANA

ORGANIZATIONS & ARCHIVES

Allen County Public Library
Historical Genealogy Department
900 Webster St.
P.O. Box 2270
Fort Wayne, IN 46801
(260) 421-1225
Fax: (260) 422-9688
<www.acpl.lib.in.us/genealogy>
Interim location (2003-approximately 2005 or 2006):
200 East Berry St.
Fort Wayne, IN 46801

Oak Park
DU
PAGE Cicero
Chicago
Aurora
COOK
Oak Lawn
Hammond
Joliet
Gary
WILL
LAKE
PORTER
LA PORTE
ST JOSEPH
South Bend
ELKHART
LA GRANGE
STEUBEN
WILLIAMS
NOBLE
DE KALB
DEFIANCE
STARKE
MARSHALL
KOSCIUSKO
WHITLEY
ALLEN
PAULDING
Fort Wayne
VAN WERT
NEWTON
JASPER
PULASKI
FULTON
WABASH
HUNTINGTON
WELLS
ADAMS
IROQUOIS
WHITE
CASS
MIAMI

ILLINOIS
BENTON
CARROLL
GRANT
BLACKFORD
JAY
MERCER
FORD
HOWARD
WARREN
TIPPECANOE
CLINTON
TIPTON
DELAWARE
Muncie
OHIO
CHAMPAIGN
VERMILION
MADISON
RANDOLPH
DARKE
Champaign
FOUNTAIN
MONTGOMERY
BOONE
Anderson
HAMILTON
INDIANA
HENRY
WAYNE
VERMILLION
HENDRICKS
MARION
Indianapolis
HANCOCK
DOUGLAS
PARKE
PUTNAM
RUSH
FAYETTE
UNION
PREBLE
EDGAR
COLES
Terre Haute
JOHNSON
SHELBY
FRANKLIN
BUTLER
CLARK
VIGO
CLAY
OWEN
MORGAN
DECATUR
Hamilton
CUMBERLAND
Bloomington
BROWN
BARTHOLOMEW
HAMILTON
DEARBORN
Cincinnati
SULLIVAN
MONROE
RIPLEY
JASPER
CRAWFORD
GREENE
JENNINGS
OHIO
BOONE
KENTON
JACKSON
SWITZERLAND
LAWRENCE
JEFFERSON
GALLATIN
RICHLAND
LAWRENCE
KNOX
DAVIESS
MARTIN
SCOTT
TRIMBLE
CARROLL
GRANT
WAYNE
ORANGE
WASHINGTON
CLARK
OWEN
EDWARDS
WABASH
PIKE
DUBOIS
HENRY
GIBSON
CRAWFORD
FLOYD
OLDHAM
KENTUCKY
SCOTT
WHITE
POSEY
VANDERBURGH
WARRICK
SPENCER
PERRY
HARRISON
Louisville
JEFFERSON
SHELBY
FRANKLIN
Frankfort
WOODFORD
Lexington
Evansville
MEADE
BULLITT
SPENCER
ANDERSON
FAYETTE
JESSAMINE
HANCOCK
GALLATIN
HENDERSON
BRECKINRIDGE
NELSON
MERCER
UNION
DAVIESS
Owensboro
OHIO
HARDIN
WASHINGTON
GARRARD
WEBSTER
MCLEAN
LARUE
MARION
BOYLE

Commission on Public Records
Indiana State Archives
6440 E. 30th St.
Indianapolis, IN 46219
(317) 591-5222
Fax: (317) 233-1085
<www.ai.org/icpr/
webfile/archives/>

Indiana Genealogical Society
P.O. Box 10507
Fort Wayne, IN 46825
<www.indgensoc.org>

Indiana Historical Society
450 W. Ohio St.
Indianapolis, IN 46202
(317) 232-1882
Fax: (317) 233-3109
<www.indianahistory.org>

Indiana State Archives
6640 E. Thirtieth St.
Indianapolis, IN 46219
(317) 591-5222
<www.state.in.us/icpr/
webfile/archives/
homepage.html>

Indiana State Library, Genealogy Division
140 N. Senate Ave., Room 250
Indianapolis, IN 46204
(317) 232-3689
Fax: (317) 232-3728
<www.statelib.lib.in.us/
WWW/INDIANA/
GENEALOGY/genmenu.
HTML>

Indiana State Library
140 N. Senate Ave.
Indianapolis, IN 46204
(317) 232-3670
Fax: (317) 232-3728
<www.statelib.lib.in.us>

RESOURCES

"Genealogical Research in Indiana"
lecture by John Newman
(Audiotapes.com, $8.50)

Illustrated Historical Atlas of the State of Indiana
by Alfred T. Andreas
(Heritage Quest, $19.95)

Indiana Genealogical Research
by George K. Schweitzer
(Genealogical Sources Unlimited, $11.95)

Indiana Place Names
by Ronald L. Baker and Marvin Carmony
(Indiana University Press, out of print)

Research in Indiana
by John D. Beatty
(National Genealogical Society, $6.50)

PERIODICALS

Genealogy
(1973-1986), Indiana Historical Society, 450 W. Ohio St., Indianapolis, IN 46202

The Hoosier Genealogist
(1961-), Indiana Historical Society, 450 W. Ohio St., Indianapolis, IN 46202

The Hoosier Journal of Ancestry
(1969-), N.K. Sexton, P.O. Box 33, Little York, IN 47139

Indiana Genealogical Society Newsletter
(1989-), Indiana Genealogical Society, P.O. Box 10507, Fort Wayne, IN 46825

Indiana Genealogist
(1990-), Indiana Genealogical Society, P.O. Box 10507, Fort Wayne, IN 46825

Indiana Magazine of History
(1905-), Department of History, Indiana University, Bloomington, IN

Indiana Queries
(1987-1993, 9 vols.) Pioneer Publications, Elk, WA

Midwestern Genealogy: From Ye Olde Genealogie Shoppe, Indianapolis, Indiana
(1983-), Ye Olde Genealogie Shoppe, P.O. Box 39128, Indianapolis, IN 46239

Southern Indiana Genealogical Society Quarterly
(1980-), Southern Indiana Genealogical Society, P.O.

Box 665, New Albany, IN 47151

Sycamore Leaves
(1971-1991), Wabash Valley Genealogical Society, P.O. Box 85, Terre Haute, IN 47808

The Tri-State Packet
(1977-), Tri-State Genealogical Society, c/o Willard Library, 21 First Ave., Evansville, IN 47710

WEB SITES

Indiana Genealogy
<members.amaonline.com/nrogers/indiana.htm>: Collection of Indiana resources on the Internet.

Indiana Genealogy
<www.ipfw.edu/ipfwhist/indiana/genealog.htm>:

Searchable database of Indiana marriages through 1850.

Indiana GenWeb
<ingenweb.org>: State and county resources, queries, surname researchers.

Indiana Mailing Lists
<www.rootsweb.com/ ~jfuller/gen_mail_ states-in.html>: State, county, and special-interest lists.

Indiana Pioneers
<ourworld.compuserve. com/homepages/ njmyers/pioneers.htm>: Read 650 names from *Year Book of the Society of Indiana Pioneers*. The book itself contains information on the place and year of birth and place of settlement in Indiana prior to 1850 for the pioneers.

Indiana Resources at RootsWeb
<resources.rootsweb. com/USA/IN>: Searchable databases, surname searches, personal Web pages.

Indiana State Library Genealogy Division Databases
<www.statelib.lib.in.us/ WWW/INDIANA/ GENEALOGY/links.HTML# Searchable>: Searchable marriage, cemetery, and mortality databases.

Vital Records Information
<vitalrec.com/in.html>: Where to obtain copies of birth and death certificates, marriage licenses, and divorce decrees.

FAMILY HISTORY CENTERS

Anderson
200 W. Forty-sixth St.
(765) 644-6417

Batesville
Township Line Road
(812) 934-3443

Bedford
1010 Twenty-second St.
(812) 275-6672

Bloomington
2411 E. Second St.
(812) 333-0050

Brownsburg
10518 East 600 North
(317) 852-5688

Columbus
3330 Thirtieth St.
(812) 376-7073

Crawfordsville
125 West Rd.
(765) 362-8006

Decatur
88 Cardinal Pass
(219) 728-4300

Evansville
8020 E. Covert Ave.
(812) 471-0191

Fishers
777 Sunblest Blvd.
(317) 842-6180

Fort Wayne
5401 St. Joe Rd.
(219) 485-9581

Griffith
300 Wirth Rd. (near Clive Avenue)
(219) 838-8189

Hebron
687 West 650 South
(219) 996-6119

Huntington
Route 24 at State Road 9
(219) 356-7171

Indianapolis
900 E. Stop 11 Rd.
(317) 888-6002

Kokomo
332 West 300 South
(765) 453-0092

Lafayette
3224 Jasper St.
(765) 463-5079

Linton
1000 West (Lone Tree Road)
(812) 847-9044

Marion
1465 E. Bradford St.
(765) 662-3311

Martinsville
100 Church St.
(765) 342-4273

Muncie
4800 Robinwood Ln.
(765) 288-9139

New Albany
1534 Slate Run Rd.
(812) 949-7532

Peru
U.S. 31 South
(765) 473-9407

Richmond
3333 Backmeyer Rd.
(765) 966-2366

South Bend
930 Park Pl.
(219) 243-1633

Terre Haute
1845 N. Center
(812) 234-0269

Valparaiso
503 Burlington Beach Rd.
(219) 464-4411

Vincennes
1940 N. Old Highway 41
(812) 882-4022

Warsaw
1101 N. Cr 175 East
(219) 269-2118

IOWA

ORGANIZATIONS & ARCHIVES

Iowa Genealogical Society
6000 Douglas Ave.
P.O. Box 7735
Des Moines, IA 50322
(515) 276-0287
Fax: (515)727-1824
<www.iowagenealogy. org>

Iowa Genealogical Society Library
6000 Douglas Ave.
Suite 145
P.O. Box 7735
Des Moines, IA 50322
(515) 276-0287
<www.iowagenealogy. org/library.htm>

State Historical Society of Iowa-Des Moines
600 E. Locust
Des Moines, IA 50319
(515) 281-5111
Fax: (515) 282-0502
<www.iowahistory.org>

State Historical Society of Iowa-Iowa City
Centennial Building
402 Iowa Ave.
Iowa City, IA 52240
(319) 335-3916
Fax: (319) 335-3935
<www.iowahistory.org>

RESOURCES

Iowa County Records Manual
(State Historical Society of Iowa, $2)

PERIODICALS

The Annals of Iowa
(1893-), State Historical
Society of Iowa at Iowa
City

The Cedar Tree
(1971-), Northeast Iowa

Genealogical Society, 503
South St., Waterloo, IA
50701

The Genie Bug
(1969-), North Central
Iowa Genealogical
Society, P.O. Box 237,
Mason City, IA 50402

Hawkeye Heritage
(1966-), Iowa
Genealogical Society, P.O.
Box 7735, Des Moines, IA
50322

**Iowa Genealogical
Society Newsletter**
(1980-), Iowa

Genealogical Society, P.O.
Box 7735, Des Moines, IA
50322

Iowa Queries
(1987-), Shirley Penna-
Oakes, P.O. Box 397,
Black Eagle, WY 59414

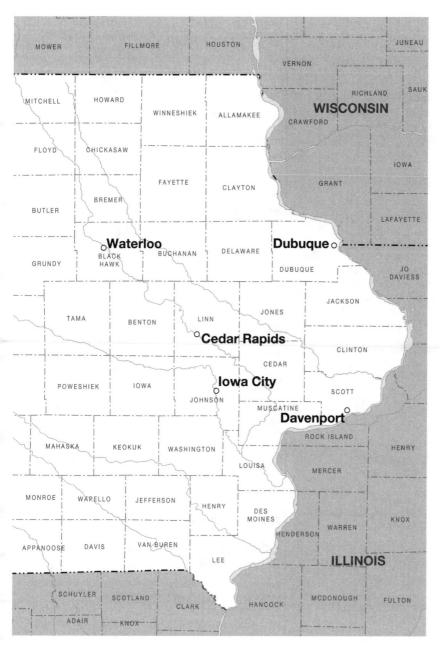

lands and treaties, links to obituaries.

Iowa GenWeb Project
<iagenweb.org>: Queries, archives, transcription projects.

Iowa Mailing Lists
<www.rootsweb.com/~jfuller/gen_mail_states-ia.html>: Network with other genealogists through state and county lists.

Iowa Resources at RootsWeb
<resources.rootsweb.com/USA/IA>: Find your ancestors in RootsWeb search engines and personal Web pages.

Vital Records Information
<vitalrec.com/ia.html>: Where to obtain copies of birth and death certificates, marriage licenses, and divorce decrees.

FAMILY HISTORY CENTERS

Ames
2524 Hoover Ave.
(515) 232-3634

Atlantic
Highways 6 and 71
(712) 243-2507

Burlington
2727 Cliff Rd.
(319) 754-7974

Cedar Falls
3006 Pleasant Dr.
(319) 266-6374

Cedar Rapids
4300 Trailridge Rd. SE
(319) 363-7178

Davenport
4929 Wisconsin Ave.
(563) 386-7547

The Palimpsest
(1920-), State Historical Society of Iowa at Iowa City

The Wahkaw
(1981-), Woodbury County Genealogical Society, P.O. Box 624, 3412 Old Lakesport Rd., Sioux City, IA 51102

WEB SITES

Iowa Counties
<iowa-counties.com>: Maps, virtual libraries, and historical resources.

Iowa Documents
<kinyon.com/iowa>: 1875 maps, county histories, and census transcriptions.

Iowa Genealogy and History Project
<crosswinds.net/~iowahistory>: Indian

Statehood: 1846
Statewide Birth and Death Records Begin: 1880
Statewide Marriage Records Begin: 1880
Address for Vital Statistics:
Iowa Department of Public Health
Vital Records Bureau
Lucas State Office Building
321 E. Twelfth St.
Des Moines, IA 50319-0075
(515) 281-4944
Fax: (515) 281-4529
<www.idph.state.ia.us/pa/vr.htm>

Available Censuses: U.S. federal censuses 1850, 1860, 1870, 1880, 1900, 1910, and 1920. Statewide indexes available for the 1850, 1860, 1870, 1880 (partial), 1900, and 1920 federal censuses. Territorial censuses: Wisconsin Territory 1836 and 1838; Iowa Territory 1840, 1844, and 1846. State censuses 1846 to 1925.

City Directories at the Family History Library Include: Davenport 1855-1863, 1866-1902, and 1906-1935; Des Moines 1866-1935, 1942, 1960, 1965, 1972, 1975, 1980, 1985, and 1990

West Des Moines
3301 Ashworth Rd.
(515) 225-0416

Dubuque
685 Fremont Ave.
(319) 583-6851

Fairfield
2143 Thirty-second St.
(515) 472-9513

Fort Dodge
1426 N. Thirty-second St.
(515) 576-6180

Glenwood
7 N. Vine St.
(712) 527-9627

Iowa City
2730 Bradford Dr.
(319) 338-5306

Logan
2629 260th St.
(712) 644-3495

Keosauqua
1579 N. Highway 1
(319) 293-3455

Knoxville
1800 W. Jackson
(641) 842-2297

Marshalltown
703 S. Twelfth St.
(515) 752-3284

Mason City
1309 S. Kentucky Ave.
(641) 424-4211

Iowa City
Scobey Road
(319) 895-6468

Muscatine
2902 Lucas St.
(319) 263-5612

Newton
1405 N. Eleventh Ave. East
(641) 792-2784

Osceola
Highway 34 East
(641) 342-6333

Ottumwa
303 W. Rochester
(641) 682-1622

Sheldon
114 N. Third
(712) 342-9932

Shenandoah
507 E. Pioneer
(712) 246-4491

Sioux City
1201 W. Clifton
(712) 255-9686

Spencer
1701 W. Eleventh
(712) 262-6172

Storm Lake
1411 E. Lakeshore Dr.
(712) 732-4527

MICHIGAN

ORGANIZATIONS & ARCHIVES

Bentley Historical Library
University of Michigan
1150 Beal Ave.
Ann Arbor, MI 48109
(734) 764-3482
<www.umich.edu/~bhl>

Burton Historical Collection
Detroit Public Library
5201 Woodward Ave.
Detroit, MI 48202
(313) 833-1480
<www.detroit.lib.mi.us/burton>

French Canadian Heritage Society of Michigan
9513 Whipple Shores Dr.
Clarkston, MI 48348
<Habitant.org/fchsm>

The Historical Society of Michigan
1305 Abbott Road
East Lansing, MI 48823
<www.hsofmich.org>

Library of Michigan
717 W. Kalamazoo St.
P.O. Box 30007
Lansing, MI 48909
(517) 373-1580
<www.libofmich.lib.mi.us>

Michigan Genealogical Council
P.O. Box 80953
Lansing, MI 48908
<www.geocities.com/Heartland/Meadows/2192>

State Archives of Michigan
Department of State
717 W. Allegan St.
Lansing, MI 48909
(517) 373-1408
<www.sos.state.mi.us/history/archive/archive.html>

RESOURCES

Index to Michigan Research in Genealogical Periodicals
by M. Quigley (Western Michigan Genealogical Society, $4)

Michigan: Atlas of Historical County Boundaries
by John H. Long and Peggy Tuck Sinko (Charles Scribners Sons, $162.50)

MICHIGAN

Statehood: 1837
Statewide Birth and Death Records Begin: 1867
Statewide Marriage Records Begin: 1867
Address for Vital Statistics:
Office of the State Registrar & Center
for Health
Michigan Department of Public Health
3423 N. Logan St.
P.O. Box 30035
Lansing, MI 48909
(517) 335-8000
<www.mdch.state.mi.us/PHA/OSR/vital_
records>

Available Censuses: U.S. federal censuses 1820,
1830, 1840, 1850, 1860, 1870, 1880, 1900, 1910,
and 1920. The 1810 census was destroyed
except for fragments of Detroit and
Michilimackinac. Statewide indexes available
for the 1820, 1830, 1840, 1850, 1860, 1870,
1880, 1900, 1910, and 1920 censuses.

**City Directories at the Family History Library
Include:** Ann Arbor 1886-1935; Detroit 1856-
1935; Grand Rapids 1856-1936; Lansing 1883,
1885, 1887, 1891, 1892, 1896, 1898, and 1900

**"An Overview of
Michigan Genealogy"**
lecture by Geneva Kebler
Wiskemann
(Audiotapes.com, $8.50)

PERIODICALS

*Detroit Society for
Genealogical Research
Magazine*
(1937-), Detroit Society
for Genealogical
Research, c/o Burton
Historical Collection,
Detroit Public Library,
5201 Woodward Ave.,
Detroit, MI 48202

Family Trails
(1967-), State
Department of
Education, Library of
Michigan, P.O. Box 30007,
Lansing, MI 48909

Michigana
(1955-), Western
Michigan Genealogical
Society, c/o Grand Rapids
Public Library, 111 Library
St. NE, Grand Rapids, MI
49503

Michigan Heritage
(1959-73), Kalamazoo
Valley Genealogical
Society, P.O. Box 405,
Comstock, MI 49041

*Michigan Historical
Collections*
(1877-1929), Michigan
Historical Commission,
Lansing, MI

Michigan History
(1917-), Michigan
Historical Center, P.O. Box
30741, Lansing, MI
48909-8241

WEB SITES

**Genealogical Death
Indexing System**
<www.mdch.state.mi.us/
pha/osr/gendisx/search2.
htm>: Database covering
1867 to 1897.

**Library of Michigan 1870
Census Index**
<envoy.libraryof
michigan.org/1870_
census>: Alphabetical list
of the family names in
each household residing
in every county and
township in Michigan in
1870.

**Michigan County Clerks
Genealogy Directory**
<www.sos.state.mi.us/
history/archive/archgene.
html>: Handy guide to
Michigan courthouse
research.

**Michigan Family History
Network**
<mifamilyhistory.org>:
More than 187,000
Michigan birth, death,
and other records online.

**Michigan Genealogy
Sites on the Internet**
<flint.lib.mi.us/fpl/
resources/genealogy/
misites.html>: Links to
archives, cemeteries, census, and military records.

**Michigan GenWeb
Project**
<www.rootsweb.com/
~migenweb>: Lookups,
research exchange, coun-
ty resources.

**Michigan Historical
Center**
<sos.state.mi.us/history/
history.html>:
Photographs, research
services, teacher
resources.

Michigan in the Civil War
<hometown.aol.com/
dlharvey/cwmireg.htm>:
Regimental rosters and
photos of Michigan mon-
uments at Gettysburg.

Michigan Mailing Lists
<www.rootsweb.com/
~jfuller/gen_mail_
states-mi.html>: State-
and county-level mailing
lists.

**Michigan Resources at
RootsWeb**
<resources.rootsweb.
com/USA/MI>: Surname
and archive searches.

Vital Records Information
<vitalrec.com/mi.html>:
Get copies of birth and
death certificates, mar-
riage licenses, and
divorce decrees.

**Wayne County Land
Records Search**
<www.waynecounty
landrecords.com>: Find
your ancestors' Detroit-
area land records.

FAMILY HISTORY
CENTERS

Adrian
140 Sand Creek Highway
(517) 263-0882

Albion/Jackson
3019 W. Morrell
(517) 784-6306

Ann Arbor
2200 Fuller Court, Suite
4-B
(734) 995-0211

Battle Creek
1312 Capital Ave. SW
(616) 964-0878

Benton Harbor
395 Jakway
(616) 925-0865

Big Rapids
1325 Woodward Ave.
(231) 796-0698

Bloomfield Hills
37425 Woodward Ave.
(248) 647-5671

Blue Water
1990 N. River Rd.
(810) 329-0039

Cadillac
8389 S. Thirty-nine Rd.
(231) 775-4585

Cheboygan
302 E. Seymour St.
(616) 627-7918

Escanaba
1315 Ninth Ave. South
(906) 789-0370

Flint
1225 Robert T Longway
(810) 232-6365

Gaylord
600 N. Elm St.
(517) 732-9626

Grand Blanc
4285 McCandlish Rd.
(810) 694-2964

Grand Rapids
2780 Leonard NE
(616) 949-3343

Hastings
600 N. Airport Rd.
(616) 948-2104

Houghton
U.S. 41 to Mill Road,
Peetsock
(906) 482-7110

Howell
1041 W. Grand River
(517) 546-2716

Iron Mountain
2100 Woodward Ave.
(906) 779-2892

Jonesville
425 Parkwood
(517) 849-2407

Kalamazoo
1112 N. Drake Rd.
(616) 342-1906

Lansing
431 E. Saginaw
(517) 332-2932

Ludington
416 E. Melendy St.
(231) 843-3358

Marquette
350 Cherry Creek Rd.
(906) 249-1511

Midland
1700 W. Sugnet Rd.
(517) 631-1120

Mount Pleasant
1404 S. Crawford Rd.
(989) 772-0240

Muskegon
1725 W. Giles Rd.
(231) 744-3283

Owosso
1588 N. Hickory
(517) 723-8656

Petoskey
707 Alcan
(231) 348-8407

Pontiac
5464 Waterford Rd.
(248) 454-0310

Riverview
18701 Grange Rd.
(734) 285-0494

Rochester
1610 Brewster
(248) 651-6836

Roseville
16965 Twelve Mile Rd.
(810) 773-4560

South Haven
610 Green St.
(616) 637-6610

Sturgis
1111 Galen St.
(616) 651-4467

Traverse City
3746 Veterans Dr.
(231) 947-4646

West Branch
315 N. Fairview Rd.
(517) 345-5023

Westland
7575 N. Hix Rd.
(734) 459-4570

MINNESOTA

ORGANIZATIONS & ARCHIVES

Central Minnesota Historical Center
Centennial Hall, Room 31
St. Cloud State University
St. Cloud, MN 56301
(320) 255-3254

Immigration History Research Center
311 Andersen Library
222 Twenty-first Ave. S.
Minneapolis MN 55455
(612) 627-4208
Fax: (612) 627-4190
<www1.umn.edu/ihrc/>

Iron Range Research Center
Highway 169 West
P.O. Box 392
Chisholm, MN 55719
(218) 254-7959 or (800) 372-6437
Fax: (218) 254-5235
<www.ironrange researchcenter.org>

Minnesota Genealogical Society
5768 Olson Memorial Highway
Golden Valley, MN 55422
(763) 595-9347
<www.mngs.org>

Minnesota Historical Society
345 W. Kellogg Blvd.
St. Paul, MN 55102
(651) 296-6126

ONTARIO

Sault Ste Marie

MARQUETTE
ALGER
SCHOOLCRAFT
LUCE
CHIPPEWA
MACKINAC
DELTA

MENOMINEE

DOOR

KEWAUNEE

MANITOWOC

EMMET
CHEBOYGAN
PRESQUE ISLE
CHARLEVOIX
ANTRIM
OTSEGO
MONTMORENCY
ALPENA
LEELANAU
BENZIE
GRAND TRAVERSE
KALKASKA
CRAWFORD
OSCODA
ALCONA
MANISTEE
WEXFORD
MISSAUKEE
ROSCOMMON
OGEMAW
IOSCO
ARENAC
MASON
LAKE
OSCEOLA
CLARE
GLADWIN
HURON
BAY
OCEANA
NEWAYGO
MECOSTA
ISABELLA
MIDLAND
TUSCOLA
SANILAC
MUSKEGON
MONTCALM
GRATIOT
Saginaw
SAGINAW
MICHIGAN
KENT
Flint
LAPEER
ST. CLAIR
OTTAWA
Grand Rapids
IONIA
CLINTON
SHIAWASSEE
GENESEE
Wyoming
OAKLAND
MACOMB
Lansing
Pontiac
ALLEGAN
BARRY
EATON
INGHAM
LIVINGSTON
Farmington Hills
Kalamazoo
JACKSON
WAYNE
Detroit
VAN BUREN
KALAMAZOO
CALHOUN
Ann Arbor
Taylor
WASHTENAW
BERRIEN
CASS
ST. JOSEPH
BRANCH
HILLSDALE
LENAWEE
MONROE
Chicago
COOK
LAKE
PORTER
LA PORTE
ST JOSEPH
ELKHART
INDIANA
WILLIAMS
FULTON
LUCAS
Toledo
Gary
LA GRANGE
STEUBEN
OHIO
WOOD
OTTAWA

MINNESOTA

Statehood: 1858
Statewide Birth Records Begin: 1900
Statewide Death Records Begin: 1908
Statewide Marriage Records Begin: 1958
Address for Vital Statistics:
   Minnesota Department of Health
   Birth and Death Records
   P.O. Box 9441
   717 Delaware Street SE
   Minneapolis, MN 55440
   (612) 623-5121
   Fax: (612) 331-5776
   <www.health.state.mn.us/divs/chs/data/
   bd_1.htm>

Available Censuses: U.S. federal censuses 1850, 1860, 1870, 1880, 1900, 1910, and 1920. Statewide indexes exist for the 1850, 1860, 1870, 1880 (partial), 1900, and 1920 censuses. Portions included in the 1836, 1838, and 1840 Wisconsin territorial censuses and in the 1840 Iowa territorial census. Minnesota territorial censuses were taken in 1849, 1850, 1853, 1855, and 1857; some or all of these have been lost. State censuses (some schedules missing) are available for 1865, 1875, 1885, 1895, and 1905.

City Directories at the Family History Library Include: Duluth 1884-1935; Minneapolis 1865-1935; Rochester 1938, 1975, 1980, 1984, and 1989; St. Paul 1856-1859 and 1863-1935

Fax: (651) 297-7436
<www.mnhs.org>

Northeast Minnesota Historical Center
University of Minnesota-Duluth
Library Annex Room 202
10 University Dr.
Duluth, MN 55812
(218) 726-8526
<www.d.umn.edu/lib/collections/nemn.html>

Northwest Minnesota Historical Center
Livingston Lord Library, Room 409
Moorhead State University

1104 Seventh Ave. S
Moorhead, MN 56563
(218) 236-2346
Fax: (218) 299-5924
<www.moorhead.msus.edu/library>

Southern Minnesota Historical Center
Memorial Library
P.O. Box 8419
Mankato, MN 56002
(507) 389-1029
<www.lib.mnsu.edu/lib/archives/archives.html>

Southwest Minnesota Historical Center
Southwest State University

Social Science 141
Marshall, MN 56258
(507) 537-6176
Fax: (507) 537-6200

West Central Minnesota Historical Research Center
University of Minnesota-Morris
Rodney A. Briggs Library, Room 110
600 E. Fourth St.
Morris, MN 56267
(320) 589-6183
Fax: (320) 589-6117
<www.mrs.umn.edu/academic/history/wchrc>

RESOURCES

Continuing Your Genealogical Research in Minnesota
by Marilyn Lind (Linden Tree, $14.50)

Genealogical Resources of the Minnesota Historical Society: A Guide
by the Minnesota Historical Society Library & Archives Division (MHS Press, $6.95)

Minnesota Genealogical Reference Guide, 6th ed.,
by Paula Stuart Warren (Warren Research, $9)

Research in Minnesota
by Paula Stuart Warren (National Genealogical Society, $6.50)

They Chose Minnesota: A Survey of the State's Ethnic Groups
edited by June D. Holmquist (Minnesota Historical Society, $24.95)

PERIODICALS

German Interest Group
(1980-1992), German Interest Group of the Minnesota Genealogical Society

Minnesota Genealogical Journal
(1984-1987, 1992-), edited by Alfred J. Dahlquist, published by Park Genealogical Book, P.O. 130968, Roseville, MN 55113

Minnesota Genealogist
(1970-), Minnesota Genealogical Society, 5768 Olson Memorial Highway, Golden Valley, MN 55422

Minnesota History
(1915-), Minnesota Historical Society, 345 W. Kellogg Blvd., St. Paul, MN 55102

Prairieland Pioneer
(1984-), Prairieland Genealogical Society, History Center, Social Science 141, Southwest State University, Marshall, MN 56258

The Prairieland Register: Genealogical Records From Southwestern Minnesota
(1977-1983), Prairieland Genealogical Society, 703 N. Sixth St., Marshall, MN 56258

Scandinavian Saga
(1979-), Scandinavian-American Genealogical Society, P.O. Box 16069, St. Paul, MN 55116

WEB SITES

Biographies of Welsh Settlers in Minnesota
<estelnet.com/catalunyacymru/catala/blue_02c.htm>:
Transcribed 1895 book.

Family History Research
<mnhs.org/library/tips/family/family.html>: Tips from the Minnesota Historical Society.

History of Trapping and the Fur Trade in Minnesota
<mntrappers.com/History.html>: Trapping history beginning in the 1600s.

Minnesota Death Certificates
<people.mnhs.org/dci>: Search the Minnesota Historical Society's index of death certificates, covering 1908 through 1946.

Minnesota GenWeb Project
<www.rootsweb.com/~mngenweb>: Family reunions, lookups, maps, county resources.

Minnesota Mailing Lists
<www.rootsweb.com/~jfuller/gen_mail_states-mn.html>: Free subscriptions to state and county mailing lists.

Minnesota Resources at RootsWeb
<resources.rootsweb.com/USA/MN>: Surname searches, personal Web sites, and archived data.

Pioneering the Upper Midwest
<memory.loc.gov/ammem/umhtml/umhome.html>: Digitized page images and transcriptions from books in the Library of Congress's general collections and rare book and special collections division.

A Selective List of Sources for Minnesota Genealogy
<wilson.lib.umn.edu/reference/mn-gene.html>: Timeline and list of Minnesota microfilm and publications.

Vital Records Information
<vitalrec.com/mn.html>: Where to obtain copies of birth and death certificates, marriage licenses, and divorce decrees.

FAMILY HISTORY CENTERS

Alexandria
1427 Lake St.
(320) 763-6721

Anoka
4700 Edinbrook Terrace
(763) 425-1865

Austin
404 Thirty-first St. NW
(507) 433-9042

Bemidji
3033 Birchmont Dr.
(218) 751-9129

Brainerd
101 S. Buffalo Hills Ln.
(218) 828-4701

Buffalo
Highway 25 North
(763) 682-5612

Burnsville
9700 Nesbitt Ave. South
(952) 893-2393

Detroit Lakes
Highway 34 E. Pelican River Rd.
(218) 847-3260

Duluth
521 Upham Rd.
(218) 726-1361

Faribault
1002 Seventeenth St. SW
(507) 334-7046

Mankato
1851 Marie Ln.
(507) 625-8342

Marshall
1401 E. Lyon St.
(507) 532-4913

Minneapolis
2801 N. Douglas Dr.
(612) 544-2479

Oakdale
2140 N. Hadley
(651) 770-3213

Pipestone
701 Second Ave. SW
(507) 825-2993

Princeton
One hundredth Ave.
Highway 95
(763) 389-1289

Rochester
2300 Viola Heights Dr. NE
(507) 281-6641

St. Cloud
1420 Twenty-ninth Ave.
North
(320) 203-7717

St Paul-Edgerton
2335 Edgerton

Virginia
Thirteenth St. South and
Sixth Ave. West
(218) 749-2490

MISSOURI

ORGANIZATIONS & ARCHIVES

**Heart of America
Genealogical Society**
c/o Kansas City Public
Library
311 E. Twelfth St.
Kansas City, MO 64106
(816) 701-3400
Fax: (816) 421-7484

**Mid-Continent Public
Library**
317 W. 24 Highway
Independence, MO 64050
(816) 252-7228
<www.mcpl.lib.mo.us>

**Missouri Genealogical
Association**
P.O. Box 833
Columbia, MO 65205
<www.mosga.org>

**Missouri Historical
Society Library and
Research Center**
Jefferson Memorial
Building
225 S. Skinker Blvd.
St. Louis, MO 63112
(314) 746-4599
Fax: (314) 746-4548
<www.mohistory.org>
mailing address:
P.O. Box 11940
St. Louis, MO 63112

Missouri State Archives
P.O. Box 1747
600 W. Main St.
Jefferson City, MO 65102
(573) 751-3280
Fax: (573) 526-7333
<www.sos.state.mo.us/
archives>

**Missouri State
Genealogical Association**
P.O. Box 833
Columbia, MO 65205
(816) 747-9330
<www.mosga.org>

**St. Louis Genealogical
Society**
4 Sunnen Dr., Suite 140
P.O. Box 43010
St. Louis, MO 63143
(314) 647-8547
Fax: (314) 647-8548
<www.rootsweb.com/
~mostlogs/STINDEX.
HTM>

St. Louis Public Library
History and Genealogy
Department

MISSOURI

Statehood: 1821
Statewide Birth and Death Records Begin: 1910
Statewide Marriage Records Begin: 1948
Address for Vital Statistics:
Bureau of Vital Records
930 Wildwood
PO Box 570
Jefferson City, MO 65102
(573) 751-6400
<www.health.state.mo.us/BirthAndDeath
Records/BirthAndDeathRecords.html>

Available Censuses: U.S. federal censuses for
1830, 1840, 1850, 1860, 1870, 1880, 1900, 1910,
and 1920. Statewide indexes are available for
the 1830, 1840, 1850, 1860, 1870, 1880, 1900,
1910, and 1920 censuses. The 1810 Louisiana
territorial census included parts of Missouri.
Missouri territorial censuses exist for 1814,
1817, and 1819. The 1876 state census exists for
some counties; other state censuses mostly lost.

**City Directories at the Family History Library
Include:** Kansas City 1860-61, 1865-1935, 1940,
and 1975; Springfield 1878, 1881, and 1937; St.
Joseph 1887-1933; St. Louis 1821-60, 1863-1935,
1917, and 1942.

1301 Olive St.
St. Louis, MO 63103
(314) 241-2288
Fax: (314) 539-0393
<www.slpl.lib.mo.us>

**State Historical Society
of Missouri**
1020 Lowry St.
Columbia, MO 65201
(573) 882-7083
Fax: (573) 884-4950
<www.system.missouri.
edu/shs>

RESOURCES

*Guide to Genealogical
Research in St. Louis,*
4th ed., by Edward E.
Steele (St. Louis
Genealogical Society,
$14)

*Missouri Genealogical
Research*
by George K. Schwietzer
(Genealogical Sources
Unlimited, $11.95)

*"Missouri Settlement
Patterns"*
lecture by Marsha
Hoffman Rising
(Audiotapes.com, $8.50)

Research in Missouri
by Pamela Boyer Porter
and Ann Carter Fleming
(National Genealogical
Society, $6.50)

*Ten Thousand Missouri
Taxpayers*
by Sherida K. Eddlemon
(Heritage Books, $24)

"Tracing Your Family Tree in Missouri"
lecture by Robert E. Parkin Jr.
(Audiotapes.com, $8.50)

PERIODICALS

Kansas City Genealogist
(1960-), Heart of America Genealogical Society and Library, c/o Kansas City Public Library, 311 E. Twelfth St., Kansas City, MO 64106

Missouri Miscellany: Statewide Missouri Genealogical Records
(1973-84), Mrs. Howard W. Woodruff, Independence, MO

Missouri Pioneers: County and Genealogical Records
(1967-76), Nadine Hodges and Mrs. Howard W. Woodruff, Independence, MO

Ozar' Kin: The People Who Settled the Missouri Ozarks
(1979-), Ozarks Genealogical Society, P.O. Box 3945, Springfield, MO 65808

Pioneer Times
(1977-1993), Mid-Missouri Genealogical Society, P.O. Box 715, Jefferson City, MO 65102

The Prairie Gleaner
(1969-), West Central Missouri Genealogical Society and Library, 705 Broad St., Warrensburg, MO 64093

St. Louis Genealogical Society Quarterly
(1968-), St. Louis Genealogical Society, P.O. Box 43010, St. Louis, MO 63143.

WEB SITES

Afro-Americans in Missouri
<usgennet.org/usa/mo/topic/afro-amer>: Links to slave schedules, Underground Railroad information, black history.

Gone But Not Forgotten, Missouri Pioneers
<www.rootsweb.com/~mopionee>: Compilation of settlers in Missouri by 1890.

Index of the Civil War in Missouri
<www.usmo.com/~momollus/Mocwlink.htm>: Battles, regiments, historic sites.

Local Records Inventory Database
<www.sos.state.mo.us/CountyInventory>: Useful guide to records at the county level.

Missouri GenWeb Project
<www.rootsweb.com/~mogenweb/mo.htm>: Archive, tombstone, and census projects; county resources.

Missouri Mailing Lists
<www.rootsweb.com/~jfuller/gen_mail_states-mo.html>: Subscribe to county and state mailing lists.

Missouri Resources at RootsWeb
<resources.rootsweb.com/USA/MO>: Database and archive search engines, plus Missouri-related personal Web sites.

Suggestions for Tracing Family History

<system.missouri.edu/shs/familytr.html>: Tips from the State Historical Society of Missouri.

Vital Records Information

<vitalrec.com/mo.html>: Birth and death certificates, marriage licenses, and divorce decrees.

World War I Military Service Cards Database

<www.sos.state.mo.us/archives/ww1/default.asp>: Information about Missouri men and women who served both stateside and overseas from 1917 to 1919. The database searches abstracts of 145,000 service cards for the U.S. Army and Marines, plus digitized images of 18,500 U.S. Navy service cards.

FAMILY HISTORY CENTERS

Adam-ondi-Ahman
22379 Koala Rd.
(660) 828-4325

Aurora
Highway 39 South of P
(417) 678-4399

Ava
Route 5 Bypass
(417) 683-4525

Blue Springs
1416 S. Nineteenth St.
(816) 228-3835

Bolivar
1575 E. Mount Gilead Rd.
(417) 777-5969

Branson
224 Church Rd.
(417) 335-6833

Cameron
1100 E. Grand
(816) 632-3770

Cape Girardeau
1048 W. Cape Rock Dr.
(573) 334-7644

Clinton
18 Highway and Kitchcart Road
(660) 885-6839

Columbia
4708 Highland Parkway South
(573) 443-2048

Excelsior Springs
One-half mile south of 10 Highway on Route
(816) 637-8383

Farmington
709 S. Henry St.
(573) 756-6521

Fulton
1603 Kingswood Dr.
(573) 642-6814

Hannibal
9 Centerville Rd.
(573) 221-5147

Houston
Highway 63 and E St.
(417) 967-9389

Independence
705 W. Walnut
(816) 461-0245

Jefferson City
4618 Henwick Ln.
(573) 893-3847

Joplin
Twenty-second and Indiana
(417) 623-6506

Kansas City
13025 Wornall Rd.
(816) 941-7389

Kirksville
2000 E. Normal St.
(660) 665-1549

Lebanon
Highway YY, one-quarter mile east of N. 5 Highway
(417) 588-2928

Liberty
1130 Clayview Dr.
(816) 781-8295

Maryville
1721 S. Munn St.
(660) 582-8536

Moberly
Highway 24 East at Jones Corner
(660) 263-5829

Monett
Highway 37 and Circle Dr.
(417) 235-5147

Nevada
1101 N. Olive
(417) 667-2781

Osage Beach
One-quarter mile north of Highway 54 on KK Highway
(573) 348-3424

Platte City
2700 Ensign Dr.
(816) 858-4920

Poplar Bluff
2414 Katy Lane
(573) 785-0211

Riverview
2540 Brooklyn
(816) 924-2142

Rolla
696 Forum Dr.
(573) 364-1451

Sedalia
1115 W. Broadway
(660) 827-6720

Sikeston
827 Euclid Ave.
(573) 471-0519

Springfield
1357 S. Ingram Mill Rd.
(417) 887-8229

Springfield
4450 S. Farm Road 141
(417) 889-2835

St. Charles
66 Oak Valley Dr.
(636) 272-1834

St. Joseph
7 N. Carriage Dr.
(816) 232-2428

St. Louis
10445 Clayton Rd.
(314) 993-2328

St. Louis
6386 Howdershell Rd.
(314) 731-5373

St Louis
Highway 21 and Ridgewood
(636) 789-4323

St Robert
123 Bosa Dr.
(573) 336-5461

Stockton
South 39 Highway
(417) 276-4125

Tipton
31469 Highway 5 South
(660) 433-5872

Trenton
2930 Oklahoma Ave.
(660) 359-3352

Washington
110 E. Fourteenth St.
(636) 239-7718

West Plains
2800 Christie Dr.
(417) 257-9857

Willard
West Highway 160, 320 W. Jackson
(417) 742-3841

OHIO

ORGANIZATIONS & ARCHIVES

Bowling Green State University
Center for Archival Collections
Jerome Library
Fifth Floor
Bowling Green, OH 43403
(419) 372-2411
Fax: (419) 372-0155
<www.bgsu.edu/colleges/library/cac/cac.html>

Ohio Genealogical Society
34 Sturges Ave.
P.O. Box 2625
Mansfield, OH 44906
(419) 522-9077
Fax: (419) 522-0224
<www.ogs.org>

Ohio Genealogical Society Library
713 S. Main St.
Mansfield, OH 44907
(419) 756-7294
Fax: (419) 756-8681
<www.ogs.org/lending.htm>

Ohio Historical Society
Ohio Historical Center
1982 Velma Ave.
Columbus, OH 43211
(614) 297-2300
Fax: (614) 297-2546
<www.ohiohistory.org>

Ohio University
Archives and Special Collections
Alden Library, Fifth Floor
Athens, OH 45701
(614) 593-2710
Fax: (614) 593-0138

<www.library.ohiou.edu/libinfo/depts/archives/archives.htm>

State Library of Ohio
Genealogical Section
65 S. Front St., Room 308
Columbus, OH 43215
(614) 644-6966
Fax: (614) 728-2789
<winslo.state.oh.us/services/genealogy/index.html>

University of Cincinnati
Archives and Rare Books Department
Blegen Library
Cincinnati, OH 45221
(513) 556-1959
Fax: (513) 556-2113
<www.archives.uc.edu/arb_nf.html>

Western Reserve Historical Society
10825 East Blvd.
Cleveland, OH 44106
(216) 721-5722
Fax: (216) 721-0645
<www.wrhs.org>

Wright State University
Special Collections and Archives
Paul Laurence Dunbar Library
Dayton, OH 45435
(937) 775-2092
Fax: (937) 775-4109
<www.libraries.wright.edu/staff/dunbar>

Youngstown Historical Center of Industry and Labor
Archives-Library
P.O. Box 533
151 W. Wood St.
Youngstown, OH 44501
(330) 743-5934
Fax: (330) 743-2999
<www.ohiohistory.org/places/youngst>

OHIO

Statehood: 1803
Statewide Birth and Death Records Begin: 1908
Statewide Marriage Records Begin: 1949
Address for Vital Statistics:
Division of Vital Statistics
Ohio Department of Health
P.O. Box 15098
Columbus, OH 43215-0098
(614) 466-2531
<www.odh.state.oh.us/Birth/vitalrec.htm>

Available Censuses: U.S. federal censuses 1820, 1830, 1840, 1850, 1860, 1870, 1880, 1900, 1910, and 1920. Statewide indexes are available for the 1820, 1830, 1840, 1850, 1860, 1880 (incomplete), 1900, 1910, and 1920 censuses. Some town or county censuses taken by the state between 1798 and 1911 also available.

City Directories at the Family History Library Include: Akron 1859 and 1889-1934; Cincinnati 1861-1935; Cleveland 1837 and 1845-1935; Columbus 1843-1935; Dayton 1850 and 1856-1934; Toledo 1858, 1860, 1864, and 1866-1935; Youngstown 1882-1901

RESOURCES

Early Ohio Settlers, Purchasers of Land in East and East Central Ohio, 1800-1840
by Ellen T. Berry and David A. Berry
(Genealogical Publishing Co., $30)

Early Ohio Settlers, 1700s-1900s
(CD-ROM; Genealogy.com, $29.99)

Genealogical Research in Ohio
by Kip Sperry
(Genealogical Publishing Co., out of print)

Ohio Courthouse Records
by Diane VanSkiver Gagel
(Ohio Genealogical Society, $2.50)

Ohio Genealogical Research
by George K. Schweitzer
(Genealogical Sources Unlimited, $11.95)

Ohio Guide to Genealogical Sources
by Carol W. Bell
(Genealogical Publishing Co., $30)

Ohio, 1787-1840, Land and Tax Records
(CD-ROM; Genealogy.com, $29.99)

PERIODICALS

The Firelands Pioneer
(1858-1878, 1882-1937, 1980-), Firelands Historical Society, Norwalk, OH

Gateway to the West (1967-1978), Anita Short and Ruth Bowers, Greenville, OH

Ohio, the Cross Road of Our Nation, also known as Ohio Records and Pioneer Families (1960-), Esther Weygandt Powell, Akron, OH

The Report (1960-), Ohio Genealogical Society, 713 S. Main St., Mansfield, OH 44907

WEB SITES

Cleveland Necrology File
<www.cpl.org>: The Cleveland Public Library hosts a database of local obituaries dating from the mid-1800s to 1975.

Maggie's World of Courthouse Dust and Genealogy Fever
<homepages.rootsweb. com/~maggieoh/ mindex.html>: Extensive list of Ohio links.

Ohio Genealogy Links and Resources
<sunnet.net/pdarling/ ohio.htm>: Links to census indexes, burial records, obituaries, and

marriage records throughout Ohio.

Ohio GenWeb Project
<www.scioto.org/ OHGenWeb>: Connect to county pages, lookups, African-American research, and migrations. The site's Early Vital Records section shows when each county was formed, its parent counties, the county seat, and

the earliest dates for available birth, death, marriage, land, probate, and court records.

Ohio Mailing Lists
<www.rootsweb.com/~jfuller/gen_mail_states-oh.html>: Subscribe to free county and state mailing lists.

Ohio Online Death Certificates
<www.ohiohistory.org/dindex/search.cfm>: Database covering 1913 to 1937.

Ohio Resources at RootsWeb
<resources.rootsweb.com/USA/OH>: Queries, archives, personal Web sites.

Revolutionary War Soldiers Living in the State of Ohio in 1818-1819
<ezinfo.ucs.indiana.edu/~jetorres/ohiorev.html>: Pension list published in 1918.

Vital Records Information
<vitalrec.com/oh.html>: Where to obtain copies of birth and death certificates, marriage licenses, and divorce decrees.

FAMILY HISTORY CENTERS

Adams
1185 Grace's Run Rd.
(937) 695-0030

Akron
106 E. Howe Rd.
(330) 630-3365

Ashtabula
571 Seven Hills Rd.
(440) 993-3616

Athens
7795 Lemaster Rd.

Canton
735 Easthill St. SE
(330) 497-2441

Centerville
901 E. Whipp Rd.
(937) 434-5690

Chillicothe
553 Fourth St.
(740) 774-4533

Cincinnati
5505 Bosworth Place
(513) 531-5624

Cincinnati
695 Clough Pike
(513) 753-3464

Cincinnati
Cornell and Snider Roads
(513) 489-3036

Cleveland
25000 Westwood Rd.
(440) 777-1518

Columbus
2135 Baldwin Rd.
(614) 866-7686

Columbus
7135 Coffman Rd.
(614) 761-1898

Columbus Westland/Scioto
2400 Red Rock Blvd.
(614) 875-8606

Dayton
1500 Shiloh Springs Rd.
(937) 854-4566

Dayton
3060 Terry Dr.
(937) 878-9551

Fairfield/Hamilton
4831 Pleasant Ave.
(513) 844-8866

Findlay
2800 Crystal Ave.
(419) 424-9693

Galion
250 South Rd.
(419) 468-2088

Georgetown
State Road 125 (two miles west of)
(937) 378-3186

Kirtland
8854 Chillicothe Rd.
(440) 256-8808

Lima
1195 Brower Rd.
(419) 227-2537

Lisbon
7250 Market St.
(330) 424-3333

Mansfield
1951 Middle Bellville Rd.
(419) 756-5530

Marion
1725 Marion-Edison Rd.
(740) 389-3212

Medina
4411 Windfall Rd.
(330) 723-5200

Middletown
4930 Central Ave.
(513) 423-9642

Mount Vernon
1010 Beech St.
(740) 392-7016

Oxford
6600 Contreras Rd.
(513) 523-0643

Rootstown
2776 Hartville Rd.
(330) 584-0068

Sandusky
4511 Galloway Rd.
(419) 626-9860

Toledo
State Route 795
(419) 872-9491

Warren/Youngstown
2205 Tibbetts Wick Rd.
(330) 759-0231

Wauseon
858 S. Shoop Ave.
(419) 337-0592

West Chester
7118 Dutchland Parkway
(513) 759-6355

Westerville
307 Huber Village Blvd.
(614) 899-9968

Wilmington
State Route 73
(937) 382-1510

Wintersville
437 Powells Ln.
(740) 264-6190

Wooster
1388 Liahona Dr.
(330) 262-0506

Zanesville
3300 Kearns Dr.
(740) 454-8344

WISCONSIN

ORGANIZATIONS & ARCHIVES

Area Research Center
Superior Public Library
1530 Tower Ave.
Superior, WI 54880
(715) 394-8860
<www.ci.superior.wi.us/library>

Chalmer Davee Library
University of Wisconsin-River Falls
410 S. Third St.
River Falls, WI 54022
(715) 425-3321
<www.uwrf.edu/library/welcome.html>

Elton S. Karrmann Library
University of Wisconsin-Platteville
725 W. Main St.
Platteville, WI 53818
(608) 342-1668
<www.uwplatt.edu/~library>

Eugene W. Murphy Library
University of Wisconsin-La Crosse
1631 W. Pine St.
La Crosse, WI 54601
(608) 785-8505
Fax: (608) 785-8639
<perth.uwlax.edu/murphylibrary>

Forrest R. Polk Library
University of Wisconsin-Oshkosh
800 Algoma Blvd.
Oshkosh, WI 54901
(920) 424-4333
<www.uwosh.edu/departments/llr>

Golda Meir Library
University of Wisconsin-Milwaukee
2311 E. Hartford Ave.
Milwaukee, WI 53211
(414) 229-4785
<www.uwm.edu/Library>

Harold W. Anderson Library
University of Wisconsin-Whitewater
800 W. Main St.
Whitewater, WI 53190
(262) 472-1032
<library.uww.edu>

Milwaukee County Historical Society
910 N. Old World Third St.
Milwaukee, WI 53203
(414) 273-8288
<www.milwaukeecounty histsoc.org>

Special Collections
William D. McIntyre Library
University of Wisconsin-Eau Claire
Eau Claire, WI 54702
(715) 836-3873
<www.uwec.edu/Library/spcoll/speccoll.html>

University of Wisconsin-Green Bay
2420 Nicolet Dr.
Green Bay, WI 54311
(920) 465-2111
<www.uwgb.edu>

Wisconsin Historical Society
816 State St.
Madison, WI 53706
Archives Division: (608) 264-6460
Library Division: (608) 264-6535
Library Division Fax: (608) 264-6520
<www.wisconsinhistory.org>

Wisconsin State Genealogical Society
P.O. Box 5106
Madison, WI 53705
<www.rootsweb.com/~wsgs>
(608) 325-2609

Wisconsin State Old Cemetery Society
c/o Robert Felber, Archivist
6100 W. Mequon Rd.
Mequon, WI 53092
(414) 355-6252

Wyllie Library/Learning Center
University of Wisconsin-Parkside
900 Wood Rd.
Kenosha, WI 53141
(265) 595-2077
Fax: (265) 595-2545
<www.uwp.edu/information.services/library>

RESOURCES

"Norwegian and Norwegian-American Genealogical Resources in Wisconsin"
lecture by Blaine Hedberg
(Audiotapes.com, $8.50)

Searching for Your Wisconsin Ancestors in the Wisconsin Libraries,
3d ed., by Carol Ward Ryan (Wisconsin State Genealogical Society, $15.95)

Wisconsin Genealogical Research,
3d ed., by Linda M. Herrick (Origins, $14)

Wisconsin's Past and Present: A Historical Atlas
by Wisconsin Cartographers' Guild (University of Wisconsin Press, $39.95)

PERIODICALS

Family Finding
(1990-), Wisconsin Jewish Genealogical Society, c/o Penny Deshur, 9280 N. Fairway Dr., Milwaukee, WI 53217

French Canadian/Acadian Genealogists of Wisconsin Quarterly
(1987-), French Canadian/Acadian Genealogists of

Wisconsin, P.O. Box 414, Hales Corners, WI 53130; (414) 786-6408

Gems of Genealogy
(1975-), Bay Area Genealogical Society, P.O. Box 283, Green Bay, WI 54305

Genealogical Gems
(1982-), Fox Valley Genealogical Society, P.O. Box 1592, Appleton, WI 54913

Korzenie/Roots/Polish Genealogical Society of Wisconsin
(1989-),

Korzenie/Roots/Polish GenealogicalSociety of Wisconsin, P.O. Box 342341, Milwaukee, WI 53234

La Crosse Area Genealogical Quarterly
(1974-), La Crosse Area Genealogical Society, P.O. Box 1782, La Crosse, WI 54602

M.C.G.S. Reporter
(1969-), Milwaukee County Genealogical Society, Inc., P.O. Box 270326, Milwaukee, WI 53227

Wisconsin Families: Quarterly of the Wisconsin Genealogical Society
(1940-1941), Wisconsin Genealogical Society

Wisconsin Magazine of History
(1917-), **Wisconsin Historical Society,** 816 State St., Madison, WI 53706

Wisconsin State Genealogical Society Newsletter
(1954-),Wisconsin State Genealogical Society, c/o Mrs. Virginia Irving, 2109 Twentieth Ave., Monroe, WI 53566

Wisconsin Then and Now
(1954-1979), Wisconsin Historical Society

WEB SITES

Archdiocese of Milwaukee Catholic Cemeteries
<www.cemeteries.org/genealogy/genealogy01.asp>: Database for burials in eight southeastern Wisconsin cemeteries.

Finding Your Civil War Ancestor in Wisconsin
<execpc.com/~kap/wisc-cw.html>: Research tips and an interactive computer database of Wisconsin regiments.

Index to Wisconsin Delayed and Affidavit Birth Registrations
<www.rootsweb.com/~wsgs/delayed_birth.

htm>: Covers births prior to October 1907.

Vital Records Information
<vitalrec.com/wi.html>: How to get birth and death certificates, marriage licenses, and divorce decrees.

Wisconsin Civil War Regimental Histories
<museum.dva.state.wi.us/His_regiments.asp>: History of each Wisconsin regiment.

Wisconsin GenWeb Project
<www.rootsweb.com/~wigenweb>: Tips on starting research, links to county resources.

Wisconsin Land Records
<searches.rootsweb.com/cgi-bin/wisconsin/wisconsin.pl>: The interactive search is part of an interface to the Pre-1908 Homestead and Cash Entry Patents from the Bureau of Land Management's General Land Office (GLO) Automated Records Project.

Wisconsin Lineage Links
<execpc.com/~drg/drgll.html>: Links to Wisconsin's lineage societies.

Wisconsin Local History and Biography Articles
<www.wisconsinhistory.org/wlhba/>: Search 16,000 articles on 50,000 pages preserved in scrapbooks at the Wisconsin

Historical Society in the late 19th and 20th centuries. Most articles were published between 1860 and 1940.

Wisconsin Mailing Lists
<www.rootsweb.com/~jfuller/gen_mail_states-wi.html>: Subscribe to county and state mailing lists.

Wisconsin Resources at RootsWeb
<resources.rootsweb.com/USA/WI>: Search engines, surnames, archives.

FAMILY HISTORY CENTERS

Appleton
425 W. Parkridge Ave.
(920) 733-5358

Barron
644 S. Sixth
(715) 537-3679

Eau Claire
3335 Stein Blvd.
(715) 834-8271

Elkhorn
4615 W. Potter Rd.
(262) 723-2777

Green Bay
651 Pinehurst
(920) 406-8050

Kenosha
1444 Thirtieth Ave.
(262) 552-7816

Kettle Moraine
411 Highway 83

LaCrosse
701 Well St.
(608) 783-3619

Madison
4505 Regent St.
(608) 238-4844

Milwaukee
9600 W. Grange Ave.
(414) 425-4182

Oshkosh
2828 W. Scenic Dr.
(920) 233-6545

Parkway
9904 W. Calumet Rd.
(414) 355-2241

Shawano
910 E. Zingler Ave.
(715) 526-2946

Sheboygan
3920 Saemann Ave.
(920) 452-7314

Wausau
5405 Rib Mountain Dr.
(715) 355-4856

West Bend
120 E. Paradise Dr.
(262) 338-6123

Great Plains and Rockies

REGIONAL ROUNDUP

BY NANCY HENDRICKSON

Although the term *manifest destiny* wasn't coined until the mid-nineteenth century, the philosophy itself was embraced decades earlier. In its simplest form, Manifest Destiny justified, by divine right, the expansion of the nation from sea to shining sea. In practical terms, it enabled Americans—including, perhaps, your ancestors—to settle where they pleased, from Mexico's California to the Black Hills of the Lakota.

In 1803, Thomas Jefferson ensured white settlement of the continent by brokering the savviest real estate deal in history. For a mere fifteen million dollars, he added 828,000 square miles of land to the nation, acquiring territory from the Mississippi River to the Rockies and from the Gulf of Mexico to Canada.

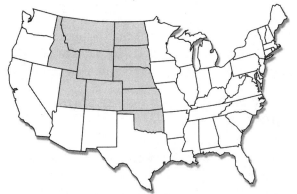

At the conclusion of Lewis and Clark's two-year exploration of the new territory, Americans headed west. At first, fur trappers and mountain men drifted across the plains into the Rockies. Then, by the 1840s, thousands of pioneers trekked along the Platte River on their way to Oregon and California. But it took the Homestead Act of 1862 to transform the Wild West into today's farm and beef belts.

The Civil War temporarily slowed westward migration, but at the war's conclusion, homesteaders poured into the Great Plains and the Rocky Mountains: The promise of free public land drew settlers from across the globe. By the time North Dakota became a state in 1889, nearly 70 percent of the U.S. inhabitants were foreign-born or had foreign-born parents.

Unfortunately, the "public land" made available to homesteaders was the same land that the tribes of the Great Plains considered home. Once the gold rushers and settlers traveled west of the Mississippi River, the stage was set for conflict. Beginning roughly with the Minnesota Sioux Uprising of 1862 and ending at Wounded Knee in 1890, the United States Army waged war against the Plains Indians. The goal—ostensibly—was to protect settlers, but Gen. Philip Sheridan's policy of surprise attacks against winter camps and the wholesale slaughter of buffalo guaranteed the taming—and settlement—of the Wild West.

If any of your ancestors were among the tens of thousands who populated the Great Plains and Rockies in the last half of the nineteenth century, you're certainly descended from hardy stock. So how do you go about tracing your frontier roots?

As with all genealogical research, start at home. Look for birth, death, and marriage records; obituaries; funeral cards; and military records—anything that details names, dates, and places.

Next, interview your relatives: Ask not only for names and dates but for any stories about the family. Often your oldest living relatives can be the source of long-forgotten tales. And, although family lore can become convoluted over time, it frequently contains grains of truth.

RESOURCES GALORE

When you move beyond "home sources," you'll find that the holdings of state historical societies are mind boggling. These societies house state census records, city directories, yearbooks, county histories, biographical sketches, and family histories—some of which exist in no other facility.

The South Dakota State Historical Society, for example, owns the largest known collection of South Dakota newspapers, consisting of one thousand titles preserved on approximately twelve thousand microfilm reels. Genealogical researchers who love delving back into newspaper records, take note: The Colorado Historical Society has copies of the *Rocky Mountain Times* dating back to 1859.

Ellie Arguimbau, archivist at the Montana Historical Society, says one of the society's most underutilized sources is the Society of Montana Pioneers' papers. These include a survey, done in 1907, which asked residents about the routes they took to reach Montana. The society also owns original homesteading diaries.

This is just a sampling, and all of the region's state historical society libraries are open to the public. If you can't do on-site research, you can have the societies provide research for you for a minimal fee; unfortunately, in most cases, such research is limited to half an hour or an hour. Fees are low and generally include the price of copies. Some of the historical society libraries participate in interlibrary loans. Check with the individual society (see the state-by-state resources later in this chapter) for more information on obtaining books or microfilms using the interlibrary loan system.

Even though you have to contact historical societies directly for specific research requests, don't overlook the societies' online resources. Some state historical societies provide Internet access to card catalogs, newspaper indexes, and historical data. The Web site of the Kansas State Historical Society <www.kshs.org>, for example, offers "History in a Nutshell," "This Day in Kansas History," and a *Guide to Kansas Research Resources*. The State Historical Society of North Dakota <www.state.nd.us/hist> lists North Dakota newspapers, grouped by county.

THE IMPORTANCE OF MILITARY RECORDS

Next, consider an ancestor's military history as a starting point for gathering genealogical data. The post-Civil War Regular Army was conspicuous for its high percentage of foreign-born soldiers. According to historian Robert Utley, a report of the adjutant general for the years 1865 to 1874 showed that half of all recruits were born in a foreign country. Of those, more than 20 percent were from Ireland and 12 percent were from Germany. Was one of your ancestors among them? If so, you may strike it rich in enlistment or pension files stored at the National Archives and Records Administration (NARA).

Bill Doty, military records expert at the

National Archives Pacific regional facility in Laguna Niguel, California, says the best place to start looking for your soldier is in microfilm publications numbered M233, T288, and M617.

Publication number M233 is a set of eighty-one microfilm rolls called "Registers of Enlistments in the United States Army, 1796-1914." The information on these rolls was compiled from enlistment papers, muster rolls of the Regular Army, and other records. These records may be the only source of information on military personnel who served in the nineteenth century and did not apply for a pension. Information on these rolls may include when and where a soldier enlisted, the period of enlistment, his place of birth, his age at the time of enlistment, his civilian occupation, a brief physical description, and his regiment. Records are arranged alphabetically by surname, then chronologically.

Publication number T288 is a set of 544 microfilm rolls called "General Index to Pension Files, 1861-1934." These files include pension applications relating to army, navy, and Marine Corps service. Although the bulk of this group comes from Civil War service, the files also include earlier and later records. Pension records include a veteran's name, rank, unit, and term of service. In addition, you can find his dependents' names, a filing date, and an application number.

According to Doty, an often underutilized source of military records is found in microfilm publication M617. This is a collection of 1,550 rolls of microfilm called "Returns from United States Military Posts, 1800-1916." The records are monthly post returns—or personnel reports—sent from the commander of a post to the adjutant general's office. Returns include morning reports; field returns; troop movements and battles or skirmishes; officers on detached duty; casualties; the number of men absent, present, or sick; and the names of officers and enlisted men. Although you won't find family information in post returns, you can find the name of your ancestor as well as his regiment and the places he served. If the name of a post changed, the new name was generally the one under which all of the returns are filed.

Military records may be requested using National Archives forms NATF 85 (pension records) and NATF 86 (enlistment records). Forms can be obtained from the National Archives by e-mail (inquire@nara.gov) or postal mail (National Archives and Records Administration, Attn: NWCTB, 700 Pennsylvania Avenue NW, Washington, DC 20408) requests. You can find additional information about forms at the NARA Web site <www.archives.gov/research_room/obtain_copies/military_and_genealogy_order_forms.html>.

WOMEN ON THE FRONTIER

The life of a homesteader was difficult at best, particularly for women. According to Elizabeth Jameson, author of *All That Glitters: Class, Conflict, and Community in Cripple Creek*, (University of Illinois Press, $23.95) homesteads were isolated, and a major problem for women was the lack of female companionship.

Often, in the first year of homesteading, a wife helped build the shelter and became part of the work team. Unfortunately, this time usually coincided with a first or second pregnancy. In fact, according to Lillian Schlissel's *Women's Diaries of the Westward Journey* (Schocken Books, $14.95), one-fifth of the women on the overland trails were pregnant.

Once a homestead was established, the "butter and egg money" wives made became a critical contribution to the family's finances and was often used to help buy seeds and other supplies. At times during the five-year homestead period, husbands would leave home to work for wages on another person's harvest or the railroad. At those times, the women and children were left alone on the land.

Jameson notes that "although some feel this

was a romantic period in history, it was the hardest period for the women. They missed kin, women friends and what they called civilized institutions."

THE RUSH FOR LAND

Most of your frontier ancestors headed west to obtain land made available by the Homestead Act of 1862. The act allowed a person to file for a quarter section (160 acres) of free land as long as certain requirements were met at the end of a five-year period. These included building a house, digging a well, and plowing ten acres.

The Homestead Act attracted a high number of immigrants. Jameson says the frontier had a higher population of foreign-born than New York City did—at times as much as 25 to 29 percent of those on the frontier were foreign-born. The frontier became home to Germans from Russia, Scandinavians, Greeks, Mexicans, Jews, and even Japanese who settled in western Nebraska to work on the sugar beet crop.

Beginning in 1889, a second land rush—immortalized in movies ranging from *Cimarron* to *Far and Away*—brought settlers to Oklahoma in droves. Oklahoma first became a U.S. possession in 1803 as part of the Louisiana Purchase. (The panhandle section, however, remained under Spanish control until 1821, then under Mexican control until 1845.) In the 1820s, the Five Civilized Tribes from the southeastern United States were relocated to Oklahoma's "Indian Territory." From then until 1889, a large part of Oklahoma Territory was set aside for resettling eastern tribes.

In 1889, the government purchased land from the Indians and opened the land to settlement. The lure of free land—a place to raise vast cattle herds or realize the promise of oil strikes—swiftly brought fifty thousand settlers into the region. In 1893, as more land was made available, another hundred thousand pioneers joined the land rush. Oklahoma was granted statehood in 1907.

Although the first federal census wasn't taken in Oklahoma until 1890, the non-Native Americans living in Indian Territory were counted in the census of 1860. These enumerations are listed under Indian Lands and are located after "Yell County, Arkansas," on census microfilms.

In 1908, Oklahoma births and deaths were registered statewide, though these records aren't complete. A mandatory registration began in 1917, but compliance was so poor that it took another ten years to obtain a true statewide registration. Oklahoma is a federal land state; records of original land transfers from the government to individuals can be found at the BLM's General Land Office Records site <www.glorecords.blm.gov>.

OTHER FRONTIER RECORDS

Many of the frontier states gained statehood fairly late in the nineteenth century. As a result, you don't have the luxury of searching the decades of census records available for Eastern and Southern states. Pre-statehood territorial census records do exist, but you may have to search more than one territory's records since boundary lines changed. For instance, parts of North Dakota were included in the 1836 Iowa Territory census and in the 1850 and 1857 Minnesota Territory censuses.

Once you know which frontier state your ancestor pioneered, your first online stop should be USGenWeb <www.usgenweb.org>. There you can find resources galore for each state and county. County resources vary, depending on the volunteer coordinator's efforts, but always include a query page and a list of surnames being researched. Be sure to check the surname list: Even if no one's searching for your surname of choice, you may find the surname of an ancestor's neighbor or in-law.

USGenWeb pages frequently contain biographies, county histories, obituaries, newspaper articles, maps, and cemetery data. You may also locate a list of people who will do free lookups in their county reference books. Some sites include a countywide search engine. On the Lincoln County, Kansas, site <skyways.lib.ks.us/genweb/lincoln>, for example, a search for "Hendrickson" returned more than eighty hits, many of which refer to my frontier family who moved into Kansas following the Civil War. Several listings were from the book *Indian Raids in Lincoln County, Kansas, 1864 and 1869*—a book I've since bought and frequently use as a reference.

While at USGenWeb, make it easy for other family researchers to find you—post your queries and surnames in each county in which your ancestors settled.

Don't know where your frontier ancestor is buried? Using an online database you may be able to find her grave site. Sites such as Interment.net: Cemetery Transcription Library <interment.net> and Cemetery Junction Directory <www.daddezio.com/cemetery> contain millions of cemetery records. Another source of cemetery records is the USGenWeb's Tombstone Transcription Project <www.rootsweb.com/~cemetery>. The project's goal is to transcribe and record tombstone inscriptions worldwide.

Often, local genealogical societies publish cemetery transcriptions in their newsletters or special publications. For example, the Red River Valley Genealogical Society <www.fargocity.com/~rrvgs>, in Fargo, North Dakota, sells cemetery records for both North Dakota and Minnesota. Other societies sell publications containing census data and land records.

To locate a genealogical society in the area where your ancestor lived, search the online directory provided by Ancestry.com and the Federation of Genealogical Societies at <www.familyhistory.com/societyhall/main.asp>. Many societies have Web sites that show lists of their publications for sale.

From 1936 to 1940, more than three hundred writers working for the Work Projects Administration compiled life histories of everyday Americans. These histories are personal recollections of pioneers and homesteaders. Although you may not find a history of your own family, you can learn about daily life on the frontier. Among the histories, for example, is that of Kansas homesteader Hernon Kyle. His narrative includes stories about wild game hunting, community activities, and local humor. The life histories are searchable by keyword or state at <lcweb2.loc.gov/ammem/wpaintro/wpahome.html>. To find Kyle's story, for example, enter the search terms "Kansas" and "homestead," then select the search criteria "match all of these words."

If you're lucky, your pioneer is mentioned in a county or township history book or in a collection of biographical sketches. Although most of these books are out of print, you have a chance of locating a copy on one of the many online bookstores specializing in rare or out-of-print books.

I found *Indian Raids in Lincoln County, Kansas* through Advanced Book Exchange <www.abebooks.com>. Here you can search by title, author, or keyword. Once your search is completed, the system displays all of the booksellers who have a copy of the book, along with the price. Prices vary greatly depending on a book's age and condition and whether it's a first edition. Other excellent online sources include Alibris <www.alibris.com>, Barnes & Noble.com <www.bn.com>, and Amazon.com <www.amazon.com>, which recently combined its rare book efforts with Bibliofind.

County histories are invaluable sources of information—both genealogical and historical. Even if one doesn't mention your ancestor, you can use it to learn about economic conditions, local gossip, folklore, local customs, and all those tidbits that put flesh on names and dates.

Your frontier ancestors were the last true American pioneers. They fought harsh weather, withstood the Indian wars, and toughed it out long enough to keep their homesteads. In many instances, their heritage may have deep European roots, but their legacy is uniquely American.

Manifest Destiny became a reality by the beginning of the twentieth century thanks to the homesteaders, trappers, soldiers, cowboys, ranchers, and schoolmarms—your ancestors—who tamed the American frontier.

ORGANIZATIONS & ARCHIVES

Center for Western Studies
Augustana College
P.O. Box 727
Sioux Falls, SD 57197
(605) 274-4007
<inst.augie.edu/CWS>

Frontier Heritage Alliance
1004 Big Goose Rd.
Sheridan, WY 82801
<www.frontierheritage.org>

University of Wyoming American Heritage Center
P.O. Box 3924
Laramie, WY 82071
(307) 766-4114
<uwadmnweb.uwyo.edu/AHC>

Western Heritage Center
2822 Montana Ave.
Billings, MT 59101

(406) 256-6809
<www.ywhc.org/home>

RESOURCES

The American West
by Dee Brown
(Macmillan, $15)

Battles and Skirmishes of the Great Sioux War, 1876-1877: The Military View
edited by Jerome A. Greene (University of Oklahoma Press, $19.95)

Beyond the Far Ridge: Pioneering in the Rocky Mountain High Country
by Edward Mark McGough (High Plains Press, $10.95)

Custer, Come at Once! The Fort Hays Years of George and Elizabeth Custer, 1867-1870
by Blaine Burkey

(Thomas More Prep, out of print)

The Far West and the Great Plains in Transition 1859-1900
by Rodman W. Paul (University of Oklahoma Press, $24.95)

Feels Like Far: A Rancher's Life on the Great Plains
by Linda M. Hasselstrom (The Lyons Press, $22.95)

The Gold Rush Widows of Little Falls
by Linda Peavy and Ursula Smith (Minnesota Historical Society Press, $14.95)

Writing the Range: Race, Class, and Culture in the Women's West
edited by Elizabeth Jameson and Susan Armitage (University of Oklahoma Press, $24.95)

WEB SITES

Buffalo Soldiers and Indian Wars
<www.buffalosoldier.net>

Crazy Horse
<www.pbs.org/weta/thewest/people/a_c/crazyhorse.htm>

Homesteading
<www.usgennet.org/usa/or/county/union/homesteading.htm>

Little Big Horn Associates
<www.lbha.org>

Mountain Men and the Fur Trade
<www.xmission.com/~drudy/amm.html>

Northern Cheyenne Sand Creek Massacre Site Project
<www.sandcreek.org>

Pioneer Sod Houses
<websteader.com/wbstdsd1.htm>

The Sioux Uprising of 1862
<www.d.umn.edu/cla/faculty/tbacig/studproj/a1041/siouxup>

Washita Battlefield National Site
<www.nps.gov/waba>

Women Pioneers of the Northern Great Plains
<memory.loc.gov/ammem/award97/ndfahtml/hult_women.html>

The Denver Public Library's genealogy holdings include 60,000 books and 85,000 microforms.

DENVER

BY SUSAN WENNER JACKSON

A gold rush brought settlers to the foothills of the Rockies in 1859, and as more gold was discovered, Denver became a booming town. Now a major metropolis with a population larger than Wyoming's, the Mile High City houses many family history resources for those with Western ancestry.

If you're ready to hit the genealogical slopes, your first peak should be the **National Archives and Records Administration–Rocky Mountain Region** [West Sixth Avenue and Kipling Street, Building 48 of the Denver Federal Center; (303) 236-0817; <www.archives.gov/facilities/co/denver.html>]. Besides its collection of all U.S. censuses and indexes for census years 1790 through 1930, this NARA facility has Revolutionary War records, pension applications, bounty land warrant applications, Indian censuses, Utah polygamy prosecution case files, and records of Colorado naturalizations. Archival holdings here date back to 1860 and come from Colorado, Montana, New Mexico,

North Dakota, South Dakota, Utah, and Wyoming. Its microfilmed records are related to the Revolutionary War, the Civil War and Reconstruction, relations between the Native Americans and the U.S. government, westward expansion, and World War II.

Prior to your visit, download the *Guide to Archival Holdings at NARA's Rocky Mountain Region (Denver)* at <www.archives.gov/facilities/co/denver/holdings.html>. The facility is about seven miles west of downtown Denver and about thirty-five miles west-southwest of the Denver International Airport. To do research at any NARA regional facility, you need to have a researcher identification card, which you can obtain upon arrival.

Is Colorado your focus? Visit both the **Colorado State Archives and Public Records** and the Colorado Historical Society. The state archives [1313 Sherman Street; (303) 866-2358; <www.archives.state.co.us/geneal.html>] hold all kinds of Colorado records: vital, court and judicial system, legislative history, business incorporation, corrections, military, school, and census. These records include the statewide marriage and divorce index (1890-1939; 1975-2001), birth and death records (before 1901), naturalization records, the 1885 Colorado state census, teacher lists and school pupil census lists for many counties, Colorado veterans' grave registrations (1862-1949), and city directories (1866-1975). The archives are in the basement of the centennial building, one block south of the state capitol building in Denver.

At the **Colorado Historical Society** [1300 Broadway; (303) 866-3682; <www.colorado history.org>], you can gain access to the Stephen H. Hart Library, one of the West's most comprehensive history libraries. Tap its vast collections of books, maps, architectural drawings, private and business correspondence, family albums, photographic prints, magazines, and newspapers. The photograph collection is nothing to sneeze at, either: 600,000 historic images of

COURTESY OF THE DENVER PUBLIC LIBRARY

Family Tree Magazine named the Denver Public Library as one of the nation's 10 best for genealogy.

Colorado's people, industries, agriculture, and communities. You can view a small portion of them at <gowest.coalliance.org>. Once you get to the historical society and find a photo you'd like to have, visit the on-site imaging studio: It provides high-quality photographic prints and scans of society images and artifacts. The library is located on the second floor of the Colorado History Museum.

Across the street is the **Denver Public Library**, where you can explore the **Western History and Genealogy Department** [10 West Fourteenth Avenue Parkway; (720) 865-1111; <www.denver.lib.co.us>]. This department offers books, manuscripts, artifacts, and photographs. The central library is also the region's only federal deposit library, containing 2.3 million documents. The library is located on the southern edge of Civic Center Park.

Denver professional genealogist Joe Beine also recommends the nearby **Clerk and Recorder's Office** [1437 Bannock Street, Room 281; (720) 865-8433; <www.denvergov.org/Clerk_and_ Recorder>], where you can do real estate and property research. This office is located in the Denver City & County Building.

As for a place to stay, you can choose from plenty of downtown hotels: **Courtyard by Marriott** [934 Sixteenth Street; (303) 571-1114], **Adam's Mark** [1550 Court Place; (800) 444-2326], **Cambridge Club Hotel** [1560 Sherman Street; (800) 877-1252], and **Oxford Hotel** [1600 Seventeenth Street; (800) 228-5838]. Denver's most historic hotel is the 1892 **Brown Palace** [321 Seventeenth Street; (303) 297-3111], whose guests have ranged from Teddy Roosevelt to the Beatles. Refuel at one of the many local restaurants and breweries, such as

- **Gallagher's Steak House** [1060 Fifteenth Street; (303) 825-6555]—continental
- **Wazee Supper Club** [1600 Fifteenth Street; (303) 623-9518]—American

Besides its genealogical collections, the city offers many museums and heritage sites to explore between research stops. The **Black American West Museum & Heritage Center** [3901 California; (303) 292-2566; <www.coax.net/people/lwf/bawmus.htm>] tells through photographs, personal artifacts, clothing, and oral histories the forgotten story of African Americans who worked as cowboys in the Old West. **Buffalo Bill Grave & Museum** [top of Lookout Mountain, exit 256 from I-70; (303) 526-0747; <www.buffalobill.org>] celebrates the life of Buffalo Bill Cody, from his days as a Pony Express rider and buffalo hunter to those as a world-renowned showman. At the **Colorado Railroad Museum** [17155 West Forty-fourth Avenue; (800) 365-6263; <www.crrm.org>], a replica of an 1880-style depot, you can relive the days when two thousand miles of narrow-gauge railroad snaked through Colorado's mountains. The museum's exhibits feature fifty thousand artifacts and photos. If you have Latinos in your family history, check out the **Museo de las Americas** [861 Santa Fe Drive; (303) 571-4401; <www.museo.org>], which focuses on the art, history, and culture of Latinos in the Americas from ancient times to the present.

OKLAHOMA CITY

BY KATHERINE HOUSE

If you're on the trail of Oklahoma ancestors or you want to learn more about the state's history, your first stop should be the **Oklahoma Museum of History** [2100 North Lincoln Boulevard; (405) 522-5248; <www.ok-history.mus.ok.us>], across the street from the state capitol. An extensive Native American exhibit features one of the few remaining rawhide tipis, circa the 1890s, from the Sioux. Learn the stories of the state's all-black towns that were settled shortly after the 1889 Land Run, and discover how your ancestors may have thrived during the 1920s oil boom and been challenged by the Dust Bowl. Admission is free.

In the same building is the **Oklahoma Historical Society**'s vast **Research Library and Archives**. The Research Library [(405) 522-5222] houses federal census records for every state up to 1900 and the complete Oklahoma census, including the 1890 Oklahoma Territory census, one of the few existing state census records from that year. Check out an online index at <www.ok-history.mus.ok.us/lib/lrdintro.htm>.

For information on homesteaders, beginning in 1889 and up to statehood in 1907, consult the seventy-two volumes of the Oklahoma Federal Land Tract Books on microfilm and *Smith's First Directory of Oklahoma Territory* for the year beginning August 1, 1890. Military records at the archives include the Confederate Civil War pension application files for Oklahoma.

Anyone researching Native American ancestors should plan on spending plenty of time in the adjacent **Oklahoma Historical Society Archives** [(405) 522-5209], which contains approximately 3.5 million documents representing sixty-six of the sixty-seven native tribes that resided in Indian Territory. (For Osage records, contact the National Archives Southwest Branch in Fort Worth, Texas.) Of special note are the Dawes Commission Rolls of the Five Civilized Tribes and the *Indian-Pioneer History*, containing thousands of interviews with Native Americans and Oklahoma pioneers conducted in the 1930s by the Work Projects Administration. The archives's newspaper collection consists of about four thousand titles on approximately thirty thousand reels of microfilm (limited indexing available). Other resources include a large vertical file collection and about 2.5 million photographic images dating as far back as the 1850s.

A new Oklahoma History Center is scheduled to open in 2004. A timetable for moving archival materials had not been developed, although the library and archives are expected to be closed for several months during the moving process. Museum displays might already be affected. Call ahead for details.

At trail's end, you'll need a place to stay. Downtown hotels—about two miles away—include the **Renaissance Oklahoma City Hotel** [10 North Broadway; (405) 228-8000] and the **Westin Oklahoma City** [One North Broadway; (800) WESTIN-1 (937-8461)]. For a quick bite to eat, go to **Deli on the Commons** [728 Culbertson Drive; (405) 524-3354]. Since you may want to rent a car anyway to navigate this sprawling city, a better bet for lodging (more selection, moderate prices) would be the area north of the airport at the junction of Interstates 44 and 40. Many major chains are represented, including **Hampton Inn** [1905 South Meridian Avenue; (800) HAMPTON (426-7866)], **Comfort Inn & Suites** [4240 West I-40 Service Road; (800) 4-CHOICE (424-6423)], and **Hilton Garden Inn** [801 South Meridian Avenue; (800) 744-1500].

One of the most popular attractions in "OKC," as residents refer to their city, is the **National Cowboy and Western Heritage Museum** [1700 Northeast Sixty-third Street; (405) 478-2250; <www.nationalcowboymuseum.org>]. Renowned for its collection of Western art, including works by Charles Russell and Frederic Remington, the museum houses the famous eighteen-foot sculpture *End of the Trail*. Researchers can use the Donald C. & Elizabeth M. Dickinson Research Center, which contains personal papers, manuscript collections, and photographs documenting the westward movement and pioneer life; call (405) 478-2250 ext. 273 or 276 to make an appointment. For information on the center and access to online catalogs, visit the Web site at <www.nationalcowboymuseum.org/fs1_r.html>.

The University of Oklahoma Libraries system in nearby Norman does not have a genealogy collection, but its **Western History Collections** [(405) 325-3641; <libraries.ou.edu/depts/westhistory>] are available to researchers. The holdings include business records, scrapbooks, diaries, photos, and maps. Parking on campus is limited.

The **Red Earth Indian Center** in the Omniplex museum complex [2100 Northeast Fifty-second; (800) 532-7652; <www.omniplex.org>] features Native American art, dance regalia, and a cradleboard collection. If your ancestors settled during the Great Land Run of 1889, visit **The Harn Homestead Museum and 1889er Museum** [313 Northeast Sixteenth Street; (405) 235-4058; <www.harnhomestead.com>], which preserves a farmhouse and other buildings from that period.

For a peek at the lives of wealthier Oklahomans, you have a few options. You can take a tour of the **Overholser Mansion** [405 Northwest Fifteenth; (405) 528-8485], the first mansion in the city, or the **Oklahoma Heritage Center** [201 Northwest Fourteenth Street; (405) 235-4458; <www.oklahomaheritage.com>], which houses a former judge's furniture and china in his onetime home.

If you have an interest in military history, save time for the **45th Infantry Division Museum** [2145 Northeast Thirty-sixth Street; (405) 424-5313; <www.45thdivisionmuseum.com>].

When it comes time to rustle up some grub, you'll find plenty of steak houses. One of the most famous is **Cattlemen's Steakhouse** [1309 South Agnew; (405) 236-0416], located in the heart of historic Stockyards City and a local institution since 1910. The **501 Ranch Steak House** [3000 W. Britton; (405) 755-3501] boasts more than one thousand wine selections. Other popular choices include **Applewoods** [2747 West Memorial Road; (405) 752-4484] and the restaurants in historic Bricktown, a renovated entertainment and dining district. For an online list, see <www.Bricktownokc.com/restaurants.html>.

SALT LAKE CITY

BY PAULA STUART WARREN AND JAMES W. WARREN

When Brigham Young founded Salt Lake City in 1847, he decided that this oasis between the Wasatch Range and the Great Salt Lake would be the "New Jerusalem." Today, more than 150 years and one million people later, the booming metropolis of Salt Lake City draws the faithful, much as Young envisioned.

Salt Lake City is a mecca for family historians, too. Tens of thousands of them make a pilgrimage there every year. The **Family History Library** (FHL), on Temple Square in the heart of the city [35 North West Temple Street; (801)

Every year, some 800,000 genealogists make the trip to Salt Lake City to research their family history.

240-2331 or (800) 453-3860 ext. 22331; <www.familysearch.org>], houses the world's largest genealogical research collection. Odds are excellent that records in the Family History Library include some pertaining to one or more of your ancestors.

The library's collection, which covers the United States and many other countries, encompasses more than 2.2 million rolls of microfilmed records; almost 750,000 microfiche; and 300,000 books; plus indexes and electronic resources. The library puts row after row of self-service microfilm, microfiche, and books at researchers' fingertips. These sources contain church, birth, marriage, death, tax, land, probate, passenger arrival and departure, and census records, among others. The collection of family histories and locality histories in microform and in books is also extensive.

You have access to this fabulous library right in your own backyard—via your local Family History Center (FHC), where you can borrow most of the microfilm resources held in Salt Lake City. More and more of the library's riches are going online at <www.familysearch.org>, where you can peruse them in your pajamas.

Since records are accessible locally, why go all the way to Salt Lake City? With proper preparation, you can accomplish in a week in Salt Lake City what might take a year of research visits to a Family History Center. At the FHL, you can move from an index to the deed or census or probate records without waiting for them to be mailed. You can browse books that contain cemetery transcriptions, will abstracts, genealogical society publications, county histories, surname directories, research guides, and more. All researchers are welcome, free of charge. Mornings and evenings are the less busy times in the library.

Plan your arrival in Salt Lake City based on the schedule you want to follow. Some people prefer to arrive midweek and take a break for research reorganization on Sunday, when the

The Family History Library in Salt Lake City is the world's largest collection of genealogy materials.

library is closed; also, midweek airfares are generally cheaper. Others prefer a Sunday-to-Sunday trip so that they travel on the day the library is closed.

If you have never visited the FHL, start by giving yourself a tour of the four research floors. Locate the reference counter, reference book area, attendant's window, film cabinets, copy center, rest rooms, telephones, and elevators. Browse the books and binders in the general reference areas. Take a similar tour on subsequent trips to reacquaint yourself with the library's layout and any changes.

Each of the library's research floors has computers that provide access to the FamilySearch system, and each has a self-service copy center for copying from books and microforms. A general reference area on each floor features frequently used map guides, address lists, indexes, lists of film numbers for selected records, how-to guides, and more. Many of these excellent resources are in-house guides that are not available elsewhere.

You should bring family group sheets and ancestor charts for ready reference. Previous research, or at least good family clues, is neces-

RICHARD PRICE/THE SALT LAKE CONVENTION & VISITORS BUREAU IMAGE LIBRARY

Salt Lake City is home to the Church of Jesus Christ of Latter-day Saints.

research plan. Check the International Genealogical Index (IGI) and Ancestral File online for clues. If you find family connections via the IGI or Ancestral File, the library is the perfect place to check the validity of or to expand upon those clues.

Some lesser-used microfilms are housed in off-site storage. To obtain these films, you must place an order on the appropriate floor at the library attendant's window. Some films are available the same day; others take longer. There is no publicly available comprehensive list of these microfilms, though eventually the online catalog may indicate which films must be ordered. Check early in your trip for your most important films. If a film isn't in the drawer, you may need to order it, someone may be using it, or it may be out for repair or repackaging. The helpful staff at the attendant's window can check the status using the call number you've gleaned from the FHL catalog.

Throughout the library are free and low-cost informational brochures on a variety of topics including the IGI; Ancestral File; Hamburg Passenger Lists; Social Security Death Index; the Family History Library Catalog; and Research Outlines about genealogy in U.S. states, Canadian provinces, and many foreign countries. These brochures may also be viewed or ordered online via FamilySearch.

Researchers may bring briefcases, laptops, pens, staplers, notebooks, and other supplies into the library. An electronic security system makes sure no one removes library material. Occasionally, bags and briefcases are checked as patrons depart the building.

Family histories in book form are held a block away on the fourth floor of the historic **Joseph Smith Memorial Building** (JSMB). Family histories in microform remain in the FHL. In addition, the JSMB houses the FamilySearch Center, with more than 180 computer workstations and individual laser printers.

The JSMB also holds a duplicate set of the

sary for determining the correct localities to search, since the FHL's records are largely locality based. Use your family information to generate an alphabetized surname list and a chronological timeline; these are timesaving tools.

Also, review FamilySearch online before your trip. Use the online FHL catalog at the FamilySearch Web site to get the call numbers for items to check at the library upon arrival and to determine what information to bring along. If you find that few records for one ancestral locality are microfilmed, you may need an alternate

1920 U.S. census. A collection of family group records is kept in more than twenty-thousand binders. **The Garden Restaurant** and **The Roof Restaurant** are in the JSMB, which is open on Monday evenings when the library is closed.

When planning your trip, make your hotel or motel reservations well in advance. Salt Lake City, surrounded by many sports and cultural venues, is a popular destination. Accommodations near the FHL include **Best Western Salt Lake Plaza Hotel** [122 West South Temple Street; (800) 780-7234], **Carlton Hotel** [140 East South Temple Street; (800) 633-3500], and **Crystal Inn** [230 West 500 South; (800) 366-4466].

Much of the downtown area is a free-fare zone for buses and light rail, which runs one block from the library all the way south to Sandy, Utah. There are motels and restaurants near some rail stations. Bus lines radiate out from the light rail, and taxicabs are usually found at the stations.

Salt Lake City's street numbering system is easy to use once you understand it. Most street names indicate how far north, south, east, or west the streets are from Temple Square, which is the heart of the system. For example, the street 400 South lies four blocks south of Temple Square, and it runs east to west.

Some hotels offer shuttle service to and from the airport; commercial shuttle services are also available. Parking is available at area hotels, the malls, and surface parking lots within a few blocks of the library. The city blocks are longer and the streets are wider than in most cities. Temple Square, across from the library, has flowers in bloom much of the year and is a peaceful place to walk.

Within two blocks of the library are a convenience store, a small grocery, two drugstores that sell food and stationery supplies, movie theaters, and two enclosed shopping malls with many of the stores and services any traveler or shopper might need. A short cab ride can take you to office supply stores, a full-service grocery

The Family History Library's collection includes more than 2.2 million rolls of microfilmed records.

store, and many restaurants.

After a long day of searching the library, you'll probably be hungry. Some nearby restaurants you might want to try are **Romano's Macaroni Grill** [110 W. Broadway (300 South, in the Peery Hotel); (801) 521-3133], **Dee's** [143 West North Temple Street; (801) 359-4414], and **Richards Street Food Court** (in Crossroads Plaza Mall, one block from the library).

Nongenealogists traveling with you won't lack for activities in Salt Lake City. The area has plenty of ski sites, golf courses, professional sporting events, movie theaters, shopping malls, museums, symphony performances, parks, and live theater. Wendover, Nevada, just two hours away, has several casinos. Your companions might scout out specialty restaurants, brewpubs, the zoo, the water park, and other places you can visit together after your day at the FHL. Be sure to take in a performance of the Mormon Tabernacle Choir on Sunday morning at Temple Square.

The **Salt Lake Convention and Visitors Bureau** <www.visitsaltlake.com> is a good contact for information on the city and its hotels, museums, restaurants, and events. *The Insiders' Guide to Salt Lake City* <www.insiders.com/saltlake> is also a helpful travel resource.

COLORADO

ORGANIZATIONS & ARCHIVES

Colorado State Archives
1313 Sherman St.
Floor 1B, Room 20
Denver, CO 80203
(303) 866-2358 or (303) 866-2390
Fax: (303) 866-2257
<www.archives.state.co.us>

Colorado Genealogical Society
P.O. Box 9218
Denver, CO 80209
(303) 571-1535
<www.rootsweb.com/~cocgs>

Colorado Historical Society
Colorado Heritage Center
1300 Broadway
Denver, CO 80203
(303) 866-3682
Fax: (303) 866-4464
<www.coloradohistory.org>

Denver Public Library
Western History and Genealogy Department
10 W. Fourteenth Ave.
Parkway
Denver, CO 80204
(720) 865-1821
<www.denver.lib.co.us>

National Archives and Records Administration-Rocky Mountain Region (Denver)
Denver Federal Center,
Building 48
West Sixth Avenue and Kipling Street
P.O. Box 25307
Denver, CO 80225-0307
(303) 236-0817
Fax: (303) 236-9297
<www.archives.gov/facilities/co/denver.html>

RESOURCES

All That Glitters: Class, Conflict, and Community in Cripple Creek
by Elizabeth Jameson
(University of Illinois Press, $23.95)

From the Grave: A Roadside Guide to Colorado's Pioneer Cemeteries
by Linda Wommack
(Caxton Press, $24.95)

COLORADO

Statehood: 1876
Statewide Birth and Death Records Begin: 1907
Statewide Marriage Records Begin: 1907
Address for Vital Statistics:
Vital Records Section
Colorado Department of Health
4300 Cherry Creek Dr. South
Denver, CO 80222
(303) 756-4464
<www.cdphe.state.co.us/hs/certs.asp>

Available Censuses: U.S. federal censuses 1880, 1900, 1910, 1920, 1930, and a special federal census taken in 1885. Indexes are available for part of the 1880 census and for the 1900 and 1920 censuses. The four territories from which Colorado was created were enumerated in an 1860 federal territorial census. The northeastern part of the state is in the "unorganized territory" portion of the 1860 Nebraska census.

City Directories at the Family History Library Include: Boulder 1883, 1916, 1936, 1940, 1962, 1965, 1971, 1975, 1978, 1983, and 1988; Colorado Springs 1902-1935; Denver 1859, 1866, and 1871-1935; Fort Collins 1922, 1931, 1936, 1938, 1960, 1966, 1968, and 1969; Greeley 1946, 1966, and1968; Pueblo 1916, 1919, 1935, 1940, 1943, 1958, 1965, 1971, 1975, 1980, 1986, and 1989

PERIODICALS

Boulder Genealogical Society Quarterly (1969-), Boulder Genealogical Society, P.O. Box 3246, Boulder, CO 80307

The Colorado Genealogist (1939-), Colorado Genealogical Society, P.O. Box 9218, Denver, CO 80209

Piñon Whispers (1980-), Southeastern Colorado Genealogical Society, P.O. Box 4207, Pueblo, CO 81003

WEB SITES

Colorado GenWeb Project <www.rootsweb.com/~cogenweb/comain.htm>: Interactive map, tips on how to write a query, county resources.

Colorado Mailing Lists <www.rootsweb.com/~jfuller/gen_mail_states-co.html>: Special-interest, state, and county lists.

Colorado Resources at RootsWeb <resources.rootsweb.com/USA/CO>: Personal Web pages, searches, obituaries.

Colorado State Archives Genealogy Guide <www.archives.state.co.us/geneal.html>: Information about available genealogy records and how to obtain them.

Genealogy Data Files, Denver Public Library <www.denver.lib.co.us/ebranch/whg/datafile.html>: Denver obituaries (1939-2000), Colorado mining fatalities, Civil War veterans.

Ghostseekers <www.ghostseekers.com>: Searchable indexes and historical links.

Rita's Colorado Genealogy Clues <coloradoclues.com>: Help for researching 1895 Colorado.

Vital Records Information <vitalrec.com/co.html>: Where to obtain copies of birth and death certificates, marriage licenses, and divorce decrees.

Western History Photography Collection <gowest.coalliance.org>: Search images from the photography collection of the Western History/Genealogy Department at the Denver Public Library.

FAMILY HISTORY CENTERS

Arvada
7080 Independence
(303) 421-0920

Aurora
950 Laredo St.
(303) 367-0570

Boulder
701 W. South Boulder Rd.
(303) 665-4685

Brighton
1454 Myrtle
(303) 659-8489

Calhan
900 Monument St.
(719) 347-0199

Canon City
1435 Elm St.
(719) 276-3038

Colorado Springs
150 Pine Ave.
(719) 634-0572

Colorado Springs-East
4955 Meadowland Blvd.
(719) 268-9185

Colorado Springs-North
8710 Lexington Dr.
(719) 534-9621

Columbine
6705 S. Webster
(303) 973-3727

Cortez
1800 E. Empire
(970) 564-1064

Delta
1679 Pioneer Rd.
(970) 874-3444

Denver
2710 S. Monaco Parkway
(303) 756-0220

Denver-North
100 E. Malley Dr.
(303) 451-7177

Durango
2 Hilltop Circle
(970) 259-1061

Eagle Valley
0934 Gypsum Creek Rd.
(970) 524-9353

Fort Collins
600 E. Swallow Dr.
(970) 226-5999

Fort Morgan
336 Cherry St.
(970) 867-9523

Frisco
161 Forest Dr.
(970) 668-5633

Glenwood Springs
409 Twenty-ninth St.
(970) 963-2531

Golden
15605 W. Thirty-second
Ave.
(303) 233-6304

Greeley
501 Forty-ninth Ave.
(970) 356-1904

La Junta
2301 Raton
(719) 384-0427

Lakewood
6465 W. Jewell Ave.
(303) 935-3003

Littleton
1939 E. Easter Ave.
(303) 798-6461

Longmont
1721 Red Cloud Rd.
(303) 772-4373

Loveland
1417 W. Twenty-ninth St.
(970) 669-6498

Manassa
716 Broadway
(719) 274-4032

Meeker
1295 W. Ninth St.
(970) 824-2763

Meeker-Ward
903 Third St.
(970) 878-5870

Montrose
2030 Stratford
(970) 249-4739

Naturita
28224 Highway 141
(970) 865-2317

Pagosa Springs
1879 Majestic Dr.
(970) 731-2623

Paonia
Fifth and Oak St.
(970) 527-4084

Parker
7160 Bayou Gulch Rd.
(720) 851-0916

Pueblo
4720 Surfwood Lane
(719) 564-0793

Rangely
123 High St.
(970) 675-8678

Redmesa-Ward
6848 State Highway 140
(970) 588-3889

Rifle
849 S. Morrow Dr.
(970) 625-1883

Salida
1140 Poncha Blvd.
(719) 539-4987

Silverton
723 Green St.
(970) 387-0162

Steamboat Springs
1155 Central Park Dr.
(970) 879-0224

Sterling
513 N. Seventh Ave.
(970) 522-6407

STATE STATS

IDAHO

Statehood: 1890
Statewide Birth and Death Records Begin: 1911
Statewide Marriage Records Begin: 1947
Address for Vital Statistics:
  Vital Statistics Unit
  Idaho Department of Health and Welfare
  450 W. State St., 1st floor
  P.O. Box 83720
  Boise, ID 83720
  (208) 334-5988
  Fax: (208) 389-9096
  <www.state.id.us/dhw>

Available Censuses: U.S. federal censuses for 1900, 1910, and 1920. Indexes are available for 1900, 1910, and 1920. Included in territorial censuses of the Oregon Territory (1850), Washington Territory (1860), and Idaho Territory (1870 and 1880). Idaho County was enumerated in the 1860 census of Spokane County, Washington. Areas of southern Idaho were included in the 1860 and 1870 censuses of Cache County, Utah. Statewide indexes are available for the 1870 and 1880 censuses.

City Directories at the Family History Library Include: Boise 1902, 1905, 1915, 1918, 1921, 1923, 1927, 1904, and 1914-1918; Pocatello 1905-1906, 1921, 1903-1906, and 1927

IDAHO

ORGANIZATIONS & ARCHIVES

Idaho Genealogical Society
P.O. Box 1854
Boise, ID 83701
(208) 384-0542
<www.lili.org/
idahogenealogy>

Idaho State Historical Society
1109 Main St.
Suite 250
Boise, ID 83702
(208) 334-2682
<www.idahohistory.net>

Idaho State Historical Society Library and Archives
Genealogical and Historical Collections
450 N. Fourth St.
Boise, ID 83702
(208) 334-3357
Fax: (208) 334-3198
<www.idahohistory.net/
library_archives.html>
Mailing address:
4620 Overland Rd.
Room 204
Boise, ID 83705

David O. McKay Library
Brigham Young University Idaho
25 South Center St.
Rexburg, ID 83460

BRITISH COLUMBIA

ALBERTA

PEND
OREILLE

BOUNDARY

LINCOLN

GLACIER

TOOLE

HILL

LIBERTY

FLATHEAD

PONDERA

SPOKANE

BONNER

TETON

CHOUTEAU

KOOTENAI

Spokane

LAKE

SANDERS

Great Falls

BENEWAH

SHOSHONE

MINERAL

MONTANA

LEWIS
AND
CLARK

CASCADE

WHITMAN

LATAH

MISSOULA

POWELL

Helena

MEAGHER

GARFIELD

CLEARWATER

NEZ
PERCE

LEWIS

GRANITE

BROADWATER

ASOTIN

RAVALLI

JEFFERSON

DEER
LODGE

GALLATIN

IDAHO

SILVER
BOW

WALLOWA

PARK

IDAHO

LEMHI

BEAVERHEAD

MADISON

UNION

ADAMS

VALLEY

PARK

BAKER

WASHINGTON

CUSTER

CLARK

FREMONT

OREGON

PAYETTE

BOISE

JEFFERSON

MADISON

TETON

GEM

BUTTE

TETON

Boise

ADA

ELMORE

CAMAS

BLAINE

BONNEVILLE

CANYON

BINGHAM

MALHEUR

GOODING

LINCOLN

CARIBOU

JEROME

MINIDOKA

POWER

OWYHEE

BANNOCK

TWIN FALLS

CASSIA

BEAR
LAKE

LINCOLN

ONEIDA

FRANKLIN

NEVADA

UTAH

HUMBOLDT

ELKO

BOX ELDER

CACHE

RICH

(208) 496-2351
Fax: (208) 356-2390
<www.lib.byui.edu>

University of Idaho Library
Special Collections Library
Moscow, ID 83844
(208) 885-6584
Fax: (208) 885-6817
<www.lib.uidaho.edu>

RESOURCES

"Along the Continental Divide: Research in Montana, Idaho, and Wyoming"
lecture by Blaine R. Bake (Audiotapes.com, $8.50)

Idaho Atlas of Historical County Boundaries
edited by John Long (Charles Scribner's Sons, $130)

PERIODICALS

The Idaho Genealogical Society Quarterly
(1958-), Idaho Genealogical Society, 325 W. State St., Boise, ID 83702

WEB SITES

Idaho GenWeb Project
<www.rootsweb.com/ ~idgenweb>: Links to county-level resources, including queries and message boards.

Idaho Mailing Lists
<www.rootsweb.com/ ~jfuller/gen_mail_ states-id.html>: State and county-level mailing lists, plus special-interest lists.

Idaho Resources at RootsWeb
<resources.rootsweb. com/USA/ID>: Archived

messages, queries, message boards.

Vital Records Information
<vitalrec.com/id.html>: Get birth and death certificates, marriage licenses, and divorce decrees.

FAMILY HISTORY CENTERS

Aberdeen-Third Ward
149 W. Central

American Falls
650 Pocatello Ave.
(208) 226-9610

Arimo
286 Henderson Ave.
(208) 254-3846

Ashton
516 N. Second
(208) 652-7548

Bancroft
311 S. Main St.
(208) 648-7337

Bear Lake
661 Washington St.
(208) 847-0340

Blackfoot
815 Mitchell Ln.
(208) 785-5022

Blackfoot-West
101 North 900 West
(208) 684-3784

Boise
3676 W. Dorian
(208) 338-3811

Bonners Ferry
1512 Alderson Ln.
(208) 267-3802

Brigham Young University-Idaho
David O. McKay Library
(208) 496-2386

Burley
224 E. Fourteenth St.
(208) 878-7286

Caldwell
3015 S. Kimball
(208) 454-8324

Carey
821 Broadford Rd.
(208) 788-9810

Carey-Ward
Main St.
(208) 823-4384

Cascade
560 N. Highway 55
(208) 382-3230

Coeur D'Alene
2293 W. Hanley Ave.
(208) 765-0150

Driggs
221 North 100 East
(208) 354-2231

Eagle
2090 N. Eagle Rd.
(208) 939-4738

Emmett
980 W. Central Rd.
(208) 365-6142

Firth
133 S. Main St.
(208) 346-6011

Fruitland
320 N. Pennsylvania Ave., Room 17-18
(208) 452-4345

Garden Valley
Highway 17 (west of post office)
(208) 462-3036

Glenns Ferry
900 U.S. Highway 30
(208) 366-2027

Grace
406 S. Main
(208) 425-3121

Grand View
Highway 78
(208) 834-2717

Grangeville
403 N Blvd.
(208) 983-2110

Idaho Falls
750 W. Elva St.
(208) 524-5291

Idaho Falls-Ammon
3000 Central Ave.
(208) 529-4087

Idaho Falls-East
1860 Kearney
(208) 524-1038

Idaho State Correctional Facility
13400 Pleasant Valley Rd.
(208) 424-3733

Island Park
Big Springs Road
(208) 558-0177

Kamiah
Highway 12
(208) 935-0831

Kellogg
902 S. Division
(208) 682-2911

Kuna
3305 W. Kuna
(208) 922-1649

Lewiston
Ninth and Preston
(208) 743-1832

Malad
1250 North 1100 West
(208) 766-2332

McCall
400 Elo Rd.
(208) 634-5910

McCammon
403 W. Sixteenth
(208) 254-3259

Meridian-East
11443 McMillian Rd.
(208) 376-0452

Meridian-South
12040 W. Amity Rd.
(208) 362-2638

Meridian-West
1985 N. Black Cat Rd.
(208) 288-1338

Moore
3100 North 3350 West
(208) 554-2806

Mountain Home
1150 N. Eighth East
(208) 587-5249

Nampa
143 Central Canyon
(208) 467-5827

Orofino
13610 Fremont Ave.
(208) 476-3914

Pocatello
156 S. Sixth Ave.
(208) 232-9262

Preston-South
55 E. First South
(208) 852-0710

Priest River
3261 Highway 2
(208) 437-2474

Pullman Washington
1657 S. Blaine
(208) 882-1769

Rexburg-East
31 W. First North
(208) 656-3273

Rigby
258 W. First North
(208) 745-8660

Rigby-East
4021 East 300 North
(208) 745-7042

Roberts
1256 East 1500 North
(208) 663-4389

Salmon
400 S. Daisy
(208) 756-2371

Sandpoint
602 Schwitzer Cutoff
Rd.
(208) 263-3327

Shelley
544 Seminary Ave.
(208) 357-3128

Shoshone
Highway 75
(208) 886-2418

Soda Springs
290 S. Third West
(208) 547-3232

St. Anthony
449 N. Second West
(208) 624-4396

St. Maries
201 S. Twenty-third St.
(208) 245-2224

Twin Falls
401 Maurice St. North
(208) 733-8073

Weiser
300 E. Main St.
(208) 549-1575

KANSAS

ORGANIZATIONS & ARCHIVES

Kansas Council of Genealogical Societies
P.O. Box 3858
Topeka, KS 66604
<skyways.lib.ks.us/genweb/kcgs>

Kansas Genealogical Society, Inc.
2601 Central Ave.
P.O. Box 103

KANSAS

Statehood: 1861
Statewide Birth and Death Records Begin: 1911
Statewide Marriage Records Begin: 1913
Address for Vital Statistics:
Office of Vital Statistics
1000 SW Jackson St.
Suite 120
Topeka, KS 66612
(785) 296-1400
<www.kdhe.state.ks.us/vital>

Available Censuses: U.S. federal censuses for 1870, 1880, 1900, 1910, and 1920. Indexes are available for part of the 1880 and all of the 1900, 1910, and 1920 censuses. An 1860 federal territorial census is available, with an index, for the Territory of Kansas. State and territorial censuses also exist for 1855, 1865, 1875, 1885, 1895, 1905, 1915, and 1925. Statewide indexes exist for the 1855, 1860, 1865, and most of the 1875 censuses.

City Directories at the Family History Library Include: Kansas City 1860-1935, 1940, 1945, 1959, 1964, 1972, 1975, 1979, 1980, and 1982; Topeka 1868-1880, 1902, 1905-1935; Wichita 1878, 1883, 1885, 1910, 1918, and 1942; suburban Wichita 1958 and 1963

Dodge City, KS 67801
(316) 225-1951
<www.dodgecity.net/kgs>

Kansas State Historical Society
6425 S.W. Sixth Ave.
Topeka, KS 66615
(785) 272-8681
Fax: (785) 272-8682
<www.kshs.org>

Kansas State Library
State Capitol Building
300 S.W. Tenth
Room 343 N
Topeka, KS 66612
(800) 432-3919 or (785) 296-3296
Fax: (785) 296-6650
<skyways.lib.ks.us/KSL>

University of Kansas
Kenneth Spencer
Research Library-Kansas
Collection
Lawrence, KS 66045
(785) 864-4334
Fax: (785) 864-5803
<spencer.lib.ku.edu/kc>

RESOURCES

Indian Raids in Lincoln County, Kansas, 1864 and 1869
by C. Bernhardt (Lincoln Sentinel, out of print)

Kansas and the Homestead Act, 1862-1905
by Lawrence Bacon Lee
(Ayer Co., $50.95)

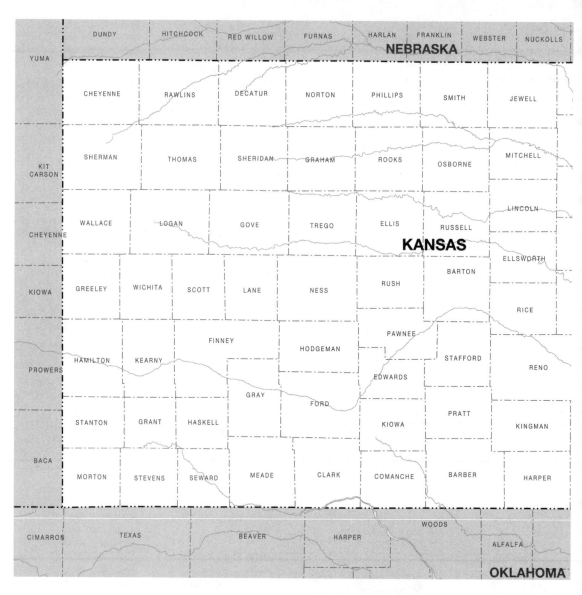

Kansas Territorial Settlers of 1860 Who Were Born in Tennessee, Virginia, North Carolina and South Carolina
by Clara Hamlett Robertson (Genealogical Publishing Co., $25)

PERIODICALS

The Descender
(1968-), Montgomery County Genealogical Society, P.O. Box 444, Coffeyville, KS 67337

The Heritage Genealogy Society Quarterly
(1972-), Heritage Genealogical Society, Wilson County, Kansas, W.A. Rankin Memorial Library, 502 Indiana, Neodesha, KS 66757

Kansas Kin Quarterly
(1963-), Riley County Kansas Genealogical Society, 2005 Claflin Rd., Manhattan, KS 66502

Midwest Historical and Genealogical Society Register
(1968-), Midwest Historical and Genealogical Society, P.O. Box 1121, Wichita, KS 67201

The Pioneer
(1977-), Douglas County Genealogical Society, P.O. Box 3664, Lawrence, KS 66046

The Seeker
(1971-), Crawford County Genealogical Society of Southeast Kansas, Pittsburg Library, 211 W. Fourth St., Pittsburg, KS 66762

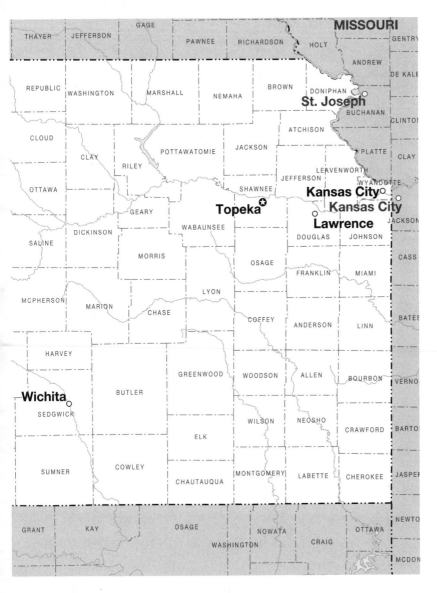

The map shows Kansas counties and cities including: THAYER, JEFFERSON, GAGE, PAWNEE, RICHARDSON, HOLT, GENTRY, MISSOURI, ANDREW, DE KALB, REPUBLIC, WASHINGTON, MARSHALL, NEMAHA, BROWN, DONIPHAN, St. Joseph, BUCHANAN, CLINTON, CLOUD, ATCHISON, CLAY, RILEY, POTTAWATOMIE, JACKSON, PLATTE, CLAY, OTTAWA, JEFFERSON, LEAVENWORTH, WYANDOTTE, SHAWNEE, Kansas City, Kansas City, GEARY, Topeka, WABAUNSEE, Lawrence, JACKSON, DICKINSON, DOUGLAS, JOHNSON, SALINE, MORRIS, OSAGE, CASS, FRANKLIN, MIAMI, MCPHERSON, MARION, LYON, CHASE, COFFEY, ANDERSON, LINN, BATES, HARVEY, GREENWOOD, WOODSON, ALLEN, BOURBON, VERNON, Wichita, BUTLER, SEDGWICK, WILSON, NEOSHO, CRAWFORD, BARTON, ELK, SUMNER, COWLEY, CHAUTAUQUA, MONTGOMERY, LABETTE, CHEROKEE, JASPER, GRANT, KAY, OSAGE, NOWATA, CRAIG, OTTAWA, NEWTON, WASHINGTON, MCDON

The Treesearcher
(1959-), Kansas Genealogical Society, P.O. Box 103, Dodge City, KS 67801

WEB SITES

Index to the 1895 Kansas State Census
<www.kshs.org/library/cens8ks.htm#indexes>: Searchable database for several counties in Kansas.

Kansas Family History
<www.ukans.edu/heritage/families/families_main.html>: Online family histories, Kansas heritage information, and an alphabetized pioneer list.

Kansas Genealogy and History
<members.aol.com/rprost/kansas.html>: Links to surnames, Civil War records, and vital records.

Kansas GenWeb Project
<skyways.lib.ks.us/genweb>: Queries, Kansas in the Civil War, history.

Kansas Heritage Server
<www.ukans.edu/heritage/heritage_main.html>: Digital preservation of records, Kansas research resources.

Kansas Mailing Lists
<www.rootsweb.com/~jfuller/gen_mail_states-ks.html>: Subscribe to county and state lists.

Kansas Resources at RootsWeb
<resources.rootsweb.com/USA/KS>: Personal Web pages and surname searches.

Vital Records Information
<vitalrec.com/ks.html>: Where to obtain copies of birth and death certificates, marriage licenses, and divorce decrees.

FAMILY HISTORY CENTERS

Burlington
604 S. Fourth
(316) 364-8077

Colby
1145 S. Franklin
(785) 462-7998

Concordia
135 1/2 W. Eighth
(785) 243-5072

Dodge City
2508 Sixth Ave.
(316) 225-6540

Emporia
2313 Graphic Arts Rd.
(316) 343-1304

Great Bend
5851 Eisenhower
(316) 793-7328

Hays
501 W. Twenty-ninth St.
(785) 625-2817

Hutchinson
18 Seventeenth Crestview Dr.
(620) 665-1187

Independence
507 Mulberry
(620) 331-7323

Iola
1420 E. Carpenter St.
(620) 365-3544

Junction City
1705 McFarland
(785) 762-8662

Kansas City
8616 Haskell
(913) 299-2876

Lawrence
3655 W. Tenth St.
(785) 843-4460

Leavenworth
1010 Limit St.
(913) 682-7729

Lenexa
7100 Hadley
(913) 722-0230

Liberal
2180 Violet
(316) 624-3544

Manhattan
2812 Marlatt Ave.
(785) 539-5445

Mound City
Highway 52 and 800 Road

Newton
1201 Grandview

Olathe
15915 W. 143rd St.
(913) 829-1775

Ottawa
1212 Willow Ln.
(785) 242-5611

Paola
Old 169 and 68 Highway
(913) 294-4411

Phillipsburg
620 S. Seventh St.
(785) 543-5851

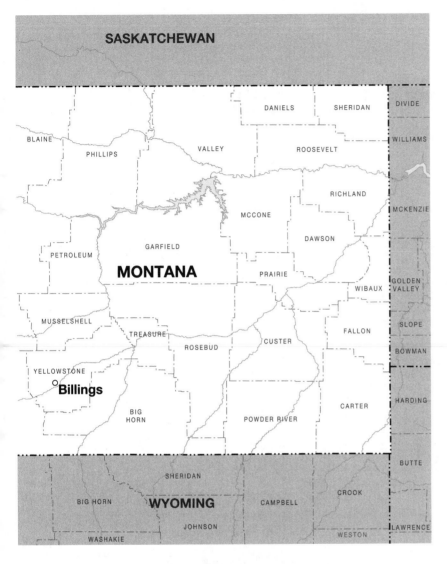

University of Montana
Maureen and Mike
Mansfield Library
32 Campus Dr. #9936
Missoula, MT 59812
(406) 243-6866
Fax: 406-243-4067
<www.lib.umt.edu>

RESOURCES

**"Along the Continental
Divide: Research in
Montana, Idaho, and
Wyoming"**
lecture by Blaine R. Bake
(Audiotapes.com, $8.50)

PERIODICALS

***Central Montana Wagon
Trails***
(1979-), Lewistown
Genealogy Society, 701
W. Main, Lewistown, MT
59457

Treasure State Lines
(1976-), Great Falls
Genealogy Society, Paris
Gibson Square, 1400 First
Ave. N., Great Falls, MT
59401

Trees and Trails
(1976-), Flathead Valley
Genealogical Society,
P.O. Box 584, Kalispell,
MT 59903

Tri-County Searcher
(1980-), Broken
Mountains Genealogical
Society, P.O. Box 261,
Chester, MT 59522

WEB SITES

Montana Genealogy
<freepages.genealogy.
rootsweb.com/~helper/
montana.htm>: Links to
Montana resources, his-
torical atlas.

Salina
845 S. Ohio
(785) 827-0058

Topeka
2401 S.W. Kingsrow Rd.
(785) 271-6818

Wichita
7011 E. Thirteenth St.
(316) 683-2951

MONTANA

ORGANIZATIONS & ARCHIVES

**Montana Historical
Society**
225 N. Roberts St.
P.O. Box 201201
Helena, MT 59620
(406) 444-2694
Fax: (406) 444-2696
<www.his.state.mt.us>

**Montana State
Genealogical Society**
P.O. Box 989
Boulder, MT 59632
<www.rootsweb.com/
~mtmsgs>

**Montana State
University**
Renne Library
P.O. Box 173320
Bozeman, MT 59717
(406) 994-3119
Fax: (406) 994-2851

MONTANA

Statehood: 1889
Statewide Birth and Death Records Begin: 1907
Statewide Marriage Records Begin: 1943
Address for Vital Statistics:
Montana Vital Records
State Department of Health
P.O. Box 4210
Helena, MT 59604
(406) 444-2685
Fax: (406) 444-1803
<vhsp.dphhs.state.mt.us/dph_l2.htm>

Available Censuses: U.S. federal censuses for 1900, 1910, and 1920. Indexes are available for the 1900 and 1920 censuses. In the 1860 census, western Montana was included in the Washington Territory and eastern Montana in the Nebraska Territory. Federal censuses for Montana Territory are available for 1870 and 1880. Indexes for the Montana portions of 1860, 1870, and 1880 are available.

City Directories at the Family History Library Include: Billings 1901-1935; Bozeman 1916, 1922, 1933, 1935, 1937, 1940, 1942, 1963, 1966, 1971, 1975, and 1980; Butte 1884 and 1890-1934; Great Falls 1903-1935; Helena 1889-1901, 1918, 1922, 1929, 1933, 1937, 1939, 1941, 1963, 1967, 1971, 1975, 1979, 1985, and 1990; Missoula 1915, 1922-23, 1934, 1936, 1938, 1940, 1943, 1959, 1964, 1970, 1975, 1980, 1986, and 1990

Montana GenWeb Project
<www.rootsweb.com/~mtgenweb>: Photo archives, online newspapers and queries, plus access to resources for Montana counties.

Montana Mailing Lists
<www.rootsweb.com/~jfuller/gen_mail_states-mt.html>: Join lists to discuss Montana state or county genealogy.

Montana Obituary Links
<www.geocities.com/~cribbswh/obit/mt.htm>:

Online newspaper listings.

Montana Resources at RootsWeb
<resources.rootsweb.com/USA/MT>: Find your family in Montana-related personal Web pages, and search for primary records.

Sons and Daughters of Montana Pioneers
<www.cowboysranch.com/SD.html>

Vital Records Information
<vitalrec.com/mt.html>:

Where to obtain copies of birth and death certificates, marriage licenses, and divorce decrees.

FAMILY HISTORY CENTERS

Belt
U.S. Highway 87
(406) 277-4442

Billings
2929 Belvedere Dr.
(406) 656-5559

Billings-East
1000 Wicks Lane
(406) 259-3348

Bozeman
2915 Colter Ave.
(406) 587-0402

Butte
3400 E. Four Mile Rd.
(406) 494-2413

Chester
580 W. Jefferson
(406) 759-5390

Choteau
1000 First St. NE
(406) 466-2725

Colstrip
115 Cherry St.
(406) 748-2039

Conrad
416 S. Kansas
(406) 278-5484

Cut Bank
414 Sixth Ave. SE
(406) 873-2806

Darby
107 Tin Cup Rd.
(406) 821-3826

Dillon
525 Barrett St.
(406) 683-2033

Ekalaka
118 Mormon Ave.
(406) 775-6583

Ennis
131 Montana Highway 287
(406) 682-4911

Eureka
1005 Osloski Rd.
(406) 296-3461

Fort Benton
2201 St. Charles
(406) 622-3662

Gardiner
1Z White Ln.
(406) 848-7509

Glasgow
800 Fourth Ave. North
(406) 228-2382

Glendive
1900 N. Anderson Ave.
(406) 365-2124

Great Falls
1401 Ninth St. NW
(406) 453-1625

Great Falls-East
1015 Fifteenth Ave. South
(406) 454-1611

Hardin
Corner of Ninth and Cody
(406) 665-3909

Havre
1315 Washington Ave.
(406) 265-7982

Helena
1610 E. Sixth Ave.
(406) 443-0716

Jordan
E. Marguerite Street
(406) 557-2307

Kalispell
1380 Whitefish Stage Rd.
(406) 752-5446

Lewistown
900 Casino Creek Dr.
(406) 538-9058

Libby
2056 U.S. Highway 2
South
(406) 293-4757

Livingston
110 W. Summit St.
(406) 222-3570

Malta
611 S. Fourth St. East
(406) 654-1207

Miles City
825 Moorehead
(406) 232-1487

Missoula
3201 Bancroft St.
(406) 543-6148

Polson
Fourth Avenue and
Highway 93
(406) 883-2565

Seeley Lake
Redwood Lane
(406) 677-2575

Sheridan
3560 Highway 287
(406) 842-5860

Sidney
1215 Fifth SW
(406) 482-3250

Stevensville
Eastside Highway and
Middle Burnt Road
(406) 777-5018

Superior
10 Moats Lane
(406) 822-4758

Thompson Falls
110 Golf St.
(406) 827-9757

Three Forks
Corner of Main and
Grove
(406) 285-3755

Townsend
916 Broadway
(406) 266-4255

NEBRASKA

ORGANIZATIONS & ARCHIVES

American Historical Society of Germans From Russia
631 D St.
Lincoln, NE 68502
(402) 474-3363
Fax: (402) 474-7229
<www.ahsgr.org>

Nebraska State Genealogical Society
P.O. Box 5608
Lincoln, NE 68505
(402) 266-8881
<www.rootsweb.com/
~nesgs>

Nebraska State Historical Society
Department of Reference Services
1500 R St.
Lincoln, NE 68501
(402) 471-4751
Fax: (402) 471-3100
<www.nebraskahistory.
org>
Mailing address:
P.O. Box 82554
Lincoln, NE 68501

PERIODICALS

Nebraska Ancestree
(1978-), Nebraska State Genealogical Society, P.O. Box 5608, Lincoln, NE 68505

The Nebraska and Midwest Genealogical Record
(1923-44), Nebraska

NEBRASKA

Statehood: 1867
Statewide Birth and Death Records Begin: 1905
Statewide Marriage Records Begin: 1909
Address for Vital Statistics:
  Department of Health and Human Services
  301 Centennial Mall South
  P.O.Box 95065
  Lincoln,NE 68509
  (402) 471-2871
  Fax: (402) 471-8230
  <www.hhs.state.ne.us/ced/nevrinfo.htm>

Available Censuses: U.S. federal censuses for 1860, 1870, 1880, 1900, 1910, and 1920. A special federal census of Nebraska for 1885 is available. Indexes are available for the 1860, 1870, 1880 (incomplete), 1900, and 1920 censuses. Territorial and state censuses exist for parts of Nebraska for 1854, 1855, 1856, 1860, 1865, and 1869.

City Directories at the Family History Library Include: Omaha 1866-1935, 1941, and 1959; Lincoln 1883-1901, 1923, 1940, 1960

Genealogical Society, Lincoln, Nebraska

Roots and Leaves
(1978-), Eastern Nebraska Genealogical Society, P.O. Box 541, Fremont, NE 68026

The Wagoner
(1978-), Northwest Genealogical Society, P.O. Box 6, Alliance, NE 69301

WEB SITES

Ancestors Lost and Found
<www.rootsweb.com/
~neresour/ancestors>:
Site dedicated to reuniting Nebraskans with old photos and memorabilia.

Nebraska GenWeb Project
<www.rootsweb.com/

~negenweb>: Online library, census projects, county resources, and queries.

Nebraska History and Record of Pioneer Days
<www.rootsweb.com/
~neresour/OLLibrary/
Journals/HPR>: Journals of the Nebraska State Historical Society beginning in 1918.

Nebraska History Resources
<www.nde.state.ne.us/SS/
nehist.html>: Links to trails, historic sites, notable Nebraskans.

Nebraska Mailing Lists
<www.rootsweb.com/
~jfuller/gen_mail_
states-ne.html>: Free subscriptions to county and state mailing lists.

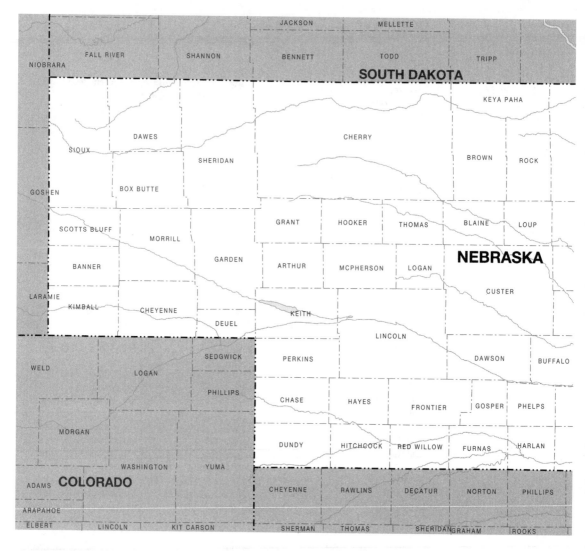

Nebraska Pioneers
<www.rootsweb.com/
~neresour/pioneer>:
Resource center on early
Nebraskan settlers.

Nebraska Resources at RootsWeb
<resources.rootsweb.
com/USA/NE>: Queries,
RootsWeb database
search engines, and tran-
scription projects.

Nebraska School Records
<idreamof.com/school/
ne.html>: Links to county
school records.

Vital Records Information
<vitalrec.com/ne.html>:
Where to obtain copies
of birth and death certificates, marriage licenses,
and divorce decrees.

FAMILY HISTORY CENTERS

Alliance
1327 Hammond Ln.
(308) 762-1308

Beatrice
326 N. Twenty-sixth St.
(402) 223-2581

Blair
2703 Sunrise Dr.
(402) 426-3299

Chadron
W. Tenth Street
(308) 432-5657

Columbus
4400 Thirty-third St.
(402) 564-6896

Gordon
800 North Ash
(308) 282-0635

Grand Island
212 W. Twenty-second
(308) 382-9418

Hastings
1725 Crane
(402) 463-3402

Kearney-Ward
510 E. Forty-sixth St.
(308) 234-3417

NORTH DAKOTA

ORGANIZATIONS & ARCHIVES

Bismarck-Mandan Historical and Genealogical Society
P.O. Box 485
Bismarck, ND 58502
<www.rootsweb.com/ ~ndbmhgs>

Chester Fritz Library
University of North Dakota
University Avenue and Centennial Drive
P.O. Box 9000
Grand Forks, ND 58202
(701) 777-2617
Fax: (701) 777-3319
<www.und.edu/dept/ library>

Germans From Russia Heritage Society
1125 W. Turnpike Ave.
Bismarck, ND 58501
(701) 223-6167
<www.grhs.com>

Institute for Regional Studies
North Dakota State University
P.O. Box 5599
Fargo, ND 58105
(701) 231-8914
Fax: (701) 237-5330
<www.lib.ndsu.nodak. edu/ndirs>

State Historical Society of North Dakota
North Dakota Heritage Center
612 E. Boulevard Ave.
Bismarck, ND 58505
(701) 328-2666
Fax: (701) 328-3710
<www.state.nd.us/hist>

Lincoln
3100 Old Cheney Rd.
(402) 423-4561

Macy
Off Highway 75
(402) 837-5204

McCook
411 Elizabeth Lane
(308) 345-5406

Nebraska City
920 Centennial Ave.
(402) 873-3500

Norfolk
100 El Camino Dr.
(402) 371-7441

North Platte
4100 W. A St.
(308) 532-0940

Omaha
11027 Martha St.
(402) 393-7641

O'Neill
130 N. Fourth St.
(402) 336-2167

Papillion
12009 S. Eighty-fourth St.
(402) 339-0461

Scottsbluff
501 Winter Creek Dr.
(308) 635-7012

Sidney
Toledo and Keller St.
(308) 254-5633

RESOURCES

Land in Her Own Name: Women As Homesteaders in North Dakota by H. Elaine Lindgren (University of Oklahoma Press, $19.95)

"Research in the Dakotas" lecture by Paula Stuart Warren (Audiotapes.com, $8.50)

Tracing Your Dakota Roots: A Guide to Genealogical Research in the Dakotas by Cathy A. Langemo and Jo Ann B. Winistorfer (Dakota Roots, $19.99)

PERIODICALS

The Dakota Homestead Historical Newsletter, formerly *Bismarck-Mandan Historical and Genealogical Society*

Quarterly (1972-), Bismarck-Mandan Historical and Genealogical Society, P.O. Box 485, Bismarck, ND 58502

Heritage Review, merged with *Der Stammbaum* (1969-), Germans From Russia Heritage Society, 1125 W. Turnpike Ave., Bismarck, ND 58501

North Central North Dakota Genealogical Record (1978-), Mouse River Loop Genealogical Society, P.O. Box 1391, Minot, ND 58702

WEB SITES

North Dakota Chronology <state.nd.us/hist/chrono. htm>: Important events in North Dakota history.

NORTH DAKOTA

Statehood: 1889
Statewide Birth and Death Records Begin: 1893
Statewide Marriage Records Begin: 1925
Address for Vital Statistics:
Division of Vital Records
600 E. Boulevard Ave.
Bismarck, ND 58505
(701) 328-2360
Fax: (701) 328-1850
<www.vitalnd.com>

Available Censuses: U.S. federal censuses for 1900, 1910, and 1920. A statewide index exists for the 1900 and 1920 censuses. North Dakota was included in the censuses of the Wisconsin (1836), Iowa (1840), Minnesota (1850), and Dakota Territories (1860, 1870, and 1880). Indexes to the censuses of the Wisconsin, Iowa, Minnesota, and Dakota Territories are available for 1836, 1840, 1850, 1860, 1870, and 1880. Censuses were also taken in 1885 (as Dakota Territory), 1905, 1915, and 1925.

City Directories at the Family History Library Include: Bismarck 1938, 1940, 1960, 1965, 1975, 1980, and 1986; Fargo 1883, 1891, 1893, and 1895-1934

North Dakota GenWeb Project
<www.rootsweb.com/~ndgenweb>: Research helps, county queries, 1890 map.

North Dakota History
<state.nd.us/hist/ndhist.htm>: An overview, beginning with pre-European contact.

North Dakota Mailing Lists
<www.rootsweb.com/~jfuller/gen_mail_states-nd.html>: Subscribe to free state and county mailing lists.

North Dakota Resources at RootsWeb
<resources.rootsweb.com/USA/ND>: Search RootsWeb-based archives and queries.

Vital Records Information
<vitalrec.com/nd.html>: Where to obtain copies of birth and death certificates, marriage licenses, and divorce decrees.

FAMILY HISTORY CENTERS

Bismarck
1500 Country West Rd.
(701) 223-6384

Dickinson
1200 Alder
(701) 264-7354

Fargo
2501 Seventeenth Ave. SW
(701) 232-4003

Grand Forks
2814 Cherry
(701) 746-6126

Minot
2025 Ninth St. NW
(701) 838-4486

Wahpeton
505 Richland St.
(701) 642-2463

Williston
1805 Twenty-sixth St. West
(701) 572-3502

ORGANIZATIONS & ARCHIVES

Museum of the Great Plains
601 NW Ferris Ave.
Lawton, OK 73507
(580) 581-3460
Fax: (580) 581-3458
<www.museum
greatplains.org>

Oklahoma Department of Libraries
Allen Wright Memorial
Library
200 N.E. Eighteenth St.
Oklahoma City, OK 73105
(405) 521-2502 or (800)
522-8116
Fax: (405) 525-7804
<www.odl.state.ok.us/
index.html>

Oklahoma Genealogical Society
P.O. Box 12986
Oklahoma City, OK 73157
<www.rootsweb.com/
~okgs>

Oklahoma Historical Society
Wiley Post Historical
Building Library Center
2100 N. Lincoln Blvd.
Oklahoma City, OK 73105
(405) 522-5209
Fax: (405) 521-2492
<www.ok-history.mus.
ok.us>

Oklahoma State Archives
Allen Wright Memorial
Library, third floor
200 N.E. Eighteenth St.
Oklahoma City, OK 73105
(405) 522-3579
Fax: (405) 522-3583
<www.odl.state.ok.us/
oar>

Gilcrease Museum
1400 N. Gilcrease
Museum Rd.
Tulsa, OK 74127
(888) 655-2278 or (918)

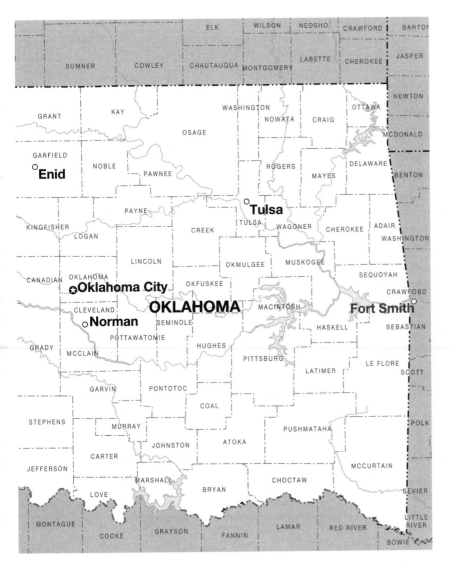

Four States Genealogist (1968-), Indian Nations Press, 812 Mayo Building, Tulsa, OK 74103

Oklahoma Genealogical Society Quarterly, formerly **The Bulletin** (1961-), Oklahoma Genealogical Society, P.O. Box 12986, Oklahoma City, OK 73157

The Texarkana U.S.A. Quarterly (1974-), Texarkana U.S.A. Genealogical Society, P.O. Box 2323, Texarkana, AK-TX 75504

The Tree Tracers (1976-), Southwest Oklahoma Genealogical Society, P.O. Box 148, Lawton, OK 73502

Tulsa Annals (1966-), Tulsa Genealogical Society, P.O. Box 585, Tulsa, OK 74101

WEB SITES

Oklahoma GenWeb Project <www.rootsweb.com/ ~okgenweb>: Stop here to find links to county resources and records.

Oklahoma History <www.oklaosf.state.ok. us/?c=8&sc=95>: Overview of Spanish Americans, Native Americans, and African Americans in Oklahoma.

Oklahoma Land Rush <www.library.cornell. edu/Reps/DOCS/ landrush.htm>: 1889 *Harper's Weekly* account of Oklahoma settlement.

596-2700
<www.gilcrease.org>

University of Oklahoma Libraries
Western History Collections
Monnet Hall, Room 452
University of Oklahoma
Norman, OK 73019
(405) 325-3641
Fax: (405) 325-6069
<libraries.ou.edu/depts/ westhistory>

RESOURCES

Exploring Your Cherokee Ancestry
by Thomas G. Mooney (Cherokee National Historical Society, $10)

"Finding Your Ancestor in Oklahoma—The Twin Territories"
lecture by Sharon Burns (Audiotapes.com, $8.50)

PERIODICALS

The Chronicles of Oklahoma
(1923-), Oklahoma Historical Society, 2100 N. Lincoln Blvd., Oklahoma City, OK 73105

Dusty Trails
(1974-1980), Genealogical Institute of Oklahoma, 3813 Cashion Place, Oklahoma City, OK 73112

OKLAHOMA

STATE STATS

Statehood: 1907
Statewide Birth and Death Records Begin: 1908
Statewide Marriage Records Begin: 1908
Address for Vital Statistics:
Vital Records Section
State Department of Health
1000 N.E. Tenth St., Room 111
P.O. Box 53551
Oklahoma City, OK 73117
(405) 271-4040
<www.health.state.ok.us/program/vital>

Available Censuses: U.S. federal censuses for 1910 and 1920. Indexes exist for both. Oklahoma was included in the 1860 census of Arkansas. The 1870 and 1880 territorial censuses have been lost and the 1890 was destroyed. For 1900, there are separate schedules and indexes for the Indian Territory and the Oklahoma Territory for 1900. In addition to the federal territorial censuses, there was a separate census of the Oklahoma Territory in 1890.

City Directories at the Family History Library Include: Oklahoma City 1905, 1916, 1941, 1960, and 1969; Tulsa 1909-1932, and 1966

Oklahoma Mailing Lists
<www.rootsweb.com/~jfuller/gen_mail_states-ok.html>: County and state lists.

Oklahoma Resources at RootsWeb
<resources.rootsweb.com/USA/OK>: Search personal Web sites, U.S. GenWeb archives, and surnames using multiple search engines.

Vital Records Information
<vitalrec.com/ok.html>: Where to obtain copies of birth and death certificates, marriage licenses, and divorce decrees.

FAMILY HISTORY CENTERS

Ada
2100 Arlington
(580) 332-5892

Ardmore
Prairie Valley Road
(405) 226-2134

Bartlesville
1501 S.E. Swan Dr.
(918) 333-3135

Chickasha
1111 Ferguson Dr.
(405) 222-0111

Claremore
1701 N. Chambers Terr.
(918) 342-0101

Cleveland
Highway 64
(918) 358-3743

Clinton
430 S. Twenty-ninth St.
(580) 323-2435

Cushing
1500 E. Ninth St.
(918) 225-3234

Elm Creek
9300 North 129 East Ave.
(918) 272-2048

Enid
419 N. Eisenhower St.
(580) 234-3313

Lawton
7202 S.W. Drakestone
(580) 536-1303

McAlester
405 W. Gene Stipe
(918) 423-3762

Muskogee
3008 E. Hancock Rd.
(918) 687-8861

Norman
1506 W. Imhoff Rd.
(405) 364-8337

Oklahoma City
5020 N.W. Sixty-third St.
(405) 721-8455

Oklahoma City-South
12915 S. Santa Fe
(405) 794-3800

Pawhuska
Fifteenth and Red Eagle
(918) 287-2107

Ponca City
2408 E. Hartford
(580) 765-3464

Sapulpa
950 Pioneer Rd.
(918) 224-7585

Seminole
2500 John St.
(405) 997-5217

Shawnee
1501 E. Independence
(405) 273-7943

Stillwater
1720 E. Virginia Ave.
(405) 377-4122

Tulsa
3640 S. New Haven
(918) 747-3966

Tulsa-East
12110 E. Seventh St.
(918) 437-5690

Woodward
2023 Main St.
(580) 256-5113

SOUTH DAKOTA

ORGANIZATIONS & ARCHIVES

Center for Western Studies
Augustana College
P.O. Box 727
Sioux Falls, SD 57197
(800) 727-2844, ext. 4007
or (605) 274-4007
Fax: (605) 274-4999
<inst.augie.edu/CWS>

I.D. Weeks Library
University of South Dakota
414 E. Clark St.
Vermillion, SD 57069
(605) 677-5371
Fax: (605) 677-5488
<www.usd.edu/library/idweeks.html>

South Dakota Genealogical Society
P.O. Box 1101
Pierre, SD 57501
(605) 224-3670
<www.rootsweb.com/~sdgenweb/gensoc/sdgensoc.html>

South Dakota State Historical Society
900 Governors Dr.
Pierre, SD 57501-2217
(605) 773-3458
Fax: 605-773-6041
<www.sdhistory.org>

RESOURCES

"Research in the Dakotas"
lecture by Paula Stuart Warren (Audiotapes.com, $8.50)

Tracing Your Dakota Roots: A Guide to Genealogical Research in the Dakotas
by Cathy A. Langemo and Jo Ann B. Winistorfer (Dakota Roots, $19.99)

PERIODICALS

Black Hills Nuggets
(1968-), Rapid City Society for Genealogical Research, P.O. Box 1495, Rapid City, SD 57709

Pioneer Pathfinder
(1975-), Sioux Valley Genealogical Society, 200 W. Sixth South, Sioux Falls, SD 57104

South Dakota Genealogical Society Quarterly
(1982-), South Dakota Genealogical Society, P.O. Box 1101, Pierre, SD 57501

The Tree Climber
(1974-), Aberdeen Area Genealogical Society, P.O. Box 493, Aberdeen, SD 57402

WEB SITES

Chronology of South Dakota History
<www.sdhistory.org/

soc_hist.htm>: Timeline of important events, such as the Lewis and Clark expedition from St. Louis to the Pacific and the formal establishment of the Dakota Territory.

History of South Dakota
<rapidweb.com/
sdhistory>: Early history of the state, including information about the Louisiana Purchase, the Lewis and Clark expedition, and the importance of the fur industry.

Mayflower **Passengers**
<rapidnet.com/~saj/
custer/mayfl.html>:
Information about South Dakota *Mayflower* descendants.

South Dakota Birth Records
<www.state.sd.us/doh/
VitalRec/birthrecords/
index.cfm>: Searchable database of birth records for people who died more than one hundred years ago.

South Dakota GenWeb Project
<www.rootsweb.com/
~sdgenweb>: Links to county sites, birth records and various historical resources

South Dakota Bureau of Land Management Database
<www.rootsweb.com/
~usgenweb/sd/land/
sdland.htm>
This database contains all homestead, mining, and timber claims, as well as cash sales and Indian allotments from 1859 to 1995.

South Dakota Mailing Lists
<www.rootsweb.com/
~jfuller/gen_mail_
states-sd.html>: Free subscriptions to county and state mailing lists.

South Dakota Resources at RootsWeb
<resources.rootsweb.
com/USA/SD >: Search RootsWeb databases and look for personal Web sites about your South Dakota family.

Vital Records Information
<www.vitalrec.com/sd.
html>: Birth and death certificates, marriage licenses, and divorce decrees.

FAMILY HISTORY CENTERS

Aberdeen
1115 Twenty-fourth Ave. NE
(605) 225-0601

Belle Fourche
1105 Todd St.
(605) 892-3700

Brookings
200 Twenty-second Ave.
(605) 692-9350

Gettysburg
530 S. Mannston St.
(605) 765-9270

Hot Springs
2133 Albany St.
(605) 745-6119

Huron
1450 Frank St. SE
(605) 352-6849

Madison
927 N. Lee Ave.
(605) 256-6335

Pierre
506 N. Jefferson
(605) 224-9117

Rapid City
2822 Canyon Lake Dr.
(605) 343-8656

Rosebud
Highway 7 West St.
(605) 747-2128

Sioux Falls
3900 S. Fairhall Ave.
(605) 361-1070

Vermillion
20 Mickelson Ave.
(605) 624-7139

Watertown
1200 Nineteenth St. NE
(605) 882-2299

Yankton
Twenty-third and
Douglas
(605) 665-5307

UTAH

ORGANIZATIONS & ARCHIVES

**Church History Library
and Church Archives**
The Church of Jesus
Christ of Latter-day Saints
50 East North Temple St.
Salt Lake City, UT 84150

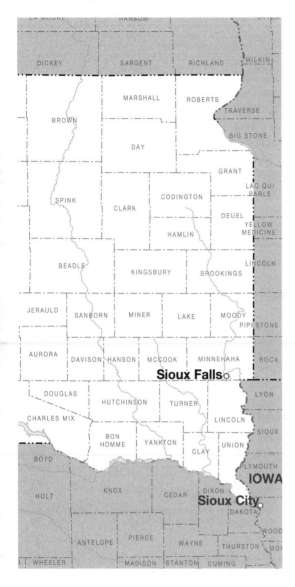

Family History Library
35 North West Temple St.
Salt Lake City, UT 84150
(800) 453-3860, ext.
22331 or (801) 240-2331
Fax: (801) 240-1584
<www.familysearch.org>

**Family History Centers
Support Unit**
50 East North Temple St.
Salt Lake City, UT 84150
(800) 346-6044

**Gerald R. Sherratt Library
Special Collections**
Southern Utah University
351 W. Center St.
Cedar City, UT 84720
(435) 586-7933
Fax: (435) 865-8152
<lib.li.suu.edu>

Harold B. Lee Library
Brigham Young
University
Provo, UT 84602

(801) 378-2926
<www.lib.byu.edu/hbll>

**J. Willard Marriott
Library**
University of Utah
295 South 1500 East
Salt Lake City, UT 84112
(801) 581-8558
Fax: (801) 585-3464
<www.lib.utah.edu/
index.phtml>

Merrill Library
Utah State University
Logan, UT 84322
(435) 797-2631
Fax: (435) 797-2880
<library.usu.edu>

**National Society of The
Sons of Utah Pioneers**
3301 E. 2920 S
Salt Lake City, UT 84109
(888) 827-2746
(801) 484-4441
Fax: (801) 484-2067
<www.sonsofutah
pioneers.org>

**Salt Lake City Public
Library**
209 East 500 South
Salt Lake City, UT 84111
(801) 524-8200
Fax: (801) 524-8289
<www.slcpl.lib.ut.us>

Stewart Library
Weber State University
2901 University Circle
Ogden, UT 84408
(877) 306-3140 or
(801) 626-6415
Fax: (801) 626-7045
<library.weber.edu>

**Utah Genealogical
Association**
P.O. Box 1144
Salt Lake City, UT 84110
(888) INFO-UGA
<www.infouga.org>

Utah State Archives
Archives Building
State Capitol

P.O. Box 141021
Salt Lake City, UT 84114
(801) 538-3013
Fax: (801) 538-3354
<www.archives.state.
ut.us>

**Utah History Information
Center**
300 Rio Grande
Salt Lake City, UT 84101
<history.utah.org>

**Utah State Historical
Society Library**
300 S. Rio Grande St.
Salt Lake City, UT 84101
(801) 533-3500
Fax: (801) 533-3503
<www.history.state.ut.
us.html>

**Utah Valley Regional
Family History Center**
Harold B. Lee Library, 2N
Brigham Young
University
Provo, UT 84602
(801) 378-6200
Fax: (801) 538-1050
<www.lib.byu.edu/dept/
uvrfhc>

RESOURCES

*Going to Salt Lake City
to Do Family History
Research*
by J. Carlyle Parker
(Marietta Publishing Co.,
$15.95)

*Your Guide to the Family
History Library*
by James W. Warren and
Paula Stuart Warren
(Betterway Books,
$19.99)

PERIODICALS

Genealogical Journal
(1972-), Utah
Genealogical Association,
P.O. Box 1144, Salt Lake
City, UT 84110

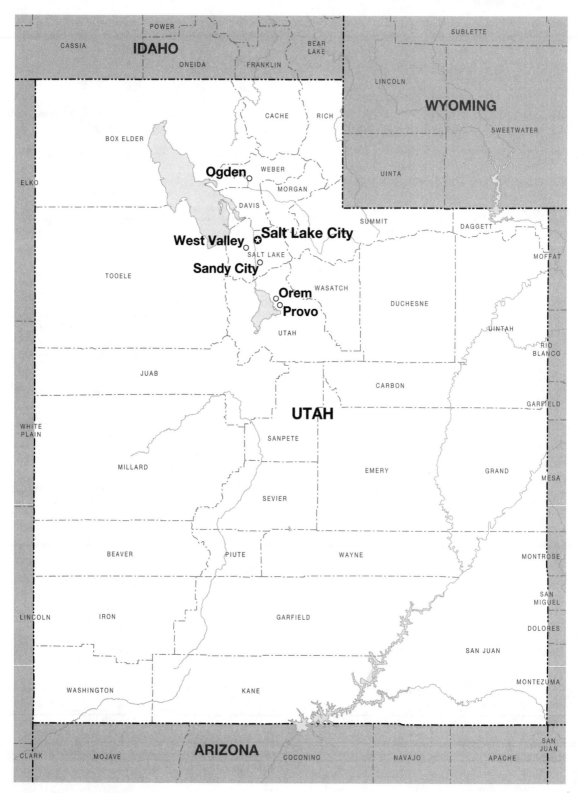

IDAHO

WYOMING

UTAH

ARIZONA

Pioneer
(1953, 1981-), National Society of the Sons of Utah Pioneers, 3301 E. 2920 S, Salt Lake City, UT 84109

Newsletter of the Utah Genealogical Association
(1971-),Utah Genealogical Association, P.O. Box 1144, Salt Lake City, UT 84110

Utah Genealogical and Historical Magazine
(1910-1940) Genealogical Society of Utah

Utah Historical Quarterly
(1928-), Utah State Historical Society, 300 S. Rio Grande, Salt Lake City, UT 84101

WEB SITES

Tracing Mormon Pioneers
<xmission.com/~nelsonb/pioneer.htm>: Step-by-step guide to tracing Mormons traveling to Utah from 1847 to 1868.

Utah GenWeb Project
<www.rootsweb.com/~utgenweb>: Links to county resources.

Utah Mailing Lists
<www.rootsweb.com/~jfuller/gen_mail_states-ut.html>: Special-interest, state, and county lists.

Utah Resources at RootsWeb
<resources.rootsweb.com/USA/UT>: Queries, message boards, mailing lists, and RootsWeb search engines.

Utah's Online Library
<pioneer.lib.ut.us>: Utah links, references, government information, virtual libraries, and more.

Vital Records Information
<vitalrec.com/ut.html>: Where to obtain copies of birth and death certificates, marriage licenses, and divorce decrees.

FAMILY HISTORY CENTERS

Alpine-North
1125 E. Alpine Blvd.
(801) 763-4580

Altamont
Main Street
(435) 454-3422

American Fork
110 E. Main
(801) 763-2014

BYU 8th
1021 South 500 West
(801) 370-6626

BYU 11th
1915 N. Canyon Rd.
(801) 378-7917

BYU 17th
800 South 800 West
(801) 378-1171

BYU 18th
945 East 700 North
(801) 370-6675

Beaver
1380 East 200 North
(435) 438-5262

Bennion
6250 South 2200 West
(801) 964-7201

Blanding
200 S. Main
(435) 678-2728

Boulder
180 East 300 North
(435) 335-7302

Bountiful-Heights
1240 East 500 North
(801) 299-4245

Bountiful-North Canyon
3350 South 100 East
(801) 299-4239

Brigham City
10 South 400 East
(435) 723-5995

Cache
50 N. Main St.
(435) 755-5594

Canyon Springs
9501 S. Poppy Ln.
(801) 576-2966

Castle Dale
290 W. Highway 29
(435) 381-2899

Castle Valley
8 Chamisa Ln.
(435) 259-7028

Cedar City
155 East 400 South
(435) 586-2296

Cedar City-North
95 North 2125 West
(435) 586-0432

Center for Family History & Genealogy-JSB
102 JSB BYU
(801) 378-8069

Center For Family History & Genealogy-KMB
BYU, KMB, Third Floor
(801) 378-1110

Circleville
195 West 200 South
(435) 577-2528

Clearfield
935 S. State St.
(801) 774-2188

Coalville
40 N. Main
(435) 336-1478

Delta
52 North 100 West
(435) 864-3312

Draper
13085 South 300 East
(801) 576-2839

Duchesne
901 North 500 East
(435) 738-5371

Dutch John
Sixth Avenue and South Boulevard

East Carbon
145 Grassy Trail Dr.
(435) 888-9989

Elberta
12800 West 15300 South

Enterprise
80 S. Center
(435) 878-2520

Ephraim
571 E. College Ave.
(435) 283-6489

Escalante
100 W. Center St.
(435) 679-8693

Escalante-Ward
80 S. Center St.
(435) 826-4217

Eureka
70 E. Main St.

Farmington
272 N. Main St.
(801) 451-1998

Ferron
35 West 200 North
(435) 384-3288

Fillmore
21 South 300 West
(435) 743-6614

Genola
11 N. Main St.
(801) 754-3965

Glendale
115 South 100 East
(435) 648-2305

Goshen
70 S. Center
(801) 667-3232

Grantsville-West
115 E. Cherry St.
(435) 884-1220

Green River
101 N. Clark St.
(435) 564-3582

Gunnison
80 W. Center
(435) 528-7347

Hanksville
59 S. Center
(435) 542-3201

Heber City
160 W. Main St.
(435) 654-2760

Helper
150 Ridgeway
(435) 472-3799

Highland
9600 North 6800 West
(801) 766-1725

Huntington
11 East 200 North
(435) 687-9090

Hurricane
37 South 200 West
(435) 635-2174

Hyrum-North
245 N. Apple Dr.
(435) 245-4551

Ivins
290 East 1060 South
(435) 634-1852

Kamas
3038 N. State Route 32
(435) 783-2921

Kanab
202 East 100 North
(435) 644-5973

Kaysville-East
201 South 600 East
(801) 543-2845

Kaysville-South
900 S. Main St.
(801) 543-2869

Kearns-Central
5823 South 4800 West
(801) 964-7470

Kearns-West
6175 W. Borax Ave.
(801) 964-7380

La Sal
401 E. Wilcox

Laketown
115 South 100 East
(435) 946-2927

Layton-Layton Hills
590 West 2000 North
(801) 774-2070

Layton-Valley View
1589 E. Gentile
(801) 543-2908

Lehi
200 N. Center St.
(801) 768-3054

Lindon
1050 East 100 North
(801) 785-7586

Loa
14 South 100 West
(435) 836-2322

Logan-Cache
105 East 500 North
(435) 755-7999

Magna-Central
8181 West 3320 South
(801) 252-2530

Magna-East
3151 South 7700 West
(801) 252-2539

Manila
First West and First North
(435) 784-3381

Manti
86 East 500 North
(435) 835-8888

Mapleton
1215 North 1000 West
(801) 489-2999

Midvale-Union Fort
7155 South 540 East
(801) 562-8085

Milford
748 West 600 South
(435) 387-2419

Moab
300 South 100 East
(435) 259-5563

Monroe-Stake
260 E. Center St.
(435) 527-4612

Montezuma Creek
300 East and Highway 263

Monticello
347 N. Second West
(435) 587-2139

Morgan
93 N. State St.
(801) 829-6261

Moroni
300 N. Center St.
(435) 436-8497

Mount Pleasant
398 S. State
(435) 462-2406

Mount Pleasant-North
461 North 300 West
(435) 462-3972

Mount Timpanogos
835 North 896 East
(801) 763-2093

Murray-Little Cottonwood
6180 Glen Oaks
(801) 264-4136

Murray-South
5735 S. Fashion Blvd.
(801) 264-4145

Murray-West
5750 S. Nena Way
(801) 264-4152

Nephi
1125 North 400 East
(435) 623-2964

Ogden
539 Twenty-fourth St.
(801) 626-1132

Orem-Geneva Heights
546 North 500 West
(801) 222-0529

Orem-Lakeridge
450 South 100 West
(801) 222-0497

Orem-Park
50 South 750 West
(801) 222-3104

Orem-Sharon Park
85 East 700 North
(801) 222-0319

Orem-Sunset Heights
1260 South 400 West
(801) 222-0449

Panguitch
290 E. Center St.
(435) 676-2201

Park City
1733 Lucky John Dr.
(435) 645-0914

UTAH

Statehood: 1896
Statewide Birth and Death Records Begin: 1905
Statewide Marriage Records Begin: 1887
Address for Vital Statistics:
 Bureau of Vital Records
 Utah State Department of Health
 288 North 1460 West St.
 P.O. Box 141012
 Salt Lake City, UT 84114
 (801) 538-6105
 <health.utah.gov/bvr>

Available Censuses: U.S. federal censuses for Utah for 1850 (1851), 1860, 1870, 1880, 1900, 1910, and 1920. Statewide indexes exist for the 1850, 1860, 1870, 1880, 1900, and 1920 censuses. Territorial censuses exist for 1856 and 1872.

City Directories at the Family History Library Include: Ogden, 1890-1935; Provo 1879, 1884, 1888, 1891, 1904, 1913-1918, 1920, 1926, 1930, 1935, 1941, 1946, 1950, 1955, 1961, 1965, 1969, 1975, 1980, 1985, 1987, and 1996; Salt Lake City 1867-1935

Parowan
87 W. Center St.
(435) 477-8077

Payson
590 S. Main
(801) 465-1349

Pleasant Grove-East
1250 East 200 South
(801) 796-4515

Pleasant Grove-Grove Creek
1176 North 730 East
(801) 785-7575

Price
85 East 400 North
(435) 637-2071

Provo-Bonneville
85 South 900 East
(801) 370-6674

Provo-Cove Point
1988 N. Cove Point Lane
(801) 370-6757

Provo-East
667 North 600 East
(801) 370-6713

Provo-Edgemont
4000 N. Timpview Dr.
(801) 222-0567

Provo-Edgemont North
4300 N. Canyon Rd.
(801) 222-3108

Provo-Grandview East
1081 West 1060 North
(801) 370-6777

Provo-North Park
1066 West 200 North
(801) 370-6638

Provo-North Park-Hispanic
376 North 700 West

Provo-South
610 West 300 South
(801) 370-6830

Provo-Sunset
1402 South 570 West
(801) 370-6844

Randolph/Woodruff
15 S. Main

Richfield
175 W. Center St.
(435) 896-8057

Riverton
12619 South 3600 West
(801) 253-7085

Roosevelt
290 West 300 North
(435) 722-9213

Salem
695 South 300 West
(801) 423-9160

Salina
98 West 400 North
(435) 529-3447

Salt Lake-Big Cottonwood
1750 E. Spring Lane
(801) 273-3719

Salt Lake-Canyon Rim
3301 East 2920 South
(801) 468-5835

Salt Lake-Emigration
680 Second Ave.
(801) 578-6661

Salt Lake-Granger South
4251 South 4800 West
(801) 964-7250

Salt Lake-Granger West
3280 South 4440 West
(801) 964-7490

Salt Lake-Hillside
1400 South 1900 East
(801) 584-3142

Salt Lake-Holladay South
4917 Viewmont St.
(801) 273-3735

Salt Lake-Hunter
3737 South 5600 West
(801) 964-3012

Salt Lake-Hunter West
7035 West 3605 South
(801) 252-2560

Salt Lake-Jordan North
3900 South 4000 West
(801) 964-7465

Salt Lake-Millcreek
4220 South 420 East
(801) 264-4052

Salt Lake-Monument Park
3125 Kennedy Dr., #607
(801) 584-3163

Salt Lake-Mt. Olympus
3862 Oakview Dr.
(801) 273-3812

Salt Lake-Olympus
2675 East 4430 South
(801) 273-3836

Salt Lake-Park
732 South 800 East
(801) 578-6719

Salt Lake-Rose Park
760 North 1200 West
(801) 578-6769

Salt Lake-South (Tongan)
4660 West 5015 South
(801) 964-7363

Salt Lake (Tongan)
3150 W. Whitehall Dr.
(801) 964-3074

Salt Lake-Wasatch
8170 Short Hills Dr.
(801) 944-2075

Salt Lake-Winder
4366 South 1500 East
(801) 273-3862

Sandy-Cottonwood Creek
1535 E. Creek Rd.
(801) 944-2140

Sandy-Crescent
10945 South 1700 East
(801) 576-2891

Sandy-Crescent Park
11350 South 1000 East
(801) 576-2949

Sandy-Crescent South
10375 S. Leilani Dr.
(801) 576-2953

Sandy-Crescent West
1265 East 11000 South
(801) 576-2971

Sandy-East
1600 Buttercup Dr.
(801) 495-7778

Sandy-Granite South
2126 E. Gyrfalcon Dr.
(801) 944-2131

Sandy-Hidden Valley
1617 East 12700 South
(801) 576-2832

Santa Clara
3040 W. Santa Clara Dr.
(435) 652-8036

Santaquin
45 South 500 West
(801) 754-3534

South Jordan
9894 South 2700 West
(801) 253-7008

Spanish Fork
420 S. Main St.
(801) 798-5535

Springville
415 South 200 East
(801) 489-2956

South Davis
3350 South 100 East
(801) 299-4239

St. George
410 South 200 East
(435) 673-4591

St. George-Green Valley
511 S. Valley View Dr.
(435) 673-7302

St George-Morningside
881 S. River Rd.
(435) 652-1425

Taylorsville-Central
4554 South 2025 West
(801) 964-3064

Taylorsville-West
4505 South 3420 West
(801) 964-3009

Tooele Valley
1025 Southwest Dr.
(435) 882-7514

Tremonton-Garland
487 East 900 North
(435) 257-7015

Tridell
Main Street Tridell
(435) 247-2340

Utah South Area FHC-Training Facility
85 N. Sixth East
(801) 356-9114

Utah South Hispanic
263 North 800 West
(801) 356-0661

Utah Valley Regional
Harold B. Lee Library, 2N
Brigham Young University
(801) 378-6200

Vernal
613 West 200 South
(435) 789-3618

Washington-Buena Vista
860 N. Fairway Dr.
(435) 627-0278

Wellington
935 E. Main
(435) 637-6717

Wendover
269 B St.

West Jordan-Bingham Creek
8539 South 2200 West
(801) 562-8154

West Jordan-Heritage
7350 South 3200 West
(801) 562-8285

West Jordan-Jordan Oak
8117 South 3905 West
(801) 280-4809

West Jordan-Oquirrh
5208 W. Cyclamen Way
(801) 964-7332

West Jordan-Prairie
5360 West 7000 South
(801) 964-7492

West Jordan-Welby
8841 South 4800 West
(801) 280-4826

WYOMING

ORGANIZATIONS & ARCHIVES

Cheyenne Genealogy Society
Laramie County Central Library
2800 Central Ave.
Cheyenne, WY 82001
<www.wyomingweb.net/genealogy>

Division of Cultural Resources
Barrett Building
Third Floor Center
2301 Central Ave.
Cheyenne, WY 82002
(307) 777-7013

Fax: (307) 777-3543
<wyospcr.state.wy.us/cr>

Laramie County Library System
Cheyenne Genealogical Society
2800 Central Ave.
Cheyenne, WY 82001
(307) 634-3561
Fax: (307) 634-2082
<www.lclsonline.org>

University of Wyoming Libraries
P.O. Box 3334
University Station
Laramie, WY 82071
(307) 766-2070
Fax: (307) 766-3062
<www-lib.uwyo.edu>

Wyoming State Historical Society
PMB 184
1740H Dell Range Blvd.
Cheyenne, WY 82009
<wyshs.org>

Wyoming State Library
Supreme Court and Library Building
2301 Capitol Ave.
Cheyenne, WY 82002
(307) 777-7283
Fax: (307) 777-6289
<www-wsl.state.wy.us>

RESOURCES

"Along the Continental Divide: Research in Montana, Idaho, and Wyoming"
lecture by Blaine R. Bake
(Audiotapes.com, $8.50)

PERIODICALS

Annals of Wyoming
(1923-), Wyoming State Archives, Barrett Building, 2301 Central Ave., Cheyenne, WY 82002

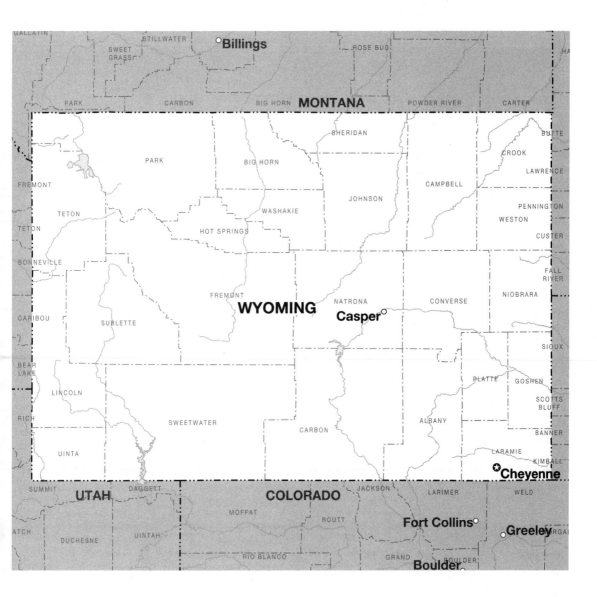

Bits and Pieces
(1965-), M.E. Brown, P.O.
Box 746, Newcastle, WY
82701

**Fremont County
Nostalgia News**
(1980-), Fremont County
Genealogical Society, c/o
Riverton Branch Library,
1330 W. Park, Riverton,
WY 82501

WEB SITES

**Diary of a Wyoming
Pioneer Woman**
<www.wyoming
companion.com/wchh.
html#Pioneer>

Vital Records Information
<vitalrec.com/wy.html>:
Where to obtain copies
of birth and death certificates, marriage licenses,
and divorce decrees.

**Wyoming GenWeb
Project**
<www.rootsweb.com/
~wygenweb>: FAQs of
Wyoming research, links
to county resources.

Wyoming Mailing Lists
<www.rootsweb.com/
~jfuller/gen_mail_
states-wy.html>: Special-
interest, state, and county lists.

Wyoming Obituary Links
<geocities.com/
~cribbswh/obit/wy.htm>:
Links to obituary tran-
scriptions from across the
state.

**Wyoming Resources at
RootsWeb**
<resources.rootsweb.
com/USA/WY>: Personal
Web sites, queries,
archives.

WYOMING

Statehood: 1890
Statewide Birth and Death Records Begin: 1909
Statewide Marriage Records Begin: 1941
Address for Vital Statistics:
Vital Records Services
Hathaway Building
Cheyenne, WY 82002
(307) 777-7591
Fax: (307) 635-4103
<wdh.state.wy.us/vital_records/
certificate.htm>

Available Censuses: Federal census reports for Wyoming Territory exist for 1870 and 1880. Uintah County in 1850 and 1860 is included in Salt Lake County, Utah. Eastern Wyoming in 1860 is under "unorganized land" in the Nebraska census reports. U.S. federal censuses exist for 1900, 1910, and 1920. Indexes are available to the 1860, 1870, 1880 (partial), 1900, 1910, and 1920 censuses. A state census exists for 1905.

City Directories at the Family History Library Include: Casper 1917, 1920, 1924, 1928, 1929, 1934, 1941, 1964, 1969, 1979, 1985, 1988; Cheyenne 1915, 1917, 1920, 1921, 1924, 1926, 1929, 1931, 1936, 1937, 1939, 1942, 1965, 1979, 1981, 1984, 1986, 1988; Sheridan 1910, 1915, 1933, 1935, 1937, 1939, 1960, 1964, 1971, 1975, 1978, 1986, 1990.

FAMILY HISTORY CENTERS

Afton
325 Jefferson St.
(307) 886-3905

Baggs
437 North St.
(307) 383-7695

Basin-Greybull
400 Highway 20 South
(307) 568-3346

Big Piney
2266 Piney Dr.
(307) 276-3251

Burlington
114 Cedar St.
(307) 762-3204

Casper
3931 W. Forty-fifth
(307) 234-3326

Cheyenne
2800 Central Ave.
(307) 634-3561

Cody
1407 Heart Mountain St.
(307) 587-3427

Cokeville
725 E. Main St.
(307) 279-3266

Douglas
Corner of Cheyenne and Warr
(307) 358-5024

Dubois
401 Miller Lane
(307) 455-3401

Evanston
1224 Morse Lee St.
(307) 789-8331

Farson
U.S. Highway 191
(307) 273-5209

Gillette
1500 O'Hara
(307) 686-9177

Glenrock
573 Lookout Dr.
(307) 436-9619

Green River
210 Shoshone Ave.
(307) 875-3972

Jackson
420 E. Broadway
(307) 733-6337

Kemmerer
512 McGovern Ave.
(307) 877-6821

Lander
Sixth and Cascade
(307) 332-5930

Laramie
3311 Hayford
(307) 755-5567

Lovell
50 W. Main
(307) 548-2963

Lusk
514 S. Linn
(307) 334-2966

Lyman
Highway 410
(307) 786-4559

Meeteetse
1716 Hays Ave.
(307) 868-2424

Pinedale
221 E. North
(307) 369-4740

Powell
527 W. Seventh
(307) 754-2110

Rawlins
117 W. Kendrick St.
(307) 324-5459

Riverton
N. Fourth West and Elizabeth Dr.
(307) 856-5290

Rock Springs
2055 Edgar St.
(307) 362-8062

Sheridan
2051 Colonial Dr.
(307) 672-8611

Thermopolis
625 S. Tenth
(307) 864-9452

Torrington
Twenty-fifth Ave. and E. E
(307) 532-5862

Wheatland
2956 South St.
(307) 322-2600

Worland
500 N. Sagebrush Dr.
(307) 347-8958

West

REGIONAL GUIDE
BY NANCY HENDRICKSON

Back in the mid-nineteenth century, long before CNN or the Internet, news of the California gold rush managed to spread east like wildfire. In Missouri, for example, Luzena Wilson and her husband "early caught the fever" and within a few days packed their belongings and walked away from the land they had worked for two years. "It sounded like such a small task," wrote Luzena, "to go out to California, and once there[,] fortune, of course, would come to us."

The Wilsons embodied the spirit of tens of thousands of Americans who poured west in the mid-1800s. Whether they were chasing free land, a better climate, good health, or gold at the end of the rainbow, they knew it could be reached by following the setting sun. If your ancestors were among them—or among any of those in the subsequent migrations, well into the twentieth century, that lured Americans to the "golden West"—you'll find a wealth of genealogical resources to help you trace them. It's not quite as small a task as the Wilsons imagined finding gold would be—your family history won't, of course, come to you—but mining for it is getting easier all the time.

TRAILS WEST

When the first Europeans traveled west to the Pacific, they had neither guidebooks nor much information about what to expect along the way. But by the time the major migrations began, published accounts helped travelers with every detail of the journey. Chances are, your westward-headed ancestors pored over one such account before leaving home.

Capt. Randolph B. Marcy's *The Prairie Traveler*, for instance, advised travelers on how to do everything from correctly packing a wagon to fording a river without drowning. He even cautioned sodbusters about the dangers of standing in front of a rifle's muzzle when pulling it out of a wagon. "Always look to your gun," he wrote, "but never let your gun look at you."

Marcy's book, which was commissioned by the War Department, took the place of Lansford W. Hastings's earlier work. Hastings painted the West in terms so glowing he was credited with single-handedly creating a land rush. Unfortunately, his prose was more effective than his directions were—one of his "shortcuts" led the Donner party to its tragic end.

The main route west was the Oregon Trail, which began on the banks of the Missouri River. Travelers arrived at a jumping-off place such as Independence or St. Joseph, Missouri, or Council Bluffs, Iowa, then waited until spring to go west. Choosing when to begin the journey could be a life-or-death decision: Leaving too early meant finding not enough grass to feed the cattle and oxen; leaving too late meant encountering winter storms through the mountains.

The trail followed the Platte River Valley to Fort Kearney, in what's now Nebraska, then to Fort Laramie, in present-day Wyoming. Between the two posts travelers encountered some of the most prominent landmarks of the journey—Courthouse Rock, Chimney Rock, and Scotts Bluff. Today, their "signatures" are still carved into the rock face at Register Cliff, located outside Guernsey, Wyoming.

After a few days' rest at Fort Laramie, the wagon trains headed toward the mountains to South Pass, crossing the Continental Divide. Near Fort Hall, California-bound settlers left the trail and headed south. Those heading to Oregon and Washington continued on, rafting down the Columbia River to Oregon City. The entire trip took four to five months.

In 1841, fewer than one hundred settlers followed the trail to Oregon, which was then claimed by both the United States and Britain. In 1847, emigration rose to four thousand; in 1848, to eleven thousand.

When the U.S. government passed the Donation Land Claims Act, guaranteeing land to people willing to settle and cultivate it, thirty thousand new farmers arrived. By 1852, an esti-mated seventy thousand were on the Oregon Trail—so many that the Indians called it "the white-topped wagon road." In all, at least 350,000 Americans traveled this route to the West. Of those, nearly a tenth died along the way, many from cholera. The rest—your ancestors—helped build the states of California, Oregon, and Washington.

EARLY ARRIVALS

A cartoon on the home page of the California Genealogical Society's Web site depicts a matronly woman staring at an ancestral portrait. "My goodness," she says, "I had no idea people from California had ancestors."

In fact, California—and the West Coast—was actually settled for decades before statehood. At one time or another, Spain, Mexico, Russia, and England each claimed California. Most settlements were Spanish, with the first missions opening in 1769 in San Diego.

When Mexico gained independence from Spain in 1821, California was included in its land booty. Ownership lasted until the close of the Mexican-American War in 1848. Although the California Republic was established in 1846, present-day California didn't become a state until 1850.

Before the gold rush of 1848, California's population was nothing to brag about. San Francisco was a shantytown with barely nine hundred people. By October 1850, however, the city had grown to twenty-five thousand and was well on its way to becoming a major supply center for the gold fields.

Like California, Oregon and Washington began under similar foreign claims. At the beginning of the nineteenth century, Russia, Spain, and Britain all claimed the territory that encompassed both of those current states. In 1848, the United States created the Oregon Territory, which included present-day Oregon, Washington, and Idaho, plus parts of Montana and Wyoming.

In 1853, the Washington Territory was carved out of the northern part of the Oregon Territory; in 1863, the Idaho Territory was created in turn from the eastern part of the Washington Territory. Oregon was granted statehood in 1859; Washington, in 1889. Knowing these boundary lines and dates can help you in your research—records for an early eastern Washington settler, for example, may be in present-day Idaho.

Were your ancestors among the first to go west? Let's look at some specific resources for your research.

ROUTE TO THE CENSUS

California was first enumerated in the federal census in 1850, followed by Oregon in 1860 and Washington in 1890. (The 1890 census was destroyed by fire, however, so the 1900 census is the earliest surviving federal census of Washington). Although the "oldest" West Coast censuses are far newer than those used to research the East, they cover the most genealogically productive years. The 1850 count was the first one to enumerate the complete household and is one of the most valuable for research based on family relationships. The censuses for 1850 and later list every person's birthplace, too. If you aren't sure where your family originated before arriving in the West, the federal census is a good jumping-off place.

You can access the federal census on microfilm through the Family History Library's (FHL) branch Family History Centers (FHCs) <www.familysearch.org> and various state archives and libraries. Federal census records are available on CD-ROMs and via subscription at Web sites such as Ancestry.com <www.ancestry.com> and Genealogy.com <www.genealogy.com>. You can also check USGenWeb (<www.usgenweb.org> and <www.us-census.org/inventory/inventory.htm>) to see if a volunteer has transcribed the census you need.

Territorial census data is also available for 1850 for the Oregon Territory (which included Washington) and for 1860, 1870, and 1880 for the Washington Territory. State and territorial census data exists for 1857 to 1892 for a few counties in Washington and for 1842 to 1905 for Oregon, but this data generally includes only the names of heads of households.

Early California census records (called *padrons*) were kept of Spanish, Mexican, and Indian residents and have been published in *The Quarterly*, a publication of the Historical Society of Southern California <www.socalhistory.org>. The FHL has microfilm of the Los Angeles *padrons* for 1790, 1836, and 1844, as well as the 1852 state census, which provided data on the entire household.

END-OF-THE-TRAIL RESOURCES

For the families who made it to the end of the Oregon Trail, you can find a wealth of resources in Portland, home to one of the largest genealogy collections on the West Coast, at the Genealogical Forum of Oregon (GFO; <www.gfo.org>). The GFO's holdings include more than twenty-two thousand volumes, thousands of rolls of microfilm, and a collection of Multnomah County marriage records. The collection's focus is the Pacific Northwest and the states where Oregon pioneers began their journeys. A valuable source at the GFO's library is the Early Oregon Settler files, which contain records of families who arrived in Oregon prior to 1900. In addition, you can investigate the microfilm records of the Oregon Donation Land Claim files (see later in this article). You can also find marriage, divorce, and death record indexes; Oregon city directories; Civil War veterans' records; county histories; and cemetery books.

The GFO sells several publications on its Web site and maintains an Internet mailing list. For someone who can't get to the GFO, a small staff of volunteers will do up to one hour of research for ten dollars plus any copying costs.

Portland is also home to the Oregon

Historical Society Library <www.ohs.org>. Founded in 1892, the library has the state's largest Oregon collection: more than a hundred thousand volumes, two million photographs, fifteen thousand maps, and eight thousand linear feet of original documents. Among the holdings are Oregon's federal censuses, provisional and territorial censuses, church registers, Sanborn fire insurance maps, and wagon train diaries. The library's biographical index contains names that appear in about fifteen western Oregon newspapers, as well as scrapbooks, local and regional histories, and Indian War pension papers.

Descendants of Washington pioneers can find treasures at the state archives <www.secstate. wa.gov/archives>, located in Olympia. The archives hold territorial census records taken between 1857 and 1892 and school censuses, which were used to count children in kindergarten through twelfth grade. The school censuses date from the late 1800s to the early 1930s.

Washington researchers may also strike genealogical gold at the Tacoma Public Library. Its collection includes censuses, city directories, county histories, passenger and cemetery lists, obituary indexes and death indexes for Washington, Oregon, and California. If you have trouble finding a Washington location, take advantage of the library's Washington Place Names Database at <www.tpl.lib.wa.us/v2/NWRoom/WaNames.htm>. This searchable database, the fruit of twenty-five years of research, can be invaluable for tracking down small or historical places. It's also rich with historical nuggets, perhaps some about your ancestors. For example, the search results for "Backman Creek" reveal that this place was named for Charles Backman, a prospector who worked in eastern Snohomish County in the 1880s and 1890s: "Backman had a 40-acre homestead claim on the south side of Darrington in 1907 but did not fulfill the conditions set out under the Homestead Act and did not perfect his title. He owned several claims in the Wellman Basin region of the county."

If you can't travel out west in person, for the cost of a letter you can buy help from the Seattle Public Library. The genealogy staff will do limited lookups in the census index, city directories, and Washington State Death Index (see <www.spl.org/quickinfo/genealogymail.html> for details).

Having difficulty locating an ancestor in records of the Oregon or California trails? Don't forget that many people came west by ship. The FHL has microfilm of passenger and crew lists of vessels that arrived in Seattle (Port Townsend) from 1890 to 1921. Unfortunately, local immigration records for ships that docked in San Francisco were destroyed in the 1906 earthquake, but the National Archives has passenger lists and indexes for vessels that arrived from 1893 to 1934. The FHL has these indexes, as well as copies of the lists for 1903 to 1918.

ANCESTORS IN THE NEWS

Local newspapers often contain gems of family information by way of obituaries and death, marriage, and birth notices. If you have problems locating your family in official records, it's well worth the effort to turn to newspapers. Besides news of vital events, you may find an article about a veteran's group your ancestor belonged to, a church function, or a community event.

If your ancestors resided in the San Francisco area, your research will probably lead you to newspapers because the city's land, court, and vital records were destroyed in fires during the "great quake" of 1906. Fortunately, the California branch of the Daughters of the American Revolution transcribed the vital statistics from the 1855 to 1874 issues of the *San Francisco Bulletin* (excluding 1869). The transcriptions were published in twenty-four volumes and are housed at the California State Library in Sacramento.

Genealogist Jim Faulkinbury is creating an index of vital records from the *San Francisco Call*. Ultimately, he expects the database to include 240,000 entries. As entries are completed, they're posted to an online searchable database at <feefhs.org/fdb2/sfcalli.html>. If you find one of your ancestors in the index, you can contact Faulkinbury to obtain a copy of the records.

In addition, the California State Library <www.library.ca.gov> owns a large collection of newspapers, including the full run of at least one paper from each of most California counties and major cities. Most are on microfilm and available for interlibrary loan.

The California Genealogical Society Library in Oakland holds the San Francisco Newspaper Index (*Chronicle* and *Examiner*), which covers 1904 to 1980, and an index to vital records printed in the *San Francisco Evening Bulletin*. The California Genealogical Society is the oldest genealogical society in California and, according to spokesman Rick Sherman, an underutilized resource for anyone doing California research.

For Oregon and Washington newspaper research, the Oregon Historical Society Library is a good starting place. The library has an alphabetical card file with abstracts of birth, marriage, and death information from early Oregon newspapers. You can find some pre-1880 Oregon newspapers at the Bancroft Library at the University of California at Berkeley <bancroft.berkeley.edu>. The Washington State Library <www.statelib. wa.gov>, which heads up the Washington State Newspaper Microfilm Project, maintains a large microfilm collection of newspapers dating from the 1870s.

YOUR CLAIM TO LAND RECORDS

Many Oregon- and Washington-bound pioneers were drawn by news of fertile ground, excellent climates, and free land. Thousands of settlers who arrived in the Oregon Territory were eligible to receive donation land claims—plots granted through the 1850 Donation Land Claim Act. The applications are genealogically rich with information, including birth, marriage, migration, and citizenship data. The Oregon State Archives has territorial land records covering 1845 to 1849.

Donation land records are on microfilm at the National Archives Pacific Alaska Region in Seattle and at the FHL (FHL film numbers 1028543 and 1490152 through 1490242). The FHL also has microfilm of land abstracts with indexes for 1852 to 1903 (FHL film numbers 847554 through 847559).

Washington donation land records exist for people who settled and cultivated land before 1855. The FHL has a register with indexes and abstracts for claims from 1855 to 1902 (FHL film number 418160). Each claim is identified by name, certificate number, and local office. You can use the register to locate the original file, which is on microfilm at the regional National Archives locations and at the FHL.

After 1862, settlers could also obtain homestead grants by living on the land, raising crops, and making improvements for five years. Homestead land was open to U.S. citizens or anyone who had filed an intention to become a citizen.

Homestead land entry case files are located at the National Archives and can include names, birth dates, marriage dates and locations, and citizenship information. To get a copy of the records, you must provide the name of the person who filed the claim, the legal land description, the land patent number and date, and the land office where the patent was issued. Microfilm of the tract books (which contain the information you need) are located at the FHL and the Oregon State Office of the Bureau of Land Management [P.O. Box 2965, 333 Southwest First Avenue, Portland, OR 97204; (503) 808-6002; <www.or.blm.gov>].

Spain granted land in California until 1822, followed by Mexico until 1846. Early Spanish land grant records are located at the California State Archives <www.ss.ca.gov/archives/archives.htm> and the Bancroft Library. The California State Archives also holds records from 1833 to 1845 in its Spanish Archives Record Group. This group is also available on microfilm at the FHL (indexes on FHL film numbers 978888 through 978890).

The United States's first general land offices in California were in Los Angeles and Benicia, established in 1853. The federal government sold public domain land through these land offices. Original tract books are located at the National Archives.

SOUTHWESTERN STATES

If your ancestors turned left before hitting the Pacific Coast and you're looking for records in the Southwest, be prepared to go far afield. This area—Arizona, Nevada, and New Mexico—represents a classic case of changing boundary lines. For instance, at one time Arizona was part of New Mexico; at another, part of Nevada. A large chunk of Nevada, however, once belonged to Utah, and a smaller part of Nevada belonged to New Mexico. Upon obtaining statehood, Nevada even took a slice of Arizona!

If your ancestors aren't in the records where you think they should be, check the records of surrounding states. Many of the early settlers of the region were chasing gold or silver or traveling the Santa Fe Trail on their way to California. Fortunes were made and lost as miners poured into Virginia City and other ore-rich towns. As the region became more settled, land disputes began to arise between ranchers and old Spanish land grant claims. Later, more violent encounters took place between homesteaders and the Apache. Nevada became a state way back in 1864, but Arizona and New Mexico were the last of the contiguous United States to become states, in 1912.

Arizona and Nevada have been included in the federal census since 1870. Statewide record-ing of births and deaths in Arizona began in 1909. Marriage records are recorded in the superior court clerk's office in the county where the marriage took place. Nevada did not require a statewide recording of vital records until 1911. The first federal New Mexico census was taken in 1850, and although some vital records were kept from as early as 1889, statewide registration didn't begin until 1920.

All three of these states are federal land states, so researchers can access records of the original transfer of land from the government to an individual at the Bureau of Land Management's General Land Office Records site at <www.glorecords.blm.gov>.

THE FINAL FRONTIERS

Your Western ancestors may have been lured by the Klondike gold strike of 1896 to head north to Alaska. Many Alaska settlers made the long trek from Washington in particular, encouraged by subsequent gold finds at Nome in 1898 and Fairbanks in 1902. The Russians had actually been there long before those settlers, beginning on Kodiak Island in 1784. Sitka, settled by the Russians in 1804, was Alaska's center of government until 1906, when the capital shifted to Juneau.

Federal census records for Alaska are available for 1900, 1910, 1920, and 1930. Territorial censuses cover 1904, 1905, 1906, and 1907 (partial). Alaska became the forty-ninth state in 1959.

The fiftieth state, Hawaii, became official later that same year, though Hawaii had a long history of self-rule by its indigenous peoples. The Hawaiian kingdom lasted until 1893; Hawaii became a U.S. territory in 1900, when the growing pineapple industry set off a different kind of gold rush that brought an influx of immigrants.

You can find Hawaiian ancestors in partial colonial censuses as far back as 1866, 1878, 1890, and 1896, along with various vital records files at the state archives covering 1840 to 1866 and 1847 to 1896. Federal census coverage begins with partial records from 1900, then includes 1910, 1920, and 1930.

YOUR ANCESTORS' DESTINY

For the tens of thousands of pioneers who reached the West Coast, thousands more lie in unmarked graves along the Oregon Trail or in the depths of the sea. Cholera, Indians, starvation, and disease all took their toll—from the "white-topped wagon road" to the ships sailing 'round the Horn. If your ancestors survived the journey, they were among America's hardiest.

The rush to the West fulfilled the dream of Manifest Destiny. Not everyone who went West found gold, either literally or metaphorically, but their journeys and their stories left a golden legacy for us to discover.

ORGANIZATIONS & ARCHIVES

The Bancroft Library
University of California, Berkeley
Berkeley, CA 94720
<bancroft.berkeley.edu>

Immigrant Genealogical Society
1310-B West Magnolia Blvd.
P. O. Box 7369
Burbank, CA 91510
(818) 848-3122
Fax: (818) 716-6300
<feefhs.org/igs/frg-igs.html>

National Archives Pacific Region
24000 Avila Rd.
Laguna Niguel, CA 92677

<www.archives.gov/facilities/ca/laguna_niguel.html>

National Archives Pacific Region
1000 Commodore Dr.
San Bruno, CA 94066
(949) 360-2641
Fax: (949) 360-2624
<www.archives.gov/facilities/ca/san_francisco.html>

National Archives Pacific Alaska Region (Anchorage)
654 West Third Ave.
Anchorage, AK 99501
(907) 271-2441
Fax: (907) 271-2442
<www.archives.gov/facilities/ak/anchorage.html>

National Archives Pacific Alaska Region (Seattle)
6125 Sand Point Way NE
Seattle, WA 98115
(206) 526-6501
Fax: (206) 526-6575
<www.archives.gov/facilities/wa/seattle.html>

Nordic Heritage Museum
3014 NW 67th St.
Seattle, WA 98117
(206) 789-5707
<www.nordicmuseum.com>

RESOURCES

"Family History on the Oregon Trail"
lecture by Katherine Scott Sturdevant
(Audiotapes.com, $8.50)

Italians of the American Northwest
by Charley Vingo (Pine Orchard, $74.95)

Oregon Country: Oregon Territory Map Changes
(Oregon Genealogical Society, $11)

The Oregon Trail: Yesterday and Today
by William E. Hill (Caxton Printers, $12.95)

San Francisco Passenger Departure Lists
volumes 1-6, by Peter E. Carr (TCI Genealogical Resources, $15.95 per volume)

"Staking Out the Northwest: Donation Land Claims"
lecture by Jennifer Blacke
(Audiotapes.com, $8.50)

Terrible Trail: The Meek Cutoff, 1845
by Keith Clark and Lowell Tiller (Maverick Publications, $14.95)

WEB SITES

Hudson's Bay Company Archives
<www.gov.mb.ca/chc/archives/hbca>: How to obtain records from this fur-trading company's posts in Oregon, Washington, and California. Records include weather reports, visitors' arrivals and departures, and daily activities.

Oregon Trail
<www.isu.edu/~trinmich/Oregontrail.html>: Fact-packed site about the great migration trail.

University of Washington Library Asahel Curtis Photo Company Collection
<content.lib.washington.edu/Acurtis>: More than 1,700 photos of Seattle, Washington State, and Alaska from the 1850s to 1940.

Western States Historical Marriage Records Index
<abish.byui.edu/specialCollections/fhc/gbsearch.htm>: Covers eastern Washington, eastern Oregon, and selected California counties.

LOS ANGELES

BY NANCY HENDRICKSON

You may think you're seeing stars once you get a load of the genealogical resources located in the mecca of the film industry. For starters, head to the **History and Genealogy Department of the Los Angeles Public Library** [630 West Fifth Street; (213) 228-7400; <www.lapl.org/central/history.html>]. There you can dive right into more than 200,000 history books and 45,000 volumes in the genealogy collection, including 10,000 genealogies. If your search leads you to the federal censuses, look here for plenty of them—including all of the censuses from 1790 through 1900 and a partial collection of those from 1910 and 1920. The library also owns many census indexes, all of the slave schedules, and Indian census records.

The library's genealogical wealth is not limited to census records. If you've never done city directory research, this is the place to start; you're sure to find an ancestor or two of yours in the five thousand rolls of microfilmed U.S. city directories from 1861 to 1960. In addition, the library has twelve hundred paper city directories. Unique to the library is its heraldry collection, one of the few in southern California. Its card index by family name can help you find books on heraldic symbols and coats of arms. While there, don't miss the ships' passenger lists, the newspaper collection, and the nearly complete rosters of soldiers who served in the Revolutionary War, the War of 1812, and the Civil War. You can also take advantage of the extensive collection of California death and marriage record indexes.

If you can't get to the Family History Library in Salt Lake City, the next best thing is a visit to the **Los Angeles Family History Center** [10741 Santa Monica Boulevard, West Los Angeles; (310) 474-9990; <www.lafhc.org>]. This is the largest satellite FHC in the United States. Established in 1964, the Los Angeles FHC serves some 6,300 researchers monthly. This facility houses all publicly available records from the federal census—census years 1790 through 1930—including printed indexes for most states for 1790 through 1870, mortality schedules for 1850 through 1880, and the complete 1900 and 1920 Soundex indexes to the census.

The Los Angeles FHC also holds thousands of microfiche. Among the most important records here on microfiche are the marriage, birth, and death indexes; Civil War Unit histories; street indexes for England and Wales; English and Irish census records; and the Daughters of the American Revolution Lineage Book index. Microfilms include eight hundred rolls of Revolutionary War pension files, the index to Union service records, and passenger lists. If your ancestors were of British Isles descent, also check out the Los Angeles FHC's civil registration indexes for England and Wales, the Ireland and Scotland Civil Registration Index, Welsh genealogies, and Irish Census Substitutes.

The **Southern California Genealogical Society Library** [417 Irving Drive, Burbank; (818) 843-7247; <www.scgsgenealogy.com>] is one of sev-

The Los Angeles Public Library was ranked as one of the nation's top 10 for genealogy.

eral smaller Los Angeles-area libraries catering to family researchers. Holdings include more than thirty thousand books, manuscripts, maps, microforms, and periodicals, as well as a large CD-ROM collection. The periodical collection alone has more than two thousand volumes. Unique to this library is a fine collection of German and French-Canadian material.

Another Burbank facility with a large non-United States collection is the library belonging to the **Immigrant Genealogical Society** [1310-B West Magnolia Boulevard; (818) 848-3122; <feefhs.org/igs/frg-igs.html>]. More than half of the five thousand books, four hundred rolls of microfilm, and three thousand microfiche in the collection are related to German genealogy. Among the society's German collection are materials not found anywhere else in the United States.

If you have Revolutionary War ancestors, head over to the **Sons of the Revolution Library** in Glendale [600 South Central Avenue; (818) 240-1775; <www.walika.com/sr>]. Established in 1893, the library has a collection that's grown from five thousand volumes to more than thirty-five thousand. It's one of the largest American Revolutionary and Colonial America collections in the western United States. (Don't miss the leopard-skin saddle pad once owned by George Washington.)

Southern California is also home to the **National Archives and Records Administration Pacific Region** facilities at Laguna Niguel [24000 Avila Road; (949) 360-2641; <www.archives. gov/facilities/ca/laguna_niguel.html>], located about seventy miles north of San Diego and fifty miles south of Los Angeles. Among the records here are those from federal agencies and courts in Arizona; southern California; and Clark County, Nevada (the remainder of the Nevada records are kept at the NARA facility in San Francisco).

While in Los Angeles, visit **El Pueblo de Los Angeles Historic Park**, a forty-four-acre park containing the oldest existing residence in the city—Avila Adobe, built in 1818 by rancher Don Francisco Avila. Other historic structures include the Old Plaza Church—the oldest church in the city—and the Sepulveda House, built in 1887. The park is bounded by Alameda, Arcadia, Spring, and Macy Streets.

Civil War buffs won't want to miss **Drum Barracks**, the only major Civil War landmark in California. From 1862 to 1866 this was the central post for the Union army in the southwest. Only two buildings—the barracks and powder magazine—remain of the more than twenty original structures. In its heyday, the post was home for up to seven thousand men. The barracks is located at 1053 Cary Avenue in nearby Wilmington.

Want a glimpse of *really* old Los Angeles? Drop by the **George C. Page Museum** [5801 Wilshire Boulevard; (323) 934-PAGE [7243]; <www.tarpits.org>] across from the famous La Brea Tar Pits. The tar pits were first discovered in 1769, and since then thousands of Ice Age fossils have been removed. The museum houses many of the major finds in its three million-item collection.

PHOENIX

BY KATHERINE HOUSE

If you're thirsty for information about ancestors from Arizona and the rest of the Southwest, Phoenix is anything but dry. The metropolitan area boasts one of the largest Family History Centers in the country, and the state library is downtown. Plan on renting a car, though: Phoenix is a sprawling metropolis, and the Family History Center is located about twelve miles from downtown.

The **Arizona State Library, Archives and Public Records** [1700 West Washington Street (in the State Capitol); <www.dlapr.lib.az.us>] has an impressive collection of interest to family history researchers; search its catalog online at <aslaprcat.lib.az.us/uhtbin/webcat>. The facility's **Genealogical Research Center** [Room 300; (602) 542-3942] houses thousands of books and periodical volumes, including immigration and naturalization record indexes and a complete collection of the *New England Historical and Genealogical Register* (begun in 1847) and the *New York Genealogical and Biographical Record* (begun in 1870). Access to online databases is also available here.

The library's **History and Archives Division** [(602) 542-4159] is a source for all the federal censuses for Arizona (1860 through 1930), as well as birth records more than seventy-five years old and death records more than fifty years old. (These birth and death records are microfilmed and uncertified, but they are much less expensive here than through the **Office of Vital Records in the Department of Health Services** [(602) 364-1300]). The archives also yields superior court records, including pre-World War II marriage licenses, wills, civil cases, criminal cases, and probate cases; brand indexes and books (useful if your relative had a ranch); plat maps; and Territorial Prison records that provide such information on inmates as photos, complete physical descriptions (including tattoos), and data on their relatives.

Other resources in the state library are a federal depository library [(602) 542-3701]; Map Collection [(602) 542-4343] for Arizona containing maps from the earliest territorial period to the present; Arizona newspapers; a photo collection of ninety thousand images; and the Arizona Collection [(602) 542-4159], which houses 105,000 books, pamphlets, manuscripts, and periodicals relating to the state and its inhabitants.

If you stay at the pricey **Crowne Plaza** Phoenix-Downtown/City Center [100 North First Street; (800) 359-7253] or the **Hyatt Regency Phoenix** [122 North Second Street; (800) 633-7313], you can take the free **Copper Square Downtown Area Shuttle** [DASH; <www.valleymetro.org/Transit/Route/dash.htm>] to the State Capitol. North of downtown, about two miles from the library and archives, are several chain hotels as well as independent motels. Try the **Los Olivos Hotel & Suites** [202 East McDowell Road; (800) 776-5560], the **Best Western Executive Park** [1100 North Central Avenue; (800) 780-7234], or the **Holiday Inn Express Hotel and Suites** [620 North Sixth Street; (800) HOLIDAY (465-4329)]. If you can take the heat and want to experience Phoenix's first-class resorts and spas, summer is the time to visit. Prices cool off as much as 50 percent from June to August, when temperatures rise to an average of one hundred degrees.

Another oasis for researchers is the **Mesa Regional Family History Center** [41 South Hobson Street, Mesa; (480) 964-1200]. It offers all federal census and Soundex indexes through 1920, sixteen thousand books, access to electronic databases, sixty-four microfilm readers, and twelve microfiche readers. This FHC is busiest in the winter, when it serves an average of 340 patrons per day. Summers and evenings are quieter.

Located within a few miles of the Mesa FHC are lots of chain hotels, including the **Best Western Mezana Inn** [250 West Main Street; (800) 780-7234], the **Courtyard by Marriott** [1221 South Westwood Avenue; (800) 228-9290], and **La Quinta Inn & Suites** [902 West Grove Avenue; (800) 221-4731]. Several fast-food restaurants, as well as **Matta's Restaurant** [Mexican food; 932 East Main Street; (480) 964-7881], are within walking distance.

If you have African-American relatives, stop by the **George Washington Carver Museum and Cultural Center** [415 East Grant Street; (602) 254-7516], inside what was once the state's only African-American high school. The museum has a small reference library with African-American genealogical resources, although the same information is available from the Family History Center in Mesa.

Another resource is Arizona State University's

Hayden Library [Cady Mall on campus; (480) 965-4932; <www.asu.edu/lib/hayden>] in Tempe. Of special note are the Chicano Research Collection and the Southwestern Autobiography Index, a database describing more than a thousand primary source materials about people in the Southwest. You can find both of these in the Luhrs Reading Room on level four.

Native Americans are among the ethnic groups that have given rise to Phoenix's development. To learn about the city's roots, visit the **Pueblo Grande Museum and Archaeological Park** [4619 East Washington Street; (877) 706-4408; <www.pueblogrande.com>], a site of prehistoric Hohokam village ruins. At **Deer Valley Rock Art Center** [3711 West Deer Valley Road; (623) 582-8007], visitors can view more than fifteen hundred ancient petroglyphs. The **Heard Museum** [2301 North Central Avenue; (602) 252-8848; <www.heard.org>] boasts an internationally acclaimed collection of Native American fine art. Those with Native American ancestors may be interested in the Heard's Billie Jane Baguley Library and Archives photo collection; it is open by appointment.

The **Phoenix Museum of History** [105 North Fifth Street (Heritage and Science Park in Copper Square); (602) 253-2734; <www.pmoh.org>], open daily, features interactive exhibits tracing the history and development of the city. The library and archives, open by appointment only, contains city directories, deeds, licenses, maps, and other useful information.

Travel thirty minutes north of downtown and back in time to the Arizona Territory, circa 1858 to 1912, at the **Pioneer Arizona Living History Museum** [3901 West Pioneer Road; (623) 465-1052; <www.pioneer-arizona.com>]. Costumed interpreters populate the town of twenty-nine buildings, which include a working blacksmith shop, a print shop, and an opera house.

Anyone with firefighters on the family tree should rush to the **Hall of Flame Museum of Firefighting** [6101 East Van Buren Street; (602) 275-3473; <www.hallofflame.org>], which houses the world's largest collection of fire apparatus, equipment, and memorabilia. The museum's library contains local fire department histories, many of them dating to the nineteenth and early twentieth centuries. Call for an appointment.

Phoenix serves up chow at a variety of restaurants; steak houses and Mexican restaurants are the specialties. A few to try:

- **Pinnacle Peak Patio Steakhouse & Microbrewery** [10426 East Jomax Road, Scottsdale; (480) 585-1599]
- **1882 Reata Pass Steakhouse** [27500 North Alma School Parkway, Scottsdale; (480) 585-7277]
- **Arriba Mexican Grill** [1812 East Camelback Road; (602) 265-9112]
- **Durant's Restaurant** [2611 North Central Avenue; (602) 264-5967]
- **El Paso Bar B Que Company** [4303 West Peoria Avenue, Glendale; (623) 931-2438]

PORTLAND

BY DIANE WEINER

As the last stop for many hardy Oregon Trail pioneers, Portland, Oregon, was founded with an adventurous spirit that's still apparent in its people and places. Today, it's a hotbed of family history activity and a perfect place to research your own ancestral trails, particularly if your family's past included a passage to the Pacific Northwest.

If you want to do extensive genealogical research in the area, plan your steps using the *Oregon Guide to Genealogical Sources* by Connie Lenzen; it is available at libraries.

Start your search for ancestors at the **Genealogical Forum of Oregon Library** [1505 Southeast Gideon; (503) 963-1932; <www.gfo.org>]. With more than twenty-two thousand volumes and thousands of reels of microfilm, it's one of the largest genealogy collections on the

West Coast. Holdings include records from all U.S. states and several foreign countries but focus on the Northwest region and states that were common starting points for Oregon Trail overlanders. If you're researching a pioneer, investigate the Early Oregon Settler Files, on families who arrived in Oregon prior to 1900, and the Oregon and Washington Donation Land Claim Abstracts, plus a complete set of the Oregon Donation Land Claim files on microfilm. You can also use indexes to Oregon marriages, deaths, and divorces, as well as original Multnomah County marriage certificates; all Oregon census records and indexes; Portland and other Oregon city directories; records on Oregon Civil War veterans; the Library Association of Portland Newspaper Index; county histories; and cemetery books. Strong collections include an extensive CD-ROM collection, published passenger lists, and the Daughters of the American Revolution collection.

The **Oregon Historical Society (OHS) Library** [1200 Southwest Park Avenue; (503) 306-5198; <www.ohs.org>] is another treasure trove of genealogical information. Search for pioneer ancestors in the Pioneer Index of recollections gathered during reunions of pioneers' descendants, or look in the Overland Journals of pioneer letters and diaries. The Biographical Index lists names that appear in Portland and Salem newspaper articles, scrapbooks, and county histories. Almost all the sources cited are at the OHS library. A Manuscript Materials file contains letters, diaries, business papers, and architectural drawings. Vital records indexes include Portland births, marriages, Oregon deaths, Portland deaths, Portland death certificates, and divorces. The library also holds some Native American records kept by federal agencies; cemetery records; federal and state census records on microfilm and in print; Grand Army of the Republic applications for headstones; Oregon Donation Land Claims; Catholic Church records; indexes to Catholic mission

records spanning the second half of the nineteenth century; local and regional city directories; and Indian Wars pension papers for veterans of the 1847 and 1855 wars with local Native American tribes. Search for news of your ancestors in the sixteen thousand rolls of microfilmed newspapers from one hundred Oregon cities (1846 to the present) and six hundred rolls from Washington, California, Idaho, Missouri, and Hawaii (mostly nineteenth-century titles). A few minutes' walk from the city center along a tree-lined street known as the Park Blocks, the library is in the Oregon History Center, also home to the Oregon Historical Society Museum. The $6 visitor's fee includes museum admission.

The **Oregon Historical Society Museum** [(503) 306-5198; <www.ohs.org>] exhibits display Portland history, Pacific Northwest maritime history, models of historical vehicles, antique quilts, and Native American artifacts. Admission is $6 for adults, $3 for students, $1.50 for children age six to twelve, and free for younger ones. Seniors visit free on Thursdays.

Looking for copies of original birth, marriage, and death certificates? Order them in person, online, or by telephone or fax from the **Oregon Center for Health Statistics** [800 Northeast Oregon Street; (503) 731-4109; <www.ohd.hr.state.or.us/chs/welcome.htm>], located in Portland. Birth and death records begin with 1903; marriage records, 1906; divorce certificates, 1925. Access to birth records less than one hundred years old is restricted, as is that to death certificates and marriage records less than fifty years old; contact the Vital Records office.

Your journey to the end of the Oregon Trail will be much easier than it was for the pioneers. From downtown Portland, you can just hop in a car and drive twenty to thirty minutes south to Oregon City. The **End of the Oregon Trail Interpretive Center**'s trademark wagon-shaped buildings stand where the Oregon Country's first elected governor, George Abernathy, allowed newly arrived pioneers to camp and graze their oxen behind his house. A trail guide leads visitors safely through the Missouri Provisioner's Depot, a mixed-media presentation, exhibits such as Pioneer Family of the Month, and a trades and crafts store. Call (503) 657-9336 or visit <www.endoftheoregontrail.org> for tour schedules and Oregon Trail information (including pioneer diaries). Admission is $6.50 for adults, $5.50 for seniors, $4 for kids age five to twelve, and free for younger children.

The **Oregon State Archives** is an hour's drive south to Salem, but it's worth the trip. This is the place to go for provisional and territorial records dating from the earliest government in Oregon (1841). County records include maps, government information, and court and land records. Check the Web site first <arcweb.sos.state.or.us> for some of the most used records, including a searchable index to Portland births (1881 to 1899), a provisional and territorial records guide, and a Genealogical Information Locator with more than 180,000 entries compiled from archives records. For more information, call (503) 373-0701.

At the end of the day, consider filling your belly at one of Portland's fine dining establishments. The MAX light rail system makes it a snap to get around for dinner. Take it downtown, for example, for Italian pasta and salad at **Pasta Veloce** [1022 Southwest Morrison; (503) 916-4388]. **McMenamins Kennedy School Courtyard Restaurant** [5736 Northeast Thirty-third; (503) 288-3286], part of a local chain of brewpubs, is located in a former grade school that also houses a movie theater and guest rooms. **Higgins** in downtown Portland [1239 Southwest Broadway; (503) 222-9070] serves Northwest cuisine made from locally grown ingredients.

If you're in a spontaneous mood, walk through Portland's trendy Northwest neighborhood, concentrated between Northwest Twenty-first and Twenty-third Avenues. Choose from a variety of eateries such as **Marrakesh Moroccan Restaurant** [1201 Northwest Twenty-first Avenue; (503) 248-9442] or **Tuscany Grill** [811 Northwest Twenty-first Avenue; (503) 243-2757]. Opt for an early dinner, as parking can be difficult in this area.

Finally, put up your feet at one of these lodgings, all within about a mile of the Genealogical Forum of Oregon library:

- **Doubletree Hotel Downtown** [310 Southwest Lincoln Street; (503) 221-0450]
- **RiverPlace Hotel** [1510 Southwest Harbor Way; (503) 228-3233]
- **Marriott** [1401 Southwest Naito Parkway; (503) 226-7600]
- **Residence Inn Riverplace** [1710 Northeast Multnomah Street; (503) 288-1400]

SAN DIEGO

BY NANCY HENDRICKSON

San Diego has a centuries-old history dating back to the time of the conquistadors. In 1542, Juan Rodriguez Cabrillo sailed into its sheltered harbor and claimed the area as a possession of Spain. Later, in 1769, San Diego became the first of twenty-one missions built along the California coast. While today the city is best known for tourist attractions such as Sea World and the San Diego Zoo, it's a major repository for papers relating to California's early history.

An amazing collection of records is stored at the Central Branch of the **San Diego Public Library** [820 E Street; (619) 236-5834; <www.sannet.gov/public-library>], just a few blocks up from Cabrillo's harbor. Two rooms hold special interest for researchers: the Genealogy Room and the California Room. The Genealogy Room has a fine collection of books—particularly DAR indexes. Of even greater interest to San Diego-area researchers is the Great Register of Voters, dating from 1866 through 1909. Some of the registers, which give a registrant's country of origin and occupation, have been indexed and placed in the Genealogy Room.

The California Room collection includes books, periodicals, diaries, letters, memoirs, newspaper clippings, and maps relating to California history, with an emphasis on San Diego. The oldest piece in the collection is a letter written in 1699. Resources relating to the gold rush and the westward movement to California are collected in depth. At last count, the California Room had 12,700 volumes; 800 periodicals; 64 drawers of clippings; and 300 maps. Among the maps are early Spanish drawings of the bay and a fine collection of the Sanborn Fire Insurance Maps. The library's newspaper collection includes archival files and microfilm of the *San Diego Herald*, which began in 1851, and the *San Diego Union*, which purchased the *Herald* in 1860. A microfiche index of the two newspapers covers the years 1851-1903 and 1930-1983.

A quick trip east of the San Diego Public Library leads to the **Family History Center** [4195 Camino del Rio South; (619) 584-7668]. One of the largest FHCs in the United States, its holdings include twenty thousand rolls of microfilm, the federal censuses from 1790 through 1920, and more than three hundred CD-ROMs from the Family Tree Maker collection. The Family History Center also has a strong collection of German and British Isles records. Books here include county histories, marriage indexes, and biographies. In addition, you can access a fine collection of genealogy society newsletters and magazines, as well as U.S. and worldwide maps.

Although the FHC is always busy, there is rarely a wait for machines. Currently, the Family History Center has sixteen microfilm readers, ten microfiche readers, two film copiers, twenty computers connected to a network server, and additional computers for using Family Tree Maker CD-ROMs.

Membership in the six hundred-strong **San Diego Genealogical Society** buys 24/7 access to the society's private library [1050 Pioneer Way, Suite E, El Cajon; (619) 588-0065; <www.rootsweb.com/~casdgs>]. The library's holdings include more than ten thousand books on basic genealogical research, state and county histories, as well as county vital statistics. The periodical collection contains a large selection of current and back issues of publications from genealogical and historical societies nationwide. In addition, the society owns dozens of Family Tree Maker CD-ROMs, the *Periodical Source Index* (PERSI), and the index to the *New England Historical and Genealogical Register* (NEHGR).

Researchers looking for San Diego ancestors should check out the society's local San Diego county records, including censuses (1850, 1852, 1860, and 1870), taxpayers, land records, church records, cemetery records, and the voter's register (1866-1879). Two current projects are the recording of outlying cemeteries in San Diego County and the indexing of seven hundred pages of mortuary records. The San Diego Genealogical Society Library has a computer station, a microfilm reader, and a copy machine. It's open to members twenty-four hours a day, seven days a week, by way of a coded-entry door lock. The public is welcome to use the library on Thursdays.

Tucked away a half hour north of San Diego proper is a genealogical gem—the **Carlsbad City Library** [1250 Carlsbad Village Drive; (760) 434-2931; <www.ci.carlsbad.ca.us/cserv/library. html>]—known mostly to local researchers. Occupying the entire second floor is the Genealogy and Local History Collection—one of the largest in southern California. The library's collection is especially strong in seventeenth-, eighteenth-, and nineteenth-century U.S. genealogy and history. Holdings include genealogies, local histories, and genealogy journals in the form of books, journals, microfilm, microfiche, and CD-ROMs.

Among the valuable resources in the Carlsbad library are (1) one of the largest census indexes in southern California and (2) microfilms of the federal censuses of 1790 through 1870 (excluding slave schedules). In addition, you can find the complete census schedules for California from 1850 through 1920.

Early California history is showcased at **Old Town San Diego State Historic Park**. Five original adobes are part of the multiblock complex, which also includes shops, a museum, and a restaurant. Among the attractions are La Casa de Estudillo, a traditional mansion built around a courtyard, a schoolhouse, a blacksmith shop, and San Diego's first newspaper office. The park is located at San Diego Avenue and Twiggs Street.

Turn-of-the-century San Diego is reflected in the **Gaslamp Quarter**, which features Victorian-style buildings from 1880 through 1910. The oldest house in the area was built in 1850 and isn't far from the three gambling halls once operated by Wyatt Earp. The Gaslamp, with more than seventy restaurants and several coffee houses and bistros, is where contemporary San Diegans go for nighttime entertainment.

The last big historical burst for San Diego came in 1915, when the city was chosen to host the Panama-California Exposition. Several buildings for the exposition were constructed in fourteen hundred-acre **Balboa Park**, all built in the Spanish Colonial Revival style. Although only two buildings were intended for permanent use, many are now used as museums. The park today is home to the **Reuben Fleet Science Center** [1875 El Prado; (619) 238-1233; <www.rhfleet.org>], the **San Diego Aerospace Museum** [2001 Pan American Plaza; (619) 234-8291; <www.aerospacemuseum.org>], the **Museum of Man** [1350 El Prado; (619) 239-2001; <www.museumofman.org>], the **San Diego Natural History Museum** [1788 El Prado; (619) 232-3821; <www.sdnhm.org>], and the **San Diego Hall of Champions** [2131 Pan American Plaza; (619) 234-2544; <www.sandiegosports.org>].

SAN FRANCISCO

BY DAVID A. FRYXELL

California's "golden gate," epitomized by the Golden Gate Bridge in San Francisco, was more than merely metaphorical to the ancestors of millions of today's Americans. For the forty-niners who came from the East seeking their fortune, California's appeal was literally golden. For immigrants from Asia, California was the gateway to a new land.

Many of these eastbound immigrants came through **Angel Island**—"the Ellis Island of the West"—the largest island in San Francisco Bay. A fishing and hunting site for the Miwok Indians for more than six thousand years, the hilly island became an immigration station in 1910. But World War I cut short the flood of Europeans who were expected to arrive via the Panama Canal. Over the next thirty years, most

Angel Island was the "Ellis Island of the West," gateway to many immigrants from Asia.

For immigrants from Asia, the Golden Gate Bridge was among their first views of their new country.

of the immigrants through Angel Island came instead from Asia—175,000 from China alone. Because of restrictions on Asian immigration, the wait at Angel Island was longer—an average of two to three weeks, though some immigrants were detained for months or even years—than that at Ellis Island.

Today, the former immigration station on Angel Island is a National Historic Landmark. A museum in the old barracks building re-creates one of the detainee dormitories and preserves poems carved into the station's walls by immigrants waiting for their chance at a new life.

The island is open from 8 A.M. to sunset year-round. Tours of historic sites are offered on weekends from April through October [call (415) 435-3522 for information], and you can take a motorized tram tour on weekends in March and daily from early April through October [(925) 426-3058]. Ferry service to the island is available from Fisherman's Wharf in San Francisco ($10.50), Tiburon, Oakland/Alameda, and Vallejo; links on the island's Web site <www.angelisland.org> give complete fare and schedule information. You can also write to the Angel Island Association, P.O. Box 866, Tiburon, CA 94920; for park ranger information, call (415) 435-1915.

You can find the heritage of those Asian-Americans throughout San Francisco, but especially in Chinatown. There, the new **Chinese American National Museum and Learning Center** [965 Clay Street; (415) 391-118; <www.chsa.org>] and the **Pacific Heritage Museum** [608 Commercial Street; (415) 399-1124] celebrate the city's Asian influences.

If your ancestors, lured by gold, came from the other direction, you should get a feel for the gold rush at the **Wells Fargo History Museum** [420 Montgomery Street; (415) 396-2619; <www.wellsfargo.com/about/museum_info.jhtml>] and the **Museum of American Money** in the Bank of California [400 California Street; (415) 765-0400]. The nearby **Jackson Square Historical District** is the best place to see buildings from the gold rush era.

San Francisco was built on seafaring as well as gold, and you can discover that heritage at the **San Francisco Maritime Museum** [at the foot of Polk Street, Fisherman's Wharf, (415) 561-7100]. Besides the models and exhibits inside, be sure to see the remarkable collection of actual ships on nearby **Hyde Street Pier** [(415) 561-7100]. The whole **Fisherman's Wharf** area is rich in the heritage of the Italian immigrants who founded the city's fishing industry in the late nineteenth century. (And if you had ancestors who spent time in prison, you may want to visit **Alcatraz**, just a short ferry ride from here, near Angel Island.)

Nearby **Fort Mason** [(415) 441-3400] reflects not only the city's military history but also its rich ethnic traditions: Almost fifty cultural groups make their home in **Fort Mason Center**, including the **Mexican Museum** [415-202-9700; <www.mexicanmuseum.org>] and **Museo ItaloAmericano** [(415) 673-2200; <www.museoitaloamericano.org>].

More state history is celebrated at the **California Historical Society** [678 Mission Street; (415) 357-1848; <www.californiahistorical society.org>]. The society's North Baker

San Francisco's seafaring heritage comes alive in the Fisherman's Wharf area.

Research Library is open by appointment only.

For actual genealogical research, your first stop should be the **Sutro Library** [480 Winston Drive; (415) 731-4477; <www.library.ca.gov>], a branch of the California State Library Association. Open free to the public, this library features the rare book and manuscript collection of Adolph Sutro and the largest genealogy collection west of Salt Lake City: 150,000 books and 65,000 microforms. Collections of city directories (more than twenty thousand), family histories, and local histories are particularly strong. (Bring your notepad—photocopying of city directories or any older books is not permitted.)

The Sutro Library is located between the north campus of San Francisco State University and the Stonestown Galleria mall. Without a car, the best way to get there is to take the Muni Metro train to the mall (almost the end of the line) and walk through the mall and out the back and downhill to the left. The library is a low-slung building tucked into a hillside on the right-hand side of Winston Drive, a challenge for cab drivers to find.

San Francisco's regular libraries, such as the San Francisco History Room and Archives in the handsome **New Main Library,** also offer much for genealogists. The New Main Library [100 Larkin Street; (415) 557-4400; <sfpl.lib.ca.us>] is located in the Civic Center area. (If you stay in the nearby Union Square hotel area, don't be tempted to stroll here through the iffy Tenderloin district.) While there, check out the exhibit of the **Museum of the City of San Francisco** <www.sfmuseum.org> in the neighboring City Hall South Light Court at Grove and Van Ness.

The Bay Area is also home to the **National Archives and Records Administration's Pacific Region** headquarters [1000 Commodore Drive; (650) 876-9001; <www.archives.gov/facilities/ca/san_francisco.html>], about twelve miles south in San Bruno, near the airport. Among the records here are those from federal agencies and courts in northern California, Hawaii, Nevada (except Clark County), the Pacific Trust

If you had "black sheep" ancestors, perhaps they spent some time on Alcatraz Island.

Territories, and American Samoa. Across the bay in Oakland is the **California Genealogical Society Library** [1611 Telegraph Avenue, Suite 200; (510) 663-1358]. It's open to the public; nonmembers pay a $5 daily fee.

Whatever resources you target, San Francisco's multifaceted public transportation system makes it easy to get around. Your best bet is probably a hotel in the **Union Square** area, which is convenient to the Muni Metro and to cable cars for Fisherman's Wharf or Chinatown. This area is also a shopper's paradise. The **San Francisco Hilton** [333 O'Farrell Street; (415) 771-1400] and the **San Francisco Marriott** [55 Fourth Street; (415) 896-1600] are obvious big-hotel choices. You can opt for a bit of history at the classic **Sir Francis Drake** [450 Powell Street; (415) 392-7755] or the **Westin St. Francis** [335 Powell Street; (415) 397-7000], built in 1904. An affordable alternative on the other side of Market Street from Union Square is the recently renovated **Pickwick Hotel** [85 Fifth Street; (415) 421-7500].

The problem with dining in San Francisco—one of the world's great restaurant cities—is the confusing variety of options. Try sampling some of the city's heritage:

- **Puccini & Pinetti** [129 Ellis Street; (415) 392-5500]—Italian
- **Aqua** [252 California Street; (415) 956-9662]—seafood
- **Yank Sing** [427 Battery; 101 Spear St., (415) 957-9300]—Chinese dim sum
- **Mifune** [1737 Post Street; (415) 922-0337]—Japanese; located in the striking **Japan Center** [Post and Buchanan Streets; (415) 922-6776] at the heart of the city's Japanese community

The other problem with dining in San Francisco, as you may discover, is that it's hard to put down your fork and get back to your genealogy.

SEATTLE
BY KATHERINE HOUSE

Microsoft and Amazon.com are among the homegrown high-tech companies that have made Seattle synonymous with the Information Age. Visitors to the Emerald City might be surprised to learn that Seattle is home to a wealth of genealogical information, too.

For those who want to get wired to their family's past, the best place to begin is the **Seattle Public Library**, which employs two genealogy librarians, one full-timer and one part-timer. Genealogy resources are housed in the Central Library, located temporarily (through late 2003) at 800 Pike Street (the intersection of Eighth Avenue and Pike Street) in the expanded section of the Washington State Convention and Trade Center [(206) 386-4625; <www.spl.org>]. The genealogical collection, which was started in 1926 and includes about twenty-seven thousand volumes, has strong holdings for Washington State, the eastern-seaboard and upper-Midwest states, as well as the major migration-route states of Tennessee, Kentucky, Missouri, Iowa, and Oregon. Before you visit, contact the library for a free brochure about its genealogical resources. No appointment is necessary to research; go to the History, Travel, and Maps Department desk on the third floor.

Parking garages are nearby. If you prefer mass transit, take a bus to the Convention Place Station. For information on navigating Seattle's excellent public transportation system, visit <transit.metrokc.gov> on the Web or call (206) 553-3000. If you want to visit several libraries and museums in a short amount of time, you should rent a car, but be prepared to endure heavy traffic.

The Central Library is scheduled to relocate in late 2003 to its new home at 1000 Fourth Avenue. At that time the library will be closed for several weeks in preparation for the move. Check the Web site or call the Quick

Information line at (206) 386-4636 for move updates.

There's no reason to be sleepless in Seattle. Dozens of hotels are within a ten-minute walk of the library, but don't expect any bargains—this is the heart of downtown. The closest hotels are the extravagant **Elliott Grand Hyatt Seattle** [721 Pine Street; (800) 633-7313] and the lower-priced **Paramount Hotel** [724 Pine Street; (206) 292-9500] and **Roosevelt Hotel** [1531 Seventh Avenue; (206) 621-1200]. Before settling in for the night, you might want to dine at one of the nearby restaurants, which include **The Cheesecake Factory** [700 Pike Street; (206) 652-5400] and **Dragonfish Asian Café** [722 Pine Street; (206) 467-7777], a top-rated Pan-Asian café.

Seattle is also home to the **National Archives and Records Administration's Pacific-Alaska Region** Seattle office [6125 Sand Point Way NE; (206) 526-6501; <www.archives.gov/facilities/wa/seattle.html>], which houses original public records for Washington, Oregon, and Idaho. You can also find all federal census records, including those for 1930; military records, including complete Revolutionary War records; pension and bounty land warrant applications; records relating to the Five Civilized Tribes; and naturalization records for much of the Pacific Northwest. A finding aid to original records is available on the Web at <www.archives.gov/facilities/wa/seattle/finding_aids.html>. To use original records, you must apply for a researcher's identification card. The facility is accessible via Metro bus routes 74 and 75.

Conveniently, the **Seattle Genealogical Society's Research Library** is located across the street [6200 Sand Point Way NE, Suite 101; (206) 522-8658; <www.rootsweb.com/~waseags>]. Call ahead because hours change near holidays and for special events and meetings. Nonmembers pay $4 per day, as well as $5 per hour to use the library's CD-ROMs, which number more than 150.

Researchers may bring a bag lunch to the National Archives. The closest restaurants are about two miles away in the University Village shopping area in the University District. Plenty of reasonably priced chain hotels are located there, too.

Also of interest to researchers is the private **Fiske Genealogical Library** [1644 Forty-third Avenue East; (206) 328-2716; <www.fiske.lib.wa.us>], specializing in materials for townships east of the Mississippi River. Affiliated with the Pioneer Association of the State of Washington, the library charges $5 per day to nonmembers.

Anyone researching ancestors who were teachers or students in Seattle's public school system will be delighted to know about the **Seattle Public Schools Archives and Records Management Center** [1330 North Ninetieth Street; (206) 252-0795; <www.seattleschools.org/area/archives>]. It's open by appointment.

If you know where to look, you can find some gems at the **University of Washington's Suzzallo and Allen Libraries** [(206) 543-0242]. Holdings of the Scandinavian Archives [(206) 543-1929], located in the Manuscripts, Special Collections, University Archives Division in the library's basement, include microfilmed Swedish-American church records for the Pacific Northwest. Call for more information about holdings and to arrange a visit.

Those with Scandinavian roots should definitely make time for the **Nordic Heritage Museum** [3014 Northwest Sixty-seventh Street, in the Ballard area north of Lake Union; (206) 789-5707; <www.nordicmuseum.com>]. It's the only museum in the country to celebrate the legacy of immigrants from all of Scandinavia. Exhibits include colorful textiles, Bibles, china, and other treasures brought from the old country. The museum's library includes a small collection of oral histories and a scattered collection of Norwegian *Bygdebøker*, local history books. The library is open Tuesdays by appointment only.

Trade with Japan and other Asian countries is big business in Seattle, and the city is home to thousands of Asian immigrants. Not surprisingly, Seattle has an impressive collection of museums, gardens, and cultural attractions that highlight its ties to the Orient. These include the **Seattle Asian Art Museum** [1400 East Prospect Street, in Volunteer Park; (206) 654-3206; <www.seattleartmuseum.org>] and the authentic **Japanese Garden** in the **Washington Park Arboretum** [1502 Lake Washington Boulevard East; (206) 684-4725; <www.seattlejapanese garden.org>], which offers a lovely outdoor respite from research.

At the **Wing Luke Asian Museum** [407 Seventh Avenue South; (206) 623-5124; <www.wingluke.org>] you can learn about ten Asian-Pacific-American ethnic groups. Wander through the surrounding Chinatown/International District and experience ethnic restaurants, as well as small grocery stores selling live chickens and ducks. Shop **Uwajimaya Village** [600 Fifth Avenue South, Suite 100; (206) 624-6248] for Asian gifts, Asian food, and Asian-language books.

Native American influences can be seen around the city, which was named after Chief Sealth. The University of Washington's **Burke Museum of Natural History and Culture** [near Northeast Forty-fifth Street and Seventeenth Avenue NE on campus; (206) 543-5590; <www.burkemuseum.org>] offers a stunning collection of Northwest Coast ceremonial masks, as does the **Seattle Art Museum** [100 University Street; (206) 654-3100; <www.seattleartmuseum.org>]. The **Daybreak Star Cultural Center** in **Discovery Park** [(206) 285-4425; <www.unitedindians.com>] displays traditional and contemporary Native American artwork.

For a broader overview of the city's history, visit the **Museum of History & Industry** [2700 Twenty-fourth Avenue East; (206)324-1126; <www.seattlehistory.org>] and the National Park Service's **Klondike Gold Rush National Historical Park** [117 South Main Street, in the Pioneer Square Historic District; (206) 553-7220; <www.nps.gov/klse>], where you can learn about the city's role in outfitting the pioneers en route to Alaska to pan for gold. Seattle's number-one attraction is the **Pike Place Market** <www.pikeplacemarket.org>, one of the oldest farmers' markets in the country and the birthplace of Starbucks (the original shop is still open).

No matter where you stay in Seattle, don't go home without eating salmon or trying some of the city's excellent ethnic restaurants. For seafood, try **Anthony's Pier 66 & Bell Street Diner** [2201 Alaskan Way, on the waterfront; (206) 448-6688] or **Ivar's Acres of Clams** [Pier 54, on the waterfront; (206) 624-6852]. **Wild Ginger Asian Restaurant & Satay Bar** [1401 Third Avenue; (206) 623-4450] receives outstanding reviews for its Chinese and southeast Asian cuisine. To experience salmon cooked Native American style, take a trip to **Tillicum Village** in **Blake Island State Park** [(206) 933-8600; <www.tillicumvillage.com>]. The four-hour adventure includes a boat trip, dinner, and a Native American stage show.

ALASKA

ORGANIZATIONS & ARCHIVES

Anchorage Genealogical Society
P.O. Box 242294
Anchorage, AK 99524

Alaska Historical Society
P.O. Box 100299
Anchorage, AK 99510
<www.alaska.net/~ahs>

Alaska State Archives
141 Willoughby Ave.
Juneau, Alaska 99801
(907) 465-2270
Fax: (907) 465-2465
<www.archives.state.ak. us>

Alaska State Library and Historical Collections
333 Willoughby Ave.
8th Floor, State Office Building
P.O. Box 110571
Juneau, AK 99811
(907) 465-2921
Fax: (907) 465-2665
<www.library.state.ak. us>

National Archives Pacific Alaska Region (Anchorage)
654 W. Third Ave.
Anchorage, AK 99501
(907) 271-2441
Fax: (907) 271-2442
<www.archives.gov/ facilities/ak/anchorage. html>

University of Alaska, Fairbanks
Elmer E. Rasmuson Library
310 Tanana Dr.
Fairbanks, AK 99775
(907) 474-7224
Fax: (907) 474-6841
<www.uaf.edu/library>

RESOURCES

Alaska Sources: A Guide to Historical Records and Information Sources
by Connie Malcolm Bradbury (Heritage Quest, $49.95)

WEB SITES

Alaska GenWeb
<www.akgenweb.org>: Begin your Northern research at this resource-rich site.

Alaska Mailing Lists
<www.rootsweb.com/ ~jfuller/gen_mail_ states-ak.html>: Subscribe to state- or county-level mailing lists, plus special-interest lists.

Alaska Resources at RootsWeb
<resources.rootsweb. com/USA/AK>: Queries, links, and search engines.

Ghosts of the Klondike Gold Rush
<www.gold-rush.org>: History and stories of the Alaska gold rush.

Vital Records Information
<vitalrec.com/ak.html>: Where to obtain copies of birth and death certificates, marriage licenses, and divorce decrees.

Yukon and Alaska Genealogy Centre
<yukonalaska.com/ pathfinder/gen>: Index of ship passenger lists and biographies of Yukon and Alaska pioneers.

ARIZONA

ORGANIZATIONS & ARCHIVES

Arizona Historical Foundation
Hayden Memorial Library
Arizona State University
Box 871006
Tempe, AZ 85287
(480) 965-3283
Fax: 480-966-1077
<www.users.qwest.net/ ~azhistoricalfdnl>

Arizona Historical Society
949 E. Second St.
Tucson, AZ 85719
(520) 628-5774
Fax: (520) 628-5695
<info-center.ccit. arizona.edu/~azhist/ general.htm#about>

Arizona State Genealogical Society
P.O. Box 42075
Tucson, AZ 85733
(520) 275-2747
<www.rootsweb.com/ ~asgs>

Arizona State Library, Archives and Public Records
State Capitol Building, Room 200
1700 W. Washington
Phoenix, AZ 85007
(602) 542-4035
Fax: (602) 542-4972
<www.dlapr.lib.az.us>

Hayden Library
Arizona State University
Box 871006
Tempe AZ 85287
(480) 965-4932
<www.asu.edu/lib/ hayden>

University of Arizona Library
1510 E. University Blvd.
Box 210055

Tucson, AZ 85721
(520) 621-2101
Fax: (520) 621-9733
<www.library.arizona.
edu/branches/spc/
homepage>

RESOURCES

**"Genealogical Research
in the Indexes of the
Documentary Relations
of the Southwest"**
lecture by James
Wadsworth
(Audiotapes.com, $8.50)

PERIODICALS

Copper State Bulletin
formerly *Southern
Arizona Genealogical
Society Journal*
(1965-), Arizona State
Genealogical Society, P.O.
Box 42075, Tucson, AZ
85733

WEB SITES

Arizona GenWeb Project
<www.rootsweb.com/
~azgenweb>: Links to
county and state
resources, queries, mes-
sage boards.

Arizona Mailing Lists
<www.rootsweb.com/
~jfuller/gen_mail_
states-az.html>: State,
county, and special-interest lists.

**Arizona Resources at
RootsWeb**
<resources.rootsweb.
com/USA/AZ>: Queries,
message boards, search-
es.

**1883 Pensioners on the
Roll**
<homepages.rootsweb.
com/~godwin/reference/
arizona1883.html>:
County-by-county list of

Arizonans who received
military pensions as of 1
January 1883. Each entry
tells the name, certificate
number, and reason for
and amount of the
pension.

Vital Records Information
<vitalrec.com/az.html>:
Where to obtain copies
of birth and death certificates, marriage licenses,
and divorce decrees.

FAMILY HISTORY CENTERS

Ajo
801 N. Cedar St.
(520) 387-6751

Bagdad
Community Dr.
(520) 633-2073

Bisbee
Melody Lane
(520) 432-3122

Buckeye
1002 E. Eason
(623) 386-4188

Casa Grande
Colorado and Sunset
(520) 836-7519

Cave Creek
38001 N. Basin Rd.
(480) 488-9224

Chandler-Alma
2252 W. Mesquite
(480) 899-4312

Chandler-West
1950 W. Galveston St.
(480) 857-8641

Chinle
Red Tag #366A
(520) 871-4605

Chino Valley/Del Rio
441 Perkinsville Rd. NW
(520) 636-4498

Clifton
112 Riverside Dr.
(928) 865-3878

Cottonwood
1377 E. Hombre Dr.
(928) 649-0116

Douglas
2800 Fifteenth St.
(520) 364-8075

Duncan
State Rd. 75 and
Fairground Rd.
(928) 359-2348

Eagar
467 N. Butler
(928) 333-4100

Elfrida
10539 N. Highway 191
(520) 642-3482

Flagstaff
625 E. Cherry St.
(928) 774-2930

Glendale
8602 N. Thirty-first Ave.
(602) 973-3216

Globe
Highway 60 and Ensign
(520) 425-9570

Holbrook
1127 Helen Ave.
(520) 524-6663

Kingman
3180 Rutherford Dr.
(928) 753-1316

Lake Havasu City
504 N. Acoma
(928) 855-8583

Mesa
41 S. Hobson
(480) 964-1200

Mesa-Salt River
6942 E. Brown Rd.
(480) 924-8958

Montana Del Sur
Southern and Seventh
Aves.
(602) 243-9413

Nogales
621 W. Green Place
(520) 281-0368

Page
313 S. Lake Powell Blvd.
(520) 645-2328

Paradise Valley
3601 E. Shea Blvd.
(602) 953-8160

Parker
Fourteenth and Reata
(520) 669-2700

Payson
900 S. Ponderosa St.
(928) 468-0249

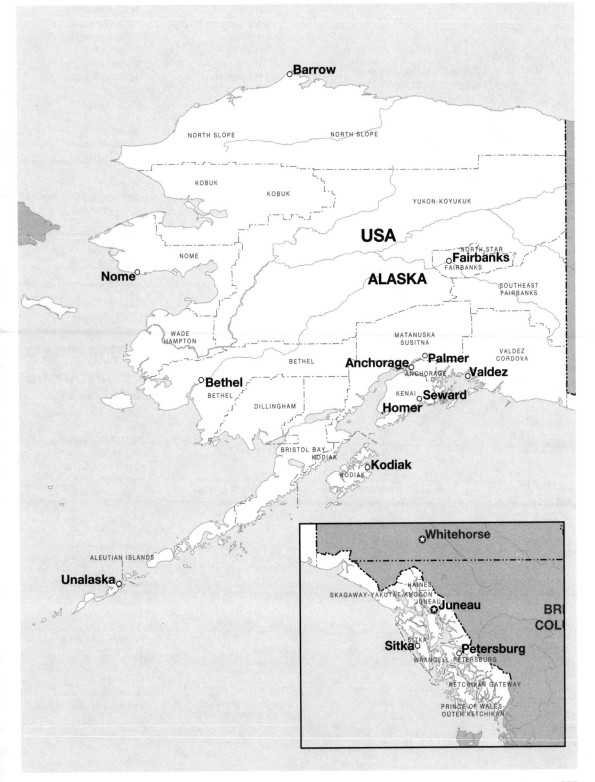

Barrow

NORTH SLOPE   NORTH SLOPE

KOBUK

KOBUK   YUKON-KOYUKUK

NOME   **USA**   NORTH STAR
                                                    Fairbanks
                                                    FAIRBANKS
Nome   **ALASKA**
                                                    SOUTHEAST
                                                    FAIRBANKS

WADE   MATANUSKA
HAMPTON   SUSITNA   **Palmer**   VALDEZ
                                                             CORDOVA
                   BETHEL   **Anchorage**   **Valdez**
                                          ANCHORAGE
Bethel   KENAI   **Seward**
BETHEL   **Homer**
           DILLINGHAM

                   BRISTOL BAY
                   KODIAK
                        KODIAK   **Kodiak**
                        KODIAK

ALEUTIAN ISLANDS

Unalaska

⭐**Whitehorse**

HAINES
SKAGAWAY-YAKUTAT-ANGOON
                   JUNEAU
                   ⭐**Juneau**   BR
                                                    COL
                   SITKA
Sitka   **Petersburg**
           WRANGELL-PETERSBURG

KETCHIKAN GATEWAY

PRINCE OF WALES-
OUTER KETCHIKAN

ARIZONA

Statehood: 1912
Statewide Birth and Death Records Begin: 1909
Statewide Marriage Records Begin: No statewide marriage registration; records exist for some counties.
Address for Vital Statistics:
Vital Records Section
Arizona Department of Health Services
P.O. Box 3887
Phoenix, AZ 85030
(602) 255-3260
<www.hs.state.az.us/vit_dir.htm>

Available Censuses: U.S. federal censuses for 1870, 1880, 1900, 1910, and 1920. Included in 1860 New Mexico census. Statewide indexes available for the 1870, 1880, 1900, 1910 (Phoenix only), and 1920 censuses. Territorial censuses available (not all complete) for 1864, 1866, 1867, 1869, 1871, 1872, and 1882. Indexes are available for 1864, 1866, 1867, and 1869.

City Directories at the Family History Library Include: Phoenix 1903, 1912, 1913, 1915-1921, 1923, 1925, 1928, 1928-32, 1935, 1964, and 1969; Tucson 1881, 1965, 1969, 1976, 1902, 1912-1914, 1917-1924, and 1926-1935

Peoria
13014 N. 108th Ave.
(623) 974-2749

Phoenix
48 E. Ashland St.
(602) 271-7015

Phoenix-Deer Valley
15018 N. Thirty-ninth Ave.
(602) 375-0878

Phoenix-East
1316 E. Cheery Lynn Rd.
(602) 266-0128

Phoenix-North
8710 N. Third Ave.
(602) 371-0649

Phoenix-West
3102 N. Eighteenth Ave.
(602) 265-7762

Polacca
394 Highway 264
(520) 737-2505

Prescott
1001 Ruth St.
(928) 778-2311

Quartzsite
Gold Star R.V. Park
(928) 927-6080

Safford-Thatcher
515 Eleventh St.
(520) 428-7927

Sahuarita
17699 S. Camino De Las Quintas
(520) 625-4104

San Manuel 1st
1002 McNab
(520) 385-4855

Scottsdale-Camelback
2202 N. Seventy-fourth St.
(480) 947-3995

Scottsdale-North
6940 E. Gold Dust
(480) 483-7629

Show Low
1401 W. Deuce of Clubs
(928) 537-2331

Sierra Vista
115 N. Highway 90
(520) 459-1284

Snowflake
284 W. First N
(928) 536-7430

Spring Valley
Highway 69 (two miles from Dordis Junction)
(928) 632-7119

St. David
Pomerene Rd., Mile Marker 306
(520) 586-2301

St. Johns
50 N. First W
(520) 337-2543

Sunsites
206 Ford St.
(520) 826-3455

Tuba City
Moenave Rd.

Tucson
500 S. Langley Ave.
(520) 298-0905

Tucson-West
3530 W. McGee
(520) 579-3493

Wickenburg
1350 W. Wickenburg Way
(520) 684-2446

Willcox
900 Encanto and Soto St.
(520) 384-2751

Winslow
205 W. Lee St.
(520) 289-5496

Woodruff
7792 Woodruff Rd.
(928) 524-2798

Yuma
4300 W. Sixteenth St.
(520) 782-6364

CALIFORNIA

ORGANIZATIONS & ARCHIVES

California Genealogical Society
1611 Telegraph Ave., Suite 100
Oakland, CA 94612
(510) 663-1358
<calgensoc.org>

The California Historical Society
678 Mission St.
San Francisco, CA 94105
(415) 357-1848
Fax: 415-357-1850
<www.california historicalsociety.org>

California State Archives
1020 O St.
Sacramento, CA 95814
(916) 653-7715
Fax: (916) 653-7363
<www.ss.ca.gov/archives/ archives.htm>

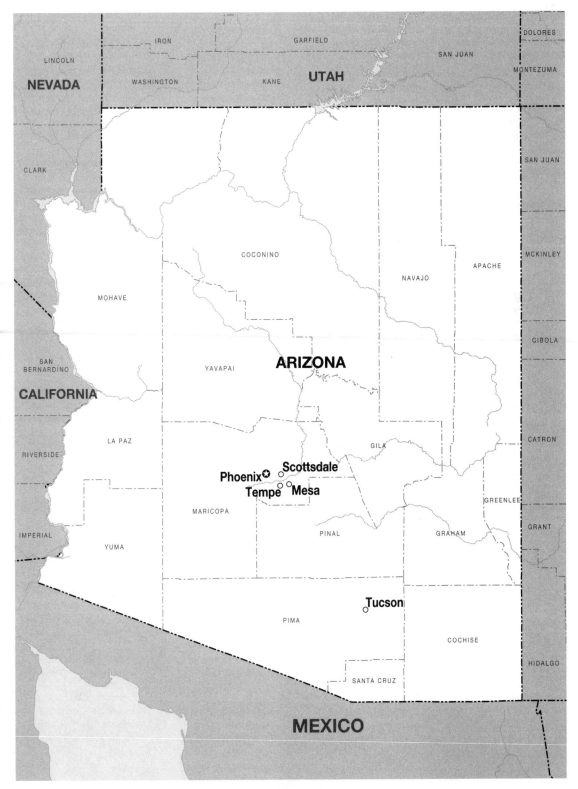

California State Library
914 Capitol Mall
Sacramento, CA 95814
(916) 654-0261
Fax: (916) 654-0241
<www.library.ca.gov>

National Archives-Pacific Region (Laguna Niguel)
24000 Avila Rd.
Laguna Niguel, CA 92677
(949) 360-2641
Fax: (949) 360-2644
<www.archives.gov/facilities/ca/laguna_niguel.html>

National Archives-Pacific Region (San Francisco)
1000 Commodore Dr.
San Bruno, CA 94066
(650) 876-9001
Fax: (650) 876-9233
<www.archives.gov/facilities/ca/san_francisco.html>

Society of California Pioneers
300 Fourth St.
San Francisco, CA 94107
(415) 957-1849
Fax: (415) 957-9858
<www.californiapioneers.org>
Mailing address:
P.O. Box 1850
San Francisco, CA 94119

Sutro Library
480 Winston Dr.
San Francisco, CA 94132
(415) 731-4477
<www.library.ca.gov>

RESOURCES

California Surname Index: Biographies From Selected Histories
by Barbara Ross Close
(California Genealogical Society, $39)

The Census of 1790: A Demographic History of Colonial California
by William Mason
(Ballena Press, out of print)

"Finding Ancestors in California's Great Register"
lecture by Betty K. Summers
(Audiotapes.com, $8.50)

An Index to the Biographies in 19th Century California County Histories
by J. Carlyle Parker (Gale Group, out of print)

Paper Trails: A Guide to Public Records in California
by Stephen B. Levine and Barbara T. Newcombe
(California Newspaper Publishers Association, $18.95)

A Useful Guide to Researching San Francisco Ancestry
by Kathleen C. Beals
(California Genealogical Society, $12)

PERIODICALS

Ash Tree Echo
(1966-), Fresno Genealogical Society, P.O. Box 1429, Fresno, CA 93716

Lifeliner
(1965-), Genealogical Society of Riverside, P.O. Box 2557, Riverside, CA 92516

Orange County California Genealogical Society Quarterly
(1964-), Orange County California Genealogical

Society, P.O. Box 1587, Orange, CA 92856

San Diego Leaves & Saplings
(1973-), San Diego Genealogical Society, 2925 Kalmia St., San Diego, CA 92104

Santa Clara County Connections
formerly *Santa Clara County Historical and Genealogical Society*
(1964-), Santa Clara County Historical and Genealogical Society, 2635 Homestead Rd., City Library, Santa Clara, CA 95051

The Searcher
(1964-), Southern California Genealogical Society, 417 Irving Dr., Burbank, CA 91504

Valley Quarterly
(1962-), San Bernardino Valley Genealogical Society, P.O. Box 2128, San Bernardino, CA 92406

WEB SITES

California County History
<csac.counties.org/counties_close_up/county_history>: Original California county list and historical maps.

California Death Records
<userdb.rootsweb.com/ca/death/search.cgi>: Covers 1940 through 1997.

California Federal Land Records
<www.rootsweb.com/~usgenweb/ca/ca-land.htm>: Links to county data.

California GenWeb Project
<cagenweb.com>: Links to California counties, queries, and message boards.

California in the Civil War
<members.aol.com/bgandersen/civ_war>: Cemeteries, battles, participants.

California Mailing Lists
<www.rootsweb.com/~jfuller/gen_mail_states-ca.html>: Subscribe to state, county, and special-interest mailing lists.

California Pioneer Project
<cpl.cagenweb.com>: List of settlers who were born in or migrated to California pre-1880.

California Resources at RootsWeb
<resources.rootsweb.com/USA/CA/>: Queries, links, and search engines.

California State Archives Local Government Records Guide
<www.ss.ca.gov/archives/level3_county.htm>: Where to obtain local government records.

Foreign-Born Voters of California, 1872
<feefhs.org/fbvca/fbvcagri.html>: About 61,700 records extracted from each county's Great Registers.

Museum of the City of San Francisco Earthquake Deaths
<www.sfmuseum.org/perished>: Lists those who died in the earthquake of 1906.

STATE STATS

CALIFORNIA

Statehood: 1850
Statewide Birth and Death Records Begin: 1905
Statewide Marriage Records Begin: 1905
Address for Vital Statistics:
Office of Vital Records and Statistics
304 S St.
Sacramento, CA 94244
(916) 445-2684
Fax: (800) 858-5553
<www.dhs.ca.gov/hisp/chs/OVR/ordercert.
htm>
Mailing address:
P.O. Box 730241
Sacramento, CA 94244

Available Censuses: U.S. federal censuses for 1850, 1860, 1870, 1880, 1900, 1910, and 1920. Statewide indexes are available for the 1850, 1860, 1870, 1880 (partial), 1900, 1910, and 1920 censuses. A state census of 1852 is available. Los Angeles censuses exist for 1790, 1836, 1844, and 1897, San Jose for 1897, San Diego for 1899, and Oakland for 1902.

City Directories at the Family History Library Include: Fresno 1926-1935, 1942, 1951-52, 1955, 1960, and 1980; Los Angeles 1873-1935, 1910, 1942; Oakland 1869-1935, 1939, 1941, 1967, and 1969; Sacramento 1851-1935, 1942, 1960, 1963-64, 1970, 1973, and 1980; San Diego 1903-1935, 1937, 1940, 1944, 1960, and 1968; San Francisco 1850-1861, 1861-1934, 1910, 1936, 1935, 1945, 1961, and 1962; San Jose 1879, 1882, 1889, 1899, 1915, 1940, 1943, 1960, 1964, and 1970

San Francisco Obituary and Death Records
<www.sfo.com/
~timandpamwolf/
sfranobi.htm>: Collection of pre-1906 death records.

San Francisco Public Library Vital Records Guide
<sfpl4.sfpl.org/INFDIR/
IS_Vital_Records.htm>: Guide to obtaining pre-1906 San Francisco vital records.

San Francisco Vital Records Information
<www.sfo.com/
~timandpamwolf/
sfranvit.htm>: Sources of birth, marriage, and death records.

Selected Guide to Sources for California Genealogy
<www.library.ca.gov/
html/genealogy.html>: What you can find in the California State Library.

Vital Records Information
<vitalrec.com/ca.html>: Where to obtain copies of birth and death certificates, marriage licenses, and divorce decrees.

FAMILY HISTORY CENTERS

Agua Dulce
35450 N. Penman Rd.
(661) 538-1644

Alpine
2425 Tavern Rd.
(619) 445-2087

Alturas
104 E. Thirteenth St.
(530) 233-2782

Anaheim
440 N. Loara
(714) 533-2772

Anderson
4075 Riverside Ave.
(530) 365-8448

Antioch
2350 Jeffrey Way
(925) 634-9004

Atascadero
2600 Ramona Dr.
(805) 466-6103

Auberry
29711 Auberry Rd.
(559) 855-8863

Auburn
1255 Bell Rd.
(530) 823-3139

Bakersfield
316 A St.
(661) 322-1976

Bakersfield-East
5600 Panorama Dr.
(661) 872-5683

Bakersfield-South
2801 S. Real Rd.
(661) 831-2036

Barstow
2571 Barstow Rd.
(760) 252-4117

Big Bear
400 E. North Shore Dr.
(909) 585-7571

Bishop
725 Keough St.
(760) 873-4881

Blythe
700 N. Broadway
(760) 922-7641

Burbank
136 N. Sunset Canyon Rd.
(818) 843-5362

Camarillo
1201 Paseo Camarillo
(805) 388-7215

Camptonville
14670 Marysville Rd.
(530) 288-1420

Canoga Park
7045 Farralone
(818) 348-8180

Carlsbad
1981 Chestnut
(760) 434-4941

Carson
22731 Main St.
(310) 835-6733

Cedarville
County Road 1 (one mile north)
(530) 279-6347

Cerritos
17909 Bloomfield Ave.
(562) 924-3676

Chico
2430 Mariposa Ave.
(530) 343-6641

Chino
3354 Eucalyptus St.
(909) 393-1936

CURRY JOSEPHINE   JACKSON   KLAMATH   LAKE   HARNEY   MALHEUR   OWYHEE

DEL NORTE   SISKIYOU

                                        MODOC   HUMBOLDT

TRINITY   WASHOE   PERSHING   LANDER

HUMBOLDT   SHASTA   LASSEN

            MENDOCINO   TEHAMA

                        GLENN   BUTTE   PLUMAS   EUREKA
                                        SIERRA
                                    NEVADA   **Reno**
LAKE   COLUSA   SUTTER   PLACER   STOREY   CHURCHILL
                    YUBA   ORMSBY
            YOLO   EL DORADO   ✪ **Carson City**
    SONOMA   NAPA ✪   AMADOR   ALPINE   DOUGLAS   **NEVADA**
Santa Rosa○   **Sacramento** CALAVERAS   LYON
Napa○   SOLANO   MINERAL
        MARIN   CONTRA   TUOLUMNE   NYE
            COSTA   SAN   MONO
San Francisco○ ○**Oakland** JOAQUIN   ESMERALDA
        SAN   ALAMEDA   STANISLAUS
        MATEO   MARIPOSA
San Jose○ SANTA   MADERA
        CLARA   MERCED   FRESNO
    SANTA   FRESNO   INYO
    CRUZ
        Salinas○ FRESNO   ○**Fresno**
            SAN
            BENITO
                                        TULARE   **CALIFORNIA**
        MONTEREY
                        KINGS

                    SAN
                    LUIS   **Bakersfield**○
                    OBISPO   KERN

                    SANTA   SAN BERNARDINO
                    BARBARA
                            VENTURA   LOS ANGELES
                        Santa Barbara○   ○**San Bernardino**

                        Los Angeles○   RIVERSIDE

                                ORANGE

                                        SAN DIEGO

                                San Diego○

                                                MEXICO

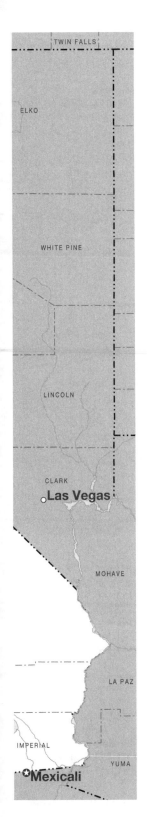

Cloverdale
1011 S. Cloverdale Blvd.
(707) 894-9238

Coalinga
404 W. Polk
(559) 935-5221

Concord
3700 Concord Blvd.
(925) 686-1766

Corning
111 Marguerite St. (at
Marguerite and
Blackburn)
(530) 824-4445

Corona
1510 Taber Rd.
(909) 735-2619

Covina
656 S. Grand Ave.
(626) 331-7117

Crescent City
1031 A St.
(707) 464-4320

Cypress
4000 Orange Ave.
(714) 821-5382

Danville
2949 Stone Valley Rd.
(925) 552-5920

Davis
850 Pioneer Ave.
(530) 662-1538

Delano
2117 Ninth Ave.
(661) 725-8031

El Cajon
1270 S. Orange Ave.
(619) 588-1426

El Centro
1280 S. Eighth St.
(760) 352-4686

El Dorado
3275 Cedar Ravine Rd.
(530) 621-1378

Elk Grove
8925 Vintage Park Dr.
(916) 688-5554

Escondido
2255 Felicita Rd.
(760) 745-1662

Etna
233 N. Highway 3
(530) 467-3341

Eureka-1st Ward
2806 Dolbeer St.
(707) 443-7411

Fairfield
2700 Camrose Dr.
(707) 425-2027

Fall River
43710 Highway 299 E
(530) 336-5202

Fillmore
1017 First St.
(805) 524-1536

Fontana
7526 Alder Ave.
(909) 829-6761

Fort Bragg
355 S. Lincoln
(707) 964-5820

Fortuna
1444 Ross Hill Rd.
(707) 725-4811

Frazier Park
6241 Frazier Mountain
Park Rd.
(661) 245-1041

Fremont
48950 Green Valley Rd.
(510) 623-7496

Fresno
1814 N. Echo Ave.
(559) 268-0888

Fresno-East
1880 E. Gettysburg
(559) 291-2448

Fresno-North
220 N. Peach
(559) 298-8768

Fresno-West
3375 W. Sierra Ave.
(559) 431-4759

Garden Grove
10332 Bolsa Ave.
(714) 554-0592

Glendale
1130 E. Wilson Ave.
(818) 241-8763

Glendora
251 S. Elwood
(626) 335-0923

Granada Hills
17101 Plummer St.
(818) 886-5953

Gridley
348 Spruce St.
(530) 846-3921

Hacienda Heights
16750 Colima Rd.
(626) 961-8765

Hanford
2400 N. Eleventh Ave.
(559) 582-8960

Hayward
3551 Decoto Rd.
(510) 713-1271

Hayward-1st Ward
2000 Highland Blvd.
(510) 538-3578

Hemet
425 N. Kirby Ave.
(909) 658-8104

Hesperia
8889 Sheepcreek Rd.
(760) 868-0883

Highland
7000 Central Ave.
(909) 864-4661

Highlands
14907 Lakeview Way
(707) 994-4929

Hollister
1670 Cienega Rd.
(831) 637-4917

Huntington Beach
8702 Atlanta Ave.
(714) 536-4736

Huntington Beach-North
5402 Heil Ave.
(714) 846-6628

Huntington Park-West
3115 S. Vermont Ave.
(323) 585-7767

Idyllwild
53830 Tollgate Rd.
(909) 659-4679

Jackson
12924 Ridge Rd.
(209) 267-1139

Jamul
14808 Lyons Valley Rd.
(619) 669-1759

Jurupa
5950 Serendipity Rd.
(909) 360-8547

Kern Valley
6400 Park Ave.
(760) 379-1658

La Crescenta
4550 Raymond Ave.
(818) 957-0925

Laguna Niguel
22851 Aliso Creek
(949) 580-1908

Lake Arrowhead
1160 Golden Rule Lane
(909) 337-9569

Lake Elsinore
18220 Dexter St.
(909) 245-4063

Lake Los Angeles
41535 170th St. E
(661) 264-2557

Lakeport
600 Sixteenth and
Hartley
(707) 263-1626

Lancaster
3140 W. Avenue K
(661) 943-1670

Lancaster-East
44330 N. Twenty-seventh
St. E
(661) 946-4675

Livermore
950 Mocho St.
(925) 447-2084

Lodi
731 N. Ham Lane
(209) 369-4148

Loma Rica
11646 Hill Rd.
(530) 743-9329

Lompoc
212 E. Central
(805) 735-4939

Long Beach
3701 Elm Ave.
(562) 988-0509

Long Beach-East
4142 Cerritos Ave.
(714) 821-6914

Loomis
3345 Margaret Dr.
(916) 652-9970

Los Altos
1300 Grant Rd.
(650) 968-1019

Los Angeles
10741 Santa Monica Blvd.
(310) 474-2202

Los Angeles-East
2316 Hillview Ave.
(323) 726-8145

Los Banos
1826 S. Center Ave.
(209) 826-0811

Manteca
6060 E. Northland
(209) 239-5516

Mariposa
5546 Highway 49 N
(209) 742-5010

McKinleyville
1660 Hartwood Dr.
(707) 839-9261

Menifee
29725 Bradley Rd.
(909) 672-0162

Menlo Park
1105 Valparaiso Ave.
(650) 325-9711

Merced
1080 E. Yosemite Ave.
(209) 722-1307

Milpitas
3110 Cropley Ave.
(408) 259-5501

Miranda
250 School Rd.
(707) 943-3071

Mission Viejo
27976 Marguerite
Parkway
(949) 364-2742

Modesto
731 El Vista Ave.
(209) 571-0370

Modesto-North
4300 Dale Rd.
(209) 545-4814

Monterey
1024 Noche Buena St.
(831) 394-1124

Moreno Valley
23300 Old Lake Dr.
(909) 247-8839

Mount Shasta
214 Adams Dr.
(530) 926-6671

Murrieta
24820 Las Brisas Rd.
(909) 698-4983

Napa
2590 Trower Ave.
(707) 257-2887

Needles
2001 El Monte
(760) 326-3363

Nevada City
615 Hollow Way St.
(530) 265-5892

Newbury Park
35 S. Wendy Dr.
(805) 499-7448

North Edwards
16509 Hillcrest St.
(760) 769-4345

Oakhurst
49967 Road 427
(559) 683-8878

Oakland
4766 Lincoln Ave.
(510) 531-3905

Ojai
411 San Antonio St.
(805) 640-8351

Orange
674 S. Yorba St.
(714) 997-7710

Oroville
2390 Monte Vista Ave.
(530) 533-2734

Palm Springs
68-487 East Palm Canyon
Highway 11
(760) 321-0974

Palmdale
2120 E. Avenue R
(661) 947-1694

Palos Verdes
5845 Crestridge
(310) 541-5644

Pasadena
770 N. Sierra Madre Villa
(626) 351-8517

Penasquitos
12835 Black Mountain
Rd.
(858) 484-1729

Pleasanton
6100 Paseo Santa Cruz
(925) 846-0149

Porterville
837 E. Morton
(559) 784-2311

Portola
683 West St.
(530) 832-4941

Poway
15750 Bernardo Heights
Parkway
(858) 487-2304

Quincy
55 Bellamy Ln.
(530) 28-5175

Rancho Cucamonga
6829 Etiwanda Ln.
(909) 899-7564

Red Bluff
545 Berrendos Ave.
(530) 527-9810

Redding
3410 Churn Creek Rd.
(530) 222-4949

Redlands
350 Wabash Ave.
(909) 794-3844

Rialto
1375 N. Willow
(909) 875-2509

Ridgecrest
1031 S. Norma St.
(760) 375-6998

Riverside
5900 Grand Ave.
(909) 784-1918

Riverside-West
4375 Jackson St.
(909) 687-5542

Rocklin
2610 Sierra Meadows Dr.

Sacramento
2745 Eastern Ave.
(916) 487-2090

San Bernardino
3860 N. Waterman Ave.
(909) 881-5355

San Diego
4195 Camino del Rio S
(619) 584-7668

San Diego-East
6767 Fifty-first St.
(619) 582-0572

San Diego-Sweetwater
3737 Valley Vista Way
(619) 472-1506

San Fernando
15555 Saticoy
(818) 779-7144

San Francisco
975 Sneath Ln.
(650) 873-1928

San Francisco-Golden Gate
1900 Pacific Ave.
(415) 771-3655

San Francisco-West
730 Sharp Park Rd.
(650) 355-4986

San Jose
4977 San Felipe Rd.
(408) 274-8592

San Lorenzo Valley
9434 Central Ave.
(831) 336-2707

San Luis Obispo
651 Foothill
(805) 543-6328

Santa Barbara
2107 Santa Barbara St.
(805) 682-2092

Santa Clara
875 Quince Ave.
(408) 241-1449

Santa Cruz
220 Elk St.
(831) 426-1078

Santa Maria
908 E. Sierra Madre
(805) 928-4722

Santa Rosa
1725 Peterson Lane
(707) 525-0399

Sea Ranch
45500 Pacific Woods Rd.
(707) 884-3255

Sequoia
36309 E. Kings Canyon
Rd.
(559) 338-2877

Simi Valley
5028 Cochran
(805) 581-2456

Solvang
2627 Janin Way
(805) 688-3443

Sonoma
16280 La Grama
(707) 996-2369

Sonora
19481 Hillsdale Dr.
(209) 536-9206

South Lake Tahoe
3460 Spruce Ave.
(530) 544-1214

Stockton
800 W. Brookside Rd.
(209) 951-7060

Susanville
905 Richmond Rd.
(530) 257-4411

Sylmar
13680 Sayre St.
(818) 833-7461

Taft
101 Church St.
(661) 765-2157

Tehachapi
600 Anita Dr.
(661) 822-7909

Thousand Oaks
3645 N. Moorpark Rd.
(805) 241-9316

Torrance
22605 Kent Ave.
(310) 791-6256

Tracy
1981 Chester Dr.
(209) 835-1816

Turlock
4300 Geer Rd.
(209) 632-9640

Twenty-Nine Palms
73002 El Paseo Dr.
(760) 367-0237

Ukiah
1337 S. Dora St.
(707) 468-5443

Upland
785 N. San Antonio
(909) 985-8821

Vacaville
480 Wrentham Dr.
(707) 451-8394

Valencia
24443 McBean Parkway
(661) 259-1347

Ventura
3501 Loma Vista Rd.
(805) 643-5607

Victorville
12100 Ridgecrest Rd.
(760) 243-5632

Visalia
825 W. Tulare Ave.
(559) 732-3712

Vista
1310 Foothill Dr.
(760) 945-6053

Wasco
2309 Ninth Place
(661) 758-2538

Weaverville
Mormon Lane
(530) 623-5226

Whittier
15265 Mulberry Dr.
(562) 946-1880

Willits
265 Margie Dr.
(707) 459-5332

Willows
810 N. Humbolt
(530) 934-4883

Yuba City
1470 Butte House Rd.
(530) 673-0113

Yucca Valley
56885 Onaga Trail
(760) 369-7430

HAWAII

ORGANIZATIONS & ARCHIVES

Bishop Museum Library
1525 Bernice St.
Honolulu, HI 96817
(808) 848-4148
Fax: (808) 847-8241
<www.bishopmuseum.
org/research/cultstud/
libarch>

**Daughters of the
American Revolution**
Aloha Chapter House

1914 Makiki Heights Dr.
Honolulu, HI 96822
(808) 949-7256
<www.geocities.com/
darhonolulu/aboutdar.
html>

**Hawaii Chinese History
Center**
111 N. King Street
Room 410
Honolulu, HI 96817
(808) 536-5948

**Hawaiian Historical
Society**
560 Kawaiahao St.
Honolulu, HI 96813
(808) 537-6271
<www.hawaiianhistory.
org>

Hawaii State Archives
Kekauluohi Building
Iolani Palace Grounds
Honolulu, HI 96813
(808) 586-0329
Fax: (808) 586-0330
<kumu.icsd.hawaii.gov/
dags/archives/welcome.
html>

Hawaii State Library
478 S. King St.
Honolulu, HI 96813
(808) 586-3500
Fax: (808) 586-3584
<www.hcc.hawaii.edu/
hspls>

**University of Hawaii at
Manoa**
Hamilton Library,
Hawaiian Collection
2550 The Mall
Honolulu, HI 96822
(808) 956- 8264
Fax: (808) 956-5968
<www2.hawaii.edu/
~speccoll/hawaii.html>

RESOURCES

*Hawaiian Genealogies:
Extracted From Hawaiian
Language Newspaper*
by Edith Kawelohea

McKinzie (Institute for
Polynesian Studies,
Brigham Young
University-Hawaii, $25)

PERIODICALS

*The Hawaiian Journal of
History*
(1967-), The Hawaiian
Historical Society

WEB SITES

**Genealogical Resources
in Hawaii**
<www.hpcug.org/
ancestors/resource.htm>:
Links and addresses.

Hawaii GenWeb Project
<www.rootsweb.com/
~higenweb/hawaii.htm>:

Links to state and county
resources.

**Hawaii *Mayflower*
Society**
<www.geocities.com/
Heartland/Ridge/4602>:
Links and resources.

Hawaii Mailing Lists
<www.rootsweb.com/
~jfuller/gen_mail_
states-hi.html>: Subscribe
to state or county-level
mailing lists, plus special-
interest lists.

**Hawaii Resources at
RootsWeb**
<resources.rootsweb.
com/USA/HI>: Archived
messages, queries, mes-
sage boards.

HAWAII

Statehood: 1959
Statewide Birth and Death Records Begin: 1842
Statewide Marriage Records Begin: 1842
Address for Vital Statistics:
Research and Statistics Office
State Department of Health
P.O. Box 3378
1250 Punchbowl St.
Honolulu, HI 96801
(808) 586-4533
<www.state.hi.us/doh/records/vr_howto.
htm>

Available Censuses: U.S. federal censuses for
1900, 1910, and 1920. Indexes are available for
the 1900 and 1920 censuses. Colonial censuses
exist for some areas for 1866, 1878 (Hilo only),
1890, and 1896 (Oahu only). Two "census files,"
1840-1866 and 1847-1866, in the Hawaii State
Archives contain miscellaneous records such as
vital record summaries, school censuses, and
population lists.

**City Directories at the Family History Library
Include:** Honolulu 1917, 1938, 1940, 1959, 1963,
and 1977

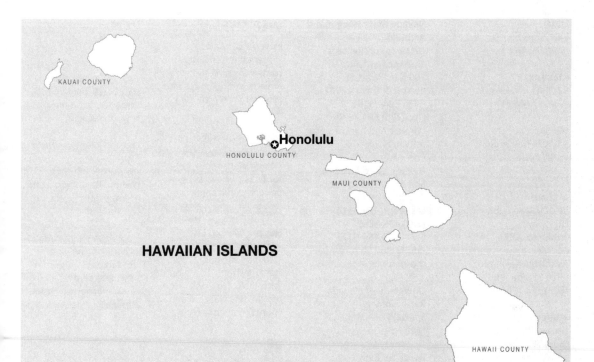

KAUAI COUNTY

⊕ Honolulu
HONOLULU COUNTY

MAUI COUNTY

HAWAIIAN ISLANDS

HAWAII COUNTY

The Royal Family of Hawaii
<www.royalty.nu/America/Hawaii.html>:
Early history, plus links to Hawaiian royalty.

Vital Records Information
<vitalrec.com/hi.html>:
Get birth and death certificates, marriage licenses, and divorce decrees.

FAMILY HISTORY CENTERS

Hana
4826 Uakea Highway
(808) 248-8445

Hanalei
5260 Kuhio Highway
(808) 826-9490

Hilo
1373 Kilauea Ave.
(808) 935-0711

Honokaa
Mamalahoa Highway
(808) 775-7348

Honolulu
1560 S. Beretania St.
(808) 955-8910

Honolulu-West
1723 Beckley St.
(808) 845-9701

Johnston Island
Chapel Annex on Arnold Ave.
(808) 421-0011

Kahului
125 W. Kamehameha Ave.
(808) 87-8841

Kaneohe
46-177 Halaulani St.
(808) 247-3134

Ka'u
Mamalahoa Highway
(808) 929-7123

Kauai
4580 Ehiku Rd.
(808) 246-9119

Keei
84-5236 Mamalahoa Highway
(808) 328-8171

Kekaha
St. Amakihi 4590
(808) 337-2222

Kihei
187 A Auhana St.
(808) 879-4366

Kohala
55-524 Hawi Rd.
(808) 889-5473

Kona
75-230 Kalani St.
(808) 329-4469

Lahaina
1594 Malo St.
(808) 667-9899

Laie
55-600 Naniloa Loop
(808) 293-2133

Lanai
348 Jacaranda St.
(808) 565-6061

Makakilo
92-900 Makakilo Dr.
(808) 672-5971

Mililani
95-1039 Meheula
Parkway
(808) 623-1712

Molokai
35-100 Maunaloa
Highway
(808) 553-5296

Pukalani/Makawao
3356 Kihapai Pl.
(808) 572-7360

Waimea
Hawaii Belt Highway 19
(808) 885-4684

Waipahu
94-210 Kahualii St.
(808) 678-0752

NEVADA

ORGANIZATIONS & ARCHIVES

Nevada Historical Society
1650 N. Virginia St.
Reno, NV 89503
(702) 688-1190
Fax: (702) 688-2917
<dmla.clan.lib.nv.us/docs/
museums/reno/his-soc.
htm>

**Nevada State
Genealogical Society**
2931 Randolph St.
Reno, NV 89515
(702) 826-1130
Mailing address:
P.O. Box 20666
Reno, NV 89502
<www.rootsweb.com/
~nvsgs>

**Nevada State Library and
Archives**
Archives and Records
Management
100 N. Stewart St.
Carson City, NV 89701
(775) 684-3310
Fax: (775) 684-3310
<dmla.clan.lib.nv.us/docs/
nsla/archives>

**Nevada State Museum
and Historical Society**
700 Twin Lakes Dr.
Las Vegas, NV 89107
(702) 486-5205
Fax: (702) 486-5172
<dmla.clan.lib.nv.us/docs/
museums/lv/vegas.htm>

**University of Nevada-
Reno Library**
Special Collections
Mail Stop 332
University Library
Reno, NV 89557
(702) 784-6500 ext. 327
Fax: (702) 784-4529
<www.library.unr.edu/
specoll/Default.htm>

RESOURCES

*Nevada Guide to
Genealogical Records*
by Diane E. Greene
(Clearfield Co., $24.95)

PERIODICALS

Chart and Quill
(1979-), Northeastern
Nevada Genealogical
Society, 1515 Idaho St.,
Elko, NV 89801

*The Nevada State
Genealogical Society
Newsletter*
(1981-), Nevada State
Genealogical Society, P.O.
Box 20666, Reno, NV
89515

WEB SITES

Nevada Genealogy
<freepages.genealogy.
rootsweb.com/~helper/
nevada.htm>: Census and
cemetery research, plus
links.

Nevada GenWeb Project
<www.rootsweb.com/
~nvgenweb>: Look here
for links to Nevada news-
papers, publications, and
research helps.

Nevada Mailing Lists
<www.rootsweb.com/
~jfuller/gen_mail_
states-nv.html>: Network
with other Nevada
researchers via state and
county mailing lists.

**Nevada Resources at
RootsWeb**
<resources.rootsweb.
com/USA/NV>: One-stop
surfing for searchable
databases, mailing lists,
and sites containing
Nevada records.

**Nevada Women's History
Project**
<www.unr.edu/wrc/
nwhp>: Read biographies
of important women in
Nevada history.

Vital Records Information
<vitalrec.com/nv.html>:
How to get copies of
birth and death certifi-
cates, marriage licenses,
and divorce decrees.

FAMILY HISTORY CENTERS

Alamo-Hiko
95 E. Broadway St.
(775) 725-3411

Austin
Main St.
(775) 964-2336

Battle Mountain
785 W. Humboldt
(775) 635-2297

Beatty
C Ave. and Lisle
(775) 553-2051

Black Mountain
19 E. Ocean Ave.
(702) 566-8190

Boulder City
916 Fifth St.
(702) 293-3304

Carson City
411 N. Saliman Rd.
(775) 884-2064

Elko-East
77 E. Spring Creek
Parkway
(775) 778-9866

Elko-West
3001 N. Fifth St.
(775) 738-4565

Ely
900 Avenue E
(775) 289-2287

Fallon-South
750 W. Richards St.
(775) 423-8888

Fernley
Highway 95A and
Mortensen
(702) 575-4474

Hawthorne
150 S. A St.
(775) 945-8241

Las Vegas
509 S. Ninth St.
(702) 382-9695

Las Vegas-East
4040 E. Wyoming Ave.
(702) 641-6219

Las Vegas-Red Rock
221 S. Lorenzi Blvd.
(702) 878-0361

Las Vegas-Warm Springs
7670 S. Bruce
(702) 361-0609

Logandale
2555 N. St. Joseph St.
(702) 398-3266

Lovelock
220 Maple Dr.
(775) 273-7380

Mesquite
100 N. Arrowhead
(702) 346-2342

Pahrump
921 E. Wilson
(775) 727-5229

Panaca
385 Main St.
(702) 728-4699

Reno
4751 Neil Rd.
(775) 826-1130

Silver Springs
Corner of Elm and
Green St.
(775) 577-0311

Smokey Valley
Highway 376 and
Jefferson Dr.
(775) 377-2060

South Lake Tahoe
3460 Spruce Ave.
(530) 544-1214

Tonopah
Smokey Valley Rd.
(702) 482-5492

Wells
First and Lake Wells St.
(775) 752-3763

Winnemucca
111 W. McArthur Ave.
(702) 623-4448

Yerington
600 N. Oregon St.
(775) 463-9587

NEW MEXICO

ORGANIZATIONS & ARCHIVES

Albuquerque Public Library
501 Copper Ave. NW
Albuquerque, NM 87102
(505) 768-51 40
Fax: (505) 768-5191
<www.cabq.gov/library>

Hispanic Genealogical Research Center of New Mexico
P.O. Box 51088
Albuquerque, NM 87181
<www.hgrc-nm.org>

Historical Society of New Mexico
P.O. Box 1912
Santa Fe, NM 87504
(505) 827-7332
Fax: (505) 827-7331
<www.hsnm.org>

New Mexico Genealogical Society
P.O. Box 8283
Albuquerque, NM 87198
(505) 828-2514
<www.nmgs.org>

New Mexico State Library
325 Don Gaspar
Santa Fe, NM 87503
(505) 827-38 52
Fax: (505) 827-3888
<www.stlib.state.nm.us>

New Mexico State Records Center

and Archives
1205 Camino Carlos Rey
Santa Fe, NM 87507
(505) 476-7900
Fax: (505) 827-7331
<www.nmcpr.state.
nm.us>

University of New Mexico Library
Special Collections
The Center for Southwest
Research General Library
Albuquerque, NM 87131
(505) 277- 6451
Fax: (505) 277-6019
<www.unm.edu/
~cswrref>

RESOURCES

"New Mexico's Historical Records: Documenting 400 Years of History"
lecture by Robert J.
Torrez (Audiotapes.com,
$8.50)

Sources of Genealogical Help in New Mexico
(Southern California
Genealogical Society,
$2.25)

PERIODICALS

New Mexico Genealogist
(1962-), New Mexico
Genealogical Society, P.O.
Box 8283, Albuquerque,
NM 87198

WEB SITES

New Mexico Genealogy
<newmexicogenealogy.
org>: Surname and query
pages and links to online
records from dozens of
sources.

New Mexico GenWeb Project
<www.rootsweb.com/
~nmgenweb>: Queries,
volunteer researchers,
county resources.

New Mexico Mailing Lists
<www.rootsweb.com/
~jfuller/gen_mail_
states-nm.html>: State
and county lists.

**New Mexico Resources at
RootsWeb**
<resources.rootsweb.
com/USA/NM>: Click here
for a variety of New
Mexico records and
resources.

Vital Records Information
<vitalrec.com/nm.html>:
Where to obtain copies
of birth and death certificates, marriage licenses,
and divorce decrees.

**FAMILY HISTORY
CENTERS**

Alamogordo
1800 Twenty-third St.
(505) 437-8772

Albuquerque
5709 Haines St. NE
(505) 266-4867

Albuquerque-East
4106 Eubank NE
(505) 293-5610

Albuquerque-West
1100 Montano Rd. NW
(505) 343-0456

Animas
10 miles north of Animas
(505) 548-2318

Carlsbad
1211 W. Church St.
(505) 885-1368

Clovis
2800 Lore St.
(505) 769-1350

Deming
1000 W. Florida
(505) 544-0286

Edgewood
2 blocks south of I-40
State Route 34
(505) 281-5384

Espanola
1101 Fairview Dr.
(505) 753-3751

Farmington
400 W. Apache
(505) 325-5813

Gallup
601 Susan Ave.
(505) 722-9502

Grants
1010 Bondad Ave.
(505) 287-2470

Hatch
210 E. Herrera
(505) 267-3036

Hobbs
3720 N. Grimes
(505) 392-6200

Las Cruces
3210 Venus St.
(505) 382-0618

Las Vegas
710 Katherine Dr.
(505) 454-0548

Los Alamos
1967 Eighteenth St.
(505) 662-3186

Los Lunas
160 James St.
(505) 865-0788

Luna
E. Main St.
(505) 547-2762

Ramah
Tietjen St. (1 block north
of Dewglo Market)
(505) 783-4536

Raton
2136 La Mesa Dr.
(505) 445-9226

Roswell
2201 W. Country Club Rd.
(505) 624-1761

Ruidoso
Mile post 14-15 on
Highway 48
(505) 336-4359

Santa Fe
410 Rodeo Rd.
(505) 982-9233

Silver City
3755 N. Swan St.
(505) 388-1068

Socorro
El Camino Real across
Sedillo
(505) 835-4806

Taos
235 Camino de la Placita
(505) 758-2018

STATE STATS

NEW MEXICO

Statehood: 1912
Statewide Birth and Death Records Begin: 1920
Statewide Marriage Records Begin: 1920
Address for Vital Statistics:
  Vital Statistics Bureau
  New Mexico Health Services
  1190 St. Francis Dr.
  Santa Fe, NM 87505
  (505) 827-2338
  Fax: (505) 984-1048

Available Censuses: U.S. federal censuses for 1850, 1860, 1870, 1880, 1900, 1910, and 1920 and a special 1885 territorial census. Statewide indexes exist for the 1850, 1860, 1870, 1880, 1900, and 1920 censuses. Spanish and Mexican colonial censuses exist for 1750, 1790, 1802, 1816, 1822, 1823, 1826, 1827, 1830, and 1845.

City Directories at the Family History Library Include: Albuquerque 1883, 1905-1935, 1923, 1940, 1960, 1965, and 1970; Santa Fe 1940, 1960, 1968, and 1983

Tres Piedras
22470 U.S. Highway 64
(505) 751-0994

Tucumcari
2400 S. Ninth St.
(505) 461-9676

White Rock
366 Grand Canyon Dr.
(505) 672-9888

OREGON

ORGANIZATIONS & ARCHIVES

Genealogical Forum of Oregon, Inc.
1505 SE Gideon
Portland, OR 97202
(503) 963-1932
<gfo.org >
Mailing address:
P.O. Box 42567
Portland, OR 97242

Multnomah County Central Library
Humanities Division
801 SW Tenth Ave.
Portland, OR 97205
(503) 988-5123
<www.multcolib.org/
agcy/cen.html>

Oregon Genealogical Society
955 Oak Alley
Eugene, Oregon 97401
(541) 345-0399
<www.rootsweb.com/
~orlncogs/ogsinfo.htm>
Mailing address:
P.O. Box 10306
Eugene, OR 97440

Oregon Historical Society
1200 SW Park Ave.
Portland, OR 97205
(503) 222-1741
Fax: (503) 221-2035

Oregon State Archives
800 Summer St. NE
Salem, OR 97310
(503) 373-0701
Fax: (503) 373-0953
<arcweb.sos.state.or.us>

Oregon State Library
State Library Building
250 Winter St. NE
Salem, OR 97310
(503) 378-4243 ext. 221
Fax: (503) 588-7119
<www.osl.state.or.us/
home>

**University of Oregon
Library**
1299 University of
Oregon
Eugene, OR 97403
(541) 346-3053
Fax: (541) 346-3485
<libweb.uoregon.edu>

RESOURCES

Early Oregon Days
by Edwin D. Culp (Caxton
Printers, $22.95)

*Genealogical Material in
Oregon Donation Land
Claims*
volumes 1-5, by Lottie
Gurley (Genealogical
Forum of Oregon, $7.25
to $9 per volume, $.75
for index)

Oregon Burial Site Guide
by Stanley R. Clarke and
Janice M. Healy (Stoney
Way, P.O. Box 5414,
Aloha, OR 97007, $98.50)

*Oregon Guide to
Genealogical Sources*
by Connie Lenzen
(Genealogical Forum of
Oregon, $25)

**"Oregon Records and
Resources"**
lecture by Connie Lenzen
(Audiotapes.com, $8.50)

Research in Oregon
by Connie Lenzen
(National Genealogical
Society, $6.50)

**"Resources at the Oregon
State Archives"**
lecture by Layne Sawyer
(Audiotapes.com, $8.50)

PERIODICALS

Beaver Briefs
(1969-), Willamette Valley
Genealogical Society, P.O.
Box 2083, Salem, OR
97308

The Bulletin
(1951-), Genealogical
Forum of Oregon, Box
42567, Portland, OR
97242

*Coos Bay Genealogical
Forum Bulletin*
(1966-), The Coos Bay
Genealogical Forum
Library, P.O. Box 1067,
North Bend, OR 97459

Mt. Hood Trackers
(1959-1977), Mt. Hood
Genealogical Forum, P.O.
Box 703, Oregon City, OR
97045

*Oregon Genealogical
Society Quarterly*
(1962-), Oregon
Genealogical Society, P.O.
Box 10306, Eugene, OR
97440

Rogue Digger
(1966-), Rogue Valley
Genealogical Society, Box
1468, Phoenix, OR 97535

WEB SITES

**Center for Columbia
River History**
<ccrh.org/content.htm>:
Oral history archives.

**City of Portland Birth
Index**
<arcweb.sos.state.or.us/
banners/genealogy.htm>:
Follow the birth index
link to search records
beginning with March
1881.

**City of Portland Death
Index**
<arcweb.sos.state.or.us/
banners/genealogy.htm>:
Follow the death index
link to search for records
of deaths between 1881
and 1917.

**Historical Oregon
Information Services**
<www.historicaloregon.
org>: This group aims to
bring information about

Oregon's history into one
place. Its Web site offers
a biweekly e-mail
newsletter and lookups
in the service's historical
and genealogical books.

**Oregon Genealogical
Information Locator**
<159.121.172.88/
genealogy/search.lasso>:
More than 195,000
entries, including vital
records, probates, and
naturalization.

Oregon Genealogy Links
<gesswhoto.com/
genealogy.html>: Links
to geographical Web
sites, cemeteries, and military and census records.

OREGON

STATE STATS

Statehood: 1859
Statewide Birth and Death Records Begin: 1903
Statewide Marriage Records Begin: 1906
Address for Vital Statistics:
   Oregon State Health Division
   Center for Health Statistics
   P.O. Box 14050
   Portland, OR 97293
   (503) 731-4095
   Fax: (503) 731-4084
   <www.ohd.hr.state.or.us./chs/certif/
   certfaqs.htm>

Available Censuses: U.S. federal censuses for
1860, 1870, 1880, 1900, 1910, and 1920.
Statewide indexes are available for the 1860,
1870, 1880, 1900, and 1920 censuses. Territorial
and state censuses also exist for a few counties
for 1842, 1843, 1845, 1849, 1850 (indexed),
1852, 1853, 1854, 1856, 1857, 1858, 1859, 1865,
1885, 1895, and 1905.

**City Directories at the Family History Library
Include:** Eugene 1921, 1960, 1962,1964,1965,
1968 and 1969; Portland 1863-1935, 1941,
1964, 1971, 1979, and 1980; Salem 1871, 1940-
1941, 1960, 1964, 1970, 1975, 1980, and 1985.

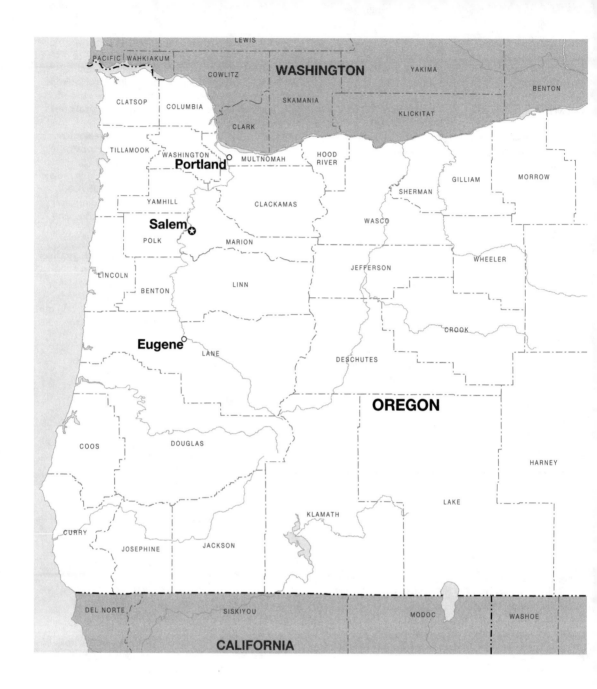

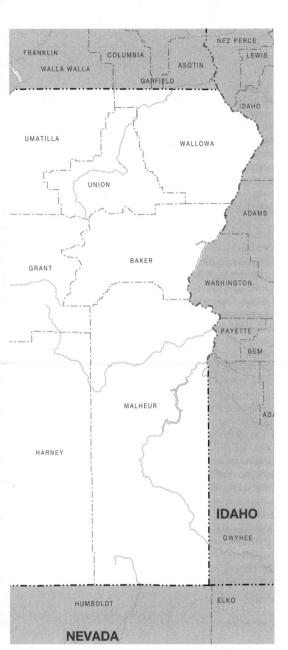

Oregon GenWeb Project
<www.rootsweb.com/
~orgenweb>: State and
county resources, Oregon
Trail history, and links to
county queries and mes-
sage boards.

**Oregon History and
Genealogy Resources**
<rootsweb.com/
~genepool/oregon.htm>:
Links to searchable data-
bases, research aids, and
resources.

Oregon Land Records
<arcweb.sos.state.or.us/
land.html>: Lists of
Oregon land records in
the Oregon State
Archives.

Oregon Mailing Lists
<lists.rootsweb.com/
index/usa/OR>: Join state,
county, or special-interest
lists.

**Oregon Resources at
RootsWeb**
<resources.rootsweb.
com/USA/OR>: Search
archived queries and
messages.
records indexes.

Oregon Trail
<www.isu.edu/~trinmich/
Oregontrail.html>: Fact-
filled site about the
Great Pioneer Trail.

**Salem Public Library
Historic Photo Database**
<photos.salemhistory.
org>: Search thousands
of photos from the mid-
1800s.

**Tribes and Villages of
Oregon**
<hanksville.org/sand/
contacts/tribal/OR.html>:
Links to Native American
reservations and councils.

**Vital Records
Information**
<vitalrec.com/or.html>:
Get birth and death cer-
tificates, marriage licenses, and divorce decrees.

FAMILY HISTORY CENTERS

Astoria
350 Niagara Ave.
(503) 325-8256

Baker
2625 Hughes Ln.
(541) 523-2397

Beaverton
4195 SW Ninety-ninth
Ave.
(503) 644-7782

Beaverton-West
17140 SW Bany Rd.
(503) 356-1385

Bend
1260 NE Thompson Dr.
(541) 382-9947

Boardman
500 Wilson Rd.
(541) 481-5050

Brookings
770 Elk Dr.
(541) 469-5754

Burns
600 N. Saginaw Ave.
(541) 573-2120

Cave Junction
309 S. Junction Ave.
(541) 592-4583

Central Point
2305 Taylor Rd.
(541) 664-5356

Chiloquin
Highway 62 and S.
Highway 422
(541) 783-2739

Coos Bay
3355 Virginia Ave.
(541) 756-3575

Corvallis
4141 NW Harrison Blvd.
(541) 758-1156

Cottage Grove
531 S. Tenth
(541) 942-2670

Elgin
755 Baltimore
(541) 437-2313

Enterprise
900 E. Greenwood St.
(541) 426-3342

Eugene-West
3550 W. Eighteenth St.
(541) 343-3741

Florence
2705 Munsel Lake Rd.
(541) 997-7268

Gold Beach
94161 Ellensburg Ave.
(541) 247-6496

Grants Pass
1969 Williams Highway
(541) 476-1926

Gresham
3600 SE 182nd Ave.
(503) 665-1524

Gresham-South
16317 SE Bluff Rd.
(503) 668-4811

Hermiston
850 SW Eleventh
(541) 567-3445

Hillsboro
2200 NE Jackson School
Rd.
(503) 640-4658

Hood River
Eighteenth and May St.
(541) 386-3539

John Day
944 E. Main St.
(541) 575-1817

Klamath Falls
6630 Alva Ave.
(541) 884-7998

La Grande
2504 N. Fir
(541) 963-5003

La Pine
52680 Day Rd.
(541) 536-5636

Lake Oswego
1271 Overlook Dr.
(503) 638-1410

Lakeview
Highway 395 N
(541) 947-2389

Lebanon
1955 Fifth St.
(541) 451-3992

Lincoln City
3565 W. Devils Lake Rd.
(541) 994-2998

McMinnville
1645 NW Baker Creek Rd.
(503) 434-5811

Medford
2900 Juanipero Way
(541) 773-3363

Milwaukie Oregon
8331 SE Cason Rd.
(503) 722-8766

Molalla
13250 S. Highway 211
(503) 829-2532

Monmouth
783 Church St.
(503) 838-2964

Myrtle Creek
871 NE Lillian St.
(541) 863-4337

Newberg
1212 Deborah Rd.
(503) 538-5505

Newport
2229 NE Crestview Dr.
(541) 265-7333

Nyssa
1309 Park Ave.
(541) 372-0228

Oakridge
76959 Lee Dr.
(541) 782-3120

Ontario
1705 NW Fourth Ave.
(541) 889-7835

Oregon City
14340 S. Donovan Rd.
(503) 655-9908

Pendleton
NW Twelfth and Gilliam
(541) 276-3117

Portland
1975 SE Thirtieth
(503) 235-9090

Portland-East
2215 NE 106th Ave.
(503) 252-1081

Prineville
333 SE Idlewood
(541) 447-1488

Rainier
27410 Parkdale Rd.
(503) 556-9694

Redmond
450 Rimrock Way
(541) 548-2436

Reedsport
2311 Longwood Dr.
(541) 271-3736

Roseburg
2001 W. Bertha
(541) 672-1237

Salem
4550 Lone Oak Rd. SE
(503) 378-0383

Salem-East
862 Forty-fifth St. NE
(503) 371-0453

Seaside
1403 S. Wahanna Rd.
(503) 738-7543

St. Helens
2735 Sykes Rd.
(503) 397-1300

Sweet Home
1155 Twenty-second Ave.
(541) 367-3360

The Dalles
1815 E. Fifteenth
(541) 298-5815

Tillamook
4200 Twelfth St.
(503) 842-2781

Tualatin
22284 SW Grahams Ferry
Rd.
(503) 692-0481

Vernonia
1350 E. Knott St.
(503) 429-7151

Willamina
900 Willamina Dr.
(503) 876-3452

Wilsonville
29350 SW Town Center
Loop E
(503) 685-7383

Woodburn
1000 Country Club Rd.
(583) 981-4731

ORGANIZATIONS & ARCHIVES

National Archives-Pacific Alaska Region (Seattle)
6125 Sand Point Way NE
Seattle, WA 98115
(206) 526-6501
Fax: (206) 526-6575
<www.archives.gov/facilities/wa/seattle.html>

Seattle Public Library
800 Pike St.
Seattle, WA 98101
(206) 386-4636
Fax: (206) 386-4632
<www.spl.lib.wa.us>

Suzzallo and Allen Libraries
University of Washington
P.O. Box 352900
Seattle, WA 98195
(206) 543-0242
Fax: (206) 685-8049
<www.lib.washington.edu/Suzzallo>

Washington State Archives
1129 Washington St. SE
Olympia, WA 98504
(360) 753-5485
Fax: (360) 664-8814
<www.secstate.wa.gov/archives>
Mailing address:
P.O. Box 40238
Olympia, WA 98504-0238

Washington State Genealogical Society
P.O. Box 1422
Olympia, WA 98507
<www.rootsweb.com/~wasgs>

Washington State Historical Society
1911 Pacific Ave.
Tacoma, WA 98402
(888) 238-4373
<www.wshs.org >

Washington State Historical Society Library
Research Center
315 N. Stadium Way
Tacoma, WA 98403
(253) 798-5914
Fax: (253) 597-4186
<www.wshs.org/text/res_wshrc.htm>

Washington State Library
Point Plaza East
6880 Capitol Blvd. S.
Tumwater, WA 98501
P.O. Box 42460
Olympia, WA 98504
(360) 704-5200
Fax: (360) 586-7575
<www.statelib.wa.gov>

RESOURCES

Germans From Russia, Index of Naturalization Records in Whitman County, Washington, 1860-1942
by Janet Margolis Damm
(Palouse Publications, $6)

Marriage Records of Territorial Pierce County, 1853-1889
(Tacoma-Pierce County Genealogical Society, $14)

Washington Atlas of Historical County Boundaries
by John Long (Charles Scribner and Sons, $130)

Washington State Atlas of Historical County Boundaries
edited by John H. Long
(Charles Scribners Sons, out of print)

"Washington State Genealogical Research"
lecture by Sarah Thorson Little (Audiotapes.com, $8.50)

PERIODICALS

The Appleland Bulletin
(1972-), Wenatchee Area Genealogical Society, P.O. Box 5280, Wenatchee, WA 98807

The Bulletin
(1963-), Eastern Washington Genealogical Society Library, P.O. Box 1826, Spokane, WA 99210

Bulletin of the Whatcom Genealogical Society
(1971-), Whatcom Genealogical Society, P.O. Box 1493, Bellingham, WA 98227

The Researcher
(1969-), Tacoma-Pierce County Genealogical Society, P.O. Box 1952, Tacoma, WA 98401

Trail Breakers
(1974-), Clark County Genealogical Society, P.O. Box 5249, Vancouver, WA 98668

Washington Heritage
formerly *Washington State Genealogical and Historical Review* (1982-), Heritage Quest, Drawer 40, Orting, WA 98630

Yakima Valley Genealogical Society Bulletin
(1973-), Yakima Valley Genealogical Society, P.O. Box 445, Yakima, WA 98907

STATE STATS

WASHINGTON

Statehood: 1889
Statewide Birth and Death Records Begin: 1907
Statewide Marriage Records Begin: 1968
Address for Vital Statistics:
　Vital Records
　P.O. Box 9709
　Olympia, WA 98507
　(360) 753-5936
　Fax: (360) 753-4135
　<www.doh.wa.gov/EHSPHL/CHS/cert.htm>

Available Censuses: U.S. federal censuses for Washington Territory for 1860, 1870, and 1880 and for the state of Washington for 1900, 1910, and 1920. Indexes are available for the 1860, 1870, 1880, 1900, and 1920 censuses. Washington is included and indexed separately in the 1850 Oregon Territory census. Territorial and state censuses also exist for some counties for various years from 1857 through 1892.

City Directories at the Family History Library Include: Seattle 1872-1935, 1911, 1913, 1917-1918, 1932, 1960, 1964, 1970, 1975, 1979; Spokane 1913, 1915, 1918, 1923, 1939, 1955, 1960, 1966, 1984

WEB SITES

Associated Catholic Cemeteries Search

<adhostnt.adhost.com/acc-seattle/accrsrch.html>: Provide your name and e-mail address in order to access the Archdiocese of Seattle's database of burial dates and locations.

The East Side Journal

<www.bcc.ctc.edu/cpsha/esj>: An index of the Kirkland, Washington, newspaper for 1918 to 1975.

Tacoma Obituaries

<search.tpl.lib.wa.us/obits>: About 367,000 individual index records, from 1930 to the present.

Vancouver Barracks Cemetery Index

<geocities.com/Eureka/4458/vanbar.html>: An alphabetized list of persons buried at the Vancouver barracks.

Vital Records Information

<vitalrec.com/wa.html>: How to order birth and death certificates, marriage licenses, and divorce decrees.

Washington GenWeb Project

<www.rootsweb.com/~wagenweb>: County- and state-level resources, queries, message boards.

Washington Mailing Lists

<www.rootsweb.com/~jfuller/gen_mail_states-wa.html>: Join state or county lists.

Washington Place Names

<www.tpl.lib.wa.us/v2/nwroom/wanames.htm>: Use the Tacoma Public Library's online tool to find obscure or obsolete locations.

Washington Resources at RootsWeb

<resources.rootsweb.com/USA/WA/>: Search archived messages and queries.

Washington State Archives

<www.secstate.wa.gov/archives/research.aspx>: Where to find property, corporation, court, census, and naturalization records.

Washington State Genealogical Resource Guide

<www.rootsweb.com/~wasgs/resguide.htm>: Historical and genealogical data for Washington counties.

FAMILY HISTORY CENTERS

Auburn
625 M St. NE
(253) 735-2009

Basin City
160 Bailie Blvd.
(509) 269-4237

Bellevue
10675 NE Twentieth St.
(425) 454-2690

Bellevue-North
4200 124th Ave. SE
(425) 562-0361

Bellingham
2925 James St.
(360) 738-1849

Bremerton
2225 N. Perry Ave.
(360) 479-9370

Bremerton
3877 Mullenix Rd. SE
(360) 895-3099

Brewster
417 S. Fourth St.
(509) 689-3218

Centralia
2195 Jackson Highway
(360) 748-1516

Chelan
195 Highway 150
(509) 682-5714

Colfax
2652 Almota Rd.
(509) 397-2988

Colville
260 E. Juniper St.
(509) 685-0207

Coulee Dam
806 Spruce
(509) 633-1781

Davenport
Lincoln and Eighth St.
(509) 725-0554

Dayton
1114 S. Third St.
(509) 382-2111

Elma
702 E. Main St.
(360) 482-5982

Ephrata
1301 Division Ave. E.
(509) 754-4762

Everett
9509 Nineteenth Ave. SE
(425) 337-0457

Federal Way
34815 Weyerhauser Way S.
(253) 874-3803

Forks
Calawah Way

Goldendale
Columbus and McKinley
(509) 773-3824

Kennewick
895 W. Gage Blvd.
(509) 628-8332

Kirkland
7910 NE 132nd St.
(425) 821-3939

Long Beach
N 1306 Washington
(360) 642-3528

Longview
1721 Thirtieth Ave.
(360) 577-8234

Lynnwood
22015 Forty-eighth Ave. W
(425) 776-6678

Maple Valley
26800 236th Pl. SE
(425) 413-7566

Morton
130 Crumb Rd.
(360) 496-2365

Moses Lake
1515 S. Division
(509) 765-8711

Mount Vernon
1700 Hazel St.
(360) 424-7723

Oak Harbor
201 NE O'Leary St.

Ocean Shores
228 Albatross NE
(306) 289-2037

Olympia
1116 Yew Ave. NE
(360) 705-4176

Omak
6 Engh Rd.
(509) 826-4802

Oroville
Highway 97 N
(509) 476-2740

Othello
Twelfth and Rainer
(509) 488-6412

Port Angeles
591 Monroe Rd.
(360) 565-8322

Port Townsend
10104 Rhody Drive Rd.
(360) 385-5191

Poulsbo
2138 Mesford Rd.
(360) 779-8655

Prosser
1835 Highland Dr.
(509) 786-3860

Puyallup
512 Valley Ave.
(253) 863-3383

Puyallup-South
13420 Ninety-fourth
Ave. E
(253) 840-1673

Quincy
1102 Second Ave. SE
(509) 787-2521

Raymond
245 Jackson
(360) 942-3939

Redmond
10115 172nd Ave. NE
(425) 861-9273

Renton-North
527 Mountain Side Blvd.
(425) 888-1098

Richland
1314 Goethals
(509) 946-6637

Ritzville
506 S. Weber Rd.
(509) 659-0932

Royal
357 Christiansen Rd.
(509) 346-2966

San Juan
1013 Lampard Rd.
(360) 378-4162

Seattle
14020 Ambaum Blvd. SW
(206) 444-6017

Seattle-North
5701 Eighth Ave. NE
(206) 522-1233

Selah
1700 Brick Rd.
(509) 925-5192

Selah-Ward
701 N. First St.
(509) 697-9527

Shelton
916 N. Twelfth St.
(360) 432-2415

Silverdale
9256 Nels Nelson Rd. NW
(360) 698-5552

Snohomish
10120 Chapel Hill Rd.
(425) 334-0754

Spokane
1717 E. Thirtieth Ave.
(509) 455-7164

Spokane-East
E. 13608 Fortieth
(509) 926-0551

Spokane-North
401 W. Regina
(509) 466-4633

Spokane-West
10405 W. Melville Rd.
(509) 455-9735

Stevenson
Maple Way and Loop Rd.
(509) 427-5927

Sunnyside
2000 E. Lincoln/Factory
Rd.
(509) 837-5002

Tacoma
5915 S. Twelfth
(253) 564-1103

Vancouver
18300 NE Eighteenth St.
(360) 944-5773

Vancouver-North
11101 NE 119th St.
(360) 253-4701

Vancouver-West
2223 NW Ninety-ninth St.
(360) 573-7881

Vashon
9330 SW 204th St.
(206) 463-1863

Wahluke
Road 24
(509) 932-4068

Walla Walla
1821 S. Second St.
(509) 529-9211

Warden
1017 S. County Rd.

Wenatchee
667 Tenth NE
(509) 884-8686

Westport
708 Englewood Ln.
(360) 268-3502

Yakima
1006 S. Sixteenth Ave.
(509) 452-3626

Yelm
14023 Clark Rd. SE
(360) 458-2460

Canada

NATIONAL GUIDE

BY MAUREEN A. TAYLOR

If you want an idea of how Canada has influenced the culture "south of the border," in the United States, just turn on your television. After the nightly news hosted by Canadian Peter Jennings, you can match wits with Canadian Alex Trebek on *Jeopardy!* and beam up a *Star Trek* rerun starring Canadian William Shatner. Flipping the dial, you might spot Canadians Mike Myers and Michael J. Fox. This Canadian presence is not just on TV: Think Celine Dion, Margaret Atwood, Wayne Gretzky, the Cirque du Soleil, *Titanic* director James Cameron. . . .

The ancestries of Canadians and people in the United States are as intermingled as our cultures. Between 1851 and 1951, for example, more than 6.5 million Canadians immigrated to the United States. Most of them never became as famous as Peter Jennings or got to command the starship *Enterprise*, but some of them may be your ancestors. In my own family, the links to Canada are only a couple of generations away. My maternal grandparents emigrated from Quebec to New England at the beginning of the twentieth century, leaving behind a portion of their extended family. They traveled back to Quebec several times to visit cousins. I remember visits where I was surrounded by another language—French—which my mother used when she didn't want the children to understand her conversations with her siblings, and the food—head cheese and blood pudding—was nothing like what we had at home. These visits helped me discover new family and a whole history I was unaware of; digging into your own Canadian roots can do the same for you.

The name *Canada* comes from the Huron-Iroquois word *kanata*, meaning "village." But this is a vast "village," formed of ten provinces and three territories (including the territory Nunavut, created in 1999). The good news for genealogists is that while Canada is physically larger than the United States, most of the population lives within a few hundred miles of the U.S. border. This makes searching for ancestors more manageable.

Before you head north, you should start closer to home, interviewing relatives and exploring family documents. Tracking down those clues is especially important in Canadian research. Since many Canadians came to the United States within the last century, it's possible to find immigration tales within a couple of recent generations. It was also quite common for people to immigrate to an area where other family already resided. If you're aware of other Canadian relations and know where in Canada they lived, start there. The closer the kinship, the more likely your ancestor came from the same place or somewhere close by.

After exhausting these home sources, create a list of books, documents, and microfilms to consult, and be sure to note where they're located. The holdings of the National Archives of Canada, the Family History Library (FHL) in Salt Lake City, the National Library of Canada, and the New England Historic Genealogical Society (NEHGS) are good places to begin. Canada's National Archives makes many of its resources available through interlibrary loan, you can borrow microfilm from the FHL through a local Family History Center, and NEHGS offers some materials on loan to members. All of these libraries have online catalogs to help you find resources.

If you're interested in only one province's records, find a regional genealogical society on the National Archives of Canada Web site <www.archives.ca/08/08_e.html>. Don't forget to look in your area for genealogical societies with a Canadian interest, such as the American-French Genealogical Society in Rhode Island. Also, consult the list of Canadian Archival Resources on the Internet <www.usask.ca/archives/menu.htm>. Angus Baxter, author of the excellent *In Search of Your Canadian Roots*, adds that Canada's public libraries are good sources of local family-history information.

As you begin your research, aim to answer these three questions:
- Why did your ancestors immigrate to or emigrate from Canada?
- Where did they first settle?
- With whom did your ancestors immigrate?

WHY CANADA?

People had many reasons for immigrating to what is now Canada. The first permanent white settlers were military men and a few hardy colonists. Disagreements between the French and British governments over Canada began when these countries created small colonies in similar territory at the same time. Armed forces protected settlers from skirmishes with native peoples but also maintained the land claims of England and France. Many of these professional soldiers stayed in Canada, establishing families and purchasing land.

In 1763, after more than a century of military encounters, England's superior sea power and the pressure of its other American colonies forced France to finally relinquish most of its claims to Canada. In 1774, England passed the Quebec Act that protected the formerly French area's Catholic religion and civil law even while ruled by Protestants.

Canada's French heritage can present a hurdle for research in some provinces, particularly Quebec. NEHGS's Michael Leclerc, author of numerous articles on French Canadian research, says record keeping in Quebec follows French customs rather than English law. Notaries kept track of a variety of transactions, including marriage intentions. The British government let Quebec's citizens retain this *coutume de Paris* (Parisian custom) to placate them after France relinquished its claims in 1763. This means that all records in Quebec are in French regardless of the language spoken by the resident. You should bone up on French words and phrases as well as record-keeping practices.

Quebec isn't the only province with a French

past. Nova Scotia (including present-day New Brunswick) was the first Canadian colony settled by immigrants from France in 1604, when it was known as Acadia. The Acadians were expelled from 1755 to 1762 when they refused to fight against Nova Scotia; many fled to Louisiana, where they began the Cajun culture. Acadian descendants can find material on their ancestors through the Confederation of Associations of Families Acadian. Its Web site <www.cafa.org> contains an index of Acadian/Cajun families.

English-speaking exiles, too, immigrated to Canada. During the American Revolution, thousands of Loyalists left the American colonies to settle in Nova Scotia, eastern Quebec, and Ontario. After the Revolution, "United Empire Loyalists" moved into the part of Nova Scotia that would become New Brunswick. The National Archives of Canada has microfilms of Loyalist papers and British military records that can help you trace these ancestors.

The American Civil War sparked Canadian unity, resulting in a confederation established by the British North America Act of 1867. But provinces were slow to join a united Canada, the last holdouts—Newfoundland and Labrador—joining in 1949. Besides soldiers and settlers, Canada's vast wilderness also attracted men who sought adventure. In fact, the original name of the Hudson's Bay Company in 1670 was the "Company of Adventurers of England trading into Hudson's Bay." Their mission was to explore and settle the areas now known as Alberta, Manitoba, Saskatchewan, and part of British Columbia. Today the company is known for its chain of retail stores rather than fur trading, but it ran frontier trading posts for two hundred years until selling its land to the Canadian government in 1869. The company archives <www.gov.mb.ca/chc/archives/hbca>, now owned by the Provincial Archives of Manitoba, is a wonderful resource for genealogists.

And don't forget Canada's native population, which numbered 300,000 at the time of European settlement. Oral histories in many Canadian families suggest marriages between settlers and native peoples. To find documentation for such stories, you need to seek out materials such as field office records for the office of Indian affairs plus affidavits for the Department of the Interior stating parentage and ethnic origin of spouse. Recently, tribes in Canada such as the Inuit banded together as a group, called The First Nations, to further joint political purposes while retaining their separate languages and culture. Genealogical documentation is required to prove membership in a First Nations tribe.

ACROSS THE BORDER AND OVER THE SEAS

While most original colonists came from either France or England, not all Canadians originated from those two countries. The nineteenth century saw an influx from Scotland and Ireland to Nova Scotia, for example. After World War II, central and southern Europeans immigrated to other areas of Canada.

The trans-Canadian railway linked the country in 1885, spurring movement to western provinces whose farmland beckoned immigrants. The railway also brought a diversity of people, from German Mennonites to a few hundred Welsh immigrants who'd spent time in Argentina. Immigration to Alberta included Mormons from Utah, Germans, Scandinavian immigrants from northern U.S. states, and Canadians from Ontario looking for better farming conditions.

The migration went in the other direction, too. My grandparents were part of one of the largest migrations from Canada, between 1871 and 1901, when more than a million Canadians seeking economic prosperity immigrated to the United States.

The family of Grant Emison, a researcher who grew up in Texas, originally immigrated to the United States, moved up to Alberta, and then returned to the United States, all within a few generations. Don't be surprised to find similar patterns within your own family. Land records, including homesteader claims at the provincial archives, can help track these mobile ancestors. Unfortunately, just knowing where your ancestors settled doesn't verify their origins. Finding passenger manifests to answer that mystery can be difficult. While Canadian officials began keeping records in 1865, not all periods are covered or complete. Many of the passenger lists to New Brunswick, for example, were destroyed in a fire at the Customs House in 1877.

There are several resources you can tap. In Nova Scotia, a new museum, Pier 21 <www.pier21.ns.ca>, has a database and microfilm archive of anyone who entered a Canadian port between 1925 and 1935. If your relatives traveled between Canada and the United States between 1895 and 1954, look for them on the passenger and immigration lists known as the St. Albans List, named after the border entry point at St. Albans, Vermont. These lists actually document individuals who crossed any part of the Canadian border, not just at Vermont. Marian Smith of the U.S. Immigration and Naturalization Service has written an online article that explains how to use these records and why they're so valuable; access this article at <www.nara.gov/publications/prologue/stalbans.html>.

TRAVELING IN GROUPS

Immigrants often traveled in groups to a new country, settling together in a particular town or neighborhood. One example of this is tiny Prince Edward Island (PEI). Because PEI remained relatively unconnected to the mainland until the Confederation Bridge replaced ferry services, this was and still is a close-knit community. Many of the families on the island descend from Scottish colonists who settled PEI and intermarried. This means that if you discover an ancestral link to the island, you're apt to find all kinds of familial connections.

When your relatives emigrated from Canada to the United States, they often followed the trails of other family members. My Bessette relatives weren't the first family members to seek out new opportunities in the United States: They let other members of the family establish themselves first, providing a foothold in the new area. Following the ancestral trail backward leads to a whole series of new places to look for records. If you hit a brick wall in tracing your Canadian roots, try going sideways. Can you find where cousins or even neighbors of your ancestors came from in Canada? Chances are, that's where your immediate kin emigrated from as well.

YOU WANT RECORDS, EH?

Once you have a general sense of where your Canadian relatives lived, learn more about the province the way it was when they arrived there. This knowledge can help you as you try to find documents. Fortunately for genealogists, each province and territory maintains an archive rich with genealogical treasure and open to the public for research. Web sites for the provincial archives outline their genealogical holdings and their policies (see listings under individual provinces). For instance, the site for the British Columbia Archives <www.bcarchives.gov.bc.ca> features searchable indexes to British Columbia birth registrations for 1872 to 1899, marriage registrations for 1872 to 1924, and death registrations for 1872 to 1979, as well as more than sixty-five thousand image files and a virtual museum. While the staff is helpful at all the facilities, you may find the research atmosphere in New Brunswick particularly welcoming. The New Brunswick provincial archives includes a special genealogical section and has published a leaflet, *Genealogical Resources at the Provincial Archives of New Brunswick*, to help researchers. Bear in mind that some of the western facilities are little more than a hundred years old. For instance, Yukon only became a separate territory in 1898. When looking for materials that pre-date formation of the province or territory, consult the archives for the region before separation.

While many of the Canadian resources, such as city directories, land records, vital records, and census documents, available to researchers are familiar, you should notice some differences. Let's look at some specific resources for genealogical research in Canada.

Censuses: Like the United States, Canada now takes a census every ten years. The first census dates from 1666, but there's a long gap in nationwide enumeration until the first Dominion census in 1871. Census documents exist on the provincial level for the seventeenth through the nineteenth centuries, though the returns are scattered. Information on the census forms varied, but after 1851 they listed all household inhabitants. The censuses up to and including the 1901 enumeration are open to the public for research. (Unfortunately, we may never get access to later returns. Statistics Canada, which compiles the census, won't release post-1901 records to the National Archives of Canada—even after the regular ninety-two-year privacy period expires. Statistics Canada believes that the Statistics Act of 1906 prohibits their release. See <www. globalgenealogy.com/Census> for more on this.) You should use city directories and similar resources to narrow your search; the censuses aren't generally indexed, so knowing your ancestor's street address can be a huge time-saver.

To access the Canadian census, you can tap microfilms available through the FHL as well as the National Archives of Canada and the NEHGS. For a preview of what the FHL has, go to <www.familysearch.org/Eng/Library/FHLC/ frameset_fhlc.asp>, click "Place Search," and type the name of a province. Scroll down the results to see all the censuses for that province accessible through the Family History Library.

Some actual census data is also accessible online, but entire census reports are not. The best place to look is at Censuslinks <censuslinks. com> (choose "Canada" from the home page), a site that connects researchers to online census material. If you're transcribing census records for a particular area, consider participating in the award-winning Canadian Genealogical Projects Registry <www.afhs.ab.ca/registry>, a project of the Alberta Family Histories Society.

Civil registration: Registering births, marriages, and deaths was a complicated affair in Canada. In most provinces and territories, legislation for formal civil registration wasn't put in place until late in the nineteenth century. This doesn't mean that vital records weren't kept; it just means they were not kept on the governmental level. In Newfoundland and Labrador, for example, church records date from 1752, while civil registration didn't start until 1892.

Religious records: Given Canada's late start with regard to official vital records, genealogists have to rely heavily on religious records of births, marriages, deaths, and so on. To use these records, you first need to determine your ancestors' religious affiliations. Among the many religious groups who settled in Canada are Catholics, Anglicans, Lutherans, Mennonites, and Quakers. Catholic records are particularly good, with women's maiden names recorded as part of the marriage records. Many of these parish records are in print courtesy of the American-French Genealogical Society <www.afgs.org>. The Toronto diocesan records are on microfilm at the Family History Library. Your search for religious records can be complicated. According to author Baxter, church registers may be housed in various places, including denominational or provincial archives, individual churches, and the National Archives.

Military records: The soldiers who accompanied colonists served the French and British governments, so finding military service records can mean crossing the ocean if you don't find answers in provincial archives. Good places to start are the Public Record Office <www.pro.gov.uk> in England (which has a helpful publication called *Tracing Your Ancestors in the Public Record Office* [Public Record Office, £12.99 or $19.95 US]) and the Bibliothèque Généalogique et d'Histoire Sociale <www.geocities.com/Eureka/1568> in France.

Eventually, if you live in the United States, you may want to go just across the border to seek your Canadian cousins in person. While you're busy researching your roots, try to plan your visit to coincide with one of the many festivals that enliven Canada all year long, from the Stratford Shakespeare Festival in Ontario to the international flavor of Folkorama in Winnipeg, Manitoba. Even the long winters don't deter Canadians from enjoying themselves—see this for yourself in Quebec City at the Winter Carnival in February when enormous ice sculptures dominate the city and the party takes to the streets. Until you can actually get there, you can always turn on *Jeopardy!* and show off your smarts to fellow Canadian Alex Trebek: "I'll take Canadian ancestors for a thousand, Alex… ."

ORGANIZATIONS & ARCHIVES

Acadian Cultural Society
P.O. Box 2304
Fitchburg, MA 01420
<www.angelfire.com/ma/1755>

American-Canadian Genealogical Society
P.O. Box 6478
Manchester, NH 03108
(603) 622-1554
<www.acgs.org>

American-French Genealogical Society
P.O. Box 830
Woonsocket, RI 02895
(401) 765-6141
<www.afgs.org>

Bibliothèque Généalogique et d'Histoire Sociale
3 Rue de Turbigo
75001 Paris, France
33 (01) 42 33 58 21
<www.geocities.com/Eureka/1568>

National Archives of Canada
395 Wellington St.
Ottawa, Ontario K1A 0N3
(866) 578-7777 (toll-free from Canada and the United States)
Reference Services: (613) 992-3884
Genealogy Reference: (613) 996-7458
<www.archives.ca/08/08_e.html>

National Library of Canada/Bibliothèque Nationale du Canada
395 Wellington St.
Ottawa, Ontario K1A 0N4
(613) 992-6969
<www.nlc-bnc.ca>

New England Historic Genealogical Society
101 Newbury St.
Boston, MA 02116
(617) 536-5740
<www.newenglandancestors.org>

RESOURCES

(all prices in U.S. dollars)

Dictionary of Canadian Place Names
by Alan Rayburn (Oxford University Press, $37.50)

Genealogist's Handbook for Atlantic Canada Research
edited by Terrence M. Punch (NEHGS, $15)

In Search of Your Canadian Roots: Tracing Your Family Tree in Canada
by Angus Baxter (Genealogical Publishing Co., $19.95)

Labouring Children: British Immigrant Apprentices to Canada, 1869-1924 (Reprints in Canadian History) by Joy Parr (University of Toronto Press, $20.95)

PERIODICALS

American-Canadian Genealogist
American-Canadian Genealogical Society, P.O. Box 6478, Manchester, NH 03108

Je Me Souviens
American-French Genealogical Society, P.O. Box 830, Woonsocket, RI 02895

Le Reveil Acadien
Acadian Cultural Society, P.O. Box 2304, Fitchburg, MA 01420

WEB SITES

Artefacts Canada
<www.chin.gc.ca/Artefacts/e_artefacts_canada.html>: Searchable database of information on museum objects and archaeological sites from the records of several museums and heritage organizations. Previously known as The National Inventories.

Black Loyalists: Our History, Our People
<collections.ic.gc.ca/blackloyalists>: Describes the first settlements of free blacks in Canada. Includes biographies of prominent Black Loyalists, descriptions and maps of Black Loyalist communities, and original historical documents.

Bob's Your Uncle, Eh!
<indexes.tpl.toronto.on.ca/genealogy/index.asp>: Genealogical search engine created by the Toronto Public Library.

Canada Research Outline
<www.familysearch.org/Eng/Search/RG/frameset_rhelps.asp>: Overview of resources for Canadian research; click on "C" for Canada, or go to separate research outlines for each province.

Canadian Encyclopedia
<www.thecanadian
encyclopedia.com>: Have
some unanswered ques-
tions about Canada? Find
the answers in this online
version of a popular ref-
erence tool.

Canadian GenWeb
<www.rootsweb.com/
~canwgw>: Links to
GenWeb projects for
each province, queries,
research tips, and more.

Canadian Mailing Lists
<www.rootsweb.com/
~jfuller/gen_mail_
country-can.html>:
Contains links to Canada-
related mailing lists.

**Digital Library of Canada
at the National Library of
Canada**
<www.nlc-bnc.ca/2/
index-e.html>: Topics

arranged in alphabetical
order, including resources
for children. The site also
contains a search feature
with a choice of English
or French.

Global Gazette
<www.globalgazette.
net>: Articles on doing
research in Canada.

Parks Canada
<parkscanada.pch.gc.ca/
parks/main_e.htm>:
Contains material about
Canada's national parks,
national historic sites,
heritage buildings, and
railway stations.
Available in English and
French.

MONTREAL

BY PETER D.A. WARWICK

The largest French-speaking city in North
America and the second-largest city in Canada,
Montreal takes its name from Mont-Royal (or
Mount Royal), the mountain on the island
where the city sits. Jacques Cartier named the
mountain in 1535. This Quebec city dates from
May 17, 1642, when a group of fifty French settlers founded Ville-Marie on a tip of land, beside
a stream flowing into the St. Lawrence River, in
what is now part of Old Montreal.

Old Montreal <vieux.montreal.qc.ca/eng/
accueila.htm> is an excellent place to get in the
mood for tracing your Quebec ancestors. This
once-walled section of Montreal was declared a
historic district in 1964. The oldest remaining
building in the city dates from 1685, and it was
built and is still owned by the Sulpician order of
the Roman Catholic Church. Other historic
buildings include Notre-Dame de Montreal,

built from 1824 to 1829 (it replaced an earlier
church), and the New York Life Building,
Montreal's first skyscraper at ten stories, built in
1888. Within the district lies **Pointe-à-Callière,
the Montreal Museum of Archaeology & History**
[350 Place Royale; (514) 872-9150; <www.
musee-pointe-a-calliere.qc.ca/indexan.
html>]. The museum is actually several buildings, including a modern museum, Montreal's
first customs house (1838), and the Youville
Pumping Station (1915). These are connected
via an underground, archaeological crypt. Here
you can see the remains of an old cemetery, the
stream that once flowed here, and the fortifica-
tions that once guarded the city. You can also
watch a multimedia show, see virtual figures
from history, and have lunch at the restaurant
inside. Pointe-à-Callière opened in 1992 following a deacde of archaeological digs on the site.

Start your genealogical research with the
Bibliothèque Centrale [1210 Rue Sherbrooke
East; (514) 872-5923; <www2.ville.montreal.
qc.ca/biblio/pageacc.htm>], and its online catalog search engine, Gulliver <gulliver.ville.
montreal.qc.ca>. The library's collection
includes microfilmed copies of the Canadian
census for Quebec, printed census materials,
gazetteers, city directories for Montreal and elsewhere in Quebec, a variety of genealogical
books (such as published genealogies and
genealogical collections), and microfilm of old
newspapers for Montreal. The Bibliothèque
Centrale is one of three libraries being merged
into the new **Bibliothèque Nationale du Québec**
[de Maisonneuve Street; (514) 873-1100;
<www.bnquebec.ca/en/qui_en/qui_present_en.
htm>]. Scheduled to open late in 2003, this public library is dedicated to collecting and conserv-
ing Quebec's and Montreal's documentary heritage, and its four million holdings include one
million books. The collections include newspapers from 1764 to the present, government publications (provincial, colonial, and federal), private papers, and photographs. Some items have

Montreal can be your headquarters for exploring your French-Canadian ancestors.

been digitized and are on the library's Web site.

The **Archives de Montreal** [275 Notre-Dame Est; (514) 872-2615 and (514) 872-1173; <www2.ville.montreal.qc.ca/archives/archives. htm>] includes photographs and documents relating to the city.

The **Stewart Museum** [20 Chemin Tour de l'Isle, Île Sainte-Hélène (in the middle of the St. Lawrence River); (514) 861-6701; <www. stewart-museum.org/map.htm>] deals with the history of Canada and its relationship with western European civilization, especially exploration and colonization. It has representative collections of the sixteenth through nineteenth centuries.

For more genealogical research, take a side trip to the **Archives Nationales du Quebec** <www.anq.gouv.qc.ca> in Sainte-Foy, a suburb of Quebec City, about three hours away from Montreal by train. There you can find copies of old provincial newspapers and microfilm of the census for Quebec. You also can find wills; records of births, deaths, and marriages; and other records.

For a taste of how your ancestors traveled, visit the **Canadian Railway Museum** [120 Rue St-Pierre; (450) 632-2410; <www.exporail.org/musee/musee_CRM.htm>] in suburban St. Constant on the south shore of the St. Lawrence River. It has Canada's largest collection of railway equipment, including steam and diesel engines, a variety of passenger equipment, and trolleys. Short train and trolley rides are available. While the archives of the Canadian Railroad Historical Association are also at the museum, the holdings are of limited use to genealogists.

Another transportation-related site, located within the city itself, is the **Lachine Canal** <www.parcscanada.gc.ca/parks/quebec/canallachine/en>. The canal was opened in 1825 and enlarged in 1848 and again in 1884. It closed in 1970 after declining in use following the completion of the St. Lawrence Seaway. In 2002, however, following the completion of a multimillion-dollar restoration project, the canal was reopened to pleasure craft. It once formed the industrial heart of Montreal and the entrance to the Great Lakes for shipping. Recreational trails now lining its banks are popular for walking and cycling.

For an overview of the city and a nice relaxing walk, visit **Mount Royal Park** <www.lemontroyal.qc.ca/en_index2.html>. Mount Royal is the dominant feature of Montreal. The park, which marked its 125th anniversary in 2002, was designed by Frederick Law Olmsted, who also designed New York's Central Park. Easily reached by public transit, the park offers opportunities to walk its trails, enjoy nature, and see the city from the highest point on the mountain. Smith House, which dates from 1858, serves as a visitor center for the park.

Montreal has an excellent transit system, the **STM** [(514) 280-5100; <www.stm.info/English/a-somm.htm>]. STM operates the city's bus, subway, and commuter rail system. The subway, called the Métro, was patterned after the Paris Métro.

Remember that Quebec is a French-speaking province. While most services are provided using both French and English, some aren't. For example, the Web sites for the archives of

Quebec, the Montreal archives, and the Montreal library are presented only in French. Announcements on the STM are also in French only.

As you'd expect in a city with a French accent, Montreal has a variety of fine restaurants. Here's a small selection:

- **Le Fripon** [436 Place Jaques-Cartier; (514) 861-1386; <www.bar-resto.com/lefripon.htm>]—fine French cuisine in the heart of Old Montreal
- **Moe's Deli & Bar** [3950 Sherbrooke Street East; (514) 253-6637; <www.bar-resto.com/moes>]—well-known establishment offering daily lunch specials and located right across from the Olympic Stadium and near the botanical gardens
- **O'Donnell's Pub** [1224 Bishop Street; (514) 877-3128; <www.bar-resto.com/odonnell/index-e.htm>]—Irish food and entertainment

For accommodations in the downtown area, check out the following:

- **Best Western Ville-Marie** [3407 Rue Peel [at the foot of Mont-Royal]; (514) 288-4141; <www.hotelvillemarie.com/index_en.html>]
- **Hotel St-Denis** [1254 Rue St-Denis; (514) 849-4526; <www.hotel-st-denis.com>]
- **L'Abri du Voyageur** [9 Rue St-Catherine Ouest; (514) 849-2922; <www.abri-voyageur.ca/english>]—a good option for those on a budget

If you prefer a bed-and-breakfast, contact the **Downtown B&B Network** [(800) 267-5180; <www.bbmontreal.qc.ca>].

OTTAWA

BY PETER D.A. WARWICK

Canada's national capital is rich in history, as you'd expect. In 1857, Queen Victoria chose Ottawa, Ontario, for the capital over such places as Montreal, Kingston, and Toronto. Back then it was primarily a lumber town; today its major businesses are government and tourism.

If you're eager to get started in your genealogical quest, head a few blocks west of the Parliament Buildings to the **National Archives of Canada** [395 Wellington Street; (866) 578-7777; (613) 996-7458 for genealogy reference; <www.archives.ca/08/08_e.html>]. Among the records held here are immigration papers; Russian immigrant papers; the census; military records; land petitions for Quebec, Lower Canada, Upper Canada, and the United Province of Canada; land grants for western Canada before the provinces were formed; records from the Canadian National Railway, and some Acadian papers. Check out ArchiviaNet <www.archives.ca/02/0201_e.html>, the online guide to the collections of the National Archives of Canada. Note that not all guides are online yet.

When you're through with the archives, head next door, in the very same building, to the **National Library of Canada** [(613) 995-9481; <www.nlc-bnc.ca/index-e.html>] for more research. A search engine allows you to search the National Library's entire online records plus the online records of thirteen hundred other libraries in Canada.

Head east along Wellington to the Rideau Canal, between Parliament Hill and the Chateau Laurier Hotel, and the **Bytown Museum** [(613) 234-4570; <www.ottawakiosk.com/bytown_museum.html>]. The museum is in the oldest stone building in Ottawa. Built in 1827, it served as a treasury and storehouse during the building of the Rideau Canal. The museum deals with Col. John By, the building of the Rideau Canal, and the early history of Ottawa. The Historical Society of Ottawa's archives are also housed there.

The **Canadian War Museum** [330 Sussex Drive; (819) 776-8600; <www.civilization.ca/cwm/cwme.asp>] covers Canada's military past, such as the two world wars and the colonial period. A new museum building is under construction west of the National Archives of

Canada. You can explore their collection and that of the Canadian Museum of Civilization, affiliated with the war museum, by browsing or doing an online search.

The **Canadian Museum of Civilization** [100 Laurier Street, Hull; (819) 776-7000; <www.civilization.ca/indexe.asp>] is located across the Ottawa River in neighboring Hull, Quebec. (Public transit service is available.) It covers Canadian history and the diverse peoples who make up Canada.

If you have any ancestors or relatives who served in the Canadian military, check out **Canada's National Military Cemetery** [280 Beechwood Avenue; <www.dnd.ca/cemetery/engraph/home_e.asp>], in the heart of Beechwood Cemetery.

Getting to all these historical attractions is easy, thanks to Ottawa's excellent public transit system, which is operated by **OC Transpo** [(613) 741-4390; <www.octranspo.com>]. Buses operate over city streets and busways. Recently, North America's only diesel-operated light-rail system opened here.

For a place to eat, try the **By Ward Market** area <www.byward-market.com>, east of the Rideau Canal. You can also still find an actual farmers' market here in an enclosed building, the oldest market in Canada. Boutiques and nightclubs are also in the area. Among the good restaurants here are

- **The Courtyard Restaurant** [21 George Street; (613) 241-1516; <www.courtyardrestaurant.com>]—opened in 1837 as a hotel; restored and opened as a restaurant in 1980
- **Ritz Clarence Street** [89 Clarence Street; (613) 789-9797; <www.ritzrestaurants.com>] —the two other restaurants in this chain are on located on Nepean Street and Elgin Street

Accommodations in the downtown area include

- **The Lord Elgin Hotel** [100 Elgin Street; (800) 267-4298; <www.lordelginhotel.ca>]
- **Best Western Victoria Park Suites** [377

O'Connor Street; (800) 465-7275; <www.vpsuites.com>]
- **The Carmichael Inn & Spa** [46 Cartier Street; (877) 416-2417; <www.carmichaelinn.com>]

TORONTO

BY PETER D.A. WARWICK

Toronto—founded in 1793 by the British, when Governor Simcoe moved the capital of Upper Canada (Ontario) here from Newark (Niagara-on-the-Lake)—is Canada's largest city today. Its old nickname, "Toronto the Good," still holds true for the genealogist. The city is filled with genealogical and historical places to visit.

To get in the historical mood, start off with a visit to the place where Toronto began—reconstructed **Fort York** [100 Garrison Road; (416) 392-6907; <www.city.toronto.on.ca/culture/fort_york.htm>]. The defending British forces blew up the fort in the American attack on April 27, 1813, during the War of 1812. The American capture of the fort and the town of York (Toronto) led the British to plan a retaliatory raid on Washington, DC, the following year.

Not far away is **The Pier: Toronto's Waterfront Museum** [245 Queens Quay West; (416) 338-7437; <www.city.toronto.on.ca/culture/the_pier.htm>]. Housed in a restored 1930 shipping warehouse, this interactive museum has a large collection of Great Lakes-related artifacts, photos, maps, books, and documents. Research in the library is by appointment only.

The **Archives of Ontario** [77 Grenville Street. one block north of College Street, off Bay Street; (416) 327-1600; <www.archives.gov.on.ca/english>] is the place to begin your search for your Ontario ancestors. Records here go back to colonial days. Be sure to check the online catalog first to save yourself time. It tells you what is in the holdings and what microfilm a particular item is on, but it does not indicate whether the name of the person you're looking for is on the item. You can even borrow microfilm via interlibrary loan. The reading room has in self-serve cabinets the most popular microfilms, such as newspapers from all over Ontario, census returns for Ontario (1842 to 1901), vital statistics, and wills.

If your ancestors came from Toronto, then head to the **City of Toronto Archives** [255 Spadina Road; (416) 397-0778; <www.city. toronto.on.ca/archives>]. It's reachable by subway and a short walk. Records date back to 1834, the year Toronto officially became a city, and include assessment rolls, city directories, diaries, maps, photographs, and much more.

For a break from records, visit nearby **Casa Loma** <www.casaloma.org>, former home of Canadian financier Sir Henry Pellatt. Finished in 1914, Casa Loma ("house on the hill") surpassed any other private home in North America at the time. Unfortunately, due to bankruptcy, Sir Henry was forced to sell the castle in 1924. It opened to the public as a museum in 1937, along with five acres of public gardens.

A treasure trove of genealogical resources awaits you at the **Toronto Public Library** [789 Yonge Street; (416) 395-5577; <www.tpl. toronto.on.ca>]. Head first to the Toronto Reference Library, one block north of Bloor and the subway. The Baldwin Room contains papers of Toronto people, businesses, and organizations, plus the John Ross Robertson Landmarks of Canada collection. Other Toronto resources available at the library include city directories, maps and plans, Toronto voters lists from 1935 to 1984, scrapbooks, and photographs. In addition, the reference library has a good selection of genealogical material for areas outside of Toronto, including the rest of Canada, the United States, and Great Britain. For example, you can access the twelve-volume *Records of the Colony of New Plymouth in New England*, which was published from 1855 to 1861. The library also has many genealogical societies' newsletters and journals, such as the *New York Genealogical and Biographical Record*.

When you're finished at the library, take the subway north to the **North York Central Library** [5120 Yonge Street; (416) 395-5535]. The Canadiana department has a large collection of genealogical materials, chiefly for Ontario, but also for other parts of Canada and the United States. Among its many resources are microfilmed copies of Canadian census returns from 1666 to 1901, directories for various Canadian cities, some county and district marriage registers for Ontario, the collection of the Ontario Genealogical Society, and some family histories. To save yourself time, before visiting check the Toronto Public Library Web site for resources here as well.

The **United Church of Canada Archives** [73 Queen's Park Crescent East; (416) 585-4563; <vicu.utoronto.ca/archives/archives.htm>] on the campus of Victoria University in downtown Toronto is another place to check out. The United Church was formed in 1925 from the union of the Presbyterian, Methodist, Congregational, and Evangelical United Brethren churches. The archives hold most local church records for Ontario, which including items such as local church histories, biographical files, and photographs.

For a taste of life as it was in pioneer Ontario, head for **Black Creek Pioneer Village** [Steeles Avenue; (416) 736-1733; <www.trca. on.ca/bcpv.html>], near York University. Open from May through December is a collection of more than thirty-five restored buildings, including a mill, a blacksmith's shop, a school, and a doctor's house.

Getting around Toronto is easy. Just hop on the **TTC** <www.city.toronto.on.ca/ttc>, Toronto's bus, subway, and streetcar network. Day passes are available. If you drive in from the United States, save yourself some problems and park at one of the suburban **GO Transit** [(800) 438-6646; <www.gotransit.com>] commuter rail stations, take the train to Union Station, and then hop on the TTC.

The problem with dining out in Toronto is having to choose from the many good restaurants. You might start with those along Bloor Street in the University Avenue/Avenue Road to Yonge Street area, such as

- **Ichi Riki** [103-120 Bloor Street East; (416) 923-2997]—has great sushi
- **Patriot** [131 Bloor Street West, second floor; (416) 922-0025]
- **Senses** [15 Bloor Street West; (416) 935-0400]

This area, easy to reach by subway and close to research sites, is also handy for lodging. Among the choices:

- **Park Hyatt Toronto** [4 Avenue Road; (416) 925-1234; <parktoronto.hyatt.com>]
- **Toronto Townhouse Bed & Breakfast** [213 Carlton Street, in the heart of Cabbagetown; (877) 500-0466; <www.toronto-townhouse. com>]
- **Town Inn Suites** [620 Church Street, near the intersection of Yonge and Bloor; (416) 964-3311; <www.towninn.com>]

VANCOUVER
BY PETER D.A. WARWICK

Named after Captain George Vancouver, the British explorer who surveyed the region in 1792, Vancouver, British Columbia, is one of Canada's most beautiful cities. It's situated at the mouth of the Fraser River and has the coastal range of mountains as a backdrop. The first permanent European settlers didn't arrive until 1865, and Vancouver became a city in 1886.

Start your voyage into your Vancouver and British Columbia roots at the **Vancouver Central Public Library** [350 West Georgia Street; (604) 331-3603; <www.vpl.vancouver.bc.ca/branches/ LibrarySquare>]. Its Special Collections area has city directories for Vancouver and the rest of British Columbia from 1860 to the present. Other parts of the library have newspapers on microfilm from Vancouver and Victoria from late 1800s, all publicly released British Columbia vital events records (births, 1872 to 1901; marriages, 1859 to 1926; deaths, 1872 to 1981), and the Canadian census (1666 to 1901). The library also has resources from other parts of Canada, the United States, and elsewhere.

Once you've exhausted the library's resources, head to the **City of Vancouver Archives** [1150 Chestnut Street; (604) 736-8561; <www. city.vancouver.bc.ca/ctyclerk/archives>]. The archives contain the private records of businesses and persons, as well as local government records. All are searchable online. The archives also hold a large, searchable collection of photographs, and a number of them are online.

To help put things in perspective, stop next door at the **Vancouver Museum** [1100 Chestnut Street; (604) 736-4431; <www.vanmuseum. bc.ca>], which covers the history of Vancouver. Exhibits include a re-creation of a traditional Edwardian home, a toy timeline for children, and the exploration and settlement of Vancouver, as well as special exhibits.

A block away lies the **Vancouver Maritime Museum** [1905 Ogden Avenue; (604) 257-8310; <www.vmm.bc.ca>], with exhibits covering the contributions of maritime arts, culture, industry, science, and history to the development of the Port of Vancouver. The St. Roch, the first ship to circumnavigate North America and the first ship to navigate the Northwest Passage in both directions, is on permanent indoor exhibit. An extensive library is also on site and available for genealogical research.

You can get a feel for the diverse history of the city by taking a walking tour of Chinatown, one of the oldest sections of Vancouver. The tour, which takes about two hours, passes buildings dating mostly from the early twentieth century. A map is available at <www.city.vancouver. bc.ca/commsvcs/planning/heritage/walks/w_ch_ map.htm>.

To relax, take a walk or bicycle ride around the one thousand-acre **Stanley Park** <www. seestanleypark.com>, the third-largest urban park in North America. It's a heavily forested area right in the heart of downtown Vancouver.

Vancouver has excellent public transit operated by **TransLink** [(604) 953-3333; <www.translink.bc.ca>]. Diesel and trolley buses, the Skytrain (a rapid transit system), and ferries to North Vancouver can take you to most places. Day passes are available.

Vancouver offers a variety of great restaurants. A few in the downtown area:

- **The Fish House in Stanley Park** [8901 Stanley Park Drive, located right in Stanley Park; (877) 681-7275; <www.fishhousestanleypark.com>]—features seafood and an oyster bar
- **Manhattan Eatery** [550 West Hastings Street, located in the Delta Vancouver Suites; (604) 899-3049; <www.manhattaneatery.com>]—features an open kitchen

- **Roy's Steak & Seafood Restaurant** [1015 Burrard Street, located in the Century Plaza Hotel; <www.century-plaza.com/roysteak.asp>]

A variety of accommodations are available. Here's a sampling:

- **Century Plaza Hotel & Spa** [1015 Burrard Street, downtown; (800) 663-1818; <www.century-plaza.com>]—has its own spa
- **Lord Stanley Hotel** [1889 Alberni Street, located close to Stanley Park; (888) 767-7829; <www.lordstanley.com>]
- **The Sylvia Hotel** [1154 Gilford Street; (604) 681-9321; <www.sylviahotel.com>]

For a directory of bed-and-breakfasts in the Vancouver area, see <www.bedandbreakfasts-bc.com/vancouver.html>.

ALBERTA

ORGANIZATIONS & ARCHIVES

Alberta Genealogical Society
Prince of Wales Armouries Heritage Centre #116
10440 108 Ave.
Edmonton, Alberta T5H 3Z9
(780) 424-4429
Fax: (780) 423-8980
<www.compusmart.ab.ca/abgensoc>

Provincial Archives of Alberta
12845 102 Ave.
Edmonton, Alberta T5N 0M6
(780) 427-1056
<www.cd.gov.ab.ca/preserving/provincial_archives>

RESOURCES

Alberta: A History in Photographs
by Faye Reineberg Holt
(Altitude Publishing, $10.95)

Alberta's North: A History, 1890-1950
by Donald Grant Wetherell (University of Alberta Press, $34.95)

Best From Alberta History
edited by Hugh A. Dempsey (Douglas and McIntyre, $10.95)

From Summit to Sea: An Illustrated History of Railroads in British Columbia and Alberta
by George Buck ($19.95)

The Rise of Agrarian Democracy : The United Farmers and Farm Women of Alberta 1909-1921
by Bradford James Rennie (University of Toronto Press, $65)

Suitable for the Wilds: Letters From Northern Alberta, 1929-1931
by Mary Percy, Dr. Jackson, Janice P. Dickin McGinnis (University of Toronto Press, $55)

PROVINCIAL STATS

ALBERTA

Date Formed: 1882
Joined Canadian Confederation: 1905
Civil Registration Began: 1889; full compliance 1898
Address for Vital Statistics:
  Government Services
  Alberta Registries, Vital Statistics
  P.O. Box 2023
  10365 97 St., Third floor
  Edmonton, Alberta T5J 4W7
  (780) 427-7013
  <www3.gov.ab.ca/gs/services/vpe/index.cfm>

City Directories at the Family History Library Include: Calgary 1961; Edmonton 1905-

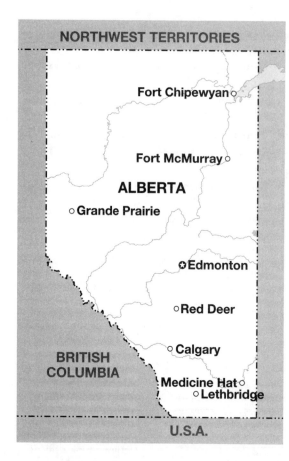

NORTHWEST TERRITORIES

Fort Chipewyan○

Fort McMurray○

ALBERTA

○Grande Prairie

✪Edmonton

○Red Deer

○Calgary

BRITISH
COLUMBIA

Medicine Hat○
○Lethbridge

U.S.A.

Talk to My Lawyer: Great Stories of Southern Alberta's Bar and Bench by James Gray (Hurtig Publishing, $24.95)

PERIODICALS

B & D Heir Lines
Brooks & District Branch of the Alberta Genealogical Society, P.O. Box 1538, Brooks, Alberta T1R 1C4

The Chinook
Alberta Family Histories Society, P.O. Box 30270, Station B, Calgary, Alberta, Canada T2M 4P1

Heritage Seekers
Grande Prairie and District Branch of the

Alberta Genealogical Society, P.O. Box 1257, Grande Prairie, Alberta T8V 4Z1

Lines of Descent
Ft. McMurray Branch of the Alberta Genealogical Society, P.O. Box 6253, Ft. McMurray, Alberta T9H 4W1

The Tree Climber
Red Deer and District Branch of the Alberta Genealogical Society, P.O. Box 922, Red Deer, Alberta T4N 5H3

Yesterday's Footprints
Lethbridge and District Branch of the Alberta Genealogical Society, 909

Third Ave. North, Room 128, Lethbridge, Alberta T1H 0H5

WEB SITES

Alberta Family Histories Society (AFHS) Genealogical Projects Registry
<www.afhs.ab.ca/ registry>

Alberta Genealogical Society Master Name Index
<www.compusmart.ab. ca/abgensoc/nameindex. html>

Alberta GenWeb Project
<www.rootsweb.com/ ~canab>

Alberta's War Memorials
<www.stemnet.nf.ca/ monuments/ab.htm>

Births, Deaths and Marriages Reported in Calgary, Alberta Newspapers, 1883-1899
<www.afhs.ab.ca/data/ announcements/ 1883-1899>

Canadian Archival Resources on the Internet–Alberta
<www.usask.ca/archives/ car/abmenu.html>

FAMILY HISTORY CENTERS

Barrhead
5215 Fifty-sixth St.
(780) 674-4208

Bow Island
309 Eighth St. West
(403) 545-2973

Brooks
40 Tenth St. West
(403) 362-2855

Calgary
2021 Seventeenth Ave. SW
(403) 571-3700

Calgary
202 Crescent Rd. NW
(403) 571-2925

Calgary
14540 Parkland Blvd. SE
(403) 571-3749

Cardston
123 Fourth Ave. West
(403) 653-3288

Cherry Grove
Main St.
(780) 594-3225

Coutts
345 3 St. West
(403) 344-3938

Drumheller
1455 Fourth Ave. NW
(403) 823-8824

Edmonton
9010 Eighty-fifth St.
(780) 469-6460

Edmonton
14325 Fifty-third Ave.
(780) 436-0136

Fairview
11328 112 Ave.
(780) 835-3501

Foremost
Third Ave. Fourth West

Fort Macleod
643 Twentieth St.
(403) 553-2556

Fort McMurray
Beaconwood Rd.
(780) 790-9151

ORGANIZATIONS & ARCHIVES

British Columbia Genealogical Society
P.O. Box 88054
Lansdowne Mall
Richmond, British
Columbia V6X 3T6
(604) 502-9119
Fax: (604) 263-4952
<www.npsnet.com/bcgs>

British Columbia Archives
655 Belleville St.
Victoria, British Columbia
V8V 1X4
(250) 387-1952
<www.bcarchives.gov.
bc.ca>

RESOURCES

British Columbia
by Anthony Hocking
(Quality Books, out of
print)

*Kanaka: The Untold
Story of Hawaiian
Pioneers in British
Columbia and the Pacific
Northwest*
by Tom Koppel
(Whitecap Books, $41.81)

*Light on the Water: Early
Photography of Coastal
British Columbia*
by R. Keith McLaren
(University of
Washington Press,
$35.00)

*Notes From the Century
Before: A Journal From
British Columbia
(Modern Library
Exploration)*
by Edward Hoagland
(Modern Library, $13.95)

PERIODICALS

AABC Newsletter
Archives Association of
British Columbia, P.O. Box
78530, University Post
Office, Vancouver, British
Columbia V6T 1Z4

*The British Columbia
Genealogist*
British Columbia
Genealogical Society, P.O.
Box 88054, Lansdowne
Mall, Richmond, British
Columbia V6X 3T6

*British Columbia
Historical News*
British Columbia
Historical Federation, P.O.
Box 5254, Victoria, British
Columbia, Station B V8R
6N4

WEB SITES

**Archives Association of
British Columbia**
<aabc.bc.ca/aabc>

**BC Geographical Names
Information System**
<www.gdbc.gov.bc.ca/
bcnames>

**British Columbia
GenWeb Project**
<www.rootsweb.com/
~canbc>

**The British Columbia
History Internet/World
Wide Web Page**
<victoria.tc.ca/Resources/
bchistory.html>

**British Columbia
Museums Association**
<www.museumsassn.
bc.ca>

**British Columbia's War
Memorials**
<www.stemnet.nf.ca/
monuments/bc.htm>

BRITISH COLUMBIA

Date Formed: 1866
Joined Canadian Confederation: 1871
Civil Registration Began: 1872
Address for Vital Statistics:
　Mailing address:
　British Columbia Vital Statistics Agency
　PO BOX 9657 STN PROV GOVT
　Victoria BC V8W 9P3
　<www.vs.gov.bc.ca/genealogy>

Office locations:

Victoria
818 Fort St.
(250) 952-2681
Fax: (250) 952-2527

Vancouver
605 Robson St., Room 250
(604) 660-2937
Fax: (604) 660-2645

Kelowna
101, 1475 Ellis St.
(250) 712-7562
Fax: (250) 712-7598

Prince George
433 Queensway
(250) 565-7105
Fax: (250) 565-7106

**City Directories at the Family History Library
Include:** Vancouver 1888, 1890, 1896, and 1959-;
Victoria 1860, 1868, 1871, 1874, and 1958

**Canadian Genealogy and
History Links–British
Columbia**
<www.islandnet.com/
~jveinot/cghl/
british-columbia.html>

**Genealogy Resources on
the Internet: British
Columbia**
<www-personal.umich.
edu/~cgaunt/canada.
html#BC>

FAMILY HISTORY CENTERS

100 Mile House
7021-93 Mile Loop Rd.
(250) 395-2421

Abbotsford
30635 Blueridge Dr.
(604) 852-8043

Bella Coola
Hagensborg
(250) 982-2458

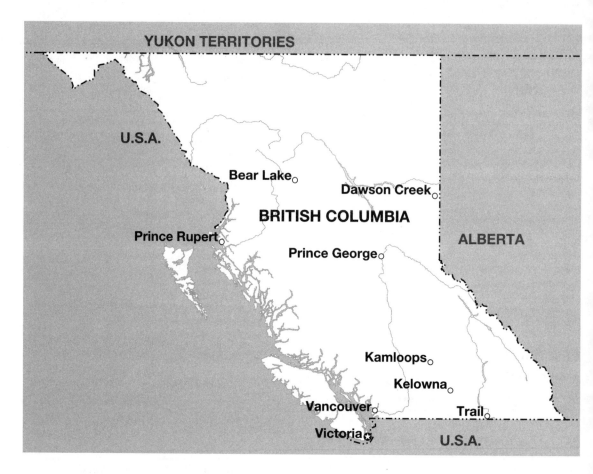

Burns Lake Francois Lake Road (250) 695-6316	**Dawson Creek** 10901 Thirteenth St. (250) 782-4921	**Nanaimo** 2424 Gleneagle Crescent (250) 758-1360	**Prince George** 4180 Fifth Ave. (250) 563-1490
Campbell River 175 Evergreen Rd. (250) 287-3858	**Duncan** 1815 Tzouhalem (250) 746-4122	**Nelson** 222 W. Richards St. (250) 352-5310	**Prince Rupert** 1225 Prince George St. (250) 624-2354
Chetwynd 5107-43 A St. (250) 788-9127	**Fort St. John** 11412 One hundredth St. (250) 785-4351	**Port McNeil** 2551 Mine Rd. (250) 956-4125	**Qualicum Beach** 591 Arbutus (250) 752-2233
Courtenay 1901 Twentieth St. (250) 334-2523	**Kamloops** 2165 Parkcrest Ave. (250) 376-2515	**Penticton** 2946 S. Main (250) 493-5580	**Quensel** 1490 Beryl St. (250) 747-2422
Cranbrook 2210 Second St. North (250) 426-4614	**Kelowna** 696 Glenmore Rd. (250) 860-1690	**Port Alberni** 4816 Compton Rd. (250) 723-9377	**Salmon Arm** 1400 Twentieth St. NE (250) 832-7923
Creston 1010 36 Ave. North (250) 428-7919	**Kitimat** 823 Kuldo Blvd. (250) 632-4720	**Powell River** 6952 Courtenay St. (604) 485-9446	**Smithers** 3974 Tenth Ave. (250) 847-9802

Sparwood
1301 Ponderosa
(250) 425-0523

Surrey
6270 126th St.
(604) 597-9695

Terrace
1744 Kenworth St.
(250) 635-9263

Trail
3585 Laburnum Dr.
(250) 368-6616

Burnaby
5280 Kincaid St.
(604) 299-8656

Vancouver
308 W. Forty-first Ave.
(604) 324-4338

Vanderhoof
Highway 27 North and
McLeod Rd.
(250) 567-9796

Vernon
1506 Thirty-fifth St.
(250) 545-1283

Victoria
701 Mann Ave.
(250) 479-3631

Williams Lake
3039 Edwards Dr.
(250) 392-4271

MANITOBA

ORGANIZATIONS & ARCHIVES

Manitoba Genealogical Society
Unit E, 1045 St. James St.
Winnipeg, Manitoba R3H 1B1
<www.mts.net/~mgsi>

Provincial Archives of Manitoba
200 Vaughn St.
Winnipeg, Manitoba R3C

1T5
(204) 945-3971
<www.gov.mb.ca/chc/archives>

RESOURCES

Dictionary of Manitoba Biography
by J.M. Bumsted
(University of Manitoba Press, $24.95)

The German Community in Winnipeg 1872 to 1919
(Immigrant Communities & Ethnic Minorities in the United States & Canada, No. 81) by Arthur Grenke (AMS Press, $55)

Homeland to Hinterland: The Changing Worlds of

the Red River Metis in the Nineteenth Century
by Gerhard John Ens
(University of Toronto Press, $26.50)

PERIODICALS

Generations
Manitoba Genealogical Society, Unit E, 1045 St.

PROVINCIAL STATS

MANITOBA

Date Formed: 1870
Joined Canadian Confederation: 1870
Civil Registration Began: 1882
Address for Vital Statistics:
Vital Statistics Agency
254 Portage Ave.
Winnipeg, Manitoba R3C 0B6
(204) 945-3701
Fax: (204) 948-3128
<www.gov.mb.ca/cca/vital>

City Directories at the Family History Library Include: Winnipeg 1960

James St., Winnipeg,
Manitoba R3H 1B1

Heritage Postings
Manitoba Mennonite
Historical Society, 169
Riverton Ave., Winnipeg,
Manitoba R2L 2E5

Leaf of the Branch
Southwest Branch of the
Manitoba Genealogical
Society, 246 Percy St.,
Brandon, Manitoba R7B
5R5

WEB SITES

**Canadian Genealogy and
History Links - Manitoba**
<www.islandnet.com/

~jveinot/cghl/manitoba.
html>

**Manitoba GenWeb
Project**
<www.rootsweb.com/
~canmb>

**Manitoba Public Library
Services**
<pls.chc.gov.mb.ca/
cgi-bin/new_main.cgi>

**Manitoba's War
Memorials**
<www.stemnet.nf.ca/mo
numents/mb.htm>

**Quintin Publications -
Manitoba**
<www.quintinpublica-
tions.com/mb.html>

FAMILY HISTORY
CENTERS

Brandon
107 Queens Ave.
(204) 726-8128

Flin Flon
198 Dominion Blvd.
(204) 687-4028

Thompson
83 Copper Rd.
(204) 677-4060

Winnipeg
45 Dalhousie Dr.
(204) 261-4271

NEW BRUNSWICK

ORGANIZATIONS
& ARCHIVES

**New Brunswick
Genealogical Society**
P. O. Box 3235, Station B
Fredericton, New
Brunswick E3A 5G9
<www.bitheads.com/
nbgs>

**Provincial Archives of
New Brunswick**
Bonar Law-Bennett
Building
23 Dineen Dr.
University of New
Brunswick
Fredericton, New
Brunswick E3B 5H1
(506) 453-2122
<www.gnb.ca/archives>

RESOURCES

*The Chignecto
Covenanters: A Regional
History of Reformed
Presbyterianism in New
Brunswick and Nova
Scotia, 1827-1905*
by Eldon Hay (McGill-
Queens University Press,
$65)

*The Development of
Elites in Acadian New
Brunswick, 1861-1881*
by Sheila M. Andrew
(McGill-Queens
University Press, $75)

*Impressions of Historic
Fredericton*
by Fernando Poyatos and
William Spray (Stoddart
Publishing $35)

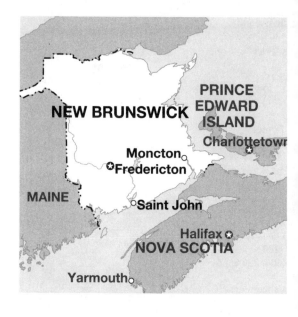

*Lost Land of Moses: The
Age of Discovery on New
Brunswick's Salmon
Rivers*
by Peter Thomas (Goose
Lane Editions, $19.95)

PERIODICALS

Generations
New Brunswick
Genealogical Society, P.O.

Box 3235, Station B,
Fredericton, New
Brunswick E3A 5G9

WEB SITES

**Canadian Archival
Resources on the
Internet–New Brunswick**
<www.usask.ca/archives/
car/nbmenu.html>

Canadian Genealogy and History Links–New Brunswick
<www.islandnet.com/
~jveinot/cghl/
new-brunswick.html>

Genealogy Resources on the Internet: New Brunswick
<www-personal.umich.
edu/~cgaunt/canada.
html#NB>

New Brunswick GenWeb
<www.rootsweb.com/
~cannb>

New Brunswick's War Memorials
<www.stemnet.nf.ca/
monuments/nb.htm>

Tribes and Bands of New Brunswick
<www.hanksville.org/
sand/contacts/tribal/NB.
html>

FAMILY HISTORY CENTERS

Moncton
2070 Mountain Rd.
(506) 856-8909

St. John
177 Manchester Ave.
(506) 672-0864

NEWFOUNDLAND & LABRADOR

ORGANIZATIONS & ARCHIVES

Newfoundland and Labrador Genealogical Society
354 Water St.,
Suite 202,
St. John's, Newfoundland
(709) 754-9525
<www3.nf.sympatico.ca/
nlgs/>
Mailing address:
Colonial Building,

PROVENCIAL STATS

NEWFOUNDLAND AND LABRADOR

Date Formed: 1832
Joined Canadian Confederation: 1949
Civil Registration Began: 1892
Address for Vital Statistics:
Vital Statistics Division
Government Services and Land
P.O. Box 8700
5 Mews Place
St. John's, Newfoundland A1B 4J6
(709) 729-3308
Fax: (709) 729-0946

Military Road
St. John's, Newfoundland
A1C 2C9

Provincial Archives of Newfoundland and Labrador
Colonial Building
Military Rd.
St. John's, Newfoundland
A1C 2C9
(709) 729-3065
<www.gov.nf.ca/panl>

RESOURCES

Canadians at Last: Canada Integrates Newfoundland as a Province
by Raymond B. Blake
(University of Toronto
Press, $55)

Family Names of the Island of Newfoundland
by E.R. Seary and Sheila
M.P. Lynch (McGill-
Queens University Press,
$49.95)

Suspended State: Newfoundland Before Canada
by Gene Long
(Breakwater Books,
$19.95)

This Marvellous Terrible Place: Images of Newfoundland and Labrador
by Yva Momatiuk and
John Eastcott (Firefly
Books, $24.95)

True Newfoundlanders: Early Homes and Families of Newfoundland and Labrador
by Margaret McBurney,
Mary Byers, and John De
Visser (Boston Mills Press,
$29)

PERIODICALS

ANLA Bulletin
Association of
Newfoundland and
Labrador Archives,
Colonial Building,
Military Rd., St. John's,
Newfoundland A1C 2C9

The Newfoundland Ancestor
Newfoundland and
Labrador Genealogical
Society, Colonial
Building, Military Road,
St. John's, Newfoundland
A1C 2C9

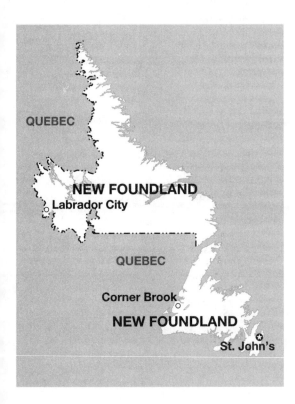

QUEBEC

NEW FOUNDLAND
Labrador City

QUEBEC

Corner Brook

NEW FOUNDLAND

St. John's

The Newfoundland Historical Society Newsletter
Newfoundland Historical Society, Colonial Building, Military Rd., St. John's, Newfoundland A1C 2C9

WEB SITES

Canadian Archival Resources on the Internet–Newfoundland and Labrador
<www.usask.ca/archives/car/nfmenu.html>

Canadian Genealogy and History Links–Newfoundland
<www.islandnet.com/~jveinot/cghl/newfoundland.html>

Genealogy Resources on the Internet: Newfoundland and Labrador
<www-personal.umich.edu/~cgaunt/canada.html#NFL>

Historical Directory of Newfoundland and Labrador Newspapers, 1806-1996
<www.mun.ca/library/cat/newspapers/papers.htm>

Labrador Straits Network
<www.labradorstraits.nf.ca>

Newfoundland and Labrador GenWeb Project
<www.huronweb.com/genweb/nf.htm>

Religion, Society and Culture in Newfoundland and Labrador
<www.ucs.mun.ca/~hrollman>

FAMILY HISTORY CENTERS

Corner Brook
19 Montgomery St.
(709) 634-9700

St. John's
Ferryland St. East
(709) 368-2601

NOVA SCOTIA

ORGANIZATIONS & ARCHIVES

Genealogical Association of Nova Scotia
P.O.Box 641, Station "Central"
Halifax, Nova Scotia B3J 2T3
(902) 454-0322
<www.chebucto.ns.ca/Recreation/GANS>

Nova Scotia Archives and Records Management
(Public Archives of Nova Scotia)
6016 University Ave.
Halifax, Nova Scotia B3H 1W4
(902) 424-6060
<www.gov.ns.ca/nsarm>

RESOURCES

Acadians of Nova Scotia: Past and Present
by Sally Ross and Alphonse Deveau (Down East Books, $17.95)

Myth, Migration and the Making of Memory: Scotia and Nova Scotia C. 1700-1990
edited by Marjory Harper and Michael E. Vance (John Donald, $29.95)

Nova Scotia, Genealogy and Local History: A Trial Bibliography
by Leonard H. Smith (Owl Books, out of print)

Scotia Heritage
by Edith L. Fletcher (E.L. Fletcher, out of print)

PERIODICALS

Collections
The Royal Nova Scotia Historical Society, P.O. Box 2622, Halifax, Nova Scotia B3J 3P7

Naidheachd A' Chlachain
Highland Village Living History Museum, 4119 Highway 223, Iona, Nova Scotia B2C 1A3

The Nova Scotia Genealogist
Genealogical Association of Nova Scotia, P.O. Box 641, Station "Central," Halifax, Nova Scotia B3J 2T3

Shelburne County Genealogical Society Newsletter
Shelburne County Genealogical Society, 168 Water St., P.O. Box 248, Shelburne, Nova Scotia B0T 1W0

WEB SITES

The Black Cultural Centre for Nova Scotia
<www.bccns.com>

Clips and Snips: Genealogical Information From the Acadian Recorder
<freepages.genealogy.rootsweb.com/~sburns>

Nova Scotia Bound
<www.geocities.com/Heartland/Meadows/8429>

Nova Scotia Census Data
<www.rootsweb.com/~casoccgs/census.html>

The Nova Scotia Genealogy Network Association
<nsgna.ednet.ns.ca>

The Nova Scotia Genealogy Resources Page
<www.chebucto.ns.ca/~ab443/genealog.html>

PROVINCIAL STATS

NOVA SCOTIA

Date Formed: 1604, as Acadia; "New Scotland" established 1621
Joined Canadian Confederation: 1867
Civil Registration Began: 1864; only marriages recorded 1877-1908
Address for Vital Statistics:
Service Nova Scotia and Municipal Relations
Vital Statistics
P.O. Box 157
1690 Hollis St.
Halifax, Nova Scotia B3J 2M9
(877) 848-2578 (in Nova Scotia)
(902) 424-4381
Fax: (902) 424-0678
<www.gov.ns.ca/bacs/vstat/>

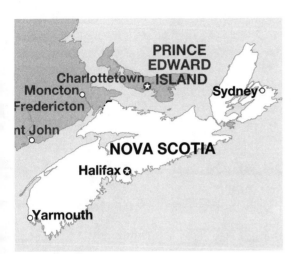

Nova Scotia GenWeb Project
<www.rootsweb.com/~canns>

Nova Scotia Vital Statistics Information
<nsgna.ednet.ns.ca/nvitals.html>

FAMILY HISTORY CENTERS

Bridgewater
337 Aberdeen Rd.
(902) 543-2099

Dartmouth
44 Cumberland Dr.
(902) 462-0628

New Glasgow
384 Abercrombie Rd.
(902) 928-0916

Sydney
230 Evergreen Dr.
(902) 539-7705

ONTARIO

ORGANIZATIONS & ARCHIVES

Archives of Ontario
77 Grenville St., Unit 300
Toronto, Ontario M5S1B3

(416) 327-1600
<www.archives.gov.on.ca>

Ontario Genealogical Society
40 Orchard View Blvd.,
Suite 102
Toronto, Ontario M4R 1B9
(416) 489-0734
Fax: (416) 489-9803
<www.ogs.on.ca>

RESOURCES

Death at Snake Hill: Secrets From a War of 1812 Cemetery
(Ontario Heritage Foundation Local History, No. 3) by Paul Litt, Ronald F. Williamson, and Joseph W.A. Whitehorn (Dundurn Press, $12.95)

Genealogy in Ontario: Searching the Records
3d ed., by Brenda Dougall Merriman (Ontario Genealogical Society, $25)

The Ojibwa of Southern Ontario
by Peter S. Schmalz (University of Toronto Press, $24.95)

Settlers of Upper Canada
(IDON EAST Corp., $39.95), CD-ROM

Toronto's Lost Villages
by Ron Brown (Polar Bear Press, out of print)

PERIODICALS

The British Isles Family History Society Chronicle
British Isles Family History Society, P.O. Box 38026, Ottawa, Ontario K2C 3Y7

Ottawa Branch News
Ottawa Branch of the Ontario Genealogical Society, P.O. Box 8346, Ottawa, Ontario K1G 3H8

The Talbot Times
Elgin County Branch of the Ontario Genealogical Society, P.O. Box 20060, St. Thomas, Ontario N5P 4H4

Toronto Tree
Toronto Branch of the Ontario Genealogical Society, P.O. Box 518, Station K, Toronto, Ontario M4P 2G9

Trails
Essex Branch of the Ontario Genealogical Society, P.O. Box 2, Station "A" Windsor, Ontario N9A 4H0

Wellington County History
Wellington County Historical Society, P.O. Box 5, Fergus, Ontario N1M 2W7

York Region Ancestors
York Region Branch of
the Ontario Genealogical
Society, Harding Post
Office, P.O. Box 32215,
Richmond Hill, Ontario
L4C 9S3

WEB SITES

**Canadian Genealogy and
History Links–Ontario**
<www.islandnet.com/
~jveinot/cghl/ontario.
html>

**Genealogy Resources on
the Internet: Ontario**
<www-personal.umich.
edu/~cgaunt/canada.
html#ONTARIO>

Ontario GenWeb Project
<www.geneofun.on.ca/
ongenweb>

Ontario History
<www.gov.on.ca/MBS/
english/about/history.
html>

Ontario Locator
<www.geneofun.on.ca/
ontariolocator>

Ontario's War Memorials
<www.stemnet.nf.ca/
monuments/on.htm>

**Upper Canada
Genealogy**
<www.uppercanada
genealogy.com>:
Resources for Ontario
research, including
records indexes, links,
and a newsletter.

FAMILY HISTORY CENTERS

Bancroft
53 Hasting St. North
(613) 332-9878

Barrie
79 Ferris Ln.
(705) 722-9152

North York
1990 Jane St.
(416) 242-7392

Bracebridge
4 Taylor Rd.
(705) 645-3262

Brampton
10062 Bramalea Rd.
(905) 799-3214

Brantford
461 Park Rd. North
(519) 753-3725

Brockville
280 Ormond St.
(613) 345-0410

Burlington
2366 Headon Rd.
(905) 335-4733

Cambridge
181 Myers Rd.
(519) 622-0092

Campbellford
25 Doxsee Ave. South
(705) 653-5233

Orleans
6255 Cumorah Dr.
(613) 837-7122

Chatham
19 Detroit Dr.
(519) 352-4627

Cornwall
500 Cornwall Centre Rd.
(613) 933-1716

Dryden
Sandy Beach Rd.
(807) 937-5289

Fort Frances
815 Keating Ave.
(807) 274-9394

Hamilton
701 Stonechurch Rd. East
(905) 385-5009

Kenora
Airport Road
(807) 548-5097

Kingston
2245 Battersea Rd.
(613) 544-8489

Kitchener
10 Lorraine St.
(519) 741-9591

PRINCE EDWARD ISLAND

Date Formed: 1769
Joined Canadian Confederation: 1873
Civil Registration Began: 1906
Address for Vital Statistics:
Vital Statistics
Department of Health and Social Services
P.O. Box 3000
35 Douses Rd.
Montague, Prince Edward Island C0A 1R0
(902) 838-0880
Fax: (902) 838-0883
<www.gov.pe.ca/vitalstatistics/index.php3>

London
1139 Riverside Dr.
(519) 473-2421

Etobicoke
95 Melbert Rd.
(416) 621-4607

North Bay
988 Airport Rd.
(705) 474-9205

Oshawa
632 Thornton Rd. North
(905) 728-3151

Ottawa
1017 Prince of Wales Dr.
(613) 224-2231

Owen Sound
490 Second Ave. SE
(519) 376-2482

Petawawa
199 Civic Centre Rd.
(613) 687-2237

Peterborough
748 Cumberland St.
(705) 745-8912

Sarnia
1400 Murphy Rd.
(519) 542-7126

Sault Ste. Marie
126 Caledon
(705) 254-5892

Simcoe
195 Victoria St.
(519) 428-2310

Smiths Falls
7283 Roger Stevens Dr.
(613) 283-8320

St. Catharines
351 Glenridge Ave.
(905) 685-5795

St. Thomas
436 Elm St.
(519) 631-2641

Timmins
500 Toke St.
(705) 264-8990

Sudbury
44 Norfork Court
(705) 525-1423

Haileybury
Edward St. Moore's Cove
(705) 672-2057

Thunder Bay
2255 Ponderosa Dr.
(807) 939-1451

Toronto-North York
24 Ferrand Dr.
(416) 422-5480

Trenton
Byrnes Ave.
(613) 392-3387

Walkerton
110 Fourth St.
(519) 881-2473

Windsor
3550 Forest Glade Dr.

Woodstock
93 Lansdowne Ave.
(519) 537-3121

PRINCE EDWARD ISLAND

ORGANIZATIONS & ARCHIVES

Prince Edward Island Genealogical Society
P.O. Box 2744
Charlottetown, Prince Edward Island C1A 8C4
<www.islandregister.com/peigs.htm>

Public Archives and Records Office
P.O. Box 100
Charlottetown, Prince Edward Island C1A 7M4
(902) 368-4290
<www2.gov.pe.ca/educ/archives/archives_index.asp>

RESOURCES

The French Regime in Prince Edward Island
by Daniel Cobb Harvey
(Reprint Services, $79)

The Historic Churches of Prince Edward Island
by H.M. Scott Smith
(Boston Mills Press, $14.95)

The Home Place: Life in Rural Prince Edward Island in the 1920s and 30s
by Jean Halliday MacKay
(Acorn Press, $15.95)

Land, Settlement, and Politics on Eighteenth-Century Prince Edward Island
by J.M. Bumsted (McGill-Queens University Press, $75)

PERIODICALS

The Island Magazine
PEI Museum and Heritage Foundation, 2 Kent St., Charlottetown, Prince Edward Island C1A 1M6

The Prince Edward Island Genealogical Society Newsletter
Prince Edward Island Genealogical Society, P.O. Box 2744, Charlottetown, Prince Edward Island C1A 8C4

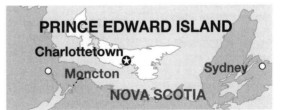

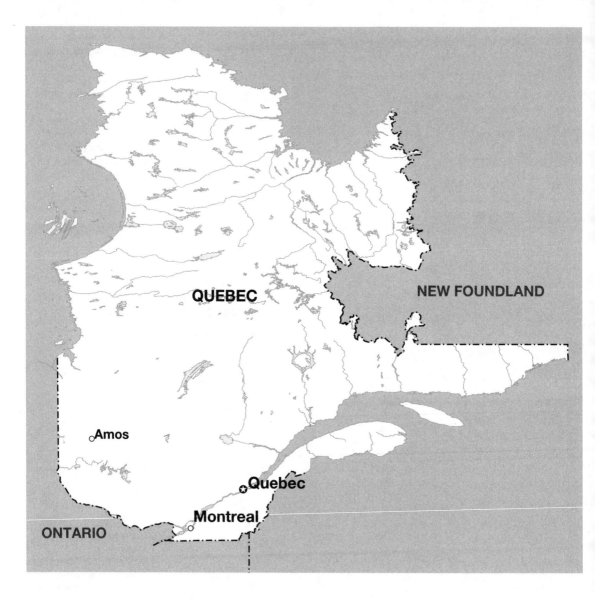

QUEBEC

NEW FOUNDLAND

○Amos

✪ Quebec

Montreal○

ONTARIO

WEB SITES

Canadian Archival Resources on the Internet–Prince Edward Island
<www.usask.ca/archives/car/pemenu.html>

Canadian Genealogy and History Links–Prince Edward Island
<www.islandnet.com/~jveinot/cghl/prince-edward-island.html>

The 1863 Lake Map of Prince Edward Island
<www.islandregister.com/lakem>

Pioneer Life on Prince Edward Island
<www.islandregister.com/life.html>

Prince Edward Island: Genealogy
<www.gov.pe.ca/infopei/Arts,_Culture_and_Heritage/Genealogy>

Prince Edward Island GenWeb Project
<www.islandregister.com/pegenweb.html>

Prince Edward Island Museum and Heritage Foundation
<museum.gov.ns.ca/mikmaq/peimuse.htm>

Prince Edward Island's War Memorials
<www.stemnet.nf.ca/monuments/pei.htm>

FAMILY HISTORY CENTERS

Charlottetown
10 Northridge Parkway
(902) 566-1013

QUEBEC

ORGANIZATIONS & ARCHIVES

Archives Nationales du Québec
1012, Avenue du Seminaire
CP 10450
Sainte-Foy, Quebec G1V 4N1
(418) 643-8904
<www.anq.gouv.qc.ca>

Quebec Family History Society
P.O. Box 1026
Pointe Claire, Quebec H9S 4H9
(514) 695-1502
<www.cam.org/~qfhs>

RESOURCES

Old Quebec, the Fortress of New France
by Gilbert Parker and Claude G. Bryan (Pelican Publishing, $30)

Opening the Gates of Eighteenth-Century Montréal
edited by Phyllis Lambert and Alan Stewart (MIT Press, $17.95)

Quebec (Exploring Canada)
by Steven Ferry (Lucent Books, $28.45)

A Register of Deceased Persons at Sea and on Grosse Ile in 1847
by Andre Charbonneau, Doris Drolet-Dube, Robert J. Grace, and Sy Tremblay (Intl.

Specialized Book Services, $16.95)

A Short History of Quebec
by John A. Dickinson and Brian J. Young (McGill-Queens University Press, $27.95)

PERIODICALS

Chateauguay Valley Historical Society Journal
Chateauguay Valley Historical Society, 745 Fairview Rd., Hinchinbrooke, Huntingdon, Quebec J0S 1H0

Connections
Quebec Family History Society, P.O. Box 1026, Pointe Claire, Quebec H9S 4H9

Shem Tov
Jewish Genealogical Society of Montreal, P.O. Box 356, Côte St. Luc, Quebec H4V 2Y5

Westmont Historical Association Newsletter
Westmont Historical Association, 4574 Sherbrooke St. West, Westmount, Quebec H3Z 1G1

WEB SITES

Annals of the Port of Quebec 1535-1900
<www.ist.uwaterloo.ca/~marj/genealogy/quebecport1901.html>

Canadian Genealogy and History Links–Quebec
<www.islandnet.com/~jveinot/cghl/quebec.html>

QUEBEC

Date Formed: 1608
Joined Canadian Confederation: 1867
Civil Registration Began: 1926
Address for Vital Statistics:
Ministère de la Justice
Direction de l'État Civil Service à la Clientele
205 Rue Montmagny
Quebec, Quebec G1N 4T2
(418) 643-3900
Fax: (418) 646-3255
<www.etatcivil.gouv.qc.ca/ENGLISH/Default.htm>

City Directories at the Family History Library Include: Montreal 1819, 1877, 1866, 1888, 1889, 1905, 1915, 1930, 1940, 1949, 1967, and 1968; Quebec 1877, 1895, and 1905

Genealogy in Quebec
<www.francogene.com/quebec>

Genealogy of Quebec's Native People and Francophone Metis
<www.francogene.com/quebec/amerin.html>

Quebec GenWeb Project
<www.rootsweb.com/~canqc/>

Quebec's War Memorials
<www.stemnet.nf.ca/monuments/pq.htm>

Tribes and Bands of Quebec
<www.hanksville.org/sand/contacts/tribal/QU.html>

FAMILY HISTORY CENTERS

Drummondville
2255 St. Georges
(819) 478-8554

Gatineau
178 De Sillery
(819) 561-2442

Montreal
1777 De Lorimier Ave.
(514) 523-6131

Lasalle
7110 Newman Blvd.
(514) 367-1615

Quebec
4500 Jacques-Crepeault
(418) 871-7771

Rimouski
130 Rue St. Germain East
(418) 722-6721

SASKATCHEWAN

ORGANIZATIONS & ARCHIVES

Saskatchewan Archives Board
Murray Building
University of Saskatchewan
3 Campus Dr.

Saskatoon, Saskatchewan
S7N 5A4
(306) 933-5832
<www.saskarchives.com>
Regina Office:
University of Regina
Regina, Saskatchewan
S4S 0A2
(306) 787-4068

**Saskatchewan
Genealogical Society**
2nd Fl., 1870 Lorne St.
P.O. Box 1894
Regina, Saskatchewan
S4P 3E1
(306) 780-9207
Fax: (306)781-6021
<www.saskgenealogy.

RESOURCES
*Exploring Family History
in Saskatchewan*
by D'Arcy Hande
(Saskatchewan Archives
Board, free download
online from <www.
saskarchives.com/web/
services-pub-bulletins.
html>)

*People Places:
Saskatchewan and Its
Names*
by Bill Barry (Canadian
Plains Research Center,
$29.95)

*Piecing the Quilt: Sources
for Women's History in
the Saskatchewan
Archives Board*
by Barbara Powell
(Canadian Plains
Research Center, $32)

PERIODICALS
Folklore
Saskatchewan History &
Folklore Society, 1860
Lorne St., Regina,
Saskatchewan S4P 2L7

*Saskatoon History
Review*
Saskatoon Heritage
Society, 831 Temperance
St., Saskatoon,
Saskatchewan S7N 0M8

WEB SITES
**Canadian Archival
Resources on the
Internet–Saskatchewan**
<www.usask.ca/archives/
car/skmenu.html>

**Canadian Genealogy and
History Links–
Saskatchewan**
<www.islandnet.com/
~jveinot/cghl/
saskatchewan.html>

**Genealogy Resources on
the Internet:
Saskatchewan**
<www-personal.umich.
edu/~cgaunt/canada.
html#SASK>

**Maps From the Atlas of
Saskatchewan: 1969 and
1999 Celebrating the
Millennium Editions**
<www.rootsweb.com/
~cansk/maps/
saskatchewanatlas.html>

**Saskatchewan Cemetery
Index**
<www.saskgenealogy.
com/cemetery/cemetery.
htm>

**Saskatchewan GenWeb
Project**
<www.rootsweb.com/
~cansk/Saskatchewan>

Saskatchewan Libraries
<www.lib.sk.ca>

**Saskatchewan's War
Memorials**
<www.stemnet.nf.ca/
monuments/sk.htm>

FAMILY HISTORY
CENTERS
Kindersley
820 First St. West
(306) 463-4808

NORTHWEST TERRITORIES

SASKATCHEWAN

Flin Flon

Prince Albert
North Battleford
Saskatoon

Regina
Swift Current

U.S.A.

PROVINCIAL STATS

SASKATCHEWAN

Date Formed: 1882
Joined Canadian Confederation: 1905
Civil Registration Began: 1878; full compliance
1920
Address for Vital Statistics:
  Vital Statistics
  1942 Hamilton St.
  Regina, Saskatchewan S4P 3V7
  (306) 787-3092
  Fax: (306) 787-2288
  <www.health.gov.sk.ca/ps_vital_statistics.
  html>

Moose Jaw
15 Woodpark Dr.
(306) 692-3246

Prince Albert
452 Thirtieth St. East
(306) 763-7874

Regina
550 Sangster Blvd.
(306) 543-2782

Saskatoon
1429 Tenth St.
(306) 343-6060

TERRITORIES

ORGANIZATIONS & ARCHIVES

Northwest Territories Archives
Prince of Wales Northern Heritage Centre
Yellowknife, Northwest Territories X1A 2L9
(403) 873-7698
<pwnhc.learnnet.nt.ca/programs/archive.htm>

Northwest Territory Genealogical Society
P.O. Box 1715
Yellowknife, Northwest Territories X1A 2P3
<www.ssimicro.com/nonprofit/nwtgs>

Yukon Archives
P.O. Box 2703
Whitehorse, Yukon Y1A 2C6
(403) 667-5321
<www.gov.yk.ca/depts/education/libarch/yukarch.html>

RESOURCES

North Canada: Yukon, Northwest Territories, Nunavut
by Geoffrey Roy (Bradt Publications, $18.95)

PERIODICALS

Under the Jack Pine
Northwest Territory Genealogical Society,

TERRITORIAL STATS

NORTHWEST, NUNAVUT, AND YUKON TERRITORIES

Date Formed
Northwest Territories: 1870
Nunavut: 1999
Yukon: 1895
Joined Canadian Confederation:
Northwest Territories: 1870
Nunavut: 1999
Yukon: 1898
Civil Registration Began:
Northwest Territories: 1925
Nunavut: 1999
Yukon: 1896; full compliance 1925

Addresses for Vital Statistics:

Northwest Territories:
Department of Health and Social Services
Government of Northwest Territories
Bag #9
Inuvik, Northwest Territories X0E 0T0
(867) 777-7420
Fax: (867) 777-3197

Nunavut:
Nunavut Health & Social Services
Bag #3
Rankin Inlet, Nunavut X0C 0G0
(867) 645-8001
Fax: (867) 645-8092
<www.gov.nu.ca/gnmain.htm>

Yukon:
Department of Health and Human Resources
Government of Yukon
P.O. Box 2703
Whitehorse, Yukon Y1A 2C6
(403) 667-5207
<www.hss.gov.yk.ca/prog/vs>

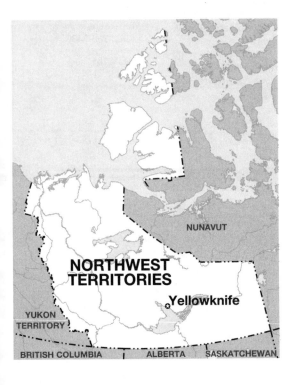

P.O. Box 1715,
Yellowknife, Northwest Territories X1A 2P3

WEB SITES

Canadian Archival Resources on the Internet–Northwest Territories
<www.usask.ca/archives/car/ntmenu.html>

Canadian Archival Resources on the Internet–Yukon Territory
<www.usask.ca/archives/car/ykmenu.html>

Canadian Genealogy and History Links–Northwest Territories
<www.islandnet.com/~jveinot/cghl/northwest-territories.html>

Canadian Genealogy and History Links–Nunavut
<www.islandnet.com/
~jveinot/cghl/nunavut.
html>

Canadian Genealogy and History Links–Yukon
<www.islandnet.com/
~jveinot/cghl/yukon.
html>

LibDex–The Library Index: Yukon
<www.libdex.com/
country/Canada-Yukon.
html>

Northwest Territories GenWeb
<www.polarnet.ca/
~taloyoak/genweb/nwt.
htm>

Tribes and Bands of the Northwest Territories
<www.hanksville.org/
sand/contacts/tribal/NWT.
html>

Tribes and Bands of the Yukon
<www.hanksville.org/
sand/contacts/tribal/YK.
html>

Yukon GenWeb
<www.rootsweb.com/
~canyk>

FAMILY HISTORY CENTERS

Whitehorse
108 Wickstrom Rd.
(867) 668-7961

Yellowknife
5016-52 Street #4
Basement
(867) 766-2435

African-American Roots

BY FRANKLIN CARTER SMITH

I n 1619, Dutch slave traders sold twenty African captives to the settlers of Jamestown, Va. For Americans with roots in Africa, this marked the beginning of your ancestors' arrival in America. By 1808, when the importation of slaves was constitutionally prohibited, the United States was home to some one million slaves. Your African ancestors were among the nation's original settlers. For nearly 240 years, slave labor helped build America, yet most of these invisible souls have yet to be identified or acknowledged. Now it's up to you, their descendants, to reconstruct the stories of their lives.

These stories of slavery went largely untold until Alex Haley's *Roots.* After the Civil War, descendants of both slaves and slaveholders suffered collective amnesia. Former slaves rarely spoke of their lives in bondage—most just wanted to forget. Today, however, African Americans embrace this heritage. African-American family reunions have become annual events, bringing together far-flung relatives, renewing interest in often forgotten ancestors and leading many to actively research their family history. Even the millions of Americans with mixed-racial ancestry—estimates of the white population with some black ancestry range from 10 to 24 percent—are digging into their heritage and exploring this lost part of their past.

Genealogy will help you reclaim the lost heritage of your slave ancestors.

COURTESY OF FRANKLIN CARTER SMITH

Because of your African ancestors' unique history in this country, your search for them will pose special challenges. You can use standard genealogical techniques, as presented in every issue of *Family Tree Magazine*, to trace back to 1870, the year of the first post-Civil War census. But when you hit the pre-Civil War years, the records are no longer in the name of your ancestors but in the names of those who owned them. Even those African Americans freed prior to the Civil War were at some point slaves or the descendants of slaves. Identifying the slaveholding families and locating their records will be the keys to your quest.

These seven steps can help you get started:

1. Start on the home front. First, do your homework. Read a good African-American genealogy guidebook, such as my new book written with Emily Anne Croom, *A Genealogist's Guide to Discovering Your African-American Ancestors* (Betterway Books, $21.99). And find a guide that covers basic techniques of research in American genealogy, such as *First Steps in Genealogy* by Desmond Walls Allen (Betterway Books, $14.99) or *Unpuzzling Your Past* by Emily Anne Croom (Betterway Books, $18.99). Dee Parmer Woodtor's interactive guide for beginners on the AfriGeneas site <www.afrigeneas.com/guide> provides tips on how and where to get started, along with suggested books and links.

Try filling out as much as you can on a pedigree chart. This will help determine just how much or how little you know about your ancestors. Collect copies of all family papers, funeral programs, photographs, and other memorabilia. Visit the family cemetery, if possible, to check ancestors' names and dates. Use the information you find in all these sources to fill in gaps on your chart.

Now decide which ancestral line to search. Consider starting with the ancestors you have the most information about or whose history is easiest to access. When you've done as much as you can on paper, find and interview the family, beginning with older family members. Failing memories and death claimed much of our history, especially from the slavery years—capture this living heritage while you can.

2. Find post-Civil War records. As for most Americans, government records are the primary source of genealogical information for African Americans—especially federal census records. Start with the most recently released census, 1930, and search back to 1870, the first census to name the recently freed slaves and show their family groups. Make sure to check the 1870 and 1880 agricultural censuses, too. And don't stop at 1870: Perhaps your ancestors were freed before the Civil War.

The U.S. Bureau of Refugees, Freedmen, and Abandoned Lands, a.k.a. the Freedmen's Bureau, was created after the Civil War to deal with the needs of the emancipated slave population. In Freedmen's Bureau records, kept from 1865 to 1872, you may find
- hospital records or registers
- labor contracts between freedmen and planters
- enrollments for local freedmen schools
- marriage registers
- lists of food rations
- reports of outrages, disputes and court cases brought by freedmen against whites
- lists of freedmen and their families
- correspondence of local field agents describing the conditions in a particular area.

You may discover other information as well. To learn more about these records, see the overview at <www.archives.gov/publications/prologue/summer_1997_freedmens_bureau_records.html>.

Civil War veterans' pension records may also hold clues. (To see if your ancestor was among the more than 250,000 slaves and free blacks who fought for the Union, search the Civil War Soldiers and Sailors System site <www.itd.nps.gov/cwss>.) As part of the pension process, applicants were required to prove their identity. In most instances, you will find their date and place of birth—which may tell you the city, county, or plantation where they were born—as well as marriage records and names and ages of parents and children. Relatives, neighbors, and friends submitted affidavits that may contain information about their relationships to the applicant, perhaps naming a plantation, owner, or family connection. Widows had to provide proof of marriage in the form of affidavits or marriage certificates, as well as previous names they may have used. Applicants had to name where they enlisted and their service history, as well as residences and occupations following the war. While some records are more helpful than others, you're sure to find some new facts or confirm others here.

State agencies are the primary repository for birth-, death-, and marriage-related records. Most states, however, didn't start officially recording births and deaths until after 1900. A rarely utilized but important document that may help determine your ancestor's whereabouts from 1865 to 1867 is the 1867 voter registration list. Check the state archives for your area of research to see if these records exist for your county.

At the local level (county, parish, township, or city), you'll find records of wills, probate, marriages, divorces, deeds, and schools. Pay special attention to the marriage records for the years immediately following the war. Many couples who were united during slavery legalized their relationships after the Civil War. The marriage bonds and certificates also may confirm the identity of other family members.

3. Zero in on 1870. Finding your ancestors in the 1870 census is the first step toward solving the mystery of their years in bondage. After the Civil War, most recently freed slaves remained near the place they'd lived before the war. Many who did relocate were reuniting with family they'd been separated from. This search will probably take you back to a county or parish somewhere in the South. From 1790 until 1900, 90 percent of African Americans lived in the South, mostly in rural areas. For many ex-slaves, the migration northeast, north, and west didn't begin until after 1900.

If your ancestors were in the North in 1870, it's possible they were freed prior to the war. Even so, you'll probably have to search for a slaveholder since most free blacks were slaves at some point. Records documenting their freedom were usually recorded in county courthouses in probate or deed records.

If you can't find your ancestors in the 1870 census, it's likely they lived in the same state, county and community in 1880. So make 1880 your focus instead. Look carefully at the community where your ancestors lived in 1870. Ask

- Who were your ancestors' neighbors?
- How old were your ancestors and their neighbors?
- Where were they born?
- Are there others in the neighborhood with the same surname as your ancestors?
- Do neighboring families have any surnames in common with your ancestors?
- Do the ages of your ancestor's children indicate they were a family before the Civil War?

Your answers will help determine if those living in the neighborhood are related or connected in other ways. Though your ancestors' surnames were crucial in recent records, the key to identifying them in your pre-Civil War search will be their first names. Pay close attention to the given names of your ancestors' family as well as those of their neighbors. Compare the names of suspected ancestors you find in any slave documents with those living in the neighborhood in 1870. This may be the only way to establish that they are one and the same.

Slaveholders rarely identified slaves by their formal given names in records; instead they used nicknames. Consider the possible variations of names that may have been used to identify an ancestor. My ancestor James Humphreys, for example, would always be listed as "Jim," Jane Green as "Jenny," Jesse Humphreys as "Jess," Martill as "Till," and Elizabeth Weathersby as "Betsy." Such a thorough and complete review of the 1870 census may reveal the identity of several new and previously unknown generations.

4. Determine the slaveholder's surname. Unlike other ethnic groups arriving in America, enslaved Africans were systematically stripped of their cultural traditions and social customs when brought to this country. As part of this process, recently arrived Africans were routinely renamed soon after being removed from the slave ship. Until the end of the Civil War, most slaves were identified by first name only. Slaves on the same plantation with the same given names were distinguished by their size, age, or color. After the Civil War, newly freed slaves had to choose surnames for official identification. Their reasons for choosing a surname varied and many would change surnames a number of times before settling on a final choice.

For some families, the reason behind the choice of a surname is already known; for others, the reason may be discovered during their research; and for the majority, the reason may never be known. If you already know the history behind your family's choice of a surname, you can eliminate years of tedious and often frustrating research. The common—and often erroneous—presumption is that most took the surnames of their most recent slaveholder. While this was sometimes true, the surname may have belonged to a prior owner or the owners of their parents or grandparents. Some randomly chose surnames with no connection to former owners.

In my research, only twice did I discover why my ancestors took their surname, and both took the name of a slaveholder. My great-great-grandfather took the name of his slaveholder-father. My family has always known this. In fact, we have his slaveholder-father's portrait painted in the late 1840s or early 1850s. My third-great-grandmother also took the name of an owner, and it was her surname that led to the identification of her owner. Though I've discovered the owners of a number of ancestors, I've still not been able to determine why they chose their surnames.

Knowing the name of the slaveholding family is essential to move your research to the next level. Those who already know this can skip ahead to step six. If this information was lost with your ancestors, start with the presumption that they took their former slaveholder's surname. First look at the neighborhood in which your ancestors lived in 1870, then broaden your search countywide, or even statewide if your ancestors' surname was unique, until you've collected a list of candidates. Be sure to include any possible spelling variations of the surname your ancestor was using. Consider going back as far as the 1850 census.

If you don't find the same or similar surnames in records from 1850 or later, proceed to the next step. Otherwise, you may narrow the pool of candidates by checking the slave censuses of 1850 and 1860 to determine if they owned slaves prior to the war. Cross-reference the ages of your ancestors with the ages of the slaves listed in the schedules. (Only age, gender, and skin color of slaves were listed in these schedules.) This will either strengthen any possible connection or eliminate unlikely candidates. When checking the 1860 and 1870 censuses, note how much real estate each slaveholder candidate owned, and compare their places of birth with your ancestors'.

If your search based on common surnames produces enough evidence to support further investigation, go to step six. If you still lack such evidence, it's time to look deeper into your ancestors' whereabouts in 1870.

5. Study your family's location. If the same-surname approach fails, studying where your ancestors lived in 1870 may hold the key to identifying a former slaveholder. Neither the newly freed slaves nor their former owners ventured far from their pre-Civil War homes immediately after the war. The black population remained heavily rural. In the economic wasteland of the South after the war, former slaves and slaveholders alike faced desperate conditions. Partly out of allegiance and partly from necessity, many former slaves and slaveholders continued their relationships. So even in 1870 your ancestors were probably still living on land owned by their former masters.

Find out who owned the land on which your ancestors lived in 1870, and you're likely to find the identity of their slaveholder as well. (If your search of Freedmen's Bureau records turns up labor contracts for your ancestors, consider yourself fortunate. The contractor and former slave owner are usually the same. In this case, proceed to step six, and start searching that family's records.) The quickest way to find out who owned the property where your ancestors may have lived is searching pre-1870 county land tax records. Land plat books also may help identify local landowners. (Check the courthouse in the county you're researching, the Family History Library <www.familysearch.org> or the state archives to see if these records exist.)

Next, cross-reference all potential slaveholder candidates with the 1850 and 1860 slave schedules to help narrow the list. If you're unable to locate or access these records, closely examine all the white families living near your ancestors in 1870. At first, consider only those white families with property. Determine if they owned land before the war, were slave owners, and lived in the same place. Your answers will help determine which families will be the focus of your search.

6. Research the "other family." Now that you've determined which slaveholding families warrant further investigation, start researching records left by them. Focus on records that either name slaves or indicate slave ownership. The number of records available will depend on whether the family was a large or small slaveholder. The most thorough and complete records were the business records of large slaveholding families. But these families made up only a small part of the slave-owning population, and finding such private records, if they still exist, could be a challenge. Estate records, on the other hand, are a matter of public record and were required for large and small slaveholder alike. Other sources likely to name your ancestor are property records, such as deeds, mortgages, and bill of sale records. Personal property tax records and state and federal census records as well as the 1850 and 1860 slave schedules can be used to help track slave ownership over time, but they are not likely to name your ancestors.

Because the lives of the slaveholder and slave families are so intertwined, you need to study the owner family's history and genealogy to fully explore your own. Slaves contributed not only to a family's financial worth but also to their status in the community. In many instances, slaves remained in the same family for generations. As valuable "property," they were transferred by inheritance, gift, or deed to sons, daughters, sisters, brothers, and grandchildren.

Once you find a slaveholder, tracking that slaveholder's genealogy back may help lead to the identity of your ancestors' parents or even grandparents, who may have been in that family for generations. Fortunately, many of these families' histories and genealogies have already been published and can be found in genealogy libraries, archives, and on the Internet.

7. Slave documents tell a story. Finding a document naming a slave ancestor or ancestors can be a cause for celebration. But your greatest reward may come from the secrets that these documents reveal about your ancestors' lives.

Estate records of slaveholding families may provide the most comprehensive picture of your ancestors' lives. It could take as little as a few months or as long as ten years to settle an estate. If you locate an estate document naming an ancestor, research the estate records to see if other ancestors are named. The quantity and quality of information found in these records also will depend on the person making the record. A meticulous record keeper may provide a wealth of information, such as entire family units, ages, births, deaths, and skin color, whereas others may provide only generic information.

These records may also provide insight into your ancestors' diet, the clothing they wore, how often they got clothing, their health, and any special skills or trade they may have had. Carefully study all related documents, not just the one on which your ancestor is named.

A research strategy alone is no guarantee that your search will be successful. But with good research skills, patience, persistence, good instincts, and lots of luck, you can go a long way toward reconstructing the lives of these invisible souls—your forgotten African-American ancestors.

ORGANIZATIONS

African-American Genealogy Group
Box 27356
Philadelphia, PA 19118
(215) 572-6063
<www.aagg.org>

Afro-American Historical and Genealogical Society
Box 73067
Washington, DC 20056
<www.rootsweb.com/~mdaahgs>

International Society of Sons and Daughters of Slave Ancestry
Box 436937
Chicago, IL 60643
<www.rootsweb.com/~ilissdsa>

National Afro-American Museum and Cultural Center
Box 578
1350 Brush Row Rd.
Wilberforce, OH 45384
(800) 752-2603
<www.ohiohistory.org/places/afroam>

Schomburg Center for Research in Black Culture
515 Malcolm X Blvd.
New York, NY 10037
(212) 491-2200
<www.nypl.org/research/sc/sc.html>

RESOURCES

African American Genealogical Research: How to Trace Your Family History
by Paul R. Begley, Alexia J. Helsley, and Steven D. Tuttle (South Carolina Department of Archives and History, $6.75)

African-American Genealogical Sourcebook
edited by Paula K. Byers (Gale Group, $112.25)

African-American Genealogy: A Bibliography and Guide to Sources
by Curt Bryan Witcher (Round Tower Books, $19.95)

African Americans in the 1870 Census
(Genealogy.com, $29.99) CD-ROM containing an alphabetical index of approximately 660,000 African Americans who were enumerated in the 1870 federal census.

Afro-Americana, 1553-1906 (Historical Society of Pennsylvania, out of print)

Bibliographic Checklist of African-American Newspapers
by Barbara K. Henritze (Genealogical Publishing Co., out of print)

Black Genealogy
by Charles L. Blockson and Ron Fry (Black Classic Press, $14.95)

Black Names in America: Origins and Usage
by Newbell Niles Puckett (G. K. Hall, out of print)

Black Roots: A Beginner's Guide to Tracing the African American Family Tree
by Tony Burroughs (Fireside, $16)

A Comprehensive Name Index for the American Slave
by Howard E. Potts (Greenwood Press, $95)

Databases for the Study of Afro-Louisiana History and Genealogy 1699-1860
edited by Gwendolyn Midlo Hall (Louisiana State University Press, $45) CD-ROM containing searchable database of individual records for 100,000 slaves.

Family Pride: The Complete Guide to Tracing African-American Genealogy
by Donna Beasley (Macmillan Publishing, $12.95)

Finding a Place Called Home: A Guide to African-American Genealogy and Historical Identity
by Dee Parmer Woodtor (Random House, $18)

Free African Americans of North Carolina and Virginia
by Paul Heinegg (Genealogical Publishing Co., out of print but available online at <www.freeafrican americans.com>)

From Slavery to Freedom: A History of African Americans
by John Hope Franklin and Alfred A. Moss Jr. (Knopf, $49.95)

A Genealogist's Guide to Discovering Your African-American Ancestors
by Franklin Carter Smith and Emily Anne Croom (Betterway Books, $21.99)

A Genealogist's Guide to Discovering Your Immigrant & Ethnic Ancestors
by Sharon DeBartolo Carmack (Betterway Books, $18.99)

Generations Past: A Selected List of Sources for Afro-American Genealogical Research
by Sandra M. Lawson (Library of Congress, out of print)

In Black and White
edited by Mary Mace Spradling (Gale Group, out of print) References twenty-one thousand African-American individuals and groups appearing in publications.

Slave Genealogy: A Research Guide with Case Studies
by David H. Streets (Heritage Books, $18.50)

Slave Narratives
(Ancestry, $39.95), CD-ROM. Firsthand accounts of more than 2,300 slaves narrated to researchers in twenty-six states. Compiled by the Works Progress Administration from 1936-1938.

A Student's Guide to African American Genealogy
by Anne E. Johnson and Adam Merton Cooper (Oryx Press, $24.95)

The Trans-Atlantic Slave Trade: A Database on CD-ROM
by David Eltis, David Richardson, Herbert S. Klein and Stephen D. Behrendt (Cambridge University Press, $125) Contains records of twenty-five thousand trans-Atlantic slave-ship voyages made between 1595 and 1866 from all over Europe.

WEB SITES

African American Cemeteries Online
<www.prairiebluff.com/aacemetery>: Online database of African-American cemeteries, categorized by state. Many include transcribed tombstones.

The African-American Genealogy Ring
<afamgenealogy.ourfamily.com>: More than one hundred linked sites for researching African-American roots.

The African-American Mosaic
<lcweb.loc.gov/exhibits/african/intro.html>: Selections from the Library of Congress's resource guide for the study of black history and culture, covering colonization, abolition, migrations, and the 1930s Works Progress Administration.

African Ancestry
<www.africanancestry.com>: Information and updates about a DNA-based test developed by Howard University researchers to help African Americans trace their African ancestry.

African Voices
<www.mnh.si.edu/africanvoices>: A lavishly designed, deep, and interactive online exhibit by the Smithsonian National Museum of Natural History. Weave through the extensive set of streaming timelines (made possible by Macromedia's Flash 4, absolutely necessary to fully enjoy this site), tour historical sites, meet individuals, and see their works.

AfriGeneas
<www.afrigeneas.com>: Finding data on African Americans prior to the 1870 census ("The Wall," as researchers call it) can be difficult, but this site proves it's not impossible. Information within tax records, diaries, plantation records and data on runaway slaves that may be helpful is indexed by last name, state and year.

Christine's Genealogy Website
<www.ccharity.com>: Christine Charity's site is an especially helpful one for researching African-American ancestors. She's got good links and information about the post-Civil War Freedmen's Bureau records, African genealogy, and related articles and databases.

Civil War Soldiers and Sailors System
<www.itd.nps.gov/cwss>: Search names and regimental histories of the Union Army's African-American units, or link to other National Park sites that interpret Civil War history.

Cyndi's List-African-American
<www.cyndislist.com/african.htm>: Cyndi's two hundred-plus African-American genealogy links are listed by category.

The Encyclopaedia Britannica Guide to Black History
<blackhistory.eb.com>: Features six hundred articles, along with historical film clips and audio recordings, hundreds of photographs and other images, related links, and more.

The Freedmen's Bureau Online
<freedmensbureau.com>: Search records from the Bureau of Refugees, Freedmen and Abandoned Lands, established by the U.S. War Department in 1865 to help freed slaves get on their feet. The bureau kept records on marriages, crimes, and labor, as well as land abandoned by Confederate owners after the war. The site also points you to related Web sites with Freedmen's Bureau information.

Genealogy Resources on the Internet—African-Ancestored Mailing Lists
<www.rootsweb.com/~jfuller/gen_mail_african.html>: Frequently updated compilation of African genealogy-related Internet mailing lists, along with descriptions and instructions on how to join each list.

Records of the Bureau of Refugees, Freedmen, and Abandoned Lands
<www.archives.gov/research_room/federal_records_guide/bureau_of_refugees_freedmen_and_abandoned_lands_rg105.html>: Guide to federal records of the Freedmen's Bureau in the National Archives.

Native American Roots

BY NANCY HENDRICKSON

I grew up in a generation that both romanticized and vilified Native Americans. Watching actors such as Jeff Chandler and Donna Reed assume Indian faces, I remained blissfully ignorant of centuries of true-life misery. Back then, claiming Native American roots would have been as unthinkable as choosing to play the Indian in those backyard gunfights.

During many of the years when I traced my own roots, I knew nothing about American Indian genealogy. Since my family was from Northern European stock, I figured I had no need to cross the threshold into researching the first Americans. But all that changed a couple of years ago, when I discovered that my great-niece came from a mix of African-American and Native American heritage.

Interest in tracing Native American roots is growing.

FROM THE NORTH AMERICAN INDIAN BY EDWARD S. CURTIS

Society's view of American Indians has changed a lot since I grew up, as shown in movie roles as well as the role-playing in America's backyards. For my great-niece—and millions of others—American Indian roots have become a source of pride. According to the 2000 census, the number of people who identified themselves solely as Indian and Alaska Native grew by 26 percent, to 2.5 million, from 1990. Add to that the option of declaring a multiracial identity, and the number in that classification jumps to 4.1 million.

As curiosity about American Indian tribes has grown, so has the interest in tracing Native American roots. Exploring this heritage will take you into new territory and away from familiar research habits. For example, the federal census won't be the backbone of your investigation. Although you might still find clues in land and military records, you will delve into regional files, federal "rolls," and a culture still deeply rooted in oral tradition. Your quest will introduce you to a realm of more than 550 federally recognized tribes whose members speak more than 250 languages.

If your search takes you to one of the "Five Civilized Tribes"—Cherokee, Chickasaw, Choctaw, Creek, and Seminole—you should appreciate the availability of records such as the Dawes Rolls, a listing of more than 100,000 tribal members. Researching smaller, less-documented tribes may take you to the National Archives and Records Administration (NARA), tribal offices, and historical societies. Your research skills will be challenged and your resourcefulness tested, but the rewards of finding your connections to this continent's first people will make it worth the effort.

Here are five steps to help you get started:

1. Start with your family. Like Alex Haley's search for his African-American roots, your search for Native American origins may have been inspired by snippets of an oral tradition or family legend. Maybe you heard someone mention an "Indian princess," or perhaps it's just a rumor of Indian blood. Whatever the case, the best place to begin your research is at home.

Because of past animosity toward Native Americans, many families hid Indian blood, and some relatives might still be uncomfortable disclosing old family stories about Indian ancestors. "It's important to talk with your family as much as possible," says Meg Hacker, director of archival operations at the NARA Southwest Region. "Obtain as much information regarding your ancestors as you can. I would recommend sitting down and talking with your family. Ask questions: Why does your family believe they are Native American? Go through family papers, Bibles, and letters, looking for birth, death, and marriage records."

Clues about Indian ancestry can surface from unexpected sources. A name you vaguely remember hearing as a child may be your first link to a shadowy past. An old tombstone may contain a reference to an "Indian" name or place. Tony Mack McClure, author of *Cherokee Proud* (Chu-Nan-Nee Books, $22.95), encourages researchers to listen carefully to every old story, "regardless of how ridiculous it may seem," and then to document every word. "A minuscule [piece] of information may seem unimportant at first, but could later prove to be the key that unlocks the mystery."

The most important mystery, of course, is the name of your ancestor's tribe—it's the key to finding records, as well as discovering your ancestors' culture and heritage. Look for that information buried in family records, vital statistics, letters, or diaries. If you don't find it there, you need to expand your research into tribal histories and migration patterns.

2. Find your ancestor's tribe. To discover your ancestor's tribe, you need to know enough about tribal history and migration to recognize an error in assumption, Hacker says. For example, if someone in your family tells you that your Native American connection is a Cherokee tribe in Michigan, realize that that scenario is impossible. The Cherokee migrated through many states, but Michigan wasn't one of them.

If your family hails from present-day New Mexico, you can probably narrow your first search down to Southwest tribes such as the Navajo or Hopi. If your ancestors lived in the area around Lake Michigan or Lake Superior, looking into Chippewa (Ojibwa) roots is a logical first step. Begin your search for your ancestor's tribe by locating the tribes that lived within the same area as your ancestor and during the same time period. *The Source: A Guidebook of American Genealogy* (Ancestry, $49.95) contains a detailed map, "Indian Tribes, Reservations and Settlements in the United States," printed in 1939. Consult *Atlas of the North American Indian* (Checkmark Books, $21.95) for maps that chronicle tribes' movements over the centuries. You can also find an excellent pre-European tribal map online: <kstrom.net/isk/maps/cultmap.html>.

3. Learn tribal culture and history. Searching for Native American roots means honing your skills as a historian. America's stormy history with indigenous tribes spanned centuries and countless conflicts. Without a basic understanding of tribal history and its historical context

FROM THE NORTH AMERICAN INDIAN BY EDWARD S. CURTIS

Geography will help you discover your ancestors' tribe. The Piegan lived in the Plains region of the United states.

within the larger perspective of American expansion, digging out your roots will be far more difficult. As a Native American researcher, you may become as adept at unraveling the ins and outs of the Grattan Massacre as a Civil War buff is at explaining the ramifications of Gettysburg.

In some cases, you need to know the migration patterns of a particular tribe or the many areas in which it was "resettled." For instance, over a 150-year time span, the Cherokee lived in the Carolinas, Georgia, Arkansas, and Oklahoma. If your family belonged to one of the Iroquois linguistic groups, you need to know that the culture was matrilineal—descended through the female line. Children belonged to

their mother's clan or tribe. Similarly, in the Ojibwa tribe, women controlled their homes and the family's property. Hopi women owned the property, and their husbands worked to benefit the wife's family.

You also might encounter surprises with naming patterns and kinship systems. At birth, a Plains Indian baby was given a name that had a connection with the clan. Later in life, however, the child often received another name that reflected his or her personality or deeds. Europeans frequently gave yet another name, an Anglo one, to the American Indians they interacted with. In the Wasco and Wishram tribes of the Interior Plateau, children received several new names during the course of their lives as they achieved higher rank or social position. Nicknames were also common.

Regional libraries and historical societies are good bets for tracking down information on the tribes in your ancestor's area. The genealogical periodicals that cover the region where your ancestor lived may contain sought-after information. One of the best indexes to these periodicals is the *Periodical Source Index* (PERSI), published by the Allen County Public Library <acpl.lib.in.us/genealogy/persi.html> in Fort Wayne, Indiana, and searchable at genealogical libraries and by subscription to Ancestry.com <www.ancestry.com>. PERSI is a subject index that covers genealogy and local history periodicals published since 1800, and it contains more than 1.8 million index entries from nearly ten thousand titles. Using PERSI, you can find articles on subjects ranging from Ojibwa decorative quillwork to Seminole Negro-Indian Scouts, 1870-81.

Equally important are firsthand narratives such as those found in *Wisdomkeepers: Meetings With Native American Spiritual Elders* (Beyond Words Publishing, $24.95). In this book, eighteen elders from different tribes discuss the location of spiritual places, the names for native homelands, historical details, and sketches of family life. Stories such as that of Hopi Thomas Banyacya can offer insight into your ancestors' culture: The Hopi believe that Big Mountain on Black Mesa in Arizona is the center of the universe and that the spiritual ceremonies performed on the mesa help determine the balance and harmony of nature. "We're the first people here," Banyacya writes in *Wisdomkeepers*. "We're the aborigines of this continent. We live here with the permission of Great Spirit."

4. Know what records are available. Most genealogists depend on federal and state census records to lay a basic foundation for their research. Tribal Indians weren't counted in early federal censuses, however. In fact, census records from 1790 to 1850 included only Indians who lived in settled areas, were taxed, and didn't claim a tribal affiliation. Indians on reservations and those who lived a nomadic existence were not taxed, and therefore not counted.

The 1860 federal census added a category called "Indian (taxed)." From 1870 to 1910, the census had an "Indian" category, but this didn't include reservation Indians until 1890. Most of that census was lost to fire, though, so 1900 is the first available census that lists most Native Americans.

Special counts were made of several tribes, with the best-known count being the Dawes Commission Rolls, taken between 1898 and 1914. These rolls listed members of the Five Civilized Tribes. Cherokee researchers should also check the Guion Miller Rolls, taken in the early twentieth century. This lists applicants for a federal fund to compensate families of Cherokee who lost land as a result of the Indian Removal Act, the 1830 law that relocated most of the Cherokee Nation to what's now Oklahoma.

Once you've identified a tribe, your search will probably take you to the National Archives and Records Administration, where you can find records from the Bureau of Indian Affairs (BIA).

NARA's collection includes special censuses and school and land records. You may also find your ancestor on annuity payrolls or land allotments. Annuities resulted from treaties or acts of Congress in which the government made annual payments to tribal members. Allotment records were created when the government allotted land to individual tribe members; these records are arranged by tribe. They usually include applications, registers of allottees' names, plat maps, and improvements made to the land.

American Indians: A Select Catalog of National Archives Microfilm Publications (available online at <www.archives.gov/publications/microfilm_catalogs/american_indian/american_indian.html> and in print) lists NARA's various Native American holdings, including the Records of the Bureau of Indian Affairs (Record Group 75). You can find a complete description of NARA's Native American holdings in *Guide to Records in the National Archives Relating to American Indians* compiled by Edward E. Hill (National Archives and Records Administration, $25, <www.archives.gov/publications/guides_and_finding_aids.html#amindians>; to order, send payment to National Archives Trust Fund, NWCC2, Department W, P.O. Box 100793, Atlanta, Georgia 30384).

Many BIA field records are now held in regional offices of the National Archives. Each NARA branch has different BIA records. For example, records relating to the Kiowa Agency are in Fort Worth, Texas; the Zuni Agency in Denver; and the Potawatomi Agency in Kansas City, Missouri. Depending on the location, you may be able to tap agency employee records, Indian index cards, vital statistics, sanitary and school records, and individual history and marriage cards.

NARA's Hacker encourages researchers to contact the National Archives regional office in the area where their tribe is located—see the listings throughout this book and <www.archives.gov/facilities> to find the appropriate location.

Write to that office, giving as much information as you have (without reciting your whole family history), and the staff will try to point you to the available records.

Another option is to contact the Bureau of Indian Affairs to obtain the phone number and address of the tribal membership office. Next, contact the tribe to see if it has records of your ancestor. You can access a tribal leaders directory (in HTML or PDF format) at <www.doi.gov/bia/areas/agency. html> or by contacting the BIA at 1849 C Street NW, Washington, DC 20240.

If your Native American ancestor served with federal troops, NARA may have a record of his veteran's benefits. The National Archives military records section has a separate alphabetical file for each American Indian veteran who served prior to 1870.

Because of the well-documented nature of the Five Civilized Tribes—so called because of their early assimilation to white culture—their records are among the easiest to find online. NARA'S Archival Research Catalog (ARC) is a database of selected microfilm and archival holdings, including several on the Oklahoma tribes. To date, about 80 percent of the Dawes Commission Rolls are online in the ARC database <www.archives.gov/research_room/arc>.

To search the Dawes Rolls for ancestors, go to the ARC database and click Search. In the keywords box, enter *enrollment* and the person's name. ARC uses boolean search syntax, so include the word *and*—for example, *enrollment and emma wicket*. Then hit Go. If the database contains information on that person, a list of hits will appear. Click on the title to see details of a particular record. When ARC has an electronic image of the record, you'll get another link that says Digital Copy Available; just click to see the card bearing your ancestor's name.

Other Native American databases on ARC:
- Descriptions of 64,177 Cherokee, Chickasaw, Creek, and Seminole applications for enrollment to the Five Civilized Tribes between 1898 and 1914. More than ten thousand of these applications have digital copies attached.
- A 634-page digitized version of Description of Final Rolls of the Citizens and Freedmen of the Five Civilized Tribes in Indian Territory. You can find names of people the Dawes Commission allowed on tribal rolls.
- A 635-page digitized Index to the Final Rolls of Citizens and Freedmen of the Five Civilized Tribes in Indian Territory.
- A 343-page index of Applications Submitted for the Eastern Cherokee Roll of 1909 (Guion Miller Roll).
- The 196-page digitized version of the Wallace Roll of Cherokee Freedmen in Indian Territory, 1890. Individuals listed were entitled to share with the Shawnee and Delaware in the per capita distribution of $75,000.
- The Kern-Clifton Roll of Cherokee Freedmen, January 16, 1867. This is a census of freedmen of the Cherokee Nation and their descendants.
- 9,618 Citizenship Applications received by the Dawes Commission, 1896.

5. Utilize online resources. Besides ARC, you have many other online resources to help you discover your Native American ancestry and heritage. As you search for your American Indian roots, make use of these three Internet tools:

- **Mailing lists:** Genealogy mailing lists are a quick and easy way for researchers to network with one another. When you join a mailing list, you receive e-mail messages sent from other list members. Mailing lists pertain to specific topics, and everyone on the list shares similar research goals. Once you've located your tribe, join in discussions at some of the nearly sixty mailing lists dedicated to Native American research at <www.rootsweb.com/~jfuller/gen_mail_natam. html> and <lists.rootsweb.com/index/other/Ethnic-Native>. Typical list topics are the Choctaw who moved from Mississippi to Oklahoma, Native American ancestry in

Michigan, and general Indian research. If you're just getting started, the NA-NEWBIES mailing list <www.accessgenealogy.com/native/nanewbies> might be a good jumping-off place.

• **Query boards:** Millions of researchers are on the Internet, and many of them routinely read queries. Query boards give you the chance to announce to the world the ancestor you're seeking, the heritage you're attempting to prove, or the brick wall you've hit. You can find dozens of query boards (also called forums) where you can post free messages requesting assistance at NativeTech.org <nativetech.org/msgboard/#genealogy>.

Other popular forums include GenForum's American Indian bulletin board <genforum.genealogy.com/ai>. And check out the recently combined Native American message boards from FamilyHistory.com and RootsWeb, now at <boards.ancestry.com> under "Topics." Once you've tracked down the general area where your ancestor lived, leave queries on the USGenWeb <www.usgenweb.org> county pages for that location.

• **Publications:** Many tribes, historical societies and individuals publish journals or newsletters about a specific tribe or about American Indian research in general. These journals may include transcripts of tribal rolls, research tips, or firsthand historical accounts.

Also look for online newsletters such as Native American Ancestry Hunting <members.aol.com/NAAHKITTY>. For a $39 annual subscription fee, you receive tips on searching, success stories, family histories, cultural information, and links to tribal resources via E-mail. Publisher Laurie Beth Duffy also maintains the free monthly NAAH Enquiries newsletter, in which you can post queries. To subscribe, send an e-mail to NAAHKITTY@aol.com, and in the subject field type "Add to NAAH ENQUIRIES mailing list." For links to more than one hundred Native American publications, check out Native American Print Media Resources <www.plumsite.com/shea/nativep.html>.

Tracing your Native American ancestors may be one of the most challenging genealogy projects of your life—and one of the most rewarding. Through your quest to unearth your family's tribal ties, you're claiming kinship with a people who felt as connected to future generations as to their own ancestors. In fact, a law of the Iroquois Confederacy required chiefs to consider the impact of their decisions on the next seven generations. As a quote often attributed to Chief Seattle puts it, "The wind that gave our grandfather his first breath also receives his last sigh, and the wind must also give our children the spirit of life." It's up to you to keep your ancestors' spirit alive by discovering their legacy.

GENERAL RESOURCES

Everyday Life Among the American Indians, 1800 to 1900
by Candy Moulton (Writer's Digest Books, $16.99)

A Genealogist's Guide to Discovering Your Immigrant & Ethnic Ancestors
by Sharon DeBartolo Carmack (Betterway Books, $18.99)

Handbook of North American Indians
edited by William C. Sturtevant (Government Printing Office, $57)

How to Research American Blood Lines: A Manual on Indian Genealogical Research
by Cecelia Svinth Carpenter (Heritage Quest, $8.95)

Indian Removal: The Emigration of the Five Civilized Tribes of Indians
by Grant Foreman (University of Oklahoma Press, $19.95)

The Indian Tribes of North America
by John R. Swanton (Smithsonian Institution Press, $35): especially helpful for learning which peoples lived where and when

Native America in the Twentieth Century: An Encyclopedia
edited by Mary B. Davis (Garland Publishing, $42.95)

Native American Genealogical Sourcebook
by Paula K. Byers (Gale Group, $95)

Native Americans Information Directory
(Gale Group, $110): includes contact information for Native American-related organizations

A Student's Guide to Native American Genealogy
(Oryx Press, $24.95)

"Tracking Native American Family History" by Curt B. Witcher and George J. Nixon in *The Source: A Guidebook of American Genealogy* (Ancestry, $49.95)

WEB SITES

About.com's Native American Culture
<nativeamculture.about.com/culture/nativeamculture>

Bureau of Indian Affairs Tribal Leaders Directory
<www.doi.gov/bia/areas/agency.html>

Cyndi's List–Native American
<www.cyndislist.com/native.htm>

Federally Recognized American Indian Tribes
<www.indians.org/Resource/FedTribes99/fedtribes99.html>

Heart of America Indian Center
<members.aol.com/Indianbrav/haic.html>

Index of Native American Resources on the Internet
<www.hanksville.org/NAresources>

Indian Scout Books
<www.indianscoutbooks.com>

Indian Tribes–Index by State
<www.kstrom.net/isk/maps/tribesbystate.html>

National Museum of the American Indian
<www.nmai.si.edu>

Native American Genealogical Research & Publishing Co.
<www.nagrpubco.net>

Native American Genealogy Resources
<www.distantcousin.com/Links/Ethnic/Native>

Native American Links
<www.accessgenealogy.com/native>

Native American Nations
<www.nativeculture.com/lisamitten/nations.html>

Native American Records and Databases
<genealogy.about.com/hobbies/genealogy/cs/indianrecords>

Native American Resource Guide
<www.usc.edu/isd/archives/ethnicstudies/indian_main.html>

Native American Resources
<www.dhc.net/~design/namerica.htm>

Native American Resources
<www.rootsweb.com/~usgwnar>

Native Web
<www.nativeweb.org/resources/genealogy_tracing_roots_>

State Historical Society of Missouri
<www.system.missouri.edu/shs/nativeam.html>

Tawodi's American Indian Genealogy
<members.aol.com/tawodi>

NORTHERN TRIBES

Territory: Area bordered by Canada on the north, the Great Lakes on the west, the Tennessee River to the south, and the Atlantic Ocean to the east. **Tribes:** Abenaki, Algonkin, Cayuga, Delaware, Huron, Iroquois, Kickapoo, Mohawk, Narraganset, Penobscot, Ottawa, Oneida, Seneca, Shawnee, Tuscarora, Wampanoag

Web Sites

Delaware Tribe of Indians
<www.delawaretribeofindians.nsn.us>

Four Huron Wampum Records
<www.canadiana.org/cgi-bin/ECO/mtq?id=592d0157c5&display=06665+0003>

Kahon:wes's Mohawk and Iroquois Index
<www.kahonwes.com/index1.htm>

Mohawk Nation Council of Chiefs
<hometown.aol.com/miketben2/miktben7.htm>

Mohawk Nation of Akwesasne
<www.peacetree.com/akwesasne>

Oneida Indian Nation
<www.oneida-nation.net>

Oneida Nation of Wisconsin
<www.oneidanation.org>

Onyota'a:ka (People of the Standing Stone)
<www.peace4turtleisland.org/pages/oneida.htm>

The Seneca Nation of Indians
<www.sni.org>

The Six Nations
<www.ratical.org/many_worlds/6Nations>

Traditional Abenaki of Mazipskwik and Related Bands
<hmt.com/abenaki>

Tuscarora and Six Nations Web Sites
<tuscaroras.com>

United Tribe of Shawnee Indians
<www.sunflower.org/~hdqrs>

Wampanoag Tribe of Gay Head
<www.wampanoagtribe.net>

The Wampum Chronicles
<www.wampumchronicles.com>

GREAT BASIN, INTERIOR PLATEAU TRIBES

Territory: Washington, Oregon, Utah, Nevada, Idaho; western half of Wyoming, Montana, and Colorado. **Tribes:** Bannock, Cayuse, Chinook, Clatsop, Duwamish, Flathead, Haida, Kutenai, Klamath, Nez Perce, Paiute, Shoshone,

Spokane, Suquamish, Tillamook, Ute, Wenatchee, Wishram, Yakama

Web Sites

Chinook
<logos.uoregon.edu/ explore/oregon/chinook.html>

Confederated Tribes of the Umatilla Indian Reservation
<www.umatilla.nsn.us>

Confederated Tribes of Warm Springs (Paiute)
<www.warmsprings. com>

Klamath Tribes
<www.klamathtribes. org/history.html>

Kuiu Thlingit Nation
<www.geocities.com/ CapitolHill/5803>

Northern Ute
<www.northernute.com>

Official Nez Perce Tribe Web Site
<www.nezperce.org>

Shoshone On-line!
<tlc.wtp.net/shoshone. htm>

Southern Ute
<www.southern-ute. nsn.us>

Spokane Tribe
<www.wellpinit.wednet. edu/spokan/spokan. html>

Suquamish Tribe
<www.suquamish.nsn. us>

Tlingit & Haida Indian Tribes of Alaska
<www.tlingit-haida.org>

SOUTHERN TRIBES

Territory: Area bordered by Kentucky and Virginia on the north, Mississippi River to the west, and the Gulf of Mexico and the Atlantic on the south and east. **Tribes:** The Five Civilized Tribes—Cherokee, Chickasaw, Choctaw, Creek, and Seminole—plus Alabama, Apalachee, Catawba, Natchez, Quapaw, Yamasee

Web Sites

All Things Cherokee
<www.allthings cherokee.com>

Beginning Your Cherokee Research
<www.tngenweb.org/ cherokee_by_blood/ cher3.htm>

Cherokee by Blood
<www.tngenweb.org/ cherokee_by_blood>

Cherokee Heritage Center
<www.cherokeeheritage. org/genealogy.html>

The Cherokee Messenger
<www.powersource.com/ cherokee>

The Cherokee Nation
<www.cherokee.org>

Cherokee National Historical Society
<www.powersource.com/ heritage/default.html>

Chickasaw Nation
<www.chickasaw.net>

Choctaw Nation of Oklahoma
<www.cableone.net/ areeves/choctaw>

Eastern Band of Cherokee
<www.cherokee-nc.com>

History of the Cherokee
<cherokeehistory.com>

Muscogee Creek Nation
<www.ocevnet.org/creek. html>

Muscogee (Creek) Nation of Oklahoma
<www.rootsweb.com/ ~itcreek>

The Official Quapaw Website
<www.geocities.com/ Athens/Aegean/1388>

Seminole Genealogy
<www.nanations.com/ seminole>

Seminole Nation of Oklahoma
<www.cowboy.net/ native/seminole>

Seminole Tribe of Florida
<www.seminoletribe. com>

Unofficial Choctaw Nation Home Page
<www.niti.net/~michael/ choctaw>

SOUTHWESTERN AND CALIFORNIA TRIBES

Territory: Most of Arizona and New Mexico, part of western and southern Texas, California. **Tribes:** Apache, Cahuilla, Chumash, Havasupai, Miwok, Modoc, Mojave, Navajo, Papago, Pima, Yaqui, Yavapai, and Yuma, plus the Pueblo tribes of the Hopi, Laguna, Taos, and Zuni

Web Sites

The Chumash Indians
<expage.com/page/ chumashindians>

The Federated Indians of Graton Rancheria
<www.coastmiwok.com>

Hopi Cultural Preservation Office
<www.nau.edu/ ~hcpo-p>

Hopi Network Message Center Index
<www.recycles.org/hopi/ guests>

Hopi the Real Thing
<www.ausbcomp.com/ redman/hopi.htm>

Links to Apache Indian Sites
<members.tripod. com/~PHILKON/ links12apache.html>

Navajo
<www.ausbcomp.com/ redman/navajo.htm>

Navajo Nation
<www.navajo.org>

New Mexico's Pueblo Indians
<members.aol.com/ chloe5/pueblos.html>

PLAINS, PRAIRIES, AND WOODLANDS TRIBES

Territory: Extended from Canada almost to Mexico; southern Alberta, Saskatchewan, and Manitoba; eastern Montana, Wyoming, and Colorado; extreme eastern part of New Mexico; North and South Dakota, Nebraska, Kansas, Oklahoma, Minnesota, Iowa, Kansas, Arkansas, and Texas Woodlands-Bounded by Lake Michigan and Lake Superior on the east and Missouri on the west; includes Illinois and parts of Wisconsin and Iowa **Tribes:** Arapaho, Arikara, Assiniboine, Blackfeet, Cheyenne, Chippewa (Ojibwa), Comanche, Crow, Fox, Illinois, Kansa, Kiowa, Mandan, Menominee, Omaha, Osage, Pawnee, Sac, Sioux, Winnebago

Web Sites

Blackfeet Nation
<www.blackfeetnation.com>

Cheyenne-Arapaho Lands
<rebelcherokee.tripod.com/itcheyenne_arapaho.html>

Cheyenne Genealogy
<www.mcn.net/~hmscook/roots/cheyenne.html>

Comanche Language and Cultural Preservation Committee
<www.comanchelanguage.org>

Fort Peck Assiniboine and Sioux History
<www.montana.edu/wwwfpcc/tribes>

Great Lakes Intertribal Council
<www.glitc.org>

Great Sioux Nation
<www.eagleswatch.com/great_sioux_nation.htm>

The Illini Confederation
<members.tripod.com/~RFester>

An Introduction to Dakota Culture and History
<www.geocities.com/Athens/Acropolis/5579/dakota.html>

Lakota Dakota Information Home Page
<puffin.creighton.edu/lakota>

Mandan, Hidatsa, Arikara
<web.ndak.net/~tatlegal>

Menominee of Wisconsin
<www.menominee.nsn.us>

Northern Cheyenne
<www.ncheyenne.net>

Ojibway Culture and History
<www.geocities.com/Athens/Acropolis/5579/ojibwa.html>

Pawnee Nation of Oklahoma
<www.pawneenation.org>

Rosebud Sioux
<www.rosebudsiouxtribe.org>

The Sac and Fox Nation
<www.cowboy.net/native/sacnfox.html>

The Sault Ste. Marie Tribe of Chippewa Indians
<www.sootribe.org>

Sioux Heritage
<www.lakhota.com>

South Dakota Native American Genealogy
<www.geocities.com/Heartland/Plains/8430>

About the Contributors

Sharon DeBartolo Carmack is the author of *Your Guide to Cemetery Research* (Betterway Books, $19.99), *Organizing Your Family History Search* (Betterway Books, $17.99), *A Genealogist's Guide to Discovering Your Female Ancestors* (Betterway Books, $17.99) and *A Genealogist's Guide to Discovering Your Immigrant & Ethnic Ancestors* (Betterway Books, $18.99). She is also a contributing editor of *Family Tree Magazine*.

Crystal Conde is assistant editor of *Family Tree Magazine*.

Emily Anne Croom is the best-selling author of *Unpuzzling Your Past* (Betterway Books, $18.99), *The Genealogist's Companion & Sourcebook* (Betterway Books, $16.99), *The Sleuth Book for Genealogists* (Betterway Books, $18.99), and *The Unpuzzling Your Past Workbook: Essential Forms and Letters for All Genealogists* (Betterway Books, $15.99). She is also the co-author of *A Genealogist's Guide to Discovering Your African-American Ancestors* (Betterway Books, $21.99).

Candace L. Doriott is a Detroit freelance writer.

Lauren Eisenstodt is assistant editor of *Family Tree Magazine*.

Jim Faber is a former *Family Tree Magazine* editorial assistant.

David A. Fryxell is editor-in-chief and founder of *Family Tree Magazine*. He is also editor-in-chief of Betterway Books' genealogy books.

Nancy Hendrickson is a contributing editor of *Family Tree Magazine* and the author of *Finding Your Roots Online*, the first volume in the new *Family Tree Magazine* Library series, to be published by Betterway Books in spring 2003. She also writes the regular AncestorNews column on the *Family Tree Magazine* Web site <www.familytreemagazine.com/ancestornews/current.html>. She is a family historian, freelance writer and the author of two astronomy books.

Katherine House is a freelance writer based in Iowa City, Iowa.

Susan Wenner Jackson is a former managing editor of *Family Tree Magazine*.

Amy Leibrock is a writer in New York City, where she is currently the senior editor of *Art Business News*.

Patricia McMorrow is a Twin Cities-based writer and editor. She is a freelance writer and a former award-winning editor at newspapers in St. Paul, Minn., and San Antonio.

Darin Painter is a writer in Arlington, Virginia, and managing editor of *Print Solutions* magazine.

Melanie Rigney is editor of *Writer's Digest* magazine, editorial director of Writer's Digest

Books, and a contributing editor of *Family Tree Magazine*.

Jonathan Rollins is a freelance writer based in northern Virginia.

Franklin Carter Smith is the co-author of *A Genealogist's Guide to Discovering Your African-American Ancestors* (Betterway Books, $21.99). Smith is a library service specialist at the Houston Public Library and a former attorney.

Allison Stacy is managing editor of *Family Tree Magazine*.

Maureen A. Taylor is the author of *Preserving Your Family Photographs* (Betterway Books, $19.99) and *Uncovering Your Ancestry through Family Photographs* (Betterway Books, $18.99). She is also a contributing editor of *Family Tree Magazine*.

James W. Warren is the co-author of *Your Guide to the Family History Library* (Betterway Books,

$19.99). He is a full-time professional genealogist and lectures at seminars across the United States with his wife, Paula Stuart Warren.

Paula Stuart Warren is the co-author of *Your Guide to the Family History Library* (Betterway Books, $19.99). She is a full-time professional genealogist, writer and lecturer who lives in St. Paul, Minn. She is a certified genealogical records specialist and specializes in Midwestern research and research at national repositories.

Peter D.A. Warwick is a Canadian freelance writer and a Great Lakes historian. He has written for *Family Tree Magazine*, *Heritage Travel* and many other magazines.

Diane Weiner is a Cincinnati writer and expert in heritage albums who was formerly the "Preserving Memories" columnist for *Family Tree Magazine*.

Jessica Yerega is assistant editor of *Writer's Digest* magazine and a native of Pittsburgh.

Index

Notes
